Data-Centric Systems and Applications

For further volumes:
http://www.springer.com/series/5258

Alejandro Vaisman • Esteban Zimányi

Data Warehouse Systems

Design and Implementation

 Springer

Alejandro Vaisman
Instituto Tecnológico de Buenos Aires
Buenos Aires
Argentina

Esteban Zimányi
Université Libre de Bruxelles
Brussels
Belgium

ISBN 978-3-642-54654-9   ISBN 978-3-642-54655-6 (eBook)
DOI 10.1007/978-3-642-54655-6
Springer Heidelberg New York Dordrecht London

Library of Congress Control Number: 2014943455

To Andrés and Manuel,
who bring me joy and
happiness day after day
A.V.

To Elena,
the star that shed light upon my path,
with all my love
E.Z.

Foreword

Having worked with data warehouses for almost 20 years, I was both honored and excited when two veteran authors in the field asked me to write a foreword for their new book and sent me a PDF file with the current draft. Already the size of the PDF file gave me a first impression of a very comprehensive book, an impression that was heavily reinforced by reading the Table of Contents. After reading the entire book, I think it is quite simply the most comprehensive textbook about data warehousing on the market.

The book is very well suited for one or more data warehouse courses, ranging from the most basic to the most advanced. It has all the features that are necessary to make a good textbook. First, a running case study, based on the Northwind database known from Microsoft's tools, is used to illustrate all aspects using many detailed figures and examples. Second, key terms and concepts are highlighted in the text for better reading and understanding. Third, review questions are provided at the end of each chapter so students can quickly check their understanding. Fourth, the many detailed exercises for each chapter put the presented knowledge into action, yielding deep learning and taking students through all the steps needed to develop a data warehouse. Finally, the book shows how to implement data warehouses using leading industrial and open-source tools, concretely Microsoft's and Pentaho's suites of data warehouse tools, giving students the essential hands-on experience that enables them to put the knowledge into practice.

For the complete database novice, there is even an introductory chapter on standard database concepts and design, making the book self-contained even for this group. It is quite impressive to cover all this material, usually the topic of an entire textbook, without making it a dense read. Next, the book provides a good introduction to basic multidimensional concepts, later moving on to advanced concepts such as summarizability. A complete overview of the data warehouse and online analytical processing (OLAP) "architecture stack" is given. For the conceptual modeling of the data warehouse, a concise and intuitive graphical notation is used, a full specification of which is given in an appendix, along with a methodology for the modeling and the translation to (logical-level) relational schemas.

Later, the book provides a lot of useful knowledge about designing and querying data warehouses, including a detailed, yet easy-to-read, description of the de facto standard OLAP query language: MultiDimensional eXpressions (MDX). I certainly learned a thing or two about MDX in a short time. The chapter on extract-transform-load (ETL) takes a refreshingly different approach by using a graphical notation based on the Business Process Modeling Notation (BPMN), thus treating the ETL flow at a higher and more understandable level. Unlike most other data warehouse books, this book also provides comprehensive coverage on analytics, including data mining and reporting, and on how to implement these using industrial tools. The book even has a chapter on methodology issues such as requirements capture and the data warehouse development process, again something not covered by most data warehouse textbooks.

However, the one thing that really sets this book apart from its peers is the coverage of advanced data warehouse topics, such as spatial databases and data warehouses, spatiotemporal data warehouses and trajectories, and semantic web data warehouses. The book also provides a useful overview of novel "big data" technologies like Hadoop and novel database and data warehouse architectures like in-memory database systems, column store database systems, and right-time data warehouses. These advanced topics are a distinguishing feature not found in other textbooks.

Finally, the book concludes by pointing to a number of exciting directions for future research in data warehousing, making it an interesting read even for seasoned data warehouse researchers.

A famous quote by IBM veteran Bruce Lindsay states that "relational databases are the foundation of Western civilization." Similarly, I would say that "data warehouses are the foundation of twenty-first-century enterprises." And this book is in turn an excellent foundation for building those data warehouses, from the simplest to the most complex.

Happy reading!

Aalborg, Denmark   Torben Bach Pedersen

Preface

Since the late 1970s, relational database technology has been adopted by most organizations to store their essential data. However, nowadays, the needs of these organizations are not the same as they used to be. On the one hand, increasing market dynamics and competitiveness led to the need of having the right information at the right time. Managers need to be properly informed in order to take appropriate decisions to keep up with business successfully. On the other hand, data possessed by organizations are usually scattered among different systems, each one devised for a particular kind of business activity. Further, these systems may also be distributed geographically in different branches of the organization.

Traditional database systems are not well suited for these new requirements, since they were devised to support the day-to-day operations rather than for data analysis and decision making. As a consequence, new database technologies for these specific tasks have emerged in the 1990s, namely, data warehousing and online analytical processing (OLAP), which involve architectures, algorithms, tools, and techniques for bringing together data from heterogeneous information sources into a single repository suited for analysis. In this repository, called a data warehouse, data are accumulated over a period of time for the purpose of analyzing its evolution and discovering strategic information such as trends, correlations, and the like. Data warehousing is nowadays a well-established and mature technology used by organizations in many sectors to improve their operations and better achieve their objectives.

Objective of the Book

This book is aimed at consolidating and transferring to the community the experience of many years of teaching and research in the field of databases and data warehouses conducted by the authors, individually as well as jointly.

However, this is not a compilation of the authors' past publications. On the contrary, the book aims at being a main textbook for undergraduate and graduate computer science courses on data warehousing and OLAP. As such, it is written in a pedagogical rather than research style to make the work of the instructor easier and to help the student understand the concepts being delivered. Researchers and practitioners who are interested in an introduction to the area of data warehousing will also find in the book a useful reference. In summary, we aimed at providing an in-depth coverage of the main topics in the field, yet keeping a simple and understandable style.

We describe next the main features that make this book different from other academic ones in the field. Throughout the book, we follow a methodology that covers all the phases of the data warehousing process, from requirements specification to implementation. Regarding data warehouse design, we make a clear distinction between the three abstraction levels of the American National Standards Institute (ANSI) database architecture, that is, conceptual, logical, and physical, unlike the usual approaches, which do not distinguish clearly between the conceptual and logical levels. A strong emphasis is given to querying using the de facto standard MDX (MultiDimensional eXpressions). Though there are many practical books covering this language, academic books have largely ignored it. We also provide an in-depth coverage of the extraction, transformation, and loading (ETL) processes. Unlike other books in the field, we devote a whole chapter to study how data mining techniques can be used to exploit the data warehouse. In addition, we study how key performance indicators (KPIs) and dashboards are built on top of data warehouses. Although there are many textbooks on spatial databases, this is not the case with spatial data warehouses, which we study in this book, together with trajectory data warehouses, which allow the analysis of data produced by objects that change their position in space and time, like cars or pedestrians. We also address several issues that we believe are likely to be relevant in the near future, like new database architectures such as column-store and in-memory databases, as well as data warehousing and OLAP on the semantic web.

A key characteristic that distinguishes this book from other textbooks is that we illustrate how the concepts introduced can be implemented using existing tools. Specifically, throughout the book we develop a case study based on the well-known Northwind database using representative tools of different kinds. As an example of a commercial implementation, we used the tools provided with Microsoft SQL Server, namely, Analysis Services, Integration Services, and Reporting Services. As an example of an open-source implementation, we used the Pentaho Business Analytics suite of products, which includes Pentaho Analysis Services, an OLAP engine commonly known as Mondrian, and Pentaho Data Integration, an ETL tool commonly known as Kettle. In particular, the chapter on logical design includes a complete description of how to define an OLAP cube in both Analysis Services and Mondrian. Similarly, the chapter on physical design illustrates how to optimize SQL Server, Analysis Services, and Mondrian applications. Further, in the chapter on ETL we give a complete example of a process that loads the Northwind data warehouse, implemented using both Integration Services and Kettle. In the chapter on data analytics, we used Analysis Services for data mining and for defining key performance indicators, and we used Reporting Services to show how dashboards can be implemented. Finally, to illustrate spatial and spatiotemporal concepts, we used the GeoMondrian OLAP tool over the open-source database PostgreSQL and its spatial extension PostGIS. In this way, the reader can replicate most of the examples and queries presented in the book.

We have also included review questions and exercises for all the chapters in order to help the reader verify that the concepts in each chapter have been well understood. We strongly believe that being formal and precise in the presentation of the topics, implementing them on operational tools, and checking the acquired knowledge against an extensive list of questions and exercises provides a comprehensive learning path for the student.

In addition to the above, support material for the book has been made available online at the address http://cs.ulb.ac.be/DWSDIbook/. This includes electronic versions of the figures, slides for each chapter, solutions to the proposed exercises, and other pedagogic material that can be used by instructors using this book as a course text.

This book builds up from the book *Advanced Data Warehouse Design: From Conventional to Spatial and Temporal Applications* coauthored by one of the authors of the present work in collaboration with Elzbieta Malinowski and published by Springer in 2007. We would like to emphasize that the present book is not a new edition of the previous one but a completely new book with a different objective: While the previous book focused solely on data warehouse design, the present book provides a comprehensive coverage of the overall data warehouse process, from requirements specification to implementation and exploitation. Although approximatively 15% of the previous book was used as a starting point of the present one, this reused material has been adapted to cope with the new objectives of the book.

Organization of the Book and Teaching Paths

Part I of the book starts with Chap. 1 and provides a historical overview of data warehousing and OLAP. Chapter 2 introduces the main concepts of relational databases needed in the remainder of the book. We also introduce the case study that we will use throughout the book, which is based on the well-known Northwind database. Data warehouses and the multidimensional model are introduced in Chap. 3, as well as the tools provided by SQL Server and the Pentaho Business Analytics suite. Chapter 4 deals with conceptual data warehouse design, while Chap. 5 is devoted to logical data warehouse design. Part I closes with Chap. 6, which studies MDX and SQL/OLAP, the extension of SQL with OLAP features.

Part II covers data warehouse implementation and exploitation issues. This part starts with Chap. 7, which tackles physical data warehouse design, focusing on indexing, view materialization, and database partitioning. Chapter 8 studies conceptual modeling and implementation of ETL processes. Chapter 9 studies data analytics as a way of exploiting the data warehouse for decision making. Chapter 10 closes Part II, providing a comprehensive method for data warehouse design.

Part III covers advanced data warehouse topics. This part starts with Chap. 11, which studies spatial data warehouses and their exploitation, denoted spatial OLAP (SOLAP). This is illustrated with an extension of the Northwind data warehouse with spatial data, denoted GeoNorthwind, and we query this data warehouse with a spatial extension of the MDX language. Chapter 12 covers trajectory data warehousing. Like in Chap. 11, we illustrate the problem by extending the Northwind data warehouse with trajectory data and show how this data warehouse can be queried extending SQL with spatiotemporal data types. Chapter 13 studies how novel techniques (like the MapReduce programming model) and technologies (like column-store and in-memory databases) can be applied in the field of data warehousing to allow large amounts of data to be processed. Chapter 14 addresses OLAP analysis over semantic web data. Finally, Chap. 15 concludes the book, pointing out what we believe will be the main challenges for data warehousing in the future. Appendix A summarizes the notations used in this book.

The figure below illustrates the overall structure of the book and the interdependencies between the chapters described above. Readers may refer to this figure to tailor their use of this book to their own particular interests. The dependency graph in the figure suggests many of the possible combinations that can be devised in order to offer advanced graduate courses on data warehousing. We can see that there is a path from Chaps. 1 to 6, covering a basic course. In addition, according to the course needs and the coverage depth given to each of the topics, this basic course can be naturally extended to include any combination of physical design, ETL process, data analytics, or even spatial databases. That means the book organization gives the lecturer enough flexibility to combine topics after the basic concepts have been delivered. For example, advanced courses can include a quick overview of Chaps. 1–5, and then they can be customized in many different ways. For example, if the lecturer wants to focus on querying, she could deliver the paths starting in Chap. 6. If she wants to focus on physical issues, she can follow the paths starting in Chaps. 7 and 8.

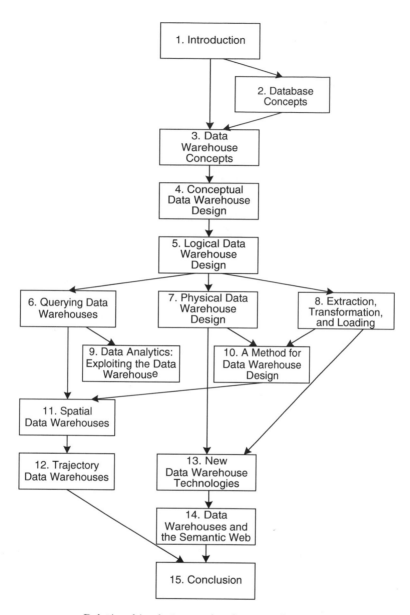

Relationships between the chapters of this book

Acknowledgments

We would like to thank Innoviris, the Brussels Institute for Research and Innovation, which funded Alejandro Vaisman's work through the OSCB project; without its financial support, this book would never have been possible. As mentioned above, some content of this book finds its roots in a previous book written by one of the authors in collaboration with Elzbieta Malinowski. We would like to thank her for all the work we did together in making the previous book a reality. This gave us the impulse for starting this new book.

Parts of the material included in this book have been previously presented in conferences or published in journals. At these conferences, we had the opportunity to discuss with research colleagues from all around the world, and we exchanged viewpoints about the subject with them. The anonymous reviewers of these conferences and journals provided us with insightful comments and suggestions that contributed significantly to improve the work presented in this book. We would like to thank Zineb El Akkaoui, with whom we have explored the use of BPMN for ETL processes in the context of her doctorate thesis. Many thanks to Benoit Foé and Julien Lusiela, who explored the spatiotemporal extension of PostGIS in the context of their master's thesis, and to Waqas Ahmed, a doctorate student of our laboratory, who helped us explore Mondrian. We are also grateful to Arthur Lesuisse, the system engineer of our department, who provided invaluable help in setting up all the computer infrastructure we needed, especially for spatializing the Northwind database. He also contributed in enhancing some of the figures of this book. We also want to thank Lorena Etcheverry, who contributed with comments, exercises, and solutions in Chap. 14.

Our special thanks to Torben Bach Pedersen, professor at Aalborg University in Denmark, who kindly agreed to write the foreword for this book, even when it was only in draft form. Finally, we would like to warmly thank Ralf Gerstner from Springer for his continued interest in this book. The enthusiastic welcome given to our book proposal gave us enormous impetus to pursue our project to its end.

Brussels, Belgium   Alejandro Vaisman, Esteban Zimányi
January 2014

About the Authors

Alejandro Vaisman is a professor at the Instituto Tecnológico de Buenos Aires. He has been a professor and chair of the master's program in data mining at the University of Buenos Aires (UBA) and professor at Universidad de la República in Uruguay. He received a BE degree in civil engineering and a BCS degree and a doctorate in computer science from the UBA under the supervision of Prof. Alberto Mendelzon from the University of Toronto (UoT). He has been a postdoctoral fellow at UoT and visiting researcher at UoT, Universidad Politécnica de Madrid, Universidad de Chile, University of Hasselt, and Université Libre de Bruxelles (ULB). His research interests are in the field of databases, business intelligence, and geographic information systems. He has authored and coauthored many scientific papers published at major conferences and in major journals.

Esteban Zimányi is a professor and a director of the Department of Computer and Decision Engineering (CoDE) of Université Libre de Bruxelles (ULB). He started his studies at the Universidad Autónoma de Centro América, Costa Rica, and received a BCS degree and a doctorate in computer science from ULB. His current research interests include data warehouses and business intelligence, semantic web, geographic information systems, and spatiotemporal databases. He has coauthored and coedited 8 books and published many papers on these topics. He is editor-in-chief of the *Journal on Data Semantics* (JoDS) published by Springer. He is coordinator of the Erasmus Mundus master's and doctorate programs on "Information Technologies for Business Intelligence" (IT4BI).

Contents

Part II   Implementation and Deployment

Part I
Fundamental Concepts

Chapter 1
Introduction

Organizations today are facing increasingly complex challenges in terms of management and problem solving in order to achieve their operational goals. This situation compels people in those organizations to utilize analysis tools that can better support their decisions. **Business intelligence** comprises a collection of methodologies, processes, architectures, and technologies that transform raw data into meaningful and useful information for decision making. Business intelligence and **decision-support systems** provide assistance to managers at various organizational levels for analyzing strategic information. These systems collect vast amounts of data and reduce them to a form that can be used to analyze organizational behavior. This data transformation comprises a set of tasks that take the data from the sources and, through extraction, transformation, integration, and cleansing processes, store the data in a common repository called a **data warehouse**. Data warehouses have been developed and deployed as an integral part of decision-support systems to provide an infrastructure that enables users to obtain efficient and accurate responses to complex queries.

A wide variety of systems and tools can be used for accessing, analyzing, and exploiting the data contained in data warehouses. From the early days of data warehousing, the typical mechanism for those tasks has been **online analytical processing (OLAP)**. OLAP systems allow users to interactively query and automatically aggregate the data contained in a data warehouse. In this way, decision makers can easily access the required information and analyze it at various levels of detail. **Data mining** tools have also been used since the 1990s to infer and extract interesting knowledge hidden in data warehouses. From the beginning of the twenty-first century, a large number of new business intelligence techniques have been developed and used to assist decision making. Thus, the business intelligence market is shifting to provide sophisticated analysis tools that go beyond the data navigation techniques that popularized the OLAP paradigm. This new paradigm is generically called **data analytics**. The business intelligence techniques used to exploit a

A. Vaisman and E. Zimányi, *Data Warehouse Systems*, Data-Centric Systems and Applications, DOI 10.1007/978-3-642-54655-6_1,
© Springer-Verlag Berlin Heidelberg 2014

data warehouse can be broadly summarized as follows (this list by no means attempts to be comprehensive):

- Reporting, such as dashboards and alerts.
- Performance management, such as metrics, key performance indicators (KPIs), and scorecards.
- Analytics, such as OLAP, data mining, time series analysis, text mining, web analytics, and advanced data visualization.

Although in this book the main emphasis will be on OLAP as a tool to exploit a data warehouse, many of these techniques will also be discussed.

In this chapter, we present an overview of the data warehousing field, covering both established topics and new developments, and indicate the chapters in the book where these subjects are covered. We give in Sect. 1.1 a historical overview of data warehousing and OLAP, starting from the early achievements. Then, we describe in Sect. 1.2 the field of spatial and spatiotemporal data warehouses, which has been increasingly used in many application domains. Finally, in Sect. 1.3 we describe new domains and challenges that are being explored in order to answer the requirements of today's analytical applications.

1.1   A Historical Overview of Data Warehousing

In the early 1990s, as a consequence of an increasingly competitive and rapidly changing world, organizations realized that they needed to perform sophisticated data analysis to support their decision-making processes. Traditional **operational** or **transactional databases** did not satisfy the requirements for data analysis, since they were designed and optimized to support daily business operations, and their primary concern was ensuring concurrent access by multiple users and, at the same time, providing recovery techniques to guarantee data consistency. Typical operational databases contain detailed data, do not include historical data, and perform poorly when executing complex queries that involve many tables or aggregate large volumes of data. Furthermore, when users need to analyze the behavior of an organization as a whole, data from several different operational systems must be integrated. This can be a difficult task to accomplish because of the differences in data definition and content. Therefore, **data warehouses** were proposed as a solution to the growing demands of decision-making users.

The classic data warehouse definition, given by Inmon, characterizes a data warehouse as a collection of subject-oriented, integrated, nonvolatile, and time-varying data to support management decisions. This definition emphasizes some salient features of a data warehouse. **Subject oriented** means that a data warehouse targets one or several subjects of analysis according to the analytical requirements of managers at various levels of the decision-making process. For example, a data warehouse in a retail company may contain data for the analysis of the inventory and sales of products. The term **integrated** expresses the fact that the contents of a data warehouse result from the integration of data from various operational and external systems. **Nonvolatile** indicates that a data warehouse accumulates data from operational systems for a long period of time. Thus, data modification and removal are not allowed in data warehouses, and the only operation allowed is the purging of obsolete data that is no longer needed. Finally, **time varying** emphasizes the fact that a data warehouse keeps track of how its data has evolved over time, for instance, to know the evolution of sales over the last months or years.

The basic concepts of databases are studied in Chap. 2. The design of operational databases is typically performed in four phases: **requirements specification, conceptual design, logical design**, and **physical design**. During the requirements specification process, the needs of users at various levels of the organization are collected. The specification obtained serves as a basis for creating a database schema capable of responding to user queries. Databases are designed using a **conceptual model**, such as the entity-relationship (ER) model, which aims at describing an application without taking into account implementation considerations. The resulting design is then translated into a **logical model**, which is an implementation paradigm for database applications. Nowadays, the most used logical model for databases is the relational model. Therefore, in the chapter we also cover two relational query languages: the relational algebra and the structured query language (SQL). Finally, physical design particularizes the logical model for a specific implementation platform in order to produce a **physical model**.

Relational databases must be highly normalized in order to guarantee consistency under frequent updates, which implies a minimum level of redundancy. This is usually achieved at the expense of a higher cost of querying, because normalization implies partitioning the database into multiple tables. Several authors have pointed out that this design paradigm is not appropriate for data warehouse applications. Data warehouses must be modeled in a way that ensures a deep understanding of the underlying data and delivers good performance for the complex queries needed for typical analysis tasks. This requires a lesser degree of normalization or, in some cases, no normalization at all. To account for these requirements, a different model was needed. Thus, multidimensional modeling was adopted for data warehouse design.

Multidimensional modeling, studied in Chap. 3, views data as consisting of facts linked to several dimensions. A **fact** represents the focus of analysis (e.g., analysis of sales in stores) and typically includes attributes called measures. **Measures** are usually numeric values that allow a quantitative evaluation of various aspects of an organization. For example, measures such as the amount or number of sales might help to analyze sales activities in various stores. **Dimensions** are used to see the measures from several perspectives. For example, a time dimension can be used to analyze changes in sales over various periods of time, whereas a location dimension can be used to analyze sales according to the geographical distribution of stores. Users may combine several analysis perspectives (i.e., dimensions) according to their needs. For example, a user may require information about sales of computer accessories (the product dimension) in July 2012 (the time dimension) at all store locations (the store dimension). Dimensions typically include attributes that form **hierarchies**, which allow users to explore measures at various levels of detail. Examples of hierarchies are month–quarter–year in the time dimension and city–state–country in the location dimension. Aggregation of measures takes place when a hierarchy is traversed. For example, moving in a hierarchy from a month level to a year level will yield aggregated values of sales for the various years.

From a methodological point of view, data warehouses must be designed analogously to operational databases, that is, following the four-step process consisting of requirements specification and conceptual, logical, and physical design. However, there is still no widely accepted conceptual model for data warehouse applications. Due to this, data warehouse design is usually performed at the logical level, leading to schemas that are difficult to understand by a typical user. We believe that a conceptual model that clearly stands on top of the logical level is required for data warehouse design. In this book, we use the **MultiDim model**, which is powerful enough to represent the complex characteristics of data warehouses at an abstraction level higher than the logical model. We study conceptual modeling for data warehouses in Chap. 4.

At the **logical level**, the multidimensional model is usually represented by relational tables organized in specialized structures called star schemas and snowflake schemas. These relational schemas relate a fact table to several dimension tables. **Star schemas** use a unique table for each dimension, even in the presence of hierarchies, which yields denormalized dimension tables. On the other hand, **snowflake schemas** use normalized tables for dimensions and their hierarchies. Then, over this relational representation of a data warehouse, an OLAP server builds a data cube, which provides a multidimensional view of the data warehouse. Logical modeling is studied in Chap. 5.

Once a data warehouse has been implemented, analytical queries must be addressed to it. MDX (MultiDimensional eXpressions) is the de facto standard language for querying a multidimensional database, although it can also be used in the definition of data cubes. Thus, MDX provides a functionality for multidimensional databases similar to the one provided by SQL (Structured Query Language) for traditional relational databases. The MDX language is studied (and compared to SQL) in Chap. 6.

The **physical level** is concerned with implementation issues. Given the size of a typical data warehouse, physical design is crucial to ensure adequate response time to the complex ad hoc queries that must be supported. Three techniques are normally used for improving system performance: materialized views, indexing, and data partitioning. In particular, bitmap indexes are used in the data warehousing context, opposite to operational databases, where B-tree indexes are typically used. A huge amount of research in these topics had been performed particularly during the second half of the 1990s. In Chap. 7, we review and study these efforts.

Although data warehouses are, in the end, a particular kind of databases, there are significant differences between the development of operational databases and data warehouses. A key one is the fact that data in a warehouse are extracted from several source systems. Thus, data must be taken from these sources, transformed to fit the data warehouse model, and loaded into the data warehouse. This process is called **extraction, transformation, and loading** (ETL), and it has been proven crucial for the success of a data warehousing project. However, in spite of the work carried out in this topic, again, there is still no consensus on a methodology for ETL design, and most problems are solved in an ad hoc manner. There exist, however, several proposals regarding ETL conceptual design. We study the design and implementation of ETL processes in Chap. 8.

Data analytics is the process of exploiting the contents of a data warehouse in order to provide essential information to the decision-making process. Three main tools can be used for this. **Data mining** consists in a series of statistical techniques that analyze the data in a warehouse in order to discover useful knowledge that is not easy to obtain from the original data. **Key performance indicators** (KPIs) are measurable organizational objectives that are used for characterizing how an organization is performing. Finally, **dashboards** are interactive reports that present the data in a warehouse, including the KPIs, in a visual way, providing an overview of the performance of an organization for decision-support purposes. We study data analytics in Chap. 9.

Designing a data warehouse is a complex endeavor that needs to be carefully carried out. As for operational databases, several phases are needed to design a data warehouse, where each phase addresses specific considerations that must be taken into account. As mentioned above, these phases are requirements specification, conceptual design, logical design, and physical design. There are three different approaches to requirements specification, which differ on how requirements are collected: from users, by analyzing source systems, or by combining both. The choice on the particular approach followed determines how the subsequent phase of conceptual design is undertaken. We study in Chap. 10 a method for data warehouse design.

By the beginning of this century, the foundational concepts of data warehouse systems were mature and consolidated. Starting from these concepts, the field has been steadily growing in many different ways. On the one hand, new kinds of data and data models have been introduced. Some of them have been successfully implemented into commercial and open-source systems. This is the case of spatial data. On the other hand, new architectures are being explored for coping with the massive amount of information that must be processed in today's decision-support systems. We comment on these issues in the next sections.

1.2   Spatial and Spatiotemporal Data Warehouses

Over the years, **spatial data** has been increasingly used in various areas, like public administration, transportation networks, environmental systems, and public health, among others. Spatial data can represent either *objects* located on the Earth's surface, such as mountains, cities, and rivers, or geographic *phenomena*, such as temperature, precipitation, and altitude. Spatial data can also represent nongeographic data, that is, data located in other spatial frames such as a human body, a house, or an engine. The amount of spatial data available is growing considerably due to technological advances in areas such as remote sensing and global navigation satellite systems (GNSS), namely, the Global Positioning System (GPS) and the Galileo system.

Management of spatial data is carried out by **spatial databases** or **geographic information systems** (GISs). Since the latter are used for storing and manipulating *geographic* objects and phenomena, we shall use the more general term *spatial databases* in the following. Spatial databases are used to store spatial data located in a two- or three-dimensional space. These systems provide a set of functions and operators for querying and manipulating spatial data. Queries may refer to spatial characteristics of individual objects, such as their area or perimeter, or may require complex operations on two or more spatial objects. **Topological relationships** between spatial objects, such as intersection, touches, and crosses, are essential in spatial applications. For example, two roads may intersect, two countries may touch because they have a common border, or a road may cross a dessert. An important characteristic of topological relationships is that they do not change when the underlying space is distorted through rotation, scaling, and similar operations.

Spatial databases offer sophisticated capabilities for the management of spatial data, including spatial index structures, storage management, and dynamic query formulation. However, similarly to conventional operational databases, they are typically targeted toward daily operations. Therefore, spatial databases are not well suited to support the decision-making process. As a consequence, a new field, called **spatial data warehouses**, emerged as a combination of the spatial database and data warehouse technologies.

Spatial data warehouses provide improved data analysis, visualization, and manipulation. This kind of analysis is called **spatial OLAP** (SOLAP), conveying a reference to the ability of exploring spatial data through map navigation and aggregation, as it is performed in OLAP with tables and charts. We study spatial data warehouses in Chap. 11.

Most applications focus on the analysis of data produced by objects like customers, suppliers, and so on, assuming that these objects are *static*, in the sense that their position in space and time is not relevant for the application at hand. Nevertheless, many applications require the analysis of data about **moving objects**, that is, objects that change their position in space and time. The possibilities and interest of mobility data analysis have expanded dramatically with the availability of positioning devices. Traffic data, for example, can be captured as a collection of sequences of positioning signals transmitted by the cars' GPS along their itineraries. Although such sequences can be very long, they are often processed by being divided in segments of movement called **trajectories**, which are the unit of interest in the analysis of movement data. Extending data warehouses to cope with trajectory data leads to the notion of **trajectory data warehouses**. These are studied in Chap. 12.

1.3 New Domains and Challenges

Nowadays, the availability of enormous amounts of data is calling for a shift in the way data warehouse and business intelligence practices have been carried out since the 1990s. It is becoming clear that for certain kinds of business intelligence applications, the traditional approach, where day-to-day business data produced in an organization are collected in a huge common repository for data analysis, needs to be revised, to account for efficiently handling large-scale data. In many emerging domains where business intelligence practices are gaining acceptance, such as social networks or geospatial data analytics, massive-scale data sources are becoming common, posing new challenges to the data warehouse research community. In addition, new database architectures are gaining momentum. Parallelism is becoming a must for large data warehouse processing. Column-store database systems (like MonetDB and Vertica) and in-memory database systems (like SAP HANA) are strong candidates for data warehouse architectures since they deliver much better performance than classic row-oriented databases for fact tables with a large number of attributes. The MapReduce programming model is also becoming increasingly popular, challenging traditional parallel database management systems architectures. Even though at the time of writing this book it is still not clear if this approach can be applied to all kinds of data warehouse and business intelligence applications, many large data warehouses have been built based on this model. As an example, the Facebook data warehouse was built using Hadoop (an open-source implementation of MapReduce). Chapter 13 discusses these new data warehousing challenges.

We already commented that the typical method of loading data into a data warehouse is through an ETL process. This process pulls data from source systems periodically (e.g., daily, weekly, or monthly), obtaining a

snapshot of the business data at a given moment in time. These data are
then used for refreshing the contents of the data warehouse. Historically,
this process has been considered acceptable, since in the early days of data
warehousing it was almost impossible to obtain real-time, continuous feeds
from production systems. Moreover, it was difficult to get consistent, reliable
results from query analysis if warehouse data were constantly changing.
However, nowadays the user requirements have changed: business intelligence
applications constantly need current and up-to-date information. In addition,
while in those early days only selected users accessed the data warehouse, in
today's web-based architectures the number of users has been constantly
growing. Moreover, modern data warehouses need to remain available 24/7,
without a time window when access could be denied. In summary, the need of
near real-time data warehousing is challenging ETL technology. To approach
real time, the time elapsed between a relevant application event and its
consequent action (called the data latency) needs to be minimized. Therefore,
to support real-time business intelligence, **real-time data warehouses** are
needed. We study these kinds of data warehouses also in Chap. 13.

The above are not the only challenges for data warehousing and OLAP in
the years to come. There is also a need to keep up with new application
requirements. For example, the web is changing the way in which data
warehouses are being designed, used, and exploited. For some data analysis
tasks (like worldwide price evolution of some product), the data contained
in a conventional data warehouse may not suffice. External data sources,
like the web, can provide useful multidimensional information, although
usually too volatile to be permanently stored. The **semantic web** aims at
representing web content in a machine-processable way. The basic layer of
the data representation for the semantic web recommended by the World
Wide Web Consortium (W3C) is the Resource Description Framework
(RDF), on top of which the Web Ontology Language (OWL) is based.
In a semantic web scenario, domain ontologies (defined in RDF or some
variant of OWL) define a common terminology for the concepts involved in a
particular domain. Semantic annotations are especially useful for describing
unstructured, semistructured, and textual data. Many applications attach
metadata and semantic annotations to the information they produce (e.g.,
in medical applications, medical imaging, and laboratory tests). Thus, large
repositories of semantically annotated data are currently available, opening
new opportunities for enhancing current decision-support systems. The data
warehousing technology must be prepared to handle semantic web data.
In this book, we study semantic web and unstructured data warehouses in
Chap. 14.

Finally, there are many interesting topics in the data warehouse domain
that are still under development. Among them, we can mention temporal
data warehouses, 3D/4D spatial data warehouses, text and multimedia data
warehouses, and graph data warehouses. Although all of them are strong
candidates to play a relevant role in the data warehousing field, due to space

reasons, in this book we decided to address mature technologies and provide brief comments on those topics in Chap. 15.

1.4   Review Questions

1.1 Why are traditional databases called operational or transactional? Why are these databases inappropriate for data analysis?

1.2 Discuss four main characteristics of data warehouses.

1.3 Describe the different components of a multidimensional model, that is, facts, measures, dimensions, and hierarchies.

1.4 What is the purpose of online analytical processing (OLAP) systems and how are they related to data warehouses?

1.5 Specify the different steps used for designing a database. What are the specific concerns addressed in each of these phases?

1.6 Explain the advantages of using a conceptual model when designing a data warehouse.

1.7 What is the difference between the star and the snowflake schemas?

1.8 Specify several techniques that can be used for improving performance in data warehouse systems.

1.9 What is the extraction, transformation, and loading (ETL) process?

1.10 What languages can be used for querying data warehouses?

1.11 Describe what is meant by the term **data analytics**. Give examples of techniques that are used for exploiting the content of data warehouses.

1.12 Why do we need a method for data warehouse design?

1.13 What is spatial data? What is spatiotemporal data? Give examples of applications for which such kinds of data are important.

1.14 Explain the differences between spatial databases and spatial data warehouses.

1.15 What is big data and how is it related to data warehousing? Give examples of technologies that are used in this context.

1.16 Describe why it is necessary to take into account web data in the context of data warehousing. Motivate your answer by elaborating an example application scenario.

Chapter 2
Database Concepts

This chapter introduces the basic database concepts, covering modeling, design, and implementation aspects. Section 2.1 begins by describing the concepts underlying database systems and the typical four-step process used for designing them, starting with requirements specification, followed by conceptual, logical, and physical design. These steps allow a separation of concerns, where requirements specification gathers the requirements about the application and its environment, conceptual design targets the modeling of these requirements from the perspective of the users, logical design develops an implementation of the application according to a particular database technology, and physical design optimizes the application with respect to a particular implementation platform. Section 2.2 presents the Northwind case study that we will use throughout the book. In Sect. 2.3, we review the entity-relationship model, a popular conceptual model for designing databases. Section 2.4 is devoted to the most used logical model of databases, the relational model. Finally, physical design considerations for databases are covered in Sect. 2.5.

The aim of this chapter is to provide the necessary knowledge to understand the remaining chapters in this book, making it self-contained. However, we do not intend to be comprehensive and refer the interested reader to the many textbooks on the subject.

2.1 Database Design

Databases constitute the core component of today's information systems. A **database** is a shared collection of logically related data, and a description of that data, designed to meet the information needs and support the activities of an organization. A database is deployed on a **database management system** (DBMS), which is a software system used to define, create, manipulate, and administer a database.

A. Vaisman and E. Zimányi, *Data Warehouse Systems*, Data-Centric Systems and Applications, DOI 10.1007/978-3-642-54655-6_2,
© Springer-Verlag Berlin Heidelberg 2014

Designing a database system is a complex undertaking typically divided into four phases, described next.

- **Requirements specification** collects information about the users' needs with respect to the database system. A large number of approaches for requirements specification have been developed by both academia and practitioners. These techniques help to elicit necessary and desirable system properties from prospective users, to homogenize requirements, and to assign priorities to them. During this phase, the active participation of users will increase their satisfaction with the delivered system and avoid errors, which can be very expensive to correct if the subsequent phases have already been carried out.
- **Conceptual design** aims at building a user-oriented representation of the database that does not contain any implementation considerations. This is done by using a **conceptual model** in order to identify the relevant concepts of the application at hand. The entity-relationship model is one of the most often used conceptual models for designing database applications. Alternatively, object-oriented modeling techniques can also be applied, based on the UML (Unified Modeling Language) notation.

  Conceptual design can be performed using two different approaches, according to the complexity of the system and the developers' experience:

  - **Top-down design:** The requirements of the various users are merged before the design process begins, and a unique schema is built. Afterward, a separation of the views corresponding to individual users' requirements can be performed. This approach can be difficult and expensive for large databases and inexperienced developers.
  - **Bottom-up design:** A separate schema is built for each group of users with different requirements, and later, during the view integration phase, these schemas are merged to form a global conceptual schema for the entire database. This is the approach typically used for large databases.

- **Logical design** aims at translating the conceptual representation of the database obtained in the previous phase into a particular **logical model** common to several DBMSs. Currently, the most common logical model is the relational model. Other logical models include the object-relational model, the object-oriented model, and the semistructured model. In this book, we focus on the relational model. To ensure an adequate logical representation, we specify a set of suitable mapping rules that transform the constructs in the conceptual model to appropriate structures of the logical model.
- **Physical design** aims at customizing the logical representation of the database obtained in the previous phase to a **physical model** targeted

to a particular DBMS platform. Common DBMSs include SQL Server, Oracle, DB2, MySQL, and PostgreSQL, among others.

A major objective of this four-level process is to provide **data independence**, that is, to ensure as much as possible that schemas in upper levels are unaffected by changes to schemas in lower levels. Two kinds of data independence are typically defined. **Logical data independence** refers to the immunity of the conceptual schema to changes in the logical schema. For example, rearranging the structure of relational tables should not affect the conceptual schema, provided that the requirements of the application remain the same. **Physical data independence** refers to the immunity of the logical schema to changes in the physical one. For example, physically sorting the records of a file on a disk does not affect the conceptual or logical schema, although this modification may be perceived by the user through a change in response time.

In the following sections, we briefly describe the entity-relationship model and the relational models to cover the most widely used conceptual and logical models, respectively. We then address physical design considerations. Before doing this, we introduce the use case we will use throughout the book, which is based on the popular Northwind relational database.[1] In this chapter, we explain the database design concepts using this example. In the next chapter, we will use a data warehouse derived from this database, over which we will explain the data warehousing and OLAP concepts.

2.2 The Northwind Case Study

The Northwind company exports a number of goods. In order to manage and store the company data, a relational database must be designed. The main characteristics of the data to be stored are the following:

- Customer data, which must include an identifier, the customer's name, contact person's name and title, full address, phone, and fax.
- Employee data, including the identifier, name, title, title of courtesy, birth date, hire date, address, home phone, phone extension, and a photo. Photos will be stored in the file system, and a path to the photo is required. Further, employees report to other employees of higher level in the company's organization.
- Geographic data, namely, the territories where the company operates. These territories are organized into regions. For the moment, only the

---

[1]This database can be downloaded from http://northwinddatabase.codeplex.com/. Notice that in this book, we do not consider the tables CustomerDemographics and CustomerCustomerDemo, which are empty, and in addition, we removed the space in the name of the table Order Details.

territory and region description must be kept. An employee can be assigned to several territories, but these territories are not exclusive to an employee: Each employee can be linked to multiple territories, and each territory can be linked to multiple employees.

- Shipper data, that is, information about the companies that Northwind hires to provide delivery services. For each one of them, the company name and phone number must be kept.
- Supplier data, including the company name, contact name and title, full address, phone, fax, and home page.
- Data about the products that Northwind trades, such as identifier, name, quantity per unit, unit price, and an indication if the product has been discontinued. In addition, an inventory is maintained, which requires to know the number of units in stock, the units ordered (i.e., in stock but not yet delivered), and the reorder level (i.e., the number of units in stock such that when it is reached, the company must produce or acquire). Products are further classified into categories, each of which has a name, a description, and a picture. Each product has a unique supplier.
- Data about the sale orders. The information required includes the identifier, the date at which the order was submitted, the required delivery date, the actual delivery date, the employee involved in the sale, the customer, the shipper in charge of its delivery, the freight cost, and the full destination address. An order can contain many products, and for each of them, the unit price, the quantity, and the discount that may be given must be kept.

2.3   Conceptual Database Design

The entity-relationship (ER) model is one of the most often used conceptual models for designing database applications. Although there is general agreement about the meaning of the various concepts of the ER model, a number of different visual notations have been proposed for representing these concepts. Appendix A shows the notations we use in this book.

Figure 2.1 shows the ER model for the Northwind database. We next introduce the main ER concepts using this figure.

Entity types are used to represent a set of real-world objects of interest to an application. In Fig. 2.1, Employees, Orders, and Customers are examples of entity types. An object belonging to an entity type is called an **entity** or an **instance**. The set of instances of an entity type is called its **population**. From the application point of view, all entities of an entity type have the same characteristics.

In the real world, objects do not live in isolation; they are related to other objects. **Relationship types** are used to represent these associations between objects. In our example, Supplies, ReportsTo, and HasCategory

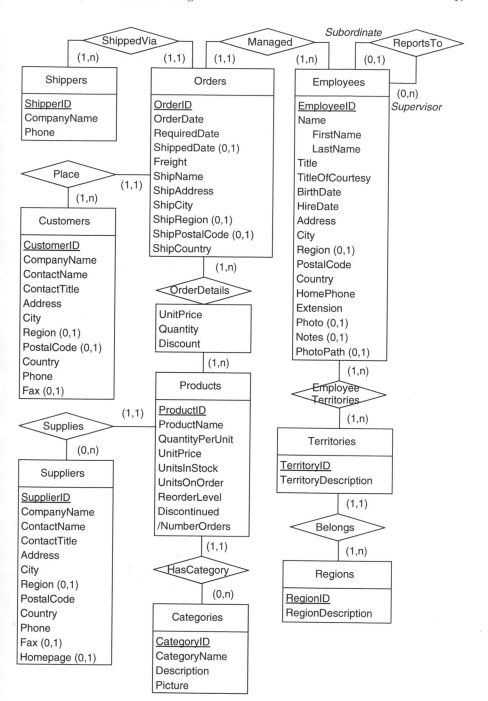

Fig. 2.1 Conceptual schema of the Northwind database

are examples of relationship types. An association between objects of a relationship type is called a **relationship** or an **instance**. The set of associations of a relationship type is called its **population**.

The participation of an entity type in a relationship type is called a **role** and is represented by a line linking the two types. Each role of a relationship type has associated with it a pair of **cardinalities** describing the minimum and maximum number of times that an entity may participate in that relationship type. For example, the role between Products and Supplies has cardinalities (1,1), meaning that each product participates exactly once in the relationship type. The role between Supplies and Suppliers has cardinality (0,n), meaning that a supplier can participate between 0 and n times (i.e., an undetermined number of times) in the relationship. On the other hand, the cardinality (1,n) between Orders and OrderDetails means that each order can participate between 1 and n times in the relationship type. A role is said to be **optional** or **mandatory** depending on whether its minimum cardinality is 0 or 1, respectively. Further, a role is said to be **monovalued** or **multivalued** depending on whether its maximum cardinality is 1 or n, respectively.

A relationship type may relate two or more object types: It is called **binary** if it relates two object types and ***n*-ary** if it relates more than two object types. In Fig. 2.1, all relationship types are binary. Depending on the maximum cardinality of each role, binary relationship types can be categorized into **one-to-one**, **one-to-many**, and **many-to-many** relationship types. In Fig. 2.1, the relationship type Supplies is a one-to-many relationship, since one product is supplied by at most one supplier, whereas a supplier may supply several products. On the other hand, the relationship type OrderDetails is many-to-many, since an order is related to one or more products, while a product can be included in many orders.

It may be the case that the same entity type is related more than once in a relationship type, as is the case for the ReportsTo relationship type. In this case, the relationship type is called **recursive**, and **role names** are necessary to distinguish between the different roles of the entity type. In Fig. 2.1, Subordinate and Supervisor are role names.

Both objects and the relationships between them have a series of structural characteristics that describe them. **Attributes** are used for recording these characteristics of entity or relationship types. For example, in Fig. 2.1, Address and Homepage are attributes of Suppliers, while UnitPrice, Quantity, and Discount are attributes of OrderDetails.

Like roles, attributes have associated **cardinalities**, defining the number of values that an attribute may take in each instance. Since most of the time the cardinality of an attribute is (1,1), we do not show this cardinality in our schema diagrams. Thus, each supplier will have exactly one Address, while they may have at most one Homepage. Therefore, its cardinality is (0,1). In this case, we say the attribute is **optional**. When the cardinality is (1,1), we say that the attribute is **mandatory**. Similarly, attributes are called **monovalued** or **multivalued** depending on whether they may take at most one or several values, respectively. In our example, all attributes are monovalued. However, if it is the case that a customer has one or more phones, then the attribute Phone will be labeled (1,n).

Further, attributes may be composed of other attributes, as shown by the attribute Name of the entity type Employees in our example, which is composed of FirstName and LastName. Such attributes are called **complex attributes**, while those that do not have components are called **simple attributes**. Finally, some attributes may be **derived**, as shown for the attribute NumberOrders of Products. This means that the number of orders in which a product participates may be derived using a formula that involves other elements of the schema and stored as an attribute. In our case, the derived attribute records the number of times that a particular product participates in the relationship OrderDetails.

A common situation in real-world applications is that one or several attributes uniquely identify a particular object; such attributes are called **identifiers**. In Fig. 2.1, identifiers are underlined; for example, EmployeeID is the identifier of the entity type Employees, meaning that every employee has a unique value for this attribute. In the figure, all entity type identifiers are simple, that is, they are composed of only one attribute, although it is common to have identifiers composed of two or more attributes.

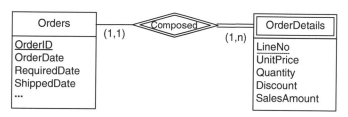

Fig. 2.2 Relationship type OrderDetails modeled as a weak entity type

Entity types that do not have an identifier of their own are called **weak entity types** and are represented with a double line on its name box. In contrast, regular entity types that do have an identifier are called **strong entity types**. In Fig. 2.1, there are no weak entity types. However, note that the relationship OrderDetails between Orders and Products can be modeled as shown in Fig. 2.2.

A weak entity type is dependent on the existence of another entity type, called the **identifying** or **owner entity type**. The relationship type that relates a weak entity type to its owner is called the **identifying relationship type** of the weak entity type. A relationship type that is not an identifying relationship type is called a **regular relationship type**. Thus, in Fig. 2.2, Orders is the owner entity type for the weak entity type OrderDetails, and Composed is its identifying relationship type. As shown in the figure, the identifying relationship type and the role that connects it to the weak entity type are distinguished by their double lines. Note that identifying relationship types have cardinality (1,1) in the role of the weak entity type and may have (0,n) or (1,n) cardinality in the role of the owner.

A weak entity type typically has a **partial identifier**, which is a set of attributes that uniquely identifies weak entities that are related to the same owner entity. An example is the attribute LineNo of OrderDetails, which stores the line number of each product in an order. Therefore, the same number can appear several times in different orders, although it is unique within each order. As shown in the figure, partial identifier attributes are underlined with a dashed line.

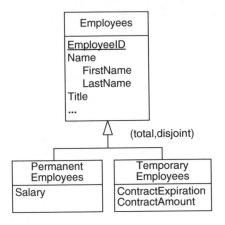

Fig. 2.3 Entity type Employees and two subtypes

Finally, owing to the complexity of conceptualizing the real world, human beings usually refer to the same concept using several different perspectives with different abstraction levels. The **generalization** (or **is-a**) **relationship** captures such a mental process. It relates two entity types, called the **supertype** and the **subtype**, meaning that both types represent the same concept at different levels of detail. The Northwind database does not include a generalization. To give an example, consider Fig. 2.3, in which we have a supertype, Employees, and two subtypes, PermanentEmployees and TemporaryEmployees. The former has an additional attribute Salary, and the latter has attributes ContractExpiration and ContractAmount.

Generalization has three essential characteristics. The first one is **population inclusion**, meaning that every instance of the subtype is also an instance of the supertype. In our example, this means that every temporary employee is also an employee of the Northwind company. The second characteristic is **inheritance**, meaning that all characteristics of the supertype (e.g., attributes and roles) are inherited by the subtype. Thus, in our example, temporary employees also have, for instance, a name and a title. Finally, the third characteristic is **substitutability**, meaning that each time an instance of the supertype is required (e.g., in an operation or in a query), an instance of the subtype can be used instead.

Generalization may also be characterized according to two criteria. On the one hand, a generalization can be either **total** or **partial**, depending on whether every instance of the supertype is also an instance of one of the subtypes. In Fig. 2.3, the generalization is total, since employees are either permanent or temporary. On the other hand, a generalization can be either **disjoint** or **overlapping**, depending on whether an instance may belong to one or several subtypes. In our example, the generalization is disjoint, since a temporary employee cannot be a permanent one.

2.4 Logical Database Design

In this section, we describe the most used logical data model for databases, that is, the relational model. We also study two well-known query languages for the relational model: the relational algebra and SQL.

2.4.1 The Relational Model

Relational databases have been successfully used for several decades for storing information in many application domains. In spite of alternative database technologies that have appeared in the last decades, the relational model is still the most often used approach for storing persistent information, particularly the information that is crucial for the day-to-day operation of an organization.

Much of the success of the relational model, introduced by Codd in 1970, is due to its simplicity, intuitiveness, and its foundation on a solid formal theory: The relational model builds on the concept of a mathematical relation, which can be seen as a table of values and is based on set theory and first-order predicate logic. This mathematical foundation allowed the design of declarative query languages and a rich spectrum of optimization techniques that led to efficient implementations. Note that in spite of this, only in the early 1980s, the first commercial relational DBMS (RDBMS) appeared.

The relational model has a simple data structure, a **relation** (or **table**) composed of one or several **attributes** (or **columns**). Thus, a **relational schema** describes the structure of a set of relations. Figure 2.4 shows a relational schema that corresponds to the conceptual schema of Fig. 2.1. As we will see later in this section, this relational schema is obtained by applying a set of translation rules to the corresponding ER schema. The relational schema of the Northwind database is composed of a set of relations, such as Employees, Customers, and Products. Each of these relations is composed of several attributes. For example, EmployeeID, FirstName, and LastName are

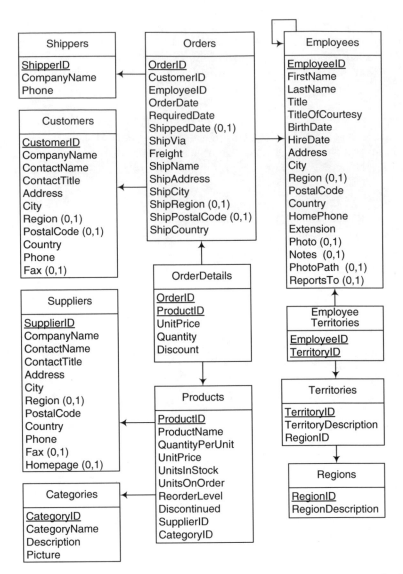

Fig. 2.4 A relational schema that corresponds to the Northwind conceptual schema in Fig. 2.1

some attributes of the relation **Employees**. In what follows, we use the notation $R.A$ to indicate the attribute A of relation R.

In the relational model, each attribute is defined over a **domain**, or **data type**, that is, a set of values with an associated set of operations, the most typical ones are integer, float, date, and string. One important restriction of the model is that attributes must be atomic and monovalued. Thus, complex attributes like Name of the entity type Employees in Fig. 2.1 must be split into atomic values, like FirstName and LastName in the table of the same name in Fig. 2.4. Therefore, a relation R is defined by a schema $R(A_1 : D_1, A_2 : D_2, \ldots, A_n : D_n)$, where R is the name of the relation, and each attribute A_i is defined over the domain D_i. The relation R is associated with a set of **tuples** (or **rows** if we see the relation as a table) $(t_1, t_2, \ldots, t_n)$. This set of tuples is a subset of the Cartesian product $D_1 \times D_2 \times \cdots \times D_n$, and it is sometimes called the **instance** or **extension** of R. The **degree** (or **arity**) of a relation is the number of attributes n of its relation schema.

The relational model allows several types of **integrity constraints** to be defined declaratively.

- An attribute may be defined as being **non-null**, meaning that **null values** (or blanks) are not allowed in that attribute. In Fig. 2.4, only the attributes marked with a cardinality (0,1) allow null values.
- One or several attributes may be defined as a **key**, that is, it is not allowed that two different tuples of the relation have identical values in such columns. In Fig. 2.4, keys are underlined. A key composed of several attributes is called a **composite key**; otherwise, it is a **simple key**. In Fig. 2.4, the table Employees has a simple key, EmployeeID, while the table EmployeeTerritories has a composite key, composed of EmployeeID and TerritoryID. In the relational model, each relation must have a **primary key** and may have other **alternate keys**. Further, the attributes composing the primary key do not accept null values.
- **Referential integrity** specifies a link between two tables (or twice the same table), where a set of attributes in one table, called the **foreign key**, references the primary key of the other table. This means that the values in the foreign key must also exist in the primary key. In Fig. 2.4, referential integrity constraints are represented by arrows from the referencing table to the table that is referenced. For example, the attribute EmployeeID in table Orders references the primary key of the table Employees. This ensures that every employee appearing in an order also appears in the table Employees. Note that referential integrity may involve foreign keys and primary keys composed of several attributes.
- Finally, a **check constraint** defines a predicate that must be valid when adding or updating a tuple in a relation. For example, a check constraint can be used to verify that in table Orders the values of attributes OrderDate and RequiredDate for a given order are such that OrderDate $\leq$ RequiredDate. Note that many DBMSs restrict check constraints to a single tuple: references to data stored in other tables or in other tuples of the same table are not allowed. Therefore, check constraints can be used only to verify simple constraints.

As can be seen, the above declarative integrity constraints do not suffice to express the many constraints that exist in any application domain. Such constraints must then be implemented using triggers. A **trigger** is a named event-condition-action rule that is automatically activated when a relation is updated. In this book, we shall see several examples of integrity constraints implemented using triggers.

Notice that triggers can also be used to compute derived attributes. Figure 2.1 shows a derived attribute NumberOrders in the entity type Products. If we want to implement this derived attribute in the table of the same name in Fig. 2.4, a trigger will update the value of the attribute each time there is an insert, update, or delete in table OrderDetails.

The translation of a conceptual schema (written in the ER or any other conceptual model) to an equivalent relational schema is called a *mapping*. This is a well-known process, implemented in most database design tools. These tools use conceptual schemas to facilitate database design and then automatically translate the conceptual schemas to logical ones, mainly into the relational model. This process includes the definition of the tables in various RDBMSs.

We now outline seven rules that are used to map an ER schema into a relational one.

Rule 1: A strong entity type E is mapped to a table T containing the simple monovalued attributes and the simple components of the monovalued complex attributes of E. The identifier of E defines the primary key of T. T also defines non-null constraints for the mandatory attributes. Note that additional attributes will be added to this table by subsequent rules.

For example, the strong entity type Products in Fig. 2.1 is mapped to the table Products in Fig. 2.4, with key ProductID.

Rule 2: Let us consider a weak entity type W, with owner (strong) entity type O. Assume W_{id} is the partial identifier of W, and O_{id} is the identifier of O. W is mapped in the same way as a strong entity type, that is, to a table T. In this case, T must also include O_{id} as an attribute, with a referential integrity constraint to attribute $O.O_{id}$. Moreover, the identifier of T is the union of W_{id} and O_{id}.

As an example, the weak entity type OrderDetails in Fig. 2.2 is mapped to the table of the same name in Fig. 2.5. The key of the latter is composed of the attributes OrderID and LineNo, where the former is a foreign key referencing table Orders.

Rule 3: A regular binary one-to-one relationship type R between two entity types E_1 and E_2, which are mapped, respectively, to tables T_1 and T_2 is mapped embedding the identifier of T_1 in T_2 as a foreign key. In addition, the simple monovalued attributes and the simple components of the monovalued complex attributes of R are also included in T_2. This table also defines non-null constraints for the mandatory attributes.

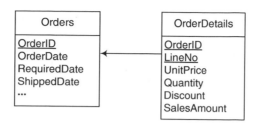

Fig. 2.5 Relationship translation of the schema in Fig. 2.2

Note that, in general, we can embed the key of T_1 in T_2, or conversely, the key of T_2 in T_1. The choice depends on the cardinality of the roles of R. In Fig. 2.1, assume the relationship Supplies has cardinalities (1,1) with Products and (0,1) with Suppliers. Embedding ProductID in table Suppliers may result in several tuples of the Suppliers relation containing null values in the ProductID column, since there can be suppliers that do not supply any product. Thus, to avoid null values, it would be preferable to embed SupplierID in table Products.

Rule 4: Consider a regular binary one-to-many relationship type R relating entity types E_1 and E_2, where T_1 and T_2 are the tables resulting from the mapping of these entities. R is mapped embedding the key of T_2 in table T_1 as a foreign key. In addition, the simple monovalued attributes and the simple components of the monovalued complex attributes of R are included in T_1, defining the corresponding non-null constraints for the mandatory attributes.

As an example, in Fig. 2.1, the one-to-many relationship type Supplies between Products and Suppliers is mapped by including the attribute SupplierID in table Products, as a foreign key, as shown in Fig. 2.4.

Rule 5: Consider a regular binary many-to-many relationship type R between entity types E_1 and E_2, such that T_1 and T_2 are the tables resulting from the mapping of the former entities. R is mapped to a table T containing the keys of T_1 and T_2, as foreign keys. The key of T is the union of these keys. Alternatively, the relationship identifier, if any, may define the key of the table. T also contains the simple monovalued attributes and the simple components of the monovalued complex attributes of R and also defines non-null constraints for the mandatory attributes.

In Fig. 2.1, the many-to-many relationship type EmployeeTerritories between Employees and Territories is mapped to a table with the same name containing the identifiers of the two tables involved, as shown in Fig. 2.4.

Rule 6: A multivalued attribute of an entity or relationship type E is mapped to a table T, which also includes the identifier of the entity or relationship type. A referential integrity constraint relates this identifier to the table associated with E. The primary key of T is composed of all of its attributes.

Suppose that in Fig. 2.1, the attribute Phone of Customers is multivalued. In this case, the attribute is mapped to a table CustomerPhone with attributes CustomerID and Phone both composing the primary key.

Rule 7: A generalization relationship between a supertype E_1 and subtype E_2 can be dealt with in three different ways:

Rule 7a: Both E_1 and E_2 are mapped, respectively, to tables T_1 and T_2, in which case the identifier of E_1 is propagated to T_2. A referential integrity constraint relates this identifier to T_1.

Rule 7b: Only E_1 is associated with a table T_1, which contains all attributes of E_2. All these attributes become optional in T_1.

Rule 7c: Only E_2 is associated with a table T_2, in which case all attributes E_1 are inherited in T_2.

As an example, the possible translations of the generalization given in Fig. 2.3 are shown in Fig. 2.6.

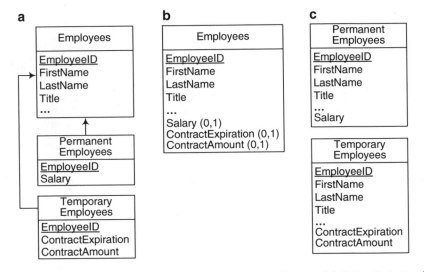

Fig. 2.6 Three possible translations of the schema in Fig. 2.3. (**a**) Using Rule 7a. (**b**) Using Rule 7b. (**c**) Using Rule 7c

Note that the generalization type (total vs. partial and disjoint vs. overlapping) may preclude one of the above three approaches. For example, the third possibility is not applicable for partial generalizations. Also, note that the semantics of the partial, total, disjoint, and overlapping characteristics are not fully captured by this translation mechanism. The conditions must be implemented when populating the relational tables. For example, assume a table T and two tables T_1 and T_2 resulting from the mapping of a total and overlapping generalization. Referential integrity does not fully capture the semantics. It must be ensured, among other conditions, that when deleting an element from T, this element is also deleted from T_1 and T_2 (since it can exist in both tables). Such constraints are typically implemented with triggers.

Applying these mapping rules to the ER schema given in Fig. 2.1 yields the relational schema shown in Fig. 2.4. Note that the above rules apply in the general case; however, other mappings are possible. For example, binary one-to-one and one-to-many relationships may be represented by a table of its own, using Rule 5. The choice between alternative representation depends on the characteristics of the particular application at hand.

It must be noted that there is a significant difference in expressive power between the ER model and the relational model. This difference may be explained by the fact that the ER model is a *conceptual* model aimed at expressing concepts as closely as possible to the users' perspective, whereas the relational model is a *logical* model targeted toward particular implementation platforms. Several ER concepts do not have a correspondence in the relational model, and thus they must be expressed using only the available concepts in the model, that is, relations, attributes, and the related constraints. This translation implies a semantic loss in the sense that data invalid in an ER schema are allowed in the corresponding relational schema, unless the latter is supplemented by additional constraints. Many of such constraints must be manually coded by the user using mechanisms such as triggers or stored procedures. Furthermore, from a user's perspective, the relational schema is much less readable than the corresponding ER schema. This is crucial when one is considering schemas with hundreds of entity or relationship types and thousands of attributes. This is not a surprise, since this was the reason for devising conceptual models back in the 1970s, that is, the aim was to better understand the semantics of large relational schemas.

2.4.2 Normalization

When considering a relational schema, we must determine whether or not the relations in the schema have potential redundancies and thus may induce anomalies in the presence of insertions, updates, and deletions.

For example, assume that in relation OrderDetails in Fig. 2.7a, each product, no matter the order, is associated with a discount percentage. Here, the discount information for a product p will be repeated for all orders in which p appears. Thus, this information will be redundant. Just associating once the product and the discount would be enough to convey the same information.

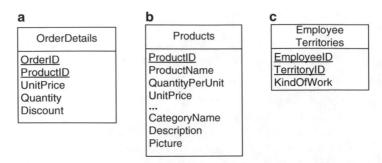

Fig. 2.7 Examples of relations that are not normalized

Consider now the relation **Products** in Fig. 2.7b, which is a variation of the relation with the same name in Fig. 2.4. In this case, we have included the category information (name, description, and picture) in the **Products** relation. It is easy to see that such information about a category is repeated for each product with the same category. Therefore, when, for example, the description of a category needs to be updated, we must ensure that all tuples in the relation **Products**, corresponding to the same category, are also updated; otherwise, there will be inconsistencies.

Finally, let us analyze the relation **EmployeeTerritories** in Fig. 2.7c, where an additional attribute **KindOfWork** has been added with respect to the relation with the same name in Fig. 2.4. Assume that an employee can do many kinds of work, independently of the territories in which she carries out her work. Thus, the information about the kind of work of an employee will be repeated as many times as the number of territories she is assigned to.

Dependencies and normal forms are used to describe the redundancies above. A **functional dependency** is a constraint between two sets of attributes in a relation. Given a relation R and two sets of attributes X and Y in R, a functional dependency $X \to Y$ holds if and only if in all the tuples of the relation, each value of X is associated with at most one value of Y. In this case, it is said that X *determines* Y. Note that a key is a particular case of a functional dependency, where the set of attributes composing the key functionally determines all of the attributes in the relation. In what follows, F will denote a set of functional dependencies and F^+ the set F augmented with the set of all functional dependencies that can be inferred from F. For example, if $A \to B$ and $B \to C$, then $A \to C$ can be inferred.

The redundancies in Fig. 2.7a, b can be expressed by means of functional dependencies. For example, in the relation **OrderDetails** in Fig. 2.7a, there is the functional dependency **ProductID** $\to$ **Discount**. Also, in the relation **Products** in Fig. 2.7b, we have the functional dependencies **ProductID** $\to$ **CategoryID** and **CategoryID** $\to$ **CategoryName**.

The redundancy in the relation **EmployeeTerritories** in Fig. 2.7c is captured by another kind of dependency. Given two sets of attributes X and Y in a relation R, a **multivalued dependency** $X \to\to Y$ holds if the value of X

determines a set of values for Y, which is independent of $R \setminus XY$, where '$\setminus$' indicates the set difference. In this case, we say that X *multidetermines* Y. In the relation in Fig. 2.7c, the multivalued dependency EmployeeID $\to\to$ KindOfWork holds, and consequently, TerritoryID $\to\to$ KindOfWork. Functional dependencies are special cases of multivalued dependencies, that is, every functional dependency is also a multivalued dependency. A multivalued dependency $X \to\to Y$ is said to be *trivial* if either $Y \subseteq X$ or $X \cup Y = R$; otherwise, it is *nontrivial*. This is straightforward since in those cases, $R \setminus XY = \varnothing$ holds.

A **normal form** is an integrity constraint aimed at guaranteeing that a relational schema satisfies particular properties. Since the beginning of the relational model in the 1970s, many types of normal forms have been defined. In addition, normal forms have also been defined for other models, such as the entity-relationship model. In the following, we consider only five normal forms that are widely used in relational databases.

As already said, the relational model allows only attributes that are atomic and monovalued. This restriction is called the **first normal form**.

The **second normal form** prevents redundancies such as those in the table OrderDetails in Fig. 2.7a. To define the second normal form, we need the concept of partial dependency, defined next:

- An attribute A in a relation schema R is called a **prime attribute** if it belongs to some key in R. Otherwise, it is called **nonprime**.
- In a relation schema R such that X is a key of R, $Z \subset X$, and Y is a nonprime attribute, a dependency of the form $Z \to Y$ is called **partial**.

A relation R is in the second normal form with respect to a set of functional dependencies F if F^+ does not contain any partial dependency. In other words, a relation schema is in the second normal form if every nonprime attribute is fully functionally dependent on every key in R. In the example of Fig. 2.7a, Product $\to$ Discount is a partial dependency. Therefore, the relation is not in the second normal form. To make the relation comply with the second normal form, the attribute Discount must be removed from the table OrderDetails and must be added to the table Products in order to store the information about the product discounts.

The **third normal form** prevents redundancies such as those in the table Products in Fig. 2.7b. In order to define the third normal form, we must define one additional concept:

- A dependency $X \to Z$ is **transitive** if there is a set of attributes Y such that the dependencies $X \to Y$ and $Y \to Z$ hold.

A relation R is in the third normal form with respect to a set of functional dependencies F if it is in the second normal form and there are no transitive dependencies between a key and a nonprime attribute in F^+. The table Product above is not in the third normal form, since there is a transitive dependency from ProductID to CategoryID and from CategoryID to

CategoryName. To make the relation comply with the third normal form, the attributes dependent on CategoryID must be removed from the table and a table Category like the one in Fig. 2.4 must be used to store the data about categories.

The **Boyce-Codd normal form** prevents redundancies originated in functional dependencies. A relation R is in the Boyce-Codd normal form with respect to a set of functional dependencies F if for every nontrivial dependency $X \to Y$ in F^+, X is a key or contains a key of R. Note that all relations in Fig. 2.4 are in the Boyce-Codd normal form.

The **fourth normal form** prevents redundancies such as those in the table EmployeeTerritories in Fig. 2.7c. A relation R is in the fourth normal form with respect to a set of functional and multivalued dependencies F if for every nontrivial dependency $X \to\to Y$ in F^+, X is a key or contains a key of R. The table above is not in the fourth normal form, since, for example, there is a multivalued dependency from EmployeeID to KindOfWork, and EmployeeID is not a key of the relation. To make the relation comply with the fourth normal form, the attribute KindOfWork must be removed from the table, and a table EmpWork(EmployeeID, KindOfWork) must be added.

2.4.3 Relational Query Languages

Data stored in a relational database can be queried using different formalisms. Two kinds of query languages are typically defined. In a *procedural* language, a query is specified indicating the operations needed to retrieve the desired result. In a *declarative* language, the user only indicates *what* she wants to retrieve, leaving to the DBMS the task of determining the equivalent procedural query that is to be executed.

In this section, we introduce the relational algebra and SQL, which we will be using in many parts of this book. While the relational algebra is a procedural query language, SQL is a declarative one.

Relational Algebra

The relational algebra is a collection of operations for manipulating relations. These operations can be of two kinds: **unary**, which receive as argument a relation and return another relation, or **binary**, which receive as argument two relations and return a relation. As the operations always return relations, the algebra is *closed*, and operations can be combined in order to compute the answer to a query. Further, another classification of the operations is as follows. **Basic** operations cannot be derived from any combination of other operations, while **derived** operations are a shorthand for a sequence of basic operations, defined in order to make queries easier to express. In what follows, we describe the relational algebra operations.

Unary Operations

The **projection** operation, denoted $\pi_{C_1,...,C_n}(R)$, returns the columns $C_1, \ldots, C_n$ from the relation R. Thus, it can be seen as a vertical partition of R into two relations: one containing the columns mentioned in the expression and the other containing the remaining columns. For the relational database given in Fig. 2.4, an example of a projection is:

$\pi_{\text{FirstName, LastName, HireDate}}(\text{Employees})$.

This operation returns the three specified attributes from the Employees table.

The **selection** operation, denoted $\sigma_\phi(R)$, returns the tuples from the relation R that satisfy the Boolean condition ϕ. In other words, it partitions a table horizontally into two sets of tuples: the ones that do satisfy the condition and the ones that do not. Therefore, the structure of R is kept in the result.

A selection operation over the relational database given in Fig. 2.4 is:

$\sigma_{\text{HireDate}\geq'01/01/1992'\wedge\text{HireDate}\leq'31/12/1994'}(\text{Employees})$.

This operation returns the employees hired between 1992 and 1994.

Since the result of a relational algebra operation is a relation, it can be used as input for another operation. To make queries easier to read, sometimes it is useful to use temporary relations to store intermediate results. We will use the notation $T \leftarrow Q$ to indicate that relation T stores the result of query Q. Thus, combining the two previous examples, we can ask for the first name, last name, and hire date of all employees hired between 1992 and 1994. The query reads:

Temp1 $\leftarrow \sigma_{\text{HireDate}\geq'01/01/1992'\wedge\text{HireDate}\leq'31/12/1994'}(\text{Employees})$
Result $\leftarrow \pi_{\text{FirstName, LastName, HireDate}}(\text{Temp1})$.

The result is given next.

FirstName	LastName	HireDate
Nancy	Davolio	1992-05-01
Andrew	Fuller	1992-08-14
Janet	Leverling	1992-04-01
...	...	...

The **rename** operation, denoted $\rho_{A_1\rightarrow B_1,...,A_k\rightarrow B_k}(R)$, returns a relation where the attributes $A_1, \ldots, A_k$ in R are renamed to $B_1, \ldots, B_k$, respectively. Therefore, the resulting relation has the same tuples as the relation R, although the schema of both relations is different.

Binary Operations

These operations are based on the set theory classic operations. We first introduce the basic binary operations, namely, union, difference, and Cartesian product, and then discuss the most used binary operation, the join, and its variants inner and outer join.

The **union** operation, denoted $R_1 \cup R_2$, takes two relations with the same schema and returns the tuples that are in R_1, in R_2, or in both, removing duplicates. If the schemas are compatible, but the attribute names differ, the attributes must be renamed before applying the operation.

The union can be used to express queries like "Identifier of employees from the UK, or who are reported by an employee from the UK," which reads:

UKEmps ← $\sigma_{Country='UK'}$(Employees)
Result1 ← $\pi_{EmployeeID}$(UKEmp)
Result2 ← $\rho_{ReportsTo \rightarrow EmployeeID}$($\pi_{ReportsTo}$(UKEmps))
Result ← Result1 ∪ Result2.

Relation UKEmps contains the employees from the UK. Result1 contains the projection of the former over EmployeeID, and Result2 contains the EmployeeID of the employees reported by an employee from the UK. The union of Result1 and Result2 yields the desired result.

The **difference** operation, denoted $R_1 \setminus R_2$, takes two relations with the same schema and returns the tuples that are in R_1 but not in R_2. As in the case of the union, if the schemas are compatible, but the attribute names differ, the attributes must be renamed before applying the operation.

We use the difference to express queries like "Identifier of employees who are not reported by an employee from the UK," which is written as follows:

Result ← $\pi_{EmployeeID}$(Employees) \ Result2.

The first term of the difference contains the identifiers of all employees. From this set, we subtract the set composed of the identifiers of all employees reported by an employee from the UK, already computed in Result2.

The **Cartesian product**, denoted $R_1 \times R_2$, takes two relations and returns a new one, whose schema is composed of all the attributes in R_1 and R_2 (renamed if necessary) and whose instance is obtained concatenating each pair of tuples from R_1 and R_2. Thus, the number of tuples in the result is the product of the cardinalities of both relations.

Although by itself the Cartesian product is usually meaningless, it is very useful when combined with a selection. For example, suppose we want to retrieve the name of the products supplied by suppliers from Brazil. To answer this query, we use the Cartesian product to combine data from the tables Products and Suppliers. For the sake of clarity, we only keep the attributes we need: ProductID, ProductName, and SupplierID from table Products, and SupplierID and Country from table Suppliers. Attribute SupplierID in one of the relations must be renamed, since a relation cannot have two attributes with the same name:

Temp1 ← $\pi_{\text{ProductID,ProductName,SupplierID}}$(Products)
Temp2 ← $\rho_{\text{SupplierID}\rightarrow\text{SupID}}(\pi_{\text{SupplierID,Country}}$(Suppliers))
Temp3 ← Temp1 × Temp2.

The Cartesian product combines each product with all the suppliers, as given in the table below.

ProductID	ProductName	SupplierID	SupID	Country
1	Chai	1	1	UK
2	Chang	1	1	UK
...	...	...	...	...
17	Alice Mutton	7	2	USA
18	Carnarvon Tigers	7	2	USA

We are only interested in the rows that relate a product to its supplier (e.g., the first two rows). The other ones are not useful (e.g., the last row combines a product supplied by supplier 7 with the country of supplier 2). We then filter the meaningless tuples, select the ones corresponding to suppliers from Brazil, and project the column we want, that is, ProductName:

Temp4 ← $\sigma_{\text{SupplierID=SupID}}$(Temp3)
Result ← $\pi_{\text{ProductName}}(\sigma_{\text{Country='Brazil'}}$(Temp4))

The **join** operation, denoted $R_1 \bowtie_\phi R_2$, where ϕ is a condition over the attributes in R_1 and R_2, takes two relations and returns a new one, whose schema consists in all attributes of R_1 and R_2 (renamed if necessary) and whose instance is obtained concatenating each pair of tuples from R_1 and R_2 that satisfy condition ϕ. The operation is basically a combination of a Cartesian product and a selection.

Using the join operation, the query "Name of the products supplied by suppliers from Brazil" will read:

Temp1 ← $\rho_{\text{SupplierID}\rightarrow\text{SupID}}$(Suppliers)
Result ← $\pi_{\text{ProductName}}(\sigma_{\text{Country='Brazil'}}$(Product $\bowtie_{\text{SupplierID=SupID}}$ Temp1)).

Note that the join combines the Cartesian product in Temp3 and the selection in Temp4 in a single operation, making the expression much more concise.

There are a number of variants of the join operation. An **equijoin** is a join $R_1 \bowtie_\phi R_2$ such that condition ϕ states the equality between *all* the attributes with the same name in R_1 and R_2. If we project the result of an equijoin over all the columns in $R_1 \cup R_2$ (i.e., all the attributes in R_1 and R_2, without duplicates), we have the **natural join**, denoted $R_1 * R_2$.

For example, the query "List all product names and category names" reads:

Temp ← Products * Categories
Result ← $\pi_{ProductName,CategoryName}$(Temp).

The first query performs the natural join between relations **Products** and **Categories**. The attributes in **Temp** are all the attributes in **Product**, plus all the attributes in **Categories**, except for **CategoryID**, which is in both relations, so only one of them is kept. The second query performs the final projection.

The joins introduced above are known as **inner joins**, since tuples that do no match the join condition are eliminated. In many practical cases, we need to keep in the result all the tuples of one or both relations, independently of whether or not they satisfy the join condition. For these cases, a set of operations, called **outer joins**, were defined. There are three kinds of outer joins: left outer join, right outer join, and full outer join.

The **left outer join**, denoted $R \bowtie S$, performs the join as defined above, but instead of keeping only the matching tuples, it keeps every tuple in R (the relation of the left of the operation). If a tuple in R does not satisfy the join condition, the tuple is kept, and the attributes of S in the result are filled with null values.

As an example, the query "Last name of employees, together with the last name of their supervisor, or null if the employee has no supervisor," reads in relational algebra:

Supervisors ← $\rho_{EmployeeID \rightarrow SupID, LastName \rightarrow SupLastName}$(Employees)
Result   ← $\pi_{EmployeeID,LastName,SupID,SupLastName}$(
              Employees $\bowtie_{ReportsTo=SupID}$ Supervisors)

The result is given in the following table.

EmployeeID	LastName	SupID	SupLastName
1	Davolio	2	Fuller
2	Fuller	NULL	NULL
3	Leverling	2	Fuller
...	...	...	...

We can see that employee 2 does not report to anybody; therefore, his supervisor data contain null values.

The **right outer join**, denoted $R \bowtie S$, is analogous to the left outer join, except that the tuples that are kept are the ones in S. The **full outer join**, denoted $R \bowtie S$, keeps all the tuples in both R and S.

Suppose that in the previous example, we also require the information of the employees who do not supervise anyone. Then, we would have:

$\pi_{EmployeeID,LastName,SupID,SupLastName}$(Employees $\bowtie_{ReportsTo=SupID}$ Supervisors)

The result is shown in the table below.

EmployeeID	LastName	SupID	SupLastName
1	Davolio	2	Fuller
2	Fuller	NULL	NULL
3	Leverling	2	Fuller
. . .	. . .	. . .	. . .
NULL	NULL	1	Davolio
NULL	NULL	3	Leverling
. . .	. . .	. . .	. . .

With respect to the left outer join shown above, the above table has, in addition, tuples of the form (NULL, NULL, SupervID, SupLastName), which correspond to employees who do not supervise any other employee.

SQL: A Query Language for Relational DBMSs

SQL (structured query language) is the most common language for creating, manipulating, and retrieving data from relational DBMSs. SQL is composed of several sublanguages. The **data definition language** (DDL) is used to define the schema of a database. The **data manipulation language** (DML) is used to query a database and to modify its content (i.e., to add, update, and delete data in a database). In what follows, we present a summary of the main features of SQL that we will use in this book. For a detailed description, we encourage the reader to check in the references provided at the end of this chapter.

Below, we show the SQL DDL command for defining table Orders in the relational schema of Fig. 2.4. The basic DDL statement is CREATE TABLE, which creates a relation and defines the data types of the attributes, the primary and foreign keys, and the constraints:

```
CREATE TABLE Orders (
    OrderID INTEGER PRIMARY KEY,
    CustomerID INTEGER NOT NULL,
    EmployeeID INTEGER NOT NULL,
    OrderDate DATE NOT NULL,
    RequiredDate DATE NOT NULL,
    ShippedDate DATE NOT NULL,
    ShippedVia INTEGER NOT NULL,
    Freight MONEY NOT NULL,
    ShipName CHARACTER VARYING (50) NOT NULL,
    ShipAddress CHARACTER VARYING (50) NOT NULL,
    ShipCity CHARACTER VARYING (50) NOT NULL,
    ShipRegion CHARACTER VARYING (50),
    ShipPostalCode CHARACTER VARYING (30),
```

```
ShipCountry CHARACTER VARYING (50) NOT NULL,
FOREIGN KEY (CustomerID) REFERENCES Customers(CustomerID),
FOREIGN KEY (ShippedVia) REFERENCES Shippers(ShipperID),
FOREIGN KEY (EmployeeID) REFERENCES Employees(EmployeeID),
CHECK (OrderDate <= RequiredDate) )
```

SQL provides a DROP TABLE statement for deleting a table and an ALTER TABLE statement for modifying the structure of a table.

The **DML** part of SQL is used to insert, update, and delete tuples from the database tables. For example, the following INSERT statement

```
INSERT INTO Shippers(CompanyName, Phone)
VALUES ('Federal Express', '02 752 75 75')
```

adds a new shipper in the Northwind database. This tuple is modified by the following UPDATE statement:

```
UPDATE Shippers
SET      CompanyName='Fedex'
WHERE  CompanyName='Federal Express'
```

Finally, the new shipper is removed in the following DELETE statement:

```
DELETE FROM Shippers WHERE CompanyName='Fedex'
```

SQL also provides statements for retrieving data from the database. The basic structure of an SQL expression is:

```
SELECT ⟨ list of attributes ⟩
FROM    ⟨ list of tables ⟩
WHERE ⟨ condition ⟩
```

where ⟨ list of attributes ⟩ indicates the attribute names whose values are to be retrieved by the query, ⟨ list of tables ⟩ is a list of the relation names that will be included in the query, and ⟨ condition ⟩ is a Boolean expression that must be satisfied by the tuples in the result. The semantics of an SQL expression

```
SELECT R.A, S.B
FROM    R, S
WHERE R.B = S.A
```

is given by the relational algebra expression

$$\pi_{R.A,S.B}(\sigma_{R.B=S.A}(R \times S)),$$

that is, the SELECT clause is analogous to a projection π, the WHERE clause is a selection σ, and the FROM clause indicates the Cartesian product $\times$ between all the tables included in the clause.

It is worth noting that an SQL query, opposite to a relational algebra one, returns a set *with duplicates* (or a bag). Therefore, the keyword DISTINCT must be used to remove duplicates in the result. For example, the query "Countries of customers" must be written:

```
SELECT DISTINCT Country
FROM    Customers
```

This query returns the set of countries of the Northwind customers, without duplicates. If the DISTINCT keyword is removed from the above query, then it would return as many results as the number of customers in the database.

As another example, the query "Identifier, first name, and last name of the employees hired between 1992 and 1994," which we presented when discussing the projection and selection operations, reads in SQL:

```
SELECT EmployeeID, FirstName, LastName
FROM    Employees
WHERE HireDate >= '1992-01-01' and HireDate <= '1994-12-31'
```

The binary operations of the relational algebra are supported in SQL: union, intersection, difference, and the different kinds of joins. Recall the query "Identifiers of employees from the UK, or who are reported by an employee from the UK." In SQL, it would read:

```
SELECT EmployeeID
FROM    Employees
WHERE Country='UK'
    UNION
SELECT ReportsTo
FROM    Employees
WHERE Country='UK'
```

Notice that the UNION in the above query removes duplicates in the result, whereas the UNION ALL will keep them, that is, if an employee is from the UK and is reported by at least one employee from the UK, it will appear twice in the result.

The join operation can be, of course, implemented as a projection of a selection over the Cartesian product of the relations involved. However, in general, it is easier and more efficient to use the join operation. For example, the query "Name of the products supplied by suppliers from Brazil" can be written as follows:

```
SELECT ProductName
FROM    Products P, Suppliers S
WHERE P.SupplierID = S.SupplierID AND Country = 'Brazil'
```

An alternative formulation of this query is as follows:

```
SELECT ProductName
FROM    Products P JOIN Suppliers S ON P.SupplierID = S.SupplierID
WHERE Country = 'Brazil'
```

On the other hand, the outer join operations must be explicitly stated in the FROM clause. For example, the query "First name and last name of employees, together with the first name and last name of their supervisor,

or null if the employee has no supervisor" can be implemented in SQL using
the LEFT OUTER JOIN operation:

```
SELECT  E.FirstName, E.LastName, S.FirstName, S.LastName
FROM    Employees E LEFT OUTER JOIN Employees S
        ON E.ReportsTo = S.EmployeeID
```

Analogously, we can use the FULL OUTER JOIN operation to also include
in the answer the employees who do not supervise anybody:

```
SELECT  E.FirstName, E.LastName, S.FirstName, S.LastName
FROM    Employees E FULL OUTER JOIN Employees S
        ON E.ReportsTo = S.EmployeeID
```

As shown in the examples above, SQL is a declarative language, that
is, we tell the system *what* we want, whereas in relational algebra, being
a procedural language, we must specify *how* we will obtain the result. In
fact, SQL query processors usually translate an SQL query into some form
of relational algebra in order to optimize it.

Aggregation and Sorting in SQL

Aggregation is used to summarize information from multiple tuples into a
single one. For this, tuples are grouped and then an aggregate function
is applied to every group. In data warehouses, particularly in OLAP,
aggregation plays a crucial role, as we will study in subsequent chapters
of this book.

Typically, DBMSs provide five basic aggregate functions, namely, COUNT,
SUM, MAX, MIN, and AVG. The COUNT function returns the number
of tuples in each group. Analogously, the functions SUM, MAX, MIN,
and AVG are applied over numeric attributes and return, respectively, the
sum, maximum value, minimum value, and average of the values in those
attributes, for each group. Note that all of these functions can be applied to
the whole table considered as a group. Further, the functions MAX and MIN
can also be used with attributes that have nonnumeric domains if a total
order is defined over the values in the domain, as is the case for strings.

The general form of an SQL query with aggregate functions is as follows:

```
SELECT    ⟨ list of grouping attributes ⟩ ⟨ list of aggr_funct(attribute) ⟩
FROM      ⟨ list of tables ⟩
WHERE     ⟨ condition ⟩
GROUP BY  ⟨ list of grouping attributes ⟩
HAVING    ⟨ condition over groups ⟩
ORDER BY  ⟨ list of attributes ⟩
```

An important restriction is that if there is a GROUP BY clause, the
SELECT clause must contain *only* aggregates or grouping attributes. The
HAVING clause is analogous to the WHERE clause, except that the condition

is applied over each group rather than over each tuple. Finally, the result can be sorted with the ORDER BY clause, where every attribute in the list can be ordered either in ascending or descending order by specifying ASC or DESC, respectively.

We next present some examples of aggregate SQL queries, more complex ones will be presented later in the book. We start with the query "Total number of orders handled by each employee, in descending order of number of orders. Only list employees that handled more than 100 orders."

```
SELECT    EmployeeID, COUNT(*) AS OrdersByEmployee
FROM      Orders
GROUP BY  EmployeeID
HAVING    COUNT(*) > 100
ORDER BY  COUNT(*) DESC
```

The result below shows that employee 4 is the one that handled the highest number of orders. Basically, to process this query, the SQL engine sorts the table Orders by EmployeeID (the attribute associated with the aggregate function) and counts the number of tuples corresponding to the same employee, by scanning the ordered table. Thus, for example, there are 156 tuples in the table Orders with EmployeeID equal to 4.

EmployeeID	OrdersByEmployee
4	156
3	127
1	123
8	104

Consider now the query "For customers from Germany, list the total quantity of each product ordered. Order the result by customer ID, in ascending order, and by quantity of product ordered, in descending order."

```
SELECT    C.CustomerID, D.ProductID, SUM(Quantity) AS TotalQty
FROM      Orders O JOIN Customers C ON O.CustomerID = C.CustomerID
          JOIN OrderDetails D ON O.OrderID = D.OrderID
WHERE     C.Country = 'Germany'
GROUP BY  C.CustomerID, D.ProductID
ORDER BY  C.CustomerID ASC, SUM(Quantity) DESC
```

This query starts by joining three tables: Orders, Customers (where we have the country information), and OrderDetails (where we have the quantity ordered for each product in each order). Then, the query selects the customers from Germany. We then group by pairs (CustomerID, ProductID), and for each group, we take the sum in the attribute Quantity. Below, we show the result and how it is built. On the table to the left, we show the result of the join, ordered by CustomerID and ProductID. This is the state of the table just before grouping takes place. Each tuple represents the appearance of a product in an order, along with the quantity of the product in the order. We can see that customer BLAUS has three orders of product 21. On the table to the right, we see the final result: there is only one tuple for BLAUS and product 21, with a total of 23 units ordered.

CustomerID	ProductID	Quantity
ALFKI	58	40
ALFKI	39	21
...	...	...
BLAUS	21	12
BLAUS	21	8
BLAUS	21	3
...	...	...

CustomerID	ProductID	TotalQty
ALFKI	58	40
ALFKI	39	21
...	...	...
BLAUS	21	23
...	...	...

Subqueries

A **subquery** (or a **nested query**) is an SQL query used within a SELECT, FROM, or WHERE clause. The external query is called the **outer query**. In the WHERE clause, this is typically used to look for a certain value in a database, and we use this value in a comparison condition through two special predicates: IN and EXISTS (and their negated versions, NOT IN and NOT EXISTS).

As an example of the IN predicate, let us consider the query "Identifier and name of products ordered by customers from Germany." The query is written as follows:

```
SELECT ProductID, ProductName
FROM    Products P
WHERE P.ProductID IN (
         SELECT D.ProductID
         FROM    Orders O JOIN Customers C ON O.CustomerID = C.CustomerID
         JOIN OrderDetails D ON O.OrderID = D.OrderID
         WHERE C.Country = 'Germany' )
```

The inner query computes the products ordered by customers from Germany. This returns a bag of product identifiers. The outer query scans the Products table, and for each tuple, it compares the product identifier with the set of identifiers returned by the inner query. If the product is in the set, the product identifier and the product name are listed.

The query above can be formulated using the EXISTS predicate, yielding what are denoted as **correlated nested queries**, as follows:

```
SELECT ProductID, ProductName
FROM   Products P
WHERE  EXISTS (
       SELECT *
       FROM   Orders O JOIN Customers C ON
              O.CustomerID = C.CustomerID JOIN
              OrderDetails D ON O.OrderID = D.OrderID
       WHERE C.Country = 'Germany' AND D.ProductID = P.ProductID )
```

Note that in the outer query, we define an alias (or variable) P. For each tuple in Products, the variable P in the inner query is instantiated with the values in such tuple; if the result set of the inner query instantiated in this way is not empty, the EXISTS predicate evaluates to true, and the values of the attributes ProductID and ProductName are listed. The process is repeated for all tuples in Products. Below, we show the result of the query, obviously the same in both ways of writing it.

ProductID	ProductName
1	Chai
2	Chang
3	Aniseed Syrup
...	...

To illustrate the NOT EXISTS predicate, consider the query "Names of customers who have not purchased any product," which is written as follows:

```
SELECT C.CompanyName
FROM   Customers C
WHERE  NOT EXISTS (
       SELECT *
       FROM   Orders O
       WHERE C.CustomerID = O.CustomerID )
```

Here, the NOT EXISTS predicate will evaluate to true if when P is instantiated in the inner query, the query returns the empty set. The result is as follows.

CompanyName
FISSA Fabrica Inter. Salchichas S.A.
Paris spécialités

Views

A **view** is just an SQL query that is stored in the database with an associated name. Thus, views are like virtual tables. A view can be created from one or many tables or other views, depending on the SQL query that defines it.

Views can be used for various purposes. They are used to structure data in a way that users find it natural or intuitive. They can also be used to restrict access to data such that users can have access only to the data they need. Finally, views can also be used to summarize data from various tables, which can be used, for example, to generate reports.

Views are created with the **CREATE VIEW** statement. To create a view, a user must have appropriate system privileges to modify the database schema. Once a view is created, it can then be used in a query as any other table.

For example, the following statement creates a view **CustomerOrders** that computes for each customer and order the total amount of the order:

```
CREATE VIEW CustomerOrders AS (
        SELECT    O.CustomerID, O.OrderID,
                  SUM(D.Quantity * D.UnitPrice) AS Amount
        FROM      Orders O, OrderDetails D
        WHERE     O.OrderID = D.OrderID
        GROUP BY O.CustomerID, O.OrderID )
```

This view is used in the next query to compute for each customer the maximum amount among all her orders:

```
SELECT    CustomerID, MAX(Amount) AS MaxAmount
FROM      CustomerOrders
GROUP BY CustomerID
```

The result of this query is as follows.

CustomerID	MaxAmount
ALFKI	1086.00
ANATR	514.40
ANTON	2156.50
AROUT	4675.00
BERGS	4210.50
...	...

As we will see in Chap. 7, views can be materialized, that is, they can be physically stored in a database.

Common Table Expressions

A **common table expression** (CTE) is a temporary table defined within an SQL statement. Such temporary tables can be seen as views within the scope of the statement. A CTE is typically used when a user does not have the necessary privileges for creating a view.

For example, the following query

```
WITH CustomerOrders AS (
       SELECT    O.CustomerID, O.OrderID,
                 SUM(D.Quantity * D.UnitPrice) AS Amount
       FROM      Orders O, OrderDetails D
       WHERE     O.OrderID = D.OrderID
       GROUP BY O.CustomerID, O.OrderID )
SELECT     CustomerID, MAX(Amount) AS MaxAmount
FROM       CustomerOrders
GROUP BY CustomerID
```

combines in a single statement the view definition and the subsequent query given in the previous section. It is worth noting that several temporary tables can be defined in the WITH clause. We will extensively use CTEs throughout this book.

2.5 Physical Database Design

The objective of **physical database design** is to specify how database records are stored, accessed, and related in order to ensure adequate performance of a database application. Physical database design is related to query processing, physical data organization, indexing, transaction processing, and concurrency management, among other characteristics. In this section, we provide a very brief overview of some of those issues that will be addressed in detail for data warehouses in Chap. 7.

Physical database design requires one to know the specificities of the given application, in particular the properties of the data and the usage patterns of the database. The latter involves analyzing the transactions or queries that are run frequently and will have a significant impact on performance, the transactions that are critical to the operations of the organization, and the periods of time during which there will be a high demand on the database (called the **peak load**). This information is used to identify the parts of the database that may cause performance problems.

There are a number of factors that can be used to measure the performance of database applications. **Transaction throughput** is the number of transactions that can be processed in a given time interval. In some systems, such as electronic payment systems, a high transaction throughput is critical. **Response time** is the elapsed time for the completion of a single transaction. Minimizing response time is essential from the user's point of view. Finally, **disk storage** is the amount of disk space required to store the database files. However, a compromise usually has to be made among these factors. From a general perspective, this compromise implies the following factors:

1. **Space-time trade-off:** It is often possible to reduce the time taken to perform an operation by using more space, and vice versa. For example,

a compression algorithm can be used to reduce the space occupied by a large file, but this implies extra time for the decompression process.

2. **Query-update trade-off:** Access to data can be made more efficient by imposing some structure upon it. However, the more elaborate the structure, the more time is taken to build it and to maintain it when its contents change. For example, sorting the records of a file according to a key field allows them to be located more easily, but there is a greater overhead upon insertions to keep the file sorted.

Further, once an initial physical design has been implemented, it is necessary to monitor the system and to tune it as a result of the observed performance and any changes in requirements. Many DBMSs provide utilities to monitor and tune the operations of the system.

As the functionality provided by current DBMSs varies widely, physical design requires one to know the various techniques for storing and finding data that are implemented in the particular DBMS that will be used.

A database is organized on **secondary storage** into one or more **files**, where each file consists of one or several **records** and each record consists of one or several **fields**. Typically, each tuple in a relation corresponds to a record in a file. When a user requests a particular tuple, the DBMS maps this logical record into a physical disk address and retrieves the record into main memory using the file access routines of the operating system.

Data are stored on a computer disk in **disk blocks** (or **pages**) that are set by the operating system during disk formatting. Transfer of data between the main memory and the disk and vice versa takes place in units of disk blocks. DBMSs store data on **database blocks** (or **pages**). One important aspect of physical database design is the need to provide a good match between disk blocks and database blocks, on which logical units such as tables and records are stored. Most DBMSs provide the ability to specify a database block size. The selection of a database block size depends on several issues. For example, most DBMSs manage concurrent access to the records using some kind of locking mechanism. If a record is locked by one transaction that aims at modifying it, then no other transaction will be able to modify this record (however, normally several transactions are able to read a record if they do not try to write it). In some DBMSs, the finest locking granularity is at the page level, not at the record level. Therefore, the larger the page size, the larger the chance that two transactions will request access to entries on the same page. On the other hand, for optimal disk efficiency, the database block size must be equal to or be a multiple of the disk block size.

DBMSs reserve a storage area in the main memory that holds several database pages, which can be accessed for answering a query without reading those pages from the disk. This area is called a **buffer**. When a request is issued to the database, the query processor checks if the required data records are included in the pages already loaded in the buffer. If so, data are read from the buffer and/or modified. In the latter case, the modified pages are marked as such and eventually written back to the disk. If the pages needed to answer the query are not in the buffer, they are read from the disk, probably replacing existing ones in the buffer (if it is full, which is normally the case) using well-known algorithms, for example, replacing the least recently used pages with the new ones. In this way, the buffer acts as a **cache** that the DBMS can access to avoid going to disk, enhancing query performance.

File organization is the physical arrangement of data in a file into records and blocks on secondary storage. There are three main types of file organization. In a **heap** (or **unordered**) file organization, records are placed in the file in the order in which they are inserted. This makes insertion very efficient. However, retrieval is relatively slow, since the various pages of the file must be read in sequence until the required record is found. **Sequential** (or **ordered**) **files** have their records sorted on the values of one or more fields, called **ordering fields**. Ordered files allow fast retrieving of records, provided that the search condition is based on the sorting attribute. However, inserting and deleting records in a sequential file are problematic, since the order must be maintained. Finally, **hash files** use a **hash function** that calculates the address of the block (or **bucket**) in which a record is to be stored, based on the value of one or more attributes. Within a bucket, records are placed in order of arrival. A **collision** occurs when a bucket is filled to its capacity and a new record must be inserted into that bucket. Hashing provides the fastest possible access for retrieving an arbitrary record given the value of its hash field. However, collision management degrades the overall performance.

Independently of the particular file organization, additional access structures called **indexes** are used to speed up the retrieval of records in response to search conditions. Indexes provide efficient ways to access the records based on the **indexing fields** that are used to construct the index. Any field(s) of the file can be used to create an index, and multiple indexes on different fields can be constructed in the same file.

There are many different types of indexes. We describe below some categories of indexes according to various criteria:

- One categorization of indexes distinguishes between **clustered** and **nonclustered indexes**, also called **primary** and **secondary indexes**. In a clustered index, the records in the data file are physically ordered according to the field(s) on which the index is defined. This is not the case for a nonclustered index. A file can have at most one clustered index and in addition can have several nonclustered indexes.
- Indexes can be **single-column** or **multiple-column**, depending on the number of indexing fields on which they are based. When a multiple-column index is created, the order of columns in the index has an impact on data retrieval. Generally, the most restrictive value should be placed first for optimum performance.
- Another categorization of indexes is according to whether they are **unique** or **nonunique**: unique indexes do not allow duplicate values, while this is not the case for nonunique indexes.

- In addition, an index can be **sparse** or **dense**: in a dense index, there is one entry in the index for every data record. This requires data files to be ordered on the indexing key. Opposite to this, a sparse index contains less index entries than data records. Thus, a nonclustered index is always dense, since it is not ordered on the indexing key.
- Finally, indexes can be **single-level** or **multilevel**. When an index file becomes large and extends over many blocks, the search time required for the index increases. A multilevel index attempts to overcome this problem by splitting the index into a number of smaller indexes and maintaining an index to the indexes. Although a multilevel index reduces the number of blocks accessed when one is searching for a record, it also has problems in dealing with insertions and deletions in the index because all index levels are physically ordered files. A **dynamic multilevel index** solves this problem by leaving some space in each of its blocks for inserting new entries. This type of index is often implemented by using data structures called **B-trees** and **B⁺-trees**, which are supported by most DBMSs.

Most DBMSs give the designer the option to set up indexes on any fields, thus achieving faster access at the expense of extra storage space for indexes, and overheads when updating. Because the indexed values are held in a sorted order, they can be efficiently exploited to handle partial matching and range searches, and in a relational system, they can speed up join operations on indexed fields.

We will see in Chap. 7 that distinctive characteristics of data warehouses require physical design solutions that are different from the ones required by DBMSs in order to support heavy transaction loads.

2.6 Summary

This chapter introduced the background database concepts that will be used throughout the book. We started by describing database systems and the usual steps followed for designing them, that is, requirements specification, conceptual design, logical design, and physical design. Then, we presented the Northwind case study, which was used to illustrate the different concepts introduced throughout the chapter. We presented the entity-relationship model, a well-known conceptual model. With respect to logical models, we studied the relational model and also gave the mapping rules that are used to translate an entity-relationship schema into a relational schema. In addition, we briefly discussed normalization, which aims at preventing redundancies and inconsistency in a relational database. Then, we presented two different languages for manipulating relational databases, namely, the relational algebra and SQL. We finished this introduction to database systems by describing several issues related to physical database design.

2.7 Bibliographic Notes

For a general overview of all the concepts covered in this chapter, we refer the reader to the textbook [49]. Other relevant database textbooks are [58, 168]. An overall view of requirements engineering is given in [217]. Conceptual database design is covered in [148] although it is based on UML [17] instead of the entity-relationship model. Logical database design is covered in [198]. A thorough overview of the components of the SQL:1999 standard is given in [133, 135], and later versions of the standard are described in [108, 132, 236]. Physical database design is detailed in [116].

2.8 Review Questions

2.1 What is a database? What is a DBMS?

2.2 Describe the four phases used in database design.

2.3 Define the following terms: entity type, entity, relationship type, relationship, role, cardinality, and population.

2.4 Illustrate with an example each of the following kinds of relationship types: binary, n-ary, one-to-one, one-to-many, many-to-many, and recursive.

2.5 Discuss different kinds of attributes according to their cardinality and their composition. What are derived attributes?

2.6 What is an identifier? What is the difference between a strong and a weak entity type? Does a weak entity type always have an identifying relationship? What is an owner entity type?

2.7 Discuss the different characteristics of the generalization relationship.

2.8 Define the following terms: relation (or table), attribute (or column), tuple (or line), and domain.

2.9 Explain the various integrity constraints that can be described in the relational model.

2.10 Discuss the basic rules for translating an ER schema into a relational schema. Give an example of a concept of the ER model that can be translated into the relational model in different ways.

2.11 Illustrate with examples the different types of redundancy that may occur in a relation. How can redundancy in a relation induce problems in the presence of insertions, updates, and deletions?

2.12 What is the purpose of functional and multivalued dependencies? What is the difference between them?

2.13 What are normal forms? Specify several normal forms that can be defined on relations. For each one of these normal forms, give an example of a relation that does not satisfy the particular normal form.

2.14 Describe the different operations of the relational algebra. Elaborate on the difference between the several types of joins. How can a join be expressed in terms of other operations of the relational algebra?

2.15 What is SQL? What are the sublanguages of SQL?

2.16 What is the general structure of SQL queries? How can the semantics of an SQL query be expressed with the relational algebra?

2.17 Discuss the differences between the relational algebra and SQL. Why is relational algebra an operational language, whereas SQL is a declarative language?

2.18 Explain what duplicates are in SQL and how they are handled.

2.19 Describe the general structure of SQL queries with aggregation and sorting. State the basic aggregation operations provided by SQL.

2.20 What are subqueries in SQL? Give an example of a correlated subquery.

2.21 What are CTEs in SQL? What are they needed for?

2.22 What is the objective of physical database design? Explain some factors that can be used to measure the performance of database applications and the trade-offs that have to be resolved.

2.23 Explain different types of file organization. Discuss their respective advantages and disadvantages.

2.24 What is an index? Why are indexes needed? Explain the various types of indexes.

2.25 What is clustering? What is it used for?

2.9 Exercises

2.1 A French horse race fan wants to set up a database to analyze the performance of the horses as well as the betting payoffs.

A racetrack is described by a name (e.g., Hippodrome de Chantilly), a location (e.g., Chantilly, Oise, France), an owner, a manager, a date opened, and a description. A racetrack hosts a series of horse races.

A horse race has a name (e.g., Prix Jean Prat), a category (i.e., Group 1, 2, or 3), a race type (e.g., thoroughbred flat racing), a distance (in meters), a track type (e.g., turf right-handed), qualification conditions (e.g., 3-year-old excluding geldings), and the first year it took place.

A meeting is held on a certain date and a racetrack and is composed of one or several races. For a meeting, the following information is kept: weather (e.g., sunny, stormy), temperature, wind speed (in km per hour), and wind direction (N, S, E, W, NE, etc.).

Each race of a meeting is given a number and a departure time and has a number of horses participating in it. The application must keep track of the purse distribution, that is, how the amount of prize money is distributed among the top places (e.g., first place: €228,000; second place: €88,000, etc.), and the time of the fastest horse.

Each race at a date offers several betting types (e.g., tiercé, quarté+), each type offering zero or more betting options (e.g., in order, in any order, and bonus for the quarté+). The payoffs are given for a betting type and a base amount (e.g., quarté+ for €2) and specify for each option the win amount and the number of winners.

A horse has a name, a breed (e.g., thoroughbred), a sex, a foaling date (i.e., birth date), a gelding date (i.e., castration date for male horses, if any), a death date (if any), a sire (i.e., father), a dam (i.e., mother), a coat color (e.g., bay, chestnut, white), an owner, a breeder, and a trainer.

A horse that participates in a race with a jockey is assigned a number and carries a weight according to the conditions attached to the race or to equalize the difference in ability between the runners. Finally, the arrival place and the margin of victory of the horses are kept by the application.

(a) Design an ER schema for this application. If you need additional information, you may look at the various existing French horse racing web sites.

(b) Translate the ER schema above into the relational model. Indicate the keys of each relation, the referential integrity constraints, and the non-null constraints.

2.2 A Formula One fan club wants to set up a database to keep track of the results of all the seasons since the first Formula One World championship in 1950.

A season is held on a year, between a starting date and an ending date, has a number of races, and is described by a summary and a set of regulations. A race has a round number (stating the ordering of the race in a season), an official name (e.g., 2013 Formula One Shell Belgian Grand Prix), a race date, a race time (expressed in both local and UTC time), a description of the weather when the race took place, the pole position (consisting of driver name and time realized), and the fastest lap (consisting of driver name, time, and lap number).

Each race of a season belongs to a Grand Prix (e.g., Belgian Grand Prix), for which the following information is kept: active years (e.g., 1950–1956, 1958, etc. for the Belgian Grand Prix), total number of races (58 races as of 2013 for the Belgian Grand Prix), and a short historical description. The race of a season is held on a circuit, described by its name (e.g., Circuit de Spa-Francorchamps), location (e.g., Spa, Belgium), type (such as race, road, street), number of laps, circuit length, race distance (the latter two expressed in kilometers), and lap record (consisting of time, driver, and year). Notice that over the years, the course of the circuits may be modified several times. For example, the Spa-Francorchamps circuit was shortened from 14 to 7 km in 1979. Further, a Grand Prix may use several circuits over the years. For example, the Belgian Grand Prix has been held alternatively in the Spa-Francorchamps, Zolder, and Nivelles circuits.

A team has a name (e.g., Scuderia Ferrari), one or two bases (e.g., Maranello, Italy), and one or two current principals (e.g., Stefano Domenicali). In addition, a team keeps track of its debut (the first Grand Prix entered), the number of races competed, the number of world championships won by constructor and by driver, the highest race finish (consisting of place and number of times), the number of race victories, the number of pole positions, and the number of fastest laps. A team competing in a season has a full name, which typically includes its current sponsor (e.g., Scuderia Ferrari Marlboro from 1997 to 2011), a chassis (e.g., F138), an engine (e.g., Ferrari 056), and a tyre brand (e.g., Bridgestone).

For each driver, the following information is kept: name, nationality, birth date and birth place, number of races entered, number championships won, number of wins, number of podiums, total points in the career, number of pole positions, number of fastest laps, highest race finish (consisting of place and number of times), and highest grid position (consisting of place and number of times). Drivers are hired by teams competing in a season as either main drivers or test drivers. Each team has two main drivers and usually two test drivers, but the number of test drivers may vary from none to six. In addition, although a main driver is usually associated with a team for the whole season, it may only participate in some of the races of the season. A team participating in a season is assigned two consecutive numbers for its main drivers, where the number 1 is assigned to the team that won the constructor's world title the previous season. Further, the number 13 is usually not given to a car, it only appeared once in the Mexican Grand Prix in 1963.

A driver participating in a Grand Prix must participate in a qualifying session, which determines the starting order for the race. The results kept for a driver participating in the qualifying session are the position and the time realized for the three parts (called Q1, Q2, and Q3). Finally, the results kept for a driver participating in a race are the following: position (may be optional), number of laps, time, the reason why the driver retired or was disqualified (both may be optional), and the number of points (scored only for the top eight finishers).

(a) Design an ER schema for this application. In particular, state the identifiers and the derived attributes. Note any unspecified require-ments and integrity constraints, and make appropriate assumptions to make the specification complete. If you need additional informa-tion, you may look at the various existing Formula One web sites.

(b) Translate the ER schema above into the relational model. Indicate the keys of each relation, the referential integrity constraints, and the non-null constraints.

2.3 For each of the relations below:

- Identify the potential redundancies.
- Identify the key(s).
- Determine its normal form.
- Propose a decomposition, if necessary.

(a) SalesManager(EmpNo, Area, FromDate, State, Country), describing the geographical areas in which sales managers operate, with the dependencies

   EmpNo, Area → FromDate
   Area → State, Country

(b) Product(ProductNo, Description, UnitPrice, VATRate, Category), which describes the products sold by a company, with the dependencies

   ProductNo → Description, UnitPrice, VATRate, Category
   Category → VATRate

(c) Assist(TeachingAssist, Professor, Course, Department), which describes the assignment of teaching assistants to professors, courses, and departments, with the dependencies

   TeachingAssist → Professor, Course, Department
   Course, Department → TeachingAssist, Professor
   Professor → Department

(d) Employee(EmpNo, Hobby, Sport), describing the hobbies and sports of employees, with the dependencies

   EmpNo →→ Hobby
   EmpNo →→ Sport

2.4 Consider the following queries to be addressed to the Northwind database. Write in relational algebra queries (a)–(g) and in SQL all the queries.

(a) Name, address, city, and region of employees.
(b) Name of employees and name of customers located in Brussels related through orders that are sent by Speedy Express.
(c) Title and name of employees who have sold at least one of the products "Gravad Lax" or "Mishi Kobe Niku."
(d) Name and title of employees as well as the name and title of the employee to whom they report.
(e) Name of products that were sold by employees or purchased by customers located in London.
(f) Name of employees and name of the city where they live for employees who have sold to customers located in the same city.

(g) Names of products that have not been ordered.
(h) Names of customers who bought all products.
(j) Name of categories and the average price of products in each category.
(k) Identifier and name of the companies that provide more than three products.
(l) Identifier, name, and total sales of employees ordered by employee identifier.
(m) Name of employees who sell the products of more than seven suppliers.

Chapter 3
Data Warehouse Concepts

This chapter introduces the basic concepts of data warehouses. A data warehouse is a particular database targeted toward decision support. It takes data from various operational databases and other data sources and transforms it into new structures that fit better for the task of performing business analysis. Data warehouses are based on a multidimensional model, where data are represented as hypercubes, with dimensions corresponding to the various business perspectives and cube cells containing the measures to be analyzed. In Sect. 3.1, we study the multidimensional model and present its main characteristics and components. Section 3.2 gives a detailed description of the most common operations for manipulating data cubes. In Sect. 3.3, we present the main characteristics of data warehouse systems and compare them against operational databases. The architecture of data warehouse systems is described in detail in Sect. 3.4. As we shall see, in addition to the data warehouse itself, data warehouse systems are composed of back-end tools, which extract data from the various sources to populate the warehouse, and front-end tools, which are used to extract the information from the warehouse and present it to users. In Sect. 3.5, we introduce the design methodology we will use throughout the book. We finish by describing in Sect. 3.6 two representative business intelligence suite of tools, SQL Server and Pentaho.

3.1 Multidimensional Model

The importance of data analysis has been steadily increasing from the early 1990s, as organizations in all sectors are being required to improve their decision-making processes in order to maintain their competitive advantage. Traditional database systems like the ones studied in Chap. 2 do not satisfy the requirements of data analysis. They are designed and tuned to support the daily operations of an organization, and their primary concern is to ensure

A. Vaisman and E. Zimányi, *Data Warehouse Systems*, Data-Centric
Systems and Applications, DOI 10.1007/978-3-642-54655-6_3,
© Springer-Verlag Berlin Heidelberg 2014

fast, concurrent access to data. This requires transaction processing and concurrency control capabilities, as well as recovery techniques that guarantee data consistency. These systems are known as **operational databases** or **online transaction processing** (**OLTP**) systems. The OLTP paradigm is focused on transactions. In the Northwind database example, a simple transaction could involve entering a new order, reserving the products ordered, and, if the reorder point has been reached, issuing a purchase order for the required products. Eventually, a user may want to know the status of a given order. If a database is indexed following one of the techniques described in the previous chapter, a typical OLTP query like the above would require accessing only a few records of the database (and normally will return a few tuples). Since OLTP systems must support heavy transaction loads, their design should prevent update anomalies, and thus, OLTP databases are highly normalized using the techniques studied in Chap. 2. Thus, they perform poorly when executing complex queries that need to join many relational tables together or to aggregate large volumes of data. Besides, typical operational databases contain detailed data and do not include historical data.

The above needs called for a new paradigm specifically oriented to analyze the data in organizational databases to support decision making. This paradigm is called **online analytical processing** (**OLAP**). This paradigm is focused on queries, in particular, analytical queries. OLAP-oriented databases should support a heavy query load. Typical OLAP queries over the Northwind database would ask, for example, for the total sales amount by product and by customer or for the most ordered products by customer. These kinds of queries involve aggregation, and thus, processing them will require, most of the time, traversing all the records in a database table. Indexing techniques aimed at OLTP are not efficient in this case: new indexing and query optimization techniques are required for OLAP. It is easy to see that normalization is not good for these queries, since it partitions the database into many tables. Reconstructing the data would require a high number of joins.

Therefore, the need for a different database model to support OLAP was clear and led to the notion of **data warehouses**, which are (usually) large repositories that consolidate data from different sources (internal and external to the organization), are updated off-line (although as we will see, this is not always the case in modern data warehouse systems), and follow the multidimensional data model. Being dedicated analysis databases, data warehouses can be designed and optimized to efficiently support OLAP queries. In addition, data warehouses are also used to support other kinds of analysis tasks, like reporting, data mining, and statistical analysis.

Data warehouses and OLAP systems are based on the **multidimensional model**, which views data in an n-dimensional space, usually called a **data cube** or a **hypercube**. A data cube is defined by dimensions and facts. **Dimensions** are perspectives used to analyze the data. For example, consider

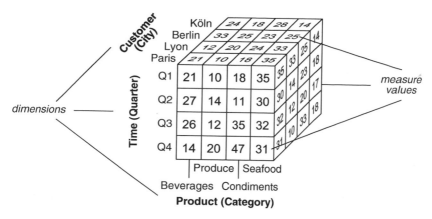

Fig. 3.1 A three-dimensional cube for sales data with dimensions Product, Time, and Customer, and a measure Quantity

the data cube in Fig. 3.1, based on a portion of the Northwind database. We can use this cube to analyze sales figures. The cube has three dimensions: Product, Time, and Customer. A **dimension level** represents the granularity, or level of detail, at which measures are represented for each dimension of the cube. In the example, sales figures are aggregated to the levels Category, Quarter, and City, respectively. Instances of a dimension are called **members**. For example, Seafood and Beverages are members of the Product dimension at the Category level. Dimensions also have associated **attributes** describing them. For example, the Product dimension could contain attributes such as ProductNumber and UnitPrice, which are not shown in the figure.

On the other hand, the **cells** of a data cube, or **facts**, have associated numeric values (we will see later that this is not always the case), called **measures**. These measures are used to evaluate quantitatively various aspects of the analysis at hand. For example, each number shown in a cell of the data cube in Fig. 3.1 represents a measure Quantity, indicating the number of units sold (in thousands) by category, quarter, and customer's city. A data cube typically contains several measures. For example, another measure, not shown in the figure, could be Amount, indicating the total sales amount.

A data cube may be **sparse** or **dense** depending on whether it has measures associated with each combination of dimension values. In the case of Fig. 3.1, this depends on whether all products are bought by all customers during the period of time considered. For example, not all customers may have ordered products of all categories during all quarters of the year. Actually, in real-world applications, cubes are typically sparse.

3.1.1 Hierarchies

We have said that the granularity of a data cube is determined by the combination of the levels corresponding to each axis of the cube. In Fig. 3.1, the dimension levels are indicated between parentheses: Category for the Product dimension, Quarter for the Time dimension, and City for the Customer dimension.

In order to extract strategic knowledge from a cube, it is necessary to view its data at several levels of detail. In our example, an analyst may want to see the sales figures at a finer granularity, such as at the month level, or at a coarser granularity, such as at the customer's country level. **Hierarchies** allow this possibility by defining a sequence of mappings relating lower-level, detailed concepts to higher-level, more general concepts. Given two related levels in a hierarchy, the lower level is called the **child** and the higher level is called the **parent**. The hierarchical structure of a dimension is called the dimension **schema**, while a dimension **instance** comprises the members at all levels in a dimension. Figure 3.2 shows the simplified hierarchies for our cube example. In the next chapter, we give full details of how dimension hierarchies are modeled. In the Product dimension, products are grouped in categories. For the Time dimension, the lowest granularity is Day, which aggregates into Month, which in turn aggregates into Quarter, Semester, and Year. Similarly, for the Customer dimension, the lowest granularity is Customer, which aggregates into City, State, Country, and Continent. It is usual to represent the top of the hierarchy with a distinguished level called All.

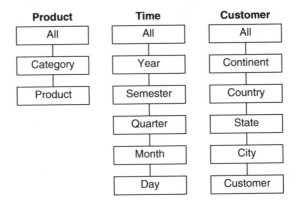

Fig. 3.2 Hierarchies of the Product, Time, and Customer dimensions

At the instance level, Fig. 3.3 shows an example of the Product dimension.[1] Each product at the lowest level of the hierarchy can be mapped to a

---

[1]Note that, as indicated by the ellipses, not all nodes of the hierarchy are shown.

corresponding category. All categories are grouped under a member called all, which is the only member of the distinguished level All. This member is used for obtaining the aggregation of measures for the whole hierarchy, that is, for obtaining the total sales for all products.

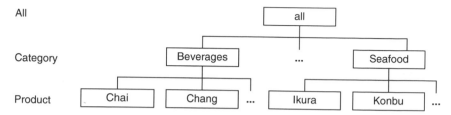

Fig. 3.3 Members of a hierarchy Product → Category

In real-world applications, there exist many kinds of hierarchies. For example, the hierarchy depicted in Fig. 3.3 is **balanced**, since there is the same number of levels from each individual product to the root of the hierarchy. In Chaps. 4 and 5, we shall study these and other kinds of hierarchies in detail, covering both their conceptual representation and their implementation in current data warehouse and OLAP systems.

3.1.2 Measures

Each measure in a cube is associated with an aggregation function that combines several measure values into a single one. Aggregation of measures takes place when one changes the level of detail at which data in a cube are visualized. This is performed by traversing the hierarchies of the dimensions. For example, if we use the Customer hierarchy in Fig. 3.2 for changing the granularity of the data cube in Fig. 3.1 from City to Country, then the sales figures for all customers in the same country will be aggregated using, for example, the SUM operation. Similarly, total sales figures will result in a cube containing one cell with the total sum of the quantities of all products, that is, this corresponds to visualizing the cube at the All level of all dimension hierarchies.

Summarizability refers to the correct aggregation of cube measures along dimension hierarchies, in order to obtain consistent aggregation results. To ensure summarizability, a set of conditions may hold. Below, we list some of these conditions

* **Disjointness of instances:** The grouping of instances in a level with respect to their parent in the next level must result in disjoint subsets. For example, in the hierarchy of Fig. 3.3, a product cannot belong to two

categories. If this were the case, each product sales would be counted twice, one for each category.

- **Completeness:** All instances must be included in the hierarchy and each instance must be related to one parent in the next level. For example, the instances of the Time hierarchy in Fig. 3.2 must contain all days in the period of interest, and each day must be assigned to a month. If this condition were not satisfied, the aggregation of the results would be incorrect, since there would be dates for which sales will not be counted.
- **Correctness:** It refers to the correct use of the aggregation functions. As explained next, measures can be of various types, and this determines the kind of aggregation function that can be applied to them.

According to the way in which they can be aggregated, measures can be classified as follows:

- **Additive measures** can be meaningfully summarized along all the dimensions, using addition. These are the most common type of measures. For example, the measure Quantity in the cube of Fig. 3.1 is additive: it can be summarized when the hierarchies in the Product, Time, and Customer dimensions are traversed.
- **Semiadditive measures** can be meaningfully summarized using addition along *some*, but not all, dimensions. A typical example is that of inventory quantities, which cannot be meaningfully aggregated in the Time dimension, for instance, by adding the inventory quantities for two different quarters.
- **Nonadditive measures** cannot be meaningfully summarized using addition across any dimension. Typical examples are item price, cost per unit, and exchange rate.

Thus, in order to define a measure, it is necessary to determine the aggregation functions that will be used in the various dimensions. This is particularly important in the case of semiadditive and nonadditive measures. For example, a semiadditive measure representing inventory quantities can be aggregated computing the average along the Time dimension and computing the sum along other dimensions. Averaging can also be used for aggregating nonadditive measures such as item price or exchange rate. However, depending on the semantics of the application, other functions such as the minimum, maximum, or count could be used instead.

In order to allow users to interactively explore the cube data at different granularities, optimization techniques based on aggregate precomputation are used. To avoid computing the whole aggregation from scratch each time the data warehouse is queried, OLAP tools implement incremental aggregation mechanisms. However, incremental aggregation computation is not always possible, since this depends on the kind of aggregation function used. This leads to another classification of measures, which we explain next.

- **Distributive measures** are defined by an aggregation function that can be computed in a distributed way. Suppose that the data are partitioned into n sets and that the aggregate function is applied to each set, giving n aggregated values. The function is distributive if the result of applying it to the whole data set is the same as the result of applying a function (not necessarily the same) to the n aggregated values. The usual aggregation functions such as the count, sum, minimum, and maximum are distributive. However, the distinct count function is not. For instance, if we partition the set of measure values $\{3, 3, 4, 5, 8, 4, 7, 3, 8\}$ into the subsets $\{3, 3, 4\}$, $\{5, 8, 4\}$, and $\{7, 3, 8\}$, summing up the result of the distinct count function applied to each subset gives us a result of 8, while the answer over the original set is 5.
- **Algebraic measures** are defined by an aggregation function that can be expressed as a scalar function of distributive ones. A typical example of an algebraic aggregation function is the average, which can be computed by dividing the sum by the count, the latter two functions being distributive.
- **Holistic measures** are measures that cannot be computed from other subaggregates. Typical examples include the median, the mode, and the rank. Holistic measures are expensive to compute, especially when data are modified, since they must be computed from scratch.

3.2 OLAP Operations

As already said, a fundamental characteristic of the multidimensional model is that it allows one to view data from multiple perspectives and at several levels of detail. The OLAP operations allow these perspectives and levels of detail to be materialized by exploiting the dimensions and their hierarchies, thus providing an interactive data analysis environment.

Figure 3.4 presents a possible scenario that shows how an end user can operate over a data cube in order to analyze data in different ways. Later in this section, we present the OLAP operations in detail. Our user starts from Fig. 3.4a, a cube containing quarterly sales quantities (in thousands) by product categories and customer cities for the year 2012.

The user first wants to compute the sales quantities by country. For this, she applies a **roll-up** operation to the Country level along the Customer dimension. The result is shown in Fig. 3.4b. While the original cube contained four values in the Customer dimension, one for each city, the new cube contains two values, each one corresponding to one country. The remaining dimensions are not affected. Thus, the values in cells pertaining to Paris and Lyon in a given quarter and category contribute to the aggregation of the corresponding values for France. The computation of the cells pertaining to Germany proceeds analogously.

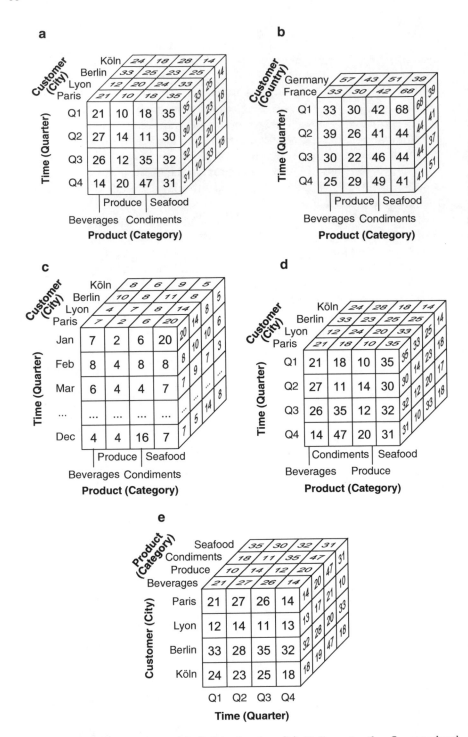

Fig. 3.4 OLAP operations. (**a**) Original cube. (**b**) Roll-up to the Country level. (**c**) Drill-down to the Month level. (**d**) Sort product by name. (**e**) Pivot

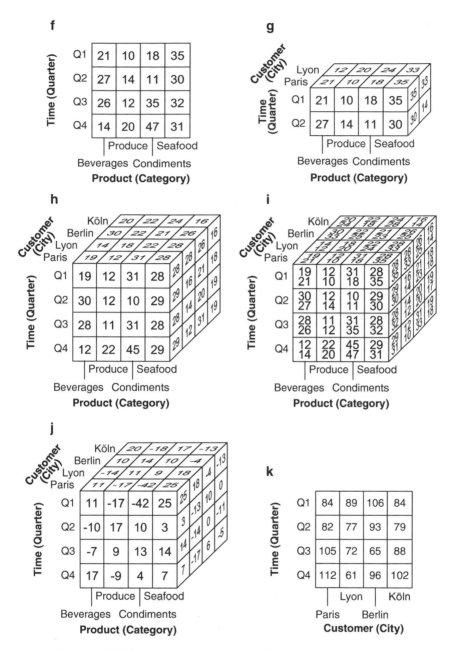

Fig. 3.4 (continued) (**f**) Slice on City='Paris'. (**g**) Dice on City='Paris' or 'Lyon' and Quarter='Q1' or 'Q2'. (**h**) Cube for 2011. (**i**) Drill-across operation. (**j**) Percentage change. (**k**) Total sales by quarter and city

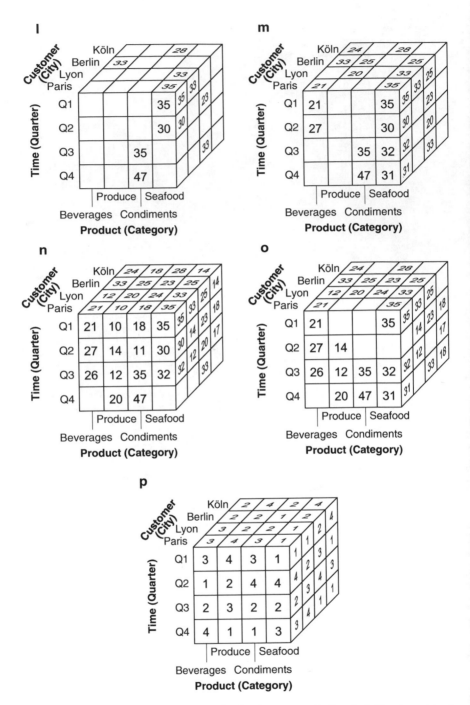

Fig. 3.4 (continued) (l) Maximum sales by quarter and city. (m) Top two sales by quarter and city. (n) Top 70% by city and category ordered by ascending quarter. (o) Top 70% by city and category ordered by descending quantity. (p) Rank quarter by category and city ordered by descending quantity

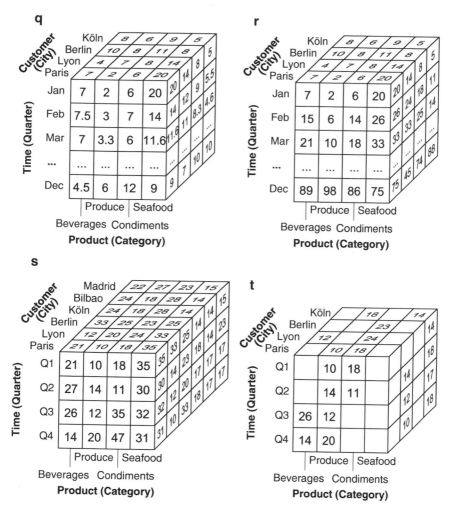

Fig. 3.4 (continued) (**q**) Three-month moving average. (**r**) Year-to-date computation. (**s**) Union of the original cube and another cube with data from Spain. (**t**) Difference of the original cube and the cube in (**m**)

Our user then notices that sales of the category Seafood in France are significantly higher in the first quarter compared to the other ones. Thus, she first takes the cube back to the City aggregation level and then applies a **drill-down** along the Time dimension to the Month level to find out whether this high value occurred during a particular month. In this way, she discovers that, for some reason yet unknown, sales in January soared both in Paris and in Lyon, as shown in Fig. 3.4c.

Our user now wants to explore alternative visualizations of the cube to better understand the data contained in it. For this, she **sorts** the products by name, as shown in Fig. 3.4d. Then, she wants to see the cube with the Time dimension on the x-axis. Therefore, she takes the original cube and rotates the axes of the cube without changing granularities. This is called **pivoting** and is shown in Fig. 3.4e.

Continuing her browsing of the original cube, the user then wants to visualize the data only for Paris. For this, she applies a **slice** operation that results in the subcube depicted in Fig. 3.4f. Here, she obtained a two-dimensional matrix, where each column represents the evolution of the sales quantity by category and quarter, that is, a collection of time series.

As her next operation, our user goes back to the original cube and builds a subcube, with the same dimensionality, but only containing sales figures for the first two quarters and for the cities Lyon and Paris. This is done with a **dice** operation, as shown in Fig. 3.4g.

Our user now wants to compare the sales quantities in 2012 with those in 2011. For this, she needs the cube in Fig. 3.4h, which has the same structure as the one for 2012 given in Fig. 3.4a. She wants to have the measures in the two cubes consolidated in a single one. Thus, she uses the **drill-across** operation that, given two cubes, builds a new one with the measures of both in each cell. This is shown in Fig. 3.4i.

The user now wants to compute the percentage change of sales between the 2 years. For this, she takes the cube resulting from the drill-across operation above, and applies to it the **add measure** operation, which computes a new value for each cell from the values in the original cube. The new measure is shown in Fig. 3.4j.

After all these manipulations, the user wants to aggregate data in various ways. Given the original cube in Fig. 3.4a, she first wants to compute to total sales by quarter and city. This is obtained by the **sum** aggregation operation, whose result is given in Fig. 3.4k. Then, the user wants to obtain the maximum sales by quarter and city, and for this, she uses the **max** operation to obtain the cube in Fig. 3.4l. After seeing the result, she decides that she needs more information; thus, she computes the top two sales by quarter and city, which is also obtained with the max operation yielding the cube in Fig. 3.4m.

In the next step, the user goes back to the original cube in Fig. 3.4a and computes the quarterly sales that amount to 70% of the total sales by city and category. She explores this in two possible ways: according to the ascending order of quarters, as shown in Fig. 3.4n, and according to the descending order of quantity, as shown in Fig. 3.4o. In both cases, she applies the **top percent** aggregation operation. She also wants to rank the quarterly sales by category and city in descending order of quantity, which is obtained in Fig. 3.4p.

Now, the user wants to apply window operations to the cube in Fig. 3.4c in order to see how monthly sales behave. She starts by requesting a 3-month moving average to obtain the result in Fig. 3.4q. Then, she asks the year-to-date computation whose result is given in Fig. 3.4r.

Finally, the user wants to add to the original cube data from Spain, which are contained in another cube. She obtains this by performing a union of the two cubes, whose result is given in Fig. 3.4s. As another operation, she also wants to remove from the original cube all sales measures except the top two sales by quarter and city. For this, she performs the difference of the original cube in Fig. 3.4a and the cube in Fig. 3.4m, yielding the result in Fig. 3.4t.

The OLAP operations illustrated in Fig. 3.4 can be defined in a way analogous to the relational algebra operations introduced in Chap. 2.

The **roll-up** operation aggregates measures along a dimension hierarchy (using an aggregate function) to obtain measures at a coarser granularity. The syntax for the roll-up operation is:

ROLLUP(CubeName, (Dimension → Level)*, AggFunction(Measure)*)

where Dimension → Level indicates to which level in a dimension the roll-up is to be performed and function AggFunction is applied to summarize the measure. When there is more than one measure in a cube, we must specify an aggregate function for each measure that will be kept in the cube. All the measures for which the aggregation is not specified will be removed from the cube. In the example given in Fig. 3.4b, we applied the operation:

ROLLUP(Sales, Customer → Country, SUM(Quantity))

When querying a cube, a usual operation is to roll up a few dimensions to particular levels and to remove the other dimensions through a roll-up to the All level. In a cube with n dimensions, this can be obtained by applying n successive ROLLUP operations. The ROLLUP* operation provides a shorthand notation for this sequence of operations. The syntax is as follows:

ROLLUP*(CubeName, [(Dimension → Level)*], AggFunction(Measure)*)

For example, the total quantity by quarter can be obtained as follows:

ROLLUP*(Sales, Time → Quarter, SUM(Quantity))

which performs a roll-up along the Time dimension to the Quarter level and the other dimensions (in this case Customer and Product) to the All level. On the other hand, if the dimensions are not specified as in

ROLLUP*(Sales, SUM(Quantity))

all the dimensions of the cube will be rolled up to the All level, yielding a single cell containing the overall sum of the Quantity measure.

A usual need when applying a roll-up operation is to count the number of members in one of the dimensions removed from the cube. For example, the following query obtains the number of distinct products sold by quarter:

ROLLUP*(Sales, Time → Quarter, COUNT(Product) AS ProdCount)

In this case, a new measure ProdCount will be added to the cube. We will see below other ways to add measures to a cube.

In many real-world situations, hierarchies are **recursive**, that is, they contain a level that rolls up to itself. A typical example is a supervision hierarchy over employees. Such hierarchies are discussed in detail in Chap. 4. The particularity of such hierarchies is that the number of levels of the hierarchy is not fixed at the schema level, but it depends on its members. The RECROLLUP operation is used to aggregate measures over recursive hierarchies by iteratively performing roll-ups over the hierarchy until the top level is reached. The syntax of this operation is as follows:

RECROLLUP(CubeName, Dimension → Level, Hierarchy, AggFct(Measure)*)

We will show an example of such an operation in Sect. 4.4.

The **drill-down** operation performs the inverse of the roll-up operation, that is, it goes from a more general level to a more detailed level in a hierarchy. The syntax of the drill-down operation is as follows:

DRILLDOWN(CubeName, (Dimension → Level)*)

where Dimension → Level indicates to which level in a dimension we want to drill down to. In our example given in Fig. 3.4c, we applied the operation

DRILLDOWN(Sales, Time → Month)

The **sort** operation returns a cube where the members of a dimension have been sorted. The syntax of the operation is as follows:

SORT(CubeName, Dimension, (Expression [{ASC | DESC | BASC | BDESC}])*)

where the members of Dimension are sorted according to the value of Expression either in ascending or descending order. In the case of ASC or DESC, members are sorted within their parent (i.e., respecting the hierarchies), whereas in the case of BASC or BDESC, the sorting is performed across all members (i.e., irrespective of the hierarchies). The ASC is the default option. For example, the following expression

SORT(Sales, Product, ProductName)

sorts the members of the Product dimension in ascending order of their name, as shown in Fig. 3.4d. Here, ProductName is supposed to be an attribute of products. When the cube contains only one dimension, the members can be sorted based on its measures. For example, if SalesByQuarter is obtained from the original cube by aggregating sales by quarter for all cities and all categories, the following expression

SORT(SalesByQuarter, Time, Quantity DESC)

sorts the members of the Time dimension on descending order of the Quantity measure.

The **pivot** (or **rotate**) operation rotates the axes of a cube to provide an alternative presentation of the data. The syntax of the operation is as follows:

PIVOT(CubeName, (Dimension → Axis)*)

where the axes are specified as {X, Y, Z, X1, Y1, Z1, ...}. Thus, the example illustrated in Fig. 3.4e is expressed by:

PIVOT(Sales, Time → X, Customer → Y, Product → Z)

The **slice** operation removes a dimension in a cube, that is, a cube of $n-1$ dimensions is obtained from a cube of n dimensions. The syntax of this operation is:

SLICE(CubeName, Dimension, Level = Value)

where the Dimension will be dropped by fixing a single Value in the Level. The other dimensions remain unchanged. The example illustrated in Fig. 3.4f is expressed by:

SLICE(Sales, Customer, City = 'Paris')

The slice operation assumes that the granularity of the cube is at the specified level of the dimension (in the example above, at the city level). Thus, a granularity change by means of a ROLLUP or DRILLDOWN operation is often needed prior to applying the slice operation.

The **dice** operation keeps the cells in a cube that satisfy a Boolean condition Φ. The syntax for this operation is

DICE(CubeName, Φ)

where Φ is a Boolean condition over dimension levels, attributes, and measures. The DICE operation is analogous to the relational algebra selection $\sigma_\Phi(R)$, where the argument is a cube instead of a relation. The example illustrated in Fig. 3.4g is expressed by:

DICE(Sales, (Customer.City = 'Paris' OR Customer.City = 'Lyon') AND
        (Time.Quarter = 'Q1' OR Time.Quarter = 'Q2'))

The **rename** operation returns a cube where some schema elements or members have been renamed. The syntax is:

RENAME(CubeName, ({SchemaElement | Member} → NewName)*)

For example, the following expression

RENAME(Sales, Sales → Sales2012, Quantity → Quantity2012)

renames the cube in Fig. 3.4a and its measure. As another example,

RENAME(Sales, Customer.all → AllCustomers)

will rename the all member of the customer dimension.

The **drill-across** operation combines cells from two data cubes that have the same schema and instances. The syntax of the operation is:

DRILLACROSS(CubeName1, CubeName2, [Condition])

The DRILLACROSS operation is analogous to a full outer join in the relational algebra. If the condition is not stated, it corresponds to an outer equijoin. Given the cubes in Fig. 3.4a, h, the cube in Fig. 3.4i is expressed by:

Sales2011-2012 ← DRILLACROSS(Sales2011, Sales2012)

Notice that a renaming of the cube and the measure, as stated above, is necessary prior to applying the drill-across operation. Notice also that the resulting cube is named Sales2011-2012. On the other hand, if in the Sales cube of Fig. 3.4c we want to compare the sales of a month with those of the previous month, this can be expressed in two steps as follows:

Sales1 ← RENAME(Sales, Quantity ← PrevMonthQuantity)
Result ← DRILLACROSS(Sales1, Sales, Sales1.Time.Month+1 = Sales.Time.Month)

In the first step, we create a temporary cube Sales1 by renaming the measure. In the second step, we perform the drill across of the two cubes by combining a cell in Sales1 with the cell in Sales corresponding to the subsequent month. As already stated, the join condition above corresponds to an outer join. Notice that the Sales cube in Fig. 3.4a contains measures for a single year. Thus, in the result above, the cells corresponding to January and December will contain a null value in one of the two measures. As we will see in Sect. 4.4, when the cube contains measures for several years, the join condition must take into account that measures of January must be joined with those of December of the preceding year. Notice also that the cube has three dimensions and the join condition in the query above pertains to only one dimension. For the other dimensions, it is supposed that an outer equijoin is performed.

The **add measure** operation adds new measures to the cube computed from other measures or dimensions. The syntax for this operation is as follows:

ADDMEASURE(CubeName, (NewMeasure = Expression, [AggFct])*)

where Expression is a formula over measures and dimension members and AggFct is the default aggregation function for the measure, SUM being the default. For example, given the cube in Fig. 3.4i, the measure shown in Fig. 3.4j is expressed by:

ADDMEASURE(Sales2011-2012, PercentageChange =
            (Quantity2011-Quantity2012)/Quantity2011)

The **drop measure** operation removes one or several measures from a cube. The syntax is as follows:

DROPMEASURE(CubeName, Measure*)

For example, given the result of the add measure above, the cube illustrated in Fig. 3.4j is expressed by:

DROPMEASURE(Sales2011-2012, Quantity2011, Quantity2012)

We have seen that the roll-up operation aggregates measures when displaying the cube at coarser level. On the other hand, we also need to aggregate measures of a cube at the current granularity, that is, without performing a roll-up operation. The syntax for this is as follows:

AggFunction(CubeName, Measure) [BY Dimension*]

Usual aggregation operations are SUM, AVG, COUNT, MIN, and MAX. In addition to these, we use extended versions of MIN and MAX, which have an additional argument that is used to obtain the n minimum or maximum values. Further, TOPPERCENT and BOTTOMPERCENT select the members of a dimension that cumulatively account for x percent of a measure. Analogously, RANK and DENSERANK are used to rank the members of a dimension according to a measure. We show next examples of these operations.

For example, the cube in Fig. 3.4a is at the Quarter and City levels. The total sales by quarter and city can be obtained by

SUM(Sales, Quantity) BY Time, Customer

This will yield the two-dimensional cube in Fig. 3.4k. On the other hand, to obtain the total sales by quarter, we can write

SUM(Sales, Quantity) BY Time

which returns a one-dimensional cube with values for each quarter. Notice that in the query above, a roll-up along the Customer dimension up to the All level is performed before applying the aggregation operation. Finally, to obtain the overall sales, we can write

SUM(Sales, Quantity)

which will result in a single cell.

Aggregation functions in OLAP can be classified in two types. **Cumulative aggregation functions** compute the measure value of a cell from several other cells. Examples of cumulative functions are SUM, COUNT, and AVG. On the other hand, **filtering aggregation functions** filter the members of a dimension that appears in the result. Examples of these functions are MIN and MAX. The distinction between these two types of aggregation functions is important in OLAP since filtering aggregation functions must compute not only the aggregated value but must also determine the dimension members that belong to the result. As an example, when asking for the best-selling employee, we must compute the maximum sales amount but also identify who is the employee that performed best.

Therefore, when applying an aggregation operation, the resulting cube will have different dimension members depending on the type of the aggregation function. For example, given the cube in Fig. 3.4a, the total overall quantity can be obtained by the expression

SUM(Sales, Quantity)

This will yield a single cell, whose coordinates for the three dimensions will be all equal to all. On the other hand, when computing the overall maximum quantity as follows

MAX(Sales, Quantity)

we will obtain the cell with value 47 and coordinates Q4, Condiments, and Paris (we suppose that cells that are hidden in Fig. 3.4a contain a smaller value for this measure). Similarly, the following expression

SUM(Sales, Quantity) BY Time, Customer

returns the total sales by quarter and customer, resulting in the cube given in Fig. 3.4k. This cube has three dimensions, where the Product dimension only contains the member all. On the other hand,

MAX(Sales, Quantity) BY Time, Customer

will yield the cube in Fig. 3.4l, where only the cells containing the maximum by time and customer will have values, while the other ones will be filled with null values. Similarly, the two maximum quantities by product and customer as shown in Fig. 3.4m can be obtained as follows:

MAX(Sales, Quantity, 2) BY Time, Customer

Notice that in the example above, we requested the two maximum quantities by time and customer. If in the cube there are two or more cells that tie for the last place in the limited result set, then the number of cells in the result could be greater than two. For example, this is the case in Fig. 3.4m for Berlin and Q1, where there are three values in the result, that is, 33, 25, and 25.

To compute top or bottom percentages, the order of the cells must be specified. For example, to compute the top 70% of the measure quantity by city and category ordered by quarter, as shown in Fig. 3.4n, we can write

TOPPERCENT(Sales, Quantity, 70) BY City, Category ORDER BY Quarter ASC

The operation computes the running sum of the sales by city and category starting with the first quarter and continues until the target percentage is reached. In the example above, the sales by city and category for the first three quarters covers 70% of the sales. Similarly, the top 70% of the measure quantity by city and category ordered by quantity, as shown in Fig. 3.4o, can be obtained by

TOPPERCENT(Sales, Quantity, 70) BY City, Category ORDER BY Quantity DESC

The rank operation also requires the specification of the order of the cells. As an example, to rank quarters by category and city order by descending quantity, as shown in Fig. 3.4p, we can write

RANK(Sales, Time) BY Category, City ORDER BY Quantity DESC

The rank and the dense rank operations differ in the case of ties. The former assigns the same rank to ties, with the next ranking(s) skipped. For example, in Fig. 3.4p, there is a tie in the quarters for Seafood and Köln, where Q2 and Q4 are in the first rank and Q3 and Q1 are in the third and fourth ranks, respectively. If the dense rank is used, then Q3 and Q1 would be in the second and third ranks, respectively.

In the examples above, the new measure value in a cell is computed from the values of other measures in the same cell. However, we often need to compute measures where the value of a cell is obtained by aggregating the measures of several nearby cells. Examples of these include moving average and year-to-date computations. For this, we need to define a subcube that is associated with each cell and perform the aggregation over this subcube. These functions correspond to the window functions in SQL that will be described in Chap. 5. For example, given the cube in Fig. 3.4c, the 3-month moving average in Fig. 3.4q can be obtained by

ADDMEASURE(Sales, MovAvg = AVG(Quantity) OVER
           Time 2 CELLS PRECEDING)

Here, the moving average for January is equal to the measure in January, since there are no previous cells. Analogously, the measure for February is the average of the values of January and February. Finally, the average for the remaining months is computed from the measure value of the current month and the two preceding ones. Notice that in the window functions, it is supposed that the members of the dimension over which the window is constructed are already sorted. For this, a sort operation can be applied prior to the application of the window aggregate function.

Similarly, to compute the year-to-date sum in Fig. 3.4r, we can write

ADDMEASURE(Sales, YTDQuantity = SUM(Quantity) OVER
           Time ALL CELLS PRECEDING)

Here, the window over which the aggregation function is applied contains the current cell and all the previous ones, as indicated by ALL CELLS PRECEDING.

The **union** operation merges two cubes that have the same schema but disjoint instances. For example, if CubeSpain is a cube having the same schema as our original cube but containing only the sales to Spanish customers, the cube in Fig. 3.4s is obtained by

UNION(Sales, SalesSpain)

The union operation is also used to display different granularities on the
same dimension. For example, if SalesCountry is the cube in Fig. 3.4b, then
the following operation

UNION(Sales, SalesCountry)

results in a cube containing sales measures summarized by city and by
country.

The **difference** operation removes the cells in a cube that exist in another
one. Obviously, the two cubes must have the same schema. For example, if
TopTwoSales is the cube in Fig. 3.4m, then the following operation

DIFFERENCE(Sales, TopTwoSales)

will result in the cube in Fig. 3.4t, which contains all sales measures except
for the top two sales by quarter and city.

Finally, the **drill-through** operation allows one to move from data at the
bottom level in a cube to data in the operational systems from which the cube
was derived. This could be used, for example, if one were trying to determine
the reason for outlier values in a data cube.

Table 3.1 summarizes the OLAP operations we have presented in this
section. In addition to the basic operations described above, OLAP tools
provide a great variety of mathematical, statistical, and financial operations
for computing ratios, variances, interest, depreciation, currency conversions,
etc.

3.3   Data Warehouses

A **data warehouse** is a repository of integrated data obtained from several
sources for the specific purpose of multidimensional data analysis. More
technically, a data warehouse is defined as a collection of subject-oriented,
integrated, nonvolatile, and time-varying data to support management
decisions. We explain next these characteristics:

- **Subject oriented** means that data warehouses focus on the analytical
  needs of different areas of an organization. These areas vary depending
  on the kind of activities performed by the organization. For example, in
  the case of a retail company, the analysis may focus on product sales
  or inventory management. In operational databases, on the contrary, the
  focus is on specific functions that applications must perform, for example,
  registering sales of products or inventory replenishment.
- **Integrated** means that data obtained from several operational and
  external systems must be joined together, which implies solving problems
  due to differences in data definition and content, such as differences
  in data format and data codification, synonyms (fields with different

Table 3.1 Summary of the OLAP operations

Operation	Purpose
Add measure	Adds new measures to a cube computed from other measures or dimensions.
Aggregation operations	Aggregate the cells of a cube, possibly after performing a grouping of cells.
Dice	Keeps the cells of a cube that satisfy a Boolean condition over dimension levels, attributes, and measures.
Difference	Removes the cells of a cube that are in another cube. Both cubes must have the same schema.
Drill-across	Merges two cubes that have the same schema and instances using a join condition.
Drill-down	Disaggregates measures along a hierarchy to obtain data at a finer granularity. It is the opposite of the roll-up operation.
Drill-through	Shows data in the operational systems from which the cube was derived.
Drop measure	Removes measures from a cube.
Pivot	Rotates the axes of a cube to provide an alternative presentation of its data.
Recursive roll-up	Performs an iteration of roll-ups over a recursive hierarchy until the top level is reached.
Rename	Renames one or several schema elements of a cube.
Roll-up	Aggregates measures along a hierarchy to obtain data at a coarser granularity. It is the opposite of the drill-down operation.
Roll-up*	Shorthand notation for a sequence of roll-up operations.
Slice	Removes a dimension from a cube by fixing a single value in a level of the dimension.
Sort	Orders the members of a dimension according to an expression.
Union	Combines the cells of two cubes that have the same schema but disjoint members.

names but the same data), homonyms (fields with the same name but different meanings), multiplicity of occurrences of data, and many others. In operational databases these problems are typically solved in the design phase.

- **Nonvolatile** means that durability of data is ensured by disallowing data modification and removal, thus expanding the scope of the data to a longer period of time than operational systems usually offer. A data warehouse gathers data encompassing several years, typically 5–10 years or beyond, while data in operational databases is often kept for only a short period of time, for example, from 2 to 6 months, as required for daily operations, and it may be overwritten when necessary.
- **Time varying** indicates the possibility of retaining different values for the same information, as well as the time when changes to these values occurred. For example, a data warehouse in a bank might store information

about the average monthly balance of clients' accounts for a period covering several years. In contrast, an operational database may not have explicit temporal support, since sometimes it is not necessary for day-to-day operations and it is also difficult to implement.

A data warehouse is aimed at analyzing the data of an entire organization. It is often the case that particular departments or divisions of an organization only require a portion of the organizational data warehouse specialized for their needs. For example, a sales department may only need sales data, while a human resources department may need demographic data and data about the employees. These departmental data warehouses are called **data marts**. However, these data marts are not necessarily private to a department; they may be shared with other interested parts of the organization.

A data warehouse can be seen as a collection of data marts. This view represents a **bottom-up** approach in which a data warehouse is built by first building the smaller data marts and then merging these to obtain the data warehouse. This can be a good approach for organizations not willing to take the risk of building a large data warehouse, which may take a long time to complete, or organizations that need fast results. On the other hand, in the classic data warehouse view, data marts are obtained from the data warehouse in a **top-down** fashion. In this approach, a data mart is sometimes just a logical view of a data warehouse.

Table 3.2 shows several aspects that differentiate operational database (or OLTP) systems from data warehouse (or OLAP) systems. We analyze next in detail some of these differences.

Typically, the users of OLTP systems are operations and employees who perform predefined operations through transactional applications, like payroll systems or ticket reservation systems. Data warehouse users, on the other hand, are usually located higher in the organizational hierarchy and use interactive OLAP tools to perform data analysis, for example, to detect salary inconsistencies or most frequently chosen tourist destinations (lines 1–2). Therefore, it is clear that data for OLTP systems should be current and detailed, while data analytics require historical, summarized data (line 3). The difference on data organization (line 4) follows from the type of use of OLTP and OLAP systems.

From a more technical viewpoint, data structures for OLTP are optimized for rather small and simple transactions, which will be carried out frequently and repeatedly. In addition, data access for OLTP requires reading and writing data files. For example, in the Northwind database application, a user may be able to frequently insert new orders, modify old ones, and delete orders if customers cancel them. Thus, the number of records accessed by an OLTP transaction is usually small (e.g., the records involved in a particular sales order). On the other hand, data structures for OLAP must support complex aggregation queries, thus requiring access to all the records in one or more tables, which will translate in long, complex SQL queries. Furthermore,

Table 3.2 Comparison between operational databases and data warehouses

Aspect	Operational databases	Data warehouses
1 User type	Operators, office employees	Managers, executives
2 Usage	Predictable, repetitive	Ad hoc, nonstructured
3 Data content	Current, detailed data	Historical, summarized data
4 Data organization	According to operational needs	According to analysis needs
5 Data structures	Optimized for small transactions	Optimized for complex queries
6 Access frequency	High	From medium to low
7 Access type	Read, insert, update, delete	Read, append only
8 Number of records per access	Few	Many
9 Response time	Short	Can be long
10 Concurrency level	High	Low
11 Lock utilization	Needed	Not needed
12 Update frequency	High	None
13 Data redundancy	Low (normalized tables)	High (denormalized tables)
14 Data modeling	UML, ER model	Multidimensional model

OLAP systems are not so frequently accessed as OLTP systems. For example, a system handling purchase orders is frequently accessed, while performing analysis of orders may not be that frequent. Also, data warehouse records are usually accessed in read mode (lines 5–8). From the above, it follows that OLTP systems usually have a short query response time, provided the appropriate indexing structures are defined, while complex OLAP queries can take a longer time to complete (line 9).

OLTP systems have normally a high number of concurrent accesses and therefore require locking or other concurrency management mechanisms to ensure safe transaction processing (lines 10–11). On the other hand, OLAP systems are read only, and therefore queries can be submitted and computed concurrently, with no locking or complex transaction processing requirements. Further, the number of concurrent users in an OLAP system is usually low.

Finally, OLTP systems are constantly being updated online through transactional applications, while OLAP systems are updated off-line periodically. This leads to different modeling choices. OLTP systems are modeled using UML or some variation of the ER model studied in Chap. 2. Such models lead to a highly normalized schema, adequate for databases that support frequent transactions, to guarantee consistency and reduce redundancy. OLAP designers use the multidimensional model, which, at the logical level (as we will see in Chap. 5), leads in general to a denormalized database schema, with a high level of redundancy, which favors query processing (lines 12–14).

3.4   Data Warehouse Architecture

We are now ready to present a general data warehouse architecture that will
be used throughout the book. This architecture, depicted in Fig. 3.5, consists
of several tiers:

- The **back-end tier** is composed of **extraction, transformation, and
  loading (ETL) tools**, used to feed data into the data warehouse from
  operational databases and other **data sources**, which can be **internal** or
  external from the organization, and a **data staging area**, which is an
  intermediate database where all the data integration and transformation
  processes are run prior to the loading of the data into the data warehouse.
- The **data warehouse tier** is composed of an **enterprise data warehouse** and/or several **data marts** and a **metadata repository** storing
  information about the data warehouse and its contents.
- The **OLAP tier** is composed of an **OLAP server**, which provides a
  multidimensional view of the data, regardless of the actual way in which
  data are stored in the underlying system.
- The **front-end tier** is used for data analysis and visualization. It contains
  client tools such as **OLAP tools**, **reporting tools**, **statistical tools**,
  and **data mining tools**.

We now describe in detail the various components of the above architecture.

3.4.1   Back-End Tier

In the back-end tier, the process commonly known as **extraction, transformation, and loading** is performed. As the name indicates, it is a three-step
process as follows:

- **Extraction** gathers data from multiple, heterogeneous data sources.
  These sources may be operational databases but may also be files in various
  formats; they may be **internal** to the organization or **external** to it.
  In order to solve interoperability problems, data are extracted whenever
  possible using application programming interfaces (APIs) such as ODBC
  (Open Database Connectivity) and JDBC (Java Database Connectivity).
- **Transformation** modifies the data from the format of the data sources
  to the warehouse format. This includes several aspects: *cleaning*, which
  removes errors and inconsistencies in the data and converts it into a
  standardized format; *integration*, which reconciles data from different data
  sources, both at the schema and at the data level; and *aggregation*, which
  summarizes the data obtained from data sources according to the level of
  detail, or granularity, of the data warehouse.

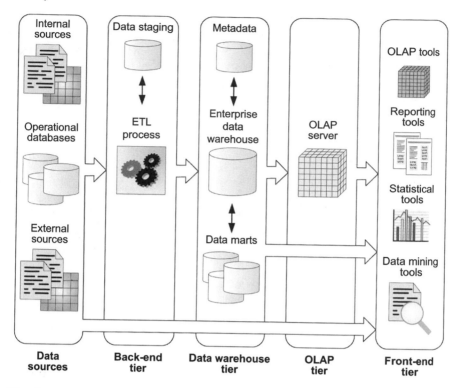

Fig. 3.5 Typical data warehouse architecture

- **Loading** feeds the data warehouse with the transformed data. This also includes **refreshing** the data warehouse, that is, propagating updates from the data sources to the data warehouse at a specified frequency in order to provide up-to-date data for the decision-making process. Depending on organizational policies, the refresh frequency may vary from monthly to several times a day or even near to real time.

ETL processes usually require a data staging area, that is, a database in which the data extracted from the sources undergoes successive modifications to eventually be ready to be loaded into the data warehouse. Such a database is usually called **operational data store**.

3.4.2 Data Warehouse Tier

The data warehouse tier in Fig. 3.5 depicts an enterprise data warehouse and several data marts. As we have explained, while an **enterprise data warehouse** is centralized and encompasses an entire organization, a **data**

mart is a specialized data warehouse targeted toward a particular functional or departmental area in an organization. A data mart can be seen as a small, local data warehouse. Data in a data mart can be either derived from an enterprise data warehouse or collected directly from data sources.

Another component of the data warehouse tier is the metadata repository. **Metadata** can be defined as "data about data." Metadata has been traditionally classified into technical and business metadata. **Business metadata** describes the meaning (or semantics) of the data and organizational rules, policies, and constraints related to the data. On the other hand, **technical metadata** describes how data are structured and stored in a computer system and the applications and processes that manipulate such data.

In the data warehouse context, technical metadata can be of various natures, describing the data warehouse system, the source systems, and the ETL process. In particular, the metadata repository may contain information such as the following:

- Metadata describing the structure of the data warehouse and the data marts, both at the conceptual/logical level (which includes the facts, dimensions, hierarchies, derived data definitions) and at the physical level (such as indexes, partitions, and replication). In addition, these metadata contain security information (user authorization and access control) and monitoring information (such as usage statistics, error reports, and audit trails).
- Metadata describing the data sources, including their schemas (at the conceptual, logical, and/or physical levels), and descriptive information such as ownership, update frequencies, legal limitations, and access methods.
- Metadata describing the ETL process, including data lineage (i.e., tracing warehouse data back to the source data from which it was derived), data extraction, cleaning, transformation rules and defaults, data refresh and purging rules, and algorithms for summarization.

3.4.3   OLAP Tier

The OLAP tier in the architecture of Fig. 3.5 is composed of an OLAP server, which presents business users with multidimensional data from data warehouses or data marts.

Most database products provide OLAP extensions and related tools allowing the construction and querying of cubes, as well as navigation, analysis, and reporting. However, there is not yet a standardized language for defining and manipulating data cubes, and the underlying technology differs between the available systems. In this respect, several languages are worth mentioning. XMLA (XML for Analysis) aims at providing a common language for exchanging multidimensional data between client applications and OLAP servers. Further, MDX (MultiDimensional eXpressions) is a query language for OLAP databases. As it is supported by a number of OLAP vendors, MDX became a de facto standard for querying OLAP systems. The SQL standard has also been extended for providing analytical capabilities; this extension is referred to as SQL/OLAP. In Chap. 6, we present a detailed study of both MDX and SQL/OLAP.

3.4.4   Front-End Tier

The front-end tier in Fig. 3.5 contains client tools that allow users to exploit the contents of the data warehouse. Typical client tools include the following:

- **OLAP tools** allow interactive exploration and manipulation of the warehouse data. They facilitate the formulation of complex queries that may involve large amounts of data. These queries are called **ad hoc queries**, since the system has no prior knowledge about them.
- **Reporting tools** enable the production, delivery, and management of reports, which can be paper-based reports or interactive, web-based reports. Reports use **predefined queries**, that is, queries asking for specific information in a specific format that are performed on a regular basis. Modern reporting techniques include key performance indicators and dashboards.
- **Statistical tools** are used to analyze and visualize the cube data using statistical methods.
- **Data mining tools** allow users to analyze data in order to discover valuable knowledge such as patterns and trends; they also allow predictions to be made on the basis of current data.

In Chap. 9, we show some of the tools used to exploit the data warehouse, like data mining tools, key performance indicators, and dashboards.

3.4.5   Variations of the Architecture

Some of the components in Fig. 3.5 can be missing in a real environment.

In some situations, there is only an enterprise data warehouse without data marts, or alternatively, an enterprise data warehouse does not exist. Building an enterprise data warehouse is a complex task that is very costly in time and resources. In contrast, a data mart is typically easier to build than an enterprise warehouse. However, this advantage may turn into a problem when several data marts that were independently created need to be integrated into a data warehouse for the entire enterprise.

In some other situations, an OLAP server does not exist and/or the client tools directly access the data warehouse. This is indicated by the arrow connecting the data warehouse tier to the front-end tier. This situation is illustrated in Chap. 6, where the same queries for the Northwind case study are expressed both in MDX (targeting the OLAP server) and in SQL (targeting the data warehouse). An extreme situation is where there is neither a data warehouse nor an OLAP server. This is called a **virtual data warehouse**, which defines a set of views over operational databases that are materialized for efficient access. The arrow connecting the data sources to the front-end tier depicts this situation. Although a virtual data warehouse is easy to build, it does not provide a real data warehouse solution, since it does not contain historical data, does not contain centralized metadata, and does not have the ability to clean and transform the data. Furthermore, a virtual data warehouse can severely impact the performance of operational databases.

Finally, a data staging area may not be needed when the data in the source systems conforms very closely to the data in the warehouse. This situation typically arises when there is one data source (or only a few) having high-quality data. However, this is rarely the case in real-world situations.

3.5 Data Warehouse Design

Like in operational databases (studied in Sect. 2.1), there are two major methods for the design of data warehouses and data marts. In the **top-down approach**, the requirements of users at different organizational levels are merged before the design process starts, and one schema for the entire data warehouse is built, from which data marts can be obtained. In the **bottom-up approach**, a schema is built for each data mart, according to the requirements of the users of each business area. The data mart schemas produced are then merged in a global warehouse schema. The choice between the top-down and the bottom-up approach depends on many factors that will be studied in Chap. 10 in this book.

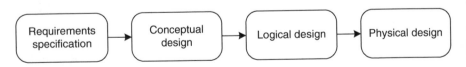

Fig. 3.6 Phases in data warehouse design

There is still no consensus on the phases that should be followed for data warehouse design. Most of the books in the data warehouse literature follow a bottom-up, practitioner's approach to design based on the relational model, using the star, snowflake, and constellation schemas, which we will study in detail in Chap. 5. In this book, we follow a different, model-based approach for data warehouse design, which follows the traditional phases for designing operational databases described in Chap. 2, that is, requirements specification, conceptual design, logical design, and physical design. These phases are shown in Fig. 3.6. In Chap. 10, which studies the design method in detail, we will see that there are important differences between the design phases for databases and data warehouses, arising from their different nature. Also note that although, for simplicity, the phases in Fig. 3.6 are depicted consecutively, actually there are multiple interactions between them. Finally, we remark that the phases in Fig. 3.6 may be applied to define either the schema of the overall schema of the organizational data warehouse or the schemas of individual data marts.

A distinctive characteristic of the method presented in this book is the importance given to the requirements specification and conceptual design phases. For these phases, we can follow two approaches, which we explain in detail in Chap. 10. In the **analysis-driven approach**, key users from different organizational levels provide useful input about the analysis needs. On the other hand, in the **source-driven approach**, the data warehouse schema is obtained by analyzing the data source systems. In this approach, normally, the participation of users is only required to confirm the correctness of the data structures that are obtained from the source systems or to identify some facts and measures as a starting point for the design of multidimensional schemas. Finally, the **analysis/source-driven approach** is a combination of the analysis- and source-driven approaches, aimed at matching the users' analysis needs with the information that the source systems can provide. This is why this approach is also called top-down/bottom-up analysis.

3.6 Business Intelligence Tools

Nowadays, the offer in business intelligence tools is quite large. The major database providers, such as Microsoft, Oracle, IBM, and Teradata, have their own suite of business intelligence tools. Other popular tools include SAP, MicroStrategy, and Targit. In addition to the above commercial tools, there are also open-source tools, of which Pentaho is the most popular one.

In this book, we have chosen two representative suites of tools for illustrating the topics presented: Microsoft's SQL Server tools and Pentaho Business Analytics. In this section, we briefly describe these tools, while the bibliographic notes section at the end of this chapter provides references to other well-known business intelligence tools.

3.6.1   Overview of Microsoft SQL Server Tools

Microsoft SQL Server provides an integrated platform for building analytical applications. It is composed of three main components, described below:

- **Analysis Services** is an OLAP tool that provides analytical and data mining capabilities. It is used to define, query, update, and manage OLAP databases. The MDX (MultiDimensional eXpressions) language is used to retrieve data. Users may work with OLAP data via client tools (Excel or other OLAP clients) that interact with Analysis Services' server component. We will study these in Chaps. 5 and 6 when we define and query the data cube for the Northwind case study. Further, Analysis Services provides several data mining algorithms and uses the DMX (Data Mining eXtensions) language for creating and querying data mining models and obtaining predictions. We will study these in Chap. 9 when we exploit the Northwind data warehouse for data analytics.
- **Integration Services** supports ETL processes, which are used for loading and refreshing data warehouses on a periodic basis. Integration Services is used to extract data from a variety of data sources; to combine, clean, and summarize this data; and, finally, to populate a data warehouse with the resulting data. We will explain in detail Integration Services when we describe the ETL for the Northwind case study in Chap. 8.
- **Reporting Services** is used to define, generate, store, and manage reports. Reports can be built from various types of data sources, including data warehouses and OLAP cubes. Reports can be personalized and delivered in a variety of formats. Users can view reports with a variety of clients, such as web browsers or other reporting clients. Clients access reports via Reporting Services' server component. We will explain Reporting Services when we build dashboards for the Northwind case study in Chap. 9.

SQL Server provides two tools for developing and managing these components. **SQL Server Data Tools** (SSDT) is a development platform integrated with Microsoft Visual Studio. SQL Server Data Tools supports Analysis Services, Reporting Services, and Integration Services projects. On the other hand, **SQL Server Management Studio** (SSMS) provides integrated management of all SQL Server components.

The underlying model across these tools is called the **Business Intelligence Semantic Model** (BISM). This model comes in two modes, the multidimensional and tabular modes, where, as their name suggest, the difference among them stems from their underlying paradigm (multidimensional or relational). From the *data model* perspective, the multidimensional mode has powerful capabilities for building advanced business intelligence applications and supports large data volumes. On the other hand, the tabular mode is simpler to understand and quicker to build than the multidimensional data mode. Further, the data volumes supported by the tabular mode are smaller than those of the multidimensional mode in Analysis Services. From the *query language* perspective, each of these modes has an associated query language, MDX and DAX (Data Analysis Expressions), respectively. Finally, from the *data access* perspective, the multidimensional mode supports data access in MOLAP (multidimensional OLAP), ROLAP (relational OLAP), or HOLAP (hybrid OLAP), which will be described in Chap. 5. On the other hand, the tabular mode accesses data through xVelocity, an in-memory, column-oriented database engine with compression capabilities. We will cover such databases in Chap. 13. The tabular mode also allows the data to be retrieved directly from relational data sources.

In this book, we cover only the multidimensional mode of BISM as well as the MDX language.

3.6.2 Overview of Pentaho Business Analytics

Pentaho Business Analytics is a suite of business intelligence products. It comes in two versions: an enterprise edition that is commercial and a community edition that is open source. The main components are the following:

- **Pentaho Business Analytics Platform** serves as the connection point for all other components. It enables a unified, end-to-end solution from data integration to visualization and consumption of data. It also includes a set of tools for development, deployment, and management of applications.
- **Pentaho Analysis Services**, also known as **Mondrian**, is a relational OLAP server. It supports the MDX (multidimensional expressions) query language and the XML for Analysis and olap4j interface specifications. It reads from SQL and other data sources and aggregates data in a memory cache.
- **Pentaho Data Mining** uses the Waikato Environment for Knowledge Analysis (Weka) to search data for patterns. Weka consists of machine learning algorithms for a broad set of data mining tasks. It contains functions for data processing, regression analysis, classification methods, cluster analysis, and visualization.
- **Pentaho Data Integration**, also known as **Kettle**, consists of a data integration (ETL) engine and GUI (graphical user interface) applications that allow users to define data integration jobs and transformations. It supports deployment on single node computers as well as on a cloud or a cluster.
- **Pentaho Report Designer** is a visual report writer that can query and use data from many sources. It consists of a core reporting engine, capable of generating reports in several formats based on an XML definition file.

In addition, several design tools are provided, which are described next:

- **Pentaho Schema Workbench** provides a graphical interface for designing OLAP cubes for Mondrian. The schema created is stored as an XML file on disk.
- **Pentaho Aggregation Designer** operates on Mondrian XML schema files and the database with the underlying tables described by the schema to generate precalculated, aggregated answers to speed up analysis work and MDX queries executed against Mondrian.
- **Pentaho Metadata Editor** is a tool that simplifies the creation of reports and allows users to build metadata domains and relational data models. It acts as an abstraction layer from the underlying data sources.

3.7   Summary

In this chapter, we introduced the multidimensional model, which is the basis for data warehouse systems. We defined the notion of online analytical processing (OLAP) systems as opposite to online transaction processing (OLTP) systems. We then studied the data cube concept and its components: dimensions, hierarchies, and measures. In particular, we presented several classifications of measures and defined the notions of measure aggregation and summarizability. Then, we defined a set of OLAP operations, like roll-up and drill-down, that are used to interactively manipulate a data cube. We then described data warehouse systems and highlighted their differences with respect to traditional database systems. As data warehouse systems include many different components, we discussed the basic architecture of data warehouse systems and several variants of it that may be considered. We finished this chapter by giving an overview of two representative sets of tools: Microsoft SQL Server tools and Pentaho Business Analytics.

3.8   Bibliographic Notes

Basic data warehouse concepts can be found in the classic books by Kimball [103] and by Inmon [90, 91]. In particular, the definition of data warehouses we gave in Sect. 3.3 is from Inmon.

The notion of hypercube underlying the multidimensional model was studied in [72], where the ROLLUP and the CUBE operations were defined for SQL. Hierarchies in OLAP are studied, among other works, in [22, 123]. The notion of summarizability of measures was defined in [115] and has been studied, for example, in [84–86]. Other classification of measures are given in

[72, 103]. More details on these concepts are given in Chap. 5, where we also give further references.

There is not yet a standard definition of the OLAP operations, in a similar way as the relational algebra operations are defined for the relational algebra. Many different algebras for OLAP have been proposed in the literature, each one defining different sets of operations. A comparison of these OLAP algebras is given in [181], where the authors advocate the need for a reference algebra for OLAP. The definition of the operations we presented in this chapter was inspired from [32].

There are many books that describe the various business intelligence tools. We next give some references for commercial and open-source tools. For SQL Server, the series of books devoted to Analysis Services [79], Integration Services [105], and Reporting Services [209] cover extensively these components. The business intelligence tools from Oracle are covered in [175, 218], while those of IBM are covered in [147, 225]. SAP BusinessObjects is presented in [81, 83], while MicroStrategy is covered in [50, 139]. For Pentaho, the book [18] gives an overall description of the various components of the Pentaho Business Intelligence Suite, while Mondrian is covered in the book [10], Kettle in [26, 179], Reporting in [57], and Weka in [228]. The book [157] is devoted to Big Data Analytics using Pentaho. On the academic side, a survey of open-source tools for business intelligence is given in [199].

3.9 Review Questions

3.1 What is the meaning of the acronyms OLAP and OLTP?

3.2 Using an example of an application domain that you are familiar with, describe the various components of the multidimensional model, that is, facts, measures, dimensions, and hierarchies.

3.3 Why are hierarchies important in data warehouses? Give examples of various hierarchies.

3.4 Discuss the role of measure aggregation in a data warehouse. How can measures be characterized?

3.5 Give an example of a problem that may occur when summarizability is not verified in a data warehouse.

3.6 Describe the various OLAP operations using the example you defined in Question 3.2.

3.7 What is an operational database system? What is a data warehouse system? Explain several aspects that differentiate these systems.

3.8 Give some essential characteristics of a data warehouse. How do a data warehouse and a data mart differ? Describe two approaches for building a data warehouse and its associated data marts.

3.9 Describe the various components of a typical data warehouse architecture. Identify variants of this architecture and specify in what situations they are used.

3.10 Briefly describe the multidimensional model implemented in Analysis Services.

3.10   Exercises

3.1 A data warehouse of a telephone provider consists of five dimensions: caller customer, callee customer, time, call type, and call program and three measures: number of calls, duration, and amount.

Define the OLAP operations to be performed in order to answer the following queries. Propose the dimension hierarchies when needed.

(a) Total amount collected by each call program in 2012.
(b) Total duration of calls made by customers from Brussels in 2012.
(c) Total number of weekend calls made by customers from Brussels to customers in Antwerp in 2012.
(d) Total duration of international calls started by customers in Belgium in 2012.
(e) Total amount collected from customers in Brussels who are enrolled in the corporate program in 2012.

3.2 A data warehouse of a train company contains information about train segments. It consists of six dimensions, namely, departure station, arrival station, trip, train, arrival time, and departure time, and three measures, namely, number of passengers, duration, and number of kilometers.

Define the OLAP operations to be performed in order to answer the following queries. Propose the dimension hierarchies when needed.

(a) Total number of kilometers made by Alstom trains during 2012 departing from French or Belgian stations.
(b) Total duration of international trips during 2012, that is, trips departing from a station located in a country and arriving at a station located in another country.
(c) Total number of trips that departed from or arrived at Paris during July 2012.
(d) Average duration of train segments in Belgium in 2012.
(e) For each trip, average number of passengers per segment, which means take all the segments of each trip and average the number of passengers.

3.3 Consider the data warehouse of a university that contains information about teaching and research activities. On the one hand, the information about teaching activities is related to dimensions department, professor, course, and time, the latter at a granularity of academic semester. Measures for teaching activities are number of hours and number of credits. On the other hand, the information about research activities is related to dimensions professor, funding agency, project, and time, the latter twice for the start date and the end date, both at a granularity of day. In this case, professors are related to the department to which they are affiliated. Measures for research activities are the number of person months and amount.

Define the OLAP operations to be performed in order to answer the following queries. For this, propose the necessary dimension hierarchies.

(a) By department the total number of teaching hours during the academic year 2012–2013.
(b) By department the total amount of research projects during the calendar year 2012.
(c) By department the total number of professors involved in research projects during the calendar year 2012.
(d) By professor the total number of courses delivered during the academic year 2012–2013.
(e) By department and funding agency the total number of projects started in 2012.

Chapter 4
Conceptual Data Warehouse Design

The advantages of using conceptual models for designing databases are well known. Conceptual models facilitate communication between users and designers since they do not require knowledge about specific features of the underlying implementation platform. Further, schemas developed using conceptual models can be mapped to various logical models, such as relational, object-relational, or object-oriented models, thus simplifying responses to changes in the technology used. Moreover, conceptual models facilitate the database maintenance and evolution, since they focus on users' requirements; as a consequence, they provide better support for subsequent changes in the logical and physical schemas.

In this chapter, we focus our study on conceptual modeling for data warehouses. In particular, we base our presentation in the MultiDim model, which can be used to represent the data requirements of data warehouse and OLAP applications. The definition of the model is given in Sect. 4.1. Since hierarchies are essential for exploiting data warehouse and OLAP systems to their full capabilities, in Sect. 4.2, we consider various kinds of hierarchies that exist in real-world situations. We classify these hierarchies, giving a graphical representation of them and emphasizing the differences between them. We also present advanced aspects of conceptual modeling in Sect. 4.3. Finally, in Sect. 4.4, we revisit the OLAP operations that we presented in Chap. 2 by addressing a set of queries to the Northwind data warehouse.

4.1 Conceptual Modeling of Data Warehouses

As studied in Chap. 2, the conventional database design process includes the creation of database schemas at three different levels: conceptual, logical, and physical. A **conceptual schema** is a concise description of the users' data requirements without taking into account implementation details.

A. Vaisman and E. Zimányi, *Data Warehouse Systems*, Data-Centric Systems and Applications, DOI 10.1007/978-3-642-54655-6_4, © Springer-Verlag Berlin Heidelberg 2014

Conventional databases are generally designed at the conceptual level using some variation of the well-known entity-relationship (ER) model, although the Unified Modeling Language (UML) is being increasingly used. Conceptual schemas can be easily translated to the relational model by applying a set of mapping rules.

Within the database community, it has been acknowledged for several decades that conceptual models allow better communication between designers and users for the purpose of understanding application requirements. A conceptual schema is more stable than an implementation-oriented (logical) schema, which must be changed whenever the target platform changes. Conceptual models also provide better support for visual user interfaces; for example, ER models have been very successful with users due to their intuitiveness.

However, there is no well-established and universally adopted conceptual model for multidimensional data. Due to this lack of a generic, user-friendly, and comprehensible conceptual data model, data warehouse design is usually directly performed at the logical level, based on star and/or snowflake schemas (which we will study in Chap. 5), leading to schemas that are difficult to understand by a typical user. Providing extensions to the ER and the UML models for data warehouses is not really a solution to the problem, since ultimately they represent a reflection and visualization of the underlying relational technology concepts and, in addition, reveal their own problems. Therefore, conceptual data warehousing modeling requires a model that clearly stands on top of the logical level.

In this chapter, we use the MultiDim model, which is powerful enough to represent at the conceptual level all elements required in data warehouse and OLAP applications, that is, dimensions, hierarchies, and facts with associated measures. The graphical notation of the MultiDim model is shown in Fig. 4.1. As we can see, the notation resembles the one of the ER model, which we presented in Chap. 2. A more detailed description of our notation is given in Appendix A.

In order to give a general overview of the model, we shall use the example in Fig. 4.2, which illustrates the conceptual schema of the Northwind data warehouse. This figure includes several types of hierarchies, which will be presented in more detail in the subsequent sections. We next introduce the main components of the model.

A **schema** is composed of a set of dimensions and a set of facts.

A **dimension** is composed of either one level or one or more hierarchies. A hierarchy is in turn composed of a set of levels (we explain below the notation for hierarchies). There is no graphical element to represent a dimension; it is depicted by means of its constituent elements.

A **level** is analogous to an entity type in the ER model. It describes a set of real-world concepts that, from the application perspective, have similar characteristics. For example, Product and Category are some of the levels in Fig. 4.2. Instances of a level are called **members**. As shown in Fig. 4.1a,

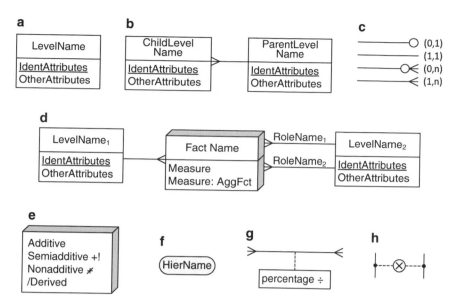

Fig. 4.1 Notation of the MultiDim model. (**a**) Level. (**b**) Hierarchy. (**c**) Cardinalities. (**d**) Fact with measures and associated levels. (**e**) Types of measures. (**f**) Hierarchy name. (**g**) Distributing attribute. (**h**) Exclusive relationships

a level has a set of **attributes** that describe the characteristics of their members. In addition, a level has one or several **identifiers** that uniquely identify the members of a level, each identifier being composed of one or several attributes. For example, in Fig. 4.2, CategoryID is an identifier of the Category level. Each attribute of a level has a type, that is, a domain for its values. Typical value domains are integer, real, and string. We do not include type information for attributes in the graphical representation of our conceptual schemas.

A **fact** (Fig. 4.1d) relates several levels. For example, the Sales fact in Fig. 4.2 relates the Employee, Customer, Supplier, Shipper, Order, Product, and Time levels. As shown in Fig. 4.1d, the same level can participate several times in a fact, playing different **roles**. Each role is identified by a name and is represented by a separate link between the corresponding level and the fact. For example, in Fig. 4.2, the Time level participates in the Sales fact with the roles OrderDate, DueDate, and ShippedDate. Instances of a fact are called **fact members**. The **cardinality** of the relationship between facts and levels, as shown in Fig. 4.1c, indicates the minimum and the maximum number of fact members that can be related to level members. For example, in Fig. 4.2, the Sales fact is related to the Product level with a one-to-many cardinality, which means that one sale is related to only one product and that each product can have many sales. On the other hand, the Sales fact is related to the Order level with a one-to-one cardinality, which means that

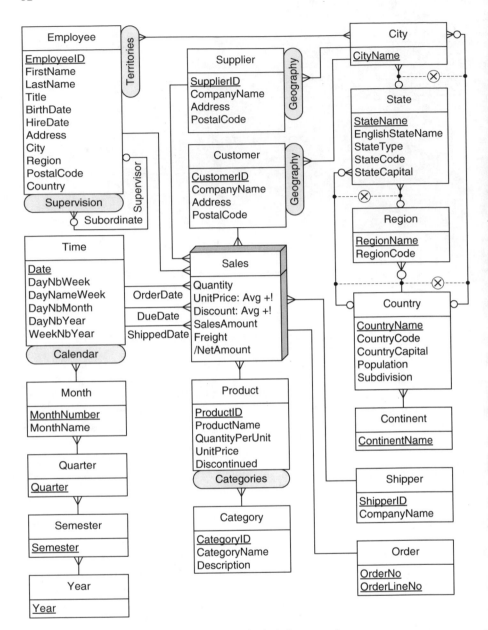

Fig. 4.2 Conceptual schema of the Northwind data warehouse

every sale is related to only one order line and that each order line has only one sale.

A fact may contain attributes commonly called **measures**. These contain data (usually numerical) that are analyzed using the various perspectives represented by the dimensions. For example, the Sales fact in Fig. 4.2 includes the measures Quantity, UnitPrice, Discount, SalesAmount, Freight, and Net-Amount. The identifier attributes of the levels involved in a fact indicate the granularity of the measures, that is, the level of detail at which measures are represented.

Measures are aggregated along dimensions when performing roll-up operations. As shown in Fig. 4.1d, the aggregation function associated with a measure can be specified next to the measure name, where the SUM aggregation function is assumed by default. In Chap. 3, we classified measures as **additive**, **semiadditive**, or **nonadditive**. As shown in Fig. 4.1e, we assume by default that measures are additive, that is, they can be summarized along all dimensions. For semiadditive and nonadditive measures, we include the symbols '+!' and '≠', respectively. For example, in Fig. 4.2 the measures Quantity and UnitPrice are, respectively, additive and semiadditive measures. Further, measures and level attributes may be **derived**, where they are calculated on the basis of other measures or attributes in the schema. We use the symbol '/' for indicating derived measures and attributes. For example, in Fig. 4.2, the measure NetAmount is derived.

A **hierarchy** comprises several related levels, as in Fig. 4.1b. Given two related levels of a hierarchy, the lower level is called the **child** and the higher level is called the **parent**. Thus, the relationships composing hierarchies are called **parent-child relationships**. The **cardinalities** in parent-child relationships, as shown in Fig. 4.1c, indicate the minimum and the maximum number of members in one level that can be related to a member in another level. For example, in Fig. 4.2, the child level Product is related to the parent level Category with a one-to-many cardinality, which means that every product belongs to only one category and that each category can have many products.

A dimension may contain several hierarchies, each one expressing a particular criterion used for analysis purposes; thus, we include the **hierarchy name** (Fig. 4.1f) to differentiate them. If a single level contains attributes forming a hierarchy, such as the attributes City, Region, and Country in the Employee dimension in Fig. 4.2, this means that the user is not interested in employing this hierarchy for aggregation purposes.

Levels in a hierarchy are used to analyze data at various *granularities* or levels of detail. For example, the Product level contains specific information about products, while the Category level may be used to see these products from the more general perspective of the categories to which they belong. The level in a hierarchy that contains the most detailed data is called the **leaf level**. The name of the leaf level defines the dimension name, except for the case where the same level participates several times in a fact, in which case the role name defines the dimension name. These are called **role-playing dimensions**. The level in a hierarchy representing the most general data is called the **root level**. It is usual (but not mandatory) to represent the root of a hierarchy using a distinguished level called All, which contains a single member, denoted all. The decision of including this level in multidimensional schemas is left to the designer. In the remainder, we do not show the All level in the hierarchies (except when we consider it necessary for clarity of presentation), since we consider that it is meaningless in conceptual schemas.

The identifier attributes of a parent level define how child members are grouped. For example, in Fig. 4.2, CategoryID in the Category level is an identifier attribute; it is used for grouping different product members during the roll-up operation from the Product to the Category levels. However, in the case of many-to-many parent-child relationships, it is also needed to determine how to distribute the measures from a child to its parent members. For this, a **distributing attribute** (Fig. 4.1g) may be used, if needed. For example, in Fig. 4.2, the relationship between Employee and City is many-to-many, that is, the same employee can be assigned to several cities. A distributing attribute can be used to store the percentage of time that an employee devotes to each city.

Finally, it is sometimes the case that two or more parent-child relationships are **exclusive**. This is represented using the symbol '⊗', as shown in Fig. 4.1h. An example is given in Fig. 4.2, where states can be aggregated either into regions or into countries. Thus, according to their type, states participate in only one of the relationships departing from the State level.

The reader may have noticed that many of the concepts of the MultiDim model are similar to those used in Chap. 3, when we presented the multidimensional model and the data cube. This suggests that the MultiDim model stays on top of the logical level, hiding from the user the implementation details. In other words, the model represents a conceptual data cube. Therefore, we will call the model in Fig. 4.2 as the Northwind data cube.

4.2 Hierarchies

Hierarchies are key elements in analytical applications, since they provide the means to represent the data under analysis at different abstraction levels. In real-world situations, users must deal with complex hierarchies of various kinds. Even though we can model complex hierarchies at a conceptual level, as we will study in this section, logical models of data warehouse and OLAP systems only provide a limited set of kinds of hierarchies. Therefore, users are often unable to capture the essential semantics of multidimensional applications and must limit their analysis to considering only the predefined kinds of hierarchies provided by the tools in use. Nevertheless, a data warehouse designer should be aware of the problems that the various kinds of hierarchies introduce and be able to deal with them. In this section, we discuss several kinds of hierarchies that can be represented by means of the MultiDim model, although the classification of hierarchies that we will provide is independent of the conceptual model used to represent them. Since many of the hierarchies we study next are not present in the Northwind data cube of Fig. 4.2, we will introduce new ad hoc examples when needed.

4.2.1   Balanced Hierarchies

A **balanced hierarchy** has only one path at the schema level, where all levels are mandatory. An example is given by hierarchy Product → Category in Fig. 4.2. At the instance level, the members form a tree where all the branches have the same length, as shown in Fig. 4.3. All parent members have at least one child member, and a child member belongs exactly to one parent member. For example, in Fig. 4.3, each category is assigned at least one product, and a product belongs to only one category.

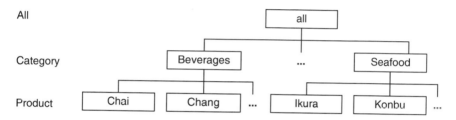

Fig. 4.3 Example of instances of the balanced hierarchy Product → Category in Fig. 4.2 (repeated from Fig. 3.3)

4.2.2   Unbalanced Hierarchies

An **unbalanced hierarchy** has only one path at the schema level, where at least one level is not mandatory. Therefore, at the instance level, there can be parent members without associated child members. Figure 4.4a shows a hierarchy schema in which a bank is composed of several branches, where a branch may have agencies; further, an agency may have ATMs. As a consequence, at the instance level, the members represent an unbalanced tree, that is, the branches of the tree have different lengths, since some parent members do not have associated child members. For example, Fig. 4.4b shows a branch with no agency and several agencies with no ATM. As in the case of balanced hierarchies, the cardinalities in the schema imply that every child member should belong to at most one parent member. For example, in Fig. 4.4, every agency belongs to one branch.

Unbalanced hierarchies include a special case that we call **recursive hierarchies**, also called **parent-child hierarchies**. In this kind of hierarchy, the same level is linked by the two roles of a parent-child relationship (note the difference between the notions of parent-child hierarchies and relationships).

a

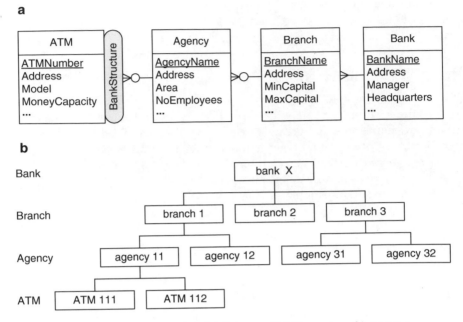

b

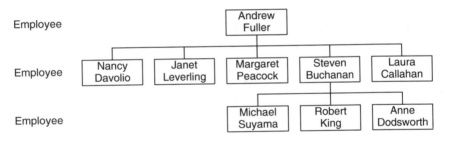

Fig. 4.4 An unbalanced hierarchy. (**a**) Schema. (**b**) Examples of instances

Fig. 4.5 Instances of the parent-child hierarchy in the Northwind data warehouse

An example is given by dimension **Employee** in Fig. 4.2, which represents an organizational chart in terms of the employee–supervisor relationship. The **Subordinate** and **Supervisor** roles of the parent-child relationship are linked to the **Employee** level. As seen in Fig. 4.5, this hierarchy is unbalanced since employees with no subordinate will not have descendants in the instance tree.

4.2.3 Generalized Hierarchies

Sometimes, the members of a level are of different types. A typical example arises with customers, which can be either companies or persons. Such a situation is usually captured in an ER model using the generalization relationship studied in Chap. 2. Further, suppose that measures pertaining to customers must be aggregated differently according to the customer type, where for companies the aggregation path is Customer → Sector → Branch, while for persons it is Customer → Profession → Branch. To represent such kinds of hierarchies, the MultiDim model has the graphical notation shown in Fig. 4.6a, where the common and specific hierarchy levels and also the parent-child relationships between them are clearly represented. Such hierarchies are called **generalized hierarchies**.

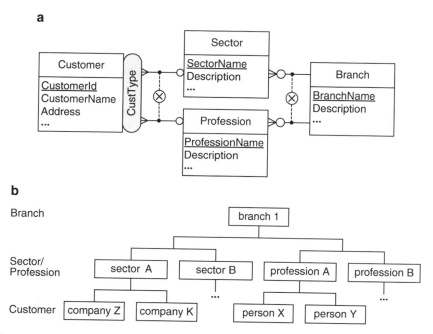

Fig. 4.6 A generalized hierarchy. (**a**) Schema. (**b**) Examples of instances

At the schema level, a generalized hierarchy contains multiple exclusive paths sharing at least the leaf level; they may also share some other levels, as shown in Fig. 4.6a. This figure shows the two aggregation paths described above, one for each type of customer, where both belong to the same hierarchy. At the instance level, each member of the hierarchy belongs to only one path, as can be seen in Fig. 4.6b. We use the symbol '⊗' to indicate that the paths are exclusive for every member. Such a notation is equivalent to the *xor* annotation used in UML. The levels at which the alternative paths split and join are called, respectively, the **splitting** and **joining levels**.

The distinction between splitting and joining levels in generalized hierarchies is important to ensure correct measure aggregation during roll-up operations, a property called summarizability, which we discussed in Chap. 3.

Generalized hierarchies are, in general, not summarizable. For example, not all customers are mapped to the **Profession** level. Thus, the aggregation mechanism should be modified when a splitting level is reached in a roll-up operation.

In generalized hierarchies, it is not necessary that splitting levels are joined. An example is the hierarchy in Fig. 4.7, which is used for analyzing international publications. Three kinds of publications are considered: journals, books, and conference proceedings. The latter can be aggregated to the conference level. However, there is not a common joining level for all paths.

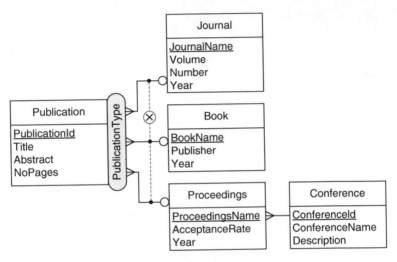

Fig. 4.7 A generalized hierarchy without a joining level

Generalized hierarchies include a special case commonly referred to as **ragged** hierarchies. An example is the hierarchy City → State → Region → Country → Continent given in Fig. 4.2. As can be seen in Fig. 4.8, some countries, such as Belgium, are divided into regions, whereas others, such as Germany, are not. Furthermore, small countries like the Vatican have neither regions nor states. A ragged hierarchy is a generalized hierarchy where alternative paths are obtained by skipping one or several intermediate levels. At the instance level, every child member has only one parent member, although the path length from the leaves to the same parent level can be different for different members.

4.2.4 Alternative Hierarchies

Alternative hierarchies represent the situation where at the schema level, there are several nonexclusive hierarchies that share at least the leaf level.

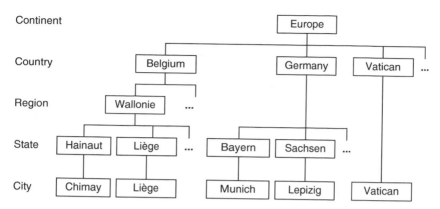

Fig. 4.8 Examples of instances of the ragged hierarchy in Fig. 4.2

An example is given in Fig. 4.9a, where the Time dimension includes two hierarchies corresponding to different groupings of months into calendar years and fiscal years. Figure 4.9b shows an instance of the dimension (we do not show members of the Time level), where it is supposed that fiscal years begin in February. As it can be seen, the hierarchies form a graph, since a child member is associated with more than one parent member and these parent members belong to different levels. Alternative hierarchies are needed when we want to analyze measures from a unique perspective (e.g., time) using alternative aggregations.

Note the difference between generalized and alternative hierarchies (see Figs. 4.6 and 4.9). Although the two kinds of hierarchies share some levels, they represent different situations. In a generalized hierarchy, a child member is related to *only one* of the paths, whereas in an alternative hierarchy, a child member is related to *all paths*, and the user must choose one of them for analysis.

4.2.5 Parallel Hierarchies

Parallel hierarchies arise when a dimension has several hierarchies associated with it, accounting for different analysis criteria. Further, the component hierarchies may be of different kinds.

Parallel hierarchies can be **dependent** or **independent** depending on whether the component hierarchies share levels. Figure 4.10 shows an example of a dimension that has two parallel independent hierarchies. The hierarchy ProductGroups is used for grouping products according to categories or departments, while the hierarchy DistributorLocation groups them according to distributors' divisions or regions. On the other hand, the

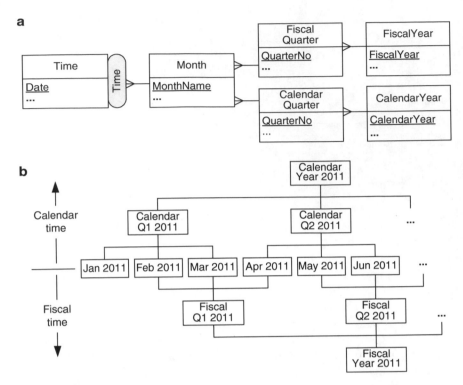

Fig. 4.9 An alternative hierarchy. (a) Schema. (b) Examples of instances

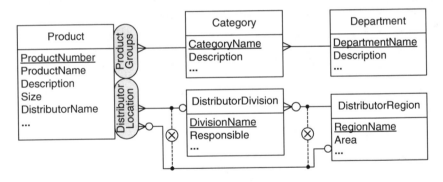

Fig. 4.10 An example of parallel independent hierarchies

parallel dependent hierarchies given in Fig. 4.11 represent a company that requires sales analysis for stores located in several countries. The hierarchy StoreLocation represents the geographic division of the store address, while the hierarchy SalesOrganization represents the organizational division of the company. Since the two hierarchies share the State level, this level plays different roles according to the hierarchy chosen for the analysis. Sharing levels in a conceptual schema reduces the number of its elements without losing its semantics, thus improving readability. In order to unambiguously define the levels composing the various hierarchies, the hierarchy name must be included in the sharing level for hierarchies that *continue beyond* that level. This is the case of StoreLocation and SalesOrganization indicated on level State.

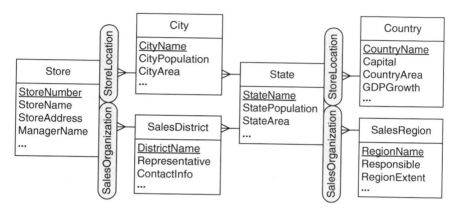

Fig. 4.11 An example of parallel dependent hierarchies

Even though both alternative and parallel hierarchies share some levels and may be composed of several hierarchies, they represent different situations and should be clearly distinguishable at the conceptual level. This is done by including only one (for alternative hierarchies) or several (for parallel hierarchies) hierarchy names, which account for various analysis criteria. In this way, the user is aware that in the case of alternative hierarchies, it is not meaningful to combine levels from different component hierarchies, whereas this can be done for parallel hierarchies. For example, for the schema in Fig. 4.11, the user can safely issue a query "Sales figures for stores in city A that belong to the sales district B."

Further, in parallel dependent hierarchies, a leaf member may be related to various different members in a shared level, which is not the case for alternative hierarchies that share levels. For instance, consider the schema in Fig. 4.12, which refers to the living place and the territory assignment of sales employees. It should be obvious that traversing the hierarchies Lives and Territory from the Employee to the State level will lead to different states for employees who live in one state and are assigned to another. As a consequence of this, aggregated measure values can be reused for shared levels in alternative hierarchies, whereas this is not the case for parallel dependent hierarchies. For example, suppose that the amount of sales generated by employees E1, E2, and E3 are $50, $100, and $150, respectively. If all employees live in state A, but only E1 and E2 work in this state, aggregating

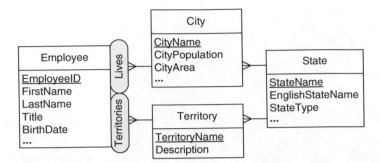

Fig. 4.12 Parallel dependent hierarchies leading to different parent members of the shared level

the sales of all employees to the State level following the Lives hierarchy gives a total amount of $300, whereas the corresponding value will be equal to $150 when the Territories hierarchy is traversed. Note that both results are correct, since the two hierarchies represent different analysis criteria.

4.2.6 Nonstrict Hierarchies

In the hierarchies studied so far, we have assumed that each parent-child relationship has a one-to-many cardinality, that is, a child member is related to at most one parent member and a parent member may be related to several child members. However, many-to-many relationships between parent and child levels are very common in real-life applications. For example, a diagnosis may belong to several diagnosis groups, 1 week may span 2 months, a product may be classified into various categories, etc.

A hierarchy that has *at least* one many-to-many relationship is called **nonstrict**; otherwise, it is called **strict**. The fact that a hierarchy is strict or not is orthogonal to its kind. Thus, the hierarchies previously presented can be either strict or nonstrict. We next analyze some issues that arise when dealing with nonstrict hierarchies.

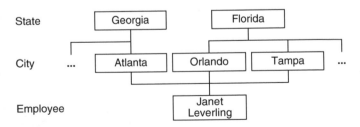

Fig. 4.13 Examples of instances of the nonstrict hierarchy in Fig. 4.2

Figure 4.2 shows a nonstrict hierarchy where an employee may be assigned to several cities. Some instances of this hierarchy are shown in Fig. 4.13. Here, the employee **Janet Leverling** is assigned to three cities that belong to two states. Therefore, since at the instance level a child member may have more than one parent member, the members of the hierarchy form an acyclic graph. Note the slight abuse of terminology. We use the term "nonstrict hierarchy" to denote an acyclic classification graph. We use this term for several reasons. Firstly, the term "hierarchy" conveys the notion that users need to analyze measures at different levels of detail; the term "acyclic classification graph" is less clear in this sense. Further, the term "hierarchy" is already used by practitioners, and there are tools that support many-to-many parent-child relationships. Finally, this notation is customary in data warehouse research.

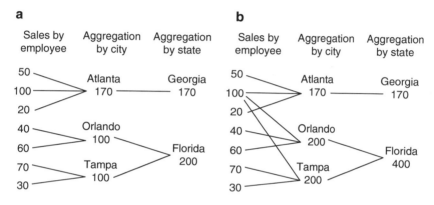

Fig. 4.14 Double-counting problem when aggregating a sales amount measure in Fig. 4.13. (**a**) Strict hierarchy. (**b**) Nonstrict hierarchy

Nonstrict hierarchies induce the problem of **double counting** of measures when a roll-up operation reaches a many-to-many relationship. Let us consider the example in Fig. 4.14, which illustrates sales by employees with aggregations along City and State levels (defined in Fig. 4.13), and employee Janet Leverling with total sales equal to 100. Figure 4.14a shows a situation where the employee has been assigned to Atlanta, in a strict hierarchy scenario. The sum of sales by territory and by state can be calculated straightforwardly, as the figure shows. Figure 4.14b shows a nonstrict hierarchy scenario, where the employee has been assigned the territories Atlanta, Orlando, and Tampa. This approach causes incorrect aggregated results, since the employee's sales are counted three times instead of only once.

One solution to the double-counting problem consists in transforming a nonstrict hierarchy into a strict one by creating a new member for each set of parent members participating in a many-to-many relationship. In our example, a new member that represents the three cities Atlanta, Orlando, and

Tampa will be created. However, in this case, a new member must also be created in the state level, since the three cities belong to two states. Another solution would be to ignore the existence of several parent members and to choose one of them as the primary member. For example, we may choose the city of Atlanta. However, neither of these solutions correspond to the users' analysis requirements, since in the former, artificial categories are introduced, and in the latter, some pertinent analysis scenarios are ignored.

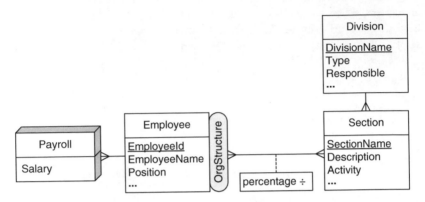

Fig. 4.15 A nonstrict hierarchy with a distributing attribute

An alternative approach to the double-counting problem would be to indicate how measures are distributed between several parent members for many-to-many relationships. For example, Fig. 4.15 shows a nonstrict hierarchy where employees may work in several sections. The schema includes a measure that represents an employee's overall salary, that is, the sum of the salaries paid in each section. Suppose that an attribute stores the percentage of time for which an employee works in each section. In this case, we depict this attribute in the relationship with an additional symbol '÷', indicating that it is a **distributing attribute** determining how measures are divided between several parent members in a many-to-many relationship.

Choosing an appropriate distributing attribute is important in order to avoid approximate results when aggregating measures. For example, suppose that in Fig. 4.15, the distributing attribute represents the percentage of time that an employee works in a specific section. If the employee has a higher position in one section and although she works less time in that section, she may earn a higher salary. Thus, applying the percentage of time as a distributing attribute for measures representing an employee's overall salary may not give an exact result. Note also that in cases where the distributing attribute is unknown, it can be approximated by considering the total number of parent members with which the child member is associated. In the example of Fig. 4.14, since we have three cities with which the employee

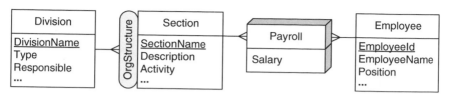

Fig. 4.16 Transforming a nonstrict hierarchy into a strict hierarchy with an additional dimension

Janet Leverling is associated, one-third of the value of the measure will be accounted for each city.

Figure 4.16 shows another solution to the problem of Fig. 4.15 where we transformed a nonstrict hierarchy into independent dimensions. However, this solution corresponds to a different conceptual schema, where the focus of analysis has been changed from employees' salaries to employees' salaries by section. Note that this solution can only be applied when the exact distribution of the measures is known, for instance, when the amounts of salary paid for working in the different sections are known. It cannot be applied to nonstrict hierarchies without a distributing attribute, as in Fig. 4.13.

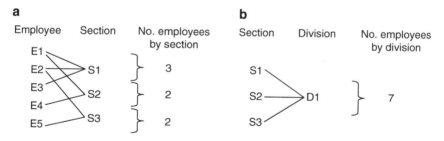

Fig. 4.17 Double-counting problem for a nonstrict hierarchy

Nevertheless, although the solution in Fig. 4.16 aggregates correctly the Salary measure when applying the roll-up operation from the Section to the Division level, the problem of double counting of the same employee will occur. Suppose that we want to use the schema in Fig. 4.16 to calculate the number of employees by section or by division; this value can be calculated by counting the instances of employees in the fact. The example in Fig. 4.17a considers five employees who are assigned to various sections. Counting the number of employees who work in each section gives correct results. However, the aggregated values for each section cannot be reused for calculating the number of employees in every division, since some employees (E1 and E2 in Fig. 4.17a) will be counted twice and the total result will give a value equal to 7 (Fig. 4.17b) instead of 5.

In summary, nonstrict hierarchies can be handled in several ways:

- Transforming a nonstrict hierarchy into a strict one:
  - Creating a new parent member for each group of parent members linked to a single child member in a many-to-many relationship.
  - Choosing one parent member as the primary member and ignoring the existence of other parent members.
  - Transforming the nonstrict hierarchy into two independent dimensions.
- Including a distributing attribute.
- Calculating approximate values of a distributing attribute.

Since each solution has its advantages and disadvantages and requires special aggregation procedures, the designer must select the appropriate solution according to the situation at hand and the users' requirements.

4.3 Advanced Modeling Aspects

In this section, we discuss particular modeling issues, namely, facts with multiple granularities and many-to-many dimensions, and show how they can be represented in the MultiDim model.

4.3.1 Facts with Multiple Granularities

Sometimes, it is the case that measures are captured at **multiple granularities**. An example is given in Fig. 4.18, where, for instance, sales for the USA might be reported per state, while European sales might be reported per city. As another example, consider a medical data warehouse for analyzing patients, where there is a diagnosis dimension with levels diagnosis, diagnosis family, and diagnosis group. A patient may be related to a diagnosis at the lowest granularity but may also have (more imprecise) diagnoses at the diagnosis family and diagnosis group levels.

As can be seen in Fig. 4.18, this situation can be modeled using exclusive relationships between the various granularity levels. Obviously, the issue in this case is to get correct analysis results when fact data are registered at multiple granularities.

4.3.2 Many-to-Many Dimensions

In a **many-to-many dimension**, several members of the dimension participate in the same fact member. An example is shown in Fig. 4.19. Since an

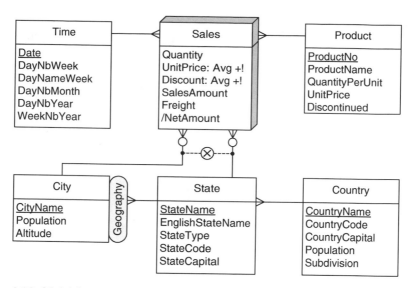

Fig. 4.18 Multiple granularities for the Sales fact

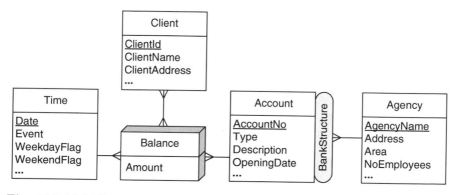

Fig. 4.19 Multidimensional schema for the analysis of bank accounts

account can be jointly owned by several clients, aggregation of the balance according to the clients will count this balance as many times as the number of account holders. For example, as shown in Fig. 4.20, suppose that at some point in time T1 there are two accounts A1 and A2 with balances of, respectively, 100 and 500. Suppose further that both accounts are shared between several clients: account A1 is shared by C1, C2, and C3 and account A2 by C1 and C2. The total balance of the two accounts is equal to 600; however, aggregation (e.g., according to the Time or the Client dimension) gives a value equal to 1,300.

The problem of **double counting** introduced above can be analyzed through the concept of **multidimensional normal forms** (MNFs). MNFs determine the conditions that ensure correct measure aggregation in the presence of the complex hierarchies studied in this chapter. The first multidimensional normal form (1MNF) requires each measure to be uniquely identified by the set of associated leaf levels. The 1MNF is the basis for correct schema design. To analyze the schema in Fig. 4.19 in terms of the 1MNF, we need to find out the functional dependencies that exist between the leaf levels and the measures. Since the balance depends on the specific account and the time when it is considered, the account and the time determine the balance. Therefore, the schema in Fig. 4.19 does not satisfy the 1MNF, since the measure is not determined by all leaf levels, and thus the fact must be decomposed.

Time	Account	Client	Balance
T1	A1	C1	100
T1	A1	C2	100
T1	A1	C3	100
T1	A2	C1	500
T1	A2	C2	500

Fig. 4.20 An example of double-counting problem in a many-to-many dimension

Let us recall the notion of multivalued dependency we have seen in Chap. 2. There are two possible ways in which the **Balance** fact in Fig. 4.19 can be decomposed. In the first one, the same joint account may have different clients assigned to it during different periods of time, and thus the time and the account multidetermine the clients. This situation leads to the solution shown in Fig. 4.21a, where the original fact is decomposed into two facts, that is, **AccountHolders** and **Balance**. If the joint account holders do not change over time, clients are multidetermined just by the accounts (but not the time). In this case, the link relating the **Time** level and the **AccountHolders** fact can be eliminated. Alternatively, this situation can be modeled with a nonstrict hierarchy as shown in Fig. 4.21b.

Even though the solutions proposed in Fig. 4.21 eliminate the double-counting problem, the two schemas in Fig. 4.21 require programming effort for queries that ask for information about individual clients. The difference lies in the fact that in Fig. 4.21a, a drill-across operation (see Sect. 3.2) between the two facts is needed, while in Fig. 4.21b, special procedures for aggregation in nonstrict hierarchies must be applied. In the case of Fig. 4.21a, since the two facts represent different granularities, queries with drill-across operations are complex, demanding a conversion either from a finer to a coarser granularity (e.g., grouping clients to know who holds a specific balance in an account) or vice versa (e.g., distributing a balance between different account holders). Note also that the two schemas in Fig. 4.21 could represent the information about the percentage of ownership of accounts by customers (if this is

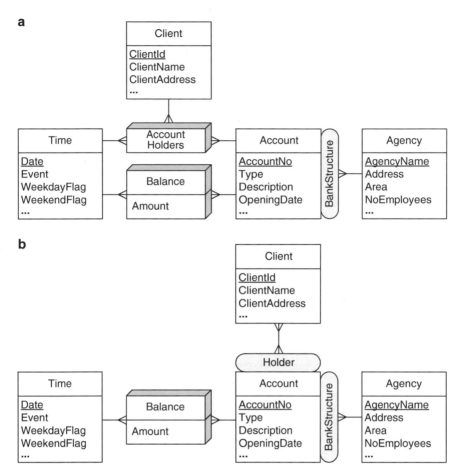

Fig. 4.21 Two possible decompositions of the fact in Fig. 4.19. (**a**) Creating two facts. (**b**) Including a nonstrict hierarchy

known). This could be represented by a measure in the AccountHolders fact in Fig. 4.21a and by a distributing attribute in the many-to-many relationship in Fig. 4.21b.

Another solution to this problem is shown in Fig. 4.22. In this solution, an additional level is created, which represents the groups of clients participating in joint accounts. In the case of the example in Fig. 4.20, two groups should be created: one that includes clients C1, C2, and C3 and another with clients C1 and C2. Note, however, that the schema in Fig. 4.22 is not in the 1MNF, since the measure Balance is not determined by all leaf levels, that is, it is only determined by Time and Account. Therefore, the schema must be decomposed leading to schemas similar to those in Fig. 4.21, with the difference that in this case, the Client level in the two schemas in Fig. 4.21 is replaced by a nonstrict hierarchy composed of the ClientGroup and the Client levels.

Finally, to avoid many-to-many dimensions, we can choose one client as the primary account owner and ignore the other clients. In this way, only one client will be related to a specific balance, and the schema in Fig. 4.19 can be used without any problems related to double counting of measures. However, this solution may not represent the real-world situation and may exclude from the analysis the other clients of joint accounts.

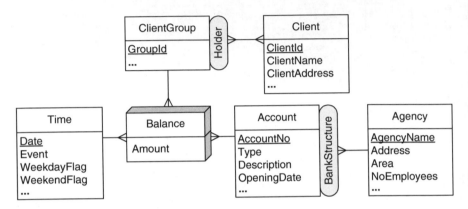

Fig. 4.22 Alternative decomposition of the fact in Fig. 4.19

In summary, many-to-many dimensions in multidimensional schemas can be avoided by using one of the solutions presented in Fig. 4.21. The choice between these alternatives depends on the functional and multivalued dependencies existing in the fact, the kinds of hierarchies in the schema, and the complexity of the implementation.

4.4   Querying the Northwind Cube Using the OLAP Operations

We conclude the chapter showing how the OLAP operations studied in Chap. 3 can be used to answer a series of queries addressed to the Northwind cube in Fig. 4.2. The idea of this section is to show how these operations can be used to express queries over a conceptual model, independently of the actual underlying implementation.

Query 4.1. Total sales amount per customer, year, and product category.

ROLLUP*(Sales, Customer → Customer, OrderDate → Year,
        Product → Category, SUM(SalesAmount))

The ROLLUP* operation is used to specify the levels at which each of the dimensions Customer, OrderDate, and Product are rolled up. For the other dimensions in the cube, a roll-up to All is performed. The SUM operation is applied to aggregate the measure SalesAmount. All other measures of the cube are removed from the result.

Query 4.2. Yearly sales amount for each pair of customer country and supplier countries.

```
ROLLUP*(Sales, OrderDate → Year, Customer → Country,
        Supplier → Country, SUM(SalesAmount))
```

As in the previous query, a roll-up to the specified levels is performed while performing a SUM operation to aggregate the measure SalesAmount.

Query 4.3. Monthly sales by customer state compared to those of the previous year.

```
Sales1 ← ROLLUP*(Sales, OrderDate → Month, Customer → State,
        SUM(SalesAmount))
Sales2 ← RENAME(Sales1, SalesAmount ← PrevYearSalesAmount)
Result ← DRILLACROSS(Sales2, Sales1,
        Sales2.OrderDate.Month = Sales1.OrderDate.Month AND
        Sales2.OrderDate.Year+1 = Sales1.OrderDate.Year AND
        Sales2.Customer.State = Sales1.Customer.State)
```

Here, we first apply a ROLLUP operation to aggregate the measure Sales-Amount. Then, a copy of the resulting cube, with the measure renamed as PrevYearSalesAmount, is kept in the cube Sales2. The two cubes are joined with the DRILLACROSS operation, where the join condition ensures that cells corresponding to the same month of two consecutive years and to the same client state are merged in a single cell in the result. Although we include the join condition for the Customer dimension, since it is an equijoin, this is not mandatory—it is assumed by default for all the dimensions not mentioned in the join condition. In the following, we do not include the equijoins in the conditions in the DRILLACROSS operations.

Query 4.4. Monthly sales growth per product, that is, total sales per product compared to those of the previous month.

```
Sales1 ← ROLLUP*(Sales, OrderDate → Month, Product → Product,
        SUM(SalesAmount))
Sales2 ← RENAME(Sales1, SalesAmount ← PrevMonthSalesAmount)
Sales3 ← DRILLACROSS(Sales2, Sales1,
        ( Sales1.OrderDate.Month > 1 AND
          Sales2.OrderDate.Month+1 = Sales1.OrderDate.Month AND
          Sales2.OrderDate.Year = Sales1.OrderDate.Year ) OR
        ( Sales1.OrderDate.Month = 1 AND Sales2.OrderDate.Month = 12 AND
          Sales2.OrderDate.Year+1 = Sales1.OrderDate.Year ) )
Result ← ADDMEASURE(Sales3, SalesGrowth =
        SalesAmount - PrevMonthSalesAmount )
```

As in the previous query, we first apply a ROLLUP operation, make a copy of the resulting cube, and join the two cubes with the DRILLACROSS operation. However, here the join condition is more involved than in the previous query, since two cases must be considered. In the first one, for the months starting from February (Month > 1), the cells to be merged must be consecutive and belong to the same year. In the second case, the cell corresponding to January must be merged with the one of December from the previous year. Finally, in the last step, we compute a new measure SalesGrowth as the difference between the sales amount of the two corresponding months.

Query 4.5. Three best-selling employees.

Sales1 ← ROLLUP*(Sales, Employee → Employee, SUM(SalesAmount))
Result ← MAX(Sales1, SalesAmount, 3)

Here, we roll up all the dimensions of the cube, except Employee, to the All level, while aggregating the measure SalesAmount. Then, the MAX operation is applied while specifying that cells with the top three values of the measure are kept in the result.

Query 4.6. Best-selling employee per product and year.

Sales1 ← ROLLUP*(Sales, Employee → Employee,
                Product → Product, OrderDate → Year, SUM(SalesAmount))
Result ← MAX(Sales1, SalesAmount) BY Product, OrderDate

In this query, we roll up the dimensions of the cube as specified. Then, the MAX operation is applied after grouping by Product and OrderDate.

Query 4.7. Countries that account for top 50% of the sales amount.

Sales1 ← ROLLUP*(Sales, Customer → Country, SUM(SalesAmount))
Result ← TOPPERCENT(Sales1, Customer, 50) ORDER BY SalesAmount DESC

Here, we roll up the Customer dimension to Country level and the other dimensions to the All level. Then, the TOPPERCENT operation selects the countries that cumulatively account for top 50% of the sales amount.

Query 4.8. Total sales and average monthly sales by employee and year.

Sales1 ← ROLLUP*(Sales, Employee → Employee, OrderDate → Month,
                SUM(SalesAmount))
Result ← ROLLUP*(Sales1, Employee → Employee, OrderDate → Year,
                SUM(SalesAmount), AVG(SalesAmount))

Here, we first roll up the cube to the Employee and Month levels by summing the SalesAmount measure. Then, we perform a second roll-up to the Year level to obtain to overall sales and the average of monthly sales.

Query 4.9. Total sales amount and total discount amount per product and month.

Sales1 ← ADDMEASURE(Sales, TotalDisc = Discount * Quantity * UnitPrice)
Result ← ROLLUP*(Sales1, Product → Product, OrderDate → Month,
                SUM(SalesAmount), SUM(TotalDisc))

Here, we first compute a new measure TotalDisc from three other measures. Then, we roll up the cube to the Product and Month levels.

Query 4.10. Monthly year-to-date sales for each product category.

Sales1 ← ROLLUP*(Sales, Product → Category, OrderDate → Month,
SUM(SalesAmount))
Result ← ADDMEASURE(Sales1, YTD = SUM(SalesAmount) OVER
OrderDate BY Year ALL CELLS PRECEDING)

Here, we start by performing a roll-up to the category and month levels. Then, a new measure is created by applying the SUM aggregation function to a window composed of all preceding cells of the same year. Notice that it is supposed that the members of the Time dimension are ordered according to the calendar time.

Query 4.11. Moving average over the last 3 months of the sales amount by product category.

Sales1 ← ROLLUP*(Sales, Product → Category, OrderDate → Month,
SUM(SalesAmount))
Result ← ADDMEASURE(Sales1, MovAvg = AVG(SalesAmount) OVER
OrderDate 2 CELLS PRECEDING)

In the first roll-up, we aggregate the SalesAmount measure by category and month. Then, we compute the moving average over a window containing the cells corresponding to the current month and the two preceding months.

Query 4.12. Personal sales amount made by an employee compared with the total sales amount made by herself and her subordinates during 1997.

Sales1 ← SLICE(Sales, OrderDate.Year = 1997)
Sales2 ← ROLLUP*(Sales1, Employee → Employee, SUM(SalesAmount))
Sales3 ← RENAME(Sales2, PersonalSales ← SalesAmount)
Sales4 ← RECROLLUP(Sales2, Employee → Employee, Supervision,
SUM(SalesAmount))
Result ← DRILLACROSS(Sales4, Sales3)

In the first step, we restrict the data in the cube to the year 1997. Then, in the second step, we perform the aggregation of the sales amount measure by employee, thus obtaining the sales figures independently of the supervision hierarchy. Then, in the third step, the obtained measure is renamed. In the fourth step, we apply the recursive roll-up, which performs an iteration over the supervision hierarchy by aggregating children to parent until the top level is reached. Finally, the last step obtains the cube with both measures.

Query 4.13. Total sales amount, number of products, and sum of the quantities sold for each order.

ROLLUP*(Sales, Order → Order, SUM(SalesAmount),
COUNT(Product) AS ProductCount, SUM(Quantity))

Here, we roll up all the dimensions, except Order, to the All level, while adding the SalesAmount and Quantity measures and counting the number of products.

Query 4.14. For each month, total number of orders, total sales amount, and average sales amount by order.

Sales1 ← ROLLUP*(Sales, OrderDate → Month, Order → Order,
        SUM(SalesAmount))
Result ← ROLLUP*(Sales1, OrderDate → Month, SUM(SalesAmount),
        AVG(SalesAmount) AS AvgSales, COUNT(Order) AS OrderCount)

In the query above, we first roll up to the Month and Order levels. Then, we perform another roll-up to remove the Order dimension and obtain the requested measures.

Query 4.15. For each employee, total sales amount, number of cities, and number of states to which she is assigned.

ROLLUP*(Sales, Employee → State, SUM(SalesAmount), COUNT(DISTINCT City)
        AS NoCities, COUNT(DISTINCT State) AS NoStates)

Recall that Territories is a nonstrict hierarchy in the Employee dimension. In this query, we roll up to the State level while adding the SalesAmount measure and counting the number of distinct cities and states. Notice that the ROLLUP* operation takes into account the fact that the hierarchy is nonstrict and avoids the double-counting problem to which we referred in Sect. 4.2.6.

4.5 Summary

This chapter focused on conceptual modeling for data warehouses. As is the case for databases, conceptual modeling allows user requirements to be represented while hiding actual implementation details, that is, regardless of the actual underlying data representation. To explain conceptual multidimensional modeling, we used the MultiDim model, which is based on the entity-relationship model and provides an intuitive graphical notation. It is well known that graphical representations facilitate the understanding of application requirements by users and designers.

We have presented a comprehensive classification of hierarchies, taking into account their differences at the schema and at the instance level. We started by describing balanced, unbalanced, and generalized hierarchies, all of which account for a single analysis criterion. Recursive (or parent-child) and ragged hierarchies are special cases of unbalanced and generalized hierarchies, respectively. Then, we introduced alternative hierarchies, which are composed of several hierarchies defining various aggregation paths for the same analysis criterion. We continued with parallel hierarchies, which are composed of several hierarchies accounting for different analysis criteria. When parallel hierarchies share a level, they are called dependent; otherwise, they are called independent. All the above hierarchies can be either strict or nonstrict, depending on whether they contain many-to-many relationships between parent and child levels. Nonstrict hierarchies define graphs at the instance level. We then presented advanced modeling aspects, namely, facts with multiple granularities and many-to-many dimensions. These often arise in practice but are frequently overlooked in the data warehouse literature. In Chap. 5, we will study how all these concepts can be implemented at the logical level. We concluded showing how the OLAP operations introduced in Chap. 3 can be applied over the conceptual model, using as example a set of queries over the Northwind data cube.

4.6 Bibliographic Notes

Conceptual data warehouse design was first introduced by Golfarelli et al. [65]. A detailed description of conceptual multidimensional models can be found in [203]. Many multidimensional models have been proposed in the literature. Some of them provide graphical representations based on the ER model (e.g., [184, 205]), as is the case of the MultiDim model, while others are based on UML (e.g., [1, 120, 204]). Other models propose new notations (e.g., [67, 88, 207]), while others do not refer to a graphical representation (e.g., [86, 160, 166]). There is great variation in the kinds of hierarchies supported by current multidimensional models. A detailed comparison of how the various multidimensional models cope with hierarchies is given in [126, 158]. Multidimensional normal forms were defined in [113, 114].

   The Object Management Group (OMG) has proposed the Common Warehouse Model (CWM)[1] as a standard for representing data warehouse and OLAP systems. This model provides a framework for representing metadata about data sources, data targets, transformations, and analysis, in addition to processes and operations for the creation and management of warehouse data. The CWM model is represented as a layered structure consisting of a number of submodels. One of these submodels, the resource layer, defines models that can be used for representing data in data warehouses and includes the relational model as one of them. Further, the analysis layer presents a metamodel for OLAP, which includes the concepts of a dimension and a hierarchy. In the CWM, it is possible to represent all of the kinds of hierarchies presented in this chapter.

---

[1]http://www.omg.org/docs/formal/03-03-02.pdf

4.7   Review Questions

4.1 Discuss the following concepts: dimension, level, attribute, identifier, fact, role, measure, hierarchy, parent-child relationship, cardinalities, root level, and leaf level.

4.2 Explain the difference, at the schema and at the instance level, between balanced and unbalanced hierarchies.

4.3 Give an example of a recursive hierarchy. Explain how to represent an unbalanced hierarchy with a recursive one.

4.4 Explain the usefulness of generalized hierarchies. To which concept of the entity-relationship model are these hierarchies related?

4.5 What is a splitting level? What is a joining level? Does a generalized hierarchy always have a joining level?

4.6 Explain why ragged hierarchies are a particular case of generalized hierarchies.

4.7 Explain in what situations alternative hierarchies are used.

4.8 Describe the difference between parallel dependent and parallel independent hierarchies.

4.9 Illustrate with examples the difference between generalized, alternative, and parallel hierarchies.

4.10 What is the difference between strict and nonstrict hierarchies?

4.11 Illustrate with an example the problem of double counting of measures for nonstrict hierarchies. Describe different solutions to this problem.

4.12 What is a distributing attribute? Explain the importance of choosing an appropriate distributing attribute.

4.13 What does it mean to have a fact with multiple granularities?

4.14 Relate the problem of double counting to the functional and multivalued dependencies that hold in a fact.

4.15 Why must a fact be decomposed in the presence of dependencies? Show an example of a fact that can be decomposed differently according to the dependencies that hold on it.

4.8   Exercises

4.1 Design a MultiDim schema for an application domain that you are familiar with. Make sure that the schema has a fact with associated levels and measures, at least two hierarchies, one of them with an exclusive relationship, and a parent-child relationship with a distributing attribute.

4.2 Design a MultiDim schema for the telephone provider application in Ex. 3.1.

4.3 Design a MultiDim schema for the train application in Ex. 3.2.

4.4 Design a MultiDim schema for the university application given in Ex. 3.3 taking into account the different granularities of the time dimension.

4.5 Design a MultiDim schema for the French horse race application given in Ex. 2.1. With respect to the races, the application must be able to display different statistics about the prizes won by owners, by trainers, by jockeys, by breeders, by horses, by sires (i.e., fathers), and by damsires (i.e., maternal grandfathers). With respect to the bettings, the application must be able to display different statistics about the payoffs by type, by race, by racetrack, and by horses.

4.6 In each of the dimensions of the multidimensional schema of Ex. 4.5, identify the hierarchies (if any) and determine its type.

4.7 Design a MultiDim schema for the Formula One application given in Ex. 2.2. With respect to the races, the application must be able to display different statistics about the prizes won by drivers, by teams, by circuit, by Grand Prix, and by season.

4.8 Consider a time dimension composed of two alternative hierarchies: (a) day, month, quarter, and year and (b) day, month, bimonth, and year. Design the conceptual schema of this dimension and show examples of instances.

4.9 Consider the well-known Foodmart cube whose schema is given in Fig. 4.23. Write using the OLAP operations the following queries[2]:

(a) All measures for stores.

(b) All measures for stores in the states of California and Washington summarized at the state level.

(c) All measures for stores in the states of California and Washington summarized at the city level.

(d) All measures, including the derived ones, for stores in the state of California summarized at the state and the city levels.

(e) Sales average in 1997 by store state and store type.

(f) Sales profit by store and semester in 1997.

(g) Sales profit percentage by quarter and semester in 1997.

(h) Sales profit by store for the first quarter of each year.

(i) Unit sales by city and percentage of the unit sales of the city with respect to its state.

(j) Unit sales by city and percentage of the unit sales of the city with respect to its country.

(k) For promotions other than "No Promotion," unit sales and percentage of the unit sales of the promotion with respect to all promotions.

(l) Unit sales by promotion, year, and quarter.

---

[2]The queries of this exercise are based on a document written by Carl Nolan entitled "Introduction to Multidimensional Expressions (MDX)."

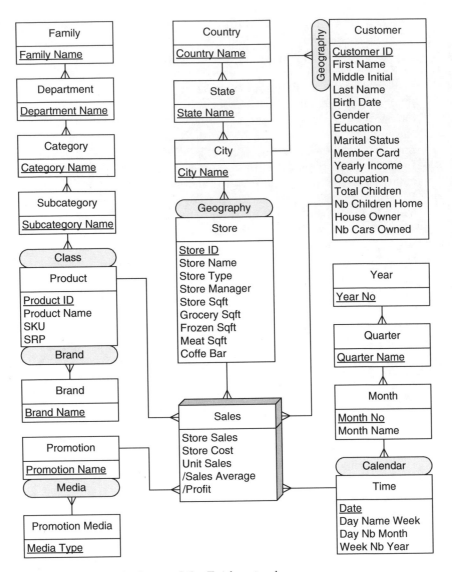

Fig. 4.23 Conceptual schema of the Foodmart cube

(m) Unit sales by promotion and store, for stores in the states of California and Washington.

(n) Sales profit by month and sales profit growth with respect to the previous month.

(o) Sales profit by month and sales profit growth with respect to the same month of the previous year.

(p) Sales profit by month and percentage profit growth with respect to the previous month.

(q) For every month in 1997, unit sales and unit sales difference with respect to the opening month of the quarter.

(r) Monthly year-to-date sales by product subcategory in 1997.

(s) Unit sales by product subcategory, customer state, and quarter.

(t) Sales profit in 1997 by store type and store city, for cities whose unit sales in 1997 exceeded 25,000.

(u) Sales profit in 1997 by store type and store city, for cities whose profit percentage in 1997 is less than the one of their state.

(v) All measures for store cities between Beverly Hills and Spokane (in the USA) sorted by name regardless of the hierarchy.

(w) All measures for store cities sorted by descending order of sales count regardless of the hierarchy.

(x) All measures for the top-five store cities based on sales count.

(y) All measures for the top-five store cities based on sales count and all measures for all the other cities combined.

(z) Store cities whose sales count accounts for 50% of the overall sales count.

(aa) For store cities whose sales count accounts for 50% of the overall sales count, unit sales by store type.

(bb) Unit sales and number of customers by product subcategory.

(cc) Number of customers and number of female customers by store.

(dd) For each product subcategory, maximum monthly unit sales in 1997 and the month when that occurred.

(ee) For 1997 and by brand, total unit sales, monthly average of unit sales, and number of months involved in the computation of the average.

Chapter 5
Logical Data Warehouse Design

Conceptual models are useful to design database applications since they favor the communication between the stakeholders in a project. However, conceptual models must be translated into logical ones for their implementation on a database management system. In this chapter, we study how the conceptual multidimensional model studied in the previous chapter can be represented in the relational model. We start in Sect. 5.1 by describing the three logical models for data warehouses, namely, relational OLAP (ROLAP), multidimensional OLAP (MOLAP), and hybrid OLAP (HOLAP). In Sect. 5.2, we focus on the relational representation of data warehouses and study four typical implementations: the star, snowflake, starflake, and constellation schemas. In Sect. 5.3, we present the rules for mapping a conceptual multidimensional model (in our case, the MultiDim model) to the relational model. Section 5.4 discusses how to represent the time dimension. Sections 5.5 and 5.6 study how hierarchies, facts with multiple granularities, and many-to-many dimensions can be implemented in the relational model. Section 5.7 is devoted to the study of slowly changing dimensions, which arise when dimensions in a data warehouse are updated. In Sect. 5.8, we study how a data cube can be represented in the relational model and how it can be queried in SQL using the SQL/OLAP extension. Finally, to show how these concepts are applied in practice, in Sects. 5.9 and 5.10, we show how the Northwind cube can be implemented, respectively, in Microsoft Analysis Services and in Mondrian.

5.1 Logical Modeling of Data Warehouses

There are several approaches for implementing a multidimensional model, depending on how the data cube is stored. These approaches are:

A. Vaisman and E. Zimányi, *Data Warehouse Systems*, Data-Centric
Systems and Applications, DOI 10.1007/978-3-642-54655-6_5,
© Springer-Verlag Berlin Heidelberg 2014

- **Relational OLAP (ROLAP)**, which stores data in relational databases and supports extensions to SQL and special access methods to efficiently implement the multidimensional data model and the related operations.
- **Multidimensional OLAP (MOLAP)**, which stores data in specialized multidimensional data structures (e.g., arrays) and implements the OLAP operations over those data structures.
- **Hybrid OLAP (HOLAP)**, which combines both approaches.

In ROLAP systems, multidimensional data are stored in relational tables. Further, in order to increase performance, aggregates are also precomputed in relational tables (we will study aggregate computation in Chap. 7). These aggregates, together with indexing structures, take a large space from the database. Moreover, since multidimensional data reside in relational tables, OLAP operations must be performed on such tables, yielding usually complex SQL statements. Finally, in ROLAP systems, all data management relies on the underlying relational DBMS. This has several advantages since relational databases are well standardized and provide a large storage capacity.

In MOLAP systems, data cubes are stored in multidimensional arrays, combined with hashing and indexing techniques. Therefore, the OLAP operations can be implemented efficiently, since such operations are very natural and simple to perform. Data management in MOLAP is performed by the multidimensional engine, which generally provides less storage capacity than ROLAP systems. Normally, typical index structures (e.g., B-trees, or R-trees) are used to index sparse dimensions (e.g., a product or a store dimension), and dense dimensions (like the time dimension) are stored in lists of multidimensional arrays. Each leaf node of the index tree points to such arrays, providing efficient cube querying and storage, since the index in general fits in main memory. Normally, MOLAP systems are used to query data marts where the number of dimensions is relatively small (less than ten, as a popular rule of thumb). For high-dimensionality data, ROLAP systems are used. Finally, MOLAP systems are proprietary, which reduces portability.

While MOLAP systems offer less storage capacity than ROLAP systems, they provide better performance when multidimensional data are queried or aggregated. Thus, HOLAP systems benefit from the storage capacity of ROLAP and the processing capabilities of MOLAP. For example, a HOLAP server may store large volumes of detailed data in a relational database, while aggregations are kept in a separate MOLAP store.

Current OLAP tools support a combination of the above models. Nevertheless, most of these tools rely on an underlying data warehouse implemented on a relational database management system. For this reason, in what follows, we study the relational OLAP implementation in detail.

5.2 Relational Data Warehouse Design

One possible relational representation of the multidimensional model is based on the **star schema**, where there is one central **fact table**, and a set of **dimension tables**, one for each dimension. An example is given in Fig. 5.1, where the fact table is depicted in gray and the dimension tables are depicted in white. The fact table contains the foreign keys of the related dimension tables, namely, ProductKey, StoreKey, PromotionKey, and TimeKey, and the measures, namely, Amount and Quantity. As shown in the figure, **referential integrity** constraints are specified between the fact table and each of the dimension tables.

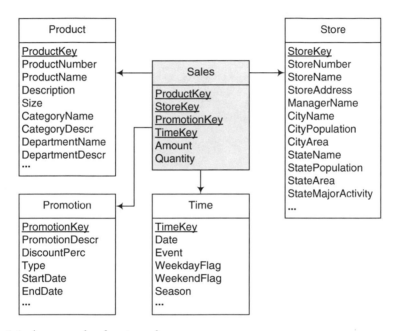

Fig. 5.1 An example of a star schema

In a star schema, the dimension tables are, in general, not normalized. Therefore, they may contain redundant data, especially in the presence of hierarchies. This is the case for dimension Product in Fig. 5.1 since all products belonging to the same category will have redundant information for the attributes describing the category and the department. The same occurs in dimension Store with the attributes describing the city and the state.

On the other hand, fact tables are usually normalized: their key is the union of the foreign keys since this union functionally determines all the measures, while there is no functional dependency between the foreign key attributes. In Fig. 5.1, the fact table Sales is normalized, and its key is composed by ProductKey, StoreKey, PromotionKey, and TimeKey.

A **snowflake schema** avoids the redundancy of star schemas by normalizing the dimension tables. Therefore, a dimension is represented by several tables related by **referential integrity** constraints. In addition, as in the case of star schemas, referential integrity constraints also relate the fact table and the dimension tables at the finest level of detail.

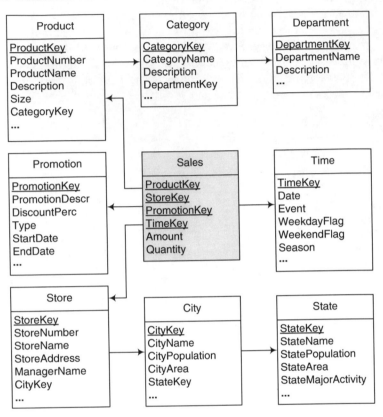

Fig. 5.2 An example of a snowflake schema

An example of a snowflake schema is given in Fig. 5.2. Here, the fact table is exactly the same as in Fig. 5.1. However, the dimensions Product and Store are now represented by normalized tables. For example, in the Product dimension, the information about categories has been moved to the table Category, and only the attribute CategoryKey remained in the original table. Thus, only the value of this key is repeated for each product of the same category, but the information about a category will only be stored once, in table Category. Normalized tables are easy to maintain and optimize storage space. However, performance is affected since more joins need to be performed when executing queries that require hierarchies to be traversed. For example, the query "Total sales by category" for the star schema in Fig. 5.1 reads in SQL as follows:

```
SELECT      CategoryName, SUM(Amount)
FROM        Product P, Sales S
WHERE       P.ProductKey = S.ProductKey
GROUP BY    CategoryName
```

while in the snowflake schema in Fig. 5.2, we need an extra join, as follows:

```
SELECT      CategoryName, SUM(Amount)
FROM        Product P, Category C, Sales S
WHERE       P.ProductKey = S.ProductKey AND P.CategoryKey = C.CategoryKey
GROUP BY    CategoryName
```

A **starflake schema** is a combination of the star and the snowflake schemas, where some dimensions are normalized while others are not. We would have a starflake schema if we replace the tables Product, Category, and Department in Fig. 5.2, by the dimension table Product of Fig. 5.1, and leave all other tables in Fig. 5.2 (like dimension table Store) unchanged.

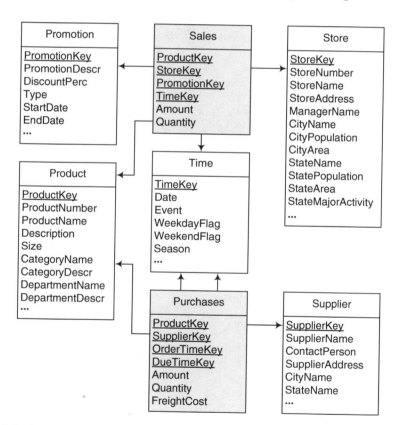

Fig. 5.3 An example of a constellation schema

Finally, a **constellation schema** has multiple fact tables that share dimension tables. The example given in Fig. 5.3 has two fact tables Sales and

Purchases sharing the Time and Product dimension. Constellation schemas may include both normalized and denormalized dimension tables.

We will discuss further star and snowflake schemas when we study logical representation of hierarchies later in this chapter.

5.3   Relational Implementation of the Conceptual Model

In Chap. 2, we presented a set of rules that can be applied to translate an ER model to the relational model. Analogously, we can define a set of rules to translate the conceptual model we use in this book (the MultiDim model) into the relational model using either the star or snowflake schema. In this section and the following one, we study such mapping rules.

Since the MultiDim model is based on the ER model, its mapping to the relational model is based on the rules described in Sect. 2.4.1, as follows:

Rule 1: A level L, provided it is not related to a fact with a one-to-one relationship, is mapped to a table T_L that contains all attributes of the level. A surrogate key may be added to the table; otherwise, the identifier of the level will be the key of the table. Note that additional attributes will be added to this table when mapping relationships using Rule 3 below.

Rule 2: A fact F is mapped to a table T_F that includes as attributes all measures of the fact. Further, a surrogate key may be added to the table. Note that additional attributes will be added to this table when mapping relationships using Rule 3 below.

Rule 3: A relationship between either a fact F and a dimension level L, or between dimension levels L_P and L_C (standing for the parent and child levels, respectively), can be mapped in three different ways, depending on its cardinalities:

Rule 3a: If the relationship is one-to-one, the table corresponding to the fact (T_F) or to the child level (T_C) is extended with all the attributes of the dimension level or the parent level, respectively.

Rule 3b: If the relationship is one-to-many, the table corresponding to the fact (T_F) or to the child level (T_C) is extended with the surrogate key of the table corresponding to the dimension level (T_L) or the parent level (T_P), respectively, that is, there is a foreign key in the fact or child table pointing to the other table.

Rule 3c: If the relationship is many-to-many, a new table T_B (standing for bridge table) is created that contains as attributes the surrogate keys of the tables corresponding to the fact (T_F) and the dimension level (T_L), or the parent (T_P) and child levels (T_C), respectively. The key of the table is the combination of both surrogate keys. If the relationship has a distributing attribute, an additional attribute is added to the table to store this information.

In the above rules, surrogate keys are generated for each dimension level in a data warehouse. The main reason for this is to provide independence from the keys of the underlying source systems because such keys can change across time. Another advantage of this solution is that surrogate keys are usually represented as integers in order to increase efficiency, whereas keys from source systems may be represented in less efficient data types such as strings. Nevertheless, the keys coming from the source systems should also be kept in the dimensions to be able to match data from sources with data in the warehouse. Obviously, an alternative solution is to reuse the keys from the source systems in the data warehouse.

Notice that a fact table obtained by the mapping rules above will contain the surrogate key of each level related to the fact with a one-to-many relationship, one for each role that the level is playing. The key of the table is composed of the surrogate keys of all the participating levels. Alternatively, if a surrogate key is added to the fact table, the combination of the surrogate keys of all the participating levels becomes an alternate key.

As we will see in Sect. 5.5, more specialized rules are needed for mapping the various kinds of hierarchies that we studied in Chap. 4.

Applying the above rules to the Northwind conceptual data cube given in Fig. 4.2 yields the tables shown in Fig. 5.4. The Sales table includes eight foreign keys, that is, one for each level related to the fact with a one-to-many relationship. Recall from Chap. 4 that in **role-playing dimensions**, a dimension plays several roles. This is the case for the dimension Time where, in the relational model, each role will be represented by a foreign key. Thus, OrderDateKey, DueDateKey, and ShippedDateKey are foreign keys to the Time dimension table in Fig. 5.4. Note also that dimension Order is related to the fact with a one-to-one relationship. Therefore, the attributes of the dimension are included as part of the fact table. For this reason, such a dimension is called a **fact** (or **degenerate**) **dimension**. The fact table also contains five attributes representing the measures: UnitPrice, Quantity, Discount, SalesAmount, and Freight. Finally, note that the many-to-many parent-child relationship between Employee and Territory is mapped to the table Territories, containing two foreign keys.

With respect to keys, in the Northwind data warehouse of Fig. 5.4, we have illustrated the two possibilities for defining the keys of dimension levels, namely, generating surrogate keys and keeping the database key as data warehouse key. For example, Customer has a surrogate key CustomerKey and a database key CustomerID. On the other hand, SupplierKey in Supplier is a database key. The choice of one among these two solutions is addressed in the ETL process that we will see in Chap. 8.

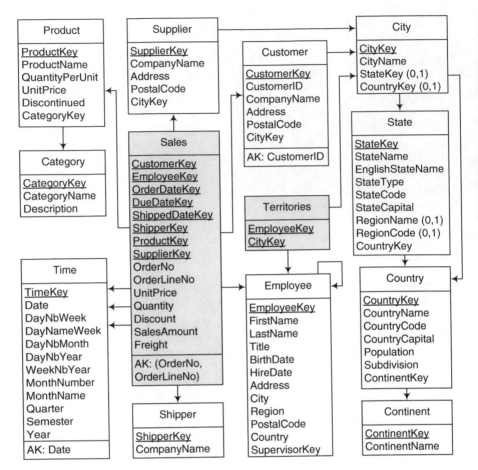

Fig. 5.4 Relational representation of the Northwind data warehouse in Fig. 4.2

5.4   Time Dimension

A data warehouse is, in the end, a historical database. Therefore, a time dimension is present in almost all data warehouses. Time information is included both as foreign keys in a fact table, indicating the time when a fact took place, and as a time dimension, containing the aggregation levels, that is, the different ways in which facts can be aggregated across time.

In OLTP database applications, temporal information is usually derived from attributes of type **DATE** using the functions provided by the database system. For example, a typical OLTP application would not explicitly store whether a particular date is a holiday: this would be computed on the fly using appropriate functions. Also, the fact that a particular date belongs to a week, a month, and so on is not explicitly stored. On the other hand, in a data warehouse, such information is stored as attributes in the time dimension since OLAP queries are highly demanding, and there is no time to perform such computations each time a fact must be summarized. For example, a query like "Total sales during weekends," posed over the schema of Fig. 5.1, would be easily evaluated with the following SQL query:

```
SELECT SUM(SalesAmount)
FROM    Time T, Sales S
WHERE  T.TimeKey = S.TimeKey AND T.WeekendFlag
```

The granularity of the time dimension varies depending on their use. For example, if we are interested in monthly data, we would define the time dimension with a granularity that will correspond to a month. Thus, the time dimension table of a data warehouse spanning 5 years will have $5 \times 12 = 60$ tuples. On the other hand, if we are interested in more detailed data, we could define the time dimension with a granularity that corresponds to a second. Thus, the same data warehouse as above will have a time dimension with $5 \times 12 \times 30 \times 24 \times 3{,}600 = 155{,}520{,}000$ tuples. The time dimension has the particularity that it can be (and in practice it is) populated automatically.

Finally, note that time dimension may have more than one hierarchy (recall our calendar/fiscal year example in Fig. 4.9). Further, even if we use a single hierarchy, we must be careful to satisfy the summarizability conditions. For example, a day aggregates correctly over a month and a year level (a day belongs to exactly 1 month and 1 year), whereas a week may correspond to 2 different months, and thus the week level cannot be aggregated over the month level in a time dimension hierarchy.

5.5 Logical Representation of Hierarchies

The general mapping rules given in the previous section do not capture the specific semantics of all of the kinds of hierarchies described in Sect. 4.2. In addition, for some kinds of hierarchies, alternative logical representations exist. In this section, we consider in detail the logical representation of the various kinds of hierarchies studied in Chap. 4.

5.5.1 Balanced Hierarchies

As we have seen, in a conceptual multidimensional schema, the levels of dimension hierarchies are represented independently, and these levels are linked by parent-child relationships. Therefore, applying the mapping rules given in Sect. 5.3 to balanced hierarchies leads to **snowflake schemas** described before in this chapter: each level is represented as a separate table, which includes the key and the attributes of the level, as well as foreign keys for the parent-child relationships. For example, applying Rules 1 and 3b to

the Categories hierarchy in Fig. 4.2 yields a snowflake structure with tables
Product and Category shown in Fig. 5.5a.

Nevertheless, if **star schemas** are required, it is necessary to represent
hierarchies using flat tables, where the key and the attributes of all levels
forming a hierarchy are included in a single table. This structure can be
obtained by denormalizing the tables that represent several hierarchy levels.
As an example, the Time dimension of Fig. 4.2 can be represented in a single
table containing all attributes, as shown in Fig. 5.5b.

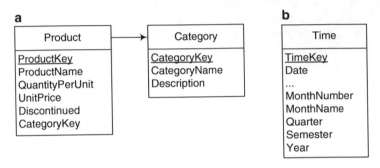

Fig. 5.5 Relations for a balanced hierarchy. (**a**) Snowflake structure. (**b**) Flat table

As we have seen in Sect. 5.2, **snowflake schemas** better represent
hierarchical structures than star schemas, since every level can be easily
distinguished and, further, levels can be reused between different hierarchies.
Additionally, in this representation, specific attributes can be included in
the different levels of a hierarchy. For example, the Product and Category
tables in Fig. 5.5a have specific attributes. However, snowflake schemas are
less performant for querying due to the joins that are needed for combining
the data scattered in the various tables composing a hierarchy.

On the other hand, **star schemas** facilitate query formulation since
fewer joins are needed for expressing queries, owing to denormalization.
Additionally, much research has been done to improve system performance
for processing star queries. However, star schemas have some drawbacks.
For example, they do not model hierarchies adequately since the hierarchy
structure is not clear. For example, for the Store dimension in Fig. 5.1, it is not
clear which attributes can be used for hierarchies. As can also be seen in the
figure, it is difficult to clearly associate attributes with their corresponding
levels, making the hierarchy structure difficult to understand.

5.5.2 Unbalanced Hierarchies

Since unbalanced hierarchies do not satisfy the summarizability conditions
(see Sect. 3.1.2), the mapping described in Sect. 5.3 may lead to the problem

of excluding from the analysis the members of nonleaf levels that do not have an associated child. For instance, since in Fig. 4.4a all measures are associated with the ATM level, these measures will be aggregated into the higher levels only for those agencies that have ATMs and, similarly, only for those branches that have agencies. To avoid this problem, an unbalanced hierarchy can be transformed into a balanced one using placeholders (marked PH1, PH2, ..., PHn in Fig. 5.6) or null values in missing levels. Then, the logical mapping for balanced hierarchies may be applied.

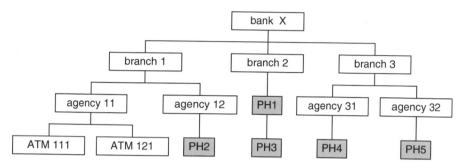

Fig. 5.6 Transformation of the unbalanced hierarchy in Fig. 4.4b into a balanced one using placeholders

The above transformation has the following consequences. First, the fact table contains measures belonging to all levels whose members can be a leaf at the instance level. For example, measures for the ATM level and for the Agency level will be included in the fact table for those members that do not have an ATM. This has the problem that users must be aware that they have to deal with fact data at several different granularities. Further, when for a child member there are two or more consecutive parent levels missing, measure values must be repeated for aggregation purposes. For example, this would be the case for branch 2 in Fig. 5.6 since two placeholders are used for two consecutive missing levels. In addition, the introduction of meaningless values requires additional storage space. Finally, special interface must be developed to hide placeholders from users.

Recall from Sect. 4.2.2 that **parent-child hierarchies** are a special case of unbalanced hierarchies. Mapping these hierarchies to the relational model yields tables containing all attributes of a level and an additional foreign key relating child members to their corresponding parent. For example, the table Employee in Fig. 5.4 shows the relational representation of the parent-child hierarchy in Fig. 4.2. Although such a table represents the semantics of parent-child hierarchies, operations over it are more complex. In particular, recursive queries are necessary for traversing a parent-child hierarchy. Recursive queries are allowed both in SQL and in MDX.

5.5.3 Generalized Hierarchies

Generalized hierarchies account for the case where dimension members are of different kinds, and each kind has a specific aggregation path. For example, in Fig. 4.6, customers can be either companies or persons, where companies are aggregated through the path Customer → Sector → Branch, while persons are aggregated through the path Customer → Profession → Branch.

As was the case for balanced hierarchies, two approaches can be used for representing generalized hierarchies at the logical level: create a table for each level, leading to snowflake schemas, or create a single flat table for all the levels, where null values are used for attributes that do not pertain to specific members (e.g., tuples for companies will have null values in attributes corresponding to persons). Alternatively, a mix of these two approaches can be followed: create one table for the common levels and another table for the specific ones. Finally, we could also use separate fact and dimension tables for each path. In all these approaches, we must keep metadata about which tables compose the different aggregation paths, while we need to specify additional constraints to ensure correct queries (e.g., to avoid grouping Sector with Profession in Fig. 4.6).

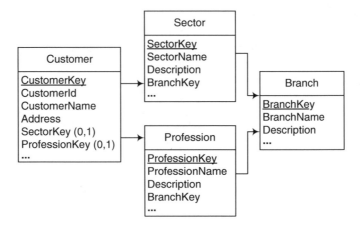

Fig. 5.7 Relations for the generalized hierarchy in Fig. 4.6

Applying the mapping described in Sect. 5.3 to the generalized hierarchy in Fig. 4.6 yields the relations shown in Fig. 5.7. Even though this schema clearly represents the hierarchical structure, it does not allow one to traverse only the common levels of the hierarchy (e.g., to go from Customer to Branch). To ensure this possibility, we must add the following mapping rule:

Rule 4: A table corresponding to a splitting level in a generalized hierarchy has an additional attribute which is a foreign key of the next joining level, provided it exists. The table may also include a discriminating attribute that indicates the specific aggregation path of each member.

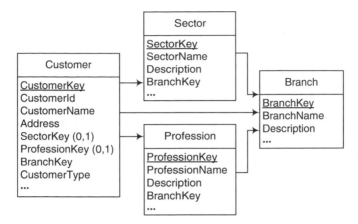

Fig. 5.8 Improved relational representation of the generalized hierarchy in Fig. 4.6

An example of the relations for the hierarchy in Fig. 4.6 is given in Fig. 5.8. The table Customer includes two kinds of foreign keys: one that indicates the next specialized hierarchy level (SectorKey and ProfessionKey), which is obtained by applying Rules 1 and 3b in Sect. 5.3; the other kind of foreign key corresponds to the next joining level (BranchKey), which is obtained by applying Rule 4 above. The discriminating attribute CustomerType, which can take the values Person and Company, indicates the specific aggregation path of members to facilitate aggregations. Finally, **check constraints** must be specified to ensure that only one of the foreign keys for the specialized levels may have a value, according to the value of the discriminating attribute:

```
ALTER TABLE Customer ADD CONSTRAINT CustomerTypeCK
      CHECK ( CustomerType IN ('Person', 'Company') )
ALTER TABLE Customer ADD CONSTRAINT CustomerPersonFK
      CHECK ( (CustomerType != 'Person') OR
( ProfessionKey IS NOT NULL AND SectorKey IS NULL ) )
ALTER TABLE Customer ADD CONSTRAINT CustomerCompanyFK
      CHECK ( (CustomerType != 'Company') OR
( ProfessionKey IS NULL AND SectorKey IS NOT NULL ) )
```

The schema in Fig. 5.8 allows one to choose alternative paths for analysis. One possibility is to use the paths that include the specific levels, for example, Profession or Sector. Another possibility is to only access the levels that are common to all members, for example, to analyze all customers, whatever their type, using the hierarchy Customer and Branch. As with the snowflake structure, one disadvantage of this structure is the necessity to apply join operations between several tables. However, an important advantage is the expansion of the analysis possibilities that it offers.

The mapping above can also be applied to **ragged hierarchies** since these hierarchies are a special case of generalized hierarchies. This is illustrated in Fig. 5.4 where the City level has two foreign keys to the State and Country levels. Nevertheless, since in a ragged hierarchy there is a unique path where some levels can be skipped, another solution is to embed the attributes of an optional level in the splitting level. This is illustrated in Fig. 5.4, where the level State has two optional attributes corresponding to the Region level. Finally, another solution would be to transform the hierarchy at the instance level by including placeholders in the missing intermediate levels, as it is done for unbalanced hierarchies in Sect. 5.5.2. In this way, a ragged hierarchy is converted into a balanced hierarchy and a star or snowflake structure can be used for its logical representation.

5.5.4 Alternative Hierarchies

For alternative hierarchies, the traditional mapping to relational tables can be applied. This is shown in Fig. 5.9 for the conceptual schema in Fig. 4.9. Note that even though generalized and alternative hierarchies can be easily distinguished at the conceptual level (see Figs. 4.6a and 4.9), this distinction cannot be made at the logical level (compare Figs. 5.7 and 5.9).

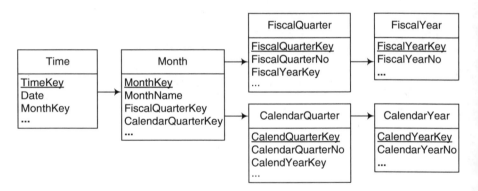

Fig. 5.9 Relations for the alternative hierarchy in Fig. 4.9

5.5.5 Parallel Hierarchies

As parallel hierarchies are composed of several hierarchies, their logical mapping consists in combining the mappings for the specific types of hierarchies. For example, Fig. 5.10 shows the result of applying this mapping to the schema shown in Fig. 4.11.

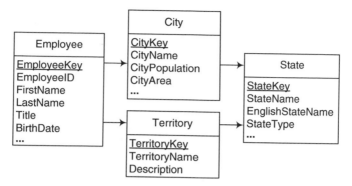

Fig. 5.10 Relations for the parallel dependent hierarchies in Fig. 4.12

Note that shared levels in parallel dependent hierarchies are represented in one table (State, in this example). Since these levels play different roles in each hierarchy, we can create views in order to facilitate queries and visualization. For example, in Fig. 5.10, table States contains all states where an employee lives, works, or both. Therefore, aggregating along the path Employee → City → State will yield states where no employee lives. If we do not want these states in the result, we can create a view named StateLives containing only the states where at least one employee lives.

Finally, note also that both alternative and parallel dependent hierarchies can be easily distinguished at the conceptual level (Figs. 4.9 and 4.12); however, their logical-level representations (Figs. 5.9 and 5.10) look similar in spite of several characteristics that differentiate them, as explained in Sect. 4.2.5.

5.5.6 Nonstrict Hierarchies

The mapping rules specified in Sect. 5.3, applied to nonstrict hierarchies, creates relations representing the levels and an additional relation (called a **bridge table**) representing the many-to-many relationship between them. An example for the hierarchy in Fig. 4.15 is given in Fig. 5.11, where the bridge table EmplSection represents the many-to-many relationship. If the parent-child relationship has a distributing attribute (as in Fig. 4.15), the bridge table will include an additional attribute for storing the values required for measure distribution. However, in order to aggregate measures correctly, a special aggregation procedure that uses this distributing attribute must be implemented.

Recall from Sect. 4.2.6 that another solution is to transform a nonstrict hierarchy into a strict one by including an additional dimension in the fact,

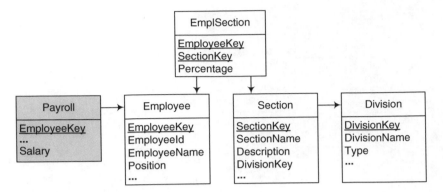

Fig. 5.11 Relations for the nonstrict hierarchy in Fig. 4.15

as shown in Fig. 4.16. Then, the corresponding mapping for a strict hierarchy can be applied. The choice between the two solutions may depend on various factors, namely,

- Data structure and size: Bridge tables require less space than creating additional dimensions. In the latter case, the fact table grows if child members are related to many parent members. The additional foreign key in the fact table also increases the space required. In addition, for bridge tables, information about the parent-child relationship and distributing attribute (if it exists) must be stored separately.
- Performance and applications: For bridge tables, join operations, calculations, and programming effort are needed to aggregate measures correctly, while in the case of additional dimensions, measures in the fact table are ready for aggregation along the hierarchy. Bridge tables are thus appropriate for applications that have a few nonstrict hierarchies. They are also adequate when the information about measure distribution does not change with time. On the contrary, additional dimensions can easily represent changes in time of measure distribution.

Finally, still another option consists in transforming the many-to-many relationship into a one-to-many relationship by defining a "primary" relationship, that is, to convert the nonstrict hierarchy into a strict one, to which the corresponding mapping for simple hierarchies is applied (as explained in Sect. 4.3.2).

5.6   Advanced Modeling Aspects

In this section, we discuss how facts with multiple granularities and many-to-many dimensions can be represented in the relational model.

5.6.1   Facts with Multiple Granularities

Two approaches can be used for the logical representation of facts with multiple granularities. The first one consists in using multiple foreign keys, one for each alternative granularity, in a similar way as it was explained for generalized hierarchies in Sect. 5.5.3. The second approach consists in removing granularity variation at the instance level with the help of placeholders, in a similar way as explained for unbalanced hierarchies in Sect. 5.5.2.

Consider the example of Fig. 4.18, where measures are registered at multiple granularities. Figure 5.12 shows the relational schema resulting from the first solution above, where the Sales fact table is related to both the City and the State levels through referential integrity constraints. In this case, both attributes CityKey and StateKey are optional, and constraints must be specified to ensure that only one of the foreign keys may have a value.

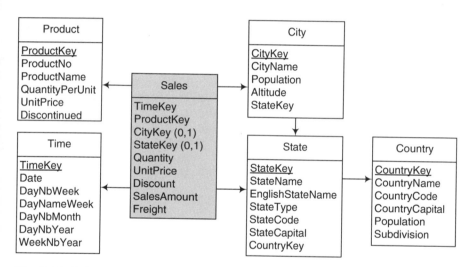

Fig. 5.12 Relations for the fact with multiple granularities in Fig. 4.18

Figure 5.13 shows an example of instances for the second solution above, where placeholders are used for facts that refer to nonleaf levels. There are two possible cases illustrated by the two placeholders in the figure. In the first case, a fact member points to a nonleaf member that has children. In this case, placeholder PH1 represents all cities other than the existing children. In the second case, a fact member points to a nonleaf member without children. In this case, placeholder PH2 represents all (unknown) cities of the state.

Obviously, in both solutions, the issue is to guarantee the correct summarization of measures. In the first solution, when aggregating at the state level, we need to perform a union of two subqueries, one for each

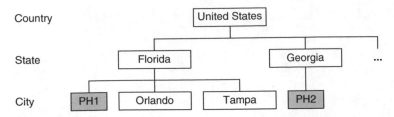

Fig. 5.13 Using placeholders for the fact with multiple granularities in Fig. 4.18

alternative path. In the second solution, when aggregating at the city level, we obtain the placeholders in the result.

5.6.2 Many-to-Many Dimensions

The mapping to the relational model given in Sect. 5.3, applied to many-to-many dimensions, creates relations representing the fact, the dimension levels, and an additional bridge table representing the many-to-many relationship between the fact table and the dimension. Figure 5.14 shows the relational representation of the many-to-many dimension in Fig. 4.19. As can be seen, a bridge table BalanceClient relates the fact table Balance with the dimension table Client. Note also that a surrogate key was added to the Balance fact table so it can be used in the bridge table for relating facts with clients.

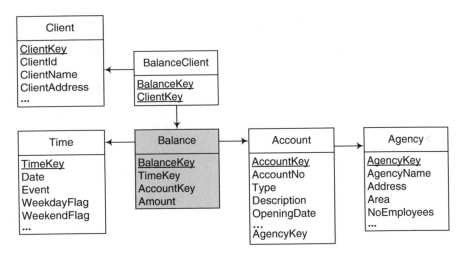

Fig. 5.14 Relations for the many-to-many dimension in Fig. 4.19

We have seen in Sect. 4.3.2 several solutions to decompose a many-to-many dimension according to the dependencies that hold on the fact table. In this case, after the decomposition, the traditional mapping to the relational model can be applied to the resulting decomposition.

5.7   Slowly Changing Dimensions

So far, we have assumed that new data that arrives to the warehouse only corresponds to facts, which means dimensions are stable, and their data do not change. However, in many real-world situations, dimensions can change both at the structure and the instance level. Structural changes occur, for example, when an attribute is deleted from the data sources and therefore it is no longer available. As a consequence, this attribute should also be deleted from the dimension table. Changes at the instance level can be of two kinds. First, when a correction must be made to the dimension tables due to an error, the new data should replace the old one. Second, when the contextual conditions of an analysis scenario change, the contents of dimension tables must change accordingly. We cover these two latter cases in this section.

We will introduce the problem by means of a simplified version of the Northwind data warehouse. In this simplified version, we consider a Sales fact table related only to the dimensions Time, Employee, Customer, and Product, and a SalesAmount measure. We assume a star (denormalized) representation of table Product, and thus category data are embedded in this table. Below, we show instances of the Sales fact table and the Product dimension table.

TimeKey	EmployeeKey	CustomerKey	ProductKey	SalesAmount
t1	e1	c1	p1	100
t2	e2	c2	p1	100
t3	e1	c3	p3	100
t4	e2	c4	p4	100

ProductKey	ProductName	Discontinued	CategoryName	Description
p1	prod1	No	cat1	desc1
p2	prod2	No	cat1	desc1
p3	prod3	No	cat2	desc2
p4	prod4	No	cat2	desc2

As we said above, new tuples will be entered into the Sales fact table as new sales occur. But also other updates are likely to occur. For example, when a new product starts to be commercialized by the company, a new tuple in Product must be inserted. Also, data about a product may be wrong, and in this case, the corresponding tuples must be corrected. Finally, the category of a product may need to be changed, not just as a result of erroneous data but as a result of a new commercial or administrative policy. Assuming that these kinds of changes are not at all frequent, when the dimensions are designed so that they support them, they are called *slowly changing dimensions*.

In the scenario above, consider a query asking for the total sales per employee and product category, expressed as follows:

```
SELECT    E.EmployeeKey, P.CategoryName, SUM(SalesAmount)
FROM      Sales S, Product P
WHERE     S.ProductKey = P.ProductKey
GROUP BY  E.EmployeeKey, P.CategoryName
```

This query would return the following table:

EmployeeKey	CategoryName	SalesAmount
e1	cat1	100
e2	cat1	100
e1	cat2	100
e2	cat2	100

Suppose now that, at an instant t after t4 (the date of the last sale shown in the fact table above), the category of product prod1 changed to cat2, which means there is a reclassification of the product with respect to its category. The trivial solution of updating the category of the product to cat2 will, in general, produce erroneous results since there is no track of the previous category of a product. For example, if the user poses the same query as above, and the fact table has not been changed in the meantime, she would expect to get the same result, but since all the sales occurred before the reclassification, she would get the following result:

EmployeeKey	CategoryKey	SalesAmount
e1	cat2	200
e2	cat2	200

This result is incorrect since the products affected by the category change were already associated with sales data. Opposite to this, if the new category would be the result of an error correction (i.e., the actual category of prod1 is cat2), this result would be correct. In the former case, obtaining the correct answer requires to guarantee the preservation of the results obtained when prod1 had category cat1 and make sure that the new aggregations will be computed with the new category.

Three basic ways of handling slowly changing dimensions have been proposed in the literature. The simplest one, called type 1, consists in overwriting the old value of the attribute with the new one. Note that in spite of the simplicity of the approach, we lose the history of the attribute. This approach is appropriate when the modification is due to an error in the dimension data.

In the second solution, called type 2, the tuples in the dimension table are versioned, and a new tuple is inserted each time a change takes place. Thus, the tuples in the fact table will match the correct tuple in the dimension table. In our example, we would enter a new row for product prod1 in the Product table, with its new category cat2. Thus, all sales prior to t will contribute to the aggregation to cat1, while the ones that occurred after t will contribute to cat2. This solution requires the table Product to be extended with two attributes indicating the validity interval of the tuple, let us call them From and To. In our example, the table Product would look like the following:

Product Key	Product Name	Discontinued	Category Name	Description	From	To
p1	prod1	No	cat1	desc1	2010-01-01	2011-12-31
p11	prod1	No	cat2	desc2	2012-01-01	9999-12-31
p2	prod2	No	cat1	desc1	2012-01-01	9999-12-31
p3	prod3	No	cat2	desc2	2012-01-01	9999-12-31
p4	prod4	No	cat2	desc2	2012-01-01	9999-12-31

In the table above, the first two tuples correspond to the two versions of product prod1, with ProductKey values p1 and p11. The value 9999-12-31 in the To attribute indicates that the tuple is still valid; this is a usual notation in temporal databases. Note that since the same product participates in the fact table with as many surrogates as there are attribute changes, to ensure correct manipulation, it is necessary to keep track of all the tuples that pertain to the same product. For example, counting the number of different products sold by the company over specific time periods cannot be done by just counting the appearance of a particular product in the fact table. Notice that since a new record is inserted every time an attribute value changes, the dimension can grow considerably, decreasing the performance during join operations with the fact table. More sophisticated techniques have been proposed to address this, and below we will comment on them.

In the type 2 approach, sometimes an additional attribute is added to explicitly indicate which is the current row. The table below shows an attribute denoted RowStatus, telling which is the current value for product prod1.

Product Key	Product Name	Discontinued	Category Name	Description	From	To	Row Status
p1	prod1	No	cat1	desc1	2010-01-01	2011-12-31	Expired
p11	prod1	No	cat2	desc2	2012-01-01	9999-12-31	Current
...	...	...	...	...	...	...	...

The type 2 approach for a snowflake (normalized) representation is handled in similar way as above. Let us consider a snowflake representation for the

Product dimension where the categories of the product are represented in a table Category.

Product Key	Product Name	Discontinued	Category Key
p1	prod1	No	c1
p2	prod2	No	c1
p3	prod3	No	c2
p4	prod4	No	c2

Category Key	Category Name	Description
c1	cat1	desc1
c2	cat2	desc2
c3	cat3	desc3
c4	cat4	desc4

Now assume that, as before, product prod1 changes its category to cat2. In the case of a solution of type 2, we add two temporal attributes to the Product table. Then, applying the change above, we obtain

Product Key	Product Name	Discontinued	Category Key	From	To
p1	prod1	No	c1	2010-01-01	2011-12-31
p11	prod1	No	c2	2012-01-01	9999-12-31
p2	prod2	No	c1	2010-01-01	9999-12-31
p3	prod3	No	c2	2010-01-01	9999-12-31
p4	prod4	No	c2	2011-01-01	9999-12-31

and the Category table remains unchanged. However, if the change occurs at an upper level in the hierarchy, for example, a description is changed, this change needs to be propagated downward in the hierarchy. For example, suppose that the description of category cat1 changes, as reflected in the following table:

Category Key	Category Name	Description	From	To
c1	cat1	desc1	2010-01-01	2011-12-31
c11	cat1	desc11	2012-01-01	9999-12-31
c2	cat2	desc2	2012-01-01	9999-12-31
c3	cat3	desc3	2010-01-01	9999-12-31
c4	cat4	desc4	2010-01-01	9999-12-31

This change must be propagated to the Product table so that all sales prior to the change refer to the old version of category cat1 (with key c1), while the new sales must point to the new version (with key c11), as shown below:

Product Key	Product Name	Discontinued	Category Key	From	To
p1	prod1	No	c1	2010-01-01	2011-12-31
p11	prod1	No	c11	2012-01-01	9999-12-31
p2	prod2	No	c1	2010-01-01	9999-12-31
p3	prod3	No	c2	2010-01-01	9999-12-31
p4	prod4	No	c2	2011-01-01	9999-12-31

The third solution to the problem of slowly changing dimensions, called type 3, consists in introducing an additional column for each attribute subject to change, which will hold the new value of the attribute. In our case, attributes CategoryName and Description changed since when product prod1 changes category from cat1 to cat2, the associated description of the category also changes from desc1 to desc2. The following table illustrates this solution:

Product Key	Product Name	Discontinued	Category Name	New Category	Description	New Description
p1	prod1	No	**cat1**	**cat2**	**desc1**	**desc2**
p2	prod2	No	cat1	Null	desc1	Null
p3	prod3	No	cat2	Null	desc2	Null
p4	prod4	No	cat2	Null	desc2	Null

Note that only the two more recent versions of the attribute can be represented in this solution and that the validity interval of the tuples is not stored.

It is worth noticing that it is possible to apply the three solutions above, or combinations of them, to the same dimension. For example, we may apply a correction (type 1) together with tuple versioning (type 2) or with attribute addition (type 3) for various attributes of a dimension table.

In addition to these three classic approaches to handle slowly changing dimensions, more sophisticated (although more difficult to implement) solutions have been proposed. We briefly comment on them next.

The type 4 approach aims at handling very large dimension tables and attributes that change frequently. This situation can make the dimension tables to grow to a point that even browsing the dimension can become very slow. Thus, a new dimension, called a **minidimension**, is created to store the most frequently changing attributes. For example, assume that in the Product dimension there are attributes SalesRanking and PriceRange, which are likely to change frequently, depending on the market conditions. Thus, we will create a new dimension called ProductFeatures, with key ProductFeaturesKey, and the attributes SalesRanking and PriceRange, as follows:

Product FeaturesKey	Sales Ranking	Price Range
pf1	1	1–100
pf2	2	1–100
...	...	...
pf200	7	500–600

As can be seen, there will be one row in the minidimension for each unique combination of SalesRanking and PriceRange encountered in the data, not one row per product.

The key ProductFeaturesKey must be added to the fact table Sales as a foreign key. In this way, we prevent the dimension to grow with every change in the sales ranking score or price range of a product, and the changes are actually captured by the fact table. For example, assume that product prod1 initially has sales ranking 2 and price range 1–100. A sale of this product will be entered in the fact table with a value of ProductFeaturesKey equal to pf2. If later the sales ranking of the product goes up to 1, the subsequent sales will be entered with ProductFeaturesKey equal to pf1.

The type 5 approach is an extension of type 4, where the primary dimension table is extended with a foreign key to the minidimension table. In the current example, the Product dimension will look as follows:

Product Key	Product Name	Discontinued	CurrentProduct FeaturesKey
p1	prod1	No	pf1
...	...	...	...

As can be seen, this allows us to analyze the current feature values of a dimension without accessing the fact table. The foreign key is a type 1 attribute, and thus, when any feature of the product changes, the current ProductFeaturesKey value is stored in the Product table. On the other hand, the fact table includes the foreign keys ProductKey and ProductFeaturesKey, where the latter points to feature values that were current *at the time of the sales*. However, the attribute CurrentProductFeaturesKey in the Product dimension would allow us to roll up historical facts based on the current product profile.

The type 6 approach extends a type 2 dimension with an additional column containing the current value of an attribute. Consider again the type 2 solution above, where the Product dimension is extended with attributes From and To indicating the validity interval of the tuple. Further, we add an attribute CurrentCategoryKey that contains the current value of the Category attribute as follows:

Product Key	Product Name	Discontinued	Category Key	From	To	Current CategoryKey
p1	prod1	No	c1	2010-01-01	2011-12-31	c11
p11	prod1	No	c11	2012-01-01	9999-12-31	c11
p2	prod2	No	c1	2010-01-01	9999-12-31	c1
p3	prod3	No	c2	2010-01-01	9999-12-31	c2
p4	prod4	No	c2	2011-01-01	9999-12-31	c2

With this solution, the CategoryKey attribute can be used to group facts based on the product category that was in effect when the facts occurred, while the CurrentCategoryKey attribute can be used to group facts based on the current product category.

Finally, the type 7 approach delivers similar functionality as the type 6 solution in the case that there are many attributes in the dimension table for which we need to support both current and historical perspectives. In a type 6 solution that would require one additional column in the dimension table for each of such attributes, these columns will contain the current value of the attributes. Instead, a type 7 solution would add to the fact table an additional foreign key of the dimension table containing not the surrogate key, but the natural key (ProductName in our example), provided it is a *durable* one. In our example, the Product dimension will be exactly the same as in the type 2 solution, but the fact table would look as follows:

TimeKey	EmployeeKey	CustomerKey	ProductKey	Product Name	SalesAmount
t1	e1	c1	p1	prod1	100
t2	e2	c2	p11	prod1	100
t3	e1	c3	p3	prod3	100
t4	e2	c4	p4	prod4	100

The ProductKey column can be used for historical analysis based on the product values effective when the fact occurred. In order to support current analysis, we need an additional view, called CurrentProduct, which keeps only current values of the Product dimension as follows:

Product Name	Discontinued	Category Key
prod1	No	c2
prod2	No	c1
prod3	No	c2
prod4	No	c2

A variant of this approach uses the surrogate key as the key of the current dimension, thus eliminating the need of handling two different foreign keys in the fact table.

Leading data warehouse platforms provide some support for slowly changing dimensions, typically type 1 to type 3. However, as we have seen, the proposed solutions are not satisfactory. In particular, they require considerable programming effort for their correct manipulation. As we will discuss in Chap. 15, temporal data warehouses have been proposed as a more general solution to this problem. They aim at providing a temporal update semantics to the data warehouse.

5.8 SQL/OLAP Operations

In this section, we show how the data cube, a multidimensional structure, can be represented in the relational model. We also show how to implement the OLAP operations in SQL using the extension called SQL/OLAP.

5.8.1 Data Cube

A relational database is not the best data structure to hold data that is, in nature, multidimensional. Consider a simple cube Sales, with two dimensions, Product and Customer, and a measure, SalesAmount, as depicted in Fig. 5.15a. This data cube contains all possible (2^2) aggregations of the cube cells, namely, SalesAmount by Product, by Customer, and by both Product and Customer, in addition to the base nonaggregated data. Computing such aggregates can be easily done by performing matrix arithmetic. This explains why MOLAP systems, which store data in special arrays, deliver good performance.

a

	c1	c2	c3	Total
p1	100	105	100	305
p2	70	60	40	170
p3	30	40	50	120
Total	200	205	190	595

b

ProductKey	CustomerKey	SalesAmount
p1	c1	100
p1	c2	105
p1	c3	100
p2	c1	70
p2	c2	60
p2	c3	40
p3	c1	30
p3	c2	40
p3	c3	50

Fig. 5.15 (a) A data cube with two dimensions, Product and Customer. (b) A fact table representing the same data

Consider now the corresponding Sales fact table depicted in Fig. 5.15b. Computing all possible aggregations along the two dimensions, Product and Customer, involves scanning the whole relation. A possible way to compute this in SQL is to use the NULL value as follows:

```
SELECT     ProductKey, CustomerKey, SalesAmount
FROM       Sales
    UNION
SELECT     ProductKey, NULL, SUM(SalesAmount)
FROM       Sales
GROUP BY ProductKey
    UNION
SELECT     NULL, CustomerKey, SUM(SalesAmount)
FROM       Sales
GROUP BY CustomerKey
    UNION
SELECT     NULL, NULL, SUM(SalesAmount)
FROM       Sales
```

The result is given in Fig. 5.16. Note that each tuple in the table represents a cell in the data cube. For example, the fourth tuple represents the total sales amount to customer c1. The penultimate tuple represents the total sales amount of product p3. Finally, the last tuple represents the total sales amount of all products to all customers. In this example, for clarity, we did not include hierarchies. However, cubes with hierarchies can be analyzed analogously.

ProductKey	CustomerKey	SalesAmount
p1	c1	100
p2	c1	70
p3	c1	30
NULL	c1	200
p1	c2	105
p2	c2	60
p3	c2	40
NULL	c2	205
p1	c3	100
p2	c3	40
p3	c3	50
NULL	c3	190
p1	NULL	305
p2	NULL	170
p3	NULL	120
NULL	NULL	595

Fig. 5.16 Data cube corresponding to the fact table in Fig. 5.15b

5.8.2 ROLLUP, CUBE, and GROUPING SETS

Computing a cube with n dimensions in the way described above would require 2^n GROUP BY statements, which is not very efficient. For this reason, SQL/OLAP extends the GROUP BY clause with the ROLLUP and CUBE operators. The former computes group subtotals in the order given by a list of attributes. The latter computes all totals of such a list. Over the grouped tuples, the HAVING clause can be applied, as in the case of a typical GROUP BY. The syntax of both statements applied to our example above are

```
SELECT    ProductKey, CustomerKey, SUM(SalesAmount)
FROM      Sales
GROUP BY ROLLUP(ProductKey, CustomerKey)
```

```
SELECT    ProductKey, CustomerKey, SUM(SalesAmount)
FROM      Sales
GROUP BY CUBE(ProductKey, CustomerKey)
```

The tables in Fig. 5.17a, b show, respectively, the result of the GROUP BY
ROLLUP and the GROUP BY CUBE queries above. In the case of roll-up, in
addition to the detailed data, we can see the total amount by product and
the overall total. For example, the total sales for product p1 is 305. If we also
need the totals by customer, we would need the cube computation, performed
by the second query.

a

ProductKey	CustomerKey	SalesAmount
p1	c1	100
p1	c2	105
p1	c3	100
p1	NULL	305
p2	c1	70
p2	c2	60
p2	c3	40
p2	NULL	170
p3	c1	30
p3	c2	40
p3	c3	50
p3	NULL	120
NULL	NULL	595

b

ProductKey	CustomerKey	SalesAmount
p1	c1	100
p2	c1	70
p3	c1	30
NULL	c1	200
p1	c2	105
p2	c2	60
p3	c2	40
NULL	c2	205
p1	c3	100
p2	c3	40
p3	c3	50
NULL	c3	190
NULL	NULL	595
p1	NULL	305
p2	NULL	170
p3	NULL	120

Fig. 5.17 Operators. GROUP BY ROLLUP (**a**) and GROUP BY CUBE (**b**)

Actually, the ROLLUP and CUBE operators are simply shorthands for a
more powerful operator, called GROUPING SETS, which is used to precisely
specify the aggregations to be computed. For example, the ROLLUP query
above can be written using GROUPING SETS as follows:

```
SELECT    ProductKey, CustomerKey, SUM(SalesAmount)
FROM      Sales
GROUP BY GROUPING SETS((ProductKey, CustomerKey), (ProductKey), ())
```

Analogously, the CUBE query would read:

```
SELECT    ProductKey, CustomerKey, SUM(SalesAmount)
FROM      Sales
GROUP BY GROUPING SETS((ProductKey, CustomerKey),
          (ProductKey), (CustomerKey), ())
```

5.8.3 Window Functions

A very common OLAP need is to compare detailed data with aggregate values. For example, we may need to compare the sales of a product to a customer against the maximum sales of this product to any customer. Thus, we could obtain the relevance of each customer with respect to the sales of the product. SQL/OLAP provides the means to perform this through a feature called **window partitioning**. This query would be written as follows:

```
SELECT ProductKey, CustomerKey, SalesAmount, MAX(SalesAmount) OVER
          (PARTITION BY ProductKey) AS MaxAmount
FROM    Sales
```

The result of the query is given in Fig. 5.18. The first three columns are obtained from the initial Sales table. The fourth one is obtained as follows. For each tuple, a window is defined, called *partition*, containing all the tuples pertaining to the same product. The attribute SalesAmount is then aggregated over this group using the corresponding function (in this case MAX), and the result is written in the MaxAmount column. Note that the first three tuples, corresponding to product p1, have a MaxAmount of 105, that is, the maximum amount sold of this product to customer c2.

ProductKey	CustomerKey	SalesAmount	MaxAmount
p1	c1	100	105
p1	c2	105	105
p1	c3	100	105
p2	c1	70	70
p2	c2	60	70
p2	c3	40	70
p3	c1	30	50
p3	c2	40	50
p3	c3	50	50

Fig. 5.18 Sales of products to customers compared with the maximum amount sold for that product

A second SQL/OLAP feature, called **window ordering**, is used to order the rows within a partition. This feature is useful, in particular, to compute rankings. Two common aggregate functions applied in this respect are ROW_NUMBER and RANK. For example, the next query shows how does each product rank in the sales of each customer. For this, we can partition the table by customer and apply the ROW_NUMBER function as follows:

```
SELECT ProductKey, CustomerKey, SalesAmount, ROW_NUMBER() OVER
          (PARTITION BY CustomerKey ORDER BY SalesAmount DESC) AS RowNo
FROM    Sales
```

The result is shown in Fig. 5.19a. The first tuple, for example, was evaluated by opening a window with all the tuples of customer c1, ordered by the sales amount. We see that product p1 is the one most demanded by customer c1.

a

Product Key	Customer Key	Sales Amount	RowNo
p1	c1	100	1
p2	c1	70	2
p3	c1	30	3
p1	c2	105	1
p2	c2	60	2
p3	c2	40	3
p1	c3	100	1
p3	c3	50	2
p2	c3	40	3

b

Product Key	Customer Key	Sales Amount	Rank
p1	c2	105	1
p1	c3	100	2
p1	c1	100	2
p2	c1	70	1
p2	c2	60	2
p2	c3	40	3
p3	c3	50	1
p3	c2	40	2
p3	c1	30	3

Fig. 5.19 (a) Ranking of products in the sales of customers. (b) Ranking of customers in the sales of products

We could instead partition by product and study how each customer ranks in the sales of each product, using the function RANK.

```
SELECT ProductKey, CustomerKey, SalesAmount, RANK() OVER
       (PARTITION BY ProductKey ORDER BY SalesAmount DESC) AS Rank
FROM   Sales
```

As shown in the result given in Fig. 5.19b, the first tuple was evaluated opening a window with all the tuples with product p1, ordered by the sales amount. We can see that customer c2 is the one with highest purchases of p1, and customers c3 and c1 are in the second place, with the same ranking.

A third kind of feature of SQL/OLAP is **window framing**, which defines the size of the partition. This is used to compute statistical functions over time series, like moving averages. To give an example, let us assume that we add two columns, Year and Month, to the Sales table. The following query computes the 3-month moving average of sales by product.

```
SELECT ProductKey, Year, Month, SalesAmount, AVG(SalesAmount) OVER
       (PARTITION BY ProductKey ORDER BY Year, Month
       ROWS 2 PRECEDING) AS MovAvg
FROM   Sales
```

The result is shown in Fig. 5.20a. For each tuple, the query evaluator opens a window that contains the tuples pertaining to the current product. Then, it orders the window by year and month and computes the average over the current tuple and the preceding two ones, provided they exist. For example, in the first tuple, the average is computed over the current tuple (there is no preceding tuple), while in the second tuple, the average is computed over the current tuple, and the preceding one. Finally, in the third tuple, the average is computed over the current tuple and the two preceding ones.

a

Product Key	Year	Month	Sales Amount	MovAvg
p1	2011	10	100	100
p1	2011	11	105	102.5
p1	2011	12	100	101.67
p2	2011	12	60	60
p2	2012	1	40	50
p2	2012	2	70	56.67
p3	2012	1	30	30
p3	2012	2	50	40
p3	2012	3	40	40

b

Product Key	Year	Month	Sales Amount	YTD
p1	2011	10	100	100
p1	2011	11	105	205
p1	2011	12	100	305
p2	2011	12	60	60
p2	2012	1	40	40
p2	2012	2	70	110
p3	2012	1	30	30
p3	2012	2	50	80
p3	2012	3	40	120

Fig. 5.20 (a) Three-month moving average of the sales per product. (b) Year-to-date sum of the sales per product

As another example, the following query computes the year-to-date sum of sales by product.

```
SELECT ProductKey, Year, Month, SalesAmount, AVG(SalesAmount) OVER
       (PARTITION BY ProductKey, Year ORDER BY Month
        ROWS UNBOUNDED PRECEDING) AS YTD
FROM   Sales
```

The result is shown in Fig. 5.20b. For each tuple, the query evaluator opens a window that contains the tuples pertaining to the current product and year ordered by month. Unlike in the previous query, the aggregation function SUM is applied to all the tuples before the current tuple, as indicated by ROWS UNBOUNDED PRECEDING.

It is worth noting that queries that use window functions can be expressed without them, although the resulting queries are harder to read and may be less efficient. For example, the query above computing the year-to-date sales can be equivalently written as follows:

```
SELECT ProductKey, Year, Month, SalesAmount, AVG(SalesAmount) AS YTD
FROM   Sales S1, Sales S2
WHERE  S1.ProductKey = S2.ProductKey AND
       S1.Year = S2.Year AND S1.Month >= S2.Month
```

Of course, there are many other functions provided in the SQL/OLAP extension, which the interested reader can find in the standard.

5.9   Definition of the Northwind Cube in Analysis Services

We introduce next the main concepts of Analysis Services using as example the Northwind cube. In this section, we consider a simplified version of the Northwind cube where the ragged geography hierarchy was transformed into a regular one. The reason for this was to simplify both the schema definition and the associated MDX and SQL queries that we will show in the next chapter. More precisely, we did not include sales data about cities that roll up to the country level, such as Singapore. Therefore, we dropped the foreign key CountryKey in table City. Moreover, we did not consider the Region level. As a result, the hierarchy City → State → Country → Continent becomes balanced.

To define a cube in Analysis Services, we use SQL Server Data Tools introduced in Chap. 3. The various kinds of objects to be created are described in detail in the remainder of this section.

5.9.1   Data Sources

A data warehouse retrieves its data from one or several data stores. A **data source** contains connection information to a data store, which includes the location of the server, a login and password, a method to retrieve the data, and security permissions. Analysis Services supports data sources that have a connectivity interface through OLE DB or .NET Managed Provider. If the source is a relational database, then SQL is used by default to query the database. In our example, there is a single data source that connects to the Northwind data warehouse.

5.9.2   Data Source Views

A **data source view** (DSV) defines the relational schema that is used for populating an Analysis Services database. This schema is derived from the schemas of the various data sources. Indeed, some transformations are often needed in order to load data from sources into the warehouse. For example, common requirements are to select some columns from a table, to add a new derived column to a table, to restrict table rows on the basis of some specific criteria, and to merge several columns into a single one. These operations can be performed in the DSV by replacing a source table with a **named query** written in SQL or by defining a **named calculation**, which adds a derived column defined by an SQL expression. Further, if the source systems do not specify the primary keys and the relationships between tables using foreign keys, these can be defined in the DSV.

Analysis Services allows the user to specify friendly names for tables and columns. In order to facilitate visibility and navigation for large data warehouses, it also offers the possibility to define customizable views within a DSV, called **diagrams**, that show only certain tables.

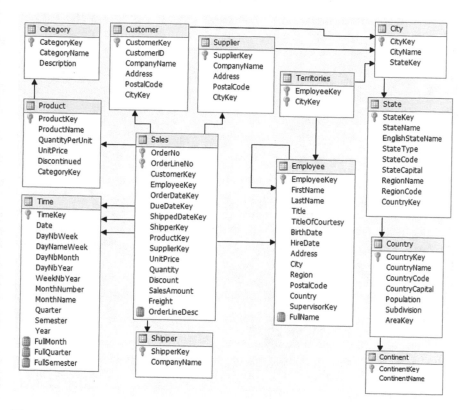

Fig. 5.21 The data source view for the Northwind cube

The DSV, based on the Northwind data warehouse of Fig. 5.4, is given in Fig. 5.21. We can see the Sales fact table and the associated dimension tables (recall that the ragged geography hierarchy was transformed into a regular one). The figure also shows several named calculations, which are identified by a special icon at the left of the attribute name. As we will see later, these named calculations are used for defining and browsing the dimensions. The calculations are:

- In the Employee dimension table, the named calculation FullName combines the first and last name with the expression

FirstName + ' ' + LastName

- In the Time dimension table, the named calculations FullMonth, FullQuarter, and FullSemester, are defined, respectively, by the expressions

  MonthName + ' ' + CONVERT(CHAR(4),Year)
  'Q' + CONVERT(CHAR(1), Quarter) + ' ' + CONVERT(CHAR(4), Year)
  'S' + CONVERT(CHAR(1), Semester) + ' ' + CONVERT(CHAR(4), Year)

  These calculations combine the month, quarter, or semester with the year.
- In the Sales fact table, the named calculation OrderLineDesc combines the order number and the order line using the expression

  CONVERT(CHAR(5),OrderNo) + ' - ' + CONVERT(CHAR(1),OrderLineNo)

5.9.3   Dimensions

Analysis Services supports several types of dimensions as follows:

- A **regular dimension** has a direct one-to-many link between a fact table and a dimension table. An example is the dimension Product.
- A **reference dimension** is indirectly related to the fact table through another dimension. An example is the Geography dimension, which is related to the Sales fact table through the Customer and Supplier dimensions. In this case, Geography may be defined as a reference dimension for the Sales fact table. Reference dimensions can be chained together, for instance, one can define another reference dimension from the Geography dimension.
- In a **role-playing dimension**, a single fact table is related to a dimension table more than once, as studied in Chap. 4. Examples are the dimensions OrderDate, DueDate, and ShippedDate, which all refer to the Time dimension. A role-playing dimension is stored once and used multiple times.
- A **fact dimension**, also referred to as **degenerate dimension**, is similar to a regular dimension, but the dimension data are stored in the fact table. An example is the dimension Order.
- In a **many-to-many dimension**, a fact is related to multiple dimension members and a member is related to multiple facts. In the Northwind data warehouse, there is a many-to-many relationship between Employees and Cities, which is represented in the bridge table Territories. This table must be defined as a fact table in Analysis Services, as we will see later.

Dimensions must be defined either from a DSV, which provides data for the dimension, or from preexisting templates provided by Analysis Services. A typical example of the latter is the time dimension, which does not need to be defined from a data source. Dimensions can be built from one or more tables.

In order to define dimensions, we need to discuss how hierarchies are handled in Analysis Services. In the next section, we provide a more detailed discussion on this topic. In Analysis Services, there are two types of hierarchies. **Attribute hierarchies** correspond to a single column in a dimension table, for instance, attribute ProductName in dimension Product. On the other hand, **multilevel** (or **user-defined**) **hierarchies** are derived from two or more attributes, each attribute being a level in the hierarchy, for instance, Product and Category. An attribute can participate in more than one multilevel hierarchy, for instance, a hierarchy Product and Brand in addition to the previous one. Analysis Services supports three types of multilevel hierarchies, depending on how the members of the hierarchy are related to each other: balanced, ragged, and parent-child hierarchies. We will explain how to define these hierarchies in Analysis Services later in this section.

We illustrate next how to define the different kinds of dimensions supported by Analysis Services using the Northwind cube. We start with a **regular dimension**, namely, the Product dimension, shown in Fig. 5.22. The right pane defines the tables in the DSV from which the dimension is created. The attributes of the dimension are given in the left pane. Finally, the hierarchy Categories, composed of the Category and Product levels, is shown in the central pane. The attributes CategoryKey and ProductKey are used for defining these levels. However, in order to show friendly names when browsing the hierarchy, the NameColumn property of these attributes are set to CategoryName and ProductName, respectively.

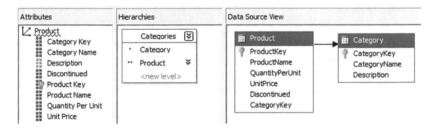

Fig. 5.22 Definition of the Product dimension

Figure 5.23 shows some members of the Product dimension. As shown in the figure, the names of products and categories are displayed in the dimension browser. Notice that a member called Unknown is shown at the bottom of the figure. In fact, every dimension has an Unknown member. If a key error is encountered while processing a fact table, which means that a corresponding key cannot be found in the dimension, the fact value can be assigned to the Unknown member for that dimension. The Unknown member can be made visible or hidden using the dimension property UnknownMember. When set to be visible, the member is included in the results of the MDX queries.

Fig. 5.23 Browsing the hierarchy of the Product dimension

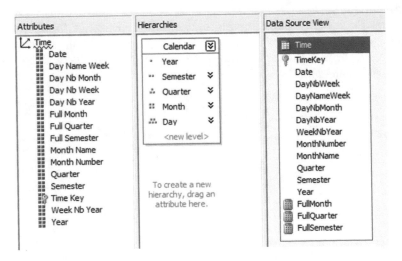

Fig. 5.24 Definition of the Time dimension

We next explain how the Time dimension is defined in Analysis Services. As shown in Fig. 5.24, the dimension has the hierarchy denoted Calendar, which is defined using the attributes Year, Semester, Quarter, MonthNumber, and TimeKey. Since specific MDX functions can be used with time dimensions, the Type property of the dimension must be set to Time. Further, Analysis Services needs to identify which attributes in a time dimension correspond to the typical subdivision of time. This is done by defining the Type property of the attributes of the dimension. Thus, the attributes DayNbMonth, Month-

Number, Quarter, Semester, and Year are, respectively, of type DayOfMonth, MonthOfYear, QuarterOfYear, HalfYearOfYear, and Year.

Attributes in hierarchies must have a one-to-many relationship to their parents in order to ensure correct roll-up operations. For example, a quarter must roll up to its semester. In Analysis Services, this is stated by defining a key for each attribute composing a hierarchy. By default, this key is set to the attribute itself, which implies that, for example, years are unique. Nevertheless, in the Northwind data warehouse, attribute MonthNumber has values such as 1 and 2, and thus, a given value appears in several quarters. Therefore, it is necessary to specify that the key of the attribute is a combination of MonthNumber and Year. This is done by defining the KeyColumns property of the attribute, as shown in Fig. 5.25. Further, in this case, the NameColumn property must also be set to the attribute that is shown when browsing the hierarchy, that is, FullMonth. This should be done similarly for attributes Quarter and Semester.

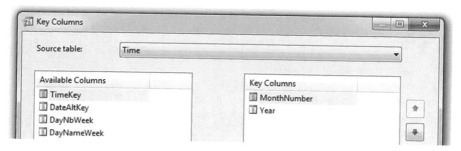

Fig. 5.25 Definition of the key for attribute MonthNumber in the Calendar hierarchy

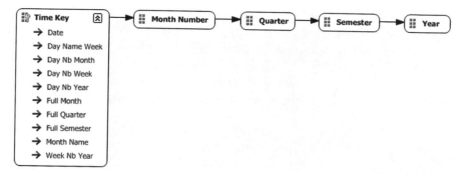

Fig. 5.26 Definition of the relationships in the Calendar hierarchy

When creating a user-defined hierarchy, it is necessary to establish the relationships between the attributes composing such hierarchy. These relationships correspond to functional dependencies. The relationships for the Time dimension are given in Fig. 5.26. In Analysis Services, there are two types of relationships, flexible and rigid. Flexible relationships can evolve across time (e.g., a product can be assigned to a new category), while rigid ones cannot (e.g., a month is always related to its year). The relationships shown in Fig. 5.26 are rigid, as indicated by the solid arrowhead.

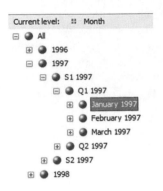

Fig. 5.27 Browsing the hierarchy in the Time dimension

Figure 5.27 shows some members of the Calendar hierarchy. As can be seen, the named calculations FullSemester, FullQuarter, and FullMonth are displayed when browsing the hierarchy.

The definition of the **fact dimension** Order follows similar steps than for the other dimensions, except that the source table for the dimension is the fact table. The key of the dimension will be composed of the combination of the order number and the line number. Therefore, the named calculation OrderLineDesc will be used in the NameColumn property when browsing the dimension. Also, we must indicate Analysis Services that this is a degenerate dimension when defining the cube. We will explain this in Sect. 5.9.5.

Finally, in **many-to-many dimensions**, like in the case of City and Employee, we also need to indicate that the bridge table Territories is actually defined as a fact table, so Analysis Services can take care of the double-counting problem. This is also done when defining the cube.

5.9.4 Hierarchies

What we have generically called hierarchies in Chap. 4 and in the present one in Analysis Services are denoted as user-defined or multilevel hierarchies. Multilevel hierarchies are defined by means of dimension attributes, and these attributes may be stored in a single table or in several tables of a snowflake schema. Therefore, both the star and the snowflake and schema representation are supported in Analysis Services.

Balanced hierarchies are supported by Analysis Services. Examples of these hierarchies in the Northwind cube are the Time and the Product dimensions studied above.

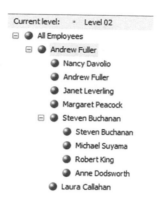

Fig. 5.28 Browsing the Supervision hierarchy in the Employee dimension

Analysis Services does not support **unbalanced hierarchies**. We have seen in Sect. 5.5.2 several solutions to cope with them. On the other hand, Analysis Services supports **parent-child hierarchies**, which are a special case of unbalanced hierarchies. We have seen that such hierarchies define a hierarchical relationship between the members of a dimension. An example is the Supervision hierarchy in the Employee dimension. As can be seen in Fig. 5.21, in the underlying dimension table, the column SupervisorKey is a foreign key referencing EmployeeKey. When defining the dimension, the Usage property for the attributes of the dimension determines how they will be used. In our case, the value of such property will be Parent for the SupervisorKey attribute, will be Regular for all other attributes except EmployeeKey, and will be Key for the attribute EmployeeKey. Figure 5.28 shows the members of the Supervision hierarchy, where the named calculation FullName is displayed when browsing the hierarchy.

In parent-child hierarchies, the hierarchical structure between members is taken into account when measures are aggregated. Thus, for example, the total sales amount of an employee would be her personal sales amount plus the total sales amount of all employees under her in the organization. Each member of a parent-child hierarchy has a system-generated child member that contains the measure values directly associated with it, independently of its descendants. These are referred to as **data members**. The MembersWithData property of the parent attribute controls the visibility of data members: they are shown when the property is set to NonLeafDataVisible, while they are hidden when it is set to NonLeafDataHidden. We can see in Fig. 5.28 that the data members are visible since both Andrew Fuller and Steven Buchanan appear twice in the hierarchy. The MembersWithDataCaption property of the parent attribute can be used to define a naming template for generating names of data members.

Analysis Services does not support **generalized hierarchies**. If the members differ in attributes and in hierarchy structure, the common solution is to define one hierarchy for the common levels and another hierarchy for each of the exclusive paths containing the specific levels. This is the case for most of the OLAP tools in the market. On the other hand, Analysis Services supports the particular case of **ragged hierarchies**. As we have already seen, in a ragged hierarchy, the parent of a member may be in a level which is not immediately above it. In a table corresponding to a ragged hierarchy, the missing members can be represented in various ways: with null values or empty strings or they can contain the same value as their parent.

In Analysis Services, a ragged hierarchy is defined using all of its levels, that is, the longest path. To support the display of ragged hierarchies, the HideMemberIf property of a level allows missing members to be hidden. The possible values for this property and their associated behaviors are as follows:

- Never: Level members are never hidden.
- OnlyChildWithNoName: A level member is hidden when it is the only child of its parent and its name is null or an empty string.
- OnlyChildWithParentName: A level member is hidden when it is the only child of its parent and its name is the same as the name of its parent.
- NoName: A level member is hidden when its name is empty.
- ParentName: A level member is hidden when its name is identical to that of its parent.

In order to display ragged hierarchies correctly, the MDX Compatibility property in the connection string from a client application must be set to 2. If it is set to 1, a placeholder member is exposed in a ragged hierarchy.

With respect to **alternative hierarchies**, in Analysis Services, several hierarchies can be defined on a dimension, and they can share levels. For example, the alternative hierarchy in Fig. 4.9 will be represented by two distinct hierarchies: the first one composed of Time → Month → CalendarQuarter → CalendarYear and another one composed of Time → Month → FiscalQuarter → FiscalYear.

Analysis Services supports **parallel hierarchies**, whether dependent or independent. Levels can be shared among the various component hierarchies.

Finally, to represent **nonstrict hierarchies** in Analysis Services, it is necessary to represent the corresponding bridge table as a fact table, as it was explained in Sect. 5.9.3. In the relational representation of the

Northwind cube given in Fig. 5.4, there is a many-to-many relationship between employees and cities represented by the table Territories. Such a table must be defined as a fact table in the corresponding cube. In this case, using the terminology of Analysis Services, the City dimension has a many-to-many relationship with the Sales measure group, through the Employee intermediate dimension and the Territories measure group.

5.9.5 Cubes

In Analysis Services, a cube is built from one or several DSVs. A cube consists of one or more dimensions from dimension tables and one or more **measure groups** from fact tables. A measure group is composed by a set of **measures**. The facts in a fact table are mapped as measures in a cube. Analysis Services allows multiple fact tables in a single cube. In this case, the cube typically contains multiple measure groups, one from each fact table.

Figure 5.29 shows the definition of the Northwind cube in Analysis Services. As can be seen in Fig. 5.29a, Analysis Services adds a new measure to each measure group, in our case Sales Count and Territories Count, which counts the number fact members associated with each member of each dimension. Thus, Sales Count would count the number of sales for each customer, supplier, product, and so on. Similarly, Territories Count would count the number of cities associated with each employee.

Figure 5.30 shows the relationships between dimensions and measure groups in the cube. With respect to the Sales measure group, all dimensions except the last two are regular dimensions, they do not have an icon to the left of the attribute relating the dimension and the measure group. On the other hand, Geography is a many-to-many dimension linked to the measure group through the Territories fact table. Finally, Order is a fact dimension linked to the measure group through the Order No attribute.

Analysis Services supports the usual additive aggregation functions SUM, MIN, MAX, COUNT, and DISTINCT COUNT. It also supports **semiadditive measures**, that is, measures that can be aggregated in some dimensions but not in others. Recall that we defined such measures in Sect. 3.1.2. Analysis Services provides several functions for semiadditive measures, namely, AverageOfChildren, FirstChild, LastChild, FirstNonEmpty, and LastNonEmpty, among other ones.

The aggregation function associated with each measure must be defined with the AggregationFunction property. The default aggregation measure is SUM, and this is suitable for all measures in our example, except for Unit Price and Discount. Since these are semiadditive measures, their aggregation should be AverageOfChildren, which computes, for a member, the average of its children.

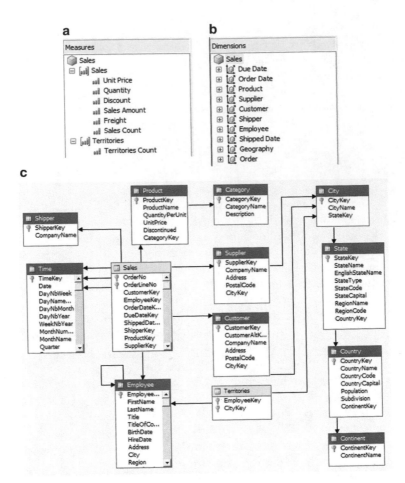

Fig. 5.29 Definition of the Northwind cube in Analysis Services. (**a**) Measure groups. (**b**) Dimensions. (**c**) Schema of the cube

The FormatString property is used to state the format in which the measures will be displayed. For example, measures Unit Price, Sales Amount, and Freight are of type money, and thus, their format will be $###,###.00, where a '#' displays a digit or nothing, a '0' displays a digit or a zero, and ',' and '.' are, respectively, thousand and decimal separators. The format string for measures Quantity and Sales Count will be ###,##0. Finally, the format string for measure Discount will be 0.00%, where the percent symbol '%' specifies that the measure is a percentage and includes a multiplication by a factor of 100.

Further, we can define the default measure of the cube, in our case Sales Amount. As we will see in Chap. 6, if an MDX query does not specify the measure to be displayed, then the default measure will be used.

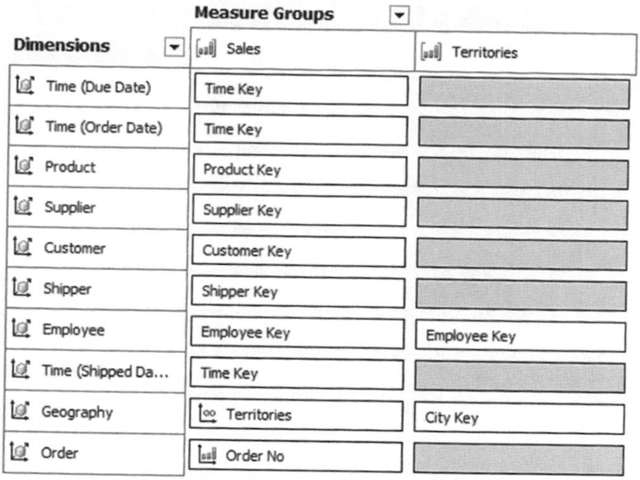

Fig. 5.30 Definition of the dimensions of the Northwind cube

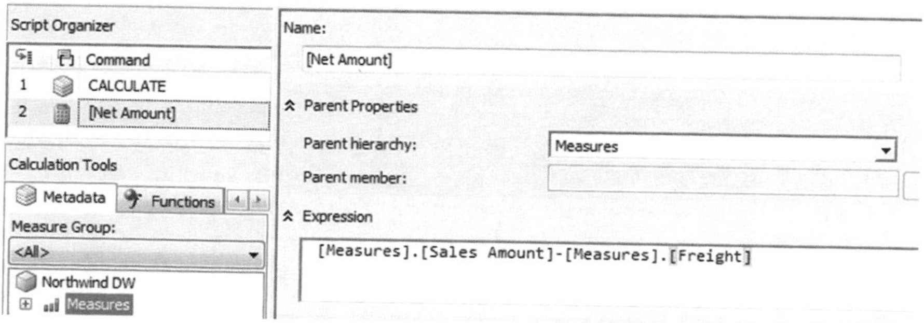

Fig. 5.31 Definition of the Net Amount derived measure

The derived measure Net Amount is defined as shown in Fig. 5.31. As can be seen in the figure, the measure will be a calculated member in the Measures dimension. The defining expression is the difference between the Sales Amount and the Freight measures.

Figure 5.32 shows an example of browsing the Northwind cube in Excel using the PivotTable tools. In the figure, the customer hierarchy is displayed on rows, the time hierarchy is displayed on columns, and the sales amount measure is displayed on cells. Thus, the figure shows the yearly sales of customers at different levels of the geography hierarchy, including the individual sales of a shop located in San Francisco.

◢	A	B	C	D	E
1	Sales Amount	Column Labels ▼			
2	Row Labels ▼	⊞1996	⊞1997	⊞1998	Grand Total
3	⊞Europe	113290,8904	351142,6916	219090,1785	683523,7605
4	⊟North America	49524,655	154427,8604	103073,3274	307025,8428
5	⊞Canada	7283,0801	30589,2604	9539,475	47411,8155
6	⊞Mexico	4687,9	12700,8275	3734,9	21123,6275
7	⊟United States	37553,6749	111137,7725	89798,9524	238490,3998
8	⊞Alaska	4675,8	3951,3749	4792,8876	13420,0625
9	⊟California		1698,4025	1378,07	3076,4725
10	⊟San Francisco		1698,4025	1378,07	3076,4725
11	Let's Stop N Shop		1698,4025	1378,07	3076,4725
12	⊞Idaho	10338,2649	56241,075	35674,5099	102253,8498
13	⊞Montana		1426,74	326	1752,74
14	⊞New Mexico	9923,78	19383,75	19982,5499	49290,0799
15	⊞Oregon	1828	15150,975	11011,135	27990,11
16	⊞Washington	2938,2	10810,4551	15516,8	29265,4551
17	⊞Wyoming	7849,63	2475	1117	11441,63
18	⊞South America	29034,32	64629,0564	60942,879	154606,2554
19	Grand Total	191849,8654	570199,6084	383106,3849	1145155,859

⊮ ◀ ▶ ⊯   By Customer and Time

Fig. 5.32 Browsing the Northwind cube in Excel

5.10   Definition of the Northwind Cube in Mondrian

Mondrian is an open-source relational online analytical processing (ROLAP) server. It is also known as Pentaho Analysis Services and is a component of the Pentaho Business Analytics suite. In this section, we describe Mondrian 4.0, which is the latest version at the time of writing this book.

In Mondrian, a **cube schema** written in an XML syntax defines a mapping between the physical structure of the relational data warehouse and the multidimensional cube. A cube schema contains the declaration of cubes, dimensions, hierarchies, levels, measures, and calculated members. A cube schema does not define the data source; this is done using a JDBC connection string. We give next the overall structure of a cube schema definition in Mondrian using the Northwind cube:

```
1    <Schema name='NorthwindDW' metamodelVersion='4.0'
2            description='Sales cube of the Northwind company'>
3        <PhysicalSchema>
4            ...
5        </PhysicalSchema>
6        <Dimension name='Time' table='Time' ...>
7            ...
8        </Dimension>
9        <Cube name='Sales'>
10           <Dimensions>
11               ...
12           </Dimensions>
```

```
13        <MeasureGroups>
14           <MeasureGroup name='Sales' table='Sales'>
15              <Measures>
16                 . . .
17              </Measures>
18              <DimensionLinks>
19                 . . .
20              </DimensionLinks>
21           </MeasureGroup>
22        </MeasureGroups>
23     </Cube>
24  </Schema>
```

The Schema element (starting in line 1) defines all other elements in the
schema. The PhysicalSchema element (lines 3–5) defines the tables that are
the source data for the dimensions and cubes, and the foreign key links
between these tables. The Dimension element (lines 6–8) defines the **shared
dimension** Time, which is used several times in the Northwind cube for
the role-playing dimensions OrderDate, DueDate, and ShippingDate. Shared
dimensions can also be used in several cubes. The Cube element (lines 9–23)
defines the Sales cube. A cube schema contains dimensions and measures,
the latter organized in measure groups. The Dimensions element (lines 10–
12) defines the dimensions of the cube. The measure groups are defined
using the element MeasureGroups (lines 13–22). The measure group Sales
(lines 14–21) defines the measures using the Measures element (lines 15–17).
The DimensionLinks element (lines 18–20) defines how measures relate to
dimensions. We detail next each of the elements introduced above.

5.10.1   Schemas and Physical Schemas

The Schema element is the topmost element of a cube schema. It is the
container for all its schema elements. A schema has a name and may have
other attributes such as description and the version of Mondrian in which it
is written. A schema always includes a PhysicalSchema element and one or
more Cube elements. Other common elements are Dimension (to define shared
dimensions) and Role for access control.

The PhysicalSchema element defines the **physical schema**, which states
the tables and columns in the database that provide data for the dimensions
and cubes in the data warehouse. The physical schema isolates the logical data
warehouse schema from the underlying database. For example, a dimension
can be based upon a table that can be a real table or an SQL query in the
database. Similarly, a measure can be based upon a column that can be a

real column or a column calculated using an SQL expression. The general structure of the physical schema of the Northwind cube is given next:

```
1   <PhysicalSchema>
2       <Table name='Employee' keyColumn='EmployeeKey'>
3           <ColumnDefs>
4               <ColumnDef name='EmployeeKey' type='Integer' />
5               <ColumnDef name='FirstName' type='String' />
6               <ColumnDef name='LastName' type='String' />
7               ...
8               <CalculatedColumnDef name='FullName' type='String'>
9                   <ExpressionView>
10                      <SQL dialect='generic'>
11                          <Column name='FirstName' /> ||' '||
12                          <Column name='LastName' />
13                      </SQL>
14                      <SQL dialect='SQL Server'>
15                          <Column name='FirstName' /> + ' ' +
16                          <Column name='LastName' />
17                      </SQL>
18                  </ExpressionView>
19              </CalculatedColumnDef>
20          </ColumnDefs>
21      </Table>
22      ...
23      <Link source='City' target='Employee' foreignKeyColumn='CityKey' />
24      ...
25  </PhysicalSchema>
```

The Table element defines the table Employee (lines 2–21). The columns of the table are defined within the ColumnDefs element, and each column is defined using the ColumnDef element. The definition of the **calculated column** FullName is given in line 8 using the CalculatedColumnDef element. The column will be populated using the values of the columns FirstName and LastName in the underlying database. The ExpressionView element is used to handle the various SQL dialects, which depend on the database system. As can be seen, concatenation of strings is expressed in standard SQL using '||', while it is expressed in SQL Server using '+'. In the case of **snowflake schemas**, the physical schema also declares the foreign key links between the tables using the Link element. In the example above, the link between the tables Employee and City is defined in line 23.

5.10.2   Cubes, Dimensions, Attributes, and Hierarchies

A cube is defined by a Cube element and is a container for a set of dimensions and measure groups, as shown in the schema definition at the beginning of this section (lines 9–23).

A dimension is a collection of attributes and hierarchies. For example, the general structure of the Time dimension in the Northwind cube is given next:

```
1   <Dimension name='Time' table='Time' type='TIME'>
2      <Attributes>
3         <Attribute name='Year' keyColumn='Year' levelType='TimeYears' />
4         ...
5         <Attribute name='Month' levelType='TimeMonths'
6            nameColumn='FullMonth' orderByColumn='MonthNumber' />
7            <Key>
8               <Column name='Year' />
9               <Column name='MonthNumber' />
10           </Key>
11        </Attribute>
12        ...
13     </Attributes>
14     <Hierarchies>
15        <Hierarchy name='Calendar' hasAll='true'>
16           <Level attribute='Year' />
17           ...
18           <Level attribute='Month' />
19           ...
20        </Hierarchy>
21     </Hierarchies>
22  </Dimension>
```

The Time dimension is defined in line 1, where attribute type states that this is a time dimension. This would not be the case for the other dimensions such as Customer. In lines 2–13, we define the attributes of the dimension, while the **multilevel hierarchies** are defined in lines 14–21. An Attribute element describes a data value, and it corresponds to a column in the relational model. In line 3, we define the attribute Year based on the column Year, while in lines 5–11, we define the attribute Month based on the column MonthNumber. The nameColumn attribute specifies the column that holds the name of members of the attribute, in this case the calculated column FullMonth, which has values such as September 1997. Further, the orderByColumn attribute specifies the column that specifies the sort order, in this case the column MonthNumber.

The Calendar hierarchy is defined in lines 15–20 using the element Hierarchy. The hasAll='true' statement indicates that the All level is included in the hierarchy. As the attribute of each level in a hierarchy must have a one-to-many relationship with the attribute of the next level, a key must be defined for attributes. For example, since attribute MonthNumber can take the same value for different years, the key of the attribute is defined as a combination of attributes MonthNumber and Year in lines 7–10. This guarantees that all values of the attribute Month are distinct. The key of attribute Year is specified as the column Year using the attribute keyColumn in line 3.

As we will see in Chap. 6, MDX has several operators that specifically operate over the time dimension. To support these operators, we need to tell Mondrian which attributes define the subdivision of the time periods to which the level corresponds. We indicate this with the attribute levelType in the Attribute element. Values for this attribute can be TimeYears, TimeHalfYears, TimeQuarters, TimeMonths, and so on.

We give next examples of attribute definition of the Product dimension:

```
1    <Attribute name='Unit Price' caption='Prix Unitaire'
2        description='Le prix unitaire de ce produit' keyColumn='UnitPrice' />
3    <Attribute name='Product Name' caption='Nom du Produit'
4        description='Le nom de ce produit' keyColumn='ProductName' />
```

The example shows three properties of the Attribute element. A caption is to be displayed on the screen to a user, whereas the name is intended to be used in code, particularly in an MDX statement. Usually, the name and caption are the same, although the caption can be localized (shown in the language of the user, as in the example) while the name is the same in all languages. Finally, a description is displayed in many user interfaces (such as Pentaho Analyzer) as tooltips when the mouse is moved over an element. Name, caption, and description are not unique to attributes; the other elements that may appear on user's screen also have them, including Schema, Cube, Measure, and Dimension.

Mondrian implicitly creates **attribute hierarchies**, even if a hierarchy is not defined explicitly for the attribute. For example, if in dimension Employee an attribute is defined as follows:

```
1    <Attributes>
2        <Attribute name='Last Name' keyColumn='LastName' />
3        ...
4    </Attributes>
```

this is interpreted as if the following hierarchy has been defined in the dimension:

```
1    <Hierarchy name='Last Name'>
2        <Level attribute='Last Name' />
3    </Hierarchy>
```

When a schema has more than one cube, these cubes may have several dimensions in common. If these dimensions have the same definitions, they are declared once and can be used in as many cubes as needed. In Mondrian, these are called **shared dimensions**. Further, we have seen that dimensions can be used more than once in the same cube. In the Northwind cube, the Time dimension is used three times to represent the order, due, and shipped dates of orders. We have seen that these are called **role-playing dimensions**.

Role-playing dimensions are defined in Mondrian using the concept of shared dimensions as we show below, where the shared dimension is Time:

```
1   <Cube name='Sales'>
2      <Dimensions>
3         <Dimension name='Order Date' source='Time' />
4         <Dimension name='Due Date' source='Time' />
5         <Dimension name='Shipped Date' source='Time' />
6         <Dimension name='Employee' table='Employee' key='Employee Key'>
7            ...
8         </Dimension>
9      </Dimensions>
10        ...
11  </Cube>
```

As we have seen, snowflake dimensions involve more than one table. For example, the Product dimension involves tables Product and Category. When defining dimensions based on **snowflake schemas** in Mondrian, it is necessary to define in which table we can find the dimension attributes, as shown next:

```
1   <Dimension name='Product' table='Product' key='Product Key'>
2      <Attributes>
3         <Attribute name='Category Name' keyColumn='CategoryName'
4            table='Category' />
5            ...
6         <Attribute name='Product Name' keyColumn='ProductName' />
7            ...
8      </Attributes>
9      <Hierarchies>
10        <Hierarchy name='Categories' hasAll='true'>
11           <Level name='Category' attribute='Category Name' />
12           <Level name='Product' attribute='Product Name' />
13        </Hierarchy>
14     </Hierarchies>
15  </Dimension>
```

As can be seen above, the definition of attribute Category Name states that it comes from table Category (lines 3–4). On the other hand, when defining the attribute Product Name the table is not specified, by default it will be found in the table defined in the Dimension element, that is, the Product table.

We show next how a **parent-child** (or **recursive**) **hierarchy** can be defined in Mondrian using the Supervision hierarchy in the Employee dimension:

```
1   <Dimension name='Employee' table='Employee' key='Employee Key'>
2      <Attributes>
3         <Attribute name='Employee Key' keyColumn='EmployeeKey' />
4            ...
5         <Attribute name='Supervisor Key' keyColumn='SupervisorKey' />
6      </Attributes>
```

```
7    <Hierarchies>
8      <Hierarchy name='Supervision' hasAll='true'>
9        <Level name='Employee' attribute='Employee Key'
10            parentAttribute='Supervisor Key' nullParentValue='NULL' />
11     </Hierarchy>
12   </Hierarchies>
13 </Dimension>
```

The parentAttribute attribute in line 10 states the name of the attribute that references the parent member in a parent-child hierarchy. The nullParentValue attribute indicates the value determining the top member of the hierarchy, in this case a null value. As in Analysis Services, each member of a parent-child hierarchy has a shadow member, called its **data member**, that keeps the measure values directly associated with it.

As we studied in this chapter and in the previous one, **ragged hierarchies** allow some levels in the hierarchy to be skipped when traversing it. The Geography hierarchy in the Northwind data warehouse shows an example. It allows one to handle, for example, the case of Israel, which does not have states or regions, and the cities belong directly to the country. As in Analysis Services, Mondrian creates hidden members, for example, a dummy state and a dummy region for Israel, to which any city in Israel belongs. Thus, if we ask for the parent member of Tel Aviv, Mondrian will return Israel, the dummy members will be hidden. In short, in Mondrian, when we define a ragged hierarchy, we must tell which members must be hidden. This is done with the hideMemberIf attribute, as shown next:

```
1   <Dimension name='Customer' table='Customer' />
2     <Attributes>
3       <Attribute name='Continent' table='Continent'
4          keyColumn='ContinentKey' />
5       <Attribute name='Country' table='State' keyColumn='CountryKey' />
6       <Attribute name='Region' table='State' keyColumn='RegionName' />
7       <Attribute name='State' table='State' keyColumn='StateKey' />
8       <Attribute name='City' table='City' keyColumn='CityKey' />
9       <Attribute name='Customer' keyColumn='CustomerKey' />
10        ...
11    </Attributes>
12    <Hierarchies>
13      <Hierarchy name='Geography' />
14        <Level attribute name='Continent' />
15        <Level attribute name='Country' />
16        <Level attribute name='Region' hideMemberIf='IfBlankName' />
17        <Level attribute name='State' hideMemberIf='IfBlankName' />
18        <Level attribute name='City' />
19        <Level attribute name='Customer' />
20      </Hierarchy>
21    </Hierarchies>
22 </Dimension>
```

In the schema above, hideMemberIf='IfBlankName' tells that a member in this level does not appear if its name is null, empty, or a whitespace. Other values for the **hideMemberIf** attribute are Never (the member always appears, the default value) and IfParentName (the member appears unless its name matches the one of its parent).

We next show how a **fact** (or **degenerate**) **dimension** can be defined in Mondrian. Such a dimension has no associated dimension table, and thus, all the columns in the dimension are in the fact table. In the case of the Northwind cube, there is a fact dimension Order, composed by the order number and the order line number corresponding to the fact. To represent this dimension, we may write:

```
1   <Dimension name='Order' table='Sales'>
2       <Attributes>
3           <Attribute name='Order No' keyColumn='OrderNo'>
4           <Attribute name='Order Line' keyColumn='OrderLine'>
5       </Attributes>
6   </Dimension>
```

Note that the table associated with the dimension is the Sales fact table.

5.10.3 Measures

As in Analysis Services, in Mondrian the measures are also considered dimensions: every cube has an implicit Measures dimension (we will see this in detail in Chap. 6). The Measures dimension has a single hierarchy, also called Measures, which has a single level, in turn also called Measures. The measures of the Sales cube are defined as follows:

```
1    <Cube name='Sales'>
2        <Dimensions .../>
3        <MeasureGroups>
4            <MeasureGroup name='Sales' table='Sales'>
5                <Measures>
6                    <Measure name='Unit Price' column='UnitPrice'
7                        aggregator='avg' formatString='$#,##0.00' />
8                    <Measure name='Sales Count' aggregator='count' />
9                    ...
10               </Measures>
11               <DimensionLinks>
12                   <ForeignKeyLink dimension='Customer'
13                       foreignKeyColumn='CustomerKey' />
14                   <ForeignKeyLink dimension='OrderDate'
15                       foreignKeyColumn='OrderDateKey' />
16                   ...
17                   <FactLink dimension='Order' />
18               </DimensionLinks>
19           </MeasureGroup>
20       </MeasureGroups>
21       <CalculatedMember name='Net Amount' dimension='Measures'
22           formula='[Measures].[Sales Amount]-[Measures].[Freight]'>
```

```
23        <CalculatedMemberProperty name='FORMAT_STRING'
24           value='$#,##0.00' />
25        </CalculatedMember>
26    </Cube>
```

As can be seen, a **measure** is defined within a **measure group** using a
Measure element (lines 5 and 6). Each measure has a name and an aggregator,
describing how to roll up values. The available aggregators are those provided
in SQL, that is, SUM, MIN, MAX, AVG, COUNT, and DISTINCT COUNT. A
column attribute defines the values to be aggregated. This is required for all
aggregators except COUNT. A COUNT aggregator without a column, as for
the Sales Count measure in line 9, counts rows.

Mondrian supports **calculated measures**, which are calculated from
other measures using an MDX formula. An example is shown for the measure
Net Amount (lines 20–24). The dimensions are linked to the measures through
the ForeignKeyLink element or, in the case of a fact dimension, through the
FactLink element (lines 10–17).

Figure 5.33 shows an example of browsing the Northwind cube in Saiku,
an open-source analytics client. In the figure, the countries of customers and
the categories of products are displayed on rows, the years are displayed on
columns, and the sales amount measure is displayed on cells. Saiku also allows
the user to write MDX queries directly on an editor.

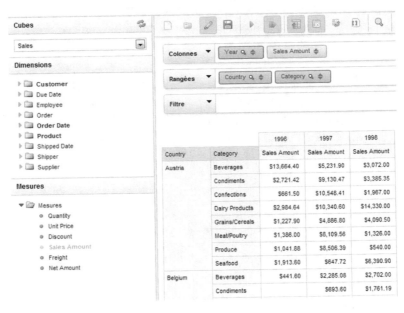

Fig. 5.33 Browsing the Northwind cube in Saiku

5.11   Summary

In this chapter, we have studied the problem of logical design of data warehouses, specifically relational data warehouse design. Several alternatives were discussed: the star, snowflake, starflake, and constellation schemas. Like in the case of operational databases, we provided rules for translating conceptual multidimensional schemas to logical schemas. Particular importance was given to the representation of the various kinds of hierarchies that can occur in practice. The problem of slowly changing dimensions was also addressed in detail. We then explained how the OLAP operations can be implemented on the relational model using the SQL language and also reviewed the advanced features SQL provides through the SQL/OLAP extension. We concluded the chapter showing how we can implement the Northwind data cube over Microsoft Analysis Services and Mondrian, starting from the Northwind data warehouse.

5.12   Bibliographic Notes

A comprehensive reference to data warehouse modeling can be found in the book by Kimball and Ross [103]. A work by Jagadish et al. [95] discusses the uses of hierarchies in data warehousing. Complex hierarchies like the ones discussed in this chapter were studied, among other works, in [84, 87, 159, 160]. The problem of summarizability is studied in the classic paper of Lenz and Shoshani [115] and in [85, 86]. Following the ideas of Codd for the relational model, there have been attempts to define normal forms for multidimensional databases [114]. Regarding SQL, analytics and OLAP are covered in the books [27, 132]. There is a wide array of books on Analysis Services that describe in detail the functionalities and capabilities of this tool [71, 79, 163, 182, 183]. Finally, a description of Mondrian can be found in the books [10, 18].

5.13   Review Questions

5.1 Describe the differences between the following concepts:

(a) Relational OLAP (ROLAP), multidimensional OLAP (MOLAP), and hybrid OLAP (HOLAP).
(b) Star schema, snowflake schema, starflake schema, and constellation schema.

5.2 Discuss the mapping rules for translating a MultiDim schema into a relational schema. Are these rules similar to those used for translating an ER schema into a relational schema?

5.3 Explain how a balanced hierarchy can be mapped into either normalized or denormalized tables. Discuss the advantages and disadvantages of these alternative mappings.

5.4 How do you transform at the logical level an unbalanced hierarchy into a balanced one?

5.5 Describe different approaches for representing generalized hierarchies at the logical level.

5.6 Is it possible to distinguish between generalized, alternative, and parallel dependent hierarchies at the logical level?

5.7 Explain how a nonstrict hierarchy can be represented in the relational model.

5.8 Analyze and discuss the pros and cons of the alternatives for representing slowly changing dimensions.

5.9 Define the kinds of SQL/OLAP window functions: partitioning, window ordering, and window framing. Write, in English, queries of each class over the Northwind data warehouse.

5.10 Identify the kind of hierarchies that can be directly represented in Analysis Services.

5.11 Identify the kind of hierarchies that can be directly represented in Mondrian.

5.12 Discuss how snowflake schemas are represented in Analysis Services and in Mondrian.

5.14   Exercises

5.1 Consider the data warehouse of a telephone provider given in Ex. 3.1. Draw a star schema diagram for the data warehouse.

5.2 For the star schema obtained in the previous exercise, write in SQL the queries given in Ex. 3.1.

5.3 Consider the data warehouse of the train application given in Ex. 3.2. Draw a snowflake schema diagram for the data warehouse with hierarchies for the train and station dimensions.

5.4 For the snowflake schema obtained in the previous exercise, write in SQL the queries given in Ex. 3.2.

5.5 Consider the university data warehouse described in Ex. 3.3. Draw a constellation schema for the data warehouse taking into account the different granularities of the time dimension.

5.6 For the constellation schema obtained in the previous exercise, write in SQL the queries given in Ex. 3.3.

5.7 Translate the MultiDim schema obtained for the French horse race application in Ex. 4.5 into the relational model.

5.8 Translate the MultiDim schema obtained for the Formula One application in Ex. 4.7 into the relational model.

5.9 The Research and Innovative Technology Administration (RITA)[1] coordinates the US Department of Transportation's (DOT) research programs. It collects several statistics about many kinds of transportation means, including the information about flight segments between airports summarized by month.[2]

There is a set of tables T_T100I_Segment_All_Carrier_XXXX, one by year, ranging from 1990 up until now. These tables include information about the scheduled and actually departured flights, the number of seats sold, the freight transported, and the distance traveled, among other ones. The schema and description of these tables is given in Table 5.1. A set of lookup tables given in Table 5.2 include information about airports, carriers, and time. The schemas of these lookup tables are composed of just two columns called Code and Description. The mentioned web site describes all tables in detail.

From the information above, construct an appropriate data warehouse schema. Analyze the input data and motivate the choice of your schema.

5.10 Implement in Analysis Services the MultiDim schema obtained for the French horse race application in Ex. 4.5 and the relational data warehouse obtained in Ex. 5.7.

5.11 Implement in Mondrian the MultiDim schema obtained for the Formula One application in Ex. 4.7 and the relational data warehouse obtained in Ex. 5.8.

---

[1] http://www.transtats.bts.gov/

[2] http://www.transtats.bts.gov/DL_SelectFields.asp?Table_ID=261

Table 5.1 Attributes of the tables T_T100I_Segment_All_Carrier_XXXX

Summaries	
DepScheduled	Departures scheduled
DepPerformed	Departures performed
Payload	Available payload (pounds)
Seats	Available seats
Passengers	Non-stop segment passengers transported
Freight	Non-stop segment freight transported (pounds)
Mail	Non-stop segment mail transported (pounds)
Distance	Distance between airports (miles)
RampTime	Ramp to ramp time (minutes)
AirTime	Airborne time (minutes)
Carrier	
UniqueCarrier	Unique carrier code. When the same code has been used by multiple carriers, a numeric suffix is used for earlier users, for example, PA, PA(1), PA(2). Use this field for analysis across a range of years
AirlineID	An identification number assigned by US DOT to identify a unique airline (carrier). A unique airline (carrier) is defined as one holding and reporting under the same DOT certificate regardless of its code, name, or holding company/corporation
UniqueCarrierName	Unique carrier name. When the same name has been used by multiple carriers, a numeric suffix is used for earlier users, for example, Air Caribbean, Air Caribbean (1)
UniqCarrierEntity	Unique entity for a carrier's operation region
CarrierRegion	Carrier's operation region. Carriers report data by operation region
Carrier	Code assigned by IATA and commonly used to identify a carrier. As the same code may have been assigned to different carriers over time, the code is not always unique. For analysis, use the unique carrier code
CarrierName	Carrier name
CarrierGroup	Carrier group code. Used in legacy analysis
CarrierGroupNew	Carrier group new
Origin	
OriginAirportID	Origin airport, Airport ID. An identification number assigned by US DOT to identify a unique airport. Use this field for airport analysis across a range of years because an airport can change its airport code and airport codes can be reused
OriginAirportSeqID	Origin airport, Airport Sequence ID. An identification number assigned by US DOT to identify a unique airport at a given point of time. Airport attributes, such as airport name or coordinates, may change over time
OriginCityMarketID	Origin airport, City Market ID. City Market ID is an identification number assigned by US DOT to identify a city market. Use this field to consolidate airports serving the same city market
Origin	Origin airport

(continued)

Table 5.1 (continued)

OriginCityName	Origin city
OriginCountry	Origin airport, country
OriginCountryName	Origin airport, country name
OriginWAC	Origin airport, world area code
Destination	
DestAirportID	Destination airport, Airport ID. An identification number assigned by US DOT to identify a unique airport. Use this field for airport analysis across a range of years because an airport can change its airport code and airport codes can be reused
DestAirportSeqID	Destination airport, Airport Sequence ID. An identification number assigned by US DOT to identify a unique airport at a given point of time. Airport attributes, such as airport name or coordinates, may change over time
DestCityMarketID	Destination airport, City Market ID. City Market ID is an identification number assigned by US DOT to identify a city market. Use this field to consolidate airports serving the same city market
Dest	Destination airport
DestCityName	Destination city
DestCountry	Destination airport, country
DestCountryName	Destination airport, country name
DestWAC	Destination airport, world area code
Aircraft	
AircraftGroup	Aircraft group
AircraftType	Aircraft type
AircraftConfig	Aircraft configuration
Time Period	
Year	Year
Quarter	Quarter
Month	Month
Other	
DistanceGroup	Distance intervals, every 500 Miles, for flight segment
Class	Service Class

Table 5.2 Lookup tables for the table T_T100I_Segment_All_Carrier_XXXX

L_STRCRAFT_CONFIG	L_CITY_MARKET_ID
L_STRCRAFT_GROUP	L_COUNTRY_CODE
L_STRCRAFT_TYPE	L_DISTANCE_GROUP_500
L_STRLINE_ID	L_MONTHS
L_STRPORT	L_QUARTERS
L_STRPORT_ID	L_REGION
L_STRPORT_SEQ_ID	L_SERVICE_CLASS
L_CARRIER_GROUP	L_UNIQUE_CARRIER_ENTITIES
L_CARRIER_GROUP_NEW	L_UNIQUE_CARRIERS
L_CARRIER_HISTORY	L_WORLD_AREA_CODES

Chapter 6
Querying Data Warehouses

Just as SQL is a language for manipulating relational databases, MDX (Multi-Dimensional eXpressions) is a language for defining and querying multidimensional databases. Although at first sight it may appear that MDX resembles SQL, they are significantly different from each other. While SQL operates over tables, attributes, and tuples, MDX works over data cubes, dimensions, hierarchies, and members (at the instance level). MDX is a de facto standard supported by many OLAP tool providers.

MDX supports two distinct modes. On the one hand, it can be used as an expression language to design OLAP cubes, that is, to define and manipulate data in order to calculate values, to add business logic to the cubes, to define custom roll-ups and actions, to define security settings, and so on. On the other hand, it can be used as a query language to retrieve data from cubes. In this chapter, we address MDX as a query language.

In Sect. 6.1, we describe the main functionalities of MDX. Starting from simple queries, we progressively introduce more complex features, like navigation capabilities that are used to drill down or roll up along hierarchies. Functions that are used to analyze time series are also discussed. Finally, aggregation functions are addressed, going from the typical ones to more involved functions like moving averages, for instance. We apply all these functions and concepts in Sect. 6.2, where we query the Northwind data cube using MDX. Generally speaking, MDX queries over cubes can also be expressed as SQL queries over the underlying data warehouse. Thus, in Sect. 6.3 we write the same queries presented in Sect. 6.2 as SQL queries over the Northwind data warehouse instead of over the Northwind multidimensional data cube. In Sect. 6.4, we compare the main features of both languages, based on an analysis of the alternatives discussed in the two formerly mentioned sections.

A. Vaisman and E. Zimányi, *Data Warehouse Systems*, Data-Centric
Systems and Applications, DOI 10.1007/978-3-642-54655-6_6,
© Springer-Verlag Berlin Heidelberg 2014

6.1   Introduction to MDX

6.1.1   Tuples and Sets

Two fundamental concepts in MDX are tuples and sets. Intuitively, a tuple identifies a single cell in a multidimensional cube. A tuple is defined by stating one member from one or several dimensions of the cube.

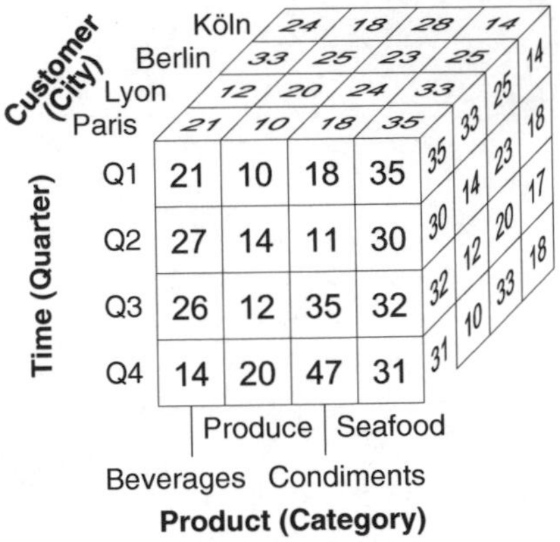

Fig. 6.1 A simple three-dimensional cube with one measure

Consider, for example, the cube given in Fig. 6.1. The cell in the top left corner with value 21 corresponds to the sales of beverages in Paris in the first quarter. To identify such cell, we just need to provide the coordinates of each dimension as follows:

(Product.Category.Beverages, Time.Quarter.Q1, Customer.City.Paris)

Notice that in the above expression, we stated the coordinate for each of the three dimensions in the format Dimension.Level.Member. As we will see later, in MDX there are several ways to specify a member of a dimension. In particular, the order of the members is not significant, and the previous tuple can also be stated as follows:

(Time.Quarter.Q1, Product.Category.Beverages, Customer.City.Paris)

Since a tuple points to a single cell, then it follows that each member in the tuple must belong to a different dimension.

A set is a collection of tuples defined using the same dimensions. For example, the following set

{ (Product.Category.Beverages, Time.Quarter.Q1, Customer.City.Paris)
  (Product.Category.Beverages, Time.Quarter.Q1, Customer.City.Lyon) }

points to the previous cell with value 21 and the one behind it with value 12. It is worth noting that a set may have one or even zero tuples.

A tuple does not need to specify a member from every dimension. Thus, the tuple

(Customer.City.Paris)

points to the slice of the cube composed of the sixteen front cells of the cube, that is, the sales of product categories in Paris, while the tuple

(Customer.City.Paris, Product.Category.Beverages)

points to the four cells at the front and left of the cube, that is, the sales of beverages in Paris. If a member for a particular dimension is not specified, then the default member for the dimension is implied. Typically, the default member is the All member, which has the aggregated value for the dimension. However, as we will see later, the default member can be also the current member in the scope of a query.

Let us see now how tuples interact with hierarchies. Suppose that in our cube we have a hierarchy in the customer dimension with levels Customer, City, State, and Country. In this case, the following tuple

(Customer.Country.France, Product.Category.Beverages, Time.Quarter.Q1)

uses the aggregated member France and therefore points to the single cell that holds the value for the total sales of beverages in France in the first quarter.

In MDX, measures act much like dimensions. Suppose that in our cube we have three measures UnitPrice, Discount, and SalesAmount. In this case, the Measures dimension, which exists in every cube, contains three members, and thus, we can specify the measure we want as in the following tuple:

(Customer.Country.France, Product.Category.Beverages, Time.Quarter.Q1, Measures.SalesAmount)

If a measure is not specified, then a default measure will be used.

6.1.2 Basic Queries

The syntax of a typical MDX query is as follows:

```
SELECT  ⟨ axis specification ⟩
FROM    ⟨ cube ⟩
[ WHERE ⟨ slicer specification ⟩ ]
```

As can be seen, at a first glance, MDX resembles SQL, but as we will see in this chapter, the two languages differ in several significant ways.

The axis specification states the axes of a query as well as the members selected for each of these axis. There can be up to 128 axes in an MDX query. Each axis has a number: 0 for the x-axis, 1 for the y-axis, 2 for the z-axis, and so on. The first axes have predefined names, namely, COLUMNS, ROWS, PAGES, CHAPTERS, and SECTIONS. Otherwise, the axes can be referenced using the AXIS(number) or the number naming convention, where AXIS(0) corresponds to COLUMNS, AXIS(1) corresponds to ROWS, and so on. It is worth noting that query axes cannot be skipped, that is, a query that includes an axis must not exclude lower-numbered axes. For example, a query cannot have a ROWS axis without a COLUMNS axis.

The slicer specification on the WHERE clause is optional. If not specified, the query returns the default measure for the cube. Unless we want to display the Measures dimension, most queries have a slicer specification.

The simplest form of an axis specification consists in taking the members of the required dimension, including those of the special Measures dimension, as follows:

```
SELECT  [Measures].MEMBERS ON COLUMNS,
        [Customer].[Country].MEMBERS ON ROWS
FROM    Sales
```

This query displays all the measures for customers summarized at the country level. In MDX the square brackets are optional, except for a name with embedded spaces, with numbers, or that is an MDX keyword, where they are required. In the following, we omit unnecessary square brackets. The result of this query is given next.

	Unit Price	Quantity	Discount	Sales Amount	Freight	Sales Count
Austria	$84.77	4,644	21.71%	$115,328.31	$6,827.10	114
Belgium	$64.65	1,242	9.72%	$30,505.06	$1,179.53	49
Denmark	$70.28	1,156	17.94%	$32,428.94	$1,377.75	45
Finland	$54.41	848	9.09%	$17,530.05	$827.45	51
France	$64.51	3,052	11.76%	$77,056.01	$3,991.42	172
Germany	$79.54	8,670	19.26%	$219,356.08	$10,459.01	309
Ireland						
...	...	...	...	...	...	...

Notice that there is no customer from Ireland and therefore the corresponding row has only null values. In order to remove such values, the NONEMPTY function must be used:

```
SELECT  Measures.MEMBERS ON COLUMNS,
        NONEMPTY(Customer.Country.MEMBERS) ON ROWS
FROM    Sales
```

Alternatively, the **NON EMPTY** keyword can be used as in the following query:

```
SELECT Measures.MEMBERS ON COLUMNS,
       NON EMPTY Customer.Country.MEMBERS ON ROWS
FROM   Sales
```

Although in this case the use of the **NONEMPTY** function and the **NON EMPTY** keyword yields the same result, there are slight differences between both, which go beyond this introduction to MDX.

Notice also that the derived measure **NetAmount** does not appear in the result. If we want this to happen, we should use the **ALLMEMBERS** keyword:

```
SELECT Measures.ALLMEMBERS ON COLUMNS,
       Customer.Country.MEMBERS ON ROWS
FROM   Sales
```

The **ADDCALCULATEDMEMBERS** function can also be used for this purpose.

6.1.3 Slicing

Consider now the query below, which shows all measures by year:

```
SELECT Measures.MEMBERS ON COLUMNS,
       [Order Date].Year.MEMBERS ON ROWS
FROM   Sales
```

The query returns the following result:

	Unit Price	Quantity	Discount	Sales Amount	Freight	Sales Count
All	$134.14	46,388	27.64%	$1,145,155.86	$58,587.49	1,931
1996	$99.55	8,775	21.95%	$191,849.87	$9,475.00	371
1997	$116.63	23,461	25.89%	$570,199.61	$29,880.49	982
1998	$205.38	14,152	35.74%	$383,106.38	$19,232.00	578

To restrict the result to Belgium, we can write the following query:

```
SELECT Measures.MEMBERS ON COLUMNS,
       [Order Date].Year.MEMBERS ON ROWS
FROM   Sales
WHERE  (Customer.Country.Belgium)
```

The added condition does not change what is returned on the axes (i.e., the years and the measure names), but only the values returned in each cell. In this example, the query returns the values of all measures for all years but only for customers who live in Belgium.

Multiple members from *different* hierarchies can be added to the **WHERE** clause. The following query shows the values of all measures for all years for customers who live in Belgium and who bought products in the category beverages:

```
SELECT  Measures.MEMBERS ON COLUMNS,
        [Order Date].Year.MEMBERS ON ROWS
FROM    Sales
WHERE   (Customer.Country.Belgium, Product.Categories.Beverages)
```

To use multiple members from the *same* hierarchy, we need to include a set in the WHERE clause. For example, the following query shows the values of all measures for all years for customers who bought products in the category beverages and live in either Belgium or France:

```
SELECT  Measures.MEMBERS ON COLUMNS,
        [Order Date].Year.MEMBERS ON ROWS
FROM    Sales
WHERE   ( { Customer.Country.Belgium, Customer.Country.France },
        Product.Categories.Beverages)
```

Using a set in the WHERE clause implicitly aggregates values for all members in the set. In this case, the query shows aggregated values for Belgium and France in each cell.

Consider now the following query, which requests the sales amount of customers by country and by year:

```
SELECT  [Order Date].Year.MEMBERS ON COLUMNS,
        Customer.Country.MEMBERS ON ROWS
FROM    Sales
WHERE   Measures.[Sales Amount]
```

Here, we specified in the WHERE clause the measure to be displayed. If no measure is stated, then the default measure is used. The result is given below:

	All	1996	1997	1998
Austria	$115,328.31	$24,467.52	$55,759.04	$35101.7502
Belgium	$30,505.06	$5,865.10	$9,075.48	$15,564.48
Denmark	$32,428.93	$2,952.40	$25,192.53	$4,284.00
Finland	$17,530.05	$2,195.760	$13,077.29	$2,257.00
...	...	...	...	...

The WHERE clause can combine measures and dimensions. For example, the following query will show a result similar to the one given above, but now with the figures restricted to the category beverages:

```
SELECT  [Order Date].Year.MEMBERS ON COLUMNS,
        Customer.Country.MEMBERS ON ROWS
FROM    Sales
WHERE   (Measures.[Sales Amount], Product.Category.[Beverages])
```

If a dimension appears in a slicer, it cannot be used in any axis in the SELECT clause. We will see later that the FILTER function can be used to filter members of dimensions appearing in an axis.

6.1.4   Navigation

The result of the query above contains aggregated values for all the years, including the All column. If we wanted to display only the values for the individual years (and not the All member), we would use the CHILDREN function instead as follows:

SELECT [Order Date].Year.CHILDREN ON COLUMNS, . . .

The attentive reader may wonder why the member All does not appear in the *rows* of the above result. The reason is that the expression

Customer.Country.MEMBERS

we used in the query is a shorthand notation for

Customer.Geography.Country.MEMBERS

and thus it selects the members of the Country level of the Geography hierarchy of the Customer dimension. Since the All member is the topmost member of the hierarchy, above the members of the Continent level, it is not a member of the Country level and does not appear in the result. Let us explain this further. As we have seen in Chap. 5, every attribute of a dimension defines an attribute hierarchy. Thus, there is an All member in each hierarchy of a dimension, for both the user-defined hierarchies and the attribute hierarchies. Since the dimension Customer has an attribute hierarchy Company Name, if in the above query we use the expression

Customer.[Company Name].MEMBERS

the result will contain the All member, in addition to the names of all the customers. Using CHILDREN instead will not show the All member.

Instead of taking the members of a dimension, a single member or an enumeration of members of a dimension can be selected. An example is given in the following query:

SELECT [Order Date].Year.MEMBERS ON COLUMNS,
        { Customer.Country.France,Customer.Country.Italy } ON ROWS
FROM   Sales
WHERE Measures.[Sales Amount]

This expression queries the sales amount of customers by year summarized for France and Italy. In the above query, the set in the row axis could be also stated using expressions such as the following ones:

Customer.France
Customer.Geography.France
Customer.Geography.Country.France

The latter expression uses fully qualified or unique names, namely, the dimension, hierarchy, and level to which the specific member belongs. When member names are uniquely identifiable, fully qualified member names are not required. Nevertheless, to remove any ambiguities in formulating expressions, the use of unique names is recommended.

To retrieve the states of the countries above, we may use the function CHILDREN as follows:

```
SELECT  [Order Date].Year.MEMBERS ON COLUMNS,
        NON EMPTY { Customer.France.CHILDREN,
        Customer.Italy.CHILDREN } ON ROWS
FROM    Sales
WHERE   Measures.[Sales Amount]
```

The result is shown below, where the first two lines correspond to departments in France and the last two lines correspond to provinces in Italy.

	All	1996	1997	1998
Bas-Rhin	$18,534.07	$9,986.20	$7,817.87	$730.00
Bouches-du-Rhône	$19,373.10	$2,675.88	$10,809.36	$5,887.86
...	...	...	...	...
Reggio Emilia	$6,641.83	$80.10	$3,000.84	$3,560.89
Torino	$1,545.70		$249.70	$1,296.00

The MEMBERS and CHILDREN functions seen above do not provide the ability to drill down to a lower level in a hierarchy. For this, the function DESCENDANTS can be used. For example, the following query shows the sales amount for German cities:

```
SELECT  [Order Date].Year.MEMBERS ON COLUMNS,
        NON EMPTY DESCENDANTS(Customer.Germany, Customer.City)
        ON ROWS
FROM    Sales
WHERE   Measures.[Sales Amount]
```

The result of the above query is given next.

	All	1996	1997	1998
Mannheim	$2,381.80		$1,079.80	$1,302.00
Stuttgart	$8,705.23	$2,956.60	$4,262.83	$1,485.80
München	$26,656.56	$9,748.04	$11,829.78	$5,078.74
...	...	...	...	...

By default, the function DESCENDANTS displays only members at the level specified as its second argument. An optional flag as third argument states whether to include or exclude descendants or children before and after the specified level as follows:

- SELF, which is the default, displays values for the City level as above.
- BEFORE displays values from the state level up to the Country level.
- SELF_AND_BEFORE displays values from the City level up to the Country level.
- AFTER displays values from the Customer level, since it is only level after City.
- SELF_AND_AFTER displays values from the City and Customer levels.
- BEFORE_AND_AFTER displays values from the Country level to the Customer level, excluding the former.
- SELF_BEFORE_AFTER displays values from the Country level to the Customer level.
- LEAVES displays values from the City level as above, since this is the only leaf level between Country and City. On the other hand, if LEAVES is used without specifying the level, as in the following query

DESCENDANTS(Customer.Geography.Germany, ,LEAVES)

then the leaf level, that is, Customer, will be displayed.

The ASCENDANTS function returns a set that includes all the ancestors of a member and the member itself. For example, the following query asks for the sales amount for the customer Du monde entier and all its ancestors in the Geography hierarchy, that is, at the City, State, Country, Continent, and All levels:

```
SELECT  Measures.[Sales Amount] ON COLUMNS,
        ASCENDANTS(Customer.Geography.[Du monde entier]) ON ROWS
FROM    Sales
```

The result of the query is as follows:

	Sales Amount
Du monde entier	$1,548.70
Nantes	$4,720.86
Loire-Atlantique	$4,720.86
France	$77,056.01
Europe	$683,523.76
All Customers	$1,145,155.86

The function ANCESTOR can be used to obtain the result for an ancestor at a specified level, as shown next:

```
SELECT  Measures.[Sales Amount] ON COLUMNS,
        ANCESTOR(Customer.Geography.[Du monde entier],
        Customer.Geography.State) ON ROWS
FROM    Sales
```

Here, only the line corresponding to Loire-Atlantique in the table above will be shown.

6.1.5   Cross Join

As said above, an MDX query can display up to 128 axes. However, most
OLAP tools are only able to display two axes, that is, two-dimensional tables.
In this case, a cross join can be used to combine several dimensions in a single
axis. Suppose that we want to obtain the sales amount for product categories
by country and by quarter. In order to view this query in a matrix format, we
need to combine the customer and time dimensions in a single axis through
the CROSSJOIN function as shown next:

```
SELECT  Product.Category.MEMBERS ON COLUMNS,
        CROSSJOIN(Customer.Country.MEMBERS,
        [Order Date].Calendar.Quarter.MEMBERS) ON ROWS
FROM    Sales
WHERE   Measures.[Sales Amount]
```

Alternatively, we can use the cross join operator '*':

```
SELECT  Product.Category.MEMBERS ON COLUMNS,
        Customer.Country.MEMBERS *
        [Order Date].Calendar.Quarter.MEMBERS ON ROWS
FROM    Sales
WHERE   Measures.[Sales Amount]
```

The result of the query is as follows:

		Beverages	Condiments	Confections	...
Austria	Q3 1996	$708.80	$884.00	$625.50	...
Austria	Q4 1996	$12,955.60	$703.60	$36.00	...
Austria	Q1 1997		$3,097.50	$1,505.22	...
Austria	Q2 1997	$1,287.50	$1,390.95	$3,159.00	...
...	...	...	...	...	...

More than two cross joins can be applied, as shown in the following query:

```
SELECT  Product.Category.MEMBERS ON COLUMNS,
        Customer.Country.MEMBERS *
        [Order Date].Calendar.Quarter.MEMBERS *
        Shipper.[Company Name].MEMBERS ON ROWS
FROM    Sales
WHERE   Measures.[Sales Amount]
```

This query yields the result displayed below:

			Beverages	Condiments	Confections	...
Austria	Q3 1996	All	$708.80	$884.00	$625.50	...
Austria	Q3 1996	Federal Shipping	$100.80		$625.50	...
Austria	Q3 1996	Speedy Express	$608.00	$884.00		...
Austria	Q3 1996	United Package				...
Austria	Q4 1996	All	$12,955.60	$703.60	$36.00	...
...	...	...	...	...	...	...

6.1.6 Subqueries

As stated above, the WHERE clause applies a slice to the cube. In the queries so far, we have used this clause to select the measure to be displayed. But this can also be used for dimensions. If we were only interested in the sales amount for the beverages and condiments product categories, we could write the following query:

```
SELECT Measures.[Sales Amount] ON COLUMNS,
        [Order Date].Calendar.Quarter.MEMBERS ON ROWS
FROM    Sales
WHERE { Product.Category.Beverages, Product.Category.Condiments }
```

Instead of using a slicer in the WHERE clause of above query, we can define a subquery in the FROM clause as follows:

```
SELECT Measures.[Sales Amount] ON COLUMNS,
        [Order Date].Calendar.Quarter.MEMBERS ON ROWS
FROM    ( SELECT { Product.Category.Beverages,
                Product.Category.Condiments } ON COLUMNS
        FROM    Sales )
```

This query displays the sales amount for each quarter in a subquery which only mentions the beverages and condiments product categories. As we can see in the query above, different from SQL, in the outer query we can mention attributes that are not selected in the subquery.

Nevertheless, there is a fundamental difference between these two approaches. When we include the product category hierarchy in the WHERE clause, it cannot appear on any axis, but this is not the case in the subquery approach as the following query shows:

```
SELECT Measures.[Sales Amount] ON COLUMNS,
        [Order Date].Calendar.Quarter.MEMBERS *
        Product.Category.MEMBERS ON ROWS
FROM    ( SELECT { Product.Category.Beverages,
                Product.Category.Condiments } ON COLUMNS
        FROM    Sales )
```

The answer of this query is given next.

		Sales Amount
Q3 1996	Beverages	$8,996.98
Q3 1996	Condiments	$4,003.30
Q4 1996	Beverages	$32,937.70
Q4 1996	Condiments	$10,778.16
...	...	...

We can see that the members of the **Category** hierarchy now are only the beverages and condiments categories and not the other categories which are present in the original Northwind cube. Thus, the structure of the cube itself has been altered.

The subquery may include more than one dimension, as the following example shows:

```
SELECT Measures.[Sales Amount] ON COLUMNS,
       [Order Date].Calendar.Quarter.MEMBERS *
       Product.Category.MEMBERS ON ROWS
FROM  ( SELECT ( { Product.Category.Beverages,
                   Product.Category.Condiments },
                 { [Order Date].Calendar.[Q1 1997],
                   [Order Date].Calendar.[Q2 1997] } ) ON COLUMNS
        FROM   Sales )
```

whose answer is as follows:

		Sales Amount
Q1 1997	Beverages	$33,902.08
Q1 1997	Condiments	$9,912.22
Q2 1997	Beverages	$21,485.53
Q2 1997	Condiments	$10,875.70

We can also nest several subquery expressions, which are used to express complex multistep filtering operations, as it is done in the following query, which asks for the sales amount by quarter for the top two selling countries for the beverages and condiments product categories:

```
SELECT Measures.[Sales Amount] ON COLUMNS,
       [Order Date].Calendar.[Quarter].Members ON ROWS
FROM  ( SELECT TOPCOUNT(Customer.Country.MEMBERS, 2,
                Measures.[Sales Amount]) ON COLUMNS
        FROM ( SELECT { Product.Category.Beverages,
                        Product.Category.Condiments } ON COLUMNS
               FROM   Sales ) )
```

This query uses the **TOPCOUNT** function, which sorts a set in descending order with respect to the expression given as third parameter and returns the specified number of elements with the highest values. Notice that although we could have used a single nesting, the expression above is easier to understand.

6.1.7 Calculated Members and Named Sets

A powerful concept in MDX is that of calculated members and named sets. Calculated members are used to define new members in a dimension or new measures. These are defined using the following clause in front of the SELECT statement:

WITH MEMBER Parent.MemberName AS ⟨ expression ⟩

where Parent refers to the parent of the new calculated member and MemberName is its name. Similarly, named sets are used to define new sets as follows:

WITH SET SetName AS ⟨ expression ⟩

Calculated members and named sets defined using the WITH clause as above are within the scope of a query. They can be defined instead within the scope of a session, and thus, they will be visible to all queries in that session or within the scope of a cube. In these cases, a CREATE statement must be used. In the sequel, we will only show examples of calculated members and named sets defined within queries.

Calculated members and named sets are computed at run time, and therefore, there is no penalty in the processing of the cube or in the number of aggregations to be stored. The most common use of calculated members is to define a new measure that relates already defined measures. For example, a measure that calculates the percentage profit of sales can be defined as follows:

```
WITH MEMBER Measures.Profit% AS
       (Measures.[Sales Amount] - Measures.[Freight]) /
       (Measures.[Sales Amount]), FORMAT_STRING = '#0.00%'
SELECT { [Sales Amount], Freight, Profit% } ON COLUMNS,
       Customer.Country ON ROWS
FROM   Sales
```

Here, FORMAT_STRING specifies the display format to use for the new calculated member. In the format expression above, a '#' displays a digit or nothing, while a '0' displays a digit or a zero. The use of the percent symbol '%' specifies that the calculation returns a percentage and includes a multiplication by a factor of 100. The result of the query follows:

	Sales Amount	Freight	Profit%
Austria	$115,328.31	$6,827.10	94.08%
Belgium	$30,505.06	$1,179.53	96.13%
Denmark	$32,428.94	$1,377.75	95.75%
Finland	$17,530.05	$827.45	95.28%
...	...	...	...

In the above example, we created a calculated member in the **Measures** dimension. It is also possible to create a calculated member in a dimension, as shown in the following example:

```
WITH MEMBER Product.Categories.[All].[Meat & Fish] AS
        Product.Categories.[Meat/Poultry] + Product.Categories.[Seafood]
SELECT { Measures.[Unit Price], Measures.Quantity, Measures.Discount,
        Measures.[Sales Amount] } ON COLUMNS,
        Category.ALLMEMBERS ON ROWS
FROM    Sales
```

The query above creates a calculated member equal to the sum of the **Meat/Poultry** and **Seafood** categories. This member is a child of the **All** member of the hierarchy **Categories** of the **Product** dimension. It will thus belong to the **Category** level of the **Categories** hierarchy. The following table shows the result of the query:

	Unit Price	Quantity	Discount	Sales Amount
...	...	...	...	...
Meat/Poultry	$50.25	3,897	7.48%	$139,428.18
Produce	$41.24	2,710	5.09%	$90,216.14
Seafood	$27.64	7,070	8.25%	$122,307.02
Meat & Fish	$77.89	10,967	15.73%	$261,735.20

In the following query, we define a named set **Nordic Countries** composed of the countries Denmark, Finland, Norway, and Sweden:

```
WITH SET [Nordic Countries] AS
        { Customer.Country.Denmark, Customer.Country.Finland,
        Customer.Country.Norway, Customer.Country.Sweden }
SELECT Measures.MEMBERS ON COLUMNS,
        [Nordic Countries] ON ROWS
FROM    Sales
```

The result of the query is as follows:

	Unit Price	Quantity	Discount	Sales Amount	Freight	Sales Count
Denmark	$70.28	1,156	17.94%	$32,428.94	$1,377.75	45
Finland	$54.41	848	9.09%	$17,530.05	$827.45	51
Norway	$97.95	152	0.00%	$5,321.15	$257.45	15
Sweden	$68.73	2,149	19.57%	$51,292.64	$3,032.12	94

In the above example, the named set is defined by enumerating its members, and thus, it is a static name set even if defined in the scope of a session or a cube, since its result must not be reevaluated upon updates of the cube. On the contrary, a dynamic named set is evaluated any time there are changes to the scope. As an example of a dynamic named set, the following query displays several measures for the top five selling products:

```
WITH SET TopFiveProducts AS
        TOPCOUNT ( Product.Categories.Product.MEMBERS, 5,
        Measures.[Sales Amount] )
SELECT { Measures.[Unit Price], Measures.Quantity, Measures.Discount,
        Measures.[Sales Amount] } ON COLUMNS,
        TopFiveProducts ON ROWS
FROM    Sales
```

The result of the query is shown below:

	Unit Price	Quantity	Discount	Sales Amount
Côte de Blaye	$256.63	623	4.78%	$141,396.74
Raclette Courdavault	$53.17	1,369	3.96%	$65,658.45
Thüringer Rostbratwurst	$115.24	596	6.21%	$63,657.02
Tarte au sucre	$46.56	1,068	5.53%	$46,643.97
Camembert Pierrot	$34.32	1,498	7.21%	$44,200.68

6.1.8 Relative Navigation

It is often necessary to relate the value of a member to those of other members in a hierarchy. MDX has many methods that can be applied to a member to traverse a hierarchy, the most common ones are PREVMEMBER, NEXTMEMBER, CURRENTMEMBER, PARENT, FIRSTCHILD, and LASTCHILD. Suppose we want to calculate the sales of a member of the Geography hierarchy as a percentage of the sales of its parent, as shown in the following query:

```
WITH MEMBER Measures.[Percentage Sales] AS
        (Measures.[Sales Amount], Customer.Geography.CURRENTMEMBER) /
        (Measures.[Sales Amount],
        Customer.Geography.CURRENTMEMBER.PARENT),
        FORMAT_STRING = '#0.00%'
SELECT { Measures.[Sales Amount], Measures.[Percentage Sales] }
        ON COLUMNS, DESCENDANTS(Customer.Europe,
        Customer.Country, SELF_AND_BEFORE) ON ROWS
FROM    Sales
```

In the WITH clause, the CURRENTMEMBER function returns the current member along a dimension during an iteration, while the PARENT function returns the parent of a member. In the SELECT clause, the measures for European countries are displayed. The expression defining the calculated member can be abbreviated as follows:

```
(Measures.[Sales Amount]) / (Measures.[Sales Amount],
        Customer.Geography.CURRENTMEMBER.PARENT)
```

where the current member of the hierarchy will be used by default if not specified. The result of the query is as follows:

	Sales Amount	Percentage Sales
Europe	$683,523.76	59.69%
Austria	$115,328.31	16.87%
Belgium	$30,505.06	4.46%
Denmark	$32,428.94	4.74%
Finland	$17,530.05	2.56%
...	...	...

As can be seen, for example, sales in Austria represent 16.87% of European sales, while European sales represent 59.69% of the overall sales. The problem with the above calculated measure is that it works well for all members of the Geography hierarchy, at any level, except for the All member, since it does not have a parent. Therefore, we must add a conditional expression in the definition of the measure as follows:

```
WITH MEMBER Measures.[Percentage Sales] AS
        IIF((Measures.[Sales Amount],
        Customer.Geography.CURRENTMEMBER.PARENT)=0, 1,
        (Measures.[Sales Amount]) / (Measures.[Sales Amount],
        Customer.Geography.CURRENTMEMBER.PARENT)),
        FORMAT_STRING = '#0.00%'
SELECT ...
```

The IIF function has three parameters: the first one is a Boolean condition, the second one is the value returned if the condition is true, and the third one is the value returned if the condition is false. Thus, since the All member has no parent, the value of the measure sales amount for its parent will be equal to 0, and in this case a value of 1 will be given for the percentage sales.

The GENERATE function iterates through the members of a set, using a second set as a template for the resultant set. Suppose we want to display the sales amount by category for all customers in Belgium and France. To avoid enumerating in the query all customers for each country, the GENERATE function can be used as follows:

```
SELECT  Product.Category.MEMBERS ON COLUMNS,
        GENERATE({Customer.Belgium, Customer.France},
        DESCENDANTS(Customer.Geography.CURRENTMEMBER,
        [Company Name])) ON ROWS
FROM    Sales
WHERE   Measures.[Sales Amount]
```

The result of the query is given next.

	Beverages	Condiments	Confections	Dairy Products	...
Maison Dewey	$108.00	$680.00	$2,659.38	$2,972.00	...
Suprêmes délices	$3,108.08	$1,675.60	$4,820.20	$5,688.00	...
Blondesddsl père et fils	$3,975.92		$1,939.00	$2,872.00	...
Bon app'	$877.50	$2,662.48	$2,313.67	$1,912.43	...
La maison d'Asie	$1,499.15	$525.90	$2,085.90	$757.76	...
Du monde entier	$194.00		$60.00	$201.60	...
...	...	...	...	...	...

The PREVMEMBER function can be used to show growth over a time period. The following query displays net sales and the incremental change from the previous time member for all months in 1996:

```
WITH MEMBER Measures.[Net Sales Growth] AS
      (Measures.[Net Sales]) -
      (Measures.[Net Sales], [Order Date].Calendar.PREVMEMBER),
      FORMAT_STRING = '$###,##0.00; $-###,##0.00'
SELECT { Measures.[Net Sales], Measures.[Net Sales Growth] } ON COLUMNS,
      DESCENDANTS([Order Date].Calendar.[1996],
      [Order Date].Calendar.[Month]) ON ROWS
FROM   Sales
```

The format expression above defines two formats, the first one for positive numbers and the second one for negative numbers. Using NEXTMEMBER in the expression above would show net sales for each month compared with those of the following month. The result of the query is given next.

	Net Sales	Net Sales Growth
July 1996	$25,982.68	$25,982.68
August 1996	$21,849.97	$-4,132.71
September 1996	$19,698.94	$-2,151.03
October 1996	$32,586.14	$12,887.20
November 1996	$42,337.16	$9,751.03
December 1996	$39,919.97	$-2,417.19

As shown above, the net sales growth for the first month is equivalent to the net sales. Since the cube only holds sales starting from July 1996, the growth for the first month cannot be measured. In this case, a value of zero is used for the previous period that is beyond the range of the cube.

In the query above, instead of the PREVMEMBER function, we can use the LAG(n) function, which returns the member located a specified number of positions preceding a specific member along the member dimension. If the number given is negative, a subsequent member is returned; if it is zero, the current member is returned. Thus, PREV, NEXT, and CURRENT can be replaced with LAG(1), LAG(-1), and LAG(0), respectively. A similar function called LEAD exists, such that LAG(n) is equivalent to LEAD(-n).

6.1.9   Time Series Functions

Time period analysis is an essential component of business intelligence applications. For example, one could want to examine the sales of a month or quarter compared to those of the same month or quarter last year. MDX provides a powerful set of time series functions for time period analysis. While their most common use is with a time dimension, most of them can also be used with any other dimension.

The PARALLELPERIOD function is used to compare values of a specified member with those of a member in the same relative position in a prior period. For example, one would compare values from one quarter with those of the same quarter in the previous year. In the previous query, we used the PREVMEMBER function to compute the growth with respect to the previous month. The PARALLELPERIOD function can be used to compute the growth with respect to the same period in the previous year, as shown next:

```
WITH MEMBER Measures.[Previous Year] AS
     (Measures.[Net Sales],
     PARALLELPERIOD([Order Date].Calendar.Quarter, 4)),
     FORMAT_STRING = '$###,##0.00'
MEMBER Measures.[Net Sales Growth] AS
     Measures.[Net Sales] - Measures.[Previous Year],
     FORMAT_STRING = '$###,##0.00; $-###,##0.00'
SELECT { [Net Sales], [Previous Year], [Net Sales Growth] } ON COLUMNS,
     [Order Date].Calendar.Quarter ON ROWS
FROM   Sales
```

Here, the PARALLELPERIOD selects the member that is four quarters (i.e., a year) prior to the current quarter. The query result is as follows:

	Net Sales	Previous Year	Net Sales Growth
Q3 1996	$67,531.59		$67,531.59
Q4 1996	$114,843.27		$114,843.27
Q1 1997	$125,174.40		$125,174.40
Q2 1997	$121,518.78		$121,518.78
Q3 1997	$133,636.32	$67,531.59	$66,104.73
Q4 1997	$159,989.61	$114,843.27	$45,146.34
Q1 1998	$259,322.36	$125,174.40	$134,147.95
Q2 1998	$104,552.03	$121,518.78	$-16,966.75

As can be seen, the net sales growth for the third quarter of 1997 is the difference between the net sales in that quarter and the net sales of the third quarter of 1996. Notice that the net sales growth for the first four quarters is equal to the net sales. As already said, since the Northwind cube contains sales data starting from July 1996, the net sales for the first four quarters shown in the result above is null. In this case, a value of zero is used for parallel periods beyond the range of the cube.

The functions OPENINGPERIOD and CLOSINGPERIOD return, respectively, the first or last sibling among the descendants of a member at a specified level. For example, the difference between the sales quantity of a month and that of the opening month of the quarter can be obtained as follows:

```
WITH MEMBER Measures.[Quantity Difference] AS
      (Measures.[Quantity]) - (Measures.[Quantity],
      OPENINGPERIOD([Order Date].Calendar.Month,
      [Order Date].Calendar.CURRENTMEMBER.PARENT))
SELECT { Measures.[Quantity], Measures.[Quantity Difference] } ON COLUMNS,
      [Order Date].Calendar.[Month] ON ROWS
FROM   Sales
```

In deriving the calculated member Quantity Difference, the opening period at the month level is taken for the quarter to which the month corresponds. If CLOSINGPERIOD is used instead, the query will show sales based on the final month of the specified season, as shown next.

	Quantity	Quantity Difference
July 1996	1,425	
August 1996	1,221	-204
September 1996	882	-543
October 1996	1,602	
November 1996	1,649	47
December 1996	1,996	394
...	...	...

The PERIODSTODATE function returns a set of periods (members) from a specified level starting with the first period and ending with a specified member. For example, the following expression defines a set containing all the months up to and including June 1997:

```
PERIODSTODATE([Order Date].Calendar.Year,
            [Order Date].Calendar.[June 1997])
```

Suppose now that we want to define a calculated member that displays year-to-date information, for example, the monthly year-to-date sales. For this, in addition to PERIODSTODATE, we need to use the SUM function, which returns the sum of a numeric expression evaluated over a set. For example, the sum of sales amount for Italy and Greece can be displayed with the following expression:

```
SUM({Customer.Country.Italy, Customer.Country.Greece},
   Measures.[Sales Amount])
```

We can now compute the monthly year-to-date sales. In the expression below, the measure to be displayed is the sum of the current time member over the year level:

```
SUM(PERIODSTODATE([Order Date].Calendar.Year,
       [Order Date].Calendar.CURRENTMEMBER), Measures.[Sales Amount])
```

Similarly, by replacing Year by Quarter in the above expression, we can obtain quarter-to-date sales. For example, the following query shows year-to-date and quarter-to-date sales:

```
WITH MEMBER Measures.YTDSales AS
          SUM(PERIODSTODATE([Order Date].Calendar.Year,
          [Order Date].Calendar.CURRENTMEMBER), Measures.[Sales Amount])
      MEMBER Measures.QTDSales AS
          SUM(PERIODSTODATE([Order Date].Calendar.Quarter,
          [Order Date].Calendar.CURRENTMEMBER), Measures.[Sales Amount])
SELECT { Measures.[Sales Amount], Measures.YTDSales, Measures.QTDSales }
       ON COLUMNS, [Order Date].Calendar.Month.MEMBERS ON ROWS
FROM   Sales
```

The result of the query is as follows:

	Sales Amount	YTDSales	QTDSales
July 1996	$27,246.10	$27,246.10	$27,246.10
August 1996	$23,104.98	$50,351.07	$50,351.07
September 1996	$20,582.40	$70,933.47	$70,933.47
October 1996	$33,991.56	$104,925.04	$33,991.56
November 1996	$44,365.42	$149,290.46	$78,356.98
December 1996	$42,559.41	$191,849.87	$120,916.40
January 1997	$57,187.26	$57,187.26	$57,187.26
February 1997	$36,275.14	$93,462.39	$93,462.39
...	...	...	...

As can be seen above, the Northwind data warehouse contains sales data starting in July 1996. Thus, the value of both measures YTDSales and QTDSales for August 1996 is the sum of the measure Sales Amount of July 1996 and August 1996. Similarly, the value of measure YTDSales for December 1996 is the sum of Sales Amount from July 1996 to December 1996. This is to be contrasted with the value of measure QTDSales for December 1996, which is the sum of Sales Amount from October 1996 to December 1996.

The xTD (YTD, QTD, MTD, and WTD) functions refer to year-, quarter-, month-, and week-to-date periods. They are only applicable to a time dimension (which was not the case for the other functions we have seen so far). The xTD functions are equivalent to the PeriodsToDate function with a level specified. YTD specifies a year level, QTD specifies a quarter level, and so on. For example, in the query above, the measure YTDSales can be defined instead by the following expression:

```
SUM(YTD([Order Date].Calendar.CURRENTMEMBER),
    Measures.[Sales Amount])
```

Moving averages are used to solve very common business problems. They are well suited to track the behavior of temporal series, such as financial indicators or stock market data. As these data change very rapidly, moving averages are used to smooth out the variations and discover general trends. However, choosing the period over which smoothing is performed is essential, because if the period is too long, the average will be flat and will not be useful to discover any trend, whereas a too short period will show too many peaks and troughs to highlight general trends.

The LAG function we have seen in the previous section, combined with the range operator ':', helps us to write moving averages in MDX. The range operator returns a set of members made of two given members and all the members in between. Thus, for computing the 3-month moving average of the number of orders, we can write the following query:

```
WITH MEMBER Measures.MovAvg3Months AS
        AVG([Order Date].Calendar.CURRENTMEMBER.LAG(2):
        [Order Date].Calendar.CURRENTMEMBER,
        Measures.[Order No]), FORMAT_STRING = '###,##0.00'
SELECT  { Measures.[Order No], Measures.MovAvg3Months } ON COLUMNS,
        [Order Date].Calendar.Month.MEMBERS ON ROWS
FROM    Sales
WHERE   (Measures.MovAvg3Months)
```

The AVG function, like SUM, returns the average of an expression evaluated over a set. The LAG(2) function obtains the month preceding the current one by 2 months. The range operator returns the set containing the 3 months over which the average of the number of orders is computed. The answer of this query is given next.

	Order No	MovAvg3Months
July 1996	21	21.00
August 1996	25	23.00
September 1996	21	22.33
October 1996	25	23.67
November 1996	25	23.67
December 1996	29	26.33
...	...	...

As can be seen, the average for July 1996 is equal to the number of orders, as there are no prior data, while the average for August 1996 will be computed from the data from July and August 1996. From September 2006 onward, the average will be computed from the current month and the prior 2 months.

6.1.10   Filtering

As its name suggests, filtering is used to reduce the number of axis members that are displayed. This is to be contrasted with slicing, as specified in the WHERE clause, since slicing does not affect selection of the axis members, but rather the values that go into them.

We have already seen the most common form of filtering, where the members of an axis that have no values are removed with the NON EMPTY clause. The FILTER function can be used for more specific filtering. This function filters a set according to a specified condition. Suppose we want to show sales amount in 1997 by city and by product category. If one were only interested in viewing top-performing cities, defined by those whose sales amount exceeds $25,000, a filter would be defined as follows:

```
SELECT  Product.Category.MEMBERS ON COLUMNS,
        FILTER(Customer.City.MEMBERS, (Measures.[Sales Amount],
        [Order Date].Calendar.[1997]) > 25000) ON ROWS
FROM    Sales
WHERE   (Measures.[Net Sales Growth], [Order Date].Calendar.[1997])
```

As shown in the result below, only five cities satisfy the condition.

	Beverages	Condiments	Confections	Dairy Products	···
Graz	$-2,370.58	$6,114.67	$8,581.51	$7,171.01	···
Cunewalde	$6,966.40	$2,610.51	$8,821.85	$7,144.74	···
London	$2,088.23	$683.88	$1,942.56	$83.13	···
Montréal	$9,142.78	$2,359.90	$213.93	$3,609.16	···
Boise	$1,871.10	$94.84	$4,411.46	$6,522.61	···

As another example, the following query shows customers that in 1997 had profit margins below the state average:

```
WITH MEMBER Measures.[Profit%] AS
        (Measures.[Sales Amount] - Measures.[Freight]) /
        (Measures.[Sales Amount]), FORMAT_STRING = '#0.00%'
MEMBER Measures.[Profit%City] AS
        (Measures.[Profit%],
        Customer.Geography.CURRENTMEMBER.PARENT),
        FORMAT_STRING = '#0.00%'
SELECT { Measures.[Sales Amount], Measures.[Freight], Measures.[Net Sales],
        Measures.[Profit%], Measures.[Profit%City] } ON COLUMNS,
        FILTER(NONEMPTY(Customer.Customer.MEMBERS),
        (Measures.[Profit%]) < (Measures.[Profit%City])) ON ROWS
FROM    Sales
WHERE   [Order Date].Calendar.[1997]
```

The result of this query is shown below:

	Sales Amount	Freight	Net Sales	Profit%	Profit%City
France restauration	$920.10	$30.34	$889.76	96.70%	97.40%
Princesa Isabel Vinhos	$1,409.20	$86.85	$1,322.35	93.84%	95.93%
Around the Horn	$6,406.90	$305.59	$6,101.31	95.23%	95.58%
North/South	$604.00	$33.46	$570.54	94.46%	95.58%
Seven Seas Imports	$9,021.24	$425.03	$8,596.21	95.29%	95.58%
...	...	...	...	...	...

Here, Profit% computes the profit percentage of the current member, and Profit%City applies Profit% to the parent of the current member, that is, the profit of the state to which the city belongs.

6.1.11 Sorting

In cube queries, all the members in a dimension have a hierarchical order. For example, consider the query below:

```
SELECT  Measures.MEMBERS ON COLUMNS,
        Customer.Geography.Country.MEMBERS ON ROWS
FROM    Sales
```

The answer of this query is given next.

	Unit Price	Quantity	Discount	Sales Amount	Freight	Sales Count
Austria	$84.77	4,644	21.71%	$115,328.31	$6,827.10	114
Belgium	$64.65	1,242	9.72%	$30,505.06	$1,179.53	49
Denmark	$70.28	1,156	17.94%	$32,428.94	$1,377.75	45
Finland	$54.41	848	9.09%	$17,530.05	$827.45	51
France	$64.51	3,052	11.76%	$77,056.01	$3,991.42	172
...	...	...	...	...	...	...

The countries are displayed in the hierarchical order determined by the Continent level (the topmost level of the Geography hierarchy), that is, first the European countries, then the North American countries, and so on. If we wanted the countries sorted by their name, we can use the ORDER function, whose syntax is given next:

```
ORDER(Set, Expression [, ASC | DESC | BASC | BDESC])
```

The expression can be a numeric or string expression. The default sort order is ASC. The 'B' prefix indicates that the hierarchical order can be broken. The hierarchical order first sorts members according to their position in the hierarchy, and then it sorts each level. The nonhierarchical order sorts members in the set independently of the hierarchy. In the previous query, the set of countries can be ordered regardless of the hierarchy in the following way:

```
SELECT  Measures.MEMBERS ON COLUMNS,
        ORDER(Customer.Geography.Country.MEMBERS,
        Customer.Geography.CURRENTMEMBER.NAME, BASC) ON ROWS
FROM    Sales
```

Here, the property NAME returns the name of a level, dimension, member, or hierarchy. A similar property, UNIQUENAME, returns the corresponding unique name. The answer to this query will show the countries in alphabetical order, that is, Argentina, Australia, Austria, and so on.

It is often the case that the ordering is based on an actual measure. In the query above, the countries can be ordered based on the sales amount as follows:

```
SELECT  Measures.MEMBERS ON COLUMNS,
        ORDER(Customer.Geography.Country.MEMBERS,
        Measures.[Sales Amount], BDESC) ON ROWS
FROM    Sales
```

Ordering on multiple criteria is difficult to express in MDX. Indeed, unlike in SQL, the ORDER function allows a *single* expression for sorting. Suppose, for instance, that we want to analyze the sales amount by continent and category. Further, suppose that we want to order the result first by continent name and then by category name. For this we need to use the GENERATE function:

```
SELECT  Measures.[Sales Amount] ON COLUMNS,
        NON EMPTY GENERATE(
        ORDER( Customer.Geography.Continent.ALLMEMBERS,
        Customer.Geography.CURRENTMEMBER.NAME, BASC ),
        ORDER( { Customer.Geography.CURRENTMEMBER } *
        Product.Categories.Category.ALLMEMBERS,
        Product.Categories.CURRENTMEMBER.NAME, BASC ) ) ON ROWS
FROM    Sales
```

In the first argument of the GENERATE function, we sort the continents in ascending order of their name. In the second argument, we cross join the current continent with the categories sorted in ascending order of their name. This query will give the following answer:

		Sales Amount
Europe	Beverages	$120,361.83
Europe	Condiments	$60,517.12
Europe	Confections	$95,690.12
Europe	Dairy Products	$137,315.75
Europe	Grains/Cereals	$48,781.57
...	...	...

6.1.12   Top and Bottom Analysis

When displaying information such as the best-selling cities based on sales amount, a usual requirement is to limit the query to, say, the top three. The HEAD function returns the first members in the set based on the number that one requests. A similar function TAIL returns a subset from the end of the set. The query "Top three best-selling store cities" is expressed as follows:

```
SELECT  Measures.MEMBERS ON COLUMNS,
        HEAD(ORDER(Customer.Geography.City.MEMBERS,
        Measures.[Sales Amount], BDESC), 3) ON ROWS
FROM    Sales
```

This query yields the following answer:

	Unit Price	Quantity	Discount	Sales Amount	Freight	Sales Count
Cunewalde	$101.46	3,616	21.40%	$103,597.43	$4,999.77	77
Boise	$90.90	4,809	32.41%	$102,253.85	$6,570.58	113
Graz	$88.00	4,045	23.57%	$93,349.45	$5,725.79	92

Alternatively, the function TOPCOUNT can be used to answer the previous query:

```
SELECT  Measures.MEMBERS ON COLUMNS,
        TOPCOUNT(Customer.Geography.City.MEMBERS, 3,
        Measures.[Sales Amount]) ON ROWS
FROM    Sales
```

As a more elaborated example, suppose that we want to display the top three cities based on sales amount together with their combined sales and the combined sales of all the other cities. This can be written as follows:

```
WITH SET SetTop3Cities AS TOPCOUNT(
        Customer.Geography.City.MEMBERS, 3, [Sales Amount])
MEMBER Customer.Geography.[Top 3 Cities] AS
        AGGREGATE(SetTop3Cities)
MEMBER Customer.Geography.[Other Cities] AS
        (Customer.[All]) - (Customer.[Top 3 Cities])
SELECT  Measures.MEMBERS ON COLUMNS,
        { SetTop3Cities, [Top 3 Cities], [Other Cities], Customer.[All] } ON ROWS
FROM    Sales
```

The query starts by selecting the three best-selling cities and denotes this set SetTop3Cities. Then, it adds two members to the Geography hierarchy. The first one, denoted Top 3 Cities, contains the aggregation of the measures of the elements in the set SetTop3Cities. The other member, denoted Other Cities, contains the difference between the measures of the member Customer.[All] and the measures of the member Top 3 Cities. The AGGREGATE function aggregates each measure using the aggregation operator specified for each measure. Thus, for measures Unit Price and Discount, the average is used, while for the other measures, the sum is applied. The result of the query is given below. We can see the values for each one of the top three cities, the aggregated values for the top three cities, and the aggregated values of the other cities.

	Unit Price	Quantity	Discount	Sales Amount	Freight	Sales Count
Cunewalde	$101.46	3,616	21.40%	$103,597.43	$4,999.77	77
Boise	$90.90	4,809	32.41%	$102,253.85	$6,570.58	113
Graz	$88.00	4,045	23.57%	$93,349.45	$5,725.79	92
Top 3 Cities	$95.46	12,470	26.69%	$299,200.73	$17,296.14	282
Other Cities	$38.68	33,918	0.95%	$845,955.13	$41,291.35	1,649
All Customers	$134.14	46,388	27.64%	$1,145,155.86	$58,587.49	1,931

Other functions exist for top filter processing. The TOPPERCENT and TOPSUM functions return the top elements whose cumulative total is at least a specified percentage or a specified value, respectively. For example, the next query displays the list of cities whose sales count accounts for 30% of all the sales.

```
SELECT  Measures.[Sales Amount] ON COLUMNS,
        { TOPPERCENT(Customer.Geography.City.MEMBERS, 30,
        Measures.[Sales Amount]), Customer.Geography.[All] } ON ROWS
FROM    Sales
```

The result of the query is as follows:

	Sales Amount
Cunewalde	$103,597.43
Boise	$102,253.85
Graz	$93,349.45
London	$51,169.01
Albuquerque	$49,290.08
All Customers	$1,145,155.86

As can be seen, the sum of the sales of the cities in the answer amounts to 34% of the total sales amount.

There is also an analogous series of BOTTOM functions, returning the bottom items in a list. For example, in the above query we could use the BOTTOMSUM function to obtain the bottom cities whose cumulative sales amount is less than, say, $10,000.

6.1.13 Aggregation Functions

As can be expected, MDX provides many aggregation functions. We have seen already an example of the SUM and AVG functions. Other functions like MEDIAN, MAX, MIN, VAR, and STDDEV compute, respectively, the median, maximum, minimum, variance, and standard deviation of tuples in a set based on a numeric value. For example, the following query analyzes each product category to see the total, maximum, minimum, and average sales amount for a 1-month period in 1997:

```
WITH MEMBER Measures.[Maximum Sales] AS
        MAX(DESCENDANTS([Order Date].Calendar.Year.[1997],
        [Order Date].Calendar.Month), Measures.[Sales Amount])
    MEMBER Measures.[Minimum Sales] AS
        MIN(DESCENDANTS([Order Date].Calendar.Year.[1997],
        [Order Date].Calendar.Month), Measures.[Sales Amount])
    MEMBER Measures.[Average Sales] AS
        AVG(DESCENDANTS([Order Date].Calendar.Year.[1997],
        [Order Date].Calendar.Month), Measures.[Sales Amount])
SELECT { [Sales Amount], [Maximum Sales],
        [Minimum Sales], [Average Sales] } ON COLUMNS,
        Product.Categories.Category.MEMBERS ON ROWS
FROM    Sales
```

The result of the query is as follows:

	Sales Amount	Maximum Sales	Minimum Sales	Average Sales
Beverages	$237,203.91	$21,817.76	$2,109.84	$7,652.65
Condiments	$91,528.81	$5,629.70	$1,252.33	$3,842.09
Confections	$162,443.91	$11,538.61	$2,174.89	$6,798.83
Dairy Products	$221,157.31	$12,992.48	$5,584.84	$9,119.26
Grains/Cereals	$80,870.58	$6,012.65	$1,891.00	$4,193.64
Meat/Poultry	$139,428.18	$14,110.16	$1,029.00	$6,217.45
Produce	$90,216.14	$12,157.90	$1,650.00	$4,429.52
Seafood	$122,307.02	$8,448.86	$1,587.11	$5,263.19

Our next query computes the maximum sales by category as well as the month in which they occurred:

```
WITH MEMBER Measures.[Maximum Sales] AS
        MAX(DESCENDANTS([Order Date].Calendar.Year.[1997],
        [Order Date].Calendar.Month), Measures.[Sales Amount])
    MEMBER Measures.[Maximum Period] AS
        TOPCOUNT(DESCENDANTS([Order Date].Calendar.Year.[1997],
        [Order Date].Calendar.Month), 1,
        Measures.[Sales Amount]).ITEM(0).NAME
SELECT { [Maximum Sales], [Maximum Period] } ON COLUMNS,
        Product.Categories.Category.MEMBERS ON ROWS
FROM    Sales
```

Here, the **TOPCOUNT** function obtains the tuple corresponding to the maximum sales amount. Then, the **ITEM** function retrieves the first member from the specified tuple, and finally, the **NAME** function obtains the name of this member. The result of the query is given below:

	Maximum Sales	Maximum Period
Beverages	$21,817.76	January 1997
Condiments	$5,629.70	December 1997
Confections	$11,538.61	April 1997
Dairy Products	$12,992.48	November 1997
Grains/Cereals	$6,012.65	June 1997
Meat/Poultry	$14,110.16	October 1997
Produce	$12,157.90	December 1997
Seafood	$8,448.86	September 1997

The previous query can be further elaborated to obtain the maximum sales by category and by country, as well as the month in which they occurred. This can be written as follows:

```
WITH MEMBER Measures.[Maximum Sales] AS
        MAX(DESCENDANTS([Order Date].Calendar.Year.[1997],
        [Order Date].Calendar.[Month]), Measures.[Sales Amount])
MEMBER Measures.[Maximum Period] AS
        TOPCOUNT(DESCENDANTS([Order Date].Calendar.Year.[1997],
        [Order Date].Calendar.[Month]), 1,
        Measures.[Sales Amount]).ITEM(0).NAME
SELECT { [Maximum Sales], [Maximum Period] } ON COLUMNS,
        Product.Categories.Category.MEMBERS *
        Customer.Geography.Country.MEMBERS ON ROWS
FROM    Sales
```

The result of the query is given next.

		Maximum Sales	Maximum Period
Beverages	Austria	$2,149.40	December 1997
Beverages	Belgium	$514.08	March 1997
Beverages	Denmark	$10,540.00	January 1997
Beverages	Finland	$288.00	February 1997
Beverages	France	$915.75	December 1997
Beverages	Germany	$8,010.00	May 1997
...	...	...	...

The **COUNT** function counts the number of tuples in a set. This function has an optional parameter, with values **INCLUDEEMPTY** or **EXCLUDEEMPTY**, which states whether to include or exclude empty cells. For example, the **COUNT** function can be used to compute the number of customers that purchased a particular product category. This can be done by counting the number of tuples obtained by joining the sales amount and customer names. Excluding empty cells is necessary to restrict the count to those customers for which there are sales in the corresponding product category. This is shown below:

```
WITH MEMBER Measures.[Customer Count] AS
        COUNT({Measures.[Sales Amount] *
        [Customer].[Company Name].MEMBERS}, EXCLUDEEMPTY)
SELECT { Measures.[Sales Amount], Measures.[Customer Count] } ON COLUMNS,
        Product.Category.MEMBERS ON ROWS
FROM    Sales
```

The result of the query is as follows:

	Sales Amount	Customer Count
Beverages	$237,203.91	82
Condiments	$91,528.81	65
Confections	$162,443.91	79
Dairy Products	$221,157.31	80
...	...	...

6.2 Querying the Northwind Cube in MDX

In this section, we further illustrate the MDX language by revisiting the queries given in Sect. 4.4 addressed to the Northwind cube.

Query 6.1. Total sales amount per customer, year, and product category.

```
SELECT [Order Date].Year.CHILDREN ON COLUMNS,
        NON EMPTY Customer.[Company Name].CHILDREN *
        Product.[Category Name].CHILDREN ON ROWS
FROM    Sales
WHERE   Measures.[Sales Amount]
```

Here, we display the years on the column axis and we use a cross join of the Customer and Category dimensions to display both dimensions in the row axis. We use the CHILDREN function instead of MEMBERS to prevent displaying the All members of the three dimensions involved in the query. The NON EMPTY keyword is used to avoid displaying customers that never ordered articles from a particular category. Finally, we state the measure to be displayed as a slicer in the WHERE clause.

		1996	1997	1998
Alfreds Futterkiste	Beverages		$553.50	
Alfreds Futterkiste	Condiments		$938.00	$400.80
Alfreds Futterkiste	Dairy Products			$1,255.00
Alfreds Futterkiste	Produce		$513.00	$91.20
Alfreds Futterkiste	Seafood		$18.00	$503.50
...	...	...	...	...

Query 6.2. Yearly sales amount for each pair of customer country and supplier countries.

```
SELECT  [Order Date].Year.MEMBERS ON COLUMNS,
        NON EMPTY Customer.Country.MEMBERS *
        Supplier.Country.MEMBERS ON ROWS
FROM    Sales
WHERE   Measures.[Sales Amount]
```

In this query, we use a cross join of the **Customer** and **Supplier** dimensions to display the pair of countries from both dimensions in the row axis.

		All	1996	1997	1998
Austria	Denmark	$675.67	$432.00	$243.67	
Austria	Finland	$900.00		$900.00	
Austria	France	$29,307.19	$12,437.20	$4,569.99	$12,300.00
...	...	...	...	...	...

Query 6.3. Monthly sales by customer state compared to those of the previous year.

```
WITH MEMBER Measures.[Previous Year] AS
        (Measures.[Sales Amount],
        PARALLELPERIOD([Order Date].Calendar.Month,12)),
        FORMAT_STRING = '$###,##0.00'
SELECT  { Measures.[Sales Amount], Measures.[Previous Year] } ON COLUMNS,
        NON EMPTY ORDER(Customer.Geography.State.MEMBERS,
        Customer.Geography.CURRENTMEMBER.NAME, BASC) *
        [Order Date].Calendar.Month.MEMBERS ON ROWS
FROM    Sales
```

In this query, we do a cross join of the **Customer** and **Order Date** dimensions to display the states and months on the row axis. We use the ORDER function to sort the states of the customers in alphabetical order irrespective of the **Geography** hierarchy. The calculated measure **Previous Year** computes the sales amount of the same month of the previous year for the current state and month using the PARALLELPERIOD function. The format for displaying the new measure is also defined.

		Sales Amount	Previous Year
Alaska	September 1996	$3,741.30	
Alaska	October 1996	$934.50	
Alaska	February 1997	$1,755.00	
Alaska	July 1997	$565.50	
Alaska	September 1997	$1,261.88	$3,741.30
Alaska	October 1997	$1,893.00	$934.50
Alaska	January 1998	$3,638.89	
...	...	...	...

Query 6.4. Monthly sales growth per product, that is, total sales per product compared to those of the previous month.

```
WITH MEMBER Measures.[Previous Month] AS
      (Measures.[Sales Amount],
      [Order Date].Calendar.CURRENTMEMBER.PREVMEMBER),
      FORMAT_STRING = '$###,##0.00'
MEMBER Measures.[Sales Growth] AS
      (Measures.[Sales Amount]) - (Measures.[Previous Month]),
      FORMAT_STRING = '$###,##0.00; $-###,##0.00'
SELECT { Measures.[Sales Amount], Measures.[Previous Month],
      Measures.[Sales Growth] } ON COLUMNS,
      NON EMPTY ORDER(Product.Categories.Product.MEMBERS,
      Product.Categories.CURRENTMEMBER.NAME, BASC) *
      [Order Date].Calendar.Month.MEMBERS ON ROWS
FROM   Sales
```

In this query, we do a cross join of the Product and Order Date dimensions to display the products and months on the row axis. The calculated measure Previous Month computes the sales amount of the previous month of the current category and month, while the calculated measure Sales Growth computes the difference of the sales amount of the current month and the one of the previous month.

		Sales Amount	Previous Month	Sales Growth
Alice Mutton	July 1996	$936.00		$936.00
Alice Mutton	August 1996	$819.00	$936.00	$-117.00
Alice Mutton	September 1996	$1,248.00	$819.00	$429.00
Alice Mutton	October 1996	$2,948.40	$1,248.00	$1,700.40
...	...	...	...	...

Query 6.5. Three best-selling employees.

```
SELECT Measures.[Sales Amount] ON COLUMNS,
      TOPCOUNT(Employee.[Full Name].CHILDREN, 3,
      Measures.[Sales Amount]) ON ROWS
FROM   Sales
```

Here, we use the TOPCOUNT function to find the three employees who have the highest value of the sales amount measure. We use the CHILDREN function instead of MEMBERS since otherwise the All member will appear in the first position, as it contains the total sales amount of all employees.

	Sales Amount
Margaret Peacock	$217,469.14
Janet Leverling	$176,515.01
Nancy Davolio	$175,837.26

Query 6.6. Best-selling employee per product and year.

```
WITH MEMBER Measures.[Top Sales] AS
        MAX([Order Date].Calendar.CURRENTMEMBER *
        Employee.[Full Name].CHILDREN, Measures.[Sales Amount])
MEMBER Measures.[Top Employee] AS
        TOPCOUNT([Order Date].Calendar.CURRENTMEMBER *
        Employee.[Full Name].CHILDREN, 1, Measures.[Sales Amount]).
        ITEM(0).ITEM(1).NAME
SELECT { Measures.[Top Sales], Measures.[Top Employee] } ON COLUMNS,
        ORDER(Product.Categories.Product.MEMBERS,
        Product.Categories.CURRENTMEMBER.NAME,BASC) *
        [Order Date].Calendar.Year.MEMBERS ON ROWS
FROM    Sales
```

The calculated measure **Top Sales** computes the maximum value of sales amount for the current year among all employees. The calculated measure **Top Employee** uses the function TOPCOUNT to obtain the tuple composed of the current year and the employee with highest sales amount. The ITEM function retrieves the first member of the specified tuple. Since such member is a combination of year and employee, ITEM is applied again to obtain the employee. Finally, the NAME function retrieves the name of the employee.

		Top Sales	Top Employee
Alice Mutton	1996	$3,010.80	Andrew Fuller
Alice Mutton	1997	$4,689.75	Steven Buchanan
Alice Mutton	1998	$2,702.70	Nancy Davolio
Aniseed Syrup	1996	$240.00	Robert King
Aniseed Syrup	1997	$800.00	Janet Leverling
Aniseed Syrup	1998	$740.00	Anne Dodsworth
...	...	...	...

Query 6.7. Countries that account for top 50% of the sales amount.

```
SELECT Measures.[Sales Amount] ON COLUMNS,
        { Customer.Geography.[All],
        TOPPERCENT([Customer].Geography.Country.MEMBERS, 50,
        Measures.[Sales Amount]) } ON ROWS
FROM    Sales
```

In this query, we use the **TOPPERCENT** function for selecting the countries whose cumulative total is equal to the specified percentage. We can see in the answer below that the sum of the values for the three listed countries slightly exceeds 50% of the sales amount.

	Sales Amount
All Customers	$1,145,155.86
United States	$238,490.40
Germany	$219,356.08
Austria	$115,328.31

Query 6.8. Total sales and average monthly sales by employee and year.

```
WITH MEMBER Measures.[Avg Monthly Sales] AS
        AVG(DESCENDANTS([Order Date].Calendar.CURRENTMEMBER,
        [Order Date].Calendar.Month),Measures.[Sales Amount]),
        FORMAT_STRING = '$###,##0.00'
SELECT { Measures.[Sales Amount], Measures.[Avg Monthly Sales] } ON COLUMNS,
        Employee.[Full Name].CHILDREN *
        [Order Date].Calendar.Year.MEMBERS ON ROWS
FROM    Sales
```

In this query, we cross join the **Employee** and **Order Date** dimensions to display the employee name and the year on the row axis. The calculated measure **Avg Monthly Sales** computes the average of sales amount of the current employee for all months of the current year.

		Sales Amount	Avg Monthly Sales
Andrew Fuller	1996	$20,773.06	$3,462.18
Andrew Fuller	1997	$62,848.74	$5,237.40
Andrew Fuller	1998	$60,591.94	$15,147.99
Anne Dodsworth	1996	$9,894.51	$3,298.17
Anne Dodsworth	1997	$18,099.29	$1,809.93
Anne Dodsworth	1998	$39,803.96	$9,950.99
...	...	...	...

Query 6.9. Total sales amount and total discount amount per product and month.

```
WITH MEMBER Measures.[TotalDisc] AS
        Measures.Discount * Measures.Quantity * Measures.[Unit Price],
        FORMAT_STRING = '$###,##0.00'
SELECT { Measures.[Sales Amount], [TotalDisc] } ON COLUMNS,
        NON EMPTY ORDER(Product.Categories.Product.MEMBERS,
        Product.Categories.CURRENTMEMBER.NAME, BASC) *
        [Order Date].Calendar.Month.MEMBERS ON ROWS
FROM    Sales
```

In this query, we cross join the **Product** and **Order Date** dimensions to display the product and the month on the row axis. The calculated measure **TotalDisc** multiplies the discount, quantity, and unit price measures to compute the total discount amount of the current product and month.

		Sales Amount	TotalDisc
Alice Mutton	July 1996	$936.00	$0.00
Alice Mutton	August 1996	$819.00	$117.00
Alice Mutton	September 1996	$1,248.00	$0.00
Alice Mutton	October 1996	$2,948.40	$50.96
...	...	...	...

Query 6.10. Monthly year-to-date sales for each product category.

```
WITH MEMBER Measures.YTDSales AS
        SUM(PERIODSTODATE([Order Date].Calendar.[Year],
        [Order Date].Calendar.CURRENTMEMBER),
        Measures.[Sales Amount]), FORMAT_STRING = '###,##0.00'
SELECT DESCENDANTS([Order Date].[1996], [Order Date].[Month])
        ON COLUMNS, Product.[Category].MEMBERS ON ROWS
FROM    Sales
WHERE (Measures.YTDSales)
```

Here, we use the **PERIODSTODATE** function in order to select all months of the current year up to the current month. Then, the **SUM** function is applied to obtain the year-to-date aggregate value of the measure **Sales Amount**.

	July 1996	August 1996	September 1996	October 1996	...
Beverages	$3,182.50	$6,577.38	$8,996.98	$15,700.82	...
Condiments	$1,753.40	$3,141.70	$4,003.30	$8,127.62	...
Confections	$5,775.15	$10,781.92	$16,527.92	$20,056.52	...
Dairy Products	$6,838.34	$11,600.04	$14,416.04	$21,353.59	...
Grains/Cereals	$1,158.86	$1,429.46	$2,159.06	$4,530.02	...
Meat/Poultry	$2,268.72	$5,764.38	$10,055.38	$13,706.68	...
Produce	$3,868.80	$4,673.12	$5,837.92	$6,700.92	...
Seafood	$2,400.33	$6,383.07	$8,936.87	$14,748.87	...

Query 6.11. Moving average over the last 3 months of the sales amount by product category.

```
WITH MEMBER Measures.MovAvg3Months AS
        AVG([Order Date].Calendar.CURRENTMEMBER.LAG(2):
        [Order Date].Calendar.CURRENTMEMBER,
        Measures.[Sales Amount]), FORMAT_STRING = '$###,##0.00'
SELECT [Order Date].Calendar.Month.MEMBERS ON COLUMNS,
        Product.[Category].MEMBERS ON ROWS
FROM    Sales
WHERE (Measures.MovAvg3Months)
```

Here, we use the LAG function and the range operator ':' to construct the set composed of the current month and its preceding 2 months. Then, we take the average of the measure Sales Amount over these 3 months.

	July 1996	August 1996	September 1996	October 1996	...
Beverages	$3,182.50	$3,288.69	$2,998.99	$4,172.77	...
Condiments	$1,753.40	$1,570.85	$1,334.43	$2,124.74	...
Confections	$5,775.15	$5,390.96	$5,509.31	$4,760.46	...
Dairy Products	$6,838.34	$5,800.02	$4,805.35	$4,838.42	...
Grains/Cereals	$1,158.86	$714.73	$719.69	$1,123.72	...
Meat/Poultry	$2,268.72	$2,882.19	$3,351.79	$3,812.65	...
Produce	$3,868.80	$2,336.56	$1,945.97	$944.04	...

Query 6.12. Personal sales amount made by an employee compared with the total sales amount made by herself and her subordinates during 1997.

```
WITH MEMBER Measures.[Personal Sales] AS
    (Employee.Supervision.DATAMEMBER, [Measures].[Sales Amount]),
    FORMAT_STRING = '$###,##0.00'
SELECT { Measures.[Personal Sales], Measures.[Sales Amount] } ON COLUMNS,
    ORDER(Employee.Supervision.MEMBERS - Employee.Supervision.[All],
    Employee.Supervision.CURRENTMEMBER.NAME, BASC) ON ROWS
FROM    Sales
WHERE [Order Date].Calendar.Year.[1997]
```

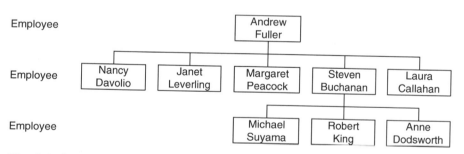

Fig. 6.2 Supervision hierarchy in the Employee dimension (repeated from Fig. 4.5)

In this query, we use the parent-child hierarchy Supervision of the Employee dimension, as depicted in Fig. 6.2. In such a hierarchy, each employee has personal sales amount values. As we have seen in Sect. 5.9.3, such value is kept in system-generated child members. This value can be accessed in MDX using the keyword DATAMEMBER as shown in the calculated measure Personal Sales of the above query. Furthermore, the value of the total sales amount for an employee at the lower level of the hierarchy (i.e., without subordinates, such as Robert King) is equal to its personal sales. For employees with subordinates, the value of the measure is the sum of her personal sales

and those of her subordinates, as is the case for Andrew Fuller and Steven
Buchanan. Notice that in this query we removed the member All from the
set of members of the Supervision hierarchy, using the set difference operator
denoted '-'. If in the query above we replace Employee.Supervision.MEMBERS
with Employee.Supervision.CHILDREN, we will obtain only the first line of
the answer corresponding to Andrew Fuller. As can be seen, parent-child
hierarchies behave to this respect differently from user-defined hierarchies.

	Personal Sales	Sales Amount
Andrew Fuller	$68,063.09	$596,630.80
Anne Dodsworth	$18,906.49	$18,906.49
Janet Leverling	$105,351.30	$105,351.30
Laura Callahan	$56,032.62	$56,032.62
Margaret Peacock	$128,809.79	$128,809.79
Michael Suyama	$38,213.37	$38,213.37
Nancy Davolio	$90,629.08	$90,629.08
Robert King	$59,908.60	$59,908.60
Steven Buchanan	$30,716.47	$147,744.92

It is worth remarking that the personal sales amount made by an employee
can also be obtained with the following query, which exploits the attribute
hierarchy [Full Name] instead of the parent-child hierarchy Supervision:

```
SELECT Measures.[Sales Amount] on COLUMNS,
       Employee.[Full Name].CHILDREN ON ROWS
FROM   Sales
WHERE  [Order Date].Calendar.Year.[1997]
```

Query 6.13. Total sales amount, number of products, and sum of the
quantities sold for each order.

```
WITH MEMBER Measures.[NbProducts] AS
     COUNT(NONEMPTY([Order].[Order No].CURRENTMEMBER *
     [Order].[Order Line].MEMBERS))
SELECT { Measures.[Sales Amount], NbProducts, Quantity } on COLUMNS,
       [Order].[Order No].CHILDREN ON ROWS
FROM   Sales
```

In this query, we use the fact (or degenerate) dimension Order, which is
defined from the fact table Sales in the data warehouse. The dimension has
two attributes, the order number and the order line, and the order number is
displayed on the rows axis. In the calculated measure NbProducts, a cross join
is used to obtain the order lines associated with the current order. By counting
the elements in this set, we can obtain the number of distinct products of
the order. Finally, the measures Sales Amount, NbProducts, and Quantity are
displayed on the column axis.

	Sales Amount	NbProducts	Quantity
10248	$342.00	2	17
10249	$1,863.40	2	49
10250	$1,552.60	3	60
10251	$654.06	3	41
...	...	...	...

Query 6.14. For each month, total number of orders, total sales amount, and average sales amount by order.

```
WITH MEMBER Measures.AvgSales AS
        Measures.[Sales Amount]/Measures.[Order No],
        FORMAT_STRING = '$###,##0.00'
SELECT { Measures.[Order No], [Sales Amount], AvgSales } ON COLUMNS,
        NON EMPTY [Order Date].Calendar.Month.MEMBERS ON ROWS
FROM    Sales
```

This query displays the months of the Order Date dimension on the row axis and the measures Order No, Sales Amount, and AvgSales on the column axis, the latter being a calculated measure. For Sales Amount, the roll-up operation computes the sum of the values in a month. For the Order No measure, since in the cube definition the aggregate function associated with the measure is DistinctCount, the roll-up operation computes the number of orders within a month. Notice that for computing the average in the calculated measure AvgSales, we divided the two measures Sales Amount and Order No. If we used instead AVG(Measures.[Sales Amount]), the result obtained will correspond to the Sales Amount. Indeed, the average will be applied to a set containing as only element the measure of the current month.

	Order No	Sales Amount	AvgSales
July 1996	21	$27,246.10	$1,297.43
August 1996	25	$23,104.98	$924.20
September 1996	21	$20,582.40	$980.11
October 1996	25	$33,991.56	$1,359.66
...	...	...	...

Query 6.15. For each employee, total sales amount, number of cities, and number of states to which she is assigned.

```
WITH MEMBER NoCities AS
        Measures.[Territories Count]
MEMBER NoStates AS
        DISTINCTCOUNT(Employee.[Full Name].CURRENTMEMBER *
        City.Geography.State.MEMBERS)
SELECT { Measures.[Sales Amount], Measures.NoCities, Measures.NoStates }
        ON COLUMNS, Employee.[Full Name].CHILDREN ON ROWS
FROM    Sales
```

Here, we exploit the many-to-many relationship between employees and cities through the bridge table Territories. We assume that we are using Analysis Services, and thus, we make use of the Territories Count measure that is automatically added to each measure when it is created, as explained in Sect. 5.9.5. We rename this measure as NoCities at the beginning of the query. Then, for the NoStates calculated measure, we perform a cross join that obtains the states to which the current employee is related and apply DISTINCTCOUNT to the result, in order to compute the number of states for such employee. Notice that a similar approach can be used for obtaining the number of cities if the measure Territories Count does not exist in the cube. Finally, the SELECT clause displays the measures.

FullName	Sales Amount	NoCities	NoStates
Andrew Fuller	$152,164.80	6	3
Anne Dodsworth	$69,046.17	7	5
Janet Leverling	$186,197.80	4	2
Laura Callahan	$122,528.86	4	3
Margaret Peacock	$224,397.30	3	2
Michael Suyama	$64,969.63	5	3
Nancy Davolio	$184,758.38	1	1
Robert King	$117,020.49	10	3
Steven Buchanan	$68,792.28	5	3

6.3   Querying the Northwind Data Warehouse in SQL

Given the schema of the Northwind data warehouse in Fig. 6.3, we revisit the queries of the previous section in SQL. This allows us to compare the expressiveness of both languages. This is of particular importance because some OLAP tools automatically translate MDX queries into SQL queries which are then sent to a relational server.

Query 6.1. Total sales amount per customer, year, and product category.

```
SELECT      C.CompanyName, T.Year, A.CategoryName,
            FORMAT(SUM(SalesAmount),'$###,##0.00') AS SalesAmount
FROM        Sales S, Customer C, Time T, Product P, Category A
WHERE       S.CustomerKey = C.CustomerKey AND
            S.OrderDateKey = T.TimeKey AND
            S.ProductKey = P.ProductKey AND P.CategoryKey = A.CategoryKey
GROUP BY    C.CompanyName, T.Year, A.CategoryName
```

Here, we join the fact tables with the involved dimension tables and aggregate the results by company, year, and category. The FORMAT function is used to format the aggregated measure.

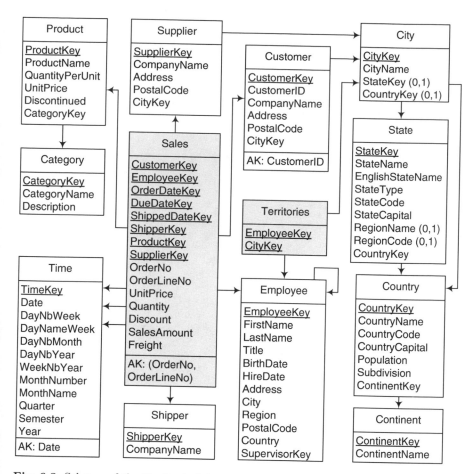

Fig. 6.3 Schema of the Northwind data warehouse (repeated from Fig. 5.4)

Query 6.2. Yearly sales amount for each pair of customer country and supplier countries.

```
SELECT    CO.CountryName AS CustomerCountry,
          SO.CountryName AS SupplierCountry, T.Year,
          FORMAT(SUM(SalesAmount),'$###,##0.00') AS SalesAmount
FROM      Sales F, Customer C, City CC, State CS, Country CO,
          Supplier S, City SC, State SS, Country SO, Time T
WHERE     F.CustomerKey = C.CustomerKey AND C.CityKey = CC.CityKey AND
          CC.StateKey = CS.StateKey AND
          CS.CountryKey = CO.CountryKey AND
          F.SupplierKey = S.SupplierKey AND S.CityKey = SC.CityKey AND
          SC.StateKey = SS.StateKey AND
          SS.CountryKey = SO.CountryKey AND F.OrderDateKey = T.TimeKey
GROUP BY  CO.CountryName, SO.CountryName, T.Year
ORDER BY  CO.CountryName, SO.CountryName, T.Year
```

Here, the tables of the geography dimension are joined twice with the fact table for obtaining the countries of the customer and the supplier.

Query 6.3. Monthly sales by customer state compared to those of the previous year.

```
CREATE FUNCTION MonthYear (@Month INT, @Year INT)
            RETURNS CHAR(14) AS
BEGIN
            DECLARE @Date CHAR(10);
            SET @Date = CAST(@Year AS CHAR(4)) + '-' +
            CAST(@Month AS CHAR(2)) + '-' + '01';
            RETURN(Datename(month,@Date) + ' ' +
            CAST(@Year AS CHAR(4)));
END
WITH MonthlySalesState AS (
            SELECT      S.StateName, T.MonthNumber, T.Year,
                        SUM(SalesAmount) AS SalesAmount
            FROM        Sales F, Customer C, City Y, State S, Time T
            WHERE       F.CustomerKey = C.CustomerKey AND
                        C.CityKey = Y.CityKey AND
                        Y.StateKey = S.StateKey AND
                        F.OrderDateKey = T.TimeKey
            GROUP BY S.StateName, T.Year, T.MonthNumber )
SELECT      M1.StateName,
            dbo.MonthYear(M1.MonthNumber,M1.Year) AS Month,
            FORMAT(M1.SalesAmount,'$###,##0.00'),
            FORMAT(M2.SalesAmount,'$###,##0.00') AS PreviousYear
FROM        MonthlySalesState M1 LEFT OUTER JOIN
            MonthlySalesState M2 ON M1.StateName = M2.StateName
            AND M1.MonthNumber = M2.MonthNumber AND
            M1.Year-1 = M2.Year
ORDER BY M1.StateName, Month
```

In this query, we define a MonthYear function that concatenates a month and a year for a more user-friendly display. In the WITH clause, we define a common table expression (see Chap. 2) which computes the monthly sales by state. In the query, the temporary table is joined twice to obtain the sales of a month and the previous month. A left outer join is used for displaying a null value in case there are no sales for the previous month.

Query 6.4. Monthly sales growth per product, that is, total sales per product compared to those of the previous month.

```
WITH MonthlySalesProd AS (
            SELECT P.ProductName, T.MonthNumber AS Month, T.Year,
                   SUM(SalesAmount) AS SalesAmount
            FROM   Sales S, Product P, Time T
            WHERE  S.ProductKey = P.ProductKey AND
                   S.OrderDateKey = T.TimeKey
            GROUP BY P.ProductName, T.Year, T.MonthNumber ),
      MonthlySalesProdComp AS (
            SELECT M1.ProductName,
```

```
             dbo.MonthYear(M1.Month,M1.Year) AS Month,
             M1.SalesAmount, M2.SalesAmount AS PreviousMonth
     FROM    MonthlySalesProd M1 LEFT OUTER JOIN
             MonthlySalesProd M2 ON
             M1.ProductName = M2.ProductName AND
             M1.Month-1 = M2.Month AND M1.Year = M2.Year
     WHERE M1.Month > 1
     UNION
     SELECT M1.ProductName,
             dbo.MonthYear(M1.Month,M1.Year) AS Month,
             M1.SalesAmount, M2.SalesAmount AS PreviousMonth
     FROM    MonthlySalesProd M1 LEFT OUTER JOIN
             MonthlySalesProd M2 ON
             M1.ProductName = M2.ProductName AND
             M1.Month+11 = M2.Month AND M1.Year-1 = M2.Year
     WHERE M1.Month=1 )
SELECT   ProductName, Month,
         FORMAT(SalesAmount,'$###,##0.00') AS SalesAmount,
         FORMAT(PreviousMonth,'$###,##0.00') AS PreviousMonth,
         FORMAT(SalesAmount - PreviousMonth,
         '$###,##0.00; $-###,##0.00') AS SalesGrowth
FROM     MonthlySalesProdComp
ORDER BY ProductName, Month
```

Here, we first define a temporary table MonthlySalesProd that computes the monthly sales by product. In the second temporary table MonthlySalesProd-Comp, the previous temporary table is used twice for obtaining through a left outer join the sales of a month and the previous month. Notice that two cases must be accounted for. In the first case, the previous month belongs to the same year, while in the second case, the previous month for January is December of the previous year. Finally, the main query is used for ordering the tuples of the second temporary table and to define their display format.

Note that the above query cannot be written with window functions, since it would combine the sales of a month with the sales of the previous *existing* month. For example, if there are no sales for February, the tuple for March will compare the sales of March and those of January.

Query 6.5. Three best-selling employees.

```
SELECT   TOP(3) E.FirstName + ' ' + E.LastName AS EmployeeName,
         FORMAT(SUM(F.SalesAmount), '$###,##0.00') AS SalesAmount
FROM     Sales F, Employee E
WHERE    F.EmployeeKey = E.EmployeeKey
GROUP BY E.FirstName, E.LastName
ORDER BY SUM(F.SalesAmount) DESC
```

In the above query, we group the sales by employee and apply the SUM aggregation to each group. The result is then sorted in descending order of the aggregated sales, and the TOP function is used to obtain the first three tuples.

Query 6.6. Best-selling employee per product and year.

```
WITH SalesProdYearEmp AS (
          SELECT    P.ProductName, T.Year,
                    SUM(S.SalesAmount) AS SalesAmount,
                    E.FirstName + ' ' + E.LastName AS EmployeeName
          FROM      Sales S, Employee E, Time T, Product P
          WHERE     S.EmployeeKey = E.EmployeeKey AND
                    S.OrderDateKey = T.TimeKey AND
                    S.ProductKey = P.ProductKey
          GROUP BY P.ProductName, T.Year, E.FirstName, E.LastName )
SELECT    ProductName, Year,
          FORMAT(SalesAmount,'$###,##0.00') AS TopSales,
          EmployeeName AS TopEmployee
FROM      SalesProdYearEmp S1
WHERE     S1.SalesAmount = (
          SELECT    MAX(SalesAmount)
          FROM      SalesProdYearEmp S2
          WHERE     S1.ProductName = S2.ProductName AND
                    S1.Year = S2.Year )
```

The WITH clause computes the total sales by product, year, and employee.
In the query, we select the tuples of this table such that the total sales equals
the maximum total sales for the product and the year.

Query 6.7. Countries that account for top 50% of the sales amount.

```
WITH SalesCountry AS (
          SELECT    CountryName, SUM(SalesAmount) AS SalesAmount
          FROM      Sales S, Customer C, City Y, State T, Country O
          WHERE     S.CustomerKey = C.CustomerKey AND
                    C.CityKey = Y.CityKey AND Y.StateKey = T.StateKey AND
                    T.CountryKey = O.CountryKey
          GROUP BY CountryName ),
     CumSalesCountry AS (
          SELECT    S.*, SUM(SalesAmount) OVER (ORDER BY
                    SalesAmount DESC ROWS UNBOUNDED PRECEDING)
                    AS CumSalesAmount
          FROM      SalesCountry S )
SELECT 'All Customers' AS CountryName,
          FORMAT(SUM(SalesAmount), '$###,##0.00') AS SalesAmount
FROM      SalesCountry
UNION
SELECT CountryName,
          FORMAT(SalesAmount, '$###,##0.00') AS SalesAmount
FROM      CumSalesCountry
WHERE CumSalesAmount <=
          (SELECT MIN(CumSalesAmount) FROM CumSalesCountry
          WHERE CumSalesAmount >=
          (SELECT 0.5 * SUM(SalesAmount) FROM SalesCountry) ) )
```

We start by defining the temporary table SalesCountry, which aggregates the
sales amount by country. In the temporary table CumSalesCountry, for each
row in SalesCountry, we define a window containing all the rows sorted in
decreasing value of sales amount and compute the sum of the current row

and all the preceding rows in the window. Finally, in the main query, we have to select the countries in CumSalesCountry whose cumulative sales amount is less or equal than the minimum value that is higher or equal to the 50% of the total sales amount.

Query 6.8. Total sales and average monthly sales by employee and year.

```
WITH MonthlySalesEmp AS (
    SELECT    E.FirstName + ' ' + E.LastName AS EmployeeName,
              T.Year, T.MonthNumber,
              SUM(SalesAmount) AS SalesAmount
    FROM      Sales S, Employee E, Time T
    WHERE     S.EmployeeKey = E.EmployeeKey AND
              S.OrderDateKey = T.TimeKey
    GROUP BY  E.FirstName, E.LastName, T.Year, T.MonthNumber )
SELECT    EmployeeName, Year,
          FORMAT(SUM(SalesAmount),'$###,##0.00') AS SalesAmount,
          FORMAT(AVG(SalesAmount),'$###,##0.00') AS AvgMonthlySales
FROM      MonthlySalesEmp
GROUP BY  EmployeeName, Year
ORDER BY  EmployeeName, Year
```

The table defined in the WITH clause computes the monthly sales by employee. In the query, we group the tuples of this table by employee and year, and the SUM and AVG functions are applied to obtain, respectively, the total yearly sales and the average monthly sales.

Query 6.9. Total sales amount and total discount amount per product and month.

```
SELECT    P.ProductName, dbo.MonthYear(T.MonthNumber,T.Year) AS Month,
          FORMAT(SUM(F.SalesAmount),'$###,##0.00') AS SalesAmount,
          FORMAT(SUM(F.UnitPrice * F.Quantity * F.Discount),
          '$###,##0.00') AS TotalDisc
FROM      Sales F, Time T, Product P
WHERE     F.OrderDateKey = T.TimeKey AND F.ProductKey = P.ProductKey
GROUP BY  P.ProductName, T.Year, T.MonthNumber
ORDER BY  P.ProductName, T.Year, T.MonthNumber
```

Here, we group the sales by product and month. Then, the SUM aggregation function is used for obtaining the total sales and the total discount amount.

Query 6.10. Monthly year-to-date sales for each product category.

```
WITH SalesByCategoryMonth AS (
    SELECT    CategoryName, Year, MonthNumber, MonthName,
              SUM(SalesAmount) AS SalesAmount
    FROM      Sales S, Product P, Category C, Time T
    WHERE     S.OrderDateKey = T.TimeKey AND
              S.ProductKey = P.ProductKey AND
              P.CategoryKey = C.CategoryKey
    GROUP BY  CategoryName, Year, MonthNumber, MonthName )
SELECT    CategoryName,
          MonthName + ' ' + CAST(Year AS CHAR(4)) AS Month,
          FORMAT(SUM(SalesAmount) OVER (PARTITION BY
```

```
           CategoryName, Year ORDER BY MonthNumber
           ROWS UNBOUNDED PRECEDING), '$###,##0.00')
           AS YTDSalesAmount
FROM       SalesByCategoryMonth
ORDER BY CategoryName, Year, MonthNumber
```

In the temporary table, we aggregate the sales amount by category and
month. In the main query, for each row in the temporary table, we define
a window containing all the rows with the same category and year, order the
rows in the window by month, and compute the sum of the current row and
all the preceding rows in the window.

Query 6.11. Moving average over the last 3 months of the sales amount by
product category.

```
WITH SalesByCategoryMonth AS (
         SELECT      CategoryName, Year, MonthNumber, MonthName,
                     SUM(SalesAmount) AS SalesAmount
         FROM        Sales S, Product P, Category C, Time T
         WHERE       S.OrderDateKey = T.TimeKey AND
                     S.ProductKey = P.ProductKey AND
                     P.CategoryKey = C.CategoryKey
         GROUP BY CategoryName, Year, MonthNumber, MonthName )
SELECT     CategoryName,
           MonthName + ' ' + CAST(Year AS CHAR(4)) AS Month,
           FORMAT(SalesAmount, '$###,##0.00') AS SalesAmount,
           FORMAT(AVG(SalesAmount) OVER (PARTITION BY
           CategoryName ORDER BY Year, MonthNumber
           ROWS 2 PRECEDING), '$###,##0.00') AS MovAvg3Months
FROM       SalesByCategoryMonth
ORDER BY CategoryName, Year, MonthNumber
```

In the temporary table, we aggregate the sales amount by category and
month. In the query, we define, for each row of the temporary table, a window
containing all the tuples with the same category, order the tuples in the
window by year and month, and compute the average of the current row and
the two preceding ones.

Query 6.12. Personal sales amount made by an employee compared with
the total sales amount made by herself and her subordinates during 1997.

```
WITH SalesByEmp1997 AS (
         SELECT      E.EmployeeKey,
                     FirstName + ' ' + LastName AS EmployeeName,
                     SUM(S.SalesAmount) AS SalesAmount
         FROM        Sales S, Employee E, Time T
         WHERE       S.EmployeeKey = E.EmployeeKey AND
                     S.OrderDateKey = T.TimeKey AND T.Year = 1997
         GROUP BY E.EmployeeKey, FirstName, LastName ),
     Supervision(SupervisorKey, SubordinateKey) AS (
         SELECT      SupervisorKey, EmployeeKey
         FROM        Employee
         WHERE       SupervisorKey IS NOT NULL
```

```
              UNION ALL
              SELECT     S.SupervisorKey, E.EmployeeKey
              FROM       Supervision S, Employee E
              WHERE      S.SubordinateKey = E.SupervisorKey )
SELECT        T2.EmployeeName,
              FORMAT(T2.SalesAmount, '$###,##0.00') AS PersonalSales,
              FORMAT(T1.TotalSubSales + T2.SalesAmount, '$###,##0.00')
              AS SalesAmount
FROM          ( SELECT    SupervisorKey, SUM(S.SalesAmount) AS TotalSubSales
              FROM       Supervision U, SalesByEmp1997 S
              WHERE      S.EmployeeKey = U.SubordinateKey
              GROUP BY SupervisorKey
              ) T1 JOIN SalesByEmp1997 T2 ON
              T1.SupervisorKey = T2.EmployeeKey
UNION
SELECT        EmployeeName,
              FORMAT(SalesAmount,'$###,##0.00') AS PersonalSales,
              FORMAT(SalesAmount,'$###,##0.00') AS SalesAmount
FROM          SalesByEmp1997 S
WHERE         NOT EXISTS (
              SELECT     *
              FROM       Supervision U
              WHERE      S.EmployeeKey = U.SupervisorKey )
```

The first temporary table SalesByEmp1997 defined in the WITH clause computes the total sales by employee. The temporary table Supervision computes with a recursive query the transitive closure of the supervision relationship. The main query is composed of the union of two queries. The first one computes the personal sales and the total sales amount for supervisors. For this, the inner query in the FROM clause computes the total amount made by the subordinates of an employee, and the additional join with the view SalesByEmp1997 is used to obtain the total sales of a supervisor in order to add the two amounts. Finally, the second query in the union takes from the SalesByEmp1997 the data from employees who are not supervisors.

Query 6.13. Total sales amount, number of products, and sum of the quantities sold for each order.

```
SELECT    OrderNo,
          FORMAT(SUM(SalesAmount),'$###,##0.00') AS SalesAmount,
          MAX(OrderLineNo) AS NbProducts, SUM(Quantity) AS Quantity
FROM      Sales
GROUP BY OrderNo
ORDER BY OrderNo
```

Recall that the sales fact table contains both the order number and the order line number, which constitute a fact dimension. In the query, we group the sales by order number, and then we apply the SUM and MAX aggregation functions for obtaining the requested values.

Query 6.14. For each month, total number of orders, total sales amount, and average sales amount by order.

```
WITH OrderAgg AS (
        SELECT      OrderNo, OrderDateKey,
                    SUM(SalesAmount) AS SalesAmount
        FROM        Sales
        GROUP BY OrderNo, OrderDateKey )
SELECT      dbo.MonthYear(MonthNumber,Year) AS Month,
            COUNT(OrderNo) AS NoOrders,
            FORMAT(SUM(SalesAmount), '$###,##0.00') AS SalesAmount,
            FORMAT(AVG(SalesAmount), '$###,##0.00') AS AvgAmount
FROM        OrderAgg O, Time T
WHERE       O.OrderDateKey = T.TimeKey
GROUP BY Year, MonthNumber
ORDER BY Year, MonthNumber
```

In the temporary table, we compute the total sales amount of each order. Notice that we also need to keep the key of the time dimension, which will be used in the main query for joining the fact table and the time dimension table. Then, by grouping the tuples by year and month, we can compute the aggregated values requested.

Query 6.15. For each employee, total sales amount, number of cities, and number of states to which she is assigned.

```
SELECT FirstName + ' ' + LastName AS FullName,
        FORMAT(SUM(SalesAmount) / COUNT(DISTINCT CityName),
        '$###,##0.00') AS TotalSales,
        COUNT(DISTINCT CityName) AS NoCities,
        COUNT(DISTINCT StateName) AS NoStates
FROM    Sales F, Employee E, Territories T, City C, State S
WHERE   F.EmployeeKey = E.EmployeeKey AND
        E.EmployeeKey = T.EmployeeKey AND
        T.CityKey = C.CityKey AND C.StateKey = S.StateKey
GROUP BY FirstName + ' ' + LastName
ORDER BY FirstName + ' ' + LastName
```

Recall that the Territories table captures the many-to-many relationship between employees and cities. Thus, the above query makes the join of the five tables and then groups the result by employee. Then, in the SELECT clause we sum the SalesAmount measure and divide it by the number of distinct CityName assigned to an employee in the Territories table. This solves the double-counting problem to which we referred in Sect. 4.2.6.

Suppose now that the Territories table have an additional attribute Percentage stating the percentage of time an employee is assigned to each city. In this case, the query above would be as follows:

```
SELECT FirstName + ' ' + LastName AS FullName,
        FORMAT(SUM(SalesAmount) * T.Percentage,
        '$###,##0.00') AS TotalSales,
        COUNT(DISTINCT CityName) AS NoCities,
        COUNT(DISTINCT StateName) AS NoStates
FROM    Sales F, Employee E, Territories T, City C, State S
WHERE   ...
```

As can be seen, the sum of the SalesAmount measure is multiplied by the percentage to account for the double-counting problem.

6.4 Comparison of MDX and SQL

In the two preceding sections, we used MDX and SQL for querying the Northwind cube. In this section, we compare the two languages.

At a first glance, the syntax of both languages seems similar. As we have shown, the functionality of both languages is also similar. Indeed, we expressed the same set of queries in both languages. However, there are some fundamental differences between SQL and MDX that we discuss next.

The main difference between SQL and MDX is the ability of MDX to reference multiple dimensions. Although it is possible to use SQL exclusively to query cubes, MDX provides commands that are designed specifically to retrieve multidimensional data with almost any number of dimensions. On the other hand, SQL refers to only two dimensions, columns and rows. Nevertheless, this fundamental difference between the two languages somehow disappears since most OLAP tools are incapable of displaying a result set with more than two dimensions. In our example queries, we used the cross join operator to combine several dimensions in one axis when we needed to analyze measures across more than two dimensions.

In SQL, the SELECT clause is used to define the column layout for a query. However, in MDX the SELECT clause is used to define several axis dimensions.

In SQL, the WHERE clause is used to *filter* the data returned by a query, whereas in MDX, the WHERE clause is used to provide a *slice* of the data returned by a query. While the two concepts are similar, they are not equivalent. In an SQL query, the WHERE clause contains an arbitrary list of items, which may or may not be returned in the result set, in order to narrow down the scope of the data that are retrieved. In MDX, however, the concept of a slice implies a reduction in the number of dimensions, and thus, each member in the WHERE clause must identify a distinct portion of data from a different dimension. Furthermore, unlike in SQL, the WHERE clause in MDX cannot filter what is returned on an axis of a query. To filter what appears on an axis of a query, we can use functions such as FILTER, NONEMPTY, and TOPCOUNT.

Let us compare the queries in MDX of Sect. 6.2 with those in SQL of Sect. 6.3.

Consider Query 6.1. A first observation is that, in SQL, the joins between tables must be explicitly indicated in the query, whereas they are implicit in MDX. Also, in SQL, an inner join will remove empty combinations, whereas in MDX, NON EMPTY must be specified to achieve this. On the other hand, outer joins are needed in SQL if we want to show empty combinations.

Furthermore, in SQL the aggregations needed for the roll-up operations must be explicitly stated through the GROUP BY and the aggregation functions in the SELECT clause, while in MDX the aggregation functions are stated in the cube definition and they are automatically performed upon roll-up operations. Finally, in SQL the display format must be stated in the query, while in MDX this is stated in the cube definition.

Consider now the comparison of measures of the current period with respect to those of a previous period, such as the previous month or the same month in the previous year. An example is given in Query 6.3. In MDX, this can be achieved with calculated members using the WITH MEMBER clause. On the other hand, in SQL this can be achieved by defining a temporary table in the WITH clause in which the aggregations needed for the roll-up operation are performed for each period, and an outer join is needed in the main query for obtaining the measure of the current period together with that of a previous period. Nevertheless, as shown in Query 6.4, obtaining the previous month in SQL is somehow complex since we must account for two cases depending on whether the previous month is in the same year or in the previous year.

Consider now top and bottom performance analysis, an example of which is given in Query 6.5. In MDX this can be obtained with functions such as TOPCOUNT, whereas in SQL, this can be achieved with the TOP function. Nevertheless, there is a fundamental difference between the two approaches. For example, in MDX, the function TOPPERCENT sorts a set in descending order, and returns a set of tuples with the highest values whose cumulative total is equal to or greater than a specified percentage. On the other hand, in SQL, stating TOP(n) PERCENT will return the percentage of the total number of tuples in the answer. We have seen in Query 6.7 how to achieve cumulative top percentages in SQL.

Query 6.8 is an example of manipulating aggregates at several granularities. In MDX this is achieved by starting at the coarser granularity and obtained the finer granularity through the DESCENDANTS function. In SQL, we computed the finer granularity in a temporary table and obtained the coarser granularity by aggregating the temporary table in the main query.

Let us consider period-to-date calculations and moving averages, as exemplified in Queries 6.10 and 6.11. In MDX, the function PERIODSTODATE is used for the former, and hierarchical navigation is used for the latter. On the other hand, in SQL these are obtained by using the window functions.

Query 6.12 is an example of aggregation in parent-child hierarchies. As can be seen, this is easily expressed in MDX, while a complex recursive query is needed to obtain similar functionality in SQL.

Queries 6.13 and 6.14 show examples of manipulating fact dimensions. Although this can be expressed quite succinctly in MDX, it is not immediate to understand how to achieve such a result. The corresponding queries in SQL are easier to write.

Finally, Query 6.15 is an example of manipulating many-to-many dimensions. As can be seen, the SQL version needs to deal with the double-counting problem while aggregating the measure.

To conclude, Table 6.1 summarizes some of the advantages and disadvantages of both languages.

Table 6.1 Comparison of MDX and SQL

MDX	SQL
Advantages	**Advantages**
• Data modeling: definition of dimensions, hierarchies, measure groups, from various data sources • Simple navigation within time dimension and hierarchies • Relatively simple expressions for often used business requests • Fast, due to the existence of aggregations	• Large user base • Easy-to-understand semantics of queries • Results are easy to visualize: scalars or 2D tables • Various ways of relating tables: joins, derived tables, correlated queries, common table expressions, etc.
Disadvantages	**Disadvantages**
• Extra effort for designing a cube and setting up aggregations • Steep learning curve: manipulating an n-dimensional space • Hard-to-grasp concepts: current context, execution phases, etc. • Some operations are difficult to express, such as ordering on multiple criteria	• Tables must be joined explicitly inside a query • Sometimes not intuitive and complex syntax for expressing analytical queries • No concept of row ordering and hierarchies: navigation dimensions may be complex • Not so performant for the types of queries used in data analysis

6.5 Summary

In this chapter, we presented the MDX language, which is used for designing and querying multidimensional databases. MDX can be used both as an expression language for defining cubes and as a query language for extracting data from cubes. We covered MDX as a query language and introduced its main functionalities through examples. After this introduction, we addressed a series of MDX queries to the Northwind cube. Then, we addressed the same queries to the Northwind data warehouse using SQL. We concluded the chapter comparing the expressiveness of MDX and SQL using both sets of queries, highlighting advantages and disadvantages.

6.6   Bibliographic Notes

MDX was first introduced in 1997 by Microsoft as part of the OLE DB for OLAP specification. After the commercial release of Microsoft OLAP Services in 1998 and Microsoft Analysis Services in 2005, MDX was adopted by the wide range of OLAP vendors, both at the server and the client side. The latest version of the OLE DB for OLAP specification was issued by Microsoft in 1999. In Analysis Services 2005, Microsoft added some MDX extensions like subqueries. This newer variant of MDX is sometimes referred to as MDX 2005. There are many books about MDX. A popular introductory one is [227], although it is somehow outdated, and more advanced books on MDX are, for example, [163, 189, 197]. MDX is also covered, although succinctly, in general books covering OLAP tools, such as [71, 79, 182].

XML for Analysis (abbreviated as XMLA) is an industry standard for communicating among analytical systems. XMLA is an application programming interface (API) based on SOAP (Simple Object Access Protocol) designed for OLAP and data mining. XMLA is maintained by XMLA Council, which is composed of many companies, with Microsoft, Hyperion, and SAS being the official XMLA Council founder members. In this chapter, we did not cover XMLA due to the fact that XMLA requests are typically generated by client tools and OLAP servers to communicate between them. XMLA is covered, for example, in the books about OLAP tools mentioned above.

Data Mining Extensions (DMX) is a query language for data mining models supported by Analysis Services. Like SQL, it supports a data definition language (DDL), a data manipulation language (DML), and a data query language. Whereas SQL statements operate on relational tables and MDX on data cubes, DMX statements operate on data mining models. DMX is used to create and train data mining models and to browse, manage, and predict against them. We will study DMX together with a data mining overview in Chap. 9. This is why we did not cover DMX in this chapter.

Self-service business intelligence is an approach to data analytics that enables business users to access and work with corporate information in order to create personalized reports and analytical queries on their own, without the involvement of IT specialists. In order to realize this vision, Microsoft introduced the Business Intelligence Semantic Model (BISM), which we introduced in Chap. 3. The BISM supports two models, the traditional multidimensional model and a new tabular model. The tabular model was designed to be simpler and easier to understand by users familiar with Excel and the relational data model. In addition, Microsoft has created a new query language to query the BISM tabular model. This language, called DAX (Data Analysis Expressions), is not a subset of MDX, but rather a new formula language that is an extension of the formula language in Excel. The DAX statements operate against an in-memory relational data store and are used to create custom measures and calculated columns. In this chapter, we did not

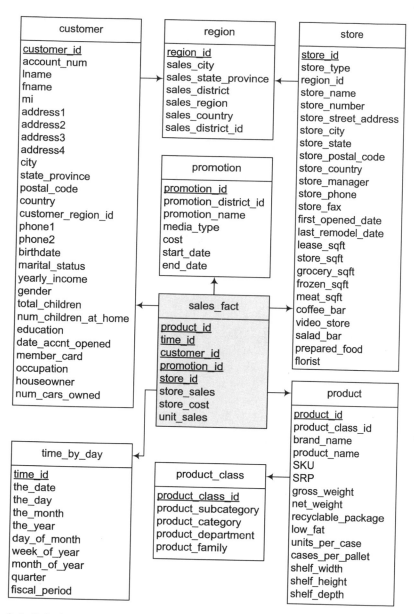

Fig. 6.4 Relational schema of the Foodmart data warehouse

cover DAX, in particular since, at the time of writing, it is mostly supported by Microsoft tools. A book entirely devoted to the BISM tabular model and DAX is [183], although these topics are also covered in the book [79] already cited above.

6.7   Review Questions

6.1 Describe what is MDX and what it is used for. Describe the two modes supported by MDX.

6.2 Define what are tuples and sets and MDX.

6.3 Describe the basic syntax of MDX queries and describe the several clauses that compose an MDX query. Which clauses are required and which are optional?

6.4 Describe conceptually how an MDX query is executed by specifying the conceptual order of executing the different clauses composing the query.

6.5 Define the slicing operation in MDX. How does this operation differ from the filtering operation specified in SQL in the WHERE clause?

6.6 Why is navigation essential for querying multidimensional databases? Give examples of navigation functions in MDX and exemplify their use in common queries.

6.7 What is a cross join in MDX? For which purpose is a cross join needed? Establish similarities and differences between the cross join in MDX and the various types of join in SQL.

6.8 What is subcubing in MDX? Does subcubing provide additional expressive power to the language?

6.9 Define calculated members and named sets. Why are they needed? State the syntax for defining them in an MDX query.

6.10 Why time series analysis is important in many business scenarios? Give examples of functionality that is provided by MDX for time series analysis.

6.11 What is filtering and how does this differ from slicing?

6.12 How you do sorting in MDX? What are the limitations of MDX in this respect?

6.13 Give examples of MDX functions that are used for top and bottom analysis. How do they differ from similar functions provided by SQL?

6.14 Describe the main differences between MDX and SQL.

6.8   Exercises

6.1 Write in MDX the queries over the Foodmart cube given in Ex. 4.9.

6.2 Consider the relational schema of the Foodmart data warehouse given in Fig. 6.4. Write in SQL the queries given in the previous exercise.

Part II
Implementation and Deployment

Chapter 7
Physical Data Warehouse Design

The physical design of data warehouses is crucial to ensure adequate query response time. There are typically three common techniques for improving performance in data warehouse systems: materialized views, indexing, and partitioning. A materialized view is a view that is physically stored in a database, which enhances query performance by precalculating costly operations such as joins and aggregations. With respect to indexing, traditional techniques used in OLTP systems are not appropriate for multidimensional data. Thus, alternative indexing mechanisms are used in data warehouses, typically bitmap and join indexes. Finally, partitioning or fragmentation divides the contents of a relation into several files, typically based on a range of values of an attribute.

In this chapter, we focus on a relational implementation of the data warehouse and the associated data cubes. We first give in Sect. 7.1 an introduction to the problems stated above. Then, in Sect. 7.2, we study the problem of computing and maintaining materialized views. In Sect. 7.3, we study the data cube maintenance problem and discuss in detail the classic algorithms in the field. Section 7.4 studies efficient ways of computing the whole data cube, while Sect. 7.4.3 studies classic algorithms aimed at materializing only a portion of the data cube. Section 7.5 studies data warehouse indexing techniques in detail, while Sect. 7.6 discusses how indexes arc used to evaluate typical data warehouse queries. Section 7.7 overviews data warehouse partitioning issues. Section 7.8 studies physical design support in SQL Server and in Analysis Services, while Sect. 7.9 briefly discusses query optimization in Analysis Services. Finally, Sect. 7.10 discusses query optimization in Mondrian.

A. Vaisman and E. Zimányi, *Data Warehouse Systems*, Data-Centric
Systems and Applications, DOI 10.1007/978-3-642-54655-6_7,
© Springer-Verlag Berlin Heidelberg 2014

7.1   Physical Modeling of Data Warehouses

In this section, we give an overview of the three classic techniques for improving data warehouse performance: materialized views, indexing, and partitioning. Later in the chapter we study these techniques in detail.

As we studied in Chap. 2, a **view** in the relational model is just a query that is stored in the database with an associated name and which can then be used like a normal table. This query can involve base tables (i.e., tables physically stored in the database) and/or other views. A **materialized view** is a view that is physically stored in a database. Materialized views enhance query performance by precalculating costly operations such as joins and aggregations and storing the results in the database. In this way, queries that only need to access materialized views will be executed faster. Obviously, the increased query performance is achieved at the expense of storage space.

A typical problem of materialized views is **updating** since all modifications to the underlying base tables must be propagated into the view. Whenever possible, updates to materialized views are performed in an incremental way, avoiding to recalculate the whole view from scratch. This implies capturing the modifications to the base tables and determining how they influence the content of the view. Much research work has been done in the area of view maintenance. We study the most classic ones in this chapter.

In a data warehouse, given that the number of aggregates grows exponentially with the number of dimensions and hierarchies, normally not all possible aggregations can be precalculated and materialized. Thus, an important problem in designing a data warehouse is the **selection of materialized views**. The goal is to select an appropriate set of views that minimizes the total query response time and the cost of maintaining the selected views, given a limited amount of resources such as storage space or materialization time. Many algorithms have been designed for selection of materialized views, and currently some commercial DBMSs provide tools that tune the selection of materialized views on the basis of previous queries to the data warehouse.

Once the views to be materialized have been defined, the queries addressed to a data warehouse must be rewritten in order to best exploit such views to improve query response time. This process, known as **query rewriting**, tries to use the materialized views as much as possible, even if they only partially fulfill the query conditions. Selecting the best rewriting for a query is a complex process, in particular for queries involving aggregations. Many algorithms have been proposed for query rewriting in the presence of materialized views. These algorithms impose various restrictions on the given query and the potential materialized views so that the rewriting can be done.

A drawback of the materialized view approach is that it requires one to anticipate the queries to be materialized. However, data warehouse queries are often ad hoc and cannot always be anticipated. As queries which are not precalculated must be computed at run time, indexing methods are required to ensure effective query processing. Traditional indexing techniques for OLTP systems are not appropriate for multidimensional data. Indeed, most OLTP transactions access only a small number of tuples, and the indexing techniques used are designed for this situation. Since data warehouse queries typically access a large number of tuples, alternative indexing mechanisms are needed.

Two common types of indexes for data warehouses are bitmap indexes and join indexes. **Bitmap indexes** are a special kind of index, particularly useful for columns with a low number of distinct values (i.e., low cardinality attributes), although several compression techniques eliminate this limitation. On the other hand, **join indexes** materialize a relational join between two tables by keeping pairs of row identifiers that participate in the join. In data warehouses, join indexes relate the values of dimensions to rows in the fact table. For example, given a fact table Sales and a dimension Client, a join index maintains for each client a list of row identifiers of the tuples recording the sales to this client. Join indexes can be combined with bitmap indexes, as we will see in this chapter.

Partitioning or **fragmentation** is a mechanism frequently used in relational databases to reduce the execution time of queries. It consists in dividing the contents of a relation into several files that can be more efficiently processed in this way. There are two ways of partitioning a relation: vertically and horizontally. **Vertical partitioning** splits the attributes of a table into groups that can be independently stored. For example, a table can be partitioned such that the most often used attributes are stored in one partition, while other less often used attributes are kept in another partition. Also, column-store database systems (that will be studied in Chap. 13) make use of this technique. **Horizontal partitioning** divides the records of a table into groups according to a particular criterion. A common horizontal partitioning scheme in data warehouses is based on time, where each partition contains data about a particular time period, for instance, a year or a range of months.

In the following sections, we study these techniques in detail.

7.2 Materialized Views

We know that a view is a derived relation defined in terms of base relations or other views, by means of the CREATE VIEW statement in SQL. A view is recomputed every time it is invoked. A materialized view, on the other hand, is a view that is physically stored in the database. This improves query performance, playing the role of a cache which can be directly accessed without looking into the base relations. But this benefit has a counterpart. When the base relations are updated, the materialized views derived from them also need to be updated. The process of updating a materialized view in response to changes in the base relations is called **view maintenance**. Under certain conditions, it is possible to compute changes to the view caused by changes in the underlying relations without recomputing the entire view from scratch. This is called **incremental view maintenance**. As this problem is central to data warehousing, we will describe it with some detail.

The view maintenance problem can be analyzed through four dimensions:

- Information: Refers to the information available for view maintenance, like integrity constraints, keys, access to base relations, and so on.
- Modification: Refers to the kinds of modifications that can be handled by the maintenance algorithm, namely, insertions, deletions, and updates; the latter are usually treated as deletions followed by insertions.
- Language: Refers to the language used to define the view, most often SQL. Aggregation and recursion are also issues in this dimension.
- Instance: Refers to whether or not the algorithm works for every instance of the database or for a subset of all instances.

For example, consider a relation Sales(ProductKey, CustomerKey, Quantity) and a materialized view TopProducts that keeps the products for which at least one customer ordered more than 150 units. The view TopProducts is defined as follows:

$$\text{TopProducts} = \pi_{\text{ProductKey}}(\sigma_{\text{Quantity}>150}(\text{Sales})).$$

It is clear that inserting a tuple like $(\text{p2}, \text{c3}, 110)$ in the table Sales would have no effect on the view, since the tuple does not satisfy the view condition. However, the insertion of the tuple $(\text{p2}, \text{c3}, 160)$ would possibly modify the view. An algorithm can easily update it without accessing the base relation, basically adding the product if it is not already in the view.

Let us now analyze the deletion of a tuple from Sales, for example, $(\text{p2}, \text{c3}, 160)$. We cannot delete p2 from the view until checking if p2 has not been ordered by some other customer in a quantity greater than 150, which requires to scan the relation Sales.

In summary, although in some cases insertion can be performed just accessing the materialized view, deletion *always* requires further information.

Consider now a view FoodCustomers which includes a join. The view contains the customers that ordered at least one product in the food category (we use the simplified and denormalized Product dimension defined in Sect. 5.7):

$$\text{FoodCustomers} = \pi_{\text{CustomerKey}}(\sigma_{\text{CategoryName}='\text{Food}'}(\text{Product}) * \text{Sales})$$

If we insert the tuple $(\text{p3}, \text{c4}, 170)$ in table Sales, we cannot know if c4 will be in the view FoodCustomers (of course assuming that it is not in the view already) unless we check in the base relations whether or not p3 is in the food category.

The above examples show the need of characterizing the kinds of view maintenance problems in terms of the kind of update and of the operations in the view definition. Two main classes of algorithms for view maintenance have been studied in the database literature:

- Algorithms using full information, which means the views and the base relations.
- Algorithms using partial information, namely, the materialized views and the key constraints.

7.2.1   Algorithms Using Full Information

Three kinds of views are addressed by these algorithms: nonrecursive views, outer-join views, and recursive views. In this section, we discuss the first two kinds and omit the discussion on recursive views, which is beyond the scope of this book.

The basic algorithm for nonrecursive views (which may include join, union, negation, and aggregation) is the **counting algorithm**. This algorithm counts the number of alternative derivations that every tuple in the view has. In this way, if we delete a tuple in a base relation, we can check whether or not we should delete it from the view. To study this kind of view, let us consider the relation FoodCustomers introduced above. The view is created as follows:

```
CREATE VIEW FoodCustomers AS (
        SELECT DISTINCT CustomerKey
        FROM   Sales S, Product P
        WHERE  S.ProductKey = P.ProductKey AND P.CategoryName = 'Food' )
```

An instance of relation Sales is depicted in Fig. 7.1a; the view FoodCustomers over this instance is shown in Fig. 7.1b. We added a column Count indicating the number of possible derivations for each tuple. For example, (c2, 2) means that customer c2 bought two products from the category food. Further, we

a

ProductKey	CustomerKey	Quantity
p1	c1	20
p1	c2	100
p2	c2	50
...	...	...

b

CustomerKey	Count
c1	1
c2	2

c

CustomerKey	Count
c1	1
c2	1

Fig. 7.1 An example of the counting algorithm. (**a**) Instance of the Sales relation. (**b**) View FoodCustomers, including the number of possible derivations of each tuple. (**c**) View FoodCustomers after the deletion of (p1, c2, 100)

suppose that the only products of the category food are p1 and p2 and the tuples shown are the only ones concerning these products.

Suppose that we delete tuple (p1, c2, 100) from Sales. Although c2 in FoodCustomers is derived from the deleted tuple, it has also an alternative derivation, through (p2, c2, 50). Thus, deleting (p1, c2, 100) does not prevent c2 to be in the view. The counting algorithm computes a relation Δ^-(FoodCustomers) which contains the tuples that can be derived from (p1, c2, 100), and therefore affected by the deletion of such tuple, and adds a -1 to each tuple. In this example, Δ^-(FoodCustomers) will contain the tuples $\{(c2, -1)\}$. Analogously, for dealing with insertions, Δ^+(FoodCustomers) extends the tuples with a 1. The updated view (shown in Fig. 7.1c) is obtained by joining Δ^-(FoodCustomers) with the materialized view FoodCustomers (using the attribute CustomerKey) and subtracting Δ^-(FoodCustomers).Count from FoodCustomers.Count. We can see that, since c2 has two possible derivations (Fig. 7.1b), it will not be removed from the view; we will only eliminate one possible derivation. If later the tuple (p2, c2, 50) gets deleted, c2 will be also eliminated from the view. On the contrary, c1 would be deleted together with (p1, c1, 20).

We analyze now views defined with an outer join. Let us consider two relations Product(ProdID, ProdName, ShipID) and Shipper(ShipID, ShipName) as depicted, respectively, in Fig. 7.2a,b. An example of outer join view is as follows:

```
CREATE VIEW ProductShipper AS (
        SELECT P.ProdID, P.ProdName, S.ShipID, S.ShipName
        FROM    Product P FULL OUTER JOIN Shipper S ON
                P.ShipID = S.ShipID )
```

This view is depicted in Fig. 7.2d. A modification Δ(Product) to a relation Product consists in insertions Δ^+(Product) and deletions Δ^-(Product). As usual, updates are considered as deletions followed by insertions. View maintenance is tackled by rewriting the full outer join as either left or right outer joins as indicated below, depending on whether we tackle the updates of the left or the right table of the full outer join. Then, we merge the result with the view to be updated:

```
SELECT P.ProdID, P.ProdName, S.ShipID, S.ShipName
FROM    $\Delta$(Product) P LEFT OUTER JOIN Shipper S ON P.ShipID = S.ShipID
```

```
SELECT P.ProdID, P.ProdName, S.ShipID, S.ShipName
FROM    Product P RIGHT OUTER JOIN $\Delta$(Shipper) S ON P.ShipID = S.ShipID
```

The first query computes the effect on the view of the changes to Product, and the second one does the same with the changes to Shipper. Consider the two relations Product and Shipper in Fig. 7.2a,b, as well as Δ^+(Product) in Fig. 7.2c containing the tuples inserted in Product. When we insert a matching tuple like (p3, MP3, s2), the projection of the left outer join with Shipper would be (p3, MP3, s2, DHL). In this case, the algorithm should

a

ProdID	ProdName	ShipID
p1	TV	s1
p2	Tablet	NULL

b

ShipID	ShipName
s1	Fedex
s2	DHL

c

ProdID	ProdName	ShipID
p3	MP3	s2
p4	PC	NULL

d

ProdID	ProdName	ShipID	ShipName
p1	TV	s1	Fedex
p2	Tablet	NULL	NULL
NULL	NULL	s2	DHL

e

ProdID	ProdName	ShipID	ShipName
p1	TV	s1	Fedex
p2	Tablet	NULL	NULL
p3	MP3	s2	DHL
p4	PC	NULL	NULL

Fig. 7.2 An example of maintenance of a full outer join view. (**a**) Table Product. (**b**) Table Shipper. (**c**) Δ^+(Product). (**d**) View ProductShipper. (**e**) Resulting view after the insertions

also delete (NULL, NULL, s2, DHL) (because (s2, DHL) now has a matching tuple), together with adding (p3, MP3, s2, DHL). If the tuple (p4, PC, NULL) is inserted into Product, the left outer join between (p4, PC, NULL) and Shipper yields (p4, PC, NULL, NULL), which is inserted into the view. Figure 7.2e shows the final state of the view.

7.2.2 Algorithms Using Partial Information

It is not always possible to maintain a view using only partial information. A view is called **self-maintainable** if it can be maintained using only the view and key constraints. This is important for data warehouses because we do not want to access base data to update summary tables. Further, we say that a view is self-maintainable with respect to a modification type T to a base relation R if the view can be self-maintained for all instances of the database in response to all modifications of type T over R.

As an example, consider again the view FoodCustomers defined above:

FoodCustomers $= \pi_{\text{CustomerKey}}(\sigma_{\text{CategoryName}='\text{Food}'}(\text{Product}) * \text{Sales})$

Suppose that c3 is in the view and we delete the tuple (p1, c3, 100) from the relation Sales. We could not delete c3 from the view without checking if this customer ordered another food product. If in the base relations we find that there is another tuple in Sales of the form (p, c3, q), such that p is in the food category, then c3 will remain in the view. Thus, the view FoodCustomers is not self-maintainable with respect to deletions on Sales. Analogously, this view is not self-maintainable with respect to insertions into any of the two base relations, because for any tuple inserted, for example, into Sales, we must check if the product is in the food category (except if c3 is already in the view, in which case nothing should be done).

We say an attribute is **distinguished** in a view V if it appears in the SELECT clause of the view definition. An attribute A belonging to a relation R is **exposed** in a view V if A is used in a predicate in V. We briefly present some well-known results in view maintenance theory:

- A select-project-join view is not self-maintainable with respect to insertions.
- A select-project-join view is self-maintainable with respect to deletions in a relation R if the key attributes from each occurrence of R in the join are either included in the view or equated to a constant in the view definition. Note that none of these conditions are satisfied in the example above.
- A left or full outer join view V defined using two relations R and S such that the keys of R and S are distinguished and all exposed attributes of R are distinguished is self-maintainable with respect to all types of modifications in S.

Consider again the outer join view defined in the previous section and the instances of Fig. 7.2:

```
CREATE VIEW ProductShipper AS (
      SELECT P.ProdID, P.ProdName, S.ShipID, S.ShipName
      FROM    Product P FULL OUTER JOIN Shipper S ON
             P.ShipID = S.ShipID )
```

Since this view satisfies the third condition above, it is self-maintainable with respect to all types of modifications in Product. Let us first compute the projection of the view over Shipper, expressed as Proj_Shipper $=$ $\pi_{ShipID,ShipName}$(Product $\bowtie$ Shipper), shown in Fig. 7.3a. Notice that the tuple (NULL, NULL) is excluded from this projection. The tables Δ^+(Product) and Δ^-(Product) denoting, respectively, the tuples inserted and deleted from Product are shown in Fig. 7.3b,c. Since the view is self-maintainable, we can join these delta tables with Proj_Shipper instead of Shipper, thus avoiding to access the base relations. The joins between delta tables and Proj_Shipper are shown in Fig. 7.3d,e. Finally, the result of both joins is merged with the original view and the side effects are addressed. For example, when inserting (p3, MP3, s2, DHL), we must delete (NULL, NULL, s2, DHL). Analogously, when deleting (p1, TV, s1, Fedex), we must insert (NULL, NULL, s1, Fedex). Figure 7.3f shows the final result.

7.3 Data Cube Maintenance

In data warehouses, materialized views that include aggregate functions are called **summary tables**. We now discuss how summary tables can be maintained with minimum access to the base data while keeping maximum

a

ShipID	ShipName
s1	Fedex
s2	DHL

b

ProdID	ProdName	ShipID
p3	MP3	s2
p4	PC	NULL

c

ProdID	ProdName	ShipID
p1	TV	s1

d

ProdID	ProdName	ShipID	ShipName
p3	MP3	s2	DHL
p4	PC	NULL	NULL

e

ProdID	ProdName	ShipID	ShipName
p1	TV	s1	Fedex

f

ProdID	ProdName	ShipID	ShipName
p2	Tablet	NULL	NULL
p3	MP3	s2	DHL
p4	PC	NULL	NULL
NULL	NULL	s1	Fedex

Fig. 7.3 An example of self-maintenance of a full outer join view. (**a**) Proj_Shipper. (**b**) Δ^+(Product). (**c**) Δ^-(Product). (**d**) Δ^+(Product) $\bowtie$ Proj_Shipper. (**e**) Δ^-(Product) $\bowtie$ Proj_Shipper. (**f**) Final result

data availability. The problem can be stated as follows: as data at the sources are added or updated, the summary tables that depend on these data must be also updated. Then, two options arise: to recompute the summary tables from scratch and to apply incremental view maintenance techniques to avoid such recomputation. Note that since summary tables remain unavailable to the data warehouse users while they are maintained, we need to reduce the time invested in their updating. In this section, we explain a representative summary table maintenance algorithm called the **summary-delta algorithm**, although many other techniques (like the ones that maintain many versions of the summary tables) exist in the literature.

Analogously to the definition of self-maintainable views, we say that an aggregate function is **self-maintainable** if the new value of the function can be computed solely from the old values and from changes to the base data. Aggregate functions must be distributive in order to be self-maintainable. The five classic aggregate functions in SQL are self-maintainable with respect to insertions, but not to deletions. In fact, MAX and MIN are not, and cannot be made, self-maintainable with respect to deletions.

The summary-delta algorithm has two main phases called propagate and refresh. The main advantage of this approach is that the propagate phase can be performed in parallel with data warehouse operations; only the refresh phase requires taking the warehouse off-line. The basic idea is to create in the propagate phase a so-called **summary-delta table** that stores the net changes to the summary table due to changes in the source data. Then, during the refresh phase, these changes are applied to the summary table.

We will explain the algorithm with a simplified version of the Sales fact table in the Northwind case study, whose schema we show next:

Sales(ProductKey, CustomerKey, TimeKey, Quantity)

Consider a view DailySalesSum defined as follows:

```
CREATE VIEW DailySalesSum AS (
       SELECT      ProductKey, TimeKey, SUM(Quantity) AS SumQuantity,
                   COUNT(*) AS Count
       FROM        Sales
       GROUP BY ProductKey, TimeKey )
```

The Count attribute is added in order to maintain the view in the presence of deletions, as we will explain later. In the propagate phase, we define two tables, Δ^+(Sales) and Δ^-(Sales), which store the insertions and deletions to the fact table, and a view where the net changes to the summary tables are stored. The latter is called a summary-delta table, which in this example is created as follows:

```
CREATE VIEW SD_DailySalesSum(ProductKey, TimeKey,
               SD_SumQuantity, SD_Count) AS
       WITH Temp AS (
               ( SELECT ProductKey, TimeKey,
                        Quantity AS _Quantity, 1 AS _Count
                 FROM    Δ+(Sales) )
               UNION ALL
               ( SELECT ProductKey, TimeKey,
                        -1 * Quantity AS _Quantity, -1 AS _Count
                 FROM    Δ-(Sales) ) )
       SELECT ProductKey, TimeKey, SUM(_Quantity), SUM(_Count)
       FROM Temp
       GROUP BY ProductKey, TimeKey
```

In the temporary table Temp of the view definition, we can see that for each tuple in Δ^+(Sales), we store a 1 in the _Count attribute, while for each tuple in Δ^-(Sales), we store a -1. Analogously, the Quantity attribute values are multiplied by 1 or -1 depending if they are retrieved from Δ^+(Sales) or Δ^-(Sales), respectively. Then, in the main SELECT clause, the SD_SumQuantity attribute contains the net sum of the quantity for each combination of ProductKey and TimeKey, while SD_Count contains the net number of tuples in the view corresponding to such combination.

During the refresh phase, we apply to the summary table the net changes stored in the summary-delta table. Below we give a general scheme of the refresh algorithm valid when the aggregate function is SUM:

Refresh Algorithm
INPUT: Summary-delta table SD_DailySalesSum
       Summary table DailySalesSum

```
OUTPUT: Updated summary table DailySalesSum
BEGIN
    For each tuple T in SD_DailySalesSum DO
        IF NOT EXISTS (
                SELECT *
                FROM    DailySalesSum D
                WHERE T.ProductKey = D.ProductKey AND
                        T.TimeKey = D.TimeKey)
            INSERT T INTO DailySalesSum
        ELSE
            IF EXISTS (
                    SELECT *
                    FROM    DailySalesSum D
                    WHERE T.ProductKey = D.ProductKey AND
                            T.TimeKey = D.TimeKey AND
                            T.SD_Count + D.Count = 0)
                DELETE T FROM DailySalesSum
            ELSE
                UPDATE DailySalesSum
                SET SumQuantity = SumQuantity + T.SD_SumQuantity,
                    Count = Count + T.SD_Count
                WHERE ProductKey = T.ProductKey AND
                        TimeKey = T.TimeKey
END
```

For each tuple T in the summary-delta table, the algorithm checks if T is already in the view. If not, it is inserted. If T is in the view and all the occurrences of a (ProductKey, TimeKey) combination are deleted (T.SD_Count + D.Count = 0), then T is deleted from the view. Otherwise, the tuple in the view corresponding to T is updated with the new sum and the new count.

Figure 7.4 shows an example using the SUM aggregate function. Figure 7.4a shows the original DailySalesSum table, Fig. 7.4b,c shows the tables containing the changes to DailySalesSum, and Fig. 7.4d shows the summary-delta table. Finally, the result of the view update is shown in Fig. 7.4e. For instance, the tuple (p4, c2, t4, 100) has been inserted, as depicted in Δ^+(Sales) (Fig. 7.4b). The tuple (p4, t4, 100, 1) in Fig. 7.4d tells the net result of the combination (p4, t4) that has to be used to update the DailySalesSum view, which yields the tuple (p4, t4, 200, 16) depicted in Fig. 7.4e.

Figure 7.5 shows an example using the MAX aggregate function. As can be seen in Fig. 7.5a, in the view DailySalesMax, we need an additional column that counts the number of tuples *that have the maximum value*, instead of counting the number of tuples that have the same combination of ProductKey and TimeKey as was the case for the SUM. The view can be created as follows:

```
CREATE VIEW DailySalesMax(ProductKey, TimeKey, MaxQuantity, Count) AS (
    SELECT ProductKey, TimeKey, MIN(Quantity), COUNT(*)
    FROM    Sales S1
    WHERE Quantity = (
            SELECT MAX(Quantity)
```

a

Product Key	Time Key	Sum Quantity	Count
p2	t2	100	10
p3	t3	100	20
p4	t4	100	15
p5	t5	100	2
p6	t6	100	1

b

Product Key	Customer Key	Time Key	Quantity
p1	c1	t1	150
p2	c1	t2	200
p2	c2	t2	100
p4	c2	t4	100
p6	c5	t6	200

c

Product Key	Customer Key	Time Key	Quantity
p2	c1	t2	10
p5	c2	t5	10
p6	c5	t6	100

d

Product Key	Time Key	SD_Sum Quantity	SD_Count
p1	t1	150	1
p2	t2	290	1
p4	t4	100	1
p5	t5	-10	-1
p6	t6	100	0

e

Product Key	Time Key	Sum Quantity	Count
p1	t1	150	1
p2	t2	390	11
p3	t3	100	20
p4	t4	200	16
p5	t5	90	1
p6	t6	200	1

Fig. 7.4 An example of the propagate and refresh algorithm with aggregate function SUM. (a) Original view DailySalesSum. (b) Δ^+(Sales). (c) Δ^-(Sales). (d) Summary-delta table SD_DailySalesSum. (e) View DailySalesSum after update

```
    FROM    Sales S2
    WHERE  S1.ProductKey = S2.ProductKey AND
                 S1.TimeKey = S2.TimeKey )
    GROUP BY ProductKey, TimeKey )
```

Figure 7.5b shows the summary-delta table. As can be seen, we need a column for keeping the maximum value in the tuples inserted or deleted, as well as another column counting the number of insertions or deletions of tuples *having the maximum value*. Thus, the first four tuples in the summary-delta table correspond to insertions, while the last three correspond to deletions since the count value is negative. The view for creating the summary-delta table is given next:

```
CREATE VIEW SD_DailySalesMax(ProductKey, TimeKey,
                 SD_MaxQuantity, SD_Count) AS (
```

a

Product Key	Time Key	Max Quantity	Count
p2	t2	150	4
p3	t3	100	5
p4	t4	50	6
p5	t5	150	5
p6	t6	100	3
p7	t7	100	2

b

Product Key	Time Key	SD_Max Quantity	SD_Count
p1	t1	100	2
p2	t2	100	2
p3	t3	100	2
p4	t4	100	2
p5	t5	100	-2
p6	t6	100	-2
p7	t7	100	-2

c

Product Key	Time Key	Max Quantity	Count
p1	t1	100	2
p2	t2	150	4
p3	t3	100	7
p4	t4	100	2
p5	t5	150	5
p6	t6	100	1
p7	t7	?	?

Fig. 7.5 An example of the propagate and refresh algorithm with aggregate function MAX. (a) Original view DailySalesMax. (b) Summary-delta table SD_DailySalesMax. (c) Updated view DailySalesMax

```
SELECT ProductKey, TimeKey, Quantity, COUNT(*)
FROM    Δ⁺(Sales) S1
WHERE  Quantity = (
            SELECT MAX(Quantity)
            FROM    Δ⁺(Sales) S2
            WHERE S1.ProductKey = S2.ProductKey AND
                  S1.TimeKey = S2.TimeKey )
GROUP BY ProductKey, TimeKey
            UNION ALL
SELECT ProductKey, TimeKey, Quantity, -1 * COUNT(*)
FROM    Δ⁻(Sales) S1
WHERE  Quantity = (
            SELECT MAX(Quantity)
            FROM    Δ⁻(Sales) S2
            WHERE S1.ProductKey = S2.ProductKey AND
                  S1.TimeKey = S2.TimeKey )
GROUP BY ProductKey, TimeKey )
```

Finally, Fig. 7.5c shows the view after the update. Let us consider first the insertions. The tuple for p1 in the summary-delta table does not have a corresponding tuple in the view, and thus, it is inserted in the view. The tuple for p2 in the summary-delta table has a maximum value smaller than that in the view so the view is not modified. The tuple for p3 in the summary-delta table has a quantity value equal to the maximum in the view so the maximum value remains the same and the counter is increased to 7. The tuple for p4 in the summary-delta table has a maximum value greater than the maximum in the view, and thus, the view must be updated with the new maximum and the new counter.

Now consider the deletions. The tuple for p5 in the summary-delta table has a quantity value smaller than the maximum in the view so the view is not modified. The tuple for p6 in the summary-delta table has a quantity value equal to the maximum in the view but with a greater count value. In this case, we decrease the counter in the view to 1. The tuple for p7 illustrates why the MAX function is not self-maintainable with respect to deletions. The maximum value and the counter in the summary-delta table are equal to those value in the view. There are two possible cases. If there are other tuples in the base table with the same combination (p7, t7), we must obtain the new maximum value and the new count from the base tables. This case is depicted in Fig. 7.5c. Otherwise, if there are no other tuples in the base table with the same combination (p7, t7), we must simply delete the tuple from the view.

The algorithm for refreshing the view DailySalesMax from the summary-delta table SD_DailySalesMax is left as an exercise.

7.4   Computation of a Data Cube

In Chap. 5, we have explained how the data cube could be computed by means of an SQL query, where the all value is represented by the null value. Computing the whole data cube in this way from the base fact and dimension tables could become extremely hard unless an adequate strategy is applied. The simplest method, consisting in performing the GROUP BY queries for each view and then taking their UNION, would be unacceptable in real-life applications. Thus, several optimization techniques have been proposed for this. We study next some of them in order to convey the main idea.

The optimization methods start with the notion of **data cube lattice**. In this lattice, each node represents a possible aggregation of the fact data, where there is an edge from node i to node j if j can be computed from i and the number of grouping attributes of i is the number of attributes of j plus one. For instance, given an aggregate view by CustomerKey and ProductKey of the Sales table of the previous section, we can compute the total sales amount by customer directly from this view, without computing it from the base table. In what follows, to avoid overloading figures, we will work with the lattice depicted in Fig. 7.6, corresponding to a four-dimensional data cube, with dimensions A, B, C, and D. In this lattice, an edge from ABC to AB means that the summary table AB can be computed from ABC. We do not include in the lattice the transitive edges, for example, edges like ABCD → AB.

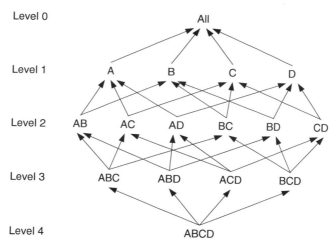

Fig. 7.6 A data cube lattice

The simplest optimizations for computing the cube lattice are:

- Smallest-parent: Computes each view from the smallest previously computed one. In the lattice of Fig. 7.6, AB can be computed from ABC, ABD, or ABCD. This method chooses the smallest of them.
- Cache-results: Caches in memory an aggregation from which other ones can be computed.
- Amortize-scans: Computes in memory as many aggregations as possible, reducing the amount of table scans.
- Share-sorts: Applies only to methods based on sorting and aims at sharing costs between several aggregations.
- Share-partitions: These are specific to algorithms based on hashing. When the hash table is too large to fit in main memory, data are partitioned and aggregation is performed for each partition that fits in memory. The partitioning cost can be shared across multiple aggregations.

Note that these methods can be contradictory. For instance, share-sorts would induce to prefer AB to be derived from ABC, while ABD could be its smallest parent. Sophisticated cube computation methods try to combine together some of these simple optimization techniques to produce an efficient query evaluation plan. We explain below a method based on sorting. Methods based on hashing follow a similar rationale. Note that most of these algorithms require the estimation of the sizes of each aggregate view in the lattice.

7.4.1 PipeSort Algorithm

The **PipeSort algorithm** gives a global strategy for computing the data cube, which includes the first four optimization methods specified above.

The algorithm includes cache-results and amortize-scans strategies by means of computing nodes with common prefixes in a single scan. This is called pipelined evaluation in database query optimization. In this way, we could compute ABCD, ABC, AB, and A in a single scan because the attribute order in the view is the sorting order in the file. For example, in the base table below, with a single scan of the first five tuples, we can compute the aggregations $(a1, b1, c1, 200)$, $(a1, b1, c2, 500)$, $(a1, b1, 700)$, $(a1, b2, 400)$, and $(a1, 1100)$.

A	B	C	D	
a1	b1	c1	d1	100
a1	b1	c1	d2	100
a1	b1	c2	d1	200
a1	b1	c2	d1	300
a1	b2	c1	d1	400
a2	b1	c1	d1	100
a2	b1	c2	d2	400
...	...	...	...	...

The input of the algorithm is a data cube lattice in which each edge e_{ij}, where node i is the parent of node j, is labeled with two costs, $S(e_{ij})$ and $A(e_{ij})$. $S(e_{ij})$ is the cost of computing j from i if i is not sorted. $A(e_{ij})$ is the cost of computing j from i if i is already sorted. Thus, $A(e_{ij}) \leq S(e_{ij})$. In addition, we consider the lattice organized into levels, where each level k contains views with exactly k attributes, starting from All, where $k = 0$. This data structure is called a *search lattice*.

The output of the algorithm is a subgraph of the search lattice such that each node has exactly one parent from which it will be computed in a certain mode, that is, sorted or not (note that in the search lattice, each node, except All, has more than one parent). If the attribute order of a node j is a prefix of the order of its parent i, then j can be computed from i without sorting the latter, and in the resulting graph, the edge will have cost $A(e_{ij})$. Otherwise, i has to be sorted to compute j and the edge will have cost $S(e_{ij})$. Note that for any node i in an output graph, there can be at most one outgoing edge marked A and many outgoing edges marked S. The goal of the algorithm is to find an output graph representing an execution plan such that the sum of the costs labeling the edges is minimum.

To obtain the minimum cost output graph, the algorithm proceeds level by level, starting from level 0 until level $N - 1$, where N is the number of levels in the search lattice. We find the best way of computing the nodes in each level k from the nodes in level $k + 1$, reducing the problem to a *weighted bipartite matching* problem as follows. Consider a pair $(k, k + 1)$ of levels. The algorithm first transforms the level $k + 1$ by making k copies of each one of its nodes. Thus, each node in level $k + 1$ will have $k + 1$ children,

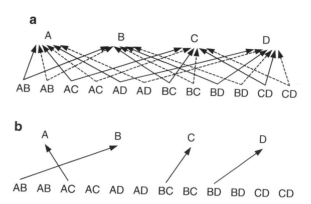

Fig. 7.7 Computation of the minimum bipartite matching between two levels in the cube lattice

that is, $k + 1$ outgoing edges. All original edges have cost $A(e_{ij})$ and all replicated edges have cost $S(e_{ij})$. Therefore, this transformed graph induces a bipartite graph (because there are edges between nodes in different levels but not between nodes in the same level). Finally, we compute the minimum cost matching in this bipartite graph such that each node j in level k will be matched to some node i in level $k + 1$. If j is connected to i by an $A()$ edge, then j determines the attribute order in which i will be sorted during its computation. If, instead, j is connected to i by an $S()$ edge, i will be sorted in order to compute j.

As an example, consider in Fig. 7.7 the graph constructed as indicated above, for levels 1 and 2 of the lattice in Fig. 7.6. Edges of type $A(e_{ij})$ are represented with solid lines, while edges of type $S(e_{ij})$ with dashed lines. Note that in Fig. 7.7a we have added a copy of each node at level 2. In Fig. 7.7b, we can see that all the views will be computed at a cost $A(e_{ij})$. For example, A will be computed from AC, B from BA, and so on.

The matching above is performed N times, where N is the number of grouping attributes, generating an evaluation plan. The heuristics is that if for every pair of levels the cost is minimum, the same occurs for the whole plan. The output lattice gives a sorting order to compute each node. As a result, the PipeSort algorithm induces the following evaluation strategy: in every chain such that a node in level k is a prefix of node in level $k + 1$ (in the output graph), all aggregations can be computed in a pipeline.

The general scheme of the PipeSort algorithm is given next:

PipeSort Algorithm
INPUT: A search lattice with the $A()$ and $S()$ edges costs
OUTPUT: An evaluation plan to compute all nodes in the search lattice
For level $k = 0$ to level $N - 1$
    Generate-Plan($k + 1 \rightarrow k$);
    For each node i in level $k + 1$

Fix the sort order of i as the order of the level k node
connected to i by an $A()$ edge;

Generate-Plan($k + 1 \rightarrow k$);
Create k additional copies of each level $k + 1$ node;
Connect each copy node to the same set of level k nodes as the original node;
Assign cost $A(e_{ij})$ to edges e_{ij} from the original nodes and cost $S(e_{ij})$
    to edges from the copy nodes;
Find the minimum cost matching on the transformed level $k + 1$ with level k;

Figure 7.8 shows an evaluation plan for computing the cube lattice of
Fig. 7.6 using the PipeSort algorithm. The minimum cost sort plan will first
sort the base fact table in CBAD order and compute CBA, CB, C, and All
aggregations in a pipelined fashion. Then, we sort the base fact table in the
BADC order and proceed as above to compute aggregates BAD, BA, and A.
We continue in the same way with ACDB and DBCA. Note how the views in
level 1 (A, B, C, and D) are computed from the views in level 2 in the way
that was indicated by the bipartite graph matching in Fig. 7.7.

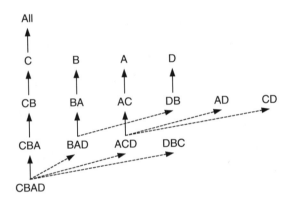

Fig. 7.8 Evaluation plan for computing the cube lattice in Fig. 7.6

7.4.2 Cube Size Estimation

We have already said that algorithms like PipeSort, and most algorithms
computing summary tables, require knowing the size of each aggregate.
However, in general this is not known in advance. Thus, we need to accurately
predict the sizes of the different aggregates. There are three classic methods
for this, although a wide array of statistical techniques could be used. The
first of these methods is purely analytical, the second is based on sampling,
and the last one on probabilistic counting.

The **analytical algorithm** is based on a result by Feller from 1957, stating
that choosing r elements (which we can assume are the tuples in a relation)
randomly from a set of n elements (which are all the different values a set

of attributes can take), the expected number of distinct elements obtained is $n - n * (1 - \frac{1}{n})^r$. This assumes that data are uniformly distributed. If it turns out not to be the case and data present some skew, we will be overestimating the size of the data cube. For instance, let us suppose a relation R(ProductKey, CustomerKey, TimeKey). If we want to estimate the size of the aggregation over ProductKey and CustomerKey, we should know the number of different values of each attribute. Then, $n = |\text{ProductKey}| * |\text{CustomerKey}|$, and r is the number of tuples in R. The main advantage of this method is its simplicity and performance. The obvious drawback of the algorithm is that it does not consult the database, and the results can be used only when we know that data are uniformly distributed.

The basic idea of the **sampling-based algorithm** is to take a random subset of the database and compute the cube over this subset. Let D be the database, S the sample, and $Cube(S)$ the size of the cube computed from S. The size of the cube will be estimated as $Cube(S) * \frac{|D|}{|S|}$. This method is simple and fast, and it has been reported that it provides satisfactory results over real-world data sets.

The **probabilistic counting algorithm** is based on the following observation: suppose we want to compute the number of tuples of the aggregation of sales by product category and shipper. We would first aggregate along the dimension Product, to generate product categories, and count the number of distinct shippers generated by this operation. For example, for the set of product-shipper pairs $\{(p1, s1), (p2, s1), (p3, s2), (p4, s4), (p5, s4)\}$, if p1 and p2 correspond to category c1 and the rest to category c2, the aggregation will have three tuples: $\{(c1, s1), (c2, s2), (c2, s4)\}$. In other words, c1 yields only one value of shipper, and c2 yields two distinct values of shipper. Thus, estimating the number of *distinct* tuples in a group (in this case, shippers by category), we can estimate the number of *tuples* in that group. This idea is used to estimate the size of a data cube by means of counting the number of distinct elements in a multiset as proposed in a well-known algorithm by Flajolet and Martin, performing this for all possible combinations of the hierarchies in the cube. The algorithm estimates the sizes of the aggregations in a cube at the cost of scanning the whole database once. However, this is cheaper than actually computing the cube, and it is proved that the error has a bound. Details of this algorithm fall beyond the scope of this book.

7.4.3 Partial Computation of a Data Cube

Generally speaking, three alternatives exist to implement a data warehouse: materialize the whole data cube (as studied in the previous section), materialize a selected portion of the cube, and not materializing any aggregation at all. Materializing the whole cube has not only the drawback of the storage space required but also the cost of refreshing the summary tables. On the other hand, it implies that any possible aggregate query will match a summary table; thus, the cost of answering the query would just be a table scan which, in addition, will often be of a small size. The "no materialization" approach is likely to be inefficient in most real-world situations. It follows that a good trade-off between these options can be to materialize only a portion of the views in the data cube. The main problem in this case is to decide which views are going to be materialized. Notice that once we decide which are the views to materialize, we can apply the techniques for cube computation and maintenance already studied in this chapter. Actually, the problem could be stated in many ways:

• How many views must we materialize to get reasonable performance?
• Given a certain amount of storage space, which views should we materialize in order to minimize the average query cost?
• If we can assume an X% performance degradation with respect to a fully materialized data cube, how much space do we save?

We next explain a classic greedy algorithm that finds, given a cube lattice, the best set of views to materialize under a certain criterion. Although the set of views returned by the algorithm may not always be the optimal one, we have chosen this algorithm as representative of a class of algorithms that aim at solving the same problem.

The algorithm makes use of a lattice that takes into account two kinds of dependencies between nodes. The first kind of dependency accounts for the case in which the attributes of a view are included in those of another view. For example, in the lattice representing the possible aggregations of the fact table Sales(ProductKey, CustomerKey, TimeKey), there is a dependency between the node (ProductKey, CustomerKey) and the node (ProductKey), stating that the latter can be computed from the former since {ProductKey} ⊆ {ProductKey, CustomerKey} holds. The second kind of dependency accounts for hierarchies. For example, given a hierarchy Month → Year, if we have an aggregation over Month, we can use it to compute the aggregation over Year without going down to the fact table. Thus, the dependency lattice represents a relation $v_i \preceq v_j$ between the views such that a view v_i can be answered using v_j. For simplicity, and without loss of generalization, in the examples of this section, we only consider the case in which the attributes of a view are included in those of another view.

The view selection algorithm is based on calculating the costs of computing the views in the lattice. A linear cost model with the following characteristics is assumed:

• The cost of answering a view v from a materialized view v_m is the number of rows in v_m.
• All queries are identical to some view in the dependency lattice.

The algorithm also requires knowing the expected number of rows for each view in the lattice. Finally, it is assumed that the lowest node in the lattice (typically, the base fact table) is always materialized.

The goal of the algorithm is to minimize the time taken to evaluate a view, constrained to materialize a fixed number of views regardless of the space available, a problem known to be NP-complete. The greedy algorithm we present below uses a heuristic that selects a sequence of views such that each choice in this sequence is the best, given what was selected before.

Let us call $C(v)$ the cost of view v, k the number of views to materialize, and S a set of materialized views. The benefit of materializing a view v not in S, relative to the materialized views already in S, is denoted $B(v, S)$, and it is computed as follows:

View Materialization Benefit Algorithm
INPUT: A lattice L, each view node labeled with its expected number of rows
    A node v, not yet selected to materialize
    A set S containing the nodes already selected to materialize
OUTPUT: The benefit of materializing v given S
BEGIN
    For each view $w \preceq v$, $w \notin S$, Bw is computed by
        Let u be the view of least cost in S such that $w \preceq u$
        If $C(v) < C(u)$, $Bw = C(u) - C(v)$, otherwise $Bw = 0$
    $B(v, S) = \sum_{w \preceq v} Bw$
END

The algorithm above works as follows. Given a view w (not yet materialized), let us denote u the (materialized) view of minimum cost from which w can be computed. Given a candidate view v selected for materialization, for each view w that depends on v, the benefit of materializing w (denoted Bw) is computed as the difference between the costs of v and u. If computing w from v is more expensive than doing it from u ($C(v) > C(u)$), materializing the candidate view does not benefit the computation of w ($Bw = 0$). The algorithm iterates over all views w, and finally, the benefit of materializing v is the sum of all individual benefits ($\sum_{w \preceq v} Bw$).

The view selection algorithm computes, in each iteration, the view v whose materialization gives the maximum benefit. The scheme of the algorithm is given next:

View Selection Algorithm
INPUT: A lattice L, each view node v labeled with its expected number of rows
    The number of views to materialize, k
OUTPUT: The set of views to materialize
BEGIN
    $S = \{$The bottom view in $L\}$
    FOR $i = 1$ TO k DO
        Select a view v not in S such that $B(v, S)$ is maximized
        $S = S \cup \{v\}$
    END DO
    S is the selection of views to materialize
END

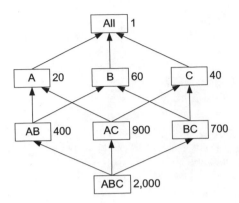

Fig. 7.9 Dependency lattice. Initially, the only view materialized is ABCD

The set S contains the views already materialized. In each one of the k iterations, the algorithm computes the benefit produced by the materialization of each of the views not yet in S. The one with the maximum benefit is added to S, and a new iteration begins.

Let us apply the algorithm to the lattice in Fig. 7.9. In addition to the node label, beside each node we indicate the cost of the view that the node represents. Assume that we can materialize three views and that the bottom view is already materialized.

Let us show how to select the first view to materialize. We need to compute the benefit of materializing each view, knowing that $S = \{ABC\}$. We start with node AB, which is a good candidate, since it offers a cost reduction of 1,600 units for each view that depends on it. For example, node A depends on AB. Currently, computing A has cost 2,000 since this is performed from ABC. If we materialize AB, the cost of computing A will drop to 400.

The benefit of materializing AB given S is given by

$$B(\mathsf{AB}, S) = \sum_{w \preceq \mathsf{AB}} Bw.$$

Thus, for each view w covered by AB, we compute $C(\mathsf{ABC}) - C(\mathsf{AB})$, because ABC is the only materialized view when the algorithm begins. That is, $C(\mathsf{ABC}) - C(\mathsf{AB})$ is the benefit of materializing AB for each view covered by AB. For example, to compute B without materializing AB, we would need to scan ABC at cost 2,000. With AB being materialized, this reduces to 400. The same occurs with all the views that have a path to All that passes through AB, that is, A, B, All, and AB itself. For C, AC, and BC, the materialization of AB is irrelevant. Then,

$$B(\mathsf{AB}, S) = 1{,}600 + 1{,}600 + 1{,}600 + 1{,}600 = 6{,}400.$$

In an analogous way,

$$B(\text{BC}, S) = \sum_{w \preceq \text{BC}} Bw = 1{,}300 \times 4 = 5{,}200,$$

which is the benefit of materializing BC for the computation of B, C, All, and BC itself. If we continue in this fashion, we will find that AB is the view to materialize because it yields the maximum benefit. Thus, when we start the second iteration, we have $S = \{\text{ABC}, \text{AB}\}$.

We now explain the second iteration. The benefit of materializing BC is $B(\text{BC}, S) = \sum_{w \preceq \text{BC}} Bw = 1{,}300 + 1{,}300 = 2{,}600$, corresponding to C and BC itself since materializing BC has no effect on the nodes that reach All through AB because they can be computed from AB at a cost of 400. For example, B can be computed from AB at cost 400; therefore, materializing BC yields no benefit for the computation of B. On the other hand, the benefit of materializing B is $B(\text{B}, S) = \sum_{w \preceq \text{B}} Bw = 340 \times 2$ since both B and All can be computed from AB at a cost $Bw = 400-60$ each. Also note that the benefit of materializing C is $B(\text{C}, S) = \sum_{w \preceq \text{C}} Bw = 1{,}960 + 400 - 40 = 2{,}320$ since the benefit for computing All is just $400 - 40$ because All can be computed from AB at a cost of 400. We will eventually choose BC in the second iteration with a benefit of 2,600.

Finally, the three views to materialize will be AB, BC, and AC, with a total benefit of 10,100. The following table shows the complete computation. Each cell in the table shows the benefit of selecting a given view in an iteration.

View	First Iteration	Second Iteration	Third Iteration
AB	**1,600 × 4 = 6,400**		
AC	1,100 × 4 = 4,400	1,100 × 2 = 2,200	1,100 × 1 = 1,100
BC	1,300 × 4 = 5,200	**1,300 x 2 = 2,600**	
A	1,980 × 2 = 3,960	380 × 2 = 760	380 × 2 = 760
B	1,940 × 2 = 3,880	340 × 2 = 680	340 × 2 = 680
C	1,960 × 2 = 3,920	1,960 + (400 - 40) = 2,320	660 + 360 = 1,020
All	1,999 × 1 = 1,999	399 × 1 = 399	399 × 1 = 399

It can be proved that the benefit of this greedy algorithm is at least 63% of the benefit of the optimal algorithm. On the other hand, even this is a classic algorithm, pedagogically interesting for presenting the problem, a clear drawback is that it does not consider the frequency of the queries over each view. Thus, in our example, even though the sum of the benefit is maximum, nothing is said about the frequency of the queries asking for A or B. This drawback has been addressed in several research papers.

7.5   Indexes for Data Warehouses

A major concern in database management systems (DBMSs) is to provide fast access to data. Given a query, a relational DBMS attempts to choose the best possible access path to the data. A popular way to speed data access is known as indexing. An index provides a quick way to locate data of interest. Almost all the queries asking for data that satisfy a certain condition are answered with the help of some index.

As an example, consider the following SQL query:

```
SELECT *
FROM    Employee
WHERE EmployeeKey = 1234
```

Without an index on attribute EmployeeKey, we should perform a complete scan of table Employee (unless it is ordered), whereas with the help of an index over such attribute, a single disk block access will do the job since this attribute is a key for the relation.

Although indexing provides advantages for fast data access, it has a drawback: almost every update on an indexed attribute also requires an index update. This suggests that designers and database administrators should be careful on defining indexes because their proliferation can lead to bad updating performance.

The most popular indexing technique in relational databases is the B^+-tree. All major vendors provide support for some variation of B^+-tree indexes. A B^+-tree index is a multilevel structure containing a root node and pointers to the next lower level in a tree. The lowest level is formed by the leaves of the tree, which in general contain a record identifier for the corresponding data. Often, the size of each node equals the size of a block, and each node holds a large number of keys, so the resulting tree has a low number of levels and the retrieval of a record can be very fast. This works well if the attribute being indexed is a key of the file or if the number of duplicate values is low.

We have seen that queries submitted to an OLAP system are of a very different nature than those of an OLTP system. Therefore, new indexing strategies are needed for OLAP systems. Some indexing requirements for a data warehouse system are as follows:

- Symmetric partial match queries: Most OLAP queries involve partial ranges. An example is the query "Total sales from January 2006 to December 2010." As queries can ask for ranges over any dimension, all the dimensions of the data cube should be symmetrically indexed so that they can be searched simultaneously.
- Indexing at multiple levels of aggregation: Since summary tables can be large or queries may ask for particular values of aggregate data, summary tables must be indexed in the same way as base nonaggregated tables.

- Efficient batch update: As already said, updates are not so critical in OLAP systems, which allows more columns to be indexed. However, the refreshing time of a data warehouse must be taken into account when designing the indexing schema. Indeed, the time needed for reconstructing the indexes after the refreshing extends the downtime of the warehouse.
- Sparse data: Typically, only 20% of the cells in a data cube are nonempty. The indexing schema must thus be able to deal efficiently with sparse and nonsparse data.

To cope with these requirements, two kinds of indexes are commonly used in data warehouse systems: bitmap indexes and join indexes. We study these indexes next.

7.5.1 Bitmap Indexes

Consider the table Product in Fig. 7.10a. For clarity, we assume a simplified example with only six products. We show next how to build a bitmap index on attributes QuantityPerUnit and UnitPrice. There are, respectively, four and five possible values for these attributes in table Product. We create a bit vector of length 6 (the number of rows in Product) for each possible attribute value, as shown in Fig. 7.10b,c. In a position i of vector j, there is a '1' if the product in row i has the value in the label of column j, and a '0' otherwise. For example, in the first row of the table in Fig. 7.10b, there is a '1' in the vector with label 25, indicating that the corresponding product (p1) has a value 25 in attribute QuantityPerUnit. Note that we have included the product key in the first column of the bitmap index to facilitate the reading, although this column is not part of the index.

Now, assume the query "Products with unit price equal to 75." A query processor will just need to know that there is a bitmap index over UnitPrice in Product and look for the bit vector with a value of 75. The vector positions where a '1' is found indicate the positions of the records that satisfy the query, in this case, the third row in the table.

For queries involving a search range, the process is a little bit more involved. Consider the query "Products having between 45 and 55 pieces per unit, and with a unit price between 100 and 200." To compute this query, we first look for the index over QuantityPerUnit and the bit vectors with labels between 45 and 55. There are two such vectors, with labels 45 and 50. The products having between 45 and 55 pieces per unit are the ones corresponding to an OR operation between these vectors. Then, we look for the index over UnitPrice and the bit vectors with labels between 100 and 200. There are three such vectors, with labels 100, 110, and 120. The products having unit price between 100 and 200 are, again, the ones corresponding to an OR operation between these vectors. We obtain the two vectors labeled OR1 and OR2 in Fig. 7.11a,b, respectively. Finally, an AND between these

a

ProductKey	ProductName	QuantityPerUnit	UnitPrice	Discontinued	CategoryKey
p1	prod1	25	60	No	c1
p2	prod2	45	60	Yes	c1
p3	prod3	50	75	No	c2
p4	prod4	50	100	Yes	c2
p5	prod5	50	120	No	c3
p6	prod6	70	110	Yes	c4

b

	25	45	50	70
p1	1	0	0	0
p2	0	1	0	0
p3	0	0	1	0
p4	0	0	1	0
p5	0	0	1	0
p6	0	0	0	1

c

	60	75	100	110	120
p1	1	0	0	0	0
p2	1	0	0	0	0
p3	0	1	0	0	0
p4	0	0	1	0	0
p5	0	0	0	0	1
p6	0	0	0	1	0

Fig. 7.10 An example of bitmap indexes for a Product dimension table. (a) Product dimension table. (b) Bitmap index for attribute QuantityPerUnit. (c) Bitmap index for attribute UnitPrice

a

	45	50	OR1
p1	0	0	0
p2	1	0	1
p3	0	1	1
p4	0	1	1
p5	0	1	1
p6	0	0	0

b

	100	110	120	OR2
p1	0	0	0	0
p2	0	0	0	0
p3	0	0	0	0
p4	1	0	0	1
p5	0	0	1	1
p6	0	1	0	1

c

	OR1	OR2	AND
p1	0	0	0
p2	1	0	0
p3	1	0	0
p4	1	1	1
p5	1	1	1
p6	0	1	0

Fig. 7.11 Finding the products having between 45 and 55 pieces per unit and with a unit price between 100 and 200. (a) OR for QuantityPerUnit. (b) OR for UnitPrice. (c) AND operation

two vectors, shown in Fig. 7.11c, gives the rows satisfying both conditions. The result is that products p4 and p5 satisfy the query.

The operation just described is the main reason of the high performance achieved by bitmapped indexing in the querying process. When performing AND, OR, and NOT operations, the system will just perform a bit comparison, and the resulting bit vector is obtained at a very low CPU cost.

The above example suggests that the best opportunities for these indexes are found where the cardinality of the attributes being indexed is low.

Otherwise, we will need to deal with large indexes composed of a large number of sparse vectors, and the index can become space inefficient. Continuing with our example, assume that the Product table contains 100,000 rows. A bitmapped index on the attribute UnitPrice will occupy $100,000 \times 6/8$ bytes $= 0.075$ MB. A traditional B-tree index would occupy approximately $100,000 \times 4 = 0.4$ MB (assume 4 bytes are required to store a record identifier). It follows that the space required by a bitmapped index is proportional to the number of entries in the index and to the number of rows, while the space required by traditional indexes depends strongly on the number of records to be indexed. OLAP systems typically index attributes with low cardinality. Therefore, one of the reasons for using bitmap indexes is that they occupy less space than B^+-tree indexes, as shown above.

There are two main reasons that make bitmap indexes not adequate in OLTP environments. On the one hand, these systems are subject to frequent updates, which are not efficiently handled by bitmap indexes. On the other hand, in database systems locking occurs at page level and not at the record level. Thus, concurrency can be heavily affected if bitmap indexes are used for operational systems, given that a locked page would lock a large number on index entries.

7.5.2 Bitmap Compression

As we have seen, bitmap indexes are typically sparse: the bit vectors have a few '1's among many '0's. This characteristic makes them appropriate for compression. We have also seen that even without compression, for low cardinality attributes, bitmap outperforms B^+-tree in terms of space. In addition, bitmap compression allows indexes to support high-cardinality attributes. The downside of this strategy is the overhead of decompression during query evaluation. Given the many textbooks on data compression and the high number of compression strategies, we next just give the idea of a simple and popular strategy, called run-length encoding (RLE). Many sophisticated techniques are based on RLE, as we comment on the bibliographic notes section of this chapter.

Run-length encoding is very popular for compressing black and white and grayscale images since it takes advantage of the fact that the bit value of an image is likely to be the same as the one of its neighboring bits. There are many variants of this technique, most of them based on how they manage decoding ambiguity. The basic idea is the following: if a bit of value v occurs n consecutive times, replace these occurrences with the number n. This sequence of bits is called a run of length n.

In the case of bitmap indexes, since the bit vectors have a few '1's among many '0's, if a bit of value '0' occurs n consecutive times, we replace these occurrences with the number n. The '1's are written as they come in the vector. Let us analyze the following sequence of bits: 0000000111000000000011. We have two runs of lengths 7 and 10, respectively, three '1's in between, and two '1's at the end. This vector can be trivially represented as the sequence of integers 7,1,1,1,10,1,1. However, this encoding can be ambiguous, since we may not be able to distinguish if a '1' is an actual bit or the length of a run. Let us see how we can handle this problem. Let us call j the number of bits needed to represent n, the length of a run. We can represent the run as a sequence of $j - 1$ '1' bits, followed by a '0', followed by n in binary format. In our example, the first run, 0000000, will be encoded as 110111, where the first two '1's correspond to the $j - 1$ part, '0' indicates the component of the run, and the last three '1's are the number 7 (the length of the run) in binary format.

Finally, the bitmap vector above is encoded as **1100111111111010101**, where the encoding is indicated in boldface and the actual bits of the vector are indicated in normal font. Note that since we know the length of the array, we could get rid of the trailing '1's to save even more space.

7.5.3 Join Indexes

It is a well-known fact that join is one of the most expensive database operations. Join indexes are particularly efficient for join processing in decision-support queries since they take advantage of the star schema design, where, as we have seen, the fact table is related to the dimension tables by foreign keys, and joins are typically performed on these foreign keys.

The main idea of join indexes consists in precomputing the join as shown in Fig. 7.12. Consider the dimension table **Product** and the fact table **Sales** from the Northwind data warehouse. We can expect that many queries require a join between both tables using the foreign key. Figure 7.12a depicts table **Product**, with an additional attribute **RowIDProd**, and Fig. 7.12b shows table **Sales** extended with an additional attribute **RowIDSales**. Figure 7.12c shows the corresponding join index, basically a table containing pointers to the matching rows. This structure can be used to efficiently answer queries requiring a join between tables **Product** and **Sales**.

A particular case of join index is the *bitmap join index*. Suppose now that a usual query asks for total sales of discontinued products. In this case, a bitmap join index can be created on table **Sales** over the attribute **Discontinued**, as shown in Fig. 7.12d. As can be seen, the sales pertaining to discontinued products (products **p2** and **p4**) have a '1' in the bit vector labeled 'Yes'. At first sight, this may appear to be strange because attribute **Discontinued** does not belong to **Sales**. Actually what happens is that the index points to the tuples in **Sales** that store sales of discontinued products. This is done by precomputing the join between both tables through the attribute **ProductKey** and then creating a bitmap index on **Sales** for each possible value of the

a

RowID Product	Product Key	Product Name	...	Discontinued	...
1	p1	prod1	...	No	...
2	p2	prod2	...	Yes	...
3	p3	prod3	...	No	...
4	p4	prod4	...	Yes	...
5	p5	prod5	...	No	...
6	p6	prod6	...	Yes	...

b

RowID Sales	Product Key	Customer Key	Time Key	Sales Amount
1	p1	c1	t1	100
2	p1	c2	t1	100
3	p2	c2	t2	100
4	p2	c2	t3	100
5	p3	c3	t3	100
6	p4	c3	t4	100
7	p5	c4	t5	100

c

RowID Sales	RowID Product
1	1
2	1
3	2
4	2
5	3
6	4
7	5

d

Yes	No
0	1
0	1
1	0
1	0
0	1
1	0
0	1

Fig. 7.12 An example of a join and a bitmap join indexes. (**a**) Product dimension table. (**b**) Sales fact table. (**c**) Join index. (**d**) Bitmap join index on attribute Discontinued

attribute Discontinued ('Yes' or 'No'). A query like the one above will be answered straightforwardly since we have precomputed the join between the two tables and the bitmap over the attribute Discontinued.

In the next section, we will show how bitmap and join indexes are used in query evaluation.

7.6 Evaluation of Star Queries

Queries over star schemas are called *star queries* since they make use of the star schema structure, joining the fact table with the dimension tables. For example, a typical star query over our simplified Northwind example in Sect. 7.3 would be "Total sales of discontinued products, by customer name and product name." This query reads in SQL:

```
SELECT    C.CustomerName, P.ProductName, SUM(S.SalesAmount)
FROM      Sales S, Customer C, Product P
WHERE     S.CustomerKey = C.CustomerKey AND
          S.ProductKey = P.ProductKey AND P.Discontinued = 'Yes'
GROUP BY  C.CustomerName, P.ProductName
```

a

Product Key	Product Name	...	Discontinued	...
p1	prod1	...	No	...
p2	prod2	...	Yes	...
p3	prod3	...	No	...
p4	prod4	...	Yes	...
p5	prod5	...	No	...
p6	prod6	...	Yes	...

b

Yes	No
0	1
1	0
0	1
1	0
0	1
1	0

c

Customer Key	Customer Name	Address	Postal Code	...
c1	cust1	35 Main St.	7373	...
c2	cust2	Av. Roosevelt 50	1050	...
c3	cust3	Av. Louise 233	1080	...
c4	cust4	Rue Gabrielle	1180	...

d

Product Key	Customer Key	Time Key	Sales Amount
p1	c1	t1	100
p1	c2	t1	100
p2	c2	t2	100
p2	c2	t3	100
p3	c3	t3	100
p4	c3	t4	100
p5	c4	t5	100

e

c1	c2	c3	c4
1	0	0	0
0	1	0	0
0	1	0	0
0	1	0	0
0	0	1	0
0	0	1	0
0	0	0	1

f

p1	p2	p3	p4	p5	p6
1	0	0	0	0	0
1	0	0	0	0	0
0	1	0	0	0	0
0	1	0	0	0	0
0	0	1	0	0	0
0	0	0	1	0	0
0	0	0	0	1	0

g

Yes	No
0	1
0	1
1	0
1	0
0	1
1	0
0	1

Fig. 7.13 An example of evaluation of star queries with bitmap indexes. (**a**) Product table. (**b**) Bitmap for Discontinued. (**c**) Customer table. (**d**) Sales fact table. (**e**) Bitmap for CustomerKey. (**f**) Bitmap for ProductKey. (**g**) Bitmap join index for Discontinued

We will study now how this query is evaluated by an engine using the indexing strategies studied above.

An efficient evaluation of our example query would require the definition of a B$^+$-tree over the dimension keys CustomerKey and ProductKey and bitmap indexes on Discontinued in the Product dimension table and on the foreign key columns in the fact table Sales. Figure 7.13a,c,d shows the Product and Customer dimension tables and the Sales fact table, while the bitmap indexes are depicted in Fig. 7.13b,e,f.

Let us describe how this query is evaluated by an OLAP engine. The first step consists in obtaining the record numbers of the records that satisfy the condition over the dimension, that is, Discontinued = 'Yes'. As shown in the bitmap index (Fig. 7.13b), such records are the ones with ProductKey values p2, p4, and p6. We then access the bitmap vectors with these labels in Fig. 7.13f, thus performing a join between Product (Fig. 7.13a) and Sales. Only the vectors labeled p2 and p4 match the search since there is no fact record for product p6. The third, fourth, and sixth rows in the fact table are the answer since they are the only ones with a '1' in the corresponding vectors in Fig. 7.13f. We then obtain the key values for the CustomerKey (c2 and c3) using the bitmap index in Fig. 7.13e. With these values we search in the B$^+$-tree index over the keys in tables Product and Customer to find the names of the products and the customer satisfying the query condition. Note that this performs the join between the dimensions and the fact table. As we can see in Figs. 7.10a and 7.13c, the records correspond to the names cust2, cust3, prod2, and prod4, respectively. Finally, the query answer is (cust2, prod2, 200) and (cust3, prod4, 100).

Note that the last join with Customer would not be needed if the query would have been of the following form:

```
SELECT      S.CustomerKey, P.ProductKey, SUM(SalesAmount)
FROM        Sales S, Product P
WHERE       S.ProductKey = P.ProductKey AND P.Discontinued = 'Yes'
GROUP BY S.CustomerKey, P.ProductKey
```

The query above only mentions attributes in the fact table Sales. Thus, the only join that needs to be performed is the one between Product and Sales.

We illustrate now the evaluation of star queries using bitmap join indexes. We have seen that the main idea is to create a bitmap index over a fact table using an attribute belonging to a dimension table, precomputing the join between both tables and building a bitmap index over the latter. Figure 7.13g shows the bitmap join index between Sales and Product over the attribute Discontinued. Finding the facts corresponding to sales of discontinued products, as required by the query under study, is now straightforward: we just need to find the vector labeled 'Yes', and look for the bits set to '1'. During query evaluation, this avoids the first step described in the previous section, when evaluating the query with bitmap indexes. This is done at the expense of the cost of (off-line) precomputation.

Note that this strategy can reduce dramatically the evaluation cost if in the SELECT clause there are no dimension attributes, and thus, we do not need to join back with the dimensions using the B$^+$-tree as explained above. Thus, the answer for the alternative query above would just require a simple scan of the Sales table, in the worst case.

7.7 Data Warehouse Partitioning

In a database, partitioning or fragmentation divides a table into smaller data sets (each one called a partition) to better support the management and processing of very large volumes of data. Partitioning can be applied to tables as well as to indexes. Further, a partitioned index can be defined over an unpartitioned table, and vice versa, a partitioned table may have unpartitioned indexes defined over it. Database vendors provide several different partitioning methods, each of them having particular design considerations.

There are two ways of partitioning a table: vertically and horizontally. **Vertical partitioning** splits the attributes of a table into groups that can be independently stored. For example, a table can be partitioned such that the most often used attributes are stored in one partition, while other less often used attributes are kept in another partition. In this way, more records can be brought into main memory, reducing their processing time. On the other hand, **horizontal partitioning** divides a table into smaller tables that have the same structure than the full table but fewer records. For example, if some queries require the most recent data while others access older data, a fact table can be horizontally partitioned according to some time frame, for example, years. An obvious advantage of this kind of partitioning is that refreshing the data warehouse is more efficient since only the last partition must be accessed.

In addition to the above, partitioning database tables into smaller data sets facilitates administrative tasks, increases query performance especially when parallel processing is applied, and enables access to a smaller subset of the data (if the user's selection does not refer to all partitions). Also, partitioning is recommended when the contents of a table need to be distributed across different servers. In the case of indexes, partitioning is advised, for example, in order to perform maintenance on parts of the data without invalidating the entire index. Finally, we remark that from an application perspective, a partitioned table is identical to a nonpartitioned table, thus partitioning is transparent for writing SQL queries and DML statements.

We next analyze further some characteristics of partitioning.

7.7.1   Queries in Partitioned Databases

There are two classic techniques of partitioning related to query evaluation. **Partition pruning** is the typical way of improving query performance using partitioning, often producing performance enhancements of several orders of magnitude. For example, a Sales fact table in a warehouse can be partitioned by month. A query requesting orders for a single month only needs to access the partition corresponding to such a month. If the Sales table contains 2 years of historical data, this query would access one partition instead of 24 ones, greatly reducing query response time.

The execution time of **joins** can also be enhanced by using partitioning. This occurs when the two tables to be joined are partitioned on the join attributes or, in the case of foreign key joins, when the reference table is partitioned on its primary key. In these cases, a large join is broken into smaller joins that occur between each of the partitions, producing significant performance gains, which can be even improved taking advantage of parallel execution.

7.7.2 Managing Partitioned Databases

Partitioning also improves the job of database and data warehouse administrators, since tables and indexes are partitioned into smaller, more manageable pieces of data. In this way, maintenance operations can be performed on these particular portions of tables. For example, a database administrator may back up just a single partition of a table instead of the whole one. In addition, partitioned database tables and indexes induce high data availability. For example, if some partitions of a table become unavailable, it is possible that most of the other partitions of the table remain on-line and available, in particular if partitions are allocated to various different devices. In this way, applications can continue to execute queries and transactions that do not need to access the unavailable partitions. Even during normal operation, since each partition can be stored in separate tablespaces, backup and recovery operations can be performed over individual partitions, independent from each other. Thus, the active parts of the database can be made available sooner than in the case of an unpartitioned table.

7.7.3 Partitioning Strategies

There are three most common partitioning strategies in database systems: range partitioning, hash partitioning, and list partitioning.

The most usual type of partitioning is **range partitioning**, which maps records to partitions based on ranges of values of the partitioning key. The temporal dimension is a natural candidate for range partitioning, although other attributes can be used. For example, if a table contains a date column defined as the partitioning key, the January 2012 partition will contain rows with key values from January 1, 2012, to January 31, 2012.

Hash partitioning maps records to partitions based on a hashing algorithm applied to the partitioning key. The hashing algorithm distributes rows among partitions in a uniform fashion, yielding, ideally, partitions of the same size. This is typically used when partitions are distributed in several devices and, in general, when data are not partitioned based on time since it is more likely to yield even record distribution across partitions.

Finally, **list partitioning** enables to explicitly control how rows are mapped to partitions specifying a list of values for the partitioning key. In this way, data can be organized in an ad hoc fashion.

Some vendors (like Oracle) support the notion of **composite partition-ing**, which combines the basic data distribution methods above. In this way, a table can be range partitioned, and each partition can be further subdivided using hash partitioning.

7.8   Physical Design in SQL Server and Analysis Services

In this section, we discuss how the theoretical concepts studied in this chapter are applied in Microsoft SQL Server. We start with the study of how materialized views are supported in these tools. We then introduce a novel kind of index provided by SQL Server called column-store index. Then, we study partitioning, followed by a description of how the three types of multidimensional data representation introduced in Chap. 5, namely, ROLAP, MOLAP, and HOLAP, are implemented in Analysis Services.

7.8.1   Indexed Views

In SQL Server, materialized views are called indexed views. Basically, an indexed view consists in the creation of a unique clustered index on a view, thus precomputing and materializing such view. We have seen that this is a mandatory optimization technique in data warehouse environments.

When we create an indexed view, it is essential to verify that the view and the base tables satisfy the many conditions required by the tool. For example, the definition of an indexed view must be deterministic, meaning that all expressions in the SELECT, WHERE, and GROUP BY clauses are deterministic. For instance, the DATEADD function is deterministic because it always returns the same result for any given set of argument values for its three parameters. On the contrary, GETDATE is not deterministic because it is always invoked with the same argument, but the value it returns changes each time it is executed. Also, indexed views may be created with the SCHEMABINDING option. This indicates that the base tables cannot be modified in a way that would affect the view definition. For example, the following statement creates an indexed view computing the total sales by employee over the Sales fact table in the Northwind data warehouse:

```
CREATE VIEW EmployeeSales WITH SCHEMABINDING AS (
        SELECT    EmployeeKey, SUM(UnitPrice * OrderQty * Discount)
                  AS TotalAmount, COUNT(*) AS SalesCount
        FROM      Sales
        GROUP BY EmployeeKey )
CREATE UNIQUE CLUSTERED INDEX CI_EmployeeSales ON
        EmployeeSales (EmployeeKey)
```

An indexed view can be used in two ways: when a query explicitly references the indexed view and when the view is not referenced in a query but the query optimizer determines that the view can be used to generate a lower-cost query plan.

In the first case, when a query refers to a view, the definition of the view is expanded until it refers only to base tables. This process is called view expansion. If we do not want this to happen, we can use the NOEXPAND hint, which forces the query optimizer to treat the view like an ordinary table with a clustered index, preventing view expansion. The syntax is as follows:

```
SELECT EmployeeKey, EmployeeName, ...
FROM   Employee, EmployeeSales WITH (NOEXPAND)
WHERE ...
```

In the second case, when the view is not referenced in a query, the query optimizer determines when an indexed view can be used in a given query execution. Thus, existing applications can benefit from newly created indexed views without changing those applications. Several conditions are checked to determine if an indexed view can cover the entire query or a part of it, for example, (a) the tables in the FROM clause of the query must be a superset of the tables in the FROM clause of the indexed view; (b) the join conditions in the query must be a superset of the join conditions in the view; and (c) the aggregate columns in the query must be derivable from a subset of the aggregate columns in the view.

7.8.2 Partition-Aligned Indexed Views

If a partitioned table is created in SQL Server and indexed views are built on this table, SQL Server automatically partitions the indexed view by using the same partition scheme as the table. An indexed view built in this way is called a partition-aligned indexed view. The main feature of such a view is that the database query processor automatically maintains it when a new partition of the table is created, without the need of dropping and recreating the view. This improves the manageability of indexed views.

We show next how we can create a partition-aligned indexed view on the Sales fact table of the Northwind data warehouse. To facilitate maintenance and for efficiency reasons, we decide to partition this fact table by year. This is done as follows.

To create a partition scheme, we need first to define the partition function. We want to define a scheme that partitions the table by year, from 1996 through 1998. The partition function is called PartByYear and takes as input

an attribute of integer type, which represents the values of the surrogate keys
for the Time dimension:

```
CREATE PARTITION FUNCTION [PartByYear] (INT)
AS RANGE LEFT FOR VALUES (184, 549, 730);
```

Here, 184, 549, and 730 are, respectively, the surrogate keys representing
the dates 31/12/1996, 31/12/1997, and 31/12/1998. These dates are the
boundaries of the partition intervals. RANGE LEFT means that the records
with values less or equal than 184 will belong to the first partition, the ones
greater than 184 and less or equal than 549 to the second, and the records
with values greater than 730 to the third partition.

Once the partition function has been defined, the partition scheme is
created as follows:

```
CREATE PARTITION SCHEME [SalesPartScheme]
    AS PARTITION [PartByYear] ALL to ( [PRIMARY] );
```

Here, PRIMARY means that the partitions will be stored in the primary
filegroup, that is, the group that contains the startup database information.
Filegroup names can be used instead (can be more than one). ALL indicates
that all partitions will be stored in the primary filegroup.

The Sales fact table is created as a partitioned table as follows:

```
CREATE TABLE Sales (CustomerKey INT, EmployeeKey INT,
    OrderDateKey INT, ... ) ON SalesPartScheme(OrderDateKey)
```

The statement ON SalesPartScheme(OrderDateKey) tells that the table will
be partitioned following the SalesPartScheme and the partition function will
have OrderDateKey as argument.

Now we create an indexed view over the Sales table, as explained in
Sect. 7.8.1. We first create the view:

```
CREATE VIEW SalesByDateProdEmp WITH SCHEMABINDING AS (
    SELECT      OrderDateKey, ProductKey, EmployeeKey, COUNT(*) AS Cnt,
                SUM(SalesAmount) AS SalesAmount
    FROM        Sales
    GROUP BY OrderDateKey, ProductKey, EmployeeKey )
```

Finally, we materialize the view:

```
CREATE UNIQUE CLUSTERED INDEX UCI_SalesByDateProdEmp
    ON SalesByDateProdEmp (OrderDateKey, ProductKey, EmployeeKey)
    ON SalesPartScheme(OrderDateKey)
```

Since the clustered index was created using the same partition scheme, this
is a partition-aligned indexed view.

7.8.3   Column-Store Indexes

SQL Server provides column-store indexes, which store data by column. In a sense, column-store indexes work like a vertical partitioning commented above and can dramatically enhance performance for certain kinds of queries. The same concepts that were explained for bitmap indexes and their use in star-join evaluation also apply to column-store indexes. We will provide a detailed study of this kind of indexes in Chap. 13.

We now show how a column-store index is defined. For this, suppose there is a materialized view Sales2012 that selects from the Sales fact table the data pertaining to 2012. Suppose that many queries request the attributes DueDateKey, EmployeeKey, and SalesAmount. In order to speed up access to the Sales2012 view, we can define a column-store index over it as follows:

```
CREATE NONCLUSTERED COLUMNSTORE INDEX CSI_Sales2012
    ON Sales2012 (DueDateKey, EmployeeKey, SalesAmount)
```

Column-store indexes have important limitations. One of them is that a table over which a column-store index is defined cannot be updated. Thus, we cannot define the index over the original Sales fact table since it is subject to updates and create instead the index over a view.

Bitmap indexes are not supported in SQL Server. Instead, SQL Server provides a so-called bitmap filter. A **bitmap filter** is a bitmap created at execution time by the query processor to filter values on tables. Bitmap filtering can be introduced in the query plan after optimization, or it can be introduced dynamically by the query optimizer during the generation of the query plan. The latter is called optimized bitmap filter and can significantly improve the performance of data warehouse queries that use star schemas by removing nonqualifying rows from the fact table early in the query plan. Note however that this is completely different from defining a bitmap index like we explained above and which is supported by other database systems like Oracle and Informix.

7.8.4   Partitions in Analysis Services

In Analysis Services, a partition is a container for a portion of the data of a measure group. Defining a partition requires to specify:

- Basic information, like name of the partition, the storage mode, and the processing mode.
- Slicing definition, which is an MDX expression specifying a tuple or a set.
- Aggregation design, which is a collection of aggregation definitions that can be shared across multiple partitions.

The data for a partition in a measure group must be exclusive of the data in any other partition in the measure group; otherwise, these data would be considered more than once. Every measure group has at least one partition, created when the measure group is defined. This initial partition is based on a single fact table in the data source view of the cube. When there are multiple partitions for a measure group, each partition can reference a different table in either the data source view or in the underlying relational data source for the cube. Also, more than one partition in a measure group can reference the same table.

Analogously to what we explained in the previous section for database tables, partitions allow large data cubes to be managed efficiently, for example, by distributing source and aggregate data of a cube across multiple hard disks and multiple servers. This improves query performance, load performance, and efficiency of cube maintenance. For example, if in the Northwind data cube we partition data by year, only the last partition will be processed when current information is added to the cube. Partitions can later be merged. For example, at the end of a year, the quarterly partitions can be merged into a single partition for the year and a new partition created for the first quarter of the new year. Thus, partitions can be configured, added, or dropped by the database administrator. Each partition is stored in a separate set of files. Aggregate data of each partition can be stored on either the instance of Analysis Services where the partition is defined or on another instance.

Finally, the storage mode of each partition can be configured independently of other partitions in the measure group, for example, using any combination of source data location, storage mode, and aggregation design. We study this feature next.

ROLAP Storage

In the **ROLAP** storage mode, the aggregations of a partition are stored in indexed views in the relational database specified as the data source of the partition. The indexed views in the data source are accessed to answer queries. In the ROLAP storage, the query response time and the processing time are generally slower than with the MOLAP or HOLAP storage modes (see below). However, ROLAP enables users to view data in real time and can save storage space when working with large data sets that are infrequently queried, such as purely historical data.

If a partition uses the ROLAP storage mode and its source data are stored in SQL Server, Analysis Services tries to create indexed views to store aggregations. When these views cannot be created, aggregation tables are not created. Indexed views for aggregations can be created if several conditions hold in the ROLAP partition and the tables in it. The more relevant ones are as follows:

*   The partition cannot contain measures that use the MIN or MAX aggregate functions.
*   Each table in the schema of the ROLAP partition must be used only once.
*   All table names in the partition schema must be qualified with the owner name, for example, [dbo].[Customer].
*   All tables in the partition schema must have the same owner.
*   The source columns of the partition measures must not be nullable.

MOLAP Storage

In the **MOLAP** storage mode, both the aggregations and a copy of the source data are stored in a multidimensional structure. Such structures are highly optimized to maximize query performance. Since a copy of the source data resides in the multidimensional structure, queries can be processed without accessing the source data of the partition.

Note however that data in a MOLAP partition reflect the most recently processed state of a partition. Thus, when source data are updated, objects in the MOLAP storage must be reprocessed to include the changes and make them available to users. Changes can be processed from scratch or, if possible, incrementally, as explained in Sect. 7.2. This update can be performed without taking the partition or cube off-line. However, if structural changes to OLAP objects are performed, the cube must be taken off-line. In these cases, it is recommended to update and process cubes on a staging server.

HOLAP Storage

The **HOLAP** storage mode combines features of the previously explained MOLAP and ROLAP modes. Like MOLAP, in HOLAP the aggregations of the partition are stored in a multidimensional data structure. However, like in ROLAP, HOLAP does not store a copy of the source data. Thus, if queries only access summary data of a partition, HOLAP works like MOLAP very efficiently. Queries that need to access unaggregated source data must retrieve it from the relational database and therefore will not be as fast as if it were stored in a MOLAP structure. However, this can be solved if the query can use cached data, that is, data that are stored in main memory rather than on disk.

In summary, partitions stored as HOLAP are smaller than the equivalent MOLAP partitions since they do not contain source data. On the other hand, they can answer faster than ROLAP partitions for queries involving summary data. Thus, this mode tries to capture the best of both worlds.

Defining Partitions in Analysis Services

We show next how MOLAP, ROLAP, and HOLAP partitions over measure
groups can be defined in Analysis Services.

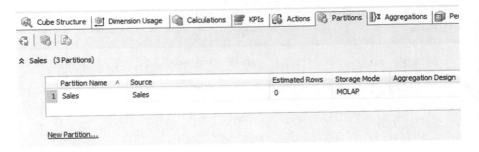

Fig. 7.14 Initial partition for the Sales measure group

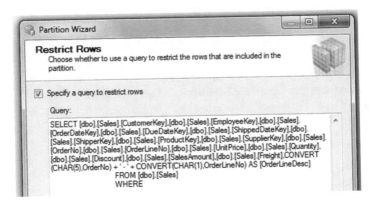

Fig. 7.15 Template query that defines a partition

Figure 7.14 shows a unique initial partition for the Sales measure group in a
data cube created from the Northwind cube. As we can see, this is a MOLAP
partition. Assume now that, for efficiency reasons, we want to partition this
measure group by year. Since in the Northwind data warehouse we have
data from 1996, 1997, and 1998, we will create one partition for each year.
We decided that the first and the last ones will be MOLAP partitions, and
the middle one, a ROLAP partition. To define the limits for the partitions,
the Analysis Services cube wizard creates an SQL query template, shown in
Fig. 7.15, which must be completed in the WHERE clause with the key range
corresponding to each partition. In order to obtain the first and last keys for

each period, a query such as the following one must be addressed to the data warehouse:

```
SELECT MIN(TimeKey), MAX(TimeKey)
FROM   Time
WHERE Date >= '1997-01-01' AND Date <= '1997-12-31'
```

The values obtained from this query can then be entered in the wizard for defining the partition for 1997.

Figure 7.16 shows the three final partitions of the measure group Sales. Note that in that figure the second partition is highlighted. Figure 7.17 shows the properties of such partition, in particular the ROLAP storage mode. This dialog box also can be used to change the storage mode.

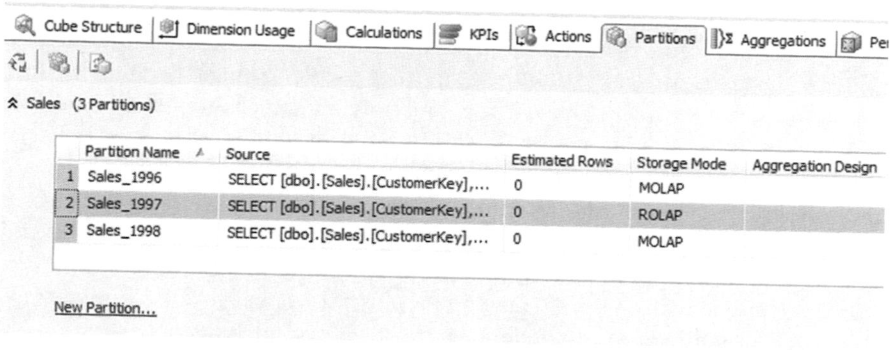

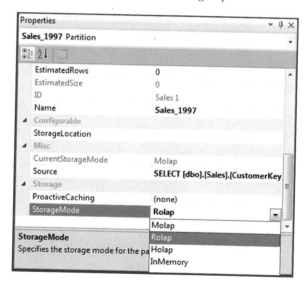

Fig. 7.16 Final partitions for the Sales measure group

Fig. 7.17 Storage mode for the Sales_1997 partition

7.9   Query Performance in Analysis Services

We now briefly describe how query performance can be enhanced in Analysis Services through several techniques.

The first step must be to optimize cube and measure group design. For this, many of the issues studied in this book apply. For example, it is suggested to use cascading attribute relationships, like Day $\rightarrow$ Month $\rightarrow$ Quarter $\rightarrow$ Year, and define user hierarchies of related attributes within each dimension. These are called natural hierarchies. The reason for this is that attributes participating in natural hierarchies are materialized on disk and are automatically considered to be aggregation candidates. Redundant relationships between attributes must be removed to assist the query execution engine in generating an appropriate query plan. Also, the cube space must be kept as small as possible, only including measure groups that are needed. Measures that are queried together must be allocated to the same measure group since if a query retrieves measures from multiple measure groups, it will require multiple storage engine operations. Large sets of measures that are not queried together must be placed into separate measure groups. Large parent-child hierarchies must be avoided, because in these hierarchies aggregations are created only for the key attribute and the top attribute. Thus, queries asking for cells at intermediate levels are calculated at query time and can be slow for large parent-child dimensions. Many-to-many dimension performance must be optimized, since it requires a run-time join between the data measure group and the intermediate measure group. Also, if possible, the size of the intermediate fact table underlying the intermediate measure group must be reduced.

Aggregations are also used by Analysis Services to enhance query performance. Thus, the most efficient aggregations for the query workload must be selected to reduce the number of records that the storage engine needs to scan on disk to evaluate a query. When designing aggregations, we must evaluate the benefits that aggregations provide when querying, against the time it takes to create and refresh such aggregations. Moreover, unnecessary aggregations can worsen query performance. A typical example is the case when a summary table matches an unusual query. This can make the summary table to be moved into the cache to be accessed faster. Since this table will be rarely used afterwards, it can deallocate a more useful table from the cache (which has a limited size), with the obvious negative effect on query. In summary, we must avoid designing a large number of aggregations since they may reduce query performance.

The Analysis Services aggregation design algorithm does not automatically consider every attribute for aggregation. Consequently, we must check the attributes that are considered for aggregation and determine if we need to suggest additional aggregation candidates, for example, because we detected that most user queries not resolved from cache are resolved by partition reads rather than aggregation reads. Analysis Services uses the Aggregation Usage property to determine which attributes it should consider for aggregation. This property can take one of four values: full (every aggregation for the cube must include this attribute), none (no aggregation uses the attribute), unrestricted (the attribute must be evaluated), and default (a rule is applied to determine if the attribute must be used). The administrator can use this property to change its value for influencing its use for aggregation.

As we have already explained, partitions must be defined to enable Analysis Services to access less data to answer a query when it cannot be answered from the data cache or from aggregations. Data must be partitioned matching common queries. Analogously to the case of measure groups, we must avoid partitioning in a way that requires most queries to be resolved from many partitions. It is recommended by the vendor that partitions contain at most 20 million records and at least 2 million records. Also, each measure group should contain fewer than 2,000 partitions. A separate ROLAP partition must be selected for real-time data and this partition must have its own measure group.

We can also optimize performance by writing efficient MDX queries and expressions. For this, run-time checks in an MDX calculation must be avoided. For example, using CASE and IF functions that must be repeatedly evaluated during query resolution will result in a slow execution. In that case, it is recommended to rewrite the queries using the SCOPE function. If possible, Non_Empty_Behavior must be used to enable the query execution engine to use the bulk evaluation mode. In addition, EXISTS rather than filtering on member properties should be used since this enables bulk evaluation mode. Too many subqueries must be avoided if possible. Also, if possible, a set must be filtered before using it in a cross join to reduce the cube space before performing such cross join.

The cache of the query engine must be used efficiently. First, the server must have enough memory to store query results in memory for reuse in subsequent queries. We must also define calculations in MDX scripts because these have a global scope that enables the cache related to these queries to be shared across sessions for the same set of security permissions. Finally, the cache must be warmed by executing a set of predefined queries using any appropriate tool.

Other techniques are similar to the ones used for tuning relational databases, like tuning memory and processor usage. For details, we refer the reader to the Analysis Services documentation.

7.10 Query Performance in Mondrian

There are three main strategies for increasing performance when using the Mondrian OLAP engine: tuning the underlying database, using materialized views (called aggregate tables), and caching.

The data used by Mondrian are stored in a database. Tuning such database is the first task to perform to enhance query performance. Since this task is independent of the Mondrian engine and also given that Mondrian can work with many kinds of databases, we do not address this issue here and focus on topics that are specific to Mondrian, namely, materialized views and caching.

7.10.1 Aggregate Tables

In Mondrian, materialized views and summary tables studied in this chapter are called **aggregate tables**. Physically, aggregate tables are created in the database and populated during the ETL process. Mondrian can be configured to use, if possible, aggregate tables when answering a query. Aggregate tables can be enabled or disabled using a file called mondrian.properties. The aggregated tables are disabled by default; they are enabled setting the properties mondrian.rolap.aggregates.Use and mondrian.rolap.aggregates.Read to true. Also, Mondrian provides a tool called Aggregation Designer to assist in creating aggregate tables. This tool reads a schema and makes recommendations for aggregate tables, generating SQL code to create and populate the tables. We show below how to declare an aggregate table for precomputing the average unit price and the total sales amount by year and product category in the Northwind cube. The table will have the following columns: Category, Year, RowCount, AvgUnitPrice, and TotalSalesAmount.

```
<Cube name ="Sales">
    <Table name = "Sales">
        <AggName name="SalesByMonthProduct">
            <AggFactCount column="RowCount" >
            <AggMeasure name="Measures.AvgUnitPrice" column="AvgUnitPrice">
            <AggMeasure name="Measures.TotalSalesAmount"
            column="TotalSalesAmount">
            <AggLevel name="Product.Category" column="Category">
            <AggLevel name="OrderDate.Year" column="Year">
        </AggName>
    </Table>
</Cube>
```

Note that this is a declaration of the aggregate table in the Mondrian OLAP server. The actual table must be created in the underlying database and populated, typically, during the ETL process.

We have studied in this book that a parent-child hierarchy can have an arbitrary depth. The classic example is the employee-supervisor relationship found in the Northwind data warehouse. In parent-child hierarchies, we normally want to aggregate measures of child members into parent members. For example, when considering an employee Andrew Fuller who is head of the Northwind company (see Fig. 6.2), we may want to report not only his sales amount but his sales amount plus the sum of the sales amount of the employees that directly and indirectly report to him (Nancy Davolio, Janet Leverling, and so on). Mondrian provides a special structure called a **closure table**, which basically contains the transitive closure of the hierarchy. This table has schema (SupervisorKey, EmployeeKey, Distance), where the third attribute contains the distance from the two employees in the hierarchy. For the hierarchy in Fig. 6.2, the closure table will contain, for example, the tuples $(2, 2, 0)$, $(2, 5, 1)$, and $(2, 6, 2)$, which correspond to (Andrew Fuller, Andrew Fuller, 0), (Andrew Fuller, Steven Buchanan, 1), and (Andrew Fuller, Michael Suyama, 2). It follows from the above that a closure table is similar to an aggregate table in the sense that it contains a redundant copy of the data in the database. Note that while an aggregate table speeds up aggregation, a closure table makes the computation of rollups along a parent-child hierarchy more efficient.

When a query matches the definition of an aggregate table, Mondrian uses such a table to answer the query instead of computing the aggregate from scratch, basically applying the theoretical concepts studied in this chapter. If more than one aggregate table matches a particular query, Mondrian must choose between them. This is done as follows: If there is an aggregate table of the same granularity as the query, Mondrian uses it. If there is no aggregate table at the desired granularity, Mondrian picks an aggregate table of lower granularity and rolls up from it. In general, Mondrian chooses the aggregate table with the fewest rows (the heuristic we have called "smallest parent").

7.10.2 Caching

Another feature provided by Mondrian to speed up query performance is caching data in main memory, to avoid accessing the database to retrieve schemas, dimension members, and facts. Mondrian provides three different kinds of caches:

- The *schema cache*, which keeps schemas in memory to avoid reading them each time a cube is loaded. This cache stores the schema in memory after it has been read for the first time and keeps it in memory until the cache is cleared. Each time the schema is updated, the cache must be cleared.
- The *member cache*, which stores dimension members in memory. The member cache must also be synchronized with the underlying data. A Service Provider Interface is used to flush the members from the cache. The member cache is populated when members of a dimension are first read, and then members are retrieved as needed. Like it is the case in

relational database systems, if the member is in memory, it does not need to be read from the database. Members are specific values in a dimension (like Customer.Country.France), and they include the root and the children. We have to give the complete path to the member since a member is not simply a value, but a value and an associated dimension level, since a member can have the same name for a given level, for different paths within the hierarchy.

- The *segment cache*, which holds data from the fact table (usually the largest table in a warehouse) and contains aggregated data, reducing the number of calculations to perform. The segment is associated with a measure, for example, **Sales Amount**, and also contains a set of predicates separated by commas (e.g., [CityName = Paris], [CategoryName = Beverages]) and a list of measure values associated with these predicates (e.g., the list of sales amounts for beverages in Paris: [120, 259, ...]). With these values in the cache, aggregations can be easily computed when a query includes the predicates in the cache. The segment cache can be *internal*, where the segments are stored in local memory, or *external*, where the segments are stored in a data grid, which increases the amount of data stored in memory by adding additional servers.

Mondrian automatically updates the caches as schemas and dimensions are read and aggregates are calculated. As usual in caching techniques, the first user to access the data is the one that populates the cache rather than getting benefits of it. However, there are techniques that populate the cache in advance, so it will be ready to benefit users from the start. This is called precaching. Normally, in Mondrian, XML for Analysis (XMLA) web service calls are used for this task (recall from Chap. 6 that XMLA is a SOAP-based standard for making web service calls).

When data sources change, the cache gets outdated with respect to the actual data, and the cache must be *flushed*. When the schema cache is flushed, its associated member and segment caches are also flushed. Most tools that use Mondrian, like Pentaho, provide a way to manually flush the cache. Pentaho provides the Enterprise Console or User Console for this. A more efficient approach is to automate cache flushing by including this task as part of the ETL process.

7.11   Summary

In this chapter, we studied the problem of physical data warehouse design. We focused on three techniques: view materialization, indexing, and partitioning. For the former, we studied the problem of incremental view maintenance, that is, how and when a view can be updated without recomputing it from scratch. In addition, we presented algorithms that compute efficiently the data cube when all possible views are materialized. Also, we showed that when full materialization is not possible, we can estimate which is the best set to be chosen for materialization given a set of constraints. We then studied two typical indexing schemes used in data warehousing, namely, bitmap and join indexes, and how they are used in query evaluation. Finally, we discussed partitioning techniques and strategies, aimed at enhancing data warehouse performance and management. The last three sections of the chapter were devoted to study physical design and query performance in Analysis Services and Mondrian, showing how the theoretical concepts studied in the first part of the chapter are applied over real-world tools.

7.12   Bibliographic Notes

A general book about physical database design is [116], while physical design for SQL Server is covered, for instance, in [35]. Most of the topics studied in this chapter have been presented in classic data warehousing papers. Incremental view maintenance has been studied in [73, 74]. The summary table algorithm is due to Mumick et al. [141]. The PipeSort algorithm, as well as other data cube computation techniques, is discussed in detail in [2]. The view selection algorithm was proposed in a classic paper by Harinarayan et al. [78]. Bitmap indexes were first introduced in [149] and bitmap join indexes in [150]. A study of the joint usage of indexing, partitioning, and view materialization in data warehouses is reported in [12]. A book on indexing structures for data warehouses is [98]. A study on index selection for data warehouses can be found in [60], while [192] surveys bitmap indexes for data warehouses. A popular bitmap compression technique, based on run-length encoding, is WAH (Word Align Hybrid) [232]. The PLWAH (Position List Word Align Hybrid) bitmap compression technique [192] was proposed as a variation of the WAH scheme, and it is reported to be more efficient than the former, particularly in terms of storage. The authors proposed this indexing scheme to support music data warehouses, which we comment in Chap. 15. Rizzi and Saltarelli [177] compare view materialization against indexing for data warehouse design. A survey of view selection methods is [128]. Finally, [10] discusses practical aspects of the Mondrian OLAP engine.

7.13   Review Questions

7.1 What is the objective of physical data warehouse design? Specify different techniques that are used to achieve such objective.

7.2 Discuss advantages and disadvantages of using materialized views.

7.3 What is view maintenance? What is incremental view maintenance?

7.4 Discuss the kinds of algorithms for incremental view maintenance, that is, using full and partial information.

7.5 Define self-maintainable aggregate functions. What is a self-maintainable view?

7.6 Explain briefly the main idea of the summary-delta algorithm for data cube maintenance.

7.7 How is data cube computation optimized? What are the kinds of optimizations that algorithms are based on?

7.8 Explain the idea of the PipeSort algorithm.

7.9 How can we estimate the size of a data cube?

7.10 Explain the algorithm for selecting a set of views to materialize. Discuss its limitations. How can they be overridden?

7.11 Compare B-tree$^+$ indexes, hash indexes, bitmap indexes, and join indexes with respect to their use in databases and data warehouses.

7.12 How do we use bitmap indexes for range queries?

7.13 Explain run length encoding.

7.14 Describe a typical indexing scheme in a star and snowflake schemas.

7.15 How are bitmap indexes used during query processing?

7.16 How do join indexes work in query processing? For which kinds of queries are they efficient? For which kinds of queries are they not efficient?

7.17 What is partitioning? Which kinds of partitioning schemes do you know?

7.18 What are the main advantages and disadvantages of partitioning?

7.19 Discuss the characteristics of storage modes in Analysis Services.

7.20 How do indexed views compare with materialized views?

7.14   Exercises

7.1 In the Northwind database, consider the relations

Employee(EmplID, FirstName, LastName, Title, ...)
Orders(OrderID, CustID, EmpID, OrderDate, ...).

Consider further a view

EmpOrders(EmpID, Name, OrderID, OrderDate)

computed from the full outer join of tables Employee and Orders, where Name is obtained by concatenating FirstName and LastName.

Define the view EmpOrders in SQL. Show an example of instances for the relations and the corresponding view. By means of examples, show how the view EmpOrders must be modified upon insertions and deletions in table Employee. Give the SQL command to compute the delta relation of the view from the delta relations of table Employee. Write an algorithm to update the view from the delta relation.

7.2 Consider a relation Connected(CityFrom, CityTo, Distance), which indicates pairs of cities that are directly connected and the distance between them, and a view OneStop(CityFrom, CityTo), which computes the pairs of cities (c1, c2) such that c2 can be reached from c1 passing through exactly one intermediate stop.

Answer the same questions as those of the previous exercise.

7.3 Consider the following tables:

Store(<u>StoreID</u>, City, State, Manager)
Order(<u>OrderID</u>, StoreID, Date)
OrderLine(<u>OrderID</u>, <u>LineNo</u>, ProductID, Quantity, Price)
Product(<u>ProductID</u>, ProductName, Category, Supplier)
Part(<u>PartID</u>, PartName, ProductID, Quantity)

and the following views:

- ParisManagers(Manager) that contains managers of stores located in Paris.
- OrderProducts(OrderID, ProductCount) that contains the number of products for each order.
- OrderSuppliers(OrderID, SupplierCount) that contains the number of suppliers for each order.
- OrderAmount(OrderID, StoreID, Date, Amount) which adds to the table Order an additional column that contains the total amount of each order.
- StoreOrders(StoreID, OrderCount) that contains the number of orders for each store.
- ProductPart(ProductID, ProductName, PartID, PartName) that is obtained from the full outer join of tables Product and Part.

Define the above views in SQL. For each of these views, determine whether the view is self-maintainable with respect to insertions and deletions. Give examples illustrating the cases that are not self-maintainable.

7.4 Consider the following tables

Professor(<u>ProfNo</u>, ProfName, Laboratory)
Supervision(<u>ProfNo,StudNo</u>)
PhDStudent(<u>StudNo</u>, StudName, Laboratory)

and a view ProfPhdStud(ProfNo, ProfName, StudNo, StudName) computed from the outer joins of these three relations.

Determine whether the view is self-maintainable. Write the SQL command for creating the view. Show a possible instance of the tables and the corresponding view. Give a delta table composed of insertions to and deletions from the table Supervision and show how the view is computed from these delta tables.

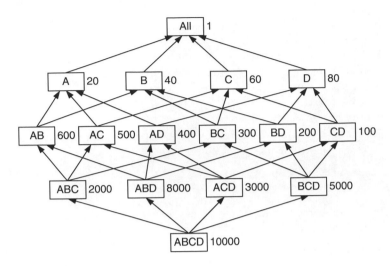

Fig. 7.18 A data cube lattice

7.5 By means of examples, explain the propagate and refresh algorithm for the aggregate functions AVG, MIN, and COUNT. For each aggregate function, write the SQL command that creates the summary-delta table from the tables containing the inserted and deleted tuples in the fact table, and write the algorithm that refreshes the view from the summary-delta table.

7.6 Suppose that a cube Sales(A, B, C, D, Amount) has to be fully materialized. The cube contains 64 tuples. Sorting takes the typical $n \log(n)$ time. Every GROUP BY with k attributes has 2^k tuples:

   (a) Compute the cube using the PipeSort algorithm.
   (b) Compute the gain of applying the PipeSort compared to the cost of computing all the views from scratch.

7.7 Consider the graph in Fig. 7.18, where each node represents a view and the numbers are the costs of materializing the view. Assuming that the bottom of the lattice is materialized, determine using the view selection algorithm the five views to be materialized first.

7.8 Consider the data cube lattice of a three-dimensional cube with dimensions A, B, and C. Extend the lattice to take into account the hierarchies $A \to A_1 \to All$ and $B \to B_1 \to B_2 \to All$. Since the lattice is complex to draw, represent it by giving the list of nodes and the list of edges.

7.9 Modify the algorithm for selecting views to materialize in order to consider the probability that each view has to completely match a given query. In other words, consider that you know the distribution of the queries, so that view A has probability $P(A)$ to match a query, view B has probability $P(B)$, etc.:

(a) How would you change the algorithm to take into account this knowledge?

(b) Suppose that in the lattice of Fig. 7.9, the view ABC is already materialized. Apply the modified algorithm to select four views to be materialized given the following probabilities for the views: $P(\mathsf{ABC}) = 0.1$, $P(\mathsf{AB}) = 0.1$, $P(\mathsf{AC}) = 0.2$, $P(\mathsf{BC}) = 0.3$, $P(\mathsf{A})) = 0.05$, $P(\mathsf{B}) = 0.05$, $P(\mathsf{C}) = 0.1$, and $P(\mathsf{All}) = 0.1$.

(c) Answer the same question as in (b) but now with the probabilities as follows: $P(\mathsf{ABC}) = 0.1$, $P(\mathsf{AB}) = 0.05$, $P(\mathsf{AC}) = 0.1$, $P(\mathsf{BC}) = 0$, $P(\mathsf{A}) = 0.2$, $P(\mathsf{B}) = 0.1$, $P(\mathsf{C}) = 0.05$, and $P(\mathsf{All}) = 0.05$, Compare the results.

7.10 Given the Employee table below, show how a bitmap index on attribute Title would look like. Compress the bitmap values using run-length encoding.

Employee Key	Employee Name	Title	Address	City	Department Key
e1	Peter Brown	Dr.	...	Brussels	d1
e2	James Martin	Mr.	...	Wavre	d1
e3	Ronald Ritchie	Mr.	...	Paris	d2
e4	Marco Benetti	Mr.	...	Versailles	d2
e5	Alexis Manoulis	Mr.	...	London	d3
e6	Maria Mortsel	Mrs.	...	Reading	d3
e7	Laura Spinotti	Mr.	...	Brussels	d4
e8	John River	Mrs.	...	Waterloo	d4
e9	Bert Jasper	Mr.	...	Paris	d5
e10	Claudia Brugman	Mrs.	...	Saint-Denis	d5

7.11 Given the Sales table below and the Employee table from Ex. 7.10, show how a join index on attribute EmployeeKey would look like.

RowID Sales	Product Key	Customer Key	Employee Key	Time Key	Sales Amount
1	p1	c1	e1	t1	100
2	p1	c2	e3	t1	100
3	p2	c2	e4	t2	100
4	p2	c3	e5	t2	100
5	p3	c3	e1	t3	100
6	p4	c4	e2	t4	100
7	p5	c4	e2	t5	100

7.12 Given the Department table below and the Employee table from Ex. 7.10, show how a bitmap join index on attribute DeptKey would look like.

Department Key	Department Name	Location
d1	Management	Brussels
d2	Production	Paris
d3	Marketing	London
d4	HumanResources	Brussels
d5	Research	Paris

7.13 Consider the tables Sales in Ex. 7.11, Employee in Ex. 7.10, and Department in Ex. 7.12.

(a) Propose an indexing scheme for the tables, including any kind of index you consider it necessary. Discuss possible alternatives according to several query scenarios. Discuss the advantages and disadvantages of creating the indexes.

(b) Consider the query:

```
SELECT    E.EmployeeName, SUM(S.SalesAmount)
FROM      Sales S, Employee E, Department D
WHERE     S.EmployeeKey = E.EmployeeKey AND
          E.DepartmentKey = D.DepartmentKey AND
          ( D.Location = 'Brussels' OR D.Location = 'Paris' )
GROUP BY E.EmployeeName
```

Explain a possible query plan that makes use of the indexes defined in (a).

Chapter 8
Extraction, Transformation, and Loading

Extraction, transformation, and loading (ETL) processes are used to extract data from internal and external sources of an organization, transform these data, and load them into a data warehouse. Since ETL processes are complex and costly, it is important to reduce their development and maintenance costs. Modeling ETL processes at a conceptual level is a way to achieve this goal. However, existing ETL tools, like Microsoft Integration Services or Pentaho Data Integration (also known as Kettle), have their own specific language to define ETL processes. Further, there is no agreed-upon conceptual model to specify such processes. In this chapter, we study the design of ETL processes using a conceptual approach. The model we use is based on the Business Process Modeling Notation (BPMN), a de facto standard for specifying business processes. The model provides a set of primitives that cover the requirements of frequently used ETL processes. Since BPMN is already used for specifying business processes, users already familiar with BPMN do not need to learn another language for defining ETL processes. Further, BPMN provides a conceptual and implementation-independent specification of such processes, which hides technical details and allows users and designers to focus on essential characteristics of such processes. Finally, ETL processes expressed in BPMN can be translated into executable specifications for ETL tools.

We start this chapter with a brief introduction of BPMN, which we give in Sect. 8.1. Then, in Sect. 8.2, we explain how we can use BPMN for conceptual modeling of ETL processes. In Sect. 8.3, we apply these concepts to the Northwind case study. We design a conceptual model for the ETL process that loads the Northwind data warehouse used in the previous chapters with data extracted from the Northwind operational database and other sources. Finally, after providing in Sect. 8.4 a brief overview of Microsoft Integration Services and Pentaho Kettle, we show in Sects. 8.5 and 8.6 how the ETL conceptual model can be implemented in both tools. A detailed specification of the process is provided, and the differences between both implementation platforms are highlighted.

A. Vaisman and E. Zimányi, *Data Warehouse Systems*, Data-Centric Systems and Applications, DOI 10.1007/978-3-642-54655-6_8, © Springer-Verlag Berlin Heidelberg 2014

8.1   Business Process Modeling Notation

A business process is a collection of related activities or tasks in an organization whose goal is to produce a specific service or product. A task can be performed by software systems, humans, or a combination of these. Business process modeling is the activity of representing the business processes of an organization so that the current processes may be analyzed and improved.

Many techniques to model business processes have been proposed over the years. Traditional techniques include Gantt charts, flowcharts, PERT diagrams, and data flow diagrams. However, the problem with these techniques is the lack of a formal semantics. On the other hand, formal techniques such as Petri Nets have a well-defined semantics but are difficult to understand by business users and, in addition, do not have the expressiveness to represent some typical situations that arise in real-world settings. Many efforts were carried out since the 1990s in the area of workflow management systems to define languages and tools for modeling and executing business processes. A standardization process resulted in BPMN released by the Object Management Group (OMG). The current version of the standard is BPMN 2.0.[1]

BPMN provides a graphical notation for defining and understanding the business processes of an organization and to communicate them in a standard manner. The rationale behind BPMN is to define a language that is usable by the business community, is constrained to support the modeling concepts that are applicable to business processes, and is useful in clearly describing complex processes. BPMN is defined using the Unified Modeling Language (UML). In addition, a precise semantics of the language and an execution semantics are also defined.

BPMN aims at tackling two conflicting requirements, namely, providing a simple mechanism for creating business process models and handling the complexity inherent to them. The approach taken to tackle these two requirements was to organize the graphical aspects of the notation into categories, so that the reader of a BPMN diagram can easily recognize the basic types of elements and understand the diagram. Within the basic categories of elements, additional variation and information can be added to support the requirements for complexity without dramatically changing the basic look and feel of the diagram. There are four basic categories of elements, namely, flow objects, connecting objects, swimlanes, and artifacts.

Flow objects are the main elements for defining a business process. There are three types of flow objects: activities, gateways, and events. An **activity** is a work performed during a process. Activities can be either single tasks

---

[1] http://www.omg.org/spec/BPMN/2.0/

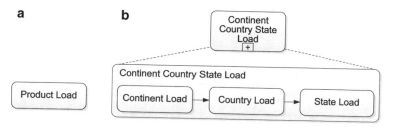

Fig. 8.1 Activities. (**a**) Single task. (**b**) Collapsed and expanded subprocess

or subprocesses, and thus they can be atomic or nonatomic. Figure 8.1a shows how a task is represented. A **subprocess** is an encapsulated process whose details we want to hide. Figure 8.1b shows that there are two ways of representing a subprocess: collapsed and expanded.

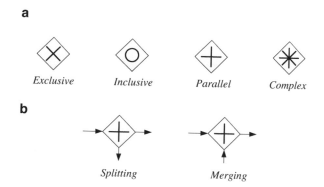

Fig. 8.2 (**a**) Different types of gateways. (**b**) Splitting and merging gateways

Gateways are used to control the sequence of activities in a process depending on *conditions*. It is worth noting that BPMN does not state how these conditions must be written; this is left to the modeler. Gateways are represented by diamond shapes. BPMN defines several types of gateways, shown in Fig. 8.2a, which are distinguished by the symbol used inside the diamond shape. All these types can be *splitting* or *merging* gateways, as shown in Fig. 8.2b, depending on the number of ingoing and outgoing branches. An **exclusive gateway** models an exclusive OR decision, that is, depending on a condition, the gateway activates exactly one of its outgoing branches. It can be represented as an empty diamond shape or a diamond shape with an 'X' inside. A default flow (see below) can be defined as one of the outgoing flows, if no other condition is true. An **inclusive gateway** triggers or merges one or more flows. In a *splitting* inclusive gateway, any combination of outgoing flows can be triggered. However, a default flow cannot be included in such a combination. In a *merging* inclusive gateway, any combination can be chosen to continue the flow. A **parallel gateway** allows the synchronization between outgoing and incoming flows as follows. A *splitting* parallel gateway is analogous to an AND operator: the incoming flow triggers one or more outgoing parallel flows. On the other hand, a *merging* parallel gateway synchronizes the flow merging all the incoming flows into a single outgoing one. Finally, **complex gateways** can represent complex conditions. For example, a merging complex gateway can model that when three out of five flows are completed, the process can continue without waiting for the completion of the other two.

Fig. 8.3 Examples of events

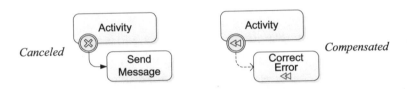

Fig. 8.4 Error handling: canceled and compensated activities

Events (see Fig. 8.3) represent something that happens that affects the sequence and timing of the workflow activities. Events may be internal or external to the task into consideration. There are three types of events, which can be distinguished depending on whether they are drawn with a single, a double, or a thick line. **Start** and **end** events indicate the beginning and ending of a process, respectively. Intermediate events include time, message, cancel, and terminate events. **Time** events can be used to represent situations when a task must wait for some period of time before continuing. **Message** events can be used to represent communication, for example, to send an e-mail indicating that an error has occurred. They can also be used for triggering a task, for example, a message may indicate that an activity can start. **Cancel** events listen to the errors in a process and notify them either by an explicit action like sending a message, as in the canceled activity shown in Fig. 8.4, or by an implicit action to be defined in the next steps of the process development. **Compensation** events can be employed to recover errors by launching specific compensation activities, which are linked to the compensation event with the association connecting object (Fig. 8.5), as shown in Fig. 8.4. Finally, **terminate** events stop the entire process, including all parallel processes.

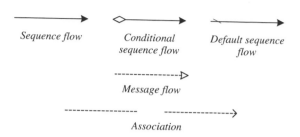

Sequence flow   Conditional   Default sequence
                     sequence flow   flow

Message flow

Association

Fig. 8.5 Connecting objects

Connecting objects are used to represent how objects are connected. There are three types of connecting objects, illustrated in Fig. 8.5, which are explained next.

A **sequence flow** represents a sequencing constraint between flow objects. It is the basic connecting object in a workflow. It states that if two activities are linked by a sequence flow, the target activity will start only when the source one has finished. If multiple sequence flows outgo from an activity, all of them will be activated after its execution. In case there is a need to control a sequence flow, it is possible to add a condition to the sequence flow by using the **conditional sequence flow**. A sequence flow may be set as the **default flow** in case of many outgoing flows. For example, as explained above, in an exclusive or an inclusive gateway, if no other condition is true, then the default flow is followed. Note that sequence flows can replace splitting and merging gateways. For example, an exclusive gateway splitting into two paths could be replaced by two conditional flows, provided the conditions are *mutually exclusive*. Inclusive gateways could be replaced by conditional flows, even when the former constraint does not apply.

A **message flow** represents the sending and receiving of messages between organizational boundaries (i.e., pools, explained below). A message flow is the only connecting object able to get through the boundary of a pool and may also connect to a flow object within that pool.

An **association** relates artifacts (like annotations) to flow objects (like activities). We give examples below. An association can indicate directionality using an open arrowhead, for example, when linking the compensation activity in case of error handling.

A **loop** (see Fig. 8.6) represents the repeated execution of a process for as long as the underlying looping condition is true. This condition must be evaluated for every loop iteration and may be evaluated at the beginning or

Fig. 8.6 Activity and subprocess loops

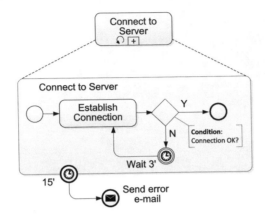

Fig. 8.7 An example of a subprocess loop

at the end of the iteration. In the example of Fig. 8.7, we represent a task of an ETL process that connects to a server. At a high abstraction level, the subprocess activity hides the details. It has the loop symbol attached (a curved arrow), indicating that the subprocess is executed repeatedly until an ending condition is reached. When we expand the subprocess, we can see what happens within it: the server waits for 3 min (this waiting task is represented by the time event). If the connection is not established, the request for the connection is launched again. After 15 min (another time event), if the connection was not reached, the task is stopped, and an error e-mail is sent (a message event).

A **swimlane** (see Fig. 8.8) is a structuring object that comprises **pools** and **lanes**. Both of them are used to define process boundaries. Only messages are allowed between two pools, not sequence flows. In other words, a workflow must be contained in only one pool. However, a pool may be subdivided into several lanes, which represent roles or services in the enterprise. Lanes within a pool do not have any special constraint, and thus sequence flows may cross a lane freely. We give an example in the next section.

Artifacts are used to add information to a diagram. There are three types of artifacts. A **data object** represents either data that are input to a process, data resulting from a process, data that needs to be collected, or data that needs to be stored. A **group** organizes tasks or processes that have some kind of significance in the overall model. A group does not affect the flow in the diagram. **Annotations** are used to add extra information to flow objects. For example, an annotation for an activity in an ETL process can indicate

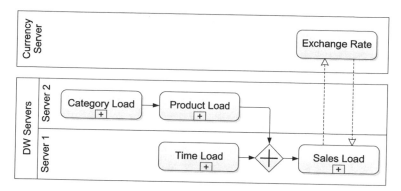

Fig. 8.8 Swimlanes: pool and lanes

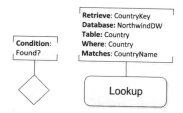

Fig. 8.9 BPMN artifacts: annotations

a gateway condition or the attributes involved in a lookup task, as shown in Fig. 8.9. Annotations may be associated with both activities and subprocesses in order to describe their semantics.

8.2 Conceptual ETL Design Using BPMN

There is no standard conceptual model for defining ETL processes. Each existing tool provides its own model, often too detailed since it takes into consideration many particular implementation issues. In this section, we show how BPMN can be customized for designing ETL processes at a conceptual level. We describe how the BPMN constructs introduced in the previous sections can be used to define the most common ETL tasks. We also introduce a BPMN-based notation for ETL. The most obvious advantage of using a conceptual approach for designing ETL processes is the ability to replicate the same process with different tools. We will illustrate this fact by describing in Sect. 8.3 the conceptual model of the ETL process that loads the Northwind data warehouse. Then, in Sects. 8.5 and 8.6, we will show how this conceptual model can be implemented, respectively, in Integration Services and Kettle.

A key point of the approach we present here is the perception of ETL processes as a combination of control and data tasks, where **control tasks** orchestrate groups of tasks and **data tasks** detail how input data are transformed and output data are produced. For example, the overall process of populating a data warehouse is a control task composed of multiple subtasks, while populating a fact or dimension table is a data task. Therefore, control tasks can be considered as workflows where arrows represent the precedence between tasks, while data tasks represent data flows where records are transferred through the arrows. Given the discussion above, designing ETL processes using business process modeling tools appears natural. We present next the conceptual model for ETL processes based on BPMN.

Control tasks represent the orchestration of an ETL process, independently of the data flowing through such process. Such tasks are represented by means of the constructs described in Sect. 8.1. For example, gateways are used to control the sequence of activities in an ETL process. The most used types of gateways in an ETL context are exclusive and parallel gateways. Events are another type of objects often used in control tasks. For instance, a cancelation event can be used to represent the situation when an error occurs and may be followed by a message event that sends an e-mail to notify the failure.

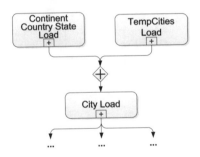

Fig. 8.10 An excerpt of a control task

Figure 8.10 shows a portion of the control task that loads the Northwind data warehouse. There are three subprocesses called Continent Country State Load, TempCities Load, and City Load, which load, respectively, the tables composing the hierarchy State → Country → Continent, a temporary table TempCities, and the table City. The first two subprocesses are the incoming flow of a parallel merging gateway. The outgoing flow of this gateway is the input to the City Load. Note that the sequence flows outgoing the City Load activity could also be modeled as a parallel splitting gateway.

Swimlanes can be used to organize ETL processes according to several strategies, namely, by *technical architecture* (such as servers to which tasks are assigned), by *business entities* (such as departments or branches), or by *user profiles* (such as manager, analyst, or designer) that give special access rights to users. For example, Fig. 8.8 illustrates the use of swimlanes for the Northwind ETL process (we will explain in detail this process later in this chapter). The figure shows some of the subprocesses that load the Product dimension table, the Time dimension table, and the Sales fact table (represented as compound activities with subprocesses); it also assumes their distribution between Server 1 and Server 2. Each one of these servers is considered as a lane contained inside the pool of data warehouse servers. We can also see that a swimlane denoted Currency Server contains a web service that receives an input currency (like US dollars), an amount, and an output currency (like euros) and returns the amount equivalent in the output currency. This could be used in the loading of the Sales fact table. Thus, flow messages are exchanged between the Sales Load activity and the Exchange Rate task which is performed by the web service. These messages go across both swimlanes.

Data tasks represent activities typically carried out to manipulate data, such as input data, output data, and data transformation. Since such data manipulation operations occur *within* an activity, data tasks can be considered as being at a lower abstraction level than control tasks. Recall that arrows in a data task represent not only a precedence relationship between its activities but also the flow of data records between them.

Data tasks can be classified into row and rowset operations. **Row operations** apply transformations to the data on a row-by-row basis. In contrast, **rowset operations** deal with a set of rows. For example, updating the value of a column is a row operation, while aggregation is a rowset operation. Data tasks can also be classified (orthogonally to the previous classification) into **unary** or ***n*-ary data tasks**, depending of the number of input flows.

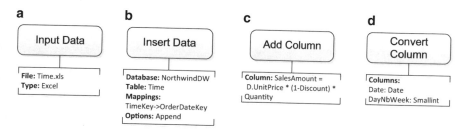

Fig. 8.11 Unary row operations. (**a**) Input data. (**b**) Insert data. (**c**) Add column. (**d**) Convert column

Figure 8.11 shows examples of unary row operations: Input Data, Insert Data, Add Column, and Convert Column. Note the annotations linked to the tasks by means of association flows. The annotations contain metadata that specify the parameters of the task. For example, in Fig. 8.11a, the annotation tells that the data is read from an Excel file called Time.xls. Similarly, the annotation in Fig. 8.11b tells that the task inserts tuples in the table Time

of the NorthwindDW database, where column TimeKey in the flow is mapped
to the attribute OrderDateKey. Further, new records will be appended to
the table. The task in Fig. 8.11c adds a column named SalesAmount to
the flow whose value is computed from the expression given. Here, it is
supposed that the values of the columns appearing in the expression are
taken from the current record. Finally, Fig. 8.11d converts the columns Date
and DayNbWeek (e.g., read from an Excel file as strings) into a Date and a
Smallint, respectively.

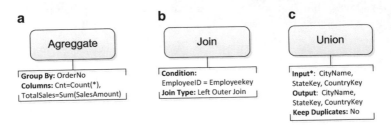

Fig. 8.12 Rowset operations. (**a**) Aggregate (unary). (**b**) Join (binary). (**c**) Union
(n-ary)

Figure 8.12 shows three rowset operations: Aggregate (unary), Join
(binary), and Union (n-ary). These operations receive a set of rows to
process altogether, rather than operating row by row. Again, annotations
complement the diagram information. For example, in the case of the Union
task, the annotation tells the name of the input and output columns and
informs if duplicates must be kept. Note that the case of the union is a
particular one: if duplicates are retained, then it becomes a row operation
since it can be done row by row. If duplicates are eliminated, then it becomes
a rowset operation because sorting is involved in the operation.

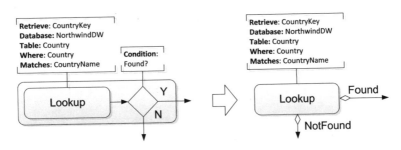

Fig. 8.13 Shorthand notation for the lookup task

A very common data task in an ETL process is the lookup, which checks
if some value is present in a file, based on a single or compound search key.

Typically, a lookup is immediately followed by an exclusive gateway with a branching condition. For conciseness, we decided to use a shorthand for these two tasks and replace this by two conditional flows. This is shown in Fig. 8.13. Table 8.1 defines the various ETL tasks and their annotations. The annotations between brackets, as in [Group By], are optional, while the annotations suffixed with an asterisk, as in Input*, can be repeated several times. Finally, the annotations separated by a vertical bar, as in Table | Query, are exclusive, one of which must be provided. In Appendix A, we give the BPMN notation for these ETL tasks.

8.3 Conceptual Design of the Northwind ETL Process

In this section, using the concepts explained in the previous ones, we present a conceptual model of the ETL process that loads the Northwind data warehouse from the operational database and other sources. Later, in Sects. 8.5 and 8.6, we show how this model can be implemented in, respectively, Microsoft Integration Services and Pentaho Kettle.

The operational data reside in a relational database, whose logical schema is shown in Fig. 8.14. These data must be mapped to a data warehouse, whose schema is given in Fig. 8.15. In addition to the operational database, some other files are needed for loading the data warehouse. We next describe these files, as well as the requirements of the process.

First, an Excel file called Time.xls contains the data needed for loading the Time dimension table. The time interval of this file covers the dates contained in the table Orders of the Northwind operational database.

We can see in Fig. 8.15 that in the Northwind data warehouse the dimension tables Customer and Supplier share the geographic hierarchy starting at the City level. Data for the hierarchy State → Country → Continent are loaded from an XML file called Territories.xml that begins as shown in Fig. 8.16a. A graphical representation of the schema of the XML file is shown in Fig. 8.16b. Here, rectangles represent XML elements, and rounded rectangles represent XML attributes. The cardinalities of the relationships are also indicated. Notice that type is an attribute of State that contains, for example, the value state for Austria. However, for Belgium it contains the value province (not shown in the figure). Notice also that EnglishStateName, RegionName, and RegionCode are optional, as indicated by the cardinality 0..1.

It is worth noting that the attribute Region of tables Customers and Suppliers in the Northwind database contains in fact a state or province name (e.g., Québec) or a state code (e.g., CA). Similarly, the attribute Country contains a country name (e.g., Canada) or a country code (e.g., USA). To identify to which state or province a city belongs, a file called Cities.txt

Table 8.1 Annotations of the ETL tasks in BPMN

Add Column: adds new derived columns to the flow	
Columns	List of Col=Expr computing the value of a new column Col added to the output flow from expression Expr

Add Column: adds new columns to the flow obtained from an SQL query	
Columns	List of column names added to the output flow
Database	Name of the database
Query	SQL query

Aggregate: adds new columns to the flow computed by aggregating values from the input flow, possibly after grouping the records	
[Group By]	List of column names from the input flow that are used for grouping. These columns are the only ones from the input flow that are also in the output flow
Columns	List of Col1=AgFct(Col2) or Col1=AgFct(*), where a new column Col1 in the output flow will be assigned the value AgFct(Col2) or AgrFct(*)

Convert Column: changes the type of columns from the flow	
Columns	List of Col:Type, where column Col in the input flow is converted to type Type in the output flow

Delete Data: deletes tuples from a database corresponding to records in the flow	
Database	Name of the database
Table	Name of the table
Where	List of column names from the input flow
Matches	List of attribute names from the table

Difference: computes the difference of two flows	
Input*	List of column names from the two input flows. Input* is used if the column names are the same for both flows, otherwise Input1 and Input2 are used, each flow defining the column names
Output	List of column names from the output flow

Drop Column: drops columns from the flow	
Columns	List of column names from the input flow that are removed from the output flow

Input Data: inserts records into the flow obtained from a file	
File	Name of the file
Type	Type of the file, such as Text, CSV, Excel, or XML
[Fields]	Name of the fields or XPath expressions

Input Data: inserts records into the flow obtained from a database	
Database	Name of the database
Table | Query	Name of the table or SQL query
[Columns]	Name of the columns

Insert Data: inserts records from the flow into a file	
File	Name of the file
Type	Type of the file
[Options]	Headers if column names are put in the first line of the file; either Empty or Append depending on whether the file is emptied before inserting the new tuples, the latter is the default

(continued)

Table 8.1 (continued)

Insert Data: inserts tuples into a database corresponding to records in the flow	
Database	Name of the database
Table	Name of the table
[Mappings]	List of Col->Attr, where column Col in the input flow is mapped to attribute Attr in the database
[Options]	Either Empty or Append depending on whether the table is emptied before inserting the new tuples, the latter is the default

Join: computes the join of two flows	
Condition	List of Col1 op Col2, where Col1 belongs to the first input flow, Col2 to the second flow, and op is a comparison operator
[Join Type]	Either Inner Join, Left Outer Join, or Full Outer Join, the first one is the default

Lookup: adds columns to the flow obtained by looking up data from a database	
Retrieve	List of column names added to the output flow
Database	Database name
Table | Query	Name of the table or SQL query
Where	List of column names from the input flow
Matches	List of attribute names from the lookup table or SQL query

Lookup: replaces column values of the flow with values obtained by looking up data from a database	
Replace	List of column names from the input flow whose values are replaced in the output flow
Database	Database name
Table | Query	Name of the table or SQL query
Where	List of column names from the input flow
Matches	List of attribute names from the lookup table or description of an SQL query

Multicast: produces several output flows from an input flow	
Input	List of column names from the input flow
Output*	List of column names from each output flow. Output* is used if the column names are the same for all flows, otherwise Output1,..., Outputn are used, each flow defining the column names

Remove Duplicates: removes duplicate records from the flow	
(None)	This task does not have any annotation

Rename Column: changes the name of columns from the flow	
Columns	List of Col->NewCol where column Col from the input flow is renamed NewCol in the output flow

Sort: sorts the records of the flow	
Columns	List of colum names from the input flow, where for each of them, either ASC or DESC is specified, the former being the default

Union: computes the union of two or more flows	
Input*	List of column names from each input flow. Input* is used if the column names are the same for all flows. Otherwise Input1, ..., Inputn are used, each flow defining the column names
Output	List of column names from the output flow
[Keep Duplicates]	Either Yes or No, the former is the default

(continued)

Table 8.1 (continued)

Update Column: replaces column values from the flow	
Columns	List of Col=Expr computing the new value of column Col from the input flow from expression Expr
[Condition]	Boolean condition that the records in the input flow must satisfy in order to be updated. If not specified all records are updated

Update Column: replaces column values from the flow	
Columns	List of column names from the input flow whose values are changed in the output flow
Database	Name of the database
Query	SQL query
[Condition]	Boolean condition that the records in the input flow must satisfy in order to be updated. If not specified all records are updated

Update Data: update tuples of a database corresponding to records in the flow	
Database	Name of the database
Table	Name of the table
Columns	List of Attr=Expr computing the new value of attribute Attr in the table from expression Expr
Where	List of column names from the input flow
Matches	List of attribute names from the table

is used. The file contains three fields separated by tabs and begins as shown in Fig. 8.17a, where the first line contains field names. In the case of cities located in countries that do not have states, as it is the case of Singapore, a null value is given for the second field. The above file is also used to identify to which state the city in the attribute TerritoryDescription of the table Territories in the Northwind database corresponds. A temporary table in the data warehouse, denoted TempCities, will be used for storing the contents of this file. The structure of the table is given in Fig. 8.17b.

It is worth noting that the keys of the operational database are reused in the data warehouse as surrogate keys for all dimensions except for dimension Customer. In this dimension, the key of the operational database is kept in the attribute CustomerID, while a new surrogate key is generated during the ETL process.

In addition, for the Sales table in the Northwind data warehouse, the following transformations are needed:

- The attribute OrderLineNo must be generated in ascending order of ProductID (in the operational database, there is no order line number).
- The attribute SalesAmount must be calculated taking into account the unit price, the discount, and the quantity.
- The attribute Freight, which in the operational database is related to the whole order, must be evenly distributed among the lines of the order.

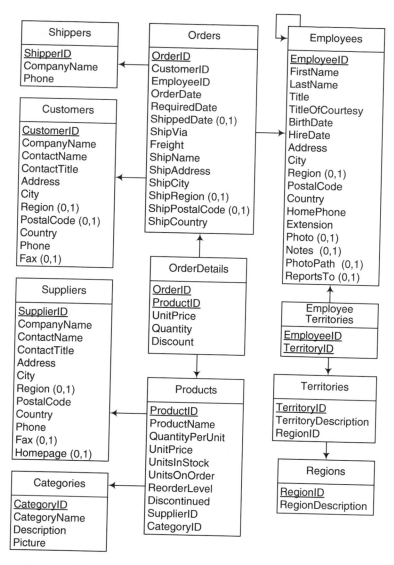

Fig. 8.14 Schema of the Northwind operational database (repeated from Fig. 2.4)

Figure 8.18 provides a general overview of the whole ETL process. The figure shows the control tasks needed to perform the transformation from the operational database and the additional files presented above and the loading of the transformed data into the data warehouse. We can see that the process starts with a start event, followed by activities (with subprocesses) that can be performed in parallel (represented by a splitting parallel gateway) which populate the dimension hierarchies. Finally, a parallel merging gateway synchronizes the flow, meaning that the loading of the **Sales** fact table

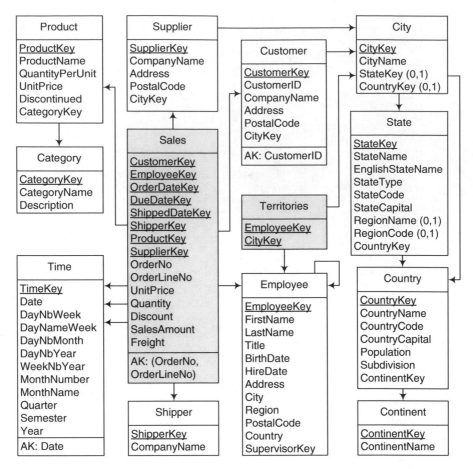

Fig. 8.15 Schema of the Northwind data warehouse (repeated from Fig. 5.4)

(activity Sales Load) can only start when all other tasks have been completed. If the process fails, a cancelation event is triggered and an error message in the form of an e-mail is dispatched.

Figure 8.19 shows the task that loads the Category table in the data warehouse. It is just composed of an input data task and an insertion data task. The former reads the table Categories from the operational database. The latter loads the table Category in the data warehouse, where the CategoryID attribute in the Categories table is mapped to the CategoryKey attribute in the Category table. Similarly, Fig. 8.20 shows the task that loads the Time table from an Excel file. It is similar to the previously explained task but includes a conversion of columns, which defines the data types of the attributes of the target table Time in the data warehouse, and the addition of a column TimeKey initialized with null values so the database can generate

a

```
<?xml version="1.0" encoding="ISO-8859-1"?>
<Continents>
  <Continent>
    <ContinentName>Europe</ContinentName>
    <Country>
      <CountryName>Austria</CountryName>
      <CountryCode>AT</CountryCode>
      <CountryCapital>Vienna</CountryCapital>
      <Population>8316487</Population>
      <Subdivision>Austria is divided into nine Bundesländer,
      or simply Länder (states; sing. Land).</Subdivision>
      <State type="state">
        <StateName>Burgenland</StateName>
        <StateCode>BU</StateCode>
        <StateCapital>Eisenstadt</StateCapital>
      </State>
      <State type="state">
        <StateName>Kärnten</StateName>
        <StateCode>KA</StateCode>
        <EnglishStateName>Carinthia</EnglishStateName>
        <StateCapital>Klagenfurt</StateCapital>
      </State>
      ...
```

b

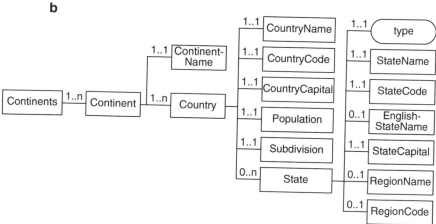

Fig. 8.16 (a) Beginning of the file Territories.xml. (b) XML schema of the file

surrogate keys for this attribute. We do not show the task that loads the TempCities table, shown in Fig. 8.17b, since it is similar to the one that loads the Categories table just described, except that the data is input from a file instead of a database.

a

City → State → Country
Aachen → North Rhine-Westphalia → Germany
Albuquerque → New Mexico → USA
Anchorage → Alaska → USA
Ann Arbor → Michigan → USA
Annecy → Haute-Savoie → France
...

b

TempCities
City
State
Country

Fig. 8.17 (a) Beginning of the file Cities.txt. (b) Associated table TempCities

The control task that loads the tables composing the hierarchy State → Country → Continent is depicted in Fig. 8.21a. As can be seen, this requires a sequence of data tasks. Figure 8.21b shows the data task that loads the Continent table. It reads the data from the XML file using the following XPath expression:

<Continents>/<Continent>/<ContinentName>

Then, a new column is added to the flow in order to be able to generate the surrogate key for the table in the data warehouse.

Figure 8.21c shows the task that loads the Country table. It reads the data from the XML file using the following XPath expressions:

<Continents>/<Continent>/<Country>/*
<Continents>/<Continent>/<ContinentName>

In this case, we need to read from the XML file not only the attributes of Country but also the ContinentName to which a country belongs. For example, when reading the Country element corresponding to Austria, we must also obtain the corresponding value of the element ContinentName, that is, Europe. Thus, the flow is now composed of the attributes CountryName, CountryCode, CountryCapital, Population, Subdivision, State, and Continent-Name (see Fig. 8.16b). The ContinentName value is then used in a lookup task for obtaining the corresponding ContinentKey from the data warehouse. Finally, the data in the flow is loaded into the warehouse. We do not show the task that loads the State table since it is similar to the one that loads the Country table just described.

The process that loads the City table is depicted in Fig. 8.22. The first task is an input data task over the table TempCities. Note that the final goal is to populate a table with a state key and a country key, one of which is null depending on the political division of the country, that is, on whether the country is divided into states or not. Thus, the first exclusive gateway tests whether State is null or not (recall that this is the optional attribute). In the first case, a lookup obtains the CountryKey. In the second case, we must match (State,Country) pairs in TempCities to values in the State and Country tables. However, as we have explained, states and countries can come in many forms;

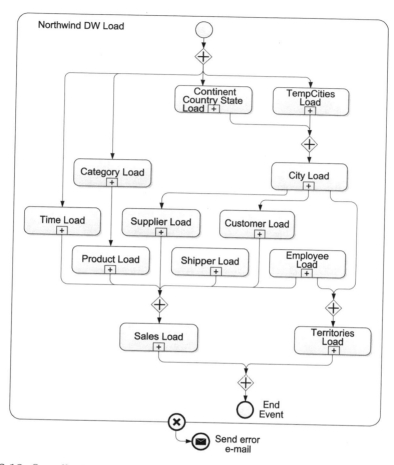

Fig. 8.18 Overall view of the conceptual ETL process for the Northwind data warehouse

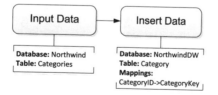

Fig. 8.19 Load of the Category dimension table

thus, we need three lookup tasks, as shown in the annotations in Fig. 8.22. The three lookups are as follows:

- The first lookup process records where State and Country correspond, respectively, to StateName and CountryName. An example is state Loire and country France.

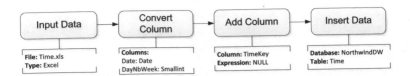

Fig. 8.20 Load of the Time dimension table

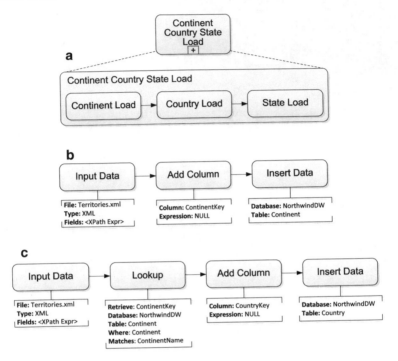

Fig. 8.21 Load of the tables for the State → Country → Continent hierarchy. (a) Associated control task. (b) Load of the Continent table. (c) Load of the Country table

- The second lookup process records where State and Country correspond, respectively, to EnglishStateName and CountryName. An example is state Lower Saxony, whose German name is Niedersachsen, together with country Germany.
- Finally, the third lookup process records where State and Country correspond, respectively, to StateName and CountryCode. An example is state Florida and country USA.

The SQL query associated with these lookups is as follows:

```
SELECT S.*, CountryName, CountryCode
FROM    State S JOIN Country C ON S.CountryKey = C.CountryKey
```

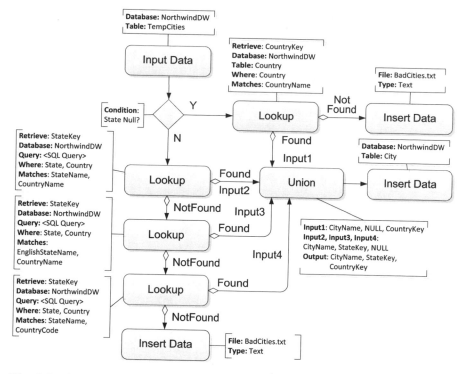

Fig. 8.22 Load of the City dimension table

Finally, a union is performed with the results of the four flows, and the table is populated with an insert data task. Note that in the City table, if a state was not found in the initial lookup (Input1 in Fig. 8.22), the attribute State will be null; on the other hand, if a state was found, it means that the city will have an associated state; therefore, the Country attribute will be null (Inputs2, Input3, and Input4 in the figure). Records for which the state and/or country are not found are stored into a BadCities.txt file.

Figure 8.23 shows the conceptual ETL process for loading the Customer table in the data warehouse. The input table Customers is read from the operational database using an input data task. Recall that the Region attribute in this table corresponds actually to a state name or a state code. Since this attribute is optional, the first exclusive gateway checks whether this attribute is null or not. If Region is null, a lookup checks if the corresponding (City, Country) pair matches a pair in TempCities and retrieves the State attribute from the latter, creating a new column. Since the value State just obtained may be null for countries without states, another exclusive gateway tests whether State is null, in which case a lookup obtains the CityKey by

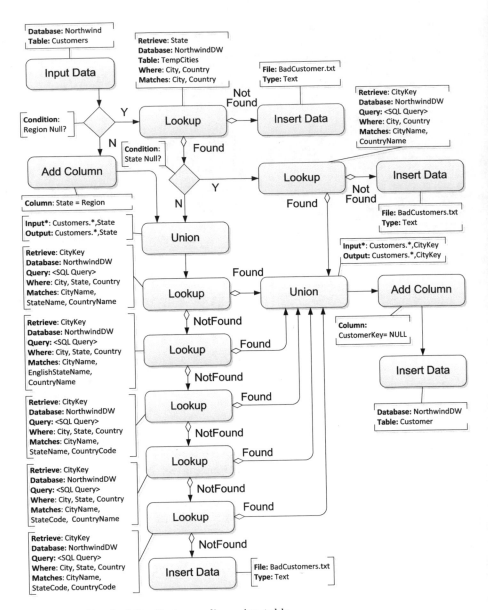

Fig. 8.23 Load of the Customer dimension table

matching values of City and Country in a lookup table defined by the following SQL query:

```
SELECT CityKey, CityName, CountryName
FROM   City C JOIN Country T ON C.CountryKey = T.CountryKey
```

Then, we send the obtained records to a union task in order to load them in the data warehouse.

Returning back to the first exclusive gateway, if the Region attribute is not null, we add a new column State initialized with the values of column Region and we make the union of these records with ones having a value of State different from null obtained in the first lookup.

Then, in a similar way as the task that loads the City table, five lookup tasks are needed, where each one tries to match a couple of values of State and Country to values in the lookup table built as a join between the City, State, and Country tables as follows:

```
SELECT  C.CityKey, C.CityName, S.StateName, S.EnglishStateName,
        S.StateCode, T.CountryName, T.CountryCode
FROM    City C JOIN State S ON C.StateKey = S.StateKey
        JOIN Country T ON S.CountryKey = T.CountryKey
```

Two additional cases are needed with respect to the City Load task:

- The fourth lookup process records where State and Country correspond, respectively, to StateCode and CountryName. An example is state BC and country Canada.
- The fifth lookup process records where State and Country correspond, respectively, to StateCode and CountryCode. An example is state AK and country USA.

Finally, we perform the union of all flows, add the column CustomerKey for the surrogate key initialized to null, and write to the target table by means of an insert data task. We omit the description of the ETL process that loads the Supplier table since it is similar to the one that loads the Customer table just described.

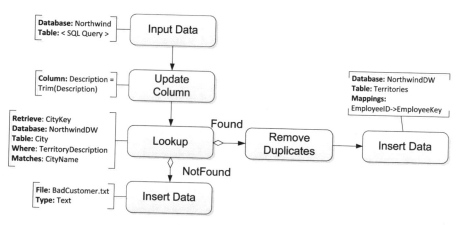

Fig. 8.24 Load of the Territories bridge table

Figure 8.24 depicts the process for loading the Territories bridge table. The input table is the following SQL query:

```
SELECT E.*, TerritoryDescription
FROM   EmployeeTerritories E JOIN Territories T ON E.TerritoryID = T.TerritoryID
```

Then, an update column task is applied to remove the leading spaces (with operation trim) from the attribute TerritoryDescription. The city key is then obtained with a lookup over the table City in the data warehouse, which adds the attribute CityKey to the flow. The data flow continues with a task that removes duplicates in the assignment of employees to cities. Indeed, in the Northwind operational database, New York appears twice in the Territories table with different identifiers, and employee number 5 is assigned to both of these versions of New York in the EmployeeTerritories table. Finally, after removing duplicates, we populate the Territories table with an insert data task, where a mapping matches the attribute EmployeeID in the database with the attribute EmployeeKey in the data warehouse.

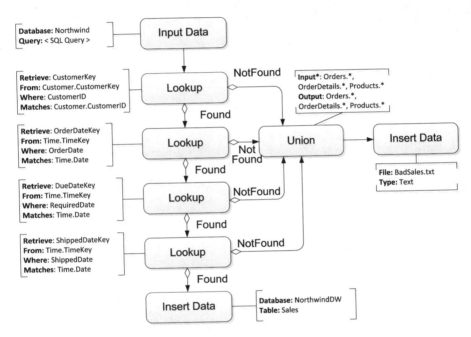

Fig. 8.25 Load of the Sales fact table

Figure 8.25 shows the conceptual ETL process for loading the Sales fact table. This task is performed once all the other tasks loading the dimension tables have been done. The process starts with an input data task that obtains data from the operational database by means of the SQL query below:

```
SELECT O.CustomerID, EmployeeID AS EmployeeKey, O.OrderDate,
       O.RequiredDate AS DueDate, O.ShippedDate,
       ShipVia AS ShipperKey, P.ProductID AS ProductKey,
       P.SupplierID AS SupplierKey, O.OrderID AS OrderNo,
       ROW_NUMBER() OVER (PARTITION BY D.OrderID
       ORDER BY D.ProductID) AS OrderLineNo,
```

```
         D.UnitPrice, Quantity, Discount,
         D.UnitPrice * (1-Discount) * Quantity AS SalesAmount,
         O.Freight/COUNT(*) OVER (PARTITION BY D.OrderID) AS Freight
FROM     Orders O, OrderDetails D, Products P
WHERE    O.OrderID = D.OrderID AND D.ProductID = P.ProductID
```

A sequence of lookups follows, which obtains the missing foreign keys for the
dimension tables. Finally, the fact table is loaded with the data retrieved.

8.4   Integration Services and Kettle

To be able to understand how the conceptual ETL design for the Northwind
data warehouse can be implemented using existing tools, in this section we
give a brief description of Microsoft Integration Services and Pentaho Data
Integration (also known as Kettle, the name we use from here on).

8.4.1   Overview of Integration Services

Integration Services is a component of SQL Server that can be used to
perform data migration tasks and in particular to implement and execute
ETL processes.

   In Integration Services, a *package* is basically a workflow containing a
collection of tasks executed in an orderly fashion. A package consists of a
control flow and, optionally, one or more *data flows*. Integration Services
provides three different types of control flow elements:

- *Tasks*, which are individual units of work that provide functionality to a
  package.
- *Containers*, which group tasks logically into units of work and are also used
  to define variables and events. Examples of containers are the Sequence
  Container and the For Loop Container.
- *Precedence constraints*, which connect tasks, containers, and executables in
  order to define the order in which these are executed within the workflow
  of a package.

   A control flow orchestrates the order of execution of package components
according to the precedence constraints defined. Among the many different
kinds of tasks supported by Integration Services, there are *data flow tasks*
(which run data flows to extract data, apply column-level transformations,
and load data), *data preparation tasks* (which copy files and directories,
download files and data, profile data for cleansing, and so on), *Analysis
Services tasks* (which create, modify, delete, and process Analysis Services

objects), and *workflow tasks* (which communicate with other processes to run packages, send and receive messages, send e-mail messages, and so on).

Creating a control flow in Integration Services requires the following steps:

- *Adding containers* that implement repeating workflows in a package.
- *Adding tasks* of the kinds mentioned above. If the package has to work with data (which is most of the times the case), the control flow must include at least one data flow task.
- *Connecting containers and tasks* using precedence constraints. Tasks or containers can be joined in a control flow dragging their connectors from one item to another. A connector between two items represents a precedence constraint, which specifies that the first one must be executed successfully before the next one in the control flow can run.
- *Adding connection managers*, which are needed when a task requires a connection to a data source.

A *data flow* extracts data into memory, transforms them, and writes them to a destination. Integration Services provides three different types of data flow components as follows:

- *Sources*, which extract data from data stores like tables and views in relational databases, files, and Analysis Services databases. Integration Services can connect with OLE DB data sources, like SQL Server, Oracle, or DB2. Also, sources can be Excel files, flat files, and XML files, among other ones.
- *Transformations*, which modify, summarize, and clean data. These transformations can split, divert, or merge the flow. Examples of transformations are **Conditional Split**, **Copy Column**, and **Aggregate**.
- *Destinations*, which load data into data stores or create in-memory data sets.

Creating a data flow includes the following steps:

- *Adding one or more sources* to extract data from files and databases and adding connection managers to connect to these sources.
- *Adding the transformations* to satisfy the package requirements.
- *Connecting data flow components*.
- *Adding one or more destinations* to load data into data stores.
- *Configuring error outputs* on components.
- *Including annotations* to document the data flow.

We illustrate all these concepts in Sect. 8.5 when we study the implementation of the Northwind ETL process in Integration Services.

8.4.2 Overview of Kettle

We now give an overview of Kettle, a tool for designing and executing ETL tasks. It is also known as Pentaho Data Integration and is a component of the Pentaho Business Analytics suite.

The main components of Kettle are as follows:

- *Transformations*, which are logical tasks consisting in steps connected by hops, defined below. Transformations are essentially data flows, and their purpose is to extract, transform, and load data.
- *Steps* are the basic components of a transformation. A step performs a specific task, such as reading data from a flat file, filtering rows, and writing to a database. The steps available in Kettle are grouped according to their function, such as input, output, scripting, and so on. Note that the steps in a transformation run *in parallel*, each one in its own thread.
- *Hops* are data paths that connect steps to each other, allowing records to pass from one step to another. Hops determine the flow of data through the steps, although not necessarily the sequence in which they run.
- *Jobs* are workflows that orchestrate the individual pieces of functionality implementing an entire ETL process. Jobs are composed of job entries, job hops, and job settings.
- *Job entries* are the primary building blocks of a job and correspond to the steps in data transformations.
- *Job hops* specify the execution order of job entries and the conditions on which they are executed based on the results of previous entries. Job hops behave differently from hops used in a transformation.
- *Job settings* are the options that control the behavior of a job and the method of logging a job's actions.

It is worth mentioning that loops are not allowed in transformations since the field values that are passed from one step to another are dependent on the previous steps, and as we said above, steps are executed in parallel. However, loops are allowed in jobs since job entries are executed sequentially.

Kettle is composed of the following components:

- *Data Integration Server*, which performs the actual data integration tasks. Its primary functions are to *execute* jobs and transformations, to define and manage *security*, to provide *content management* facilities to administer jobs and transformations in collaborative development environments, and to provide services for *scheduling* and monitoring activities.
- *Spoon*, a graphical user interface for designing jobs and transformations. The transformations can be executed locally within Spoon or in the Data Integration Server. Spoon provides a way to create complex ETL jobs without having to read or write code.

- *Pan*, a stand-alone command line tool for executing transformations. Pan reads data from and writes data to various data sources and is used also to manipulate data.
- *Kitchen*, a stand-alone command line tool for executing jobs. Jobs are usually scheduled to run in batch mode at regular intervals.
- *Carte*, a lightweight server for running jobs and transformations on a remote host. It provides similar execution capabilities as the Data Integration Server but does not provide scheduling, security, and content management facilities.

We illustrate these concepts in Sect. 8.6 when we study the implementation of the Northwind ETL process in Kettle.

8.5   The Northwind ETL Process in Integration Services

In this section, we show an implementation in Integration Services of the ETL process that loads the Northwind data warehouse. We compare this implementation with the conceptual design presented in Sect. 8.3 and show how to translate the constructs of the conceptual ETL language into the equivalent ones in Integration Services. In our implementation, the Northwind operational database and the Northwind data warehouse are located on an SQL Server database.

Figure 8.26 shows the overall ETL process. It is composed of one sequence container task (the one with the blue arrow in the left) and eleven data flow tasks. All of these tasks are connected by precedence constraints, represented by green arrows. The reader can compare this representation with the one in Fig. 8.18. Note that gateways are not present, but the semantics of the corresponding arrows is quite similar: no task can start until all precedent tasks have finished.

Several data flow tasks are simple. For example, the task that loads the Category table is given in Fig. 8.27a (compare with Fig. 8.19), where the data flow tasks are an OLE DB Source task that reads the entire table from the operational database and an OLE DB Destination task that receives the output from the previous task and stores it in the data warehouse. Similar data flows are used for loading the Product, Shipper, and Employee tables.

Another straightforward task is the data flow that loads the Time dimension table, shown in Fig. 8.27b. After loading the source Excel file, a data conversion transformation is needed to convert the data types from the Excel file into the data types of the database. We can also see that this is very similar to the conceptual specification depicted in Fig. 8.20, except that the addition of the surrogate key column is implicit in the Time Load task. We further explain this next.

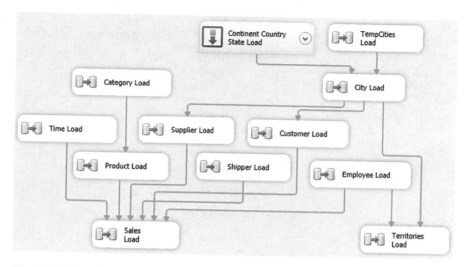

Fig. 8.26 Overall view of the ETL process in Integration Services

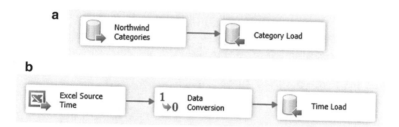

Fig. 8.27 Load of the Category (**a**) and the Time (**b**) dimension tables

As explained in Sect. 8.3, in some tables, the keys of the operational database are reused as surrogate keys in the data warehouse, while in other tables a surrogate key must be generated in the data warehouse. Therefore, the mapping of columns in the OLE DB Destination tasks should be done in one of the ways shown in Fig. 8.28. For example, for the table Category (Fig. 8.28a), we reuse the key in the operational database (CategoryID) as key in the data warehouse (CategoryKey). On the other hand, for the table Customer (Fig. 8.28b), the CustomerID key in the operational database is kept in the CustomerID column in the data warehouse, and a new value for CustomerKey is generated during the insertion in the data warehouse.

Figure 8.29 shows the data flow used for loading the table TempCities from the text file Cities.txt. A data conversion transformation is needed to convert the default types obtained from the text file into the database types.

Figure 8.30a shows the data flow that loads the hierarchy composed of the Continent, Country, and State tables. This is the Integration Services equivalent to the conceptual control flow defined in Fig. 8.21a. A Sequence

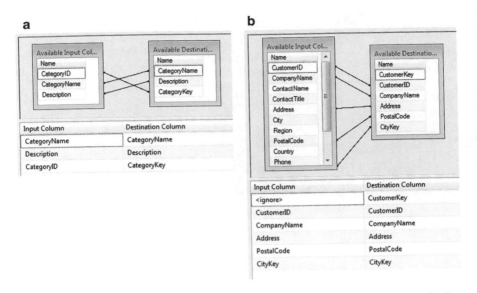

Fig. 8.28 Mappings of the source and destination columns, depending on whether the key in the operational database is reused in the data warehouse

Fig. 8.29 Load of the TempCities table

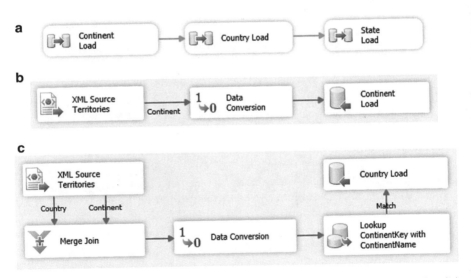

Fig. 8.30 (a) Load of the tables for the Continent → Country → State hierarchy. (b) Load of the Continent dimension table. (c) Load of the Country dimension table

Container is used for the three data flows that load the tables of the hierarchy. Since Continent is the highest level in the hierarchy, we first need to produce a key for it, so it can be later referenced from the Country level. The data flow for loading the table Continent is given in Fig. 8.30b. With respect to the conceptual model given in Fig. 8.21b, a data conversion is needed to convert the data types from the XML file into the data types of the database. This is shown in Fig. 8.31, where the ContinentName, read from the XML file, is by default of length 255, and it is converted into a string of length 20. Finally, the Continent table is loaded, and a ContinentKey is automatically generated.

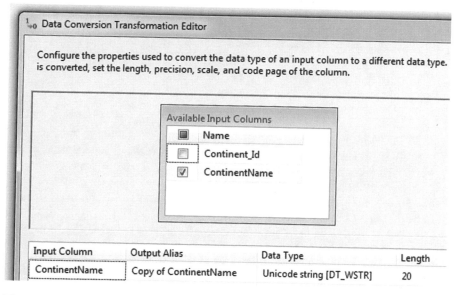

Fig. 8.31 Conversion of the data types that are input from the XML file

The data flow that loads the table Country is given in Fig. 8.30c. With respect to the conceptual model given in Fig. 8.21b, a merge join transformation is needed to obtain for a given Country the corresponding ContinentName. A data conversion transformation is needed to convert the data types from the XML file into the data types of the database. Then, a lookup transformation is needed to obtain, from the database, the ContinentKey corresponding to the ContinentName. This attribute is also added to the flow. Finally, the Country table is loaded analogously to the Continent table above. Notice that the data flow that loads the table State is similar; therefore, we omit it.

Figure 8.32 shows the data flow for loading the City table. The conceptual model for the data flow has been presented in Fig. 8.22. The data flow needs to associate to each city in the TempCities table either a StateKey or a CountryKey, depending on whether or not the corresponding country is divided in states. For this, the conditional split tests if the State is null or not.

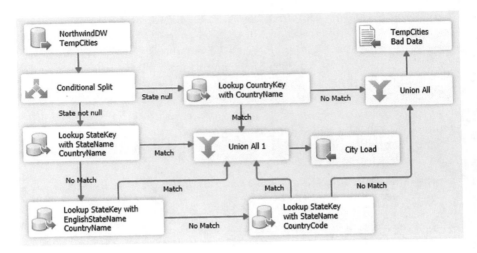

Fig. 8.32 Load of the City dimension table

In the first case, a lookup is needed for obtaining the CountryKey. This will obtain, for example, the country key for Singapore, which has no states. In the second case, as explained in Sect. 8.3, three lookup tasks are needed, where a couple of values of State and Country in TempCities must be matched with either StateName and CountryName, EnglishStateName and CountryName, or StateName and CountryCode. Since this process is similar to the one in the conceptual design, we do not repeat it here. Finally, a union of the four flows is performed (note that this task is named Union All 1 since there cannot exist two tasks with the same name), and the City table is loaded.

The task that loads the Customer table is shown in Fig. 8.33, while its conceptual schema is given in Fig. 8.23. It starts with a conditional split since some customers have a null value in Region (this attribute in fact corresponds to states). In this case, a lookup adds a column State by matching City and Country from Customers with City and Country from TempCities. Notice that the value State just obtained may be null for countries without states, and thus another conditional split (called Conditional Split 1) is needed. If State is null, then a lookup tries to find a CityKey by means of matching values of City and Country. The SQL query of the lookup task, the same as in Sect. 8.3, is as follows:

```
SELECT CityKey, CityName, CountryName
FROM    City C JOIN Country T ON C.CountryKey = T.CountryKey
```

On the other hand, for customers that have a nonnull Region, the values of this column are copied into a new column State. Analogously to the loading of City, we must perform five lookup tasks in order to retrieve the city key. Since this process is analogous to the one in the conceptual design given in Sect. 8.3, we do not repeat the details here. Finally, we perform the union of

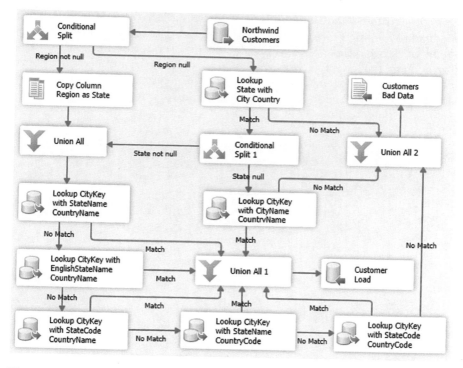

Fig. 8.33 Load of the Customer dimension table

all flows and load the data into the warehouse. A similar data flow task is used for loading the **Supplier** dimension table.

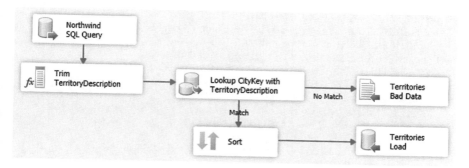

Fig. 8.34 Load of the Territories bridge table

The data flow that loads the **Territories** bridge table is shown in Fig. 8.34. This data flow is similar to the conceptual design of Fig. 8.24. It starts with an OLE DB Source task consisting in an SQL query that joins the

EmployeeTerritories and the Territories table as in Sect. 8.3. It continues with a derived column transformation that removes the trailing spaces in the values of TerritoryDescription. Then, a lookup transformation searches the corresponding values of CityKey in City. The data flow continues with a sort transformation that removes duplicates in the assignment of employees to territories, as described in Sect. 8.3. Finally, the data flow finishes by loading the data warehouse table.

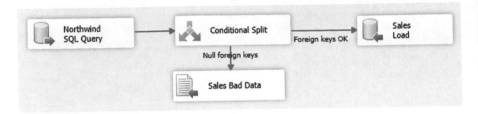

Fig. 8.35 Load of the Sales fact table

Finally, the data flow that loads the Sales table is shown in Fig. 8.35. The first OLE DB Source task includes an SQL query that combines data from the operational database and the data warehouse, as follows:

```
SELECT
    ( SELECT CustomerKey FROM dbo.Customer C
      WHERE C.CustomerID = O.CustomerID) AS CustomerKey,
    EmployeeID AS EmployeeKey,
    ( SELECT TimeKey FROM dbo.Time T
      WHERE T.Date = O.OrderDate) AS OrderDateKey,
    ( SELECT TimeKey FROM dbo.Time T
      WHERE T.Date = O.RequiredDate) AS DueDateKey,
    ( SELECT TimeKey FROM dbo.Time T
      WHERE T.Date = O.ShippedDate) AS ShippedDateKey,
    ShipVia AS ShipperKey, P.ProductID AS ProductKey,
    SupplierID AS SupplierKey, O.OrderID AS OrderNo,
    CONVERT(INT, ROW_NUMBER() OVER (PARTITION BY D.OrderID
      ORDER BY D.ProductID)) AS OrderLineNo,
    D.UnitPrice, Quantity, Discount,
    CONVERT(MONEY, D.UnitPrice * (1-Discount) * Quantity) AS SalesAmount,
    CONVERT(MONEY, O.Freight/COUNT(*) OVER
      (PARTITION BY D.OrderID)) AS Freight
  FROM   Northwind.dbo.Orders O, Northwind.dbo.OrderDetails D,
         Northwind.dbo.Products P
WHERE O.OrderID = D.OrderID AND D.ProductID = P.ProductID
```

Notice that the above query obtains data from both the Northwind operational database and the Northwind data warehouse in a single query. This is possible to do in Integration Services but not in other platforms such as in PostgreSQL. Thus, the above query performs the lookups of surrogate keys from the data warehouse in the inner queries of the SELECT clause. However, if these surrogate keys are not found, null values are returned in the result. Therefore, a conditional split transformation task selects the records obtained in the previous query with a null value in the lookup columns and stores them in a flat file. The correct records are loaded in the data warehouse.

Notice the difference of the above query with respect to the corresponding query in the conceptual model given in Fig. 8.25. While the above query implements all the necessary lookups, in the conceptual design we have chosen to implement the lookups in individual tasks, which conveys information in a clearer way. Therefore, the conceptual design is more appropriate to communicate the process steps within the project participants and also gives us the flexibility to choose the implementation that is more appropriate for the application needs.

8.6 The Northwind ETL Process in Kettle

We describe next a possible implementation in Kettle of the ETL process that loads the Northwind data warehouse. In our implementation, the Northwind operational database and the Northwind data warehouse are located on a PostgreSQL database server.

Figure 8.36 shows the overall ETL process, in Kettle terminology, a job. It is similar to the corresponding process for Integration Services shown in Fig. 8.26. Notice that we have not implemented a control flow for grouping the three tasks that load the hierarchy composed of the Continent, Country, and State tables, although this could be done in Kettle using subjobs.

Figure 8.37a shows the transformation (or flow) that loads the Category dimension table. As can be seen, it is similar to the data flow in Integration Services shown in Fig. 8.27a. On the other hand, Fig. 8.37b shows the transformation that loads the Time dimension table. Compared with the corresponding data flow shown in Fig. 8.27b, Integration Services requires an additional step for setting the appropriate data types for the attributes read, while this is specified in the transformation step (or task) that reads the CSV file in Kettle.[2]

Transformations similar to the above are needed to load the Product and Shipper tables. However, although loading the Employee table (which contains a parent-child hierarchy) in Integration Services is also similar to the other ones, this is not the case in Kettle, as Fig. 8.38 shows. In this figure, we can see the transformation that loads the Employee dimension table. We have seen in Chap. 7 that Mondrian requires a closure table that contains the

---

[2]Note that in what follows we will refer indistinctly to transformations and steps (in Kettle terminology) or flows and tasks (in Integration Services terminology), respectively, since they represent analogous concepts.

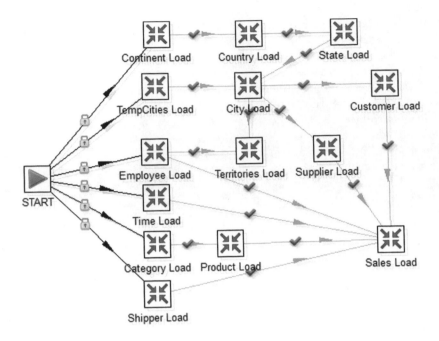

Fig. 8.36 Overall view of the ETL process in Kettle

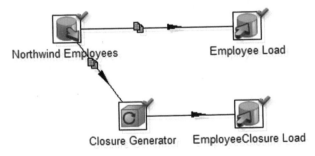

Fig. 8.37 Load of the Category (**a**) and the Time (**b**) dimension tables

Fig. 8.38 Load of the Employee dimension table

transitive closure of the Supervision hierarchy. For this reason, after reading the Employees table in the Northwind database, the rows read are sent *in parallel* to the steps that load the Employee and the EmployeeClosure tables, as shown by the icon over the arrows that represent those flows.

Fig. 8.39 Load of the Continent (**a**) and the Country (**b**) dimension tables

Figure 8.39a shows the transformation that loads the Continent dimension table. With respect to the corresponding data flow in Fig. 8.30b, we can see that the conversion task is not required in Kettle. On the other hand, the transformation that loads the Country dimension table in Fig. 8.39b differs from the corresponding transformation in Integration Services in Fig. 8.30c, since in Kettle, we can find the ContinentName associated with a given Country using an XPath expression in a similar way as was done in the conceptual design given in Sect. 8.3. On the other hand, in Integration Services, a merge join is needed for this task. After this, a lookup over the database is performed to get the ContinentKey, and finally the Country table is loaded.

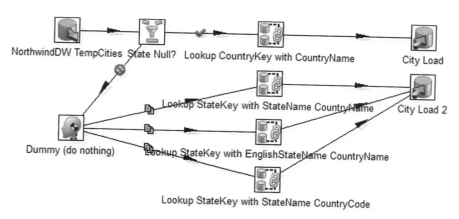

Fig. 8.40 Load of the City dimension table

Figure 8.40 shows the transformation that loads the City dimension table. It significantly differs from the corresponding transformation in Fig. 8.32 in several aspects. First, it is not possible to cascade lookup steps in Kettle as it is done with lookup tasks in Integration Services since in the latter the lookup task allows one to split the records into alternative flows depending on whether a lookup value is found or not, while there is no simple way to do this in Kettle. Thus, the cascade lookups must be implemented as a collection of parallel flows. For the same reason, in the Kettle implementation, we do not have tasks that load records for which a lookup value was not found in a text file. The loading of the City table illustrates the above limitation. In the first step, the transformation tests whether State is null or not. The rows that do not have a null value must be sent in parallel to all the subsequent lookup tasks, as shown by the icon over the arrows that represent the flows, while in Integration Services these lookup tasks are cascaded. Note that we need a dummy task from which the parallel tasks are triggered. A second important difference between the Integration Services and Kettle implementations is that in the latter there is no need to explicitly include a union task, since when a step has multiple input flows, the union of all such flows is performed. However, this requires that all the fields in the input flows have the same name and appear in the same order in the rows. For this reason, two different steps are needed for loading the City table in Kettle: one for the records containing CountryKey (task City Load) and the other for the records containing StateKey (task City Load 2).

Figure 8.41 shows the transformation that loads the Customer dimension table. Notice that there are two different steps for performing lookups, as indicated by the different icons: the one that looks for State and the other ones that look for CityKey. The former lookup type looks for values *in a single table* and sends *all* rows in the input flow to the output flow, where null values are put in the lookup fields when there is no match. After this, in order to split the flow, we can check if State is null. The second type of lookup looks

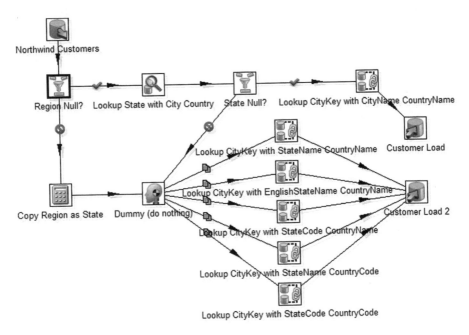

Fig. 8.41 Load of the Customer dimension table

for values *in an SQL query* and *only* sends to the output stream the rows for which a matching value is found. A dummy task is needed in Kettle for performing the union between the step that copies the column Region into a new column State and the step that filters the rows for which a value for State was found in the first lookup. For the same reasons explained above, the transformation in Fig. 8.41 differs from the corresponding one in Fig. 8.33 in that the dummy step sends the input rows to all subsequent lookup tasks. The SQL query used in the lookup step that looks for CityKey with StateName and CountryName is as follows:

```
SELECT  C.CityKey
FROM    City C JOIN State S ON C.StateKey = S.Statekey
        JOIN Country T ON S.CountryKey = T.CountryKey
WHERE   ? = CityName AND ? = StateName AND ? = CountryName
```

The '?' symbols are used as parameters that are replaced in the flow with the values of City, State, and Country that are read from the Customers table. The SQL queries for the other lookups are similar.

The implementation for the Supplier dimension table is similar so we omit its description.

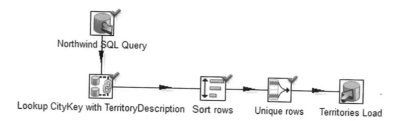

Northwind SQL Query

Lookup CityKey with TerritoryDescription   Sort rows   Unique rows   Territories Load

Fig. 8.42 Load of the Territories bridge table

Figure 8.42 shows the transformation that loads the Territories bridge table. The corresponding data flow for Integration Services is shown in Fig. 8.34. The flow starts by obtaining the assignment of employees to territories from the Northwind database using an SQL query. In the case of Kettle, there is no step that removes the trailing spaces in the TerritoryDescription column. This was taken into account in the SQL query of the subsequent lookup step as follows:

```
SELECT CityKey
FROM   City
WHERE  TRIM(?) = CityName
```

Note that a similar solution could have been applied in Integration Services. After the lookup of the CityKey, Kettle requires a sort process prior to the unique rows step. Compared with the corresponding implementation in

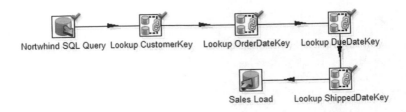

Fig. 8.43 Load of the Sales fact table

Integration Services, in the latter the sort data task includes the capability to remove duplicates, which in Kettle requires two transformation steps.

Finally, Fig. 8.43 shows the transformation that loads the Sales fact table. The corresponding flow for Integration Services is shown in Fig. 8.35. The flow starts by obtaining values from the following SQL query addressed to the Northwind database, which is the same as in the conceptual design given in Sect. 8.3:

```
SELECT O.CustomerID, EmployeeID AS EmployeeKey,
       O.OrderDate, O.RequiredDate, O.ShippedDate,
       ShipVia AS ShipperKey, P.ProductID AS ProductKey,
       P.SupplierID AS SupplierKey, O.OrderID AS OrderNo,
       ROW_NUMBER() OVER (PARTITION BY D.OrderID
       ORDER BY D.ProductID) AS OrderLineNo,
       D.UnitPrice, Quantity, Discount,
       D.UnitPrice * (1-Discount) * Quantity AS SalesAmount,
       O.Freight/COUNT(*) OVER (PARTITION BY D.OrderID) AS Freight
FROM   Orders O, OrderDetails D, Products P
WHERE  O.OrderID = D.OrderID AND D.ProductID = P.ProductID
```

In the corresponding query in Integration Services, it is possible to query both the Northwind operational database and the Northwind data warehouse in a single query, while this not possible natively in PostgreSQL. For this, additional lookup steps are needed in Kettle for obtaining the surrogate keys. As a consequence, an additional task is needed in Integration Services for removing the records with null values for surrogate keys obtained from the SQL query, while these records are automatically removed in the lookup steps in Kettle.

8.7 Summary

In this chapter, we have presented a detailed study of ETL processes, a key component of a data warehousing architecture. We have shown the usefulness of producing a conceptual model of ETL processes, independent of any implementation. In this way, deploying the model in different tools is possible. Further, information can be shared and distributed in a language that can be easily understood by the stakeholders. The conceptual model for ETL processes is based on the BPMN standard, relying on the assumption that ETL processes are similar to business processes. We illustrated the design and implementation of ETL processes with a complete example based on the Northwind case study. Thus, the reader can have a clear idea of the usual tasks that must be performed while implementing such processes. We provided three versions of the Northwind ETL process, a conceptual one using BPMN and two implementations in Microsoft Integration Services and in Pentaho Kettle. We described the differences between the three versions of this ETL process, taking into account implementation considerations in the two platforms chosen.

8.8   Bibliographic Notes

A classic reference for ETL is the book by Kimball and Caserta [102]. Various approaches for designing, optimizing, and automating ETL processes have been proposed in the last few years. A survey of ETL technology can be found in [219]. Simitsis et al. [221] represent ETL processes as a graph where nodes match to transformations, constraints, attributes, and data stores and edges correspond to data flows, inter-attribute relations, compositions, and concurrent candidates. An approach for mapping conceptual ETL design to logical ETL design was proposed in [188]. The books [105] and [26] describe in detail, respectively, Microsoft Integration Services and Pentaho Data Integration or Kettle. An introduction to business process modeling, and an overview of BPMN 2.0 are provided in [211]. This chapter is based on previous work on using BPMN as a conceptual model for ETL processes, performed by the authors and collaborators [45–48].

Although in this chapter we focused on Integration Services and Kettle, other tools are available for designing and executing ETL processes, like Oracle Data Integrator [80] or Talend Open Studio [19]. However, all existing tools provide their own language for specifying ETL processes. Their languages differ considerably in many respects, in particular since they are based on different paradigms and have different expression power.

8.9   Review Questions

8.1 What is a business process? Why do we need to model business processes?

8.2 Describe and classify the main constructs of BPMN.

8.3 What is the difference between an exclusive and an inclusive gateway?

8.4 Can we model splitting of flows without gateways? Are there cases where this is not possible?

8.5 Give examples of the use of the several kinds of BPMN events.

8.6 What is a default flow? When should we use it?

8.7 Discuss why should we or should we not need a conceptual design phase for ETL processes.

8.8 Why is BPMN appropriate for modeling ETL processes? Do you think that there are situations where this is not the case?

8.9 Explain the rationale of the methodology studied in the chapter. What are control tasks? What are data tasks?

8.10 What is the main difference between the diagrams for ETL design proposed in this chapter and the typical BPMN diagram?

8.11 Discuss the advantages and disadvantages of representing, in Integration Services, a sequence of tasks as a single SQL query (see an example in Sect. 8.5).

8.12 Compare Integration Services and Pentaho Kettle. What are the main differences between them? For each element of the former (e.g., a flow), describe the analogous one on the latter.

8.13 Discuss why it is not possible to perform a sequence of lookups in Kettle, as it is done in Integration Services.

8.10   Exercises

8.1 Design the conceptual ETL schema for loading the **Product** dimension of the Northwind data warehouse.

8.2 In the Northwind data warehouse, suppose that surrogate keys **CategoryKey** and **ProductKey** are added, respectively, to the **Category** and the **Product** tables, while the operational keys are kept in attributes **CategoryID** and **ProductID**. Modify the conceptual ETL schema obtained in Ex. 8.1 to take into account this situation.

8.3 Modify the conceptual ETL schema obtained in Ex. 8.2 to take into account a refresh scenario in which products obtained from the operational database may be already in the **Product** dimension in the data warehouse. Use a type 1 solution for the slowly changing dimension by which the attribute values obtained from the operational database are updated in the data warehouse.

8.4 Modify the conceptual ETL schema obtained in Ex. 8.3 by using a type 2 solution for the slowly changing dimension **Product** by which for the products that have changed the value of the To attribute for the current record is set to the current date and a new record is inserted in the dimension with a null value in that attribute.

8.5 Design the conceptual ETL schema for loading the **Supplier** dimension of the Northwind data warehouse.

8.6 Implement in Integration Services the conceptual schemas of Exs. 8.1 and 8.5.

8.7 Implement in Kettle the conceptual schemas of Exs. 8.1 and 8.5.

8.8 Given the operational database of the French horse race application obtained in Ex. 2.1 and the associated data warehouse obtained in Ex. 4.5, design the conceptual ETL schema that loads the data warehouse from the operational database.

8.9 Given the operational database of the Formula One application obtained in Ex. 2.2 and the associated data warehouse obtained in Ex. 4.7, design the conceptual ETL schema that loads the data warehouse from the operational database.

8.10 Given the source database in Ex. 5.9 and the schema of your solution, implement in Integration Services the ETL schema that loads the data warehouse from the sources.

8.11 Given the source database in Ex. 5.9 and the schema of your solution, implement in Kettle the ETL schema that loads the data warehouse from the sources.

Chapter 9
Data Analytics: Exploiting the Data Warehouse

Analytics can be defined as the discovery and communication of meaningful patterns in data. Organizations apply analytics to their data in order to describe, predict, and improve organizational performance. Analytics uses descriptive and predictive models to gain valuable knowledge from data and uses this insight to guide decision making. Analytics relies on data visualization to communicate insight. We can distinguish several variations of analytics depending on the kind of data to be analyzed. While data analytics copes with traditional structured data, text analytics refers to the analysis of unstructured textual sources such as those found in blogs, social networks, and the like. Web analytics refers to the collection, analysis, and reporting of web data. Finally, visual analytics combines automated analysis techniques with interactive visualizations, providing effective means to interactively explore large and complex data sets for decision making.

In this chapter, we focus on data analytics in the context of data warehousing, that is, on the exploitation of the data collected in the warehouse to support the decision-making process. We describe several tools that can be used for this purpose, namely, data mining, key performance indicators (KPIs), and dashboards. We start in Sect. 9.1 by presenting the most widely used data mining tasks and the techniques that implement them. We focus on decision trees, clustering, and association analysis and also comment on other techniques like regression and pattern analysis. Then, in Sect. 9.2, we discuss the notion of KPIs. Finally, in Sect. 9.3, we explain how dashboards are used to display KPIs and other organizational information in a way that the managers can take timely and informed decisions. In all cases, we implement these techniques over the Northwind case study using Microsoft Analysis Services.

Note that this chapter is not intended to be a comprehensive presentation of these topics as there are many books entirely devoted to each one of them. We give an introduction to these topics in the context of data warehouses and point at the end of the chapter to popular references in these domains.

A. Vaisman and E. Zimányi, *Data Warehouse Systems*, Data-Centric Systems and Applications, DOI 10.1007/978-3-642-54655-6_9, © Springer-Verlag Berlin Heidelberg 2014

9.1   Data Mining

Data mining is the analysis of often large data sets to find unsuspected interesting relationships and to summarize data in novel ways that are both understandable and useful to the users. Mining information and knowledge from large databases had become nowadays a key topic in database systems. Thus, vendors of such systems, as well as the academic community, have been giving increasing attention to the development of data mining tools. The growing capability to collect and process data, enhanced with the possibilities given by data warehousing, has generated the necessity to have tools which can help to handle this explosive growth and to extract useful information from such data, and data mining has emerged as an answer to these needs.

Data mining is a single step in a larger process called **knowledge discovery in databases**, which aims at the extraction of nontrivial, implicit, previously unknown, and potentially useful information from data in databases. The knowledge discovery process involves several steps such as data cleaning, selection, transformation, reduction, model selection, and, finally, exploitation of the extracted knowledge.

Data mining borrows from several scientific fields like artificial intelligence, statistics, neural networks, and other ones, but the need for a separate research area is justified by the size of the data collections under analysis. The information is hidden in large and often heterogeneous collections of data, located in several different sources, with users demanding friendly and effective visualization tools. On the other hand, usual data mining queries cannot be answered in plain SQL. Moreover, it is often the case that the user does not know what she is looking for, so she needs an interactive environment, which can be provided by a combination of OLAP and data mining tools.

We point out next some requirements in data mining not covered by the scientific fields from which it inherits:

- Heterogeneous data must be handled, in addition to traditional relational data. For example, textual, web, spatial, and temporal data, among others, must be supported.
- Efficient and scalable algorithms are required due to the size of the data under analysis.
- Graphical user interfaces are necessary for knowledge discovery, since it is often the case that nonexpert users interact with such systems.
- Privacy-aware data mining algorithms must be developed, since data are used in strategic planning and decision making, increasing the need for data protection, in addition to privacy regulation compliance.
- Mining at different abstraction levels also needs to be supported. Sometimes, essential knowledge that cannot be found at some level of abstraction could be discovered at finer or coarser granularity levels.

- Since data in databases are constantly being modified, discovery methods should be incremental, to be able to update results as data change, without needing to rerun the algorithms from scratch.

9.1.1 Data Mining Tasks

Data mining can be categorized into types of tasks, which correspond to various different objectives of the data analyst. Data mining tasks aim at discovering models and patterns. A **model** is a global summary of a data set. A simple model can be represented by a linear equation like

$$Y = aX + b$$

where X and Y are variables and a and b are parameters. Opposite to the global nature of a model, **patterns** make statements about restricted regions of space spanned by the variables. An example is the simple probabilistic statement

$$\text{if } X > x_1 \text{ then } \text{prob}(Y > y_1) = p_1.$$

Thus, a pattern describes a structure of a relatively small part of the data space. We next discuss the main data mining tasks.

Exploratory data analysis is an approach for data analysis that uses a variety of (mostly graphical) techniques to get insight into a data set, aimed at exploring the data without a clear idea of what we are looking for. Thus, these techniques are typically visual and interactive. A common example of an exploratory data analysis technique is to perform a scatterplot of the data set in the plane and visually analyze the characteristics of such data set. For example, if we can approximate this set of points using a line, we say that the data set is linear. The same plot can also be used to visually look for outliers.

The goal of **descriptive modeling** is to describe the data or the process that generates such data. A typical descriptive technique is **clustering**. This technique aims at putting together similar records based on the values of their attributes. For example, in commercial databases, we may want to split the records into homogeneous groups so that similar people (e.g., customers) fall in the same group. There are two possibilities in this respect. We can either define the number of groups in advance or let the algorithm discover natural groups of data.

Predictive modeling aims at building a model that predicts the value of one variable from the values of other ones. Typical techniques are **classification** and **regression**. In the former, the variable being predicted is categorical, while in the latter, the variable to be predicted is quantitative. For example, in classification, we may want to categorize insurance customers according to three levels of risk: low, medium, and high. Regression models can be used to predict the value of a commodity. The key difference between both prediction and description is that prediction has a unique variable as objective, while in descriptive problems no single variable is central to the model. In this chapter, we focus on classification.

Pattern discovery aims at revealing either a regular behavior in a data set or records that deviate from such a regular behavior. A typical example of the former is the problem of finding **sequential patterns** in a data set. In traffic analysis, for instance, we can discover frequent routes of moving objects like cars, trucks, and pedestrians. An example of finding irregular behavior is to discover fraudulent credit card transactions. Another problem related to pattern discovery arises when, given a pattern of interest, the user wants to discover similar ones in the data set. This is used, for instance, to find documents relevant to a set of keywords or images similar to a given one.

Typically, data mining algorithms have the following components:

- A model or pattern, for determining the underlying structure or functional forms that we are looking for in the data.
- A score function, to assess the quality of the model.
- Optimization and search methods, to optimize the score function and search over different models and patterns.
- Data management strategies, to handle data access efficiently during search and optimization.

In the next sections, we give a brief overview of the most important data mining techniques and algorithms used to carry out the data mining tasks described above. We will illustrate these using the Northwind data warehouse given in Fig. 5.4, to which we added two tables, depicted in Fig. 9.1, one containing customer demographic data and another containing prospective new customers. The latter will be used for prediction purposes, to forecast the probability that a new customer places an order above a certain amount.

We explain next some of the attributes of these tables. The domain of attribute BusinessType is the set {Minimart, Grocery, Supermarket, Hypermarket, Pub, Tavern, Café, Restaurant, Delicatessen}. The domain of attribute OwnershipType is the set {Soletrader, Partnership, Cooperative, Limited liability company, Unlimited liability company, Corporation, Franchise}. Attributes TotalEmployees and PermanentEmployees have the following categorical values:

- 1: 1–19
- 2: 20–49
- 3: 50–99
- 4: 100–249
- 5: 250–499
- 6: 500–999
- 7: 1,000–2,500
- 8: Over 2,500

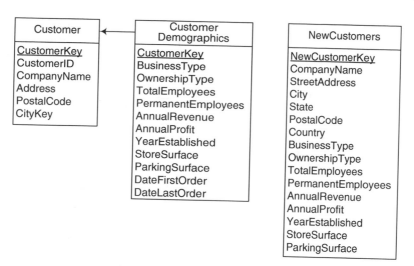

Fig. 9.1 Tables CustomerDemographics and NewCustomers added to the Northwind data warehouse given in Fig. 5.4

Attributes AnnualRevenue and AnnualProfit have the following values:

- 1: Under $10,000
- 2: $10,000–50,000
- 3: $50,000–100,000
- 4: $100,000–500,000
- 5: $500,000–1,000,000
- 6: Over $1,000,000

Attribute YearEstablished has a range of 1950–1997. Attributes StoreSurface and ParkingSurface are expressed in square meters. Finally, attributes Date-FirstOrder and DateLastOrder are derived from the Sales fact table.

9.1.2 Supervised Classification

Supervised classification is the process that allocates a set of objects in a database to different predefined classes according to a model built on the attributes of these objects. For this, a database DB is split into a **training set** E and a **test set** T. The tuples of DB and T have the same format, while the tuples in E have an additional field, which is the **class identity**, which stores the class of each tuple in the training set. These classes are used to generate a model to be used for classifying new data. Once the model is built using the training set (with labeled records), the correctness of the classification is evaluated using the test set (with unlabeled records). Typical uses of classification are credit approval (risk classification), marketing, health planning, and so on.

Classification methods were borrowed from statistics and machine learning. The most popular methods are the ones based on **decision trees**. A decision tree has three types of nodes: a *root node*, with no incoming edges and zero or more outgoing edges; *internal nodes*, with exactly one incoming edge and two or more outgoing edges; and *leaf or terminal nodes*, with exactly one incoming edge and no outgoing edges. In a decision tree, each terminal node is assigned a class label. Nonterminal nodes contain attribute test conditions to split records with different characteristics from each other.

For example, in the Northwind case study, we want to generate a very simple classification of customers, consisting in just two classes: good or bad customers, identified as 'G' and 'B', respectively. For this, we use two demographic characteristics: the year the business was established and the annual profit. To represent the first characteristic, we use the attribute YearEstablished. For the second and to keep the example simple at this stage, we use a continuous attribute called AnnualProfitCont. Recall that in Sect. 9.1 the attribute AnnualProfit has been categorized into six classes. For the current example, we use the actual continuous values. Later in this chapter, we will show an example using discrete attributes when we present Analysis Services data mining tools. Intuitively, to be classified as 'G', a customer established a long time ago (say, 20 years) requires a smaller profit than the profit required to a customer more recently established. We will see below how this classification is produced.

YearEstablished	AnnualProfitCont	Class
1977	1,000,000	G
1961	500,000	B
1978	1,300,000	B
1985	1,200,000	G
1995	1,400,000	B
1975	1,100,000	G

In this example, we can use the YearEstablished attribute to separate records first, and, in a second step, we can use the AnnualProfitCont attribute for a finer classification within the class of customers with similar amount of years in the market. The intuition behind this is that the attribute YearEstablished conveys more information about the record than the attribute AnnualProfitCont.

Once the model has been built, classifying a test record is straightforward, as this is done by traversing the tree and evaluating the conditions at each node. For example, we can build a tree like the one in Fig. 9.2, based on the training data. Then, if a record with YearEstablished = 1995 and AnnualProfitCont = 1,200,000 arrives, it will be classified as 'G', following the path: YearEstablished $\leq$ 1977 = false, AnnualProfitCont $\leq$ 1,000,000 = false. Again, the rationale here is that even if the customer has established

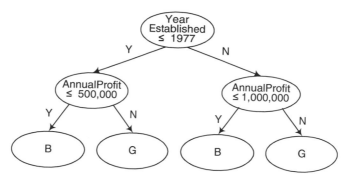

Fig. 9.2 An example of a decision tree model for the Northwind customers

relatively recently, its profit is high enough to be considered as a reliable customer.

There are many algorithms that compute a decision tree. A well-known one is the ID3 algorithm. Here, starting at the root, which initially contains all the training samples, the attribute conveying more information is used to split the nodes in a recursive fashion. Other algorithms like SPRINT and SLIQ are also used to improve the efficiency of classification in large databases. The basic process involves two steps, partitioning and pruning, as shown below. It is usual to split the data set into two halves, the first being used for partitioning and the second for pruning:

ID3 Algorithm
INPUT: A data set T
OUTPUT: A classification tree
BEGIN
   1. Build an initial tree from the training data set T
      IF all points in T belong to the same class THEN RETURN;
      Evaluate splits for every attribute;
      Use the best split for partition T into T_1 and T_2;
      ID3(T_1);
      ID3(T_2);
   2. Prune this tree to increase test accuracy.
      This removes branches that are likely to induce errors.
END

A key challenge in these algorithms is how to partition the tree nodes. This is done measuring the information conveyed by each attribute. Attributes conveying more information are selected first. There are many methods used for node partitioning. For example, the SPRINT algorithm uses the Gini index, while the SLIQ algorithm uses the notion of information entropy.

The **Gini index** for a data set T whose elements are classified into C classes is defined as follows:

$$Gini(T) = 1 - \sum_{i=1}^{C} p_i^2$$

where p_i is the relative frequency of class i in the data set T. If the set T contains n samples and a split divides T into two subsets T_1 and T_2, with sizes n_1 and n_2, respectively, the Gini index of the divided data is given by

$$Gini_{\text{Split}}(T) = \frac{n_1}{n} Gini(T_1) + \frac{n_2}{n} Gini(T_2).$$

The attribute achieving the smallest Gini index value is then chosen to split the node. Note that there are three different cases to consider, depending on the kind of attribute, namely, binary, categorical, or continuous. The latter is the case in our example. Since it would be very expensive to consider all possible values to split a node, candidate values are taken as the actual values of the attribute. Thus, for the YearEstablished attribute, we only consider the values 1961, 1977, 1978, 1995, 2010, and 2012. For instance, splitting the node using YearEstablished $= 1977$ results in a subset T_1 containing one record in class 'B' and two records in class 'G' (for the values ≤ 1977) and another subset T_2 containing two records in class 'B' and one record in class 'G' (for the values > 1977). Thus, the Gini index will be

$$Gini(T_1) = 1 - (\tfrac{1}{3})^2 - (\tfrac{2}{3})^2 = 0.444$$
$$Gini(T_2) = 1 - (\tfrac{2}{3})^2 - (\tfrac{1}{3})^2 = 0.4444$$
$$Gini_{\text{YearEstablished}=1977}(T) = \tfrac{3}{6}(0.444) + \tfrac{3}{6}(0.444) = 0.444$$

Doing the same, for example, with AnnualProfitCont $= 1{,}000{,}000$, we would obtain a Gini index of 0.495 (we leave the computation to the reader); thus, we select first the attribute YearEstablished. At a second level, we will use AnnualProfitCont for a finer classification.

9.1.3 Clustering

Clustering or unsupervised classification is the process of grouping objects into classes of similar ones. Classes are defined as collections of objects with high intraclass similarity and low interclass similarity. Let us motivate the use of clustering in the Northwind case study. In addition to the classification that we described above, which is used to predict a customer's behavior, the Northwind managers also want to have a first idea of the groups of similar customers that can be defined based on their demographic characteristics and in the purchases they had made. With this information, for example, the marketing department can prepare customized offers or packages. Note that to include information about the customer's purchases, a join between the tables Customer and CustomerDemographics and the fact table Sales must be performed, in order to generate a larger table that will be the input to the clustering algorithm containing, for example, the number of orders placed, the maximum and minimum amounts of the orders, and other data that may be useful to group similar customers. Anyway, this is only one of the many possible data preparation tasks that must be performed over the data in order to guarantee reliable results. We show a concrete example over Analysis Services later in this chapter.

Data clustering discovers distribution patterns of the data set. The most popular clustering methods are based on similarity or distance between data points. Thus, a notion of **distance** between clusters must be defined in order to evaluate the quality of a clustering model. Typically the Euclidean distance is used. We explain this next.

Let us call $d(x, y)$ the distance between two points x and y in a cluster. In addition, for a given cluster C_k, its center r_k is computed, often as the vector mean of the points in the cluster. To determine the quality of a certain clustering configuration $\mathcal{C} = C_1, \ldots, C_K$, we need to compute two functions: the **within cluster variation** $wc(\mathcal{C})$ and the **between cluster variation** $bc(\mathcal{C})$. These functions are used to measure the intraclass and interclass similarity, respectively. The within cluster variation is first computed for each cluster and then for the whole clustering configuration, as indicated below:

$$wc(C_k) = \sum_{x(i) \in C_k} d(x, r_k)^2; \quad wc(\mathcal{C}) = \sum_{k=1}^{K} wc(C_k).$$

The between cluster variation is measured by the distance between cluster centers and is computed as follows:

$$bc(\mathcal{C}) = \sum_{1 \le j \le k \le K} d(r_j, r_k)^2.$$

Finally, the quality of a clustering can be defined by the **score function** $bc(\mathcal{C})/wc(\mathcal{C})$.

Clustering algorithms are aimed at optimizing the score functions. The problem consists in searching the space of assignments of points to clusters and find the one that minimizes/maximizes the score function. The typical clustering algorithm, from which many different variants are built, is the **K-means algorithm**. Here, the number of K clusters is fixed at the start. The basic algorithm randomly picks K cluster centers and assigns each point to the cluster whose mean is closest using the Euclidean distance. For each cluster, the new center is computed and used to replace each initial cluster center value. Then, each object is assigned to the cluster with the smallest squared Euclidean distance. The cluster centers are recalculated based on the new membership assignment, and the procedure is repeated until no object changes the clusters. A scheme of the algorithm is given next:

K-Means Algorithm

INPUT: A data set T containing n data points $(x_1, \ldots, x_n)$
OUTPUT: A set of K clusters $C_1, \ldots, C_K$

```
BEGIN
    FOR k = 1, ..., K let r_k be a randomly chosen point in T;
    WHILE changes in clusters C_k happen DO
            /* Form clusters */
            FOR k = 1, ..., K DO
                C_k = {x_i ∈ T | d(r_k, x_i) ≤ d(r_j, x_i) ∀j = 1, ..., K, j ≠ k};
            END;
            /* Compute new cluster centers */
            FOR k = 1, ..., K; DO
                r_k = the vector mean of the points in C_k;
            END;
    END;
END;
```

There are several enhancements and variations of the classic clustering method. A relevant one is hierarchical clustering. The idea behind **hierarchical clustering** is to reduce or increase iteratively the number of clusters of a given model. In the first case, we have **agglomerative algorithms**; in the second one, we have **divisive algorithms**. Let us consider agglomerative algorithms. The rationale is that if two clusters are close to each other (given the distance function in use), we can merge them into a single one. The general algorithm is given below:

Agglomerative Algorithm
INPUT: A data set T containing n data points $(x_1, \ldots, x_n)$.
    A function $d(C_i, C_j)$ to measure the distance between clusters.
OUTPUT: A set of K clusters $C_1, \ldots, C_K$

```
BEGIN
    FOR k = 1, ..., n let C_i = {x_i};
    WHILE there is more than one cluster left DO
        Let C_i and C_j be the clusters minimizing the distance between
            all pairs of clusters;
        C_i = C_i ∪ C_j;
        Remove C_j;
    END;
END;
```

9.1.4   Association Rules

Association analysis aims at discovering interesting relationships hidden in large data sets. Although it can be used in many domains, it is a very popular technique for market basket analysis, for example, in the retail industry. Thus, the goal of mining association rules in databases is to discover associations between items that are present in a set of transactions. Although through this technique we can find many trivial associations, it is also possible to find unexpected associations, that is, items that are frequently purchased together although their relationship is not that obvious. Like in all data mining techniques, data preprocessing must be performed to produce the appropriate tables over which the algorithms can be applied. For example, the Northwind data warehouse is an appropriate source of data to find associations between items. Conceptually, the Sales fact table contains data of all customer purchases. Further, the OrderNo and OrderLineNo can be used to obtain the items that are purchased together. With this information, the Northwind management can discover which are the items that are frequently ordered together. We show a concrete example in Sect. 9.1.7.

Let $\mathcal{I} = \{i_1, i_2, \ldots, i_m\}$ be a set of literals, called items. A set of items is called an **itemset**. Let $\mathcal{D}$ be a set of transactions, where each transaction T is an itemset such that $T \subseteq \mathcal{I}$. Let also X be an itemset. A transaction T is said to contain X if and only if $X \subseteq T$. An **association rule** is an implication of the form $X \Rightarrow Y$, where $X \subset \mathcal{I}, Y \subset \mathcal{I}$, and $X \cap Y = \varnothing$. The rule $X \Rightarrow Y$ holds in $\mathcal{D}$ with **confidence** c, if $c\%$ of the transactions in $\mathcal{D}$ that contain X also contain Y. The rule $X \Rightarrow Y$ has **support** s in $\mathcal{D}$ if $s\%$ of the transactions in $\mathcal{D}$ contain $X \cup Y$.

We illustrate the problem with a simple but typical example. Consider the following table containing a collection of transactions corresponding to purchases in a supermarket. A transaction is identified by a TransactionID attribute and a list of items included in the transaction.

TransactionId	Items
1000	{1,2,3}
2000	{1,3}
3000	{1,4}
4000	{2,5,6}

From this data set, we can obtain at least the following rules. First, $1 \Rightarrow 3$ with support 50% and confidence 66%, which means half of the transactions include items 1 and 3, and from the three transactions that include item 1, two of them include item 3. That is, $c = \frac{2}{4}$ and $s = \frac{2}{3}$. Analogously, the rule $3 \Rightarrow 1$ also holds with support 50% (for the same reason of the previous rule) and confidence 100%. The latter is because all the transactions containing item 3 also contain item 1.

In general, algorithms for finding association rules consist in two main stages:

1. Generate the **frequent itemsets**, which finds all the itemsets that satisfy a minimum support (*minsup*) threshold.
2. Generate the association rules, which extracts all the high-confidence rules from the frequent itemsets found in the previous step. These are called **strong rules**.

The first operation above is critical since generating the rules once the frequent itemsets have been found is straightforward.

Another concept worth to be commented is the one of **interesting rules**. We say an association rule $A \Rightarrow B$ is *interesting* if its confidence exceeds a certain value or, in other words, if $\frac{P(A \cap B)}{P(A)}$ is greater than a constant d. The former is just a test of statistical independence.

The most well-known algorithms for mining association rules are the Apriori algorithm and the DHP algorithm. The main idea is to generate, in the ith iteration, the set of candidate itemsets of length i (denoted C_i) and prune the ones that do not satisfy the minimum required support. In this way, we generate the sets called large itemsets L_i, which will be used for finding the sets of candidate itemsets with length $i + 1$. To prune these sets, the Apriori principle is typically applied: if an itemset is frequent, all of its subsets must also be frequent. For instance, $\{A, B\}$ cannot be a frequent itemset if either A or B are not frequent. The DHP algorithm is similar to Apriori, but it uses hashing to test the eligibility of a k-itemset.

Let us show how the Apriori algorithm works, using the example introduced above. We first rewrite the transaction table as a table with two columns Item and Count, where column Count contains the number of times that an item appears in a transaction in the database.

Item	Count
1	3
2	2
3	2
4	1
5	1
6	1

Assume that the minimum support required is $minsup = 50\%$, which means each itemset must appear at least two times in the database of transactions, in order to be considered frequent. Initially, every item is a candidate 1-itemset C_1. However, only items 1, 2, and 3 have support at least equal to $minsup$. Thus, we delete the remaining ones (depicted in light gray in the table above) and we obtain the set of large 1-itemsets L_1. With this set we generate the new candidate itemset table C_2, depicted below.

Item	Count
{1,2}	1
{1,3}	2
{2,3}	1

Then, the only 2-itemset that satisfies $minsup$ is $\{1,3\}$. Since we cannot generate 3-itemsets (because the set would contain the subset $\{1,2\}$, which does not satisfy the minimum support), we stop here. Then, the only two rules that can be generated are $1 \Rightarrow 3$ and $3 \Rightarrow 1$.

To enhance the efficiency of the process of discovering association rules, various techniques can be applied:

1. Database scan reduction: If the candidate itemsets can be stored in main memory, some scans could be avoided and more than one large itemset could be found using the same database scan.
2. Sampling: If mining is required frequently, sampling can be a way of improving performance, with reasonable accuracy cost, if we take the reduction factor into account when computing the confidence and support. A *relaxation factor* is calculated according to the size of the sample.
3. Parallel data mining: Several algorithms supporting parallelism have been developed, in order to take advantage of parallel architectures.

As data are entered into the database, we may need to recompute the discovered association rules. In order to keep performance within required limits, incremental updating of association rules should be developed, to avoid repeating the whole mining process. The classic Fast Update algorithm (FUP) was the first one proposed to solve the problem of incremental mining of association rules. The algorithm handles insertions but is not able to deal with deletions. Although it was enhanced in sequel versions, we explain here the basic algorithm to give a general idea of how updates can be handled in association rule mining.

Let us consider a database DB and the frequent itemsets obtained from it, denoted $L - \{L_1, \ldots, L_k\}$. There is also an incremental database db, containing the new records. The goal of FUP is to reuse information to efficiently obtain the new frequent itemsets $L' = \{L'_1, \ldots, L'_k\}$ over the database $DB' = DB \cup db$. Let us assume that D is the size (number of transactions) of DB and d is the size of db. We call $X.s_{DB}$ the support of an itemset X over the database DB expressed as the number of transactions in which X appears in the database.

The FUP algorithm is based in the fact that, given an original database DB and an incremental database db, the following holds:

- A 1-itemset X frequent in DB (i.e., $X \in L_1$) becomes infrequent in DB' (i.e., $X \notin L'_1$) if and only if $X.s_{DB'} < minsup \times (D + d)$.
- A 1-itemset X infrequent in DB (i.e., $X \notin L_1$) may become frequent in DB' (i.e., $X \in L'_1$) if and only if $X.s_{db} < minsup \times d$.
- A k-itemset X whose $(k-1)$-subsets become infrequent (i.e., the subsets are in L_{k-1} but not in L'_{k-1}) must be infrequent in db.

Similarly to the Apriori algorithm, the FUP algorithm involves a number of iterations. The candidate sets at each iteration are generated based on the frequent itemsets found in the previous iteration. At the kth iteration, the db is scanned exactly once. The originally frequent itemsets $\{X | X \in L_k\}$ only have to be checked against the small increment db. To discover the new frequent itemsets, the set of candidate itemsets C_k is firstly extracted from db and then pruned according to the support count of each candidate itemset in *db* using the rules above. To explain the idea of the algorithm, next we focus on how to incrementally compute the 1-itemsets, which means the itemsets of length one. The remaining itemsets are computed analogously in subsequent iterations. To compute L_1' in the updated database DB', the FUP algorithm proceeds as follows:

- Scan *db* for all itemsets $X \in L_1$, and update their support count $X.s_{DB'}$. Then, if $X.s_{DB'} < minsup \times (D + d)$, X will not be in L_1' (in the original FUP algorithm, it is called a loser).
- In the same scan, compute the candidate set C_1 with all the items X that are in *db* but not in L_1. If $X.s_{db} < minsup \times d$, X cannot be a frequent itemset in the updated database.
- Scan the original database DB to update the support count for each $X \in C_1$. Then, we can generate L_1'.

For instance, suppose that our example database is updated with the following transactions (the incremental database *db*):

TransactionId	Items
5000	{1,2,4}
6000	{4}

The count of each item in *db* is given by

Item	Count
1	1
2	1
4	2

Recall that we require $minsup = 50\%$. Let us consider first the frequent 1-itemsets in the original database DB, which means the items in L_1. These are $I_1 = 1$ (appears three times in the database), $I_2 = 2$ (appears twice in the database), and $I_3 = 3$ (also appears twice in the database). The first step of the FUP algorithm requires a scan of *db* for all itemsets L_1 and the computation of their support with respect to DB'. For each one of these items, we have

$$I_1.s_{DB'} = 4 > 0.5 \times 6$$
$$I_2.s_{DB'} = 3 = 0.5 \times 6$$
$$I_3.s_{DB'} = 2 < 0.5 \times 6$$

Therefore, itemset I_3 will be a loser since it does not verify the support in the updated database; therefore, it is dropped. On the contrary, I_1 and I_2 will be included in L_1'.

The second step of the algorithm computes the candidate set C_1 with all the 1-itemsets in db that are not in L_1. We only have $I_4 = 4$ in this situation. Since I_4 is in both transactions in db, we have $I_4.s_{db} = 2 > 0.5 \times 2$, and thus, I_4 will be added to L'_1.

Finally, the updated support count is given in the following table, where in light gray we indicate the items I with support less than $minsup \times 6$:

Item	Count
1	4
2	3
3	2
4	3
5	1
6	1

The association analysis studied so far operates over the items in a database of transactions. However, we have seen that dimension hierarchies are a way of defining a hierarchy of concepts along which transaction items can be classified. This leads to the notion of **hierarchical association rules**. For example, in the Northwind data warehouse, products are organized into categories. Assume now that in the original transaction database in our example above, items 1 and 2 belong to category A, items 3 and 4 to category B, and items 5 and 6 to category C. The transaction table with the categories instead of the items is given below:

TransactionId	Items
1000	{A,A,B}
2000	{A,B}
3000	{A,B}
4000	{A,C,C}

Suppose now that we require $minsup = 75\%$ over the items database, we would obtain no rules as a result. However, aggregating items over categories, like in the table above, would result in the rules A $\Rightarrow$ B and B $\Rightarrow$ A since categories A and B have support larger than the minimum, namely, 1 and 0.75, respectively. That means we could not say that each time a given item X appears in the database, an item Y will appear, but we could say that each time an item of category A appears, an item of category B will be present too. This is called a hierarchical association rule. Note that combinations of items at different granularities can also appear, for example, rules like "Each time a given item X appears in the database, an item of a category C will also appear."

9.1.5   Pattern Growth Algorithm

The Apriori algorithm presented above is the most popular approach to mining association rules. However, when the minimum support is low or the length of the patterns is long, candidate generation may turn out to be inefficient. In addition, in each iteration, the database must be scanned with respect to the current candidates, which is also a costly task. To address these problems, another approach to mining frequent itemsets, called pattern growth, has been devised. The pattern growth algorithm does not generate candidate itemsets. The method uses a two-step approach: In the first step, a compact data structure, called **FP-tree**, is built to encode the database. Two scans of the database are required for this. In the second step, the frequent itemsets are extracted after traversing and partitioning the FP-tree. We sketch the idea of the algorithm next, using the same transaction database as above.

TransactionId	Itemset	Ordered Frequent Items
1000	{1,2,3}	⟨1:3, 2:2, 3:2⟩
2000	{1,3}	⟨1:3, 3:2⟩
3000	{1,4}	⟨1:3⟩
4000	{2,5,6}	⟨2:2⟩

Note that, to better illustrate the algorithm, we added a column to represent the frequent items, in descending order of support. For example, 1:3 means that item 1 has support 3 (recall that in this example, the minimum support is 2). Items 4, 5, and 6 were excluded from this new column because their support is 1. Below, we explain how these values are obtained.

The FP-tree is a data structure defined as follows:

- The nodes are of the form $i{:}c$, where i represents the item and c represents a counter.
- There is an edge (indicated as a solid line) between nodes appearing together in a transaction; a fixed order is used, so paths in the tree overlap if transactions share items.
- There is a table T containing an entry for each item in the tree.
- There is an edge (indicated as a dashed line) between nodes containing the same item (independent of the value of the counter), forming a path composed of nodes representing the same item.
- There is an edge between each entry in T to the node in the tree which is the head of the path indicated above.

Figure 9.3 shows the FP-tree of our example. We next explain how we built this tree.

The FP-tree is constructed in two passes over the database. In the *first pass*, we scan the database to find the support of each item. We discard items that are not frequent (the ones with support less than 2 in our example), and, for each transaction, we sort the frequent items in decreasing order of their support. In this way, the common prefixes can be shared between transactions.

In our example, only items 1, 2, and 3 are frequent. The first transaction in the database includes all of these items. Thus, we sort them in descending order of support, including the support count in the form $i{:}c$. We obtain the list $\langle 1{:}3,\ 2{:}2,\ 3{:}2 \rangle$, meaning that items 1, 2, and 3 have support 3, 2, and 2, respectively. We proceed analogously with the other transactions.

In the *second pass*, we construct the FP-tree as follows. We first create the root node and then perform a scan of the database, analyzing each transaction again, but *only considering the frequent items* obtained in the first pass. In our example, the first transaction produces the first branch of the tree: root $\rightarrow$ 1:1 $\rightarrow$ 2:1 $\rightarrow$ 3:1. The branch is ordered according to the third column of the table above, that is, the order defined in the first pass. The second transaction contains items 1 and 3, so it shares a common prefix with the first transaction (i.e., item 1). Thus, we increment the support count of this prefix to 2, and the branch will read root $\rightarrow$ 1:2 $\rightarrow$ 3:1. The third transaction includes only one item whose minimum support is at least 2 (again, item 1). Thus, we just increase the node count, yielding the node 1:3. Finally, the fourth transaction leads to a new branch of length 1, namely, root $\rightarrow$ 2:1. Figure 9.3 shows the final state of the FP-tree.

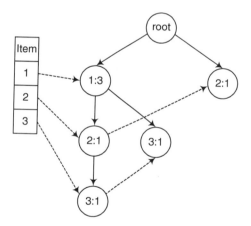

Fig. 9.3 The FP-tree for the running example

Note that this tree represents, in a compact form, the part of the database containing only items satisfying the minimum support. Each transaction is mapped to a path in the FP-tree, and the more paths that overlap, the higher the compression rate achieved. In this way, it is even possible that this tree fits in main memory. In the best case, we will have a single path in the tree.

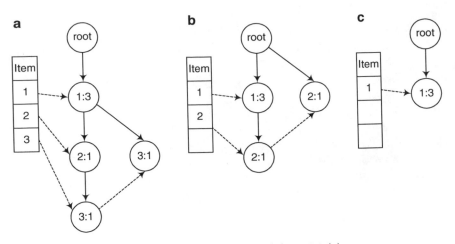

Fig. 9.4 Prefix path subtrees ending in 3 (**a**), 2 (**b**), and 1 (**c**)

In the worst case, we will have the whole database, if there are no items in common in the transactions, which is very unlikely in real-world scenarios.

To discover the frequent itemsets, the method makes use of a divide and conquer strategy. The FP-tree is divided using a bottom-up algorithm that finds subtrees such that each one of them is composed of the paths ending at the same item. These are called prefix path subtrees. There are as many subtrees as frequent items. Each subtree is built bottom-up starting from a frequent item. For instance, for the FP-tree in Fig. 9.3, the prefix path subtree ending in 3 is shown in Fig. 9.4a. The subtree is composed of all the paths that start at the root and end at a node representing item 3. We proceed analogously with items 2 and 1, yielding the subtrees of Fig. 9.4b, c. Note that the support of the items *in each subtree* is obtained by adding the values of the counters along each linked list (the one formed by the dashed lines). For example, in Fig. 9.4a, the support of item 3 is 2, because two nodes 3:1 are linked by a dashed line. Thus, item 3 is frequent, and we can now find the frequent itemsets ending in 3. For this, we need to build the corresponding *conditional subtrees* as we explain next.

For each subtree corresponding to an item i, we construct a *conditional subtree* as follows: we take each prefix path subtree for i and remove all the nodes containing i. For example, for the subtree corresponding to item 3, we traverse the tree bottom-up starting from each node for 3. We drop all the nodes for item 3 (in this case, the two nodes 3:1) and update the counters. Now, the node 1:3 becomes 1:2 (corresponding to the paths root $\rightarrow$ 1:2 $\rightarrow$ 2:1, and root $\rightarrow$ 2:1). We obtain the tree in Fig. 9.5a. From this tree we remove the infrequent nodes, in this case, node 2:1. The name 'conditional' arises from the fact that this tree contains only items that appear together with item 3. Frequent itemsets containing the item {3} are obtained combining the nodes in the conditional tree with such item. In this case, combining item 1 (from node 1:2) with the parameter of the conditional tree (in this case, item 3), we obtain the 2-itemset {1,3}. Thus, item 3 yields two frequent itemsets, {1,3} and {3}.

Then, we build the conditional FP-tree for item {2}. We traverse bottom-up the tree in Fig. 9.4b, starting from each node for 2, and update the counters. Now, the node 1:3 becomes 1:1. Then, we drop all the nodes for item 2, in this case, the two nodes 2:1. We obtain the tree in Fig. 9.5b. Since we can drop the only node in the tree because it does not have the minimum support (the node 1:1 indicates the only path remaining for item 1), we just obtain the itemset {2}.

Proceeding analogously, the conditional FP-tree for item {1} is the empty tree; thus, we just obtain the itemset {1}.

Alternatively, we could also obtain the conditional FP-trees without using the prefix path subtrees as follows. We pick *only* the transactions that contain i and remove i from such transactions. All other transactions are discarded. Then, we construct the conditional FP-trees as explained for regular FP-trees. For example, for the subtree corresponding to item 3, we pick only transactions 1000 and 2000 (the ones that contain item 3) and eliminate item 3 from the transactions. Transactions 3000 and 4000 are discarded. Thus, we keep items {1,2} (from transaction 1000) and {1} (from transaction 2000). With these items we build an FP-tree as explained above, obtaining the tree in Fig. 9.5a, from which we remove the infrequent nodes. From this tree, frequent itemsets containing the item {3} are obtained as explained above. We can proceed analogously to build the conditional FP-tree for item {2}.

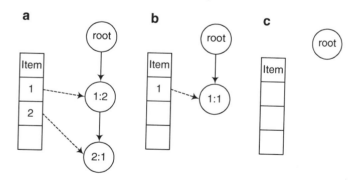

Fig. 9.5 Conditional FP-tree for items 3 (**a**), 2 (**b**), and 1 (**c**)

9.1.6 Sequential Patterns

The association rules studied above have an important characteristic: they do not consider order. As we have seen in our examples, the order in which the items were purchased was irrelevant; therefore, if a rule $1 \Rightarrow 3$ holds, then $3 \Rightarrow 1$ must also hold. However, there are many real-world situations where the order in which actions are taken is relevant for the decision maker. For instance, in our Northwind example, we may be interested not only in the items bought together but also in statements like "Customers that purchase item X frequently order item Y *afterward*, with 40% support." We can see that if the rule $1 \Rightarrow 3$ holds, not necessarily $3 \Rightarrow 1$ does since the order is now important. When order matters, we are in the case of **sequential pattern mining**, which is a particular case of association analysis.

Consider a sequence $\langle s_1, s_2, \ldots, s_n \rangle$ such that the s_i's are itemsets as defined above when studying association rules. We say that a sequence $s_1 = \langle a_1, a_2, \ldots, a_n \rangle$ is contained in another sequence $s_2 = \langle b_1, b_2, \ldots, b_m \rangle$, if there exist integers $i_1, \ldots, i_n$ such that $a_1 \subseteq b_{i_1}$, $a_2 \subseteq b_{i_2}$, $\ldots$, $a_n \subseteq b_{i_n}$, where the b_{i_j}'s are itemsets in s_2, ordered and different from each other.

For example, the sequence $\langle \{\text{Shoes}\}, \{\text{Shirt}, \text{Tie}\} \rangle$ is contained in the sequence $\langle \{\text{Belt}\}, \{\text{Shoes}\}, \{\text{Jacket}\}, \{\text{Shirt}, \text{Belt}, \text{Tie}\}, \{\text{Jacket}\} \rangle$, because the term $\{\text{Shoes}\}$ in the first sequence matches a similar term in the second one, and the term $\{\text{Shirt}, \text{Tie}\}$ in the first sequence is included in $\{\text{Shirt}, \text{Belt}, \text{Tie}\}$ in the second one. On the other hand, the sequence $\langle \{\text{Shoes}\}, \{\text{Shirt}\} \rangle$ is not contained in the sequence $\langle \{\text{Shoes}, \text{Shirt}\} \rangle$.

Let us consider the set of transactions performed by customers given in Fig. 9.6, where the transactions are ordered by customer and, for each customer, by transaction time.

We say a customer C *supports* a sequence s if s is contained in the sequence corresponding to C. The *support* s of a sequence is the fraction of total customers who support it. In this case, the problem of finding sequential patterns can be defined as follows: given a database D of customer transactions, find the maximal sequences that have a certain minimum support.

As an example, we want to find the maximal sequential patterns with support greater than 2 in the transaction database above. In this case, there will be Shoes followed by Shoes, and Shoes followed by Shirt and Tie, because we can see that customers 1 and 4 support the sequence $\langle \{\text{Shoes}\}, \{\text{Shoes}\} \rangle$, and customers 2 and 4 support the sequences $\langle \{\text{Shoes}\}, \{\text{Shirt}, \text{Tie}\} \rangle$.

Algorithms for finding sequential patterns are similar to the algorithms for discovering association rules. However, the number of candidate sequences will be much larger than the number of candidate itemsets because:

- In association rule mining, an item can appear at most once in an itemset. For example, given two items i_1 and i_2, only one 2-itemset can be generated. On the contrary, for sequential pattern mining, there are many sequences that can be generated, like $\langle \{i_1, i_2\} \rangle$, $\langle \{i_1\}, \{i_1\} \rangle$, $\langle \{i_2\}, \{i_1\} \rangle$, and so on.
- As already commented, order matters for sequences but not for itemsets. For example, $\{1, 2\}$ and $\{2, 1\}$ represent the same itemset, while

CustomerId	Time	Items
1	2012-06-02	{Shoes}
1	2013-10-03	{Shoes}
2	2013-06-01	{Shoes}
2	2013-06-15	{Jacket}
2	2013-08-14	{Shirt, Tie}
3	2012-03-02	{Shoes, Tie}
4	2013-06-02	{Shoes}
4	2013-07-12	{Shirt, Belt, Tie}
4	2013-10-21	{Shoes}
5	2013-11-06	{Shoes}

Fig. 9.6 A set of transactions of the Northwind customers

$\langle \{i_1\}, \{i_2\} \rangle$ and $\langle \{i_2\}, \{i_1\} \rangle$ correspond to different sequences and must be generated separately.

Further, the Apriori principle also holds for sequential data since any data sequence that contains a particular k-sequence must also contain all of its $(k-1)$-subsequences.

Basically, for generating sequential patterns, we enumerate all possible sequences and count their support. In this way, we first generate 1-sequences, then 2-sequences, and so on. The general form of the sequences produced is given next:

1-sequences: $\langle i_1, i_2, \ldots, i_n \rangle$
2-sequences: $\langle \{i_1, i_2\}, \{i_1, i_3\}, \ldots, \{i_{n-1}, i_n\} \rangle$,
$\qquad \langle \{i_1\}, \{i_1\} \rangle, \langle \{i_1\}, \{i_2\} \rangle, \ldots, \langle \{i_{n-1}\}, \{i_n\} \rangle$
3-sequences: $\langle \{i_1, i_2, i_3\} \rangle, \langle \{i_1, i_2, i_4\} \rangle, \ldots, \langle \{i_1, i_2\}, \{i_1\} \rangle, \ldots,$
$\qquad \langle \{i_1\}, \{i_1, i_2\} \rangle, \ldots, \langle \{i_1\}, \{i_1\}, \{i_1\} \rangle, \ldots, \langle \{i_n\}, \{i_n\}, \{i_n\} \rangle$

We can see that we first generate all sequences with just one itemset (the 1-sequences). To produce the sequences with elements containing two itemsets, we generate all possible combinations of two itemsets in the 1-sequences and eliminate the ones that do not satisfy the minimum support condition. With the remaining sequences, we do the same to generate the sequences with elements containing three itemsets and continue in the same way until no more sequences with the required support can be produced.

From the above, it follows that the same principles apply to associates rules and sequential pattern analysis; thus, we do not get into further details and direct the interested reader to the references given at the end of the chapter.

9.1.7   Data Mining in Analysis Services

In the previous section, we studied how data mining algorithms create a mining model by analyzing a data set to find hidden patterns and trends. Once the parameters of the mining model are defined, they are applied across the entire data set to extract interesting knowledge. As we have seen, the mining model can take various forms, like a decision tree that predicts whether a particular customer will buy a product, a model that forecasts sales, a set of clusters describing the customers' profiles, a set of rules that describe which products are ordered together, and so on.

The two tools that we have used to implement our examples, namely, Microsoft Analysis Services and Pentaho Business Analytics, provide data mining capabilities that implement the concepts studied above. The former also provides a query language denoted **DMX** (Data Mining eXtensions). This language can be used for querying data mining models in Analysis Services. There are two kinds of DMX queries: **content queries**, which provide details about the patterns discovered during the analysis, and **prediction queries**, which use the patterns in the model, for example, to make predictions for new data. On the other hand, Pentaho Data Mining is based on Weka (Waikato Environment for Knowledge Analysis). Weka is a machine learning and data mining software written in Java. Weka includes classification, regression, association rules, and clustering algorithms. In this section and to avoid redundancy, we use Analysis Services to illustrate how data mining concepts can be used in practice.

We next study three algorithms provided by Analysis Services, namely, decision trees, clustering, and association rules. We will present these algorithms using the Northwind case study, extended with the demographic and new customer data described in Sect. 9.1. Since the original Northwind database is not big enough to obtain meaningful results (in particular, because of the low number of customers), we have extended such data set ten times with generated data.

To create a decision tree and cluster models, we will use the Customer and CustomerDemographics dimension tables, together with the Sales fact table, to produce a view TargetCustomers. This view includes a class Boolean attribute HighValueCust which indicates that the customer had placed an order with a total amount higher than $3,500. This attribute represents the class variable whose value the model will forecast, as we explain below. The view TargetCustomers is defined as follows:

```
CREATE VIEW TargetCustomers AS
    WITH CustOrderTotal AS (
        SELECT    S.CustomerKey, S.OrderNo,
                  SUM(S.SalesAmount) AS TotalAmount
        FROM      Sales S
        GROUP BY S.CustomerKey, S.OrderNo ),
    CustMaxAmount AS (
```

```
SELECT    CustomerKey, MAX(TotalAmount) AS MaxAmount
FROM      CustOrderTotal
GROUP BY CustomerKey )
SELECT C.CustomerKey, C.CustomerID, C.CompanyName,
       C.Address, C.CityKey, D.AnnualProfit, D.AnnualRevenue,
       D.BusinessType, D.DateFirstOrder, D.DateLastOrder,
       D.OwnershipType, D.ParkingSurface, D.StoreSurface,
       D.TotalEmployees, D.PermanentEmployees, D.YearEstablished,
       CASE
            WHEN M.MaxAmount >= 3500 THEN 1
            ELSE 0
       END AS HighValueCust
FROM   Customer C, CustomerDemographics D, CustMaxAmount M
WHERE  C.CustomerKey = D.CustomerKey AND
       C.CustomerKey = M.CustomerKey
```

In addition, as we explained in Sect. 9.1, we have the table NewCustomers containing new prospective customers whose behavior we want to predict.

To create an association model for the Northwind case study, we need to define views containing orders and items. For this, we create two views: The first one, denoted AssocOrders, contains the order number and customer data. The second one, denoted AssocLineItems, contains the details of each order, which means the products that each order contains. We show next the definition of these views:

```
CREATE VIEW AssocOrders AS
       SELECT DISTINCT S.OrderNo, S.CustomerKey, O.CountryName,
              D.BusinessType
       FROM   Sales S, Time T, Customer C, CustomerDemographics D,
              City Y, State A, Country O
       WHERE  S.OrderDateKey = T.TimeKey AND Year(T.Date) = 1997 AND
              S.CustomerKey = C.CustomerKey AND
              C.CustomerKey = D.CustomerKey AND
              C.CityKey = Y.CityKey AND Y.StateKey = A.StateKey AND
              A.CountryKey = O.CountryKey
CREATE VIEW AssocLineItems AS
       SELECT OrderNo, OrderLineNo, P.ProductName
       FROM   Sales S, Time T, Product P
       WHERE  S.OrderDateKey = T.TimeKey AND Year(T.Date) = 1997 AND
              S.ProductKey = P.ProductKey
```

We are now ready to present our data mining case study for the Northwind company. We will show how to:

- Build a decision tree model to predict, given the new customer characteristics, if she is likely to place an order with an amount higher than $3,500.
- Build a clustering model to produce a profile of the current customers and predict a new customer's profile.
- Create an association rule model to predict which items will be ordered together.

Decision Trees

As we explained above, we want to build a decision tree model that predicts whether or not a new customer is likely to place an order with a total amount of more than $3,500. For this we use the TargetCustomers view. The decision tree algorithm requires us to indicate the class attribute to be predicted, the attributes that must be used as input, and the attributes that will be ignored by the algorithm but that can be used for visualization of the results. The TargetCustomers view includes the attribute HighValueCust. A value of '1' in this attribute means that the customer is a high-valued one. Otherwise, the variable takes the value '0'. This is the variable to be predicted.

Figure 9.7 shows how the attributes to be used for building the model are defined in Analysis Services, both for the decision tree model explained in this section and the clustering model explained in the next section. Note that the attribute HighValueCust is defined as PredictOnly. Also, for example, BusinessType will be used as a predictor variable; therefore, it is defined as input. Finally, Address will only be used for visualization purposes, and it is marked as Ignore.

With this input, the model is deployed. Figure 9.8 shows an excerpt of the decision tree obtained. We can see that the root (the whole data set) is first split using the attribute YearEstablished, resulting in six subsets. Then, the nodes are further split according to the distribution of the HighValueCust values. When the contents of the classes are stable, the split stops. We can see, for example, that all the records in the path YearEstablished >= 1975 and YearEstablished < 1990 → BusinessType = 'Restaurant' have HighValueCust = 1. However, if BusinessType = 'Grocery Store' the algorithm continued splitting.

Structure ∧	NWDW_Decision_Tree	NWDW_Clustering
	Microsoft_Decision_Trees	Microsoft_Clustering
Address	Ignore	Ignore
Business Type	Input	Input
City Key	Input	Input
Company Name	Ignore	Ignore
Customer Alt Key	Ignore	Ignore
Customer Key	Key	Key
Date First Order	Input	Input
Date Last Order	Input	Input
High Value Cust	PredictOnly	PredictOnly
Parking Surface	Input	Input
Permanent Employees	Input	Input
Store Surface	Input	Input
Year Established	Input	Input

Fig. 9.7 Attributes for the decision tree and the clustering models in the Northwind case study

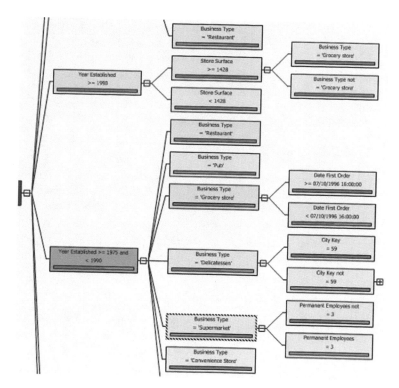

Fig. 9.8 Excerpt of the decision tree for the Northwind case study

Given a decision tree model, a DMX **content query** over it can provide statistics about the number of cases at each level of the tree or the rules at each node, while a **prediction query** maps the model to new data in order to produce recommendations and classifications. Metadata about the model can also be retrieved. For example, over the model deployed (called NWDW_DecisionTree), we can issue the following content query asking for the characteristics of an interior node in the tree (NODE_TYPE = 3):

```
SELECT NODE_NAME AS [Node], NODE_CAPTION AS [Caption],
       NODE_SUPPORT as [Support], [CHILDREN_CARDINALITY] AS [Children]
FROM   NWDW_DecisionTree.CONTENT
WHERE NODE_TYPE = 3
```

In this query, the attribute NODE_SUPPORT contains the number of records in the node, while the attribute CHILDREN_CARDINALITY tells in how many subgroups has the algorithm divided the node. This query results in the following table. We can see that, for instance, the node labeled YearEstablished >= 1975 and YearEstablished < 1990 contains 239 elements and has seven children. On the other hand, the node Business Type = 'Delicatessen' contains 43 elements and has two children.

Node	Caption	Support	Children
00000000400	Year Established < 1955	153	2
00000000401	Year Established >= 1955 and < 1960	50	2
00000000402	Year Established >= 1960 and < 1970	110	4
00000000403	Year Established >= 1970 and < 1975	71	2
00000000404	Year Established >= 1975 and < 1990	239	7
0000000040402	Business Type = 'Delicatessen'	43	2
...	...	...	...

We can then issue a prediction query that uses the decision tree model that has been produced. For this, we use the table called **NewCustomers** in Fig. 9.1. Each new customer can be input to the model to check if she is likely to place a $3,500 value order. The query uses the DMX function **PredictProbability** to display the probability of a customer with the attribute values indicated in the subquery (e.g., a store surface of 773 square meters and established in 1956), to be classified as a high-valued one (**HighValueCust = 1**):

```
SELECT  [High Value Cust], PredictProbability([High Value Cust], 1) AS [Probability],
FROM    [NWDW_Decision_Tree] NATURAL PREDICTION JOIN
        ( SELECT 'Restaurant' AS [Business Type], 5 AS [Permanent Employees],
        1956 AS [Year Established], 1 AS [Annual Profit],
        773 AS [Store Surface], 460 AS [Parking Surface] ) AS T
```

This query results in the following table, which tells that there is a probability of 75% that the customer places an order above $3,500:

High Value Cust	Probability
1	0.7551

The next query does the same, but scans the whole **NewCustomers** table using the **OPENQUERY** statement. Note that the **PREDICTION JOIN** operation is performed between the attributes in the table and the ones in the model. The final **WHERE** clause of the query filters the results to return only high-valued customers:

```
SELECT  CompanyName, BusinessType, PermanentEmployees AS [PE],
        YearEstablished AS [YE], AnnualProfit AS [AP],
        StoreSurface AS [SS], ParkingSurface AS [PS],
        PredictProbability([High Value Cust], 1) AS [Prob=1],
        PredictProbability([High Value Cust], 0) AS [Prob=0]
FROM    [NWDW_Decision_Tree] PREDICTION JOIN
        OPENQUERY(Sales,
        'SELECT CompanyName, BusinessType, PermanentEmployees,
        YearEstablished, AnnualProfit, StoreSurface, ParkingSurface
        FROM NewCustomers') AS T ON
        [NWDW_Decision_Tree].[Business Type] = T.[BusinessType] AND
```

[NWDW_Decision_Tree].[Permanent Employees] =
T.[PermanentEmployees] AND
[NWDW_Decision_Tree].[Year Established] = T.[YearEstablished] AND
[NWDW_Decision_Tree].[Store Surface] = T.[StoreSurface] AND
[NWDW_Decision_Tree].[Parking Surface] = T.[ParkingSurface]
WHERE [High Value Cust] = 1

This query results in the following table, where values in the column Prob=1 indicate the probability of being a high-valued customer:

CompanyName	BusinessType	PE	YE	AP	SS	PS	Prob=1	Prob=0
L'Amour Fou	Restaurant	4	1955	2	1178	918	0.7551	0.2448
Le Tavernier	Pub	1	1984	1	2787	438	0.5326	0.4673
Potemkine	Restaurant	5	1956	1	773	460	0.7551	0.2448
Flamingo	Restaurant	3	1960	2	2935	1191	0.6041	0.3958
Pure Bar	Pub	3	1989	2	1360	307	0.5326	0.4673
...	...	...	...	...	...	...	...	...

Clustering

We will now show how to build a clustering model to find out a customer profile structure, using the view TargetCustomers and the parameters depicted in the right-hand side of Fig. 9.7. Then, given the table of prospective customers (NewCustomers), we can predict to which profile each new customer is likely to belong. Figure 9.9 shows the result of the clustering algorithm. The shadow and thickness of the lines linking the clusters indicate the strength of the relationship between the clusters, the darker and thicker the line, the stronger the link between two clusters. The profiles of some of the clusters are given in Fig. 9.10. These profiles indicate, for example, the number of elements in each cluster and the distribution of the attribute values within each cluster. We can see, for example, that Cluster 5 contains few high-valued customers.

In clustering models, a content query asks for details about the clusters that were found. A prediction query may ask to which cluster a new data point is most likely to belong.

Once the model is built (in this case, called NWDW_Clustering), we can find out the characteristics of the clusters produced. Since in Analysis Services, the clustering structure is a tree such that below the root (NODE_TYPE=1) there is a collection of flat nodes (i.e., NODE_TYPE=5). Thus, since all clusters have a node type of 5, we can easily retrieve a list of the clusters by querying the model content for only the nodes of that type. We can also filter the nodes by support. The query shown below displays the identifier, the name, the support (the number of elements in the cluster), and the description (the

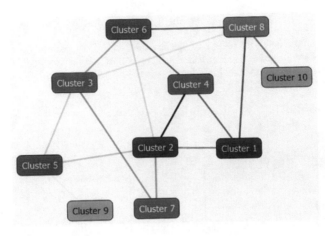

Fig. 9.9 Clustering for the Northwind customers

Attributes						
Variables	States	Populatio... Size: 678	Cluster 1 Size: 102	Cluster 2 Size: 89	Cluster 6 Size: 77	Cluster 5 Size: 74
Business Type	Restaurant Grocery Supermarket Delicatessen Other					
City Key	60 109 28 82 Other					
Date First Order	02/11/1997 16:02:12 05/11/1996 00:00:00 04/07/1996 00:00:00					
Date Last Order	06/05/1998 00:00:00 13/03/1998 00:00:00 07/06/1997 15:18:50					
High Value Cust	0 1 missing					
Parking Surface	6,034.10 1,310.00 17.00					

Fig. 9.10 Profiles of the clusters for the Northwind customers

attributes of the objects in the clusters), for all clusters of type 5 with support greater than 75:

```
SELECT NODE_NAME AS [Name], NODE_CAPTION AS [Caption],
       NODE_SUPPORT AS [Support], NODE_DESCRIPTION AS [Description]
```

FROM   NWDW_Clustering.CONTENT
WHERE NODE_TYPE = 5 AND NODE_SUPPORT > 75

The above query yields the following result:

Name	Caption	Support	Description
001	Cluster 1	102	City Key=66, City Key=74, City Key=17, City Key=7, City Key=75, City Key=33, City Key=70, City Key=3, City Key=108, City Key=59, Permanent Employees=0, 1971 <=Year Established <=1992, Business Type=Delicatessen, [...]
002	Cluster 2	89	City Key=30, City Key=49, City Key=12, City Key=2, City Key=28, Business Type=Pub, Business Type=Restaurant, [...]
006	Cluster 6	77	City Key=95, City Key=53, City Key=54, 1950 <=Year Established <=1957, Permanent Employees=6, City Key=11, Business Type=Minimart, [...]

We can also ask for the discriminating factors of clusters. The following query returns a table that indicates the primary discriminating factors between two clusters with node IDs 001 and 002:

CALL System.Microsoft.AnalysisServices.System.DataMining.Clustering.
    GetClusterDiscrimination('NWDW_Clustering', '001', '002', 0.0005, true)

The query uses a system stored procedure, although the query could also be performed manually. Attributes with positive score favor the cluster with ID 001, whereas attributes with negative values favor the cluster with ID 002. For example, if we analyze the table below with respect to Fig. 9.10, we can see that Cluster 2 contains an important proportion of records with BusinessType = 'Restaurant' compared to Cluster 1. This is explained by the score −63.7781. The result of this query is given next:

Attributes	Values	Score
Store Surface	142 - 1,924	100
Store Surface	1,925 - 7,857	-99.9999
Date Last Order	12/03/1998 - 06/05/1998	76.1429
Date Last Order	18/07/1996 - 12/03/1998	-68.3848
Business Type	Restaurant	-63.7781
...	...	...

We can use the model to make predictions about the outcome using the predictable attributes in the model, which are handled depending on whether the attribute is set to Predict or PredictOnly (Fig. 9.7). In the first case, the values for the attribute are added to the clustering model and appear as attributes in the finished model. In the second case, the values are not used to create clusters. Instead, after the model is completed, the clustering algorithm creates new values for the PredictOnly attribute based on the clusters to which each case belongs. This is our case in this example, as it can be seen in Fig. 9.7.

Our next prediction query uses the **Cluster** DMX function to return the cluster to which a new case, for which we know the business type, the total number of permanent employees, the year established, the annual profit, and the store surface, is most likely to belong. It also uses the **ClusterProbability** DMX function to return the probability of belonging to that cluster. Note that the query, again, is performed over the model not over the database (the name in the **FROM** clause is the name of the model):

```
SELECT  Cluster() AS [Cluster], ClusterProbability() AS [Probability]
FROM    [NWDW_Clustering] NATURAL PREDICTION JOIN
        ( SELECT 'Restaurant' AS [Business Type],
        2 AS [Permanent Employees], 1977 AS [Year Established],
        2 AS [Annual Profit], 400 AS [Store Surface], 860 AS [Parking Surface] )
```

This yields the following result:

Cluster	Probability
Cluster 7	0.7047

Finally, we can do the same as above, but for all the records in the **NewCustomers** database, as we have done for the decision trees model, using the **PREDICTION JOIN** and **OPENQUERY** DMX clauses, joining the model and the database table:

```
SELECT  T.CompanyName, T.BusinessType, T.ParkingSurface AS [PS],
        T.PermanentEmployees AS [PE], T.StoreSurface AS [SS],
        T.YearEstablished AS [YE], Cluster() AS [Cluster],
        ClusterProbability() as [Probability]
FROM    [NWDW_Clustering] PREDICTION JOIN OPENQUERY(Sales,
        'SELECT CompanyName, BusinessType, ParkingSurface,
        PermanentEmployees, StoreSurface, YearEstablished
        FROM NewCustomers') AS T ON
        [NWDW_Clustering].[Business Type] = T.[BusinessType] AND
        [NWDW_Clustering].[Permanent Employees] =
        T.[PermanentEmployees] AND
        [NWDW_Clustering].[Year Established] = T.[YearEstablished] AND
        [NWDW_Clustering].[Store Surface] = T.[StoreSurface] AND
        [NWDW_Clustering].[Parking Surface] = T.[ParkingSurface]
```

The result of this query is as follows:

CompanyName	BusinessType	PS	PE	SS	YE	Cluster	Probability
La Grande Epicerie	Grocery	1135	2	1788	1963	Cluster 7	0.7979
L'Amour Fou	Restaurant	918	4	1178	1955	Cluster 7	0.7806
Copenhagen Tavern	Tavern	0	3	667	1976	Cluster 8	0.5874
Au soleil	Café	542	3	374	1996	Cluster 8	0.5598
Mio Padre	Minimart	183	6	570	1965	Cluster 2	0.9943
...	...	...	..	...	...	...	...

Association Rules

We have already explained that the association model for the Northwind case study requires two views, namely, AssocOrders and AssocLineItems. Once these views are prepared, we can set the model parameters like support and confidence (called *probability* in Analysis Services) and deploy the model. In our case, we just show the results to give the look and feel of the tool and discuss the DMX commands since the number of records is still low to produce meaningful results. Figure 9.11 shows the association rules obtained, along with their probability. Figure 9.12 shows some of the itemsets obtained. For example, we can see that the products Sirop d'érable and Sir Rodney's Scones have a support of 55, which means they appear together 55 times in the database. The reader can also compare the itemsets and the corresponding rules that those itemsets yield. For example, the itemset (Sirop d'érable, Sir Rodney's Scones) produces two rules, since the order of purchasing does not matter: Sirop d'érable → Sir Rodney's Scones, and Sir Rodney's Scones → Sirop d'érable.

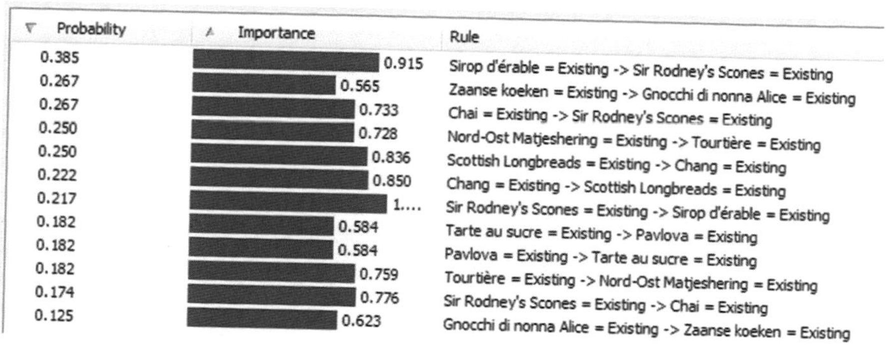

▽ Probability	↗ Importance	Rule
0.385	0.915	Sirop d'érable = Existing -> Sir Rodney's Scones = Existing
0.267	0.565	Zaanse koeken = Existing -> Gnocchi di nonna Alice = Existing
0.267	0.733	Chai = Existing -> Sir Rodney's Scones = Existing
0.250	0.728	Nord-Ost Matjeshering = Existing -> Tourtière = Existing
0.250	0.836	Scottish Longbreads = Existing -> Chang = Existing
0.222	0.850	Chang = Existing -> Scottish Longbreads = Existing
0.217	1....	Sir Rodney's Scones = Existing -> Sirop d'érable = Existing
0.182	0.584	Tarte au sucre = Existing -> Pavlova = Existing
0.182	0.584	Pavlova = Existing -> Tarte au sucre = Existing
0.182	0.759	Tourtière = Existing -> Nord-Ost Matjeshering = Existing
0.174	0.776	Sir Rodney's Scones = Existing -> Chai = Existing
0.125	0.623	Gnocchi di nonna Alice = Existing -> Zaanse koeken = Existing

Fig. 9.11 Association rules for the Northwind case study

There are two common uses of an association model: to discover information about frequent itemsets and to extract details about particular rules and itemsets. For example, we can retrieve a list of rules that were scored as being especially interesting or create a list of the most common itemsets. This information can be obtained through a DMX content query or browsing this information by using the Microsoft Association Viewer. The next content query returns details about the parameter values that were used when the model was created:

```
SELECT MINING_PARAMETERS
FROM    $system.DMSCHEMA_MINING_MODELS
WHERE MODEL_NAME = 'Association'
```

⋏ Support	▽ Size	Itemset
55	2	Sirop d'érable = Existing, Sir Rodney's Scones = Existing
44	2	Chai = Existing, Sir Rodney's Scones = Existing
44	2	Scottish Longbreads = Existing, Chang = Existing
44	2	Nord-Ost Matjeshering = Existing, Tourtière = Existing
44	2	Tarte au sucre = Existing, Pavlova = Existing
44	2	Zaanse koeken = Existing, Gnocchi di nonna Alice = Existing
352	1	Gnocchi di nonna Alice = Existing
319	1	Raclette Courdavault = Existing
275	1	Gorgonzola Telino = Existing
275	1	Boston Crab Meat = Existing
264	1	Rhönbräu Klosterbier = Existing
253	1	Sir Rodney's Scones = Existing

Fig. 9.12 Itemsets for the Northwind case study

The query returns the following result:

MINING_PARAMETERS
MAXIMUM_ITEMSET_COUNT=200000, MAXIMUM_ITEMSET_SIZE=3, MAXIMUM_SUPPORT=1, MINIMUM_SUPPORT=7.53768844221106E-03, MINIMUM_IMPORTANCE=-999999999, MINIMUM_ITEMSET_SIZE=0, MINIMUM_PROBABILITY=0.1

Our next query retrieves all the itemsets, together with a nested table (an attribute that is actually a table) that lists the products included in each itemset. The NODE_NAME column contains the unique ID of the itemset within the model. In this example, the nested table has been flattened (using the FLATTENED keyword). Thus, an itemset will generate as many rows in the result as products such itemset contains. This is the case, for instance, of nodes 74 and 75, which contain two items:

```
SELECT    FLATTENED NODE_NAME AS [Node],
          NODE_PROBABILITY AS [Probability],
          NODE_SUPPORT AS [Support],
          (SELECT  ATTRIBUTE_NAME AS [Name]
          FROM NODE_DISTRIBUTION) AS Products
FROM      Association.CONTENT
WHERE     NODE_TYPE = 7
ORDER BY NODE_NAME
```

Each itemset is contained in its own node (as indicated by NODE_TYPE = 7). This query returns the following table:

Node	Probability	Support	Products.Name
...	...	...	...
72	0.0728	319	Assoc Line Items1(Raclette Courdavault)
73	0.0804	352	Assoc Line Items1(Gnocchi di nonna Alice)
74	0.0125	55	Assoc Line Items1(Sirop d'érable)
74	0.0125	55	Assoc Line Items1(Sir Rodney's Scones)
75	0.0100	44	Assoc Line Items1(Zaanse koeken)
75	0.0100	44	Assoc Line Items1(Gnocchi di nonna Alice)
...	...	...	...

As another example, the following query returns the top 5 itemsets ordered by the support for each node. The NODE_CAPTION provides a text description of the items:

```
SELECT TOP 5 (NODE_SUPPORT), NODE_NAME, NODE_CAPTION
FROM    Association.CONTENT
WHERE NODE_TYPE = 7
```

This query returns the following table:

NODE_SUPPORT	NODE_NAME	NODE_CAPTION
352	73	Gnocchi di nonna Alice = Existing
319	72	Raclette Courdavault = Existing
275	70	Gorgonzola Telino = Existing
275	71	Boston Crab Meat = Existing
264	69	Rhönbräu Klosterbier = Existing

Finally, we can use the model to issue prediction queries, typically based on rules, to be used, for example, to make recommendations. The following query tells us what products we can recommend to a customer who has purchased a particular product. Since the column that corresponds to the products to be predicted is a nested table, we must use one SELECT clause to map the new value to the nested table column [Product Name] and another SELECT clause to map the nested table column to the case-level column, [Assoc Line Items]. Adding the keyword INCLUDE_STATISTICS to the query displays the probability and support for the recommendation:

```
SELECT FLATTENED PredictAssociation([Association].[Assoc Line Items],
       INCLUDE_STATISTICS, 3) AS [A]
FROM    [Association] NATURAL PREDICTION JOIN
       ( SELECT
       ( SELECT 'Tarte au sucre' AS [Product Name] )
       AS [Assoc Line Items] ) AS T
```

The query returns the following table:

Product Name	$SUPPORT	$PROBABILITY	$ADJUSTEDPROBABILITY
Pavlova	242	0.1818	0.6445
Gnocchi di nonna Alice	352	0.0804	0.0772
Raclette Courdavault	319	0.0728	0.0702

The adjusted probability is used by Analysis Services to "penalize" popular items during a prediction task. For example, given two items such that their predicted probability is the same and such that one of them is much popular than the other one (i.e., much more people buys the first one), we would like to recommend the less popular one. In this case, the $AdjustedProbability lifts the predicted probability. This is the case of product Pavlova in the example above, whose probability is strongly lifted.

9.2　Key Performance Indicators

Traditionally, managers use reporting tools to display statistics in order to monitor the performance of an organization. These reports, for example, display the monthly sales by employee for the current year, the sales amount by month also during the current year, the top ten orders or the top ten employees (according to the sales figures achieved), and so on. However, note that these reports lack a lot of crucial information. For example, how are sales performing against expected figures? What are the sale goals for employees? What is the sales trend? To obtain this information, business users must define a collection of indicators and display them timely in order to alert when things are getting out of the expected path. For example, they can devise a sales indicator that shows the sales over the current analysis period (e.g., quarter) and how these sales figures compare against an expected value or company goal. Indicators of this kind are called key performance indicators (KPIs).

KPIs are complex measurements used to estimate the effectiveness of an organization in carrying out their activities and to monitor the performance of their processes and business strategies. KPIs are traditionally defined with respect to a business strategy and business objectives, delivering a global overview of the company status. They are usually included in dashboards and reports (which will be discussed below), providing a detailed view of each specific area of the organization. Thus, business users can assess and manage organizational performance using KPIs. To support decision making, KPIs typically have a current value which is compared against a target value, a threshold value, and a minimum value. All these values are usually normalized, to facilitate interpretation.

9.2.1 Classification of Key Performance Indicators

There have been many proposals of classification of KPIs. The simplest one is to classify them according to the industry in which they are applied. In this way, we have, for instance, agriculture KPIs, education and training KPIs, finance KPIs, and so on. Another simple classification is based on the functionals area where they are applied. Thus, we have accounting KPIs, corporate services KPIs, finance KPIs, human resources KPIs, and so on.

KPIs can be also classified along other dimensions, for example, the temporal dimension. In this way, we have:

- Leading KPIs, which reflect expectations about what can happen in the future. An example is *expected demand.*
- Coincident KPIs, which reflect what is currently happening. An example is *number of current orders.*
- Lagging KPIs, which reflect what happened in the past. Examples include *earnings before interest and taxes* or *customer satisfaction.*

Another dimension along which we can classify KPIs refers to whether the indicator measures characteristics of the input or the output of a process. Thus, we have:

- Input KPIs, which measure resources invested in or used to generate business results. Examples include *headcount* or *cost per hour.*
- Output KPIs, which reflect the overall results or impact of the business activity to quantify performance. An example is *customer retention.*

KPIs can be also classified as qualitative or quantitative:

- Qualitative KPIs, which measure a descriptive characteristic, an opinion, or a property. An example is *customer satisfaction measured through surveys*, where even if survey data are quantitative, the measures are based on a subjective interpretation of a customer's opinions.
- Quantitative KPIs, which measure characteristics obtained through a mathematical expression. These are the most common kinds of KPIs. An example is *units per man-hour.*

KPIs can be also classified as strategic or operational:

- Strategic KPIs, which are typically reported to senior levels in the organization and at less regular intervals than the corresponding operational indicators. They have a medium- or long-term time scope.
- Operational KPIs, which are focused at lower levels in the organization and are reported more frequently than strategic indicators. They usually have a short-term time scope.

The last classification we give is based on the issues addressed by a KPI. Thus, we may have:

- Process KPIs, which refer to the efficiency or productivity of a business process. Examples are *sales growth* or *shipping efficiency.*
- Quality KPIs, which describe the quality of the production. Examples are *number of production interruptions* or *customer satisfaction.*
- Context KPIs, which are not directly influenced by the processes of the organization. Examples are *size of market* or *number of competitors.*

There are many other classifications of KPIs in the literature, although the list we have given above covers the most common ones.

9.2.2   Guidelines for Defining Key Performance Indicators

To be able to define a good set of indicators for an organization, we need to identify the sources from which we can obtain relevant information. These sources of information can be classified into primary, secondary, and external, as follows:

- Primary sources:
  - Front-line employees. They are at the core of the value chain and know what are the important factors to achieve the operational goals.
  - Managers. They provide their perspective across the value chain and their strategic knowledge.
  - Board. It defines the organizational goals and suggest specific KPIs that are highly prioritized and sometimes nonnegotiable.
  - Suppliers and customers. They bring an external perspective to what should be measured and improved.
- Secondary sources. These include strategic development plan, annual business/strategic plan, annual reports, internal operational reports, and competitor review reports.
- External sources. These include printed catalogs, on-line catalogs, annual reports of other organizations, expert advice, and questions in discussion forums.

When the sources have been identified, we can follow the steps below in order to define the indicators for the problem at hand:

1. Assemble a (preferably small) team.
2. Categorize potential metrics, basically to look at the business from many different perspectives. For example, we may want to define metrics that capture how the organization is performing from a financial perspective,

from a customer's perspective, and with respect to employee's expectations.

3. Brainstorm possible metrics to discuss many possible measures before deciding the final set.
4. Prioritize the initially defined metrics. In order to do this, for each metric, we must:

- Give its precise definition.
- Define if the indicator is leading or lagging. It is recommended to have an even number of leading and lagging metrics.
- Verify if the metric is likely to have a relevant impact.
- Check if the metric is linked to a specific set of business processes that we can drill into if it deviates from the desired values.
- Check if we have at least one to two metrics for each key category defined in the second step.

5. Perform a final filter on metrics. This consists in checking if the metric definition is unambiguous and clear to people not on the core team, if we have credible data to compute the metric, and making sure that achieving the metrics will lead to achieving our goals.
6. Set targets for the selected metrics. This is a crucial step since it is one of the biggest challenges in KPI definition. For this, historical information can be used as a guide against which the core team can look at industry benchmarks and economic conditions.

Finally, we give a set of conditions that a KPI must satisfy in order to be potentially useful. The conditions below consolidate a collection of good practices usually found in the literature:

- The metric must be specific and unambiguous, which means the definition of the indicator must be clear and easily understandable. In addition, the definition must precisely specify how the metric will be computed. In the Northwind case, for instance, an indicator called Sales Performance could be defined as the total value of the SalesAmount attribute in the Sales fact table, computed over the current quarter, divided by the value of the attribute for the same period last year. This ratio is then compared against an expected sales growth value set as a company goal.
- The indicator must be clearly owned by a department or company office, which means there must be an individual or a group that must be made clearly accountable for keeping the indicator on track.
- The metric must be measurable, which means all elements must be quantifiable.
- The indicator can be produced timely. To be useful for decision making, we must be able to produce a KPI at regular predefined intervals, in a way such that it can be analyzed together with other KPIs in the set of indicators.

- The indicator must be aligned with the company goals. KPIs should lead to the achievement of the global company goals. For example, a global goal can be to grow 10% per year.
- The number of KPIs must remain manageable, and decision makers must not be overwhelmed by a large number of indicators.

We next apply the above guidelines to define a collection of indicators for the Northwind case study.

9.2.3   KPIs for the Northwind Case Study

We now give some examples of indicators that can be appropriate for the Northwind company. We define KPIs belonging to several categories and according to the requirements of the departments that will be responsible for monitoring such indicators. For example, the sales department wants to monitor sales performance and order activity. The marketing department wants to follow shipping efficiency as an indirect way of estimating customer satisfaction. The human resources department wants to measure how sales employees are performing to estimate the end-of-year bonuses. Therefore, we propose the following KPIs:

1. *Sales performance*: Measures the monthly sales amount with respect to the same month of the previous year. *The goal consists in achieving 15% growth year over year.* It is computed over the **Sales** fact table of the Northwind data warehouse.
2. *Number of orders*: Measures the activity in terms of orders received. It is computed as the number of orders submitted per month. *The goal is to achieve a 5% monthly increase*: The indicator is computed from the **Sales** fact table of the Northwind data warehouse. Note that if we also compute this KPI weekly, we can have an idea of how orders are evolving within the current period and can take corrective measures in order to achieve the monthly goal.
3. *Shipping efficiency*: Measures the delay in the shipping of orders. Therefore, it is a measure of customer satisfaction. It is computed as the monthly average of the difference between the order and the shipped dates in the **Sales** fact table of the data warehouse. It is computed every month. *The goal is that the difference between both dates takes a value less than 7.*
4. *Shipping costs*: Measures the relative cost of shipping with respect to the sales amount. It is computed as the quotient between the freight costs and the total sales amount (the **Freight** and **SalesAmount** attributes in the **Sales** fact table) for the current month. It is computed monthly. *The goal is that the shipping cost does not exceed the 5% of the sales amount.*
5. *Salespersons reaching quota*: Measures the percentage of the employees reaching their selling quota yearly. It is computed monthly, to see how

this number is evolving during the current year. For this, we use the Sales fact table. For simplicity, we assume that the employee's quota is computed as a 15% increase over last year's sales. *The goal is that the salespersons reaching quota must be at least of 75%.*

We next show how we can define KPIs using Microsoft Analysis Services.

9.2.4 KPIs in Analysis Services

Analysis Services provides a framework for defining KPIs that exploit the business data stored in cubes. Each KPI uses a predefined set of properties to which MDX expressions are assigned. Only the metadata for the KPIs are stored by Analysis Services, whereas a set of MDX functions is available to applications for retrieving KPI values from cubes using these metadata. The Cube Designer provided in SQL Server Data Tools enables cube developers to create and test KPIs.

In Analysis Services, a cube can have a collection of KPIs. Each KPI has five properties, which are MDX expressions that return numeric values from a cube, as described next:

- Value, which returns the actual value of the KPI. It is mandatory for a KPI.
- Goal, which returns the goal of the KPI.
- Status, which returns the status of the KPI. To best represent the value graphically, this expression should return a value between −1 and 1. Client applications use this value to display a graphic indicator of the KPI value.
- Trend, which returns the trend of the KPI over time. As with Status, it should return a value between −1 and 1. Client applications use this value to display a graphic indicator of the KPI trend direction.
- Weight, which returns the weight of the KPI. If a KPI has a parent KPI, we can define weights to control the contribution of this KPI to its parent.

Analysis Services creates hidden calculated members on the Measures dimension for each KPI property above. Nevertheless, these calculated measures can be used in an MDX expression, even though they are hidden.

We show next how the *Sales performance* KPI defined in the previous section can be implemented using Analysis Services. Recall that we want to monitor the sales amount by year with respect to the goal of achieving 15% growth year over year. Let us now give more detail about what the users want. If the actual sales amount is more than 95% of the goal, the performance is considered satisfactory. If, however, the sales amount is within 85–95% of the goal, management must be alerted. If the sales amount drops under 85% of the goal, management must take immediate action to change the trend. These alerts and calls to action are commonly associated with the use of KPIs. We are also interested in the trends associated with the sales amount; if the sales amount is 20% higher than expected, this is great news and should be highlighted. Similarly, if the sales amount is 20% lower than expected, then we have to deal immediately with the situation.

The MDX query that computes the goal of the KPI is given next:

```
WITH MEMBER Measures.SalesPerformanceGoal AS
       CASE
              WHEN ISEMPTY(PARALLELPERIOD(
                     [Order Date].Calendar.Month, 12,
                     [Order Date].Calendar.CurrentMember))
                     THEN Measures.[Sales Amount]
              ELSE 1.15 *
                     ( Measures.[Sales Amount],
                     PARALLELPERIOD (
                     [Order Date].Calendar.Month, 12,
                     [Order Date].Calendar.CurrentMember))
       END,
       FORMAT_STRING = '$###,##0.00'
SELECT { [Sales Amount], SalesPerformanceGoal } ON COLUMNS,
       [Order Date].Calendar.Month.MEMBERS ON ROWS
FROM   Sales
```

In the above query, the CASE statement sets the goal to the sales of the current month if the corresponding month of the previous year is not included in the time frame of the cube. This query gives the following result:

	Sales Amount	SalesPerformanceGoal
...	...	...
June 1997	$33,843.80	$33,843.80
July 1997	$51,020.86	$32,041.18
August 1997	$45,841.67	$29,308.07
September 1997	$50,105.74	$25,270.56
October 1997	$62,651.25	$40,801.50
November 1997	$42,536.81	$52,440.05
...	...	...

As can be seen above, since the sales in the Northwind data warehouse started in July 1996, the goal until June 1997 is set to the current sales.

We can use SQL Server Data Tools for defining the above KPI, which we name **Sales Performance**. For this, we need to provide MDX expressions for each of the above properties as follows:

- Value: The measure used for defining the KPI is [Measures].[Sales Amount].
- Goal: The goal to increase 15% over last year sales amount is given by the CASE expression in the query above.
- Status: We need to choose a graphical indicator for displaying the status of the KPI. The available indicators are shown in Fig. 9.13. We select the traffic light indicator. Then, the MDX expression defined for the status

must return a value between −1 and 1. The KPI browser displays a red traffic light when the status is −1, a yellow traffic light when the status is 0, and a green traffic light when the status is 1. The MDX expression is given next:

```
CASE
    WHEN KpiValue("Sales Performance")/
        KpiGoal("Sales Performance") >= 0.95
    THEN 1
    WHEN KpiValue("Sales Performance")/
        KpiGoal("Sales Performance") < 0.85
    THEN -1
    ELSE 0
END
```

In the preceding MDX expression, the KpiValue and the KpiGoal functions retrieve, respectively, the actual value and the goal value of the Sales Performance KPI.

Fig. 9.13 Graphical indicators for displaying the status of a KPI

- Trend: Here, we choose the default indicator, that is, the standard arrow. The associated MDX expression is given next:

```
CASE
    WHEN ( KpiValue("Sales Performance") -
        KpiGoal("Sales Performance") ) /
        KpiGoal("Sales Performance") <= -0.2
    THEN -1
    WHEN ( KpiValue("Sales Performance") -
        KpiGoal("Sales Performance") ) /
        KpiGoal("Sales Performance") > 0.2
    THEN 1
    ELSE 0
END
```

This expression computes the trend of the KPI by subtracting current KPI values and last year values from the same period and divided between last year values from the same period. If there is a decrease of 20% or more, the value of the trend is −1; if there is an increase of 20% or more, the value of the trend is 1; otherwise, the value of the trend is 0.
- Weight: We leave it empty.

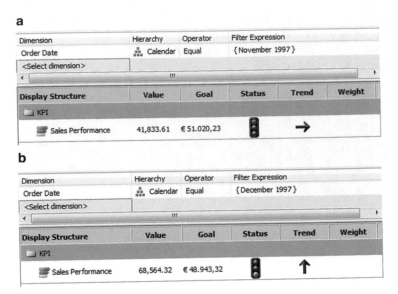

Fig. 9.14 Display of the Sales Performance KPI for November 1997 (**a**) and December 1997 (**b**)

Now that the KPI is defined, we can address the following MDX query to the Northwind cube:

```
SELECT { Measures.[Sales Amount], Measures.[Sales Performance Goal],
         Measures.[Sales Performance Trend] } ON COLUMNS,
       { [Order Date].Calendar.Month.[November 1997],
         [Order Date].Calendar.Month.[December 1997] } ON ROWS
FROM   Sales
```

The result is given next.

	Sales Amount	Sales Performance Goal	Sales Performance Trend
November 1997	$41,833.61	$51.020,23	0
December 1997	$68,564.32	$48.943,32	1

Figure 9.14 shows the KPI for November and December 1997. As can be seen, where the figures for the month of December achieved the goal, this was not the case for the month of November.

9.3 Dashboards

The most popular visualization tools in business intelligence are **dashboards**, which are collections of multiple visual components (such as charts or KPIs) on a single view. Dashboards enable organizations to effectively measure, monitor, and manage business performance. Dashboards are used to visualize organizational data and utilize different performance measurement models to identify and implement measures for all levels in the organization. There is an extensive practitioner-oriented literature on dashboards, although there is a lack of academic literature. In this section, we characterize dashboards, give some practical hints for their design, and implement a dashboard for the Northwind case study.

There are many definitions of the dashboard concept. However, since the visible part of a dashboard system is its user interface, most of them focus on its visual features. A classic definition due to Stephen Few states that a dashboard is a "visual display of the most important information needed to achieve one or more objectives, consolidated and arranged on a single screen so the information can be monitored at a glance."

Dashboards help to make fact-based decisions, using the right data, delivered reliably in an easily accessed and perceivable form. Note that decision makers require data in context to manage performance over time. Thus, although the current status of business is important, decision makers require comparisons of current values to past performance and to future objectives. We must also take into account that the time horizon and scope of data needed differ significantly based on the roles in the organization. An executive, focused on achieving enterprise-wide strategic goals, requires a high-level view across different lines of business and covering months or years. Business managers, on the other hand, must achieve daily or weekly performance goals and require not only a narrower time frame and kind of data but also, if current rates are off-target, the ability to quickly investigate the amount and cause of variation of a parameter. Business analysts have a much broader set of needs. Rather than knowing what they are looking for, they often approach performance data with ad hoc questions; therefore, they may require a time frame ranging between just a few hours up to many weeks.

9.3.1 Types of Dashboards

A well-known classification of dashboards proposes three high-level categories: strategic, operational, and analytical.

Strategic dashboards provide a quick overview of the status of an organization, assisting executive decisions such as the definition of long-term goals. Strategic dashboards, therefore, do not require real-time data: the focus is not on what is going on right now but in the past performance. Strategic dashboard data may be quantitative or qualitative. For instance, in the Northwind case study, the sales manager wants trend data on revenues and sales. Qualitatively, a human resource manager may want the top ten and worst ten salesmen. Because of their broad time horizon, strategic dashboards should have an interface that quickly guides decision makers to the answers they seek, telling if the indicator is on track.

Operational dashboards are designed to monitor the company operations. Monitoring operations requires more timely data, tracking constantly changing activities that could require immediate attention. Operational dashboards require a simple view to enable rapid visual identification of measures that are going away from the goals and require immediate action. Thus, the design of these kinds of dashboards must be very simple to avoid mistakes. The timeliness of operational data can vary. If things are on track, periodic snapshots may be sufficient. However, if a measure deviates from the goal, operational managers may want real-time data to see if the variance is an anomaly or a trend.

Analytical dashboards support interaction with the data, such as drilling down into the underlying details, to enable the exploration needed to make sense of it, which means not just to see what is going on but to examine the causes. Therefore, analytical dashboards must support what we called exploratory data analysis in Sect. 9.1.

9.3.2　Guidelines for Dashboard Design

In order to design a dashboard that complies with the needs of the intended audience, the visual elements and interactions must be carefully chosen. Factors such as placement, attention, cognitive load, and interactivity contribute greatly to the effectiveness of a dashboard.

A dashboard is meant to be viewed at a glance, so once the elements to be shown have been selected, they must be arranged in a display that can be viewed all at once in a screen, without having to scroll or navigate through multiple pages, minimizing the effort of viewing information. In addition, important information must be noticed quickly. From a designer's point of view, it is crucial to know who will be the users of the dashboard we are designing and what their goals are, in order to define to which of the above categories we defined the dashboard belongs. This information is typically obtained through user interviews.

To design a dashboard that can be effective and usable for its audience, we need to choose data visualizations that convey the information clearly, are easy to interpret, avoid excessive use of space, and are attractive and legible. For example, dashboards may provide the user with visualizations that allow data comparison. Line graphs, bar charts, and bullet bars are effective visual metaphors to use for quick comparisons. Analytical dashboards should provide interactivity, such as filtering or drill-down exploration. A scatterplot can provide more detail behind comparisons by showing patterns created by individual data points.

Operational dashboards should display any variations that would require action in a way that is quickly and easily noticeable. KPIs are used for effectively showing the comparison and drawing attention to data that indicate that action is required. A KPI must be set up to show where data falls within a specified range, so if a value falls below or above a threshold, the visual element utilizes color coding to draw attention to that value, like we showed in Sect. 9.2. Typically, red is used to show when performance has fallen below a target, green indicates good performance, and yellow can be used to show that no action is required. If multiple KPIs are used in a dashboard, the color coding must be used consistently for the different KPIs, so a user does not have to go through the extra work of decoding color codes for KPIs that have the same meaning. For example, we must use the same shade of red for all KPIs on a dashboard that show if a measure is performing below a threshold.

We must avoid to include distracting tools in a dashboard, like motion and animations. Also, using too many colors, or colors that are too bright, is distracting and must be avoided. Dashboard visualization should be easy to interpret and self-explanatory. Thus, only important text (like graph titles, category labels, or data values) should be placed on the dashboard. While a dashboard may have a small area, text should not be made so small that it is difficult to read. A good way to test readability is through test users.

9.3.3 Dashboards in Reporting Services

In this section, we illustrate how we can use Microsoft Reporting Services for building a dashboard for the Northwind company.

Reporting Services is a server-based reporting platform that provides reporting functionality for a wide range of data sources. The three main components of the Microsoft Reporting Services architecture are the client, the report server, and the report databases. The SQL Server Data Tools is typically used as the client. The report server is responsible to take a client's request to render a report or to perform a management request. The server performs functions like authentication, report and data processing, report rendering, scheduling, and delivery. Finally, there are three databases in the Reporting Services architecture: the two Reporting Services databases, denoted ReportServer and ReportServerTempDB, and the data source. The latter is the origin of the data that will populate the reports and can correspond to various providers, like SQL Server and Oracle databases, or XML, ODBC, and OLE DB data providers; the former store metadata about the reports.

Reporting Services provides many objects that can be included in a dashboard. These include various chart types, report objects like gauges (typically used with KPIs), images (for embedding standard images, such as JPEG or TIFF, in a report), maps, data bars, sparklines, and indicators. These can be put together with tabular data, as we show below.

We next describe our case study. The management of the Northwind company wants to put together in a dashboard a group of indicators to monitor the performance of several sectors of the company. The dashboard will contain the following elements:

- A graph showing the evolution of the *total sales per month*, together with the total sales in the same month for the previous year.
- To the right of the former graph, we will place a gauge to monitor the *percentual variation of total sales* with respect to the same month for the previous year. The goal is to obtain a 5% increase, and the gauge allows the manager to easily visualize if the goal has been achieved.
- Below the first graph, we will place another one conveying the *shipping costs*. The graph reports, monthly, the total freight cost with respect to the total sales. The goal is that the shipping costs must represent less than the 5% of the sales amount.
- To the right of this graph, we place a gauge showing the percentage of shipping costs with respect to the total sales from January to the end of April 1998 (data in the Northwind data warehouse range from 1996 to 1998). This is the KPI introduced in Sect. 9.2.
- In the lower part of the dashboard, we will place a table that can be used to analyze the performance of the sales force of the company and take actions if necessary. Thus, we list the three employees with the least number of sales as of April 1998. For each one of them, we compute the total sales and the percentage with respect to the expected yearly sales quota. We assume that an employee is expected to increase her sales 5% each year.

Figure 9.15 shows the definition of the dashboard in Reporting Services using SQL Server Data Tools. As can be seen in the left part of the figure, the data source of the report is the Northwind data warehouse. There are five datasets, one for each element of the dashboard. Each dataset has an associated SQL query. The one in the dialog box corresponds to the top left chart of the report, which shows the monthly sales compared with those of the previous year. Each dataset has a set of fields, shown below the dataset name, which correspond to the columns returned by the SQL query. Figure 9.16 shows the resulting dashboard. We explain below its different components.

The top left chart shows the monthly sales compared with those of the previous year. The corresponding SQL query is given next:

```
WITH MonthlySales AS (
    SELECT    DATEPART(yy, T.Date) AS Year,
              DATEPART(mm, T.Date) AS Month,
              SUBSTRING(DATENAME(mm, T.Date), 1, 3)
              AS MonthName, SUM(S.SalesAmount) AS MonthlySales
    FROM      Sales S, Time T
    WHERE     S.OrderDateKey = T.TimeKey
```

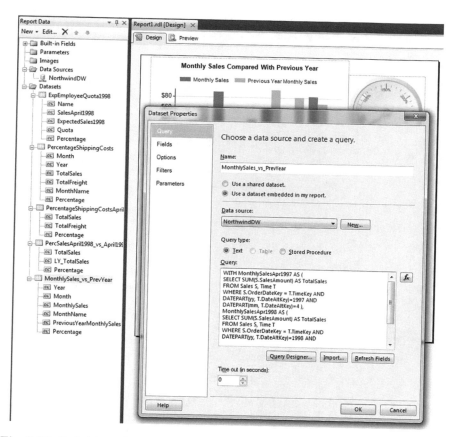

Fig. 9.15 Definition of the dashboard for the Northwind case study in Reporting Services using SQL Server Data Tools

```
        GROUP BY DATEPART(yy, T.Date), DATEPART(mm, T.Date),
                    DATENAME(mm, T.Date) )
SELECT MS.Year, MS.Month, MS.MonthName, MS.MonthlySales,
        PYMS.MonthlySales AS PreviousYearMonthlySales,
        MS.MonthlySales / PYMS.MonthlySales AS Percentage
FROM    MonthlySales MS, MonthlySales PYMS
WHERE  MS.Month = PYMS.Month AND PYMS.Year = MS.Year - 1 AND
        NOT (MS.Year = 1998 AND MS.Month = 5)
```

The above query computes the monthly sales amount in a temporary table denoted MonthlySales. In addition to the year and the month, the table obtains in the column MonthName the first three letters of the month name to be used for the labels of the x-axis of the chart. Then, the main query joins this table twice to obtain the monthly sales amount together with that of the previous year. The last line of the main query excludes the values from

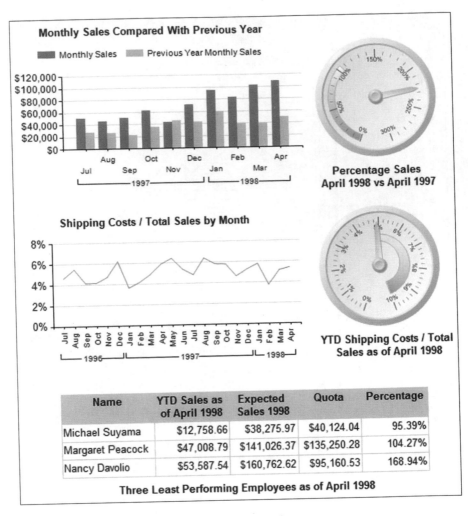

Fig. 9.16 Dashboard of the Northwind case study

May 1998 since in the Northwind data set, the sales for this month are not complete (sales stop at May 4, 1998).

The top right gauge shows the percentage of the sales in April 1998 with respect to the sales in April 1997. The gauge defines a range (shown in the left side of the scale) with a gradient from light gray to white and ranging from 0 to 105%. This corresponds to the KPI targeting a 5% increase of monthly sales amount with respect to the same month of the previous year. The query for the gauge is given next:

```
WITH MonthlySalesApr1997 AS (
        SELECT SUM(S.SalesAmount) AS TotalSales
```

```
FROM   Sales S, Time T
WHERE  S.OrderDateKey = T.TimeKey AND
       DATEPART(yy, T.Date)=1997 AND
       DATEPART(mm, T.Date)=4 ),
MonthlySalesApr1998 AS (
  SELECT SUM(S.SalesAmount) AS TotalSales
  FROM   Sales S, Time T
  WHERE  S.OrderDateKey = T.TimeKey AND
         DATEPART(yy, T.Date)=1998 AND
         DATEPART(mm, T.Date)=4 )
SELECT MS.TotalSales, LYMS.TotalSales AS LY_TotalSales,
       MS.TotalSales / LYMS.TotalSales AS Percentage
FROM   MonthlySalesApr1998 MS, MonthlySalesApr1997 LYMS
```

The above query defines two temporary tables computing, respectively, the monthly sales for April 1997 and April 1998. Each of these tables results in a single line. Then, a cross join of the two temporary tables is performed in the main query to obtain both values in a single line.

Below, we analyze the query for the center left chart, which shows the shipping costs with respect to the total sales by month:

```
SELECT   DATEPART(yy, T.Date) AS Year, DATEPART(mm, T.Date) AS Month,
         SUBSTRING(DATENAME(MM, T.Date), 1, 3) AS MonthName,
         SUM(S.SalesAmount) AS TotalSales, SUM(S.Freight) AS TotalFreight,
         SUM(S.Freight) / SUM(S.SalesAmount) AS Percentage
FROM     Sales S, Time T
WHERE    S.OrderDateKey = T.TimeKey AND NOT
         ( DATEPART(yy, T.Date) = 1998 AND DATEPART(mm, T.Date) = 5 )
GROUP BY DATEPART(yy, T.Date), DATEPART(mm, T.Date),
         DATENAME(mm, T.Date)
ORDER BY Year, Month, DATENAME(mm, T.Date)
```

In this query, we compute the total sales and the total freight cost by month, as well as the percentage between the two. As before, we exclude the values from May 1998.

The gauge in the center right of Fig. 9.16 shows the percentage of shipping costs with respect to the total sales from January to April 1998. The range of the gauge (shown at the right of the scale) reflects the KPI used for monitoring shipping costs, targeted at remaining below 5% of the sales amount. The corresponding query is given next:

```
SELECT SUM(S.SalesAmount) AS TotalSales, SUM(S.Freight) AS TotalFreight,
       SUM(S.Freight) / SUM(S.SalesAmount) AS Percentage
FROM   Sales S, Time T
WHERE  S.OrderDateKey = T.TimeKey AND DATEPART(yy, T.Date) = 1998 AND
       DATEPART(mm, T.Date) >= 1 AND DATEPART(mm, T.Date) <= 4
```

Finally, the query for the bottom table showing the three least performing selling employees as of April 1998 is given next:

```
WITH Quota1998 AS (
       SELECT   S.EmployeeKey, SUM(S.SalesAmount) * 1.05 AS Quota
```

```
            FROM      Sales S, Time T
            WHERE     S.OrderDateKey = T.TimeKey AND
                      DATEPART(yy, T.Date) = 1997
            GROUP BY S.EmployeeKey )
SELECT      TOP (3) E.FirstName + ' ' + E.LastName AS Name,
            SUM(S.SalesAmount) AS SalesApril1998,
            SUM(S.SalesAmount) * 3 AS ExpectedSales1998, Q.Quota,
            SUM(S.SalesAmount) * 3 / Q.Quota AS Percentage
FROM        Sales S, Time T, Employee E, Quota1998 Q
WHERE       S.OrderDateKey = T.TimeKey AND
            S.EmployeeKey = E.EmployeeKey AND
            S.OrderDateKey = T.TimeKey AND
            S.EmployeeKey = Q.EmployeeKey AND
            DATEPART(yy, T.Date) = 1998 AND DATEPART(mm, T.Date) <= 4
GROUP BY S.EmployeeKey, E.FirstName, E.LastName, Q.Quota
ORDER BY Percentage
```

In the temporary table Quota1998, we compute the sales quota that employees must achieve for 1998, as 5% increase of the sales amount for 1997. Then, the main query computes in the column SalesApril1998 the sales of employees from January to April 1998 and in the column ExpectedSales1998 the expected sales for 1998, calculated as three times the previous value; finally, the query computes the percentage of the expected sales and the quota.

9.4   Summary

In this chapter, we have discussed how a data warehouse can be exploited to obtain valuable and hidden information. We started describing three commonly used data mining techniques and their implementation in Analysis Services. We also applied them to the Northwind case study. Then, we studied KPIs, gave a classification of them, and provided guidelines for their definition. We also illustrated how to define KPIs for the Northwind case study in Analysis Services. We continued with the study of dashboards. We characterized different types of dashboards and gave guidelines for their definition. We concluded by illustrating how to create a dashboard for the Northwind case study using Microsoft Reporting Services.

9.5   Bibliographic Notes

There is a wide literature in data mining, where the concepts that we explained in this chapter could be studied in detail. For example, the book by Han, Kamber, and Pei [77] provides a good introduction to data mining techniques. Another good reference is the book by Tan et al. [196]. The classic Apriori algorithms can be found in [3, 190]. The latter covers association rules at different levels of granularity. The pattern growth algorithm was introduced in [76]. Sequential pattern algorithms are described in [4, 191]. Variants to make them more efficient by pruning uninteresting sequences are explained in Garofalakis et al. [59, 60]. Clustering is studied in [101], and the DBSCAN algorithm is described in [51]. The classic SLIQ and SPRINT classification algorithms are described in [131, 186], respectively.

Most of the books on KPIs and dashboards are oriented to practitioners. A typical reference on KPIs is the book by Parmenter [156]. Some references for dashboards are [55, 56, 162, 169]. Details on Microsoft Reporting Services can be found in [209].

9.6   Review Questions

9.1 What is data mining? Which disciplines does it comprise? How does data mining differentiate from statistics?

9.2 How does data mining fit into the process of knowledge discovery in databases?

9.3 Describe the main data mining tasks.

9.4 Describe the components of most data mining algorithms.

9.5 What is the main difference between supervised and unsupervised classification? Give examples of the possible uses of each technique.

9.6 What are decision trees? What is the Gini index used for?

9.7 Explain the partition algorithm for building a decision tree.

9.8 What is clustering? How would you select a good distance function? What is a score function?

9.9 Explain the K-means algorithm for clustering.

9.10 What is an association rule? Define confidence and support. What are they used for? What is an itemset? What is a frequent itemset?

9.11 Explain the Apriori algorithm for mining association rules.

9.12 Explain the concept of hierarchical association rules. How would you use them in a data mining process?

9.13 Describe the FUP algorithm for updating association rules. Give the principles on which this algorithm works and discuss its limitations.

9.14 Explain the concept of mining sequential patterns. How does it differentiate from mining association rules? What are the implications of accounting for order?

9.15 What are key performance indicators or KPIs? What are they used for? Detail the conditions a good KPI must satisfy.

9.16 Define a collection of KPIs using an example of an application domain that you are familiar with.

9.17 Explain the notion of dashboard. Compare the different definitions for dashboards.

9.18 What types of dashboards do you know? How would you use each kind?

9.19 Comment on the dashboard design guidelines.

9.20 Define a dashboard using an example of an application domain that you are familiar with.

9.7 Exercises

9.1 Consider the following training data about students:

StudID	Age	Country	FamilyIncome	Distance	Finish
s1	1	local	low	1	1
s2	0	local	medium	0	0
s3	0	local	high	1	0
s4	0	local	medium	1	0
s5	4	foreigner	medium	2	1
s6	3	foreigner	medium	1	1
s7	3	foreigner	low	1	2
s8	2	foreigner	low	1	3
s9	1	local	high	2	3
s10	0	local	high	1	2

where the classes are as follows:

- Age indicates the age at which the student started the studies. Possible values are as follows: 0 (between 17 and 21), 1 (between 22 and 26), 3 (between 27 and 32), and 4 (older than 32).
- Country can have two values: local and foreigner.
- FamilyIncome can be low, medium, and high.
- Distance indicates the distance that the student has to travel to go to university. It can take values 0 (less than 1 mile), 1 (between 1 and 3 miles), and 2 (more than 3 miles).
- Finish indicates whether the student finished her studies in the years planned for the corresponding career. It can take the values 0 (the student finished her studies on time), 1 (the student finished at most with 1-year delay), 2 (the student finished with 2 or more years of delay), and 3 (the student abandoned her studies).

(a) Manually run the ID3 algorithm to build a decision tree over the class Finish. Use the Gini index to partition the nodes.

(b) Use the K-means algorithm to generate three clusters of students.

9.2 Consider the Foodmart data warehouse of Fig. 6.4:

(a) Build a decision tree model that predicts whether a new customer is likely to order an item of a (sub)category X. Use the Customer, Product, Product_class, and Sales tables in the Foodmart data warehouse to build the data set. Add a Boolean attribute Buyer to each record: if a customer has purchased an item of (sub)category X, classify the record as 1, otherwise as 0. Add also an attribute age.

(b) Analyze the model using Analysis Services. Comment on the main characteristics, the attributes that the algorithm has selected to partition the tree, and other features you consider of interest. Modify the parameters and verify if you obtain the same model.

(c) Write a prediction query that checks for a new customer if she will order an item of the required (sub)category.

9.3 Consider again the Foodmart data warehouse:

(a) Use the Customer dimension and build a clustering model.

(b) Analyze the model using Analysis Services. Comment on the main characteristics, the number of clusters, and so on. Analyze if the partition reflects correctly the data or if you think that the model must be revised. Modify the parameters to produce other models.

(c) Write a DMX query that returns the cluster to which a new customer will most likely belong. Assume that this customer is a 35-year-old single female with university studies.

9.4 Consider the following transaction database:

TID	Items
T1	{A,B,C}
T2	{A,B,D}
T3	{B,C}
T4	{D,E,F}
T5	{E,F,G}
T6	{A,C,E}
T7	{A,B,D}
T8	{A,B,C,F}
I9	{A,D,E,F}
T10	{B,C,D,E}

(a) Manually run the Apriori algorithm to find out the frequent itemsets and rules with minimum support and confidence of 40%.

(b) Use the FUP algorithm to insert the following transactions:

TID	Items
T1	{A,K}
T2	{C,E,K}
T3	{F, G}
T4	{K,L}

Explain the algorithm step by step.

(c) Insert the necessary transactions such that at least two new frequent itemsets are discovered, keeping the same support.

9.5 Given the transaction database below, manually run the FP-growth algorithm with minimum support of 3.

TID	Items
T1	{A,B}
T2	{B,C,D}
T3	{A,C,D,E}
T4	{A,D,E}
T5	{A,B,C}
T6	{A,B,C,D}
T7	{A}
T8	{A,B,C}
T9	{A,B,D}
T10	{B,C,E}

9.6 Consider again the Foodmart data warehouse:

(a) Use the Sales table to build a transaction database for association rule mining. Use this table to produce an association rule model.
(b) Explore the model, and write a query to find out the 10 most frequent itemsets.
(c) Write a DMX query that, given the purchase of a product by a customer, selects other products to recommend her.

9.7 Use the Sales, Product, and Product_class tables to build a table containing transactions for hierarchical association rule mining. The hierarchy in the Product_class table contains the levels product_subcategory $\rightarrow$ product_category $\rightarrow$ product_department $\rightarrow$ product_family. We want to know, given a purchase of a product of a class C, which is the class of a product that will be bought together with the former one, where class is one of subcategory, category, department, or family. Using the Product_class table, produce an association rule model and analyze it.

9.8 Implement in Analysis Services the KPIs defined in Sect. 9.2.3 for the Northwind data warehouse.

9.9 The Foodmart company wants to define a collection of KPIs based on its data warehouse. The finance department wants to monitor the overall performance of the company stores, to check the percentage of the stores accountable for 85% of the total sales (the Pareto's principle). The sales department wants to monitor the evolution of the sales cost. It also wants to measure the monthly rate of new customers.
Propose KPIs that can help the departments in these tasks. Define these KPIs together with the goals that they are aimed to evaluate.

9.10 Define in Analysis Services the KPIs of Ex. 9.9.

9.11 Define in Reporting Services a dashboard to display the best five customers (the ones that purchased for the highest amount) for the last year, the best five selling products for the last year, the evolution in the last 2 years of the product sales by family, and the evolution in the last 2 years of the promotion sales against nonpromoted sales.

Chapter 10
A Method for Data Warehouse Design

Even though there is an abundant literature in the area of software development, few publications have been devoted to the development of data warehouses. Most of them are written by practitioners based on their experience in building data warehouses. On the other hand, the scientific community has proposed a variety of approaches, which in general target a specific conceptual model and are too complex to be used in real-world environments. As a consequence, there is still a lack of a methodological framework that could guide developers in the various stages of the data warehouse development process.

In this chapter, building over several existing approaches, we describe a general method for data warehouse design. We use the Northwind case study to illustrate the methodology. In Sect. 10.1, we present the existing approaches to data warehouse design. Then, in Sect. 10.2, we refer to the various phases that make up the data warehouse design process. Analogously to traditional database design, the methodology includes the phases of requirements specification, conceptual design, logical design, and physical design. The subsequent sections are devoted to more detailed descriptions of each design phase. In Sect. 10.3, we describe three different approaches to requirements specification. These approaches differ in which is the driving force for specifying requirements: users, source systems, or both. Section 10.4 covers conceptual design for data warehouses. In Sects. 10.5 and 10.6, we briefly describe the logical and physical design phases for data warehouses, extensively covered in Chaps. 5 and 7. We just provide this description to give a complete self-contained vision of the method. Section 10.7 highlights the advantages and disadvantages of the three approaches.

A. Vaisman and E. Zimányi, *Data Warehouse Systems*, Data-Centric
Systems and Applications, DOI 10.1007/978-3-642-54655-6_10,
© Springer-Verlag Berlin Heidelberg 2014

10.1   Approaches to Data Warehouse Design

A wide variety of approaches have been proposed for designing data warehouses. They differ in several aspects, such as whether they target data warehouses or data marts, the various phases that make up the design process, and the methods used for performing requirements specification and data warehouse design. This section highlights some of the essential characteristics of the current approaches according to these aspects.

A data warehouse includes data about an entire organization that help users at high management levels to take strategic decisions. However, these decisions may also be taken at lower organizational levels related to specific business areas, in which case only a subset of the data contained in a data warehouse is required. This subset is typically contained in a **data mart** (see Sect. 3.4), which has a similar structure to a data warehouse but is smaller in size. Data marts can be physically collocated with the data warehouse or they can have their own separate platform.

Like in operational databases (see Sect. 2.1), there are two major methods for the design of a data warehouse and its related data marts:

- **Top-down design:** The requirements of users at different organizational levels are merged before the design process begins, and one schema for the entire data warehouse is built. Then, separate data marts are tailored according to the characteristics of each business area or process.
- **Bottom-up design:** A separate schema is built for each data mart, taking into account the requirements of the decision-making users responsible for the corresponding specific business area or process. Later, these schemas are merged in a global schema for the entire data warehouse.

The choice between the top-down and the bottom-up approach depends on many factors, such as the professional skills of the development team, the size of the data warehouse, the users' motivation for having a data warehouse, and the financial support, among other things. The development of an enterprise-wide data warehouse using the top-down approach may be overwhelming for many organizations in terms of cost and duration. It is also a challenging activity for designers because of its size and complexity. On the other hand, the smaller size of data marts allows the return of the investment to be obtained in a shorter time period and facilitates the development processes. Further, if the user motivation is low, the bottom-up approach may deliver a data mart faster and at less cost, allowing users to quickly interact with OLAP tools and create new reports; this may lead to an increase in users' acceptance level and improve the motivation for having a data warehouse. Nevertheless, the development of these data marts requires a global data warehouse framework to be established so that the data marts are built considering their future integration into a whole data warehouse. A lack of this global framework can make such integration difficult and costly in the long term.

There is no consensus on the phases that should be followed for data warehouse design. Some authors consider that the traditional phases of developing operational databases described in Chap. 2, that is, requirements specification, conceptual design, logical design, and physical design, can also be used in developing data warehouses. Other authors ignore some of these phases, especially the conceptual design phase. Several approaches for data warehouse design have been proposed based on whether the analysis goals, the source systems, or a combination of these are used as the driving force. We next present these approaches, which we study in detail in the next sections.

The **analysis-driven approach** requires the identification of key users that can provide useful input about the organizational goals. Users play a fundamental role during requirements analysis and must be actively involved in the process of discovering relevant facts and dimensions. Users from different levels of the organization must be selected. Then, various techniques, such as interviews or facilitated sessions, are used to specify the information requirements. Consequently, the specification obtained will include the requirements of users at all organizational levels, aligned with the overall business goals. This is also called goal-driven approach.

In the **source-driven approach**, the data warehouse schema is obtained by analyzing the underlying source systems. Some of the proposed techniques require conceptual representations of the operational source systems, most of them based on the entity-relationship model, which we studied in Chap. 2. Other techniques use a relational schema to represent the source systems. These schemas should be normalized to facilitate the extraction of facts, measures, dimensions, and hierarchies. In general, the participation of users is only required to confirm the correctness of the derived structures or to identify some facts and measures as a starting point for the design of multidimensional schemas. After creating an initial schema, users can specify their information requirements. This is also called data-driven or supply-driven approach.

The **analysis/source-driven** approach is a combination of the analysis- and source-driven approaches, which takes into account what are the analysis needs from the users and what the source systems can provide. In an ideal situation, these two components should match, that is, all information that the users require for analysis purposes should be supplied by the data included in the source systems. This approach is also called top-down/bottom-up analysis.

These approaches, originally proposed for the requirements specification phase, are adapted to the other data warehouse design phases in the method that we explain in the next section.

10.2   General Overview of the Method

We next describe a general method for data warehouse design that encompasses various existing approaches from both research and practitioners. The method is based on the assumption that data warehouses are a particular type of databases dedicated to analytical purposes. Therefore, their design should follow the traditional database design phases, that is, requirements specification, conceptual design, logical design, and physical design, as shown in Fig. 10.1, which repeats, for clarity, Fig. 3.6 presented in Chap. 3. Nevertheless, there are significant differences between the design phases for databases and data warehouses, which stem from their different nature, as explained in Chap. 3. Note that although the various phases in Fig. 10.1 are depicted consecutively, actually there are multiple interactions between them, especially if an iterative development process is adopted in which the system is developed in incremental versions with increased functionality.

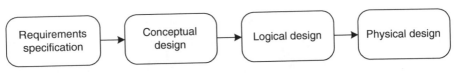

Fig. 10.1 Phases in data warehouse design (repeated from Fig. 3.6)

The phases in Fig. 10.1 may be applied to define either the overall data warehouse schema or the schemas of the individual data marts. From now on, we shall use the term "data warehouse" to mean that the concepts that we are discussing apply also to data marts if not stated otherwise.

For all the phases in Fig. 10.1, the specification of business and technical metadata is in continuous development. These include information about the data warehouse schema, the data source schemas, and the ETL processes. For example, the metadata for a data warehouse schema may provide information such as aliases used for various elements, abbreviations, currencies for monetary attributes or measures, and metric systems. The elements of the source systems should also be documented similarly. This could be a difficult task if conceptual schemas for these systems do not exist. The metadata for the ETL processes should consider several elements, such as the frequency of data refreshment. Data in a fact table may be required on a daily or monthly basis or after some specific event (e.g., after finishing a project). Therefore, users should specify a data refreshment strategy that corresponds to their analysis needs.

To illustrate the proposed method, we will use a hypothetical scenario concerning the design of the Northwind data warehouse we have been using as example throughout this book. We assume that the company wants to analyze its sales along dimensions like customers, products, geography, and so on in order to optimize the marketing strategy, for example, detecting customers that potentially could increase their orders or sales regions that are underperforming. To be able to conduct the analysis process, Northwind decided to implement a data warehouse system.

10.3 Requirements Specification

The requirements specification phase is one of the earliest steps in system development and thus entails significant problems if it is faulty or incomplete. Not much attention has been paid to the requirements analysis phase in data warehouse development, and many data warehouse projects skip this phase; instead, they concentrate on technical issues such as database modeling or query performance. As a consequence, many data warehouse projects fail to meet user needs and do not deliver the expected support for the decision-making process.

Requirements specification determines, among other things, *which* data should be available and *how* these data should be organized. In this phase, the queries of interest for the users are also determined. The requirements specification phase should lead the designer to discover the essential elements of a multidimensional schema, like the facts and their associated dimensions, which are required to facilitate future data manipulation and calculations. We will see that requirements specification for decision support and operational systems differ significantly from each other. The requirements specification phase establishes a foundation for all future activities in data warehouse development; in addition, it has a major impact on the success of data warehouse projects since it directly affects the technical aspects, as well as the data warehouse structures and applications.

We present next a general framework for the requirements specification phase. Although we separate the phases of requirements specification and conceptual design for readability purposes, these phases often overlap. In many cases, as soon as initial requirements have been documented, an initial conceptual schema starts to be sketched. As the requirements become more complete, so does the conceptual schema. For each one of the three approaches above, we first give a general description and then explain in more detail the various steps; finally, we apply each approach to the Northwind case study. We do not indicate the various iterations that may occur between steps. Our purpose is to provide a general framework to which details can be added and that can be tailored to the particularities of a specific data warehouse project.

10.3.1 Analysis-Driven Requirements Specification

In the analysis-driven approach, the driving force for developing the conceptual schema are the analysis needs of users. These requirements express

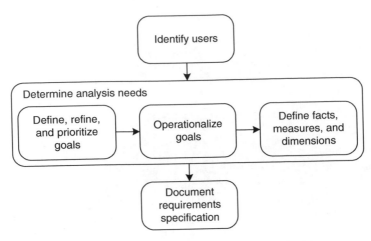

Fig. 10.2 Steps for requirements specification in the analysis-driven approach

the organizational goals and needs that the data warehouse is expected to address to support the decision-making process.

The steps in the analysis-driven approach to requirements specification are shown in Fig. 10.2 and described next.

Identify Users

Since a data warehouse provides an enterprise-wide decision-support infrastructure, users at various hierarchical levels in the organization should be considered when analyzing requirements. *Executive users* at the top organizational level typically require global, summarized information. They help in understanding high-level objectives and goals and the overall business vision. *Management users* may require more detailed information pertaining to a specific area of the organization. They provide more insight into the business processes or the tactics used for achieving the business goals. Finally, *professional users* are responsible for a specific section or set of services and may demand specific information related to their area of interest. Furthermore, the identification of potential users should also consider different entities in a horizontal division of the organization (e.g., departments). This will help in providing an overall view of the project and its scope.

Determine Analysis Needs

Analysis needs help developers understand what data should be available to respond to the users' expectations on the data warehouse system. This phase should eventually discover a collection of facts, measures, dimensions, and hierarchies. The process includes several steps, as follows.

Define, Refine, and Prioritize Goals

The starting point in determining analysis needs is the consideration of the business goals. Successful data warehouse projects assume that the goals of the company are the same for everyone and that the entire company will therefore be pursuing the same direction. Therefore, a clear specification of goals is essential to guide user needs and convert them into data elements. Since users at several different management levels participate in requirements specification, analysis needs may be expressed by considering both general and specific goals. The specific goals should be aligned with the general ones to ensure a common direction of the overall development. The goal-gathering process is conducted by means of interviews and brainstorming sessions, among other ones. The list of goals should be analyzed to detect redundancies and dependencies. For example, some goals could be combined because of their similarity, discarded because of their inconsistency, or considered as subgoals of other ones. This analysis may require additional interaction with the users to establish the final list of goals.

Operationalize Goals

Once the goals have been defined and prioritized, we need to make them concrete. Thus, for each goal identified in the previous step, a collection of representative queries must be defined through interviews with the users. These queries capture **functional requirements**, which define the operations and activities that a system must be able to perform. Each user is requested to provide, in natural language, a list of queries needed for her daily task. Initially, the vocabulary can be unrestricted. However, certain terms may have different meanings for different users. The analyst must identify and disambiguate them. For example, a term like "the best customer" should be expressed as "the customer with the highest total sales amount." A document is then produced, where for each goal there is a collection of queries, and each query is associated with a user. The process continues with query analysis and integration. Here, users review and consolidate the queries in the document above to avoid misunderstandings or redundancies. The frequency of the queries must also be estimated. Finally, a prioritization process is carried out. Since we worked with different areas of the organization, we must unify all requirements from these areas and define priorities between them. A possible priority hierarchy can be *areas* → *users* → *queries of the same user*. Intuitively, the idea is that the requirement with the least priority in an area prevails over the requirement with the highest priority in the area immediately following in importance the previous one. Obviously, other criteria could also be used. This is a cyclic process, which results in a final document containing consistent, nonredundant queries. In addition to the queries, **nonfunctional requirements** should also be elicited and specified. These are criteria that can be used to judge the operation of a system rather than specific behavior. Thus, a list of nonfunctional requirements may be associated with each query, for example, required response time and accuracy.

Define Facts, Measures, and Dimensions

In this step, the analyst tries to identify the underlying facts and dimensions from the queries above. This is typically a manual process. For example, in the documentation of this step, we can find a query "Name of top five customers with monthly average sales higher than $1,500." This query includes the following data elements: customer name, month, and sales. We should also include information about which data elements will be aggregated and the functions that must be used. If possible, this step should also specify the granularities required for the measures and information about whether they are additive, semiadditive, or nonadditive (see Sect. 3.1).

Document Requirements Specification

The information obtained in the previous step should be documented. The documentation delivered is the starting point for the **technical** and **business metadata** (see Sect. 3.4). Therefore, this document should include all elements required by the designers and also a dictionary of the terminology, organizational structure, policies, and constraints of the business, among other things. For example, the document could express in business terms what the candidate measures or dimensions actually represent, who has access to them, and what operations can be done. Note that this document will not be final since additional interactions could be necessary during the conceptual design phase in order to refine or clarify some aspects.

10.3.2 Analysis-Driven Requirements for the Northwind Case Study

We now apply the analysis-driven approach to produce a requirements specification for the Northwind data warehouse. We do not include all details about each step. We limit ourselves to illustrate only the essential aspects of the method.

Identify Users

In this example, three groups of users were identified:

1. Executive: the members of the board of directors of the Northwind company who define the overall company goals.
2. Management: managers at departmental levels, for example, marketing, regional sales, and human resources.
3. Professional: professional personnel who implement the indications of the management. Examples are marketing executive officers.

Determine Analysis Needs

This step starts with the specification of the goals. We will just address the general goal: *increase the overall company sales by 10% percent yearly*. This goal can be decomposed into *subgoals*:

1. Increase sales in underperforming regions.
2. For customers buying below their potential, increase their orders (in number of orders and individual order amount).
3. Increase sales of products selling below the company expectations.
4. Take action on employees performing below their expected quota.

In the next step, further sessions with the users are carried out to understand their demands in more detail and operationalize the goals and subgoals. As we explained above, the queries can be expressed in free natural language. Then, the terms must be aligned with a data dictionary or common vocabulary during a process of cleansing, disambiguation, and prioritization. Below, we give some examples of the queries that operationalize the goals above. We show the queries already expressed in a common vocabulary that we assume has been previously defined in a data dictionary. We omit here the process of prioritizing queries and users. We then identify potential dimensions, hierarchy levels, and measures. To facilitate reading, we use different fonts for **dimensions**, **hierarchy levels**, and *measures*.

1. Increase sales in underperforming regions:
   (a) Five best- and worst-selling (measured as total *sales* amount) pairs of **customer** and **supplier countries**.
   (b) **Countries**, **states**, and **cities** whose **customers** have the highest total *sales* amount.
   (c) Five best- and worst-selling (measured as total *sales* amount) **products** by **customer country**, **state**, and **city**.

2. For customers buying below their potential, increase their orders (in number of orders and individual order amount):

   (a) Monthly *sales* by customer compared to the corresponding *sales* (for the same customer) of the previous year.
   (b) Total number of orders by customer, time period (e.g., year), and product.
   (c) Average *unit price* per customer.

3. Increase sales of products selling below the company expectations:

   (a) Monthly *sales* for each product category for the current year.
   (b) Average *discount* percentage per product and month.
   (c) Average *quantity* ordered per product.

4. Take action on employees performing below their expected quota:

   (a) Best-selling employee per product per year with respect to *sales* amount.
   (b) Average monthly *sales* by employee and year.
   (c) Total *sales* by an employee and her subordinates during a certain time period.

Table 10.1 shows, for each query, which are the candidate dimensions, measures, and hierarchies. If priorities are considered, they will be associated with each query; it is also usual that each query is associated with the users that proposed it. In the first column from the left of the table, dimension and measure names are distinguished by their fonts. Thus, for instance, Employee is a dimension while *Quantity* is a measure. The table displays summarized information in the sense that a check mark is placed if a query mentions at least one level of one hierarchy in the second column from the left. Note also that Table 10.1 includes more hierarchy levels than the ones referenced in the goals and subgoals above. We assume that these have been discovered by means of the analysis of other queries not shown here. We will also see later that the complete design includes more dimensions and measures not displayed here for the sake of clarity. For example, we do not show here the information related to the shipping of products. Also, regarding the Time dimension, note that we did not identify the three roles it plays in the Northwind data warehouse, that is, as an order date, a shipped date, or a due date. The queries we have addressed only allow to discover the order date role; therefore, we have just called this dimension Time.

Table 10.1 does not only show the dimensions but also candidate hierarchies inferred from the queries above and company documentation. For example, in dimension Employee, we can see that there are two candidate hierarchies: Supervision and Territories. The former can be inferred, among other sources of information, from Requirement 4c, which suggests that users are interested in analyzing together employees and their supervisors as a sales force. The Territories hierarchy is derived from the documentation of the company processes, which state that employees are assigned to a given number of cities and a city may have many employees assigned

Table 10.1 Multidimensional elements of the Northwind case study obtained using the analysis-driven approach

Dimensions /measures	Hierarchies and levels	Analysis scenarios											
		1a	1b	1c	2a	2b	2c	3a	3b	3c	4a	4b	4c
Employee	**Supervision** Subordinate → Supervisor **Territories** Employee ⇆ City → State → Country → Continent	–	–	–	–	–	–	–	–	–	✓	✓	✓
Time	**Calendar** Day → Month → Quarter → Semester → Year	–	–	–	✓	✓	✓	✓	✓	–	✓	✓	✓
Product	**Categories** Product → Category	–	–	✓	–	✓	–	✓	✓	✓	✓	–	–
Customer	**Geography** Customer → City → State → Country → Continent	✓	✓	✓	✓	✓	✓	–	–	–	–	–	–
Supplier	**Geography** Supplier → City → State → Country → Continent	✓	–	–	–	–	–	–	–	–	–	–	–
Quantity	–	–	–	–	–	–	–	–	✓	–	–	–	
Discount	–	–	–	–	–	–	–	✓	–	–	–	–	
SalesAmount	–	✓	✓	✓	✓	–	–	✓	–	–	✓	✓	✓
UnitPrice	–	–	–	–	–	–	✓	–	–	–	–	–	

to it. In addition, users informed that they are interested in analyzing total sales along a geographic dimension. Note that following the previous description, the hierarchy will be nonstrict. Requirements 1a–c suggest that customers are organized geographically and that this organization is relevant for analysis. Thus, Geography is a candidate hierarchy to be associated with customers. The same occurs with suppliers. The hierarchy Categories follows straightforwardly from Requirement 3a. The remaining hierarchies are obtained analogously.

Document Requirements Specification

The information compiled is included in the specification of the users' requirements. For example, it can contain summarized information as presented in Table 10.1 and also more descriptive parts that explain each element. The requirements specification document also contains the business metadata. For the Northwind case study, there are various ways to obtain these metadata, for example, by interviewing users or administrative staff or accessing the existing company documentation. We do not detail this document here.

10.3.3   Source-Driven Requirements Specification

The source-driven approach is based on the data available at the source systems. It aims at identifying all multidimensional schemas that can be implemented starting from the available operational databases. These databases are analyzed exhaustively in order to discover the elements that can represent facts with associated dimensions, hierarchies, and measures leading to an initial data warehouse schema.

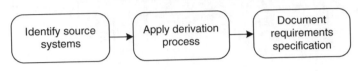

Fig. 10.3 Steps for requirements specification in the source-driven approach

We briefly describe next the steps in this approach to requirements specification, depicted in Fig. 10.3. As with the analysis-driven approach, we do not show the various iterations that could be required before the final data warehouse schema is developed.

Identify Source Systems

The aim of this step is to determine the existing operational systems that can be data providers for the warehouse. External sources are not considered at this stage; they can be included later on when the need for additional information has been identified.

This step relies on system documentation, preferably represented using the entity-relationship model or relational tables. However, in many situations, this representation may be difficult to obtain, for example, when the data sources include implicit structures that are not declared through the data definition language of the database, when redundant and denormalized structures have been added to improve query response time, when the database has not been well designed, or when the databases reside on legacy systems whose inspection is a difficult task. In such situations, reverse engineering processes can be applied. These processes are used to rebuild the logical and conceptual schemas of source systems whose documentation is missing or outdated.

It is important not only to identify the data sources but also to assess their quality. Moreover, it is often the case that the same data are available from more than one source. Reliability, availability, and update frequency of these sources may differ from each other. Thus, data sources must be analyzed to assess their suitability to satisfy nonfunctional requirements. For this, meetings with data producers are carried out where the set of data sources, the quality of their data, and their availability must be documented. At the end of the whole requirements specification process, ideally we will have for each data element the best data source for obtaining it.

Apply Derivation Process

There are many techniques to derive multidimensional elements from operational databases. All these techniques require that the operational databases are represented using either the entity-relationship or the relational model.

Facts and their associated measures are determined by analyzing the existing documentation or the structure of the databases. Facts and measures are associated with elements that are frequently updated. If the operational databases are relational, they may correspond to tables and attributes, respectively. If the operational databases are represented using the entity-relationship model, facts could be entity or relationship types, while measures may be attributes of these elements. An alternative option is to involve users who understand the operational systems and can help to determine what data can be considered as measures. Identifying facts and measures is the most important aspect of this approach since these form the basis for constructing multidimensional schemas.

Various procedures can be applied to derive dimensions and hierarchies. These procedures may be automatic, semiautomatic, or manual. The former two require knowledge about the specific conceptual models that are used for the initial schema and its subsequent transformations. The process of discovering a dimension or a leaf level of a hierarchy usually starts from identifying the static (not frequently updated) elements that are related to the facts. Then, a search for other hierarchy levels is conducted. For this purpose, starting with a leaf level of a hierarchy, every relationship in which it participates is revised. Unlike automatic or semiautomatic procedures, manual procedures allow designers to find hierarchies embedded within the same entity or table, for example, to find city and province attributes in a customer or employee entity type. However, either the presence of system experts who understand the data in the operational databases is required or the designer must have good knowledge about the business domain and the underlying systems.

Document Requirements Specification

Like in the analysis-driven approach, the requirements specification phase should be documented. The documentation should describe those elements of the source systems that can be considered as facts, measures, dimensions, and hierarchies. This will be contained in the **technical metadata**. Further, it is desirable to involve at this stage a domain expert who can help in defining business terminology for these elements and in indicating, for example, whether measures are additive, semiadditive, or nonadditive.

10.3.4   Source-Driven Requirements for the Northwind Case Study

We illustrate next the source-driven approach for the Northwind case study. We assume that the entity-relationship schema of the operational database, shown in Fig. 10.4, is available and data of appropriate quality can be obtained. We skip the step of identifying the source systems, except for the geographic data, which were obtained from external sources (typically web-based), complementing the ones in the database in the Customers, Employees, and Suppliers tables.

Apply Derivation Process

We chose a manual derivation process to provide a more general solution, although automatic or semiautomatic methods could have also been applied.

We start by identifying candidate facts. In the schema of Fig. 10.4, we can distinguish the many-to-many relationship type OrderDetails, with attributes that represent numeric data. This is a clear candidate to be a fact in a multidimensional schema. Candidate measures for this fact are the attributes UnitPrice, Quantity, and Discount. An order in Orders is associated with many products through the relationship type OrderDetails. Since users have expressed that they are interested in individual sales rather than in the whole content of an order, a fact should be associated with an order line. Thus, the products in OrderDetails may be subsumed in the Orders table so that each record in the latter now becomes a fact. We call this fact Sales. A sales fact is associated with a unique employee (in entity type Employees), shipper (in entity type Shippers), and customer (in entity type Customers). In addition, it is associated with three dates: the order date, the required date, and the shipped date. These are potential dimensions, analyzed below.

Since each sales fact is associated with an order line, we may also envision a dimension Order, with a one-to-one relationship with the fact Sales. Thus, Order is a candidate to be a fact or degenerate dimension (see Chap. 3), which can be used, for example, to determine the average sales amount of an order or the average number of items in an order.

The other many-to-many relationship type in the schema is EmployeeTerritories. Since it does not have associated attributes, initially we can consider it as candidate to be a nonstrict hierarchy rather than a fact.

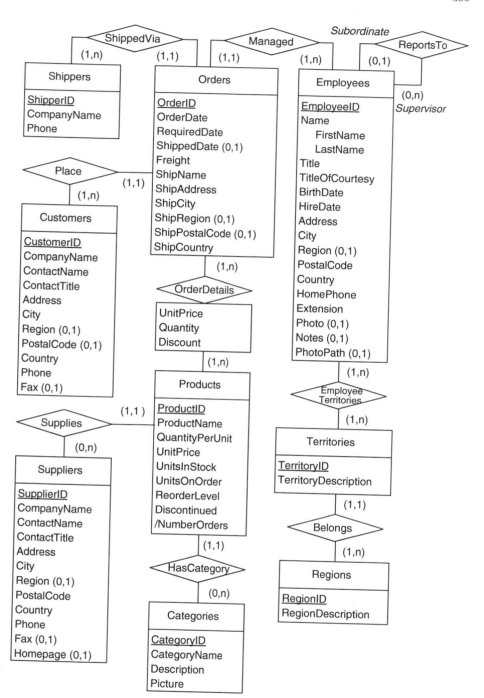

Fig. 10.4 Conceptual schema of the Northwind database (repeated from Fig. 2.1)

We now analyze potential dimensions and hierarchies. We start with the time dimension. Users have indicated that for decision making, a granularity at the level of day will suffice, and analysis by month, quarter, semester, and year are needed. The former defines, on the one hand, a Time dimension and, on the other hand, the hierarchy Date → Month → Quarter → Semester → Year. We call this hierarchy Calendar. We mentioned that each sales fact is associated with three dates, thus yielding three roles for the Time dimension, namely, OrderDate and ShippedDate (for the attribute with that name in the operational database) and DueDate (for the RequiredDate attribute).

In addition to the Time dimension, we have seen that a sales fact is associated with three other potential dimensions: Employee, Customer, and Supplier, derived from the respective many-to-one relationship types with the Orders table. A careful inspection of these geographic data showed that the data sources were incomplete. Thus, external data sources need to be checked (like Wikipedia[1] and GeoNames[2]) to complete the data. This analysis also shows that we need several different kinds of hierarchies to account for all possible political organizations of countries. Also, a detailed analysis of the data revealed that in the Northwind database, the term territories actually refers to cities, and this is the name we will adopt in the requirements process. Also, in the one-to-many relationship type Belongs between Territories and Regions, we consider the latter as a candidate to be a dimension level, yielding a candidate hierarchy City → Region. In light of the above, we define a hierarchy, called Geography, composed of the levels City → State → Region → Country. But this hierarchy should also allow other paths to be followed, like City → Country (for cities that do not belong to any state) and State → Country (for states that do not belong to any region). During conceptual design, we will show how this will be modeled. This hierarchy will be shared by the Customer and Supplier dimensions and will also be a part of the Employee dimension via the Territories hierarchy. The difference is that the latter is a nonstrict hierarchy, while Geography is a strict one.

The Products entity type induces the Product dimension, mentioned before. The Categories entity type and the HasCategory relationship type allow us to derive a hierarchy Product → Category, which we call Categories.

Finally, the entity type Employees is involved in a one-to-many recursive relationship type denoted ReportsTo. This is an obvious candidate to be a parent-child hierarchy, which we call Supervision.

Table 10.2 summarizes the result of applying the derivation process. We included the cardinalities of the relationship between the dimensions and the fact Sales. The term Employee ⇆ City indicates a many-to-many relationship between the Employee and City levels. All other relationships are many-to-one.

---

[1] http://www.wikipedia.org
[2] http://www.geonames.org

Table 10.2 Multidimensional elements in the Northwind case study obtained using the source-driven approach

Facts	Measures	Dimensions and cardinalities		Hierarchies and levels
Sales	UnitPrice Quantity Discount	Product	1:n	**Categories** Product → Category
		Supplier	1:n	**Geography** Supplier → City → State → Region → Country
		Customer	1:n	**Geography** Supplier → City → State → Region → Country
		Employee	1:n	**Supervision** Subordinate → Supervisor **Territories** Employee ⇆ City → State → Region → Country
		OrderDate	1:n	**Calendar** Date → Month → Quarter → Semester → Year
		DueDate	1:n	**Calendar** (as above)
		ShippedDate	1:n	**Calendar** (as above)
		Order	1:1	

Document Requirements Specification

Similarly to the analysis-driven approach, all information specified in the previous steps is documented here. This documentation includes a detailed description of the source schemas that serve as a basis for identifying the elements in the multidimensional schema. It may also contain elements in the source schema for which it is not clear whether they can be used as attributes or hierarchies in a dimension. For example, we considered that the address of employees will not be used as a hierarchy. If the source schemas use attributes or relation names with unclear semantics, the corresponding elements of the multidimensional schema must be renamed, specifying clearly the correspondences between the old and new names.

10.3.5 Analysis/Source-Driven Requirements Specification

The analysis/source-driven approach to requirements specification combines both of the previously described approaches, which can be used in parallel to achieve an optimal design. As illustrated in Fig. 10.5, two types of activities can be distinguished: one that corresponds to analysis needs (as described in Sect. 10.3.1) and another that represents the steps involved in creating a multidimensional schema from operational databases (as described in Sect. 10.3.3). Each type of activity results in the identification of elements for the initial multidimensional schema.

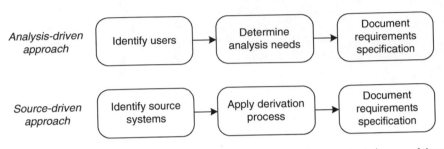

Fig. 10.5 Steps for requirements specification in the analysis/source-driven approach

10.4   Conceptual Design

Independently of whether the analysis-driven or the source-driven approach has been used, the requirements specification phase should eventually provide the necessary elements for building the initial conceptual data warehouse schema. The purpose of this schema is to represent a set of data requirements in a clear and concise manner that can be understood by the users. In the following, we detail the various steps of the conceptual-design phase and show examples of their execution. We use the MultiDim model described in Chap. 4 to define the conceptual schemas, although other conceptual models that provide an abstract representation of a data warehouse schema can also be used.

10.4.1   Analysis-Driven Conceptual Design

The design of a conceptual schema is an iterative process composed of three steps, shown in Fig. 10.6, namely, the development of the initial schema, the verification that the data in this schema are available in the source systems, and the mapping between the data in the schema and the data in the sources. In the case of missing data items, modification of the schema must be performed, which may lead to changes in the mappings. Finally, note that data can be directly obtained from the sources or can be derived from one or many sources. We next detail the three steps above.

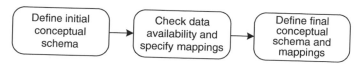

Fig. 10.6 Steps for conceptual design in the analysis-driven approach

Develop Initial Conceptual Schema

Well-specified analysis requirements lead to clearly distinguishable multidimensional elements, that is, facts, measures, dimensions, and hierarchies. We have shown this in Tables 10.1 and 10.2 as the result of the analysis- and source-driven requirements specification, respectively. Therefore, a first approximation to the conceptual schema can be developed. This schema should be validated against its potential use for analytical processing. This can be done by first revising the list of queries and analytical scenarios and also by consulting the users directly. Designers should be aware of the features of the multidimensional model in use and pose more detailed questions (if necessary) to clarify any aspect that may remain unclear. For example, a schema may contain different kinds of hierarchies, as specified in Sect. 4.2, some dimensions can play different roles, and derived attributes and measures could be needed. During this step, the refinement of the conceptual schema may require several iterations with the users.

Check Data Availability and Specify Mappings

The data contained in the source systems determines whether the proposed conceptual schema can be transformed into logical and physical schemas and be fed with the data required for analysis. All elements included in the conceptual schema are checked against the data items in the source systems. This process can be time-consuming if the underlying source systems are not documented, are denormalized, or are legacy systems. The result of this step is a specification of the mappings for all elements of the multidimensional schema that match data in the source systems. This mapping can be represented either descriptively or, more formally, using model-driven engineering techniques. This specification includes also a description of the required transformations, if they are necessary. Note that it is important to determine data availability at an early stage in data warehouse design to avoid unnecessary effort in developing logical and physical schemas for which the required data may not be available.

Develop Final Conceptual Schema and Mappings

If data are available in the source systems for all elements of the conceptual schema, the initial schema could be considered as the final schema. However, if not all multidimensional elements can be fed with data from the source systems, a new iteration with the users to modify their requirements according to the availability of data is required. As a result, a new schema should be developed and presented to the users for acceptance. The changes to the schema may require modification of existing mappings.

10.4.2   Analysis-Driven Conceptual Design for the Northwind Case Study

Develop Initial Schema

Based on the users' requirements, we developed the initial conceptual diagram shown in Fig. 10.7. This diagram was presented in Chap. 4, and we repeat it here to facilitate the presentation.

As described in the requirements phase, the main focus of analysis pertains to sales amount figures. This is represented at the conceptual level by the Sales fact in Fig. 10.7. Given that the source data are organized into orders, we need to transform order data into sales facts during the ETL process. For example, the schema in Fig. 10.7 includes the measures Quantity, UnitPrice, Discount, SalesAmount, Freight, and NetAmount. The first three measures are obtained directly from the sources, while the others must be computed during the ETL process. SalesAmount will be computed from Quantity, UnitPrice, and Discount. On the other hand, since in the operational database Freight is associated with a complete order rather than with an order line, in the data warehouse it must be distributed proportionally across the articles in the corresponding order. Finally, NetAmount is a derived measure, computed over the data cube. We remark the difference between a measure that is computed during the ETL process (SalesAmount) and a derived attribute, which is computed from the data cube (NetAmount). In addition, we specify the aggregate function to be applied to each measure. For example, average is applied to the measures UnitPrice and Discount. Note that the measures Freight and NetAmount are not included in Table 10.1 since they do not follow from Queries 1a–4c, which only represent a portion of the actual set of queries.

The Sales fact is defined between the Product, Supplier, Customer, Employee, and Time dimensions. Since the orders are associated with different time instants, the Time level participates in the Sales fact with the roles OrderDate, DueDate, and ShippedDate. According to the requirements summarized in Table 10.1, the Time dimension contains four aggregation levels, where most of the scenarios include aggregation over time. Dimension Product is related to the parent level Category with a one-to-many cardinality, defining a strict hierarchy. The level Product also contains specific information about products.

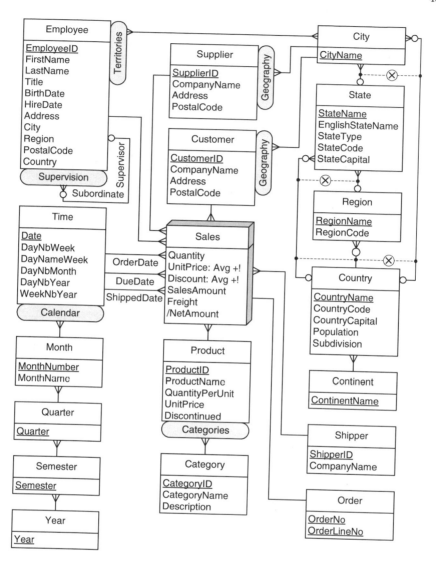

Fig. 10.7 Conceptual schema of the Northwind data warehouse (repeated from Fig. 4.2)

Also, following Table 10.1, geographic data are transformed in dimension levels, which are used in three hierarchies for the Customer, Supplier, and Employee dimensions. These hierarchies share the levels City, State, Region, Country, and Continent and are manually constructed (using the external data sources) taking into account the administrative divisions of the countries we want to represent. In addition, the many-to-many relationship between Employee and City defines a nonstrict hierarchy. This relationship was discovered analyzing the content of the source database in the requirements phase.

Finally, for human resource management (Columns 4a–4c in Table 10.1), we need to analyze sales by employee supervisors. Thus, in dimension Employee, we defined a recursive hierarchy denoted Supervision.

Check Data Availability and Specify Mappings

The next step in the method is to check the availability of data in the source systems for all elements included in the data warehouse schema. In our example, the logical schema of the data source is depicted in Fig. 10.4, thus facilitating the task of specifying mappings. In the absence of a conceptual representation of the source systems, their logical structures can be used instead. Table 10.3 shows an example of a table that specifies the way in which source tables and attributes of the operational databases are related to the levels and attributes of the data warehouse. The rightmost column indicates whether a transformation is required. For example, data representing the ProductName, QuantityPerUnit, and UnitPrice of products in the operational database can be used without any transformation in the data warehouse for the corresponding attributes of the Product level. Note that Table 10.3 is just a simplification of the information that should be collected. Additional documentation should be delivered that includes more detailed specification of the required mappings and transformations.

Develop Final Conceptual Schema and Mappings

Revision and additional consultation with users are required in order to adapt the multidimensional schema to the content of the data sources. When this has been done, the final schema and the corresponding mappings are developed. In our example, some of the issues found during the revision process were:

- We need to create and populate the dimension Time. The time interval of this dimension must cover the dates contained in the table Orders of the Northwind operational database.
- The dimensions Customer and Suppliers share the geographic hierarchy starting with City. However, this information is incomplete in the operational database. Therefore, the data for the hierarchy State, Country, and Continent must be obtained from an external source.

Metadata for the source systems, the data warehouse, and the ETL processes are also developed in this step. Besides the specification of transformations, the metadata include abstract descriptions of various features mentioned earlier in this section. For example, for each source system, its

Table 10.3 Data transformation between sources and the data warehouse

Source table	Source attribute	DW level	DW attribute	Transformation
Products	ProductName	Product	ProductName	—
Products	QuantityPerUnit	Product	QuantityPerUnit	—
Products	UnitPrice	Product	UnitPrice	—
...	...	...	...	...
Customers	CustomerID	Customer	CustomerID	✓
Customers	CompanyName	Customer	CompanyName	—
...	...	...	...	...
Orders	OrderID	Order	OrderNo	✓
Orders		Order	OrderLineNo	✓
Orders	OrderDate	Time	—	✓
...	...	...	...	...

access information must be specified (e.g., login, password, and accessibility). Also, for each element in the source schemas (e.g., the entity and relationship types), we specify its name, its alias, a description of its semantics in the application domain, and so on. The elements of the data warehouse schema are also described by names and aliases and, additionally, include information about data granularity, policies for the preservation of data changes (i.e., whether they are kept or discarded upon updates), loading frequencies, and the purging period, among other things.

10.4.3 Source-Driven Conceptual Design

In this approach, once the operational schemas have been analyzed, the initial data warehouse schema is developed. Since not all facts will be of interest for the purpose of decision support, input from users is required to identify which facts are important. Users can also refine the existing hierarchies since some of these are sometimes "hidden" in an entity type or a table. As a consequence, the initial data warehouse schema is modified until it becomes the final version accepted by the users.

The conceptual-design phase consists of three steps, shown in Fig. 10.8. We discuss next these steps.

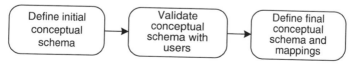

Fig. 10.8 Steps for conceptual design in the source-driven approach

Develop Initial Schema

Since the multidimensional elements have been identified in the requirements specification phase, the development of an initial data warehouse conceptual schema is straightforward. The usual practice for these kinds of schemas is to use names for the various schema elements that facilitate user understanding. However, in some cases, users are familiar with the technical names used in the source systems. Therefore, designers should develop a dictionary of names to facilitate communication with the users.

Validate Conceptual Schema with Users

The schema was obtained starting from the data sources. Thus, at this point, the participation of the users has been minimal, consisting of responding only to specific inquiries from the designer. In this step, users are incorporated in a more active role. Most of the time, these users belong to the professional or administrative level because of their knowledge of the underlying systems. The initial schema is examined in detail, and it is possible that it requires some modification for several reasons: (1) it may contain more elements than those required for the analysis purposes of the decision-making users; (2) some elements may require transformation (e.g., attributes into hierarchies); and (3) some elements could be missing even though they exist in the source systems (e.g., owing to confusing names). Note that the inclusion of new elements may require further interaction with the source systems.

Develop Final Conceptual Schema and Mappings

Users' recommendations about changes are incorporated into the initial schema, leading to a final conceptual schema that should be approved by the users. In this stage, an abstract specification of mappings and transformations (if required) between the data in the source systems and the data in the data warehouse is defined.

During all the above steps of the conceptual-design phase, a specification of the business, technical, and ETL metadata should be developed, following the same guidelines as those described for the analysis-driven approach.

10.4.4   Source-Driven Conceptual Design for the Northwind Case Study

Develop Initial Schema

The requirements elicitation phase discussed in Sect. 10.3.4 resulted in the multidimensional elements depicted in Table 10.2, namely, the facts, dimensions, and hierarchies inferred from the analysis of the operational database (Fig. 10.4). This led to the multidimensional schema shown in Fig. 10.7.

Validate Conceptual Schema with Users

The initial data warehouse schema as presented in Fig. 10.7 should be delivered to the users. In this way, they can assess its appropriateness for the analysis needs. This can lead to the modification of the schema, either by removing schema elements that are not needed for analysis or by specifying missing elements. Recall that in the source-driven approach, during the requirements elicitation the users have not participated, thus changes to the initial conceptual schema will likely be needed.

Develop Final Conceptual Schema and Mappings

The modified schema is finally delivered to the users. Given that the operational schema of the Northwind database is very simple, the mapping between the source schema and the final data warehouse schema is almost straightforward. The implementation of such a mapping was described in Chap. 8, thus we do not repeat it here. Further, since we already have the schemas for the source system and the data warehouse, we can specify metadata in a similar way to that described for the analysis-driven approach above.

10.4.5 Analysis/Source-Driven Conceptual Design

In the analysis/source-driven approach, two activities are performed, targeting both the analysis requirements of the data warehouse and the exploration of the source systems feeding the warehouse. This leads to the creation of two data warehouse schemas (Fig. 10.9). The schema obtained from the analysis-driven approach identifies the structure of the data warehouse as it emerges from the analysis requirements. The source-driven approach results in a data warehouse schema that can be extracted from the existing operational databases. After both initial schemas have been developed, they must be matched. Several aspects should be considered in this matching process, such as the terminology used and the degree of similarity between the two solutions for each multidimensional element, for example, between dimensions, levels, attributes, or hierarchies. Some solutions for this have been proposed in academic literature, although they are highly technical and complex to implement.

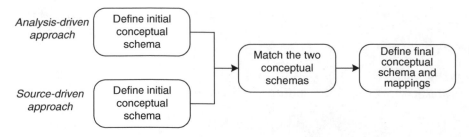

Fig. 10.9 Steps for conceptual design in the analysis/source-driven approach

An ideal situation arises when both schemas cover the same analysis aspects, that is, the users' needs are covered by the data in the operational systems and no other data are needed to expand the analysis. In this case, the schema is accepted, and mappings between elements of the source systems and the data warehouse are specified. Additionally, documentation is developed following the guidelines studied for the analysis-driven and source-driven approaches. This documentation contains metadata about the data warehouse, the source systems, and the ETL process. Nevertheless, in real-world applications, it is seldom the case that both schemas will cover the same aspects of analysis. Two situations may occur:

1. The users require less information than what the operational databases can provide. In this case, it is necessary to determine whether users may consider new aspects of analysis or whether to eliminate from the schema those facts that are not of interest to users. Therefore, another iteration of the analysis- and source-driven approaches is required, where either new users will be involved or a new initial schema will be developed.
2. The users require more information than what the operational databases can provide. In this case, the users may reconsider their needs and limit them to those proposed by the analysis-driven solution. Alternatively, the users may require the inclusion of external sources or legacy systems that were not considered in the previous iteration but contain the necessary data. Thus, new iterations of the analysis- and source-driven approaches may again be needed.

10.5   Logical Design

As illustrated in Fig. 10.10, two steps must be considered during the logical design phase: first, the transformation of the conceptual multidimensional schema into a logical schema; and second, the specification of the ETL processes, considering the mappings and transformations indicated in the previous phase. We shall refer next to these two steps.

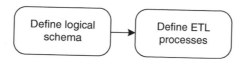

Fig. 10.10 Steps for logical design

10.5.1 Logical Schemas

After the conceptual design phase has been completed, it is necessary to apply mapping rules to the resulting conceptual schema in order to generate a logical schema. These mapping rules depend on the conceptual model used. In Sect. 5.3, we described some general mapping rules that translate the MultiDim conceptual model into the relational model. In this section, we apply these rules to the conceptual multidimensional schemas developed in the previous phase. As explained in Sect. 5.2, the logical representation of a data warehouse is often based on the relational data model using specific structures such as star and snowflake schemas. We also studied in Chap. 7 that many data warehouse applications include precomputed summary tables containing aggregated data that are stored as materialized views. However, we do not consider such tables to be part of the core logical schema.

We comment next on some design decisions taken when transforming the schema shown in Fig. 10.7 into relational tables. To facilitate the reading, we repeat the logical schema of the Northwind data warehouse in Fig. 10.11.

First, considering users' analysis needs, query performance, and data reuse, we must decide whether a star or a snowflake representation should be chosen. In Sect. 5.2, we have already stated the advantages and disadvantages of star (denormalized) or snowflake (normalized) schemas for representing dimensions with hierarchies. The following decisions were taken in our case study.

Given that the Calendar hierarchy is only used in the Time dimension, for performance reasons we denormalize these hierarchies and include them in a single table instead of mapping every level to a separate table, thus choosing a star representation for the Time dimension.

The hierarchies Territories, Geography (for customers), and Geography (for suppliers) in Fig. 10.7 share the levels City, State, Region, Country, and Continent. In order to favor the reuse of existing data, we decided to use the snowflake representation for this hierarchy, that is, we represent each one of the levels above in a separate table, except for Region, which is embedded in the table State. We explain this choice next. The hierarchy City → State → Region → Country → Continent is a ragged one (Sect. 4.2). To map this hierarchy to the relational model, we can embed all the data of the parent level in the child one (a denormalized mapping) or we can create a table for each level and an optional foreign key referencing the potential parent

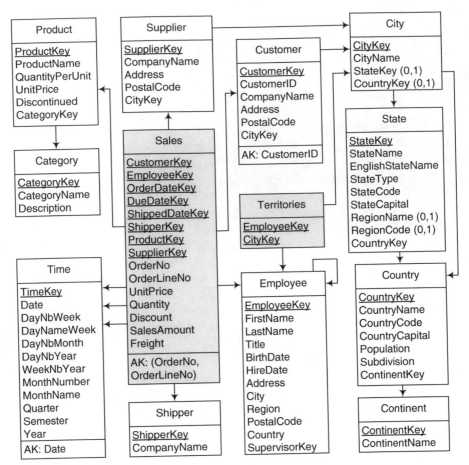

Fig. 10.11 Relational schema of the Northwind data warehouse (repeated from Fig. 5.4)

levels, as explained in Chap. 5. For the levels State and Region, we adopted the first alternative, where the attributes RegionName and RegionCode have been embedded in the State table as optional attributes. For the other levels, we have chosen the snowflaked solution. For example, in the City table, we have embedded StateKey and CountryKey as optional foreign keys. Then, if a city does directly belong to a country, we can reference the country without traversing the intermediate levels.

Territories is a nonstrict hierarchy (Sect. 4.2.6) since it contains a many-to-many relationship between the Employee and City levels. In order to represent this relationship in the relational model, we must use a bridge table. For that purpose, we create the table Territories, which references both the Employee and the City tables.

In a similar way, we define tables for the other hierarchies and levels. Finally, the fact table is created containing all measures included in the conceptual schema and referencing all participating dimensions.

10.5.2 ETL Processes

During the conceptual design phase, we identified the mappings required between the sources and the data warehouse. We also specify some transformations that could be necessary in order to match user requirements with the data available in the source systems. However, before implementing the ETL processes, several additional tasks must be specified in more detail.

In the logical design phase, all transformations of the source data should be considered. Some of them can be straightforward, for example, the separation of addresses into their components (e.g., street, city, postal code) or the extraction of date components (e.g., month and year). Note that the transformation may depend on the logical model. For example, in the relational model, each component of a department address will be represented as a separate attribute.

Other transformations may require further decisions, for instance, whether to recalculate measure values to express them in euros or dollars or to use the original currency and include the exchange rate. It should be clear that in real situations, complex data transformations may be required. Further, since the same data can be included in different source systems, the issue of inconsistencies may arise, and an appropriate strategy for resolving them must be devised. Also, developers should design the necessary data structures for all elements for which users want to keep changes, as explained in Sect. 5.7.

A preliminary sequence of execution for the ETL processes should also be determined. This ensures that all data will be transformed and included, with their consistency being checked. We do not explain here the ETL design for the Northwind data warehouse since it was studied in detail in Chap. 8.

10.6 Physical Design

As with the logical-design phase, we should consider two aspects in the physical-design phase: one related to the implementation of the data warehouse schema and another that considers the ETL processes. This is illustrated in Fig. 10.12. Since in Chap. 8 we have presented an in-depth analysis of an ETL case study, we do not extend further in this subject, and we focus on the implementation of the data warehouse schema.

During the physical design phase, the logical schema is converted into a tool-dependent physical database structure. Physical design decisions should

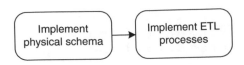

Fig. 10.12 Steps for physical design

consider both the proposed logical schema and the analytical queries specified during the process of requirements gathering. A well-developed physical design should enable to manage very large amounts of data, to refresh the data warehouse with new data from the source systems, to perform complex operations that may include joins of many tables, and to aggregate many data items. All of these depend on the facilities provided by the DBMS regarding storage methods, indexes, partitioning, parallel query execution, aggregation functions, and view materialization, among other things.

As studied in Chap. 7, **partitioning** consists in dividing a table into smaller data sets, thus providing better support for the management of very large volumes of data. For example, if it is usual that a query requests employee names, dimension Employee can be fragmented vertically to have the attributes FirstName, LastName, and City in one partition and the remaining ones in another partition. This enables more records to be retrieved into the main memory. Also, the Sales fact table could be partitioned horizontally according to time if it is usual that queries require the most recent data according to some time frame, for example, years. However, to be able to use partitioning techniques, we must have a good knowledge not only of the consequences of having partitioned dimension and fact tables but also of which method of partitioning may work better if the system we are working with supports more than one (e.g., Oracle provides four types of horizontal partitioning methods). SQL Server, as we have seen in Chap. 7, also supports partitioning. We have shown how the Sales fact table can be partitioned by year. We have also explained in Chap. 7 that in Analysis Services it is possible to partition data cubes, where the **storage modes** in the partitions can differ from each other. For example, one partition can be stored in a MOLAP mode, while another one can be stored in a ROLAP mode.

Indexing is a key feature to obtain good query performance in data warehouses. In the physical design phase, we must define which kinds of indexes we are going to use and over which attributes. In addition to the typical B-tree and hashed indexes provided by the database management systems, bitmap indexes and join indexes are used in data warehousing. We have studied that bitmap indexes are appropriate for answering typical data warehouse queries, in particular for filtering tuples using conditions over low-cardinality columns. Again, the designer should be aware of the possibilities of the DBMS that she will use. For example, we have seen in Sect. 7.8.3 that in SQL Server it is not possible to define a bitmap index over a table column, while this is possible in Oracle. We have also seen that column-store indexes, which were studied in Chap. 7, can be defined in SQL Server.

View materialization is a key feature for achieving good query performance in OLAP. Thus, during physical design, we must define which are the most common queries our system will support and, based on this study, define which are the materialized views that we need. Recall that SQL Server supports materialized views indirectly, through the feature called indexed views, basically a unique clustered index defined over a view. Since view materialization was studied in Chap. 7, we do not extend further in this topic here.

10.7 Characterization of the Various Approaches

In this section, we summarize the three approaches to data warehouse development. We discuss the many aspects that must be considered before choosing one of those approaches for a specific data warehouse project.

10.7.1 Analysis-Driven Approach

The analysis-driven approach requires the intensive participation of users from different organizational levels. In particular, the support of executive-level users is important in order to define business goals and needs. The identification of key users for requirements specification is a crucial task. It is necessary to consider several aspects:

- Users should be aware of the overall business goals to avoid situations where the requirements represent the personal perceptions of users according to their role in the organization or business unit.
- Users who would dominate the requirements specification process should be avoided or tempered in order to ensure that the information needs of different users will be considered.
- Users must be available and agree to participate during the whole process of requirements gathering and conceptual design.
- Users must have an idea of what a data warehouse system and an OLAP system can offer. If this is not the case, they should be instructed by means of explanations, demonstrations, or prototypes.

The development team requires highly qualified professionals. For example, a project manager should have very strong moderation and leadership skills. A good knowledge of information-gathering techniques and business process modeling is also required. It is important that data warehouse designers should be able to communicate with and to understand nonexpert users in order to obtain the required information and, later on, to present and describe the proposed multidimensional schema to them. This helps to avoid the situation where users describe the requirements for the data warehouse system using business terminology and the data warehouse team develops the system using a more technical viewpoint that is difficult for the users to understand.

Advantages of the analysis-driven approach are

- It provides a comprehensive and precise specification of the needs of stakeholders from their business viewpoint.
- It facilitates, through the effective participation of users, a better understanding of the facts, dimensions, and the relationships between them.
- It promotes the acceptance of the system if there is continuous interaction with potential users and decision makers.
- It enables the specification of long-term strategic goals.

However, some disadvantages of this approach can play an important role in determining its usability for a specific data warehouse project:

- The specification of business goals can be a difficult process, and its result depends on the techniques applied and the skills of the developer team.
- Requirements specification not aligned with business goals may produce a complex schema that does not support the decision processes at all organizational levels.
- The duration of the project tends to be longer than the duration of the source-driven approach. Thus, the cost of the project can also be higher.
- The users' requirements might not be satisfied by the information existing in the source systems.

10.7.2   Source-Driven Approach

In this approach, the participation of the users is not explicitly required. They are involved only sporadically, either to confirm the correctness of the structures derived or to identify facts and measures as a starting point for creating multidimensional schemas. Typically, users come from the professional or the administrative organizational level since data are represented at a low level of detail. Also, this approach requires highly skilled and experienced designers. Besides the usual modeling abilities, they should have enough business knowledge to understand the business context and its needs. They should also have the capacity to understand the structure of the underlying operational databases.

The source-driven method has several advantages:

- It ensures that the data warehouse reflects the underlying relationships in the data.
- It ensures that the data warehouse contains all necessary data from the beginning.
- It simplifies the ETL processes since data warehouses are developed on the basis of existing operational databases.

- It reduces the user involvement required to start the project.
- It facilitates a fast and straightforward development process, provided that well-structured and normalized operational systems exist.
- It allows automatic or semiautomatic techniques to be applied if the operational databases are represented using the entity-relationship model or normalized relational tables.

However, it is important to consider the following disadvantages before choosing this approach:

- Only business needs reflected in the underlying source data models can be captured.
- The system may not meet users' expectations since the company's goals and the users' requirements are not reflected at all.
- The method may not be applied when the logical schemas of the underlying operational systems are hard to understand or the data sources reside on legacy systems.
- Since it relies on existing data, this approach cannot be used to address long-term strategic goals.
- The inclusion of hierarchies may be difficult since they may be hidden in various structures, for example, in generalization relationships.
- It is difficult to motivate end users to work with large schemas developed for and by specialists.
- The derivation process can be difficult without knowledge of the users' needs since, for instance, the same data can be considered as a measure or as a dimension attribute.

10.7.3 Analysis/Source-Driven Approach

As this approach combines the analysis-driven and source-driven approaches, the recommendations regarding users and the development team given above should also be considered here. The analysis/source-driven approach has several important advantages:

- It generates a feasible solution, supported by the existing data sources, which better reflects the users' goals.
- It alerts about missing data in the operational databases that are required to support the decision-making process.
- If the source systems offer more information than what the business users initially demand, the analysis can be expanded to include new aspects not yet considered.

However, this approach has the following disadvantages:

- The development process is complicated since two schemas are required, one obtained from the definition of the analysis requirements and another derived from the underlying source systems.

- The integration process to determine whether the data sources cover the users' requirements may need complex techniques.

10.8 Summary

In this chapter, we have presented a general method for the design of data warehouses. Our proposal is close to the classic database design method and is composed of the following phases: requirements specification, conceptual design, logical design, and physical design. For the requirements specification and conceptual design phases, we have proposed three different approaches: (1) the analysis-driven approach, which focuses on analysis needs; (2) the source-driven approach, which develops the data warehouse schema on the basis of the structures of the underlying operational databases, typically represented using the entity-relationship or the relational model; and (3) the analysis/source-driven approach, which combines the first two approaches, matching the users' analysis needs with the availability of data. The next phases of the method presented correspond to those of classic database design. Therefore, a mapping of the conceptual model to a logical model is specified, followed by the definition of physical structures. The design of these structures should consider the specific features of the target DBMS with respect to the particularities of data warehouse applications.

10.9 Bibliographic Notes

Given the lack of consensus about a data warehouse design methodology, we comment in some detail the most well-known approaches to this topic. Golfarelli and Rizzi [65] presented a data warehouse design method composed of the following steps: analysis of the information system, requirements specification, conceptual design workload refinement and schema validation, logical design, and physical design. This method corresponds to the one used in traditional database design, extended with an additional phase of workload refinement in order to determine the expected data volume. Luján-Mora and Trujillo [119] presented a method for data warehouse design based on UML. This proposal deals with all data warehouse design phases from the analysis of the operational data sources to the final implementation, including the ETL processes. Jarke et al. [96] proposed the DWQ (Data Warehouse Quality) design method for data warehouses, consisting of six steps, focusing on data quality concepts.

Regarding requirements specification following the analysis-driven approach, Mazón et al. [130] propose to include business goals in data warehouse requirements analysis. These requirements are then transformed into a multidimensional model. Kimball et al. [103, 104] base their data warehouse development strategy on choosing the core business processes to model. Then, business users are interviewed to introduce the data warehouse team to the company's goals and to understand the users' expectations of the data warehouse. Even though this approach lacks formality, it has been applied in many data warehouse projects.

There are several methods for requirements analysis based on the source-driven approach: Böhnlein and Ulbrich-vom Ende [15] proposed a method for deriving logical data warehouse structures from the conceptual schemas of operational systems. Golfarelli et al. [68] presented a graphical conceptual model for data warehouses called the Dimensional Fact Model and proposed a semiautomatic process for building conceptual schemas from operational entity-relationship (ER) schemas. Cabibbo and Torlone [23] presented a design method that starts from an existing ER schema, deriving a multidimensional schema and providing an implementation of it in terms of relational tables and multidimensional arrays. Paim et al. [153] proposed a method for requirements specification consisting of the phases of requirements planning, specification, and validation. Paim and Castro [152] extended this method by including nonfunctional requirements, such as performance and accessibility. Vaisman [210] proposed a method for the specification of functional and nonfunctional requirements that integrates the concepts of requirements engineering and data quality. This method refers to the mechanisms for collecting, analyzing, and integrating requirements. Users are also involved in order to determine the expected quality of the source data. Then, data sources are selected using quantitative measures to ensure data quality. The outcome of this method is a set of documents and a ranking of the operational data sources that should satisfy the users' requirements according to various quality parameters.

As for the combination of approaches, Bonifati et al. [16] presented a method for the identification and design of data marts, which consists of three general parts: top-down analysis, bottom-up analysis, and integration. The top-down analysis emphasizes the users' requirements and requires precise identification and formulation of goals. On the basis of these goals, a set of ideal star schemas is created. On the other hand, the bottom-up analysis aims at identifying all the star schemas that can be implemented using the available source systems. This analysis requires the source systems to be represented using the ER model. The final integration phase is used to match the ideal star schemas with realistic ones based on the existing data.

10.10   Review Questions

10.1 What are the similarities and the differences between designing a database and designing a data warehouse?

10.2 Compare the top-down and the bottom-up approaches for data warehouse design. Which of the two approaches is more often used?

How does the design of a data warehouse differ from the design of a data mart?

10.3 Discuss the various phases in data warehouse design, emphasizing the objective of each phase.

10.4 Summarize the main characteristics of the analysis-driven, source-driven, and analysis/source-driven approaches for requirements specification. How do they differ from each other? What are their respective advantages and disadvantages? Identify in which situations one approach would be preferred over the others.

10.5 Using an application domain that you are familiar with, illustrate the various steps in the analysis-driven approach for requirements specification. Identify at least two different users, each one with a particular analysis goal.

10.6 Using the application domain of Question 10.5, illustrate the various steps in the source-driven approach for requirements specification. Define an excerpt of an ER schema from which some multidimensional elements can be derived.

10.7 Compare the steps for conceptual design in the analysis-driven, source-driven, and analysis/source-driven approaches.

10.8 Develop a conceptual multidimensional schema for the application domain of Question 10.5 using among the three approaches the one that you know best.

10.9 Illustrate the different aspects of the logical design phase by translating the conceptual schema developed in Question 10.8 into the relational model.

10.10 Describe several aspects that are important to consider in the physical design phase of data warehouses.

10.11   Exercises

10.1 Consider the train application described in Ex. 3.2. Using the analysis-driven approach, write the requirements specifications that would result in the MultiDim schema obtained in Ex. 4.3.

10.2 Consider the French horse race application described in Ex. 2.1. Using the source-driven approach, write the requirements specifications in order to produce the MultiDim schema obtained in Ex. 4.5.

10.3 Consider the Formula One application described in Ex. 2.2. Using the analysis/source-driven approach, write the requirements specifications in order to produce the MultiDim schema obtained in Ex. 4.7.

10.4 The ranking of universities has become an important factor in establishing the reputation of a university at the international level. Our university wants to determine what actions it should take to improve its position in the rankings. To simplify the discussion, we consider only the ranking by *The Times*. The evaluation criteria in this ranking refer to the two main areas of activities of universities, namely, research and education. However, a closer analysis shows that 60% of the criteria are related to research activities (peer review and citation/faculty scores) and 40% to the university's commitment to teaching. Therefore, we suppose that the decision-making users chose initially to analyze the situation related to research activities. To be able to conduct the analysis process, it was decided to implement a data warehouse system.

Universities are usually divided into faculties representing general fields of knowledge (e.g., medicine, engineering, sciences, and so on). These faculties comprise several departments dedicated to more specialized domains; for example, the faculty of engineering may include departments of civil engineering, mechanical engineering, and computer engineering, among others. University staff (e.g., professors, researchers, teaching assistants, administrative staff, and so on) are administratively attached to departments. In addition, autonomous structures called research centers support multidisciplinary research activities. University staff from various faculties or departments may belong to these research centers. Research projects are conducted by one or several research bodies, which may be either departments or research centers. The research department is the administrative body that coordinates all research activities at the university. It serves as a bridge between high-level executives (e.g., the Rector and the research council of the university) and researchers, as well as between researchers and external organizations, whether industrial or governmental. For example, the research department is responsible for the evaluation of research activities, for the development of strategic research plans, for promoting research activities and services, for managing intellectual property rights and patents, and for technology transfer and creation of spin-offs, among other things. In particular, the establishment of strategic research areas is based on the university's core strengths and ambitions, taking into account long-term potential and relevance. These areas are the focus of institutional initiatives and investments. On the basis of the institutional research strategy, faculties, departments, and research centers establish their own research priorities.

Suppose the university has *one general goal*: to improve its ranking considering the strategic research areas established at the university. This goal is decomposed into two subgoals related to improving the scores in two evaluation criteria of *The Times* ranking: (a) the peer review and (b) the citation per faculty criteria. The peer review criterion (40% of the ranking score) is based on interviewing selected academics from various countries to name the top institutions in the areas and subjects about which they feel able to make an informed judgment. The citation per faculty criterion (20% of the ranking score) refers to the numbers of citations of academic papers generated by staff members.

Determining the activities that could improve these evaluation criteria required the participation of users at various organizational levels. Interviews with users allowed us to conclude that, in the first step, information related to international conferences, projects, and publications was necessary to better understand the participation of the university's staff in international forums.

Participation in *international conferences* helps the university's staff to meet international colleagues working in the same or a similar area. In this way, not only can new strategic contacts be established (which may lead to international projects) but also the quality of the university's research can be improved.

Further, *international projects* promote the interaction of the university staff with peers from other universities working in the same area and thus could help to *improve the peer review score*. There are several sources of funding for research projects: the university, industry, and regional, national, and international institutions. Independently of the funding scheme, a project may be considered as being international when it involves participants from institutions in other countries.

Finally, knowledge about the international publications produced by the university's staff is essential for assessing the *citation per faculty criterion*. Publications can be of several types, namely, articles in conference proceedings or in journals, and books.

Based on the description above, we ask you to

(a) Produce a requirements specification for the design of the data warehouse using the *analysis-driven approach*. For this, you must

   - Identify users.
   - For each goal and subgoal, write a set of queries that these users would require. Refine and prioritize these queries.
   - Define facts, measures, and dimensions based on these queries.
   - Infer dimension hierarchies.
   - Build a table summarizing the information obtained.

(b) Produce a conceptual schema, using the *analysis-driven approach* and the *top-down design*. Discuss data availability conditions and how they impact on the design. Identify and specify the necessary mappings.

(c) Produce a conceptual schema, using the *analysis-driven approach*, and the *bottom-up design*. For this, you must build three data marts: one for the analysis of conferences, another one for the analysis of publications, and the third one for the analysis of research projects. Then, merge the three of them, and compare the schema produced with the one obtained through the top-down approach above.

(d) Produce a requirements specification for the design of the data warehouse using the *source-driven approach*, given the entity-

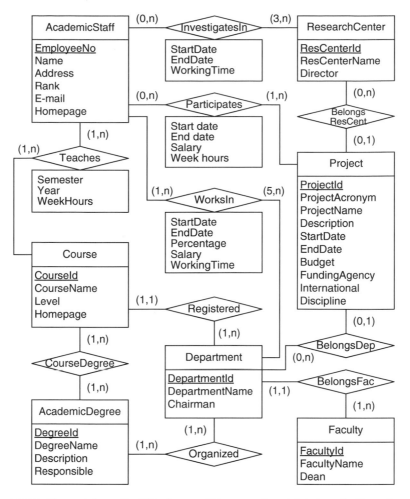

Fig. 10.13 Excerpt from the ER schema of the operational database in the university application

relationship schema of the operational database in Fig. 10.13. For this, you must

- Explain how the facts, measures, dimensions, and hierarchies are derived.
- Summarize in a table the information obtained.

(e) Produce a conceptual schema using the *source-driven approach*, deriving the schema from the one in Fig. 10.13. Validate the conceptual schema with the users, indicating if the schema includes less, more, or the exact information needed to solve our case.

Part III
Advanced Topics

Chapter 11
Spatial Data Warehouses

It is estimated that about 80% of the data stored in databases has a spatial or location component. Therefore, the location dimension has been widely used in data warehouse and OLAP systems. However, this dimension is usually represented in an alphanumeric, nonspatial manner (i.e., using solely the place name) since these systems are not able to manipulate spatial data. Nevertheless, it is well known that including spatial data in the analysis process can help to reveal patterns that are difficult to discover otherwise. Taking into account the growing demand to incorporate spatial data into the decision-making process, we present in this chapter how data warehouses can be extended with spatial data.

Section 11.1 briefly introduces some concepts related to spatial databases, providing background information for the rest of the chapter. In Sect. 11.2, we present a spatial extension of the MultiDim conceptual model and use this model to show how we can enhance the Northwind data warehouse with spatial data, leading to the GeoNorthwind data warehouse. In Sect. 11.3, we discuss implementation options for spatial data; in particular, we address the vector and raster models and how they are implemented in PostGIS, the spatial extension of the PostgreSQL database management system. Section 11.4 presents the relational representation of spatial data warehouses. Section 11.5 briefly introduces GeoMondrian, a spatial OLAP (SOLAP) server. In Sects. 11.6 and 11.7, we address analytical queries to the GeoNorthwind data warehouse expressed, respectively, in MDX and in SQL. Finally, Sect. 11.8 discusses spatial data warehouse design, complementing the methodological aspects covered in Chap. 10.

A. Vaisman and E. Zimányi, *Data Warehouse Systems*, Data-Centric
Systems and Applications, DOI 10.1007/978-3-642-54655-6_11,
© Springer-Verlag Berlin Heidelberg 2014

11.1   General Concepts of Spatial Databases

Spatial databases have been used for several decades for storing and manipulating spatial data. These data are used to describe the spatial properties of real-world phenomena. There are two complementary ways of modeling spatial data. In the **object-based** approach, space is decomposed into identifiable objects whose shapes are described. This allows us, for example, to represent a road as a line or a state as a surface. The **field-based** approach is used to represent phenomena that vary on space, associating with each point a value that characterizes a feature at that point. Typical examples are temperature, altitude, and soil cover. In order to represent these two alternative ways to model spatial features, we need appropriate data types. In this section, we describe spatial data types for both the object-based and the field-based approaches at a conceptual level.

11.1.1   Spatial Data Types

A **spatial object** corresponds to a real-world entity for which an application needs to store spatial characteristics. Spatial objects consist of a descriptive component and a spatial component. The **descriptive component** is represented using traditional data types, such as integer, string, and date; it contains general characteristics of the spatial object. For example, a state object may be described by its name, population, and capital. The **spatial component** defines the extent of the object in the space of interest.

Several spatial data types can be used to represent the spatial extent of real-world objects. At the conceptual level, we use the spatial data types defined by the MADS model, cited in the bibliographic notes at the end of the chapter. These data types provide support for two-dimensional features. They are organized in a hierarchy, shown in Fig. 11.1.

Point represents zero-dimensional geometries denoting a single location in space. A point can be used to represent, for instance, a village in a country.

Line represents one-dimensional geometries denoting a set of connected points defined by a continuous curve in the plane. A line can be used to represent, for instance, a road in a road network. A line is closed if it has no identifiable extremities (i.e., its start point is equal to its end point).

OrientedLine represents lines whose extremities have the semantics of a start point and an end point (the line has a given direction from the start point to the end point). It is a specialization of Line and can be used to represent, for instance, a river in a hydrographic network.

Surface represents two-dimensional geometries denoting a set of connected points that lie inside a boundary formed by one or more disjoint closed lines. If the boundary consists of more than one closed line, one of the closed lines

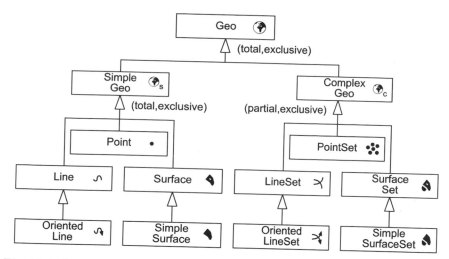

Fig. 11.1 Spatial data types

contains all the others, and the latter represent holes in the surface defined by the former line. In simpler words, a surface may have holes but no islands (no exterior islands and no islands within a hole).

SimpleSurface represents surfaces without holes. For example, the extent of a lake may be represented by a surface or a simple surface, depending on whether the lake has islands or not.

SimpleGeo is a generic spatial data type that generalizes the types Point, Line, and Surface. SimpleGeo is an abstract type, that is, it is never instantiated as such: Upon creation of a SimpleGeo value, it is necessary to specify which of its subtypes characterizes the new element. A SimpleGeo value can be used, for instance, to generically represent cities, whereas a small city may be represented by a point and a bigger city by a simple surface.

Several spatial data types are used to describe spatially homogeneous sets. PointSet represents sets of points, for instance, tourist points of interest. LineSet represents sets of lines, for example, a road network. OrientedLineSet (a specialization of LineSet) represents a set of oriented lines, for example, a river and its tributaries. SurfaceSet and SimpleSurfaceSet represent sets of surfaces with or without holes, respectively, for example, administrative regions.

ComplexGeo represents any heterogeneous set of geometries that may include sets of points, sets of lines, and sets of surfaces. ComplexGeo may be used to represent a water system consisting of rivers (oriented lines), lakes (surfaces), and reservoirs (points). ComplexGeo has PointSet, LineSet, OrientedLineSet, SurfaceSet, and SimpleSurfaceSet as subtypes.

Finally, Geo is the most generic spatial data type, generalizing the types SimpleGeo and ComplexGeo; its semantics is "this element has a spatial extent" without any commitment to a specific spatial data type. Like SimpleGeo, Geo is an abstract type. It can be used, for instance, to represent the administrative regions of a country, where regions may be either a Surface or a SurfaceSet.

It is worth noting that empty geometries are allowed, that is, geometries representing an empty set of points. This is needed in particular to express the fact that the intersection of two disjoint geometries is also a geometry, although it may be an empty one.

Spatial data types have a set of operations, which can be grouped in classes. Table 11.1 shows the most common operations.

Table 11.1 Classes of operations on spatial types

Class	Operations
Topological operations	Intersects, Disjoint, Equals, Overlaps, Contains, Within, Touches, Covers, CoveredBy, Crosses
Predicates	IsEmpty, OnBorder, InInterior
Unary operations	Boundary, Buffer, Centroid, ConvexHull
Binary operations	Intersection, Union, Difference, SymDifference
Numeric	NoComponents, Length, Area, Perimeter Distance, Direction

Topological operations are based on the well-known **topological relation-ships**, which specify how two spatial values relate to each other. They are extensively used in spatial applications since they can be used to test, for instance, whether two states have a common border, a highway crosses a state, or a city is located in a state.

The definitions of the topological relationships are based on the definitions of the boundary, the interior, and the exterior of spatial values. Intuitively, the **exterior** of a spatial value is composed of all the points of the underlying space that do not belong to the spatial value. The **interior** of a spatial value is composed of all its points that do not belong to the boundary. The **boundary** is defined for the different spatial data types as follows. A point has an empty boundary, and its interior is equal to the point. The boundary of a line is given by its extreme points, provided that they can be distinguished (e.g., a closed line has no boundary). The boundary of a surface is given by the enclosing closed line and the closed lines defining the holes.

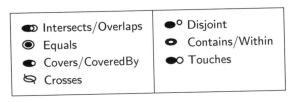

Fig. 11.2 Icons for the various topological relationships

We describe next the topological relationships; the associated icons are given in Fig. 11.2 and examples are shown in Fig. 11.3.

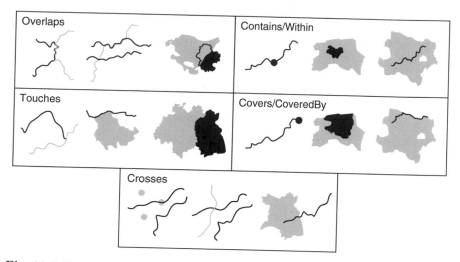

Fig. 11.3 Examples of the various topological relationships. The two objects in the relationship are drawn in *black* and in *gray*, respectively

Intersects/Disjoint: Intersects and Disjoint are inverse relationships: When one applies, the other does not. Two geometries are disjoint if the interior and the boundary of one object intersects only the exterior of the other object.

Equals: A geometry equals another one if they share exactly the same set of points.

Overlaps: Two geometries overlap if the interior of each one intersects both the interior and the exterior of the other one.

Contains/Within: Contains and Within are symmetric relationships: *a* Contains *b* if and only if *b* Within *a*. A geometry contains another one if the inner object is located in the interior of the other object and the boundaries of the two objects do not intersect.

Touches: Two geometries meet if they intersect but their interiors do not.

Covers/CoveredBy: Covers and CoveredBy are symmetric relationships: *a* Covers *b* if and only if *b* CoveredBy *a*. A geometry covers another one if it includes all points of the other, inner geometry. This means that the first geometry contains the inner one, as defined previously, but without the restriction that the boundaries of the geometries do not intersect.

Crosses: One geometry crosses another if they intersect and the dimension of this intersection is less than the greatest dimension of the geometries.

Predicates return a Boolean value. IsEmpty determines whether a geometry is empty. OnBorder and InInterior determine, respectively, whether a point belongs to the boundary or the interior of another geometry.

Unary operations take one spatial value and return a new one. Boundary returns the exterior ring of a surface. Buffer returns a geometry containing all points whose distance to the geometry passed as parameter is less than or equal to a given distance. Centroid returns the center point of a geometry. ConvexHull returns the minimum convex geometry that encloses a geometry.

Binary operations take two (or more) spatial values and return a new spatial value. Intersection, Union, Difference, and SymDifference operate as in usual set theory and return a geometry obtained by applying the corresponding operation to the geometries given as argument.

Numeric operations take one or two geometries and return a numeric value. NoComponents returns the number of disjoint maximal connected subsets of a geometry, for instance, the number of points for a point set, the number of connected components for a line set, or the number of faces for a surface. Length returns the length of a line. Area returns the area of a surface. Perimeter returns the length of the boundary of a surface. Distance determines the minimum distance among all pairs of points of two geometries. Finally, Direction returns the angle of the line between two points, measured in degrees, that is, a value between 0 and 360.

11.1.2   Continuous Fields

Continuous fields are phenomena that change continuously in space and/or time. Examples include altitude and temperature, where the former varies only in space and the latter varies in both space and time. In this chapter, we cover only nontemporal fields, leaving temporal fields for the next chapter. At a *conceptual level*, a continuous field can be represented as a function that assigns to each point in space a value of a domain, for example, an integer for altitude. Continuous fields are represented with field types, which capture the variation in space of base types (such as integers and reals). They are obtained by applying a constructor field($\cdot$). Hence, a value of type field(real) (e.g., representing altitude) is a continuous function f : point $\to$ real.

Notice that continuous fields are partial functions, that is, they could be undefined at some points in space. Consider, for example, a field AltitudeBE defining the altitude in Belgium. Since there are several enclaves and exclaves between Belgium, the Netherlands, and Germany, the altitude of an enclave of Germany within Belgium will be undefined.

Field types have associated operations, which can be grouped into several classes, as shown in Table 11.2. We discuss next some of these operations.

First, there are operations that perform the *projection into the domain and range*. Operations DefSpace and RangeValues return, respectively, the projection of a field type into its domain and range. For instance, DefSpace(AltitudeBE) and RangeValues(AltitudeBE) will result, respectively, in a region covering Belgium and the range of values [−4 m, 694 m].

Table 11.2 Classes of operations on field types

Class	Operations
Projection to domain/range	DefSpace, RangeValues
Interaction with domain/range	IsDefinedAt, HasValue, AtGeometry, At, AtMin, AtMax, Concave, Convex, Flex
Rate of change	PartialDer_x, PartialDer_y
Field aggregation	Integral, Area, Surface, FAvg, FVariance, FStDev, FMin, FMax
Lifting	All new operations inferred

Another set of operations allow the *interaction with domain and range*. The IsDefinedAt predicate checks whether the spatial function is defined at a given point or is somewhere defined at a subset of the space defined by a spatial value. Analogously, predicate HasValue checks whether the function takes somewhere (one of) the value(s) from the range given as the second argument. Operation AtGeometry restricts the function to a given subset of the space defined by a spatial value. For example, these operations can be used to restrict the AltitudeBE field to a point corresponding to the Grand Place in Brussels, to the highway E411, or to the province of Namur.

Operation At restricts the function to a point or to a point set (a range) in the range of the function. For example, this allows us to restrict the AltitudeBE field to the values between 100 and 200 m. Predicates AtMin and AtMax reduce the function to the points in space where its value is minimal or maximal, respectively. For the AltitudeBE field, these predicates will yield, respectively, a field defined at multiple points at the West of Veurne (the lowest points in Belgium), or a field defined only at the Signal de Botrange in Hautes Fagnes (the highest point in Belgium). Operations Concave and Convex restrict the function to the points where it is concave or convex, respectively. Finally, operation Flex restricts the function to the points where convexity changes.

Rate of change operations compute how a continuous field changes across space. Functions PartialDer_x and PartialDer_y give, respectively, the partial derivative of the function defining the field with respect to one of the axes x and y. For example, PartialDer_x is defined by

$$\frac{\partial f}{\partial x}(x,y) = \lim_{\delta \to 0} \frac{f(x+\delta,y) - f(x,y)}{\delta}.$$

There are three basic *field aggregation operations* that take as argument a field over numeric values (integer or real) defined over a spatial extent S and return a real value. Integral returns the volume under the surface defined by the function, Area returns the area of the spatial extent on which the function is defined, and Surface returns the area of the (curved) surface defined by the function. These operations are defined as follows:

- Integral: $\iint_S f(x, y) \, dx \, dy$.
- Area: $\iint_S dx \, dy$.
- Surface: $\iint_S \sqrt{1 + \left(\frac{\partial f}{\partial x}\right)^2 + \left(\frac{\partial f}{\partial y}\right)^2} \, dx \, dy$.

From these operations, other derived operations can be defined. These are prefixed with an 'F_' (field) in order to distinguish them from the usual aggregation operations generalized to fields, which we discuss below.

- FAvg: Integral/Area.
- FVariance: $\iint_S \frac{(f(x,y)-\text{FAvg})^2}{\text{Area}} \, dx \, dy$.
- FStDev: $\sqrt{\text{FVariance}}$.

Finally, FMin and FMax return, respectively, the minimum and maximum value taken by the function. These are obtained by Min(RangeValues(·)) and Max(RangeValues(·)), where Min and Max are the classic operations over numeric values.

All operations on basic types are generalized for field types. This is called **lifting**. An operation op for basic types is lifted to allow any of the arguments to be replaced by a field type and returns a field type. As an example, the less than ($<$) operation has lifted versions where one or both of its arguments can be field types and the result is a Boolean field type. Intuitively, the semantics of such lifted operations is that the result is computed at each point in space using the nonlifted operation. For example, applying the lifted '$<$' operation to two fields that describe the temperature at 2 days will result in a Boolean field that states at each point whether the temperature of the first field is smaller than the one in the second. When two fields are defined on different spatial extents, the result of a lifted operation is defined in the *intersection* of both extents and undefined elsewhere.

Aggregation operations are also lifted. For instance, a lifted Avg operation combines several fields, yielding a new field where the average is computed at each point in space. Lifted aggregation operations are used in particular for granularity transformations. For example, a lifted average could be used to transform a temperature field of granularity day to granularity month.

11.2   Conceptual Modeling of Spatial Data Warehouses

In this section, we explain the spatial extension of the MultiDim model. For this, we use as example the GeoNorthwind data warehouse, which is the Northwind data warehouse extended with spatial types. As shown in the schema in Fig. 11.4, pictograms are used to represent spatial information.

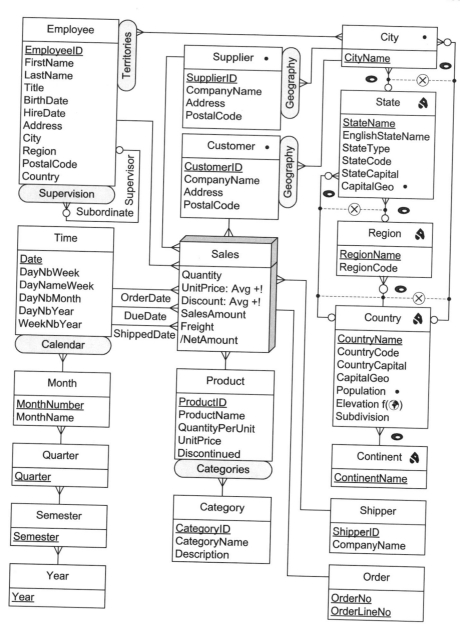

Fig. 11.4 Conceptual schema of the GeoNorthwind data warehouse

Since the spatially extended MultiDim model can contain both spatial and nonspatial elements, the definitions of schemas, levels, hierarchies, cardinalities, and facts with measures remain the same as those presented in Sect. 4.1.

A **spatial level** is a level for which the application needs to store spatial characteristics. This is captured by its **geometry**, which is represented using one of the spatial data types described in Sect. 11.1.1. In Fig. 11.4, we have seven spatial levels: Supplier, Customer, City, State, Region, Country, and Continent. On the other hand, Product and Time are nonspatial levels.

A **spatial attribute** is an attribute whose domain is a spatial data type. For example, CapitalGeo is a spatial attribute of type point, while Elevation is a spatial attribute of type field of reals. Attributes representing continuous fields are identified by the 'f(⊙)' pictogram.

A spatial level is represented using the icon of its associated spatial type to the right of the level name. A level may be spatial independent of the fact that it has spatial attributes (see Fig. 11.5). For example, depending on application requirements, a level such as State may be spatial (Fig. 11.5a,b) or not (Fig. 11.5c) and may have spatial attributes such as CapitalGeo (Fig. 11.5b,c).

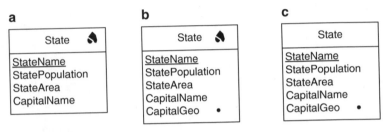

Fig. 11.5 Examples of levels with spatial characteristics. (**a**) Spatial level. (**b**) Spatial level with a spatial attribute. (**c**) Nonspatial level with a spatial attribute

A **spatial hierarchy** is a hierarchy that includes at least one spatial level. For example, in Fig. 11.4, we have two spatial hierarchies in the Supplier and Customer dimensions, which share the levels from City to Continent. Spatial hierarchies can combine nonspatial and spatial levels. Similarly, a **spatial dimension** is a dimension that includes at least one spatial hierarchy.

Two related spatial levels in a spatial hierarchy may involve a **topological constraint**, expressed using the various topological relationships given in Sect. 11.1.1. To represent them, we use the pictograms shown in Fig. 11.2. For example, in Fig. 11.4, the geometry of each state is covered by the geometry of its corresponding region or country, depending on which level a state rolls up to. Note that in Fig. 11.4, there is no topological constraint between the Supplier and City levels since the location of the supplier is obtained from its address through geocoding and the location of the city corresponds to the center of the city.

A **spatial fact** is a fact that relates several levels, two or more of which are spatial. A spatial fact may also have a **topological constraint** that must be satisfied by the related spatial levels: An icon in the fact indicates the topological relationship used for specifying the constraint. In the

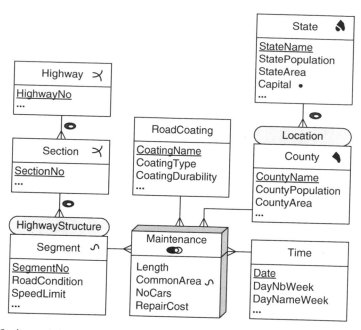

Fig. 11.6 A spatial data warehouse for analyzing the maintenance of highways

GeoNorthwind data warehouse, the Sales fact does not impose any constraint between its spatial dimensions Supplier and Customer. As an example of a spatial fact with an associated topological constraint, consider the schema of Fig. 11.6, which can be used for the analysis of highway maintenance costs. The spatial fact Maintenance relates two spatial levels: County and Segment. This fact includes an Overlaps topological constraint, indicating that a segment and a county related to a fact member must overlap.

Facts, whether spatial or not, may contain measures that represent data that are meaningful for leaf members that are aggregated when a hierarchy is traversed. Measures can be numeric or **spatial**, where the latter are represented by a geometry. Note that numeric measures can be calculated using spatial operations such as distance and area. For example, Fig. 11.6 contains two measures. Length is a numerical measure obtained using spatial operations, representing the length of the part of a highway segment that belongs to a county, and CommonArea represents the geometry of the common part.

Measures require the specification of the function used for aggregation along the hierarchies. By default, we assume sum for numerical measures and spatial union for spatial measures. For example, in Fig. 11.6, when users roll up from the County to the State level, for each state the measures Length, NoCars, and RepairCost of the corresponding counties will be summed, while the CommonArea measure will be a LineSet resulting from the spatial union of the lines representing highway segments for the corresponding counties.

In the following sections, we refer in more detail to the various spatial elements of the MultiDim model.

11.2.1   Spatial Hierarchies

All the types of hierarchies we have discussed in Sect. 4.2 apply also to spatial hierarchies. We give next some examples of them.

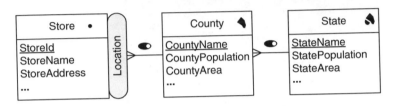

Fig. 11.7 A balanced spatial hierarchy

Figure 11.7 shows an example of a **balanced spatial hierarchy**. Note that different spatial data types are associated with the levels of the hierarchy: point for **Store**, surface for **County**, and surface set for **State**. Further, a Covers topological constraint holds in the parent-child relationships forming the hierarchy.

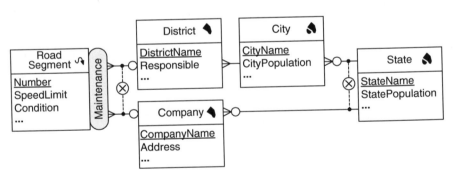

Fig. 11.8 A generalized spatial hierarchy

The example in Fig. 11.8 shows a **generalized spatial hierarchy** containing multiple exclusive paths that share some levels. In the example, a road segment is related either to a district or to a company in charge of its maintenance. The special case of **ragged hierarchies** is shown in the Geography hierarchy in the GeoNorthwind data warehouse (Fig. 11.4). In the example, a city is related either to a state or to a country. Similarly, a state is related either to a region or to a country.

Figure 11.9 shows an **alternative spatial hierarchy** composed of several nonexclusive spatial hierarchies sharing some levels. This example represents part of the set of hierarchies used by the US Census Bureau. There are two hierarchies, one representing the usual subdivision of the territory and the other is the subdivision used for American Indian, Alaska Native, and Native Hawaiian Areas (AIANNHAs).

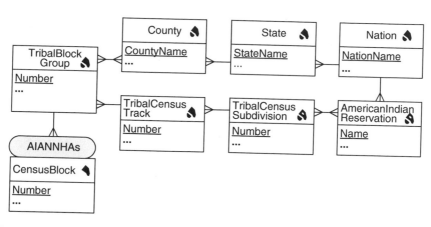

Fig. 11.9 An alternative spatial hierarchy

Figure 11.10 shows a parallel spatial hierarchy with two independent hierarchies, Location and OrganizStructure, accounting for different analysis criteria.

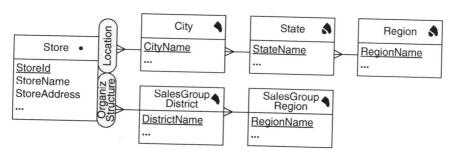

Fig. 11.10 Parallel independent spatial hierarchies

Analogous to the nonspatial case, a spatial hierarchy is nonstrict if it has at least one many-to-many relationship. Figure 11.11 shows an example. The many-to-many cardinality represents the fact that a lake may belong to more than one city. Most nonstrict hierarchies arise when a partial containment relationship exists, for example, when only part of a lake belongs to a city or when only part of a highway belongs to a state.

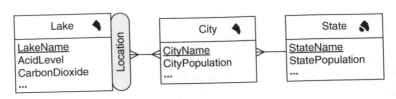

Fig. 11.11 A nonstrict spatial hierarchy

11.2.2 Spatiality and Measures

Spatial measures are measures represented by a geometry. For example, Fig. 11.6 shows a spatial measure CommonArea, which represents the geometry (a line) of the part of a highway segment belonging to a county. The MultiDim model allows spatial measures independently of the fact that there are spatial dimensions.

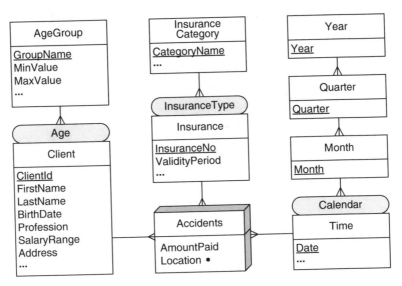

Fig. 11.12 A fact with a spatial measure

Various kinds of aggregation functions for spatial data have been defined. For example, *spatial distributive* functions include convex hull, spatial union, and spatial intersection. Examples of *spatial algebraic* functions are the center of n points and the center of gravity, and examples of *spatial holistic* functions are the equipartition and the nearest-neighbor index. In the MultiDim model, the spatial union is used by default for aggregating spatial measures, as we already explained.

Spatial measures allow richer analysis than nonspatial measures do. For example, consider the schema in Fig. 11.12, which is used for analyzing the locations of road accidents taking into account the various insurance categories (full coverage, partial coverage, and so on) and the client data. This schema includes a spatial measure representing the locations of accidents. We can use, for example, the default aggregate function (the spatial union) to roll up to the InsuranceCategory level in order to display the accident locations corresponding to each category aggregated and represented as a set of points. Other aggregation functions can also be used for this, such as the center of n points.

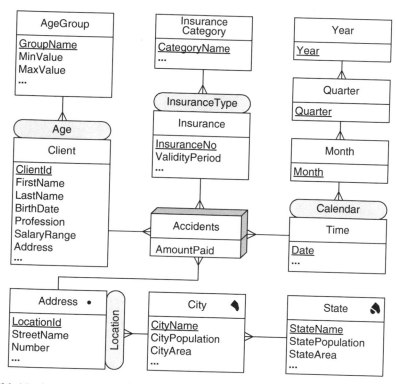

Fig. 11.13 A variant of the schema in Fig. 11.12

An alternative schema for the analysis of road accidents is shown in Fig. 11.13. In this schema, there is no spatial measure; the focus of analysis has been changed to the amount of insurance payments according to the various geographic locations. This is reflected by the spatial hierarchy Address → City → State.

Although the schemas in Figs. 11.12 and 11.13 are similar, different analyses can be performed when a location is represented as a spatial measure or as a spatial hierarchy. For example, in Fig. 11.12, the locations of accidents can be aggregated (by using spatial union) when a roll-up operation over the Time or Insurance hierarchies is executed. However, this aggregation cannot be done with the schema in Fig. 11.13. The dimensions are independent, and traversing a hierarchy along one of them does not aggregate data in another hierarchy. Further, an analysis of the amounts of insurance payments made in different geographic zones is not supported by the alternative using spatial measures since in this case only the exact locations of the accidents are known. The same occurs when we want to analyze the amount of insurance payments in some specific geographic area.

11.3   Implementation Considerations for Spatial Data

The object-based and field-based models that we presented in Sect. 11.1 are used to represent spatial data at an abstract level. Two common implementations of these abstract models are, respectively, the vector model and the raster model. Both models are implemented in PostGIS, the spatial extension to the PostgreSQL database management system, which we introduce next.

PostgreSQL is a widely used open-source, object-relational database management system. It allows us to store complex types of objects and to define new custom data types, functions, and operators to manipulate them. PostgreSQL supports various languages for writing database functions, in particular SQL, PL/PGSQL, and C. Among other advanced features, PostgreSQL supports arrays and table inheritance. As a consequence, it is easily extensible with new types and operators, which is the main reason why it was chosen as the platform for PostGIS.

PostGIS extends PostgreSQL with spatial data types, spatial operators, and spatial functions. In addition, indexing capabilities are provided by PostgreSQL through the GIST index for spatial objects.

In this section, we study how the spatial data types supporting the vector and raster models are implemented in PostGIS. First, we need to introduce some additional concepts.

11.3.1   Spatial Reference Systems

The Earth is a complex surface whose shape and dimension cannot be described with mathematical formulas. There are two main reference surfaces to approximate the shape of the Earth: the geoid and the ellipsoid.

The **geoid** is a reference model for the surface of the Earth that coincides with the mean sea level and its imaginary extension through the continents. It is used in geodesy to measure precise surface elevations. However, the geoid is not very practical to produce maps. The **ellipsoid** is a mathematically defined surface that approximates the geoid. The most common reference ellipsoid used is the one defined by the World Geodetic System in 1984 and last revised in 2004, usually referred to as WGS 84. This ellipsoid is used by the Global Positioning System (GPS). Nevertheless, different regions of the world use different reference ellipsoids, minimizing the differences between the geoid and the ellipsoid.

The ellipsoid is used to measure the location of points of interest using latitude and longitude. These are measures of the angles (in degrees) from the center of the Earth to a point on the Earth's surface. **Latitude** measures angles in the North–South direction, while **longitude** measures angles in the East–West direction. While an ellipsoid approximates the shape of the Earth, a **datum** defines where on the Earth to anchor the ellipsoid.

To produce a map, the curved reference surface of the Earth, approximated by an ellipsoid, must be transformed into the flat plane of the map by means of a **map projection**. Thus, a point on the reference surface of the Earth with geographic coordinates expressed by latitude and longitude is transformed into Cartesian (or map) coordinates (x, y) representing positions on the map plane. However, as a map projection necessarily causes deformations, different projections are used for different purposes, depending on which information is preserved, namely, shapes and angles, area, distance, or directions. These four features are conflicting (e.g., it is not possible to preserve both shapes and angles as well as area), and thus, the importance placed on each of these features dictates the choice of a particular projection.

A **spatial reference system** (SRS) assigns coordinates in a mathematical space to a location in real-world space. An SRS defines at least the units of measure of the underlying coordinate system (such as degrees or meters), the maximum and minimum coordinates (also referred to as the bounds), the default linear unit of measure, whether data are planar or spheroid, and projection information for transforming the data to other SRSs. SRSs are in general good for only a specific region of the globe. If two geometries are in the same SRS, they can be overlaid without distortion. If this is not the case, they must be transformed. As there are thousands of SRSs, each one is identified by a spatial reference system identifier (SRID).

11.3.2 Vector Model

The spatial data types described in Sect. 11.1.1 were defined at the conceptual level, describing spatial features from an abstract perspective, without taking into consideration how these will be implemented into actual systems. The **vector model** provides a collection of data types for representing spatial objects into the computer. Thus, for example, while at an abstract level a linear object is defined as an infinite collection of points, at the implementation level such a line must be approximated using points, lines, and curves as primitives. A point is represented by coordinates such as (x, y) or (x, y, z) depending on the number of dimensions of the underlying space.

More complex linear and surface objects use structures (lists, sets, or arrays) based on the point representation.

The standard ISO/IEC 13249 SQL/MM is an extension of SQL:2003 for managing multimedia and application-specific packages. Part 3 of the standard defines how to store, retrieve, and manipulate spatial data in a relational database system. It defines how zero-, one-, or two-dimensional spatial data values are represented on a two-dimensional ($\mathbb{R}^2$), three-dimensional ($\mathbb{R}^3$), or four-dimensional ($\mathbb{R}^4$) coordinate space. We describe next the spatial data types defined by SQL/MM, which are used and extended in PostGIS.

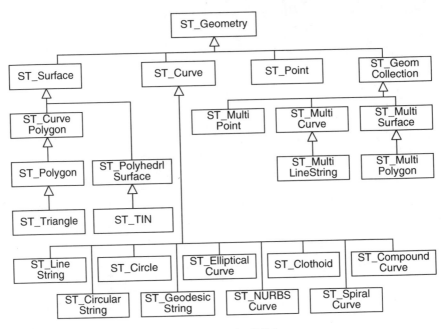

Fig. 11.14 Hierarchy of spatial types in SQL/MM

Figure 11.14 shows the type hierarchy defined in the SQL/MM standard for geometric features. ST_Geometry is the root of the hierarchy, and it is an abstract type. ST_Point represents 0-dimensional geometries. ST_Curve is an abstract type representing 1-dimensional geometries. Several subtypes of ST_Curve are defined. ST_LineString represents line segments defined by a sequence of points using linear interpolation. ST_CircularString represents arc segments defined by a sequence of points using circular interpolation. ST_CompoundCurve represents a combination of linear and circular strings. ST_Circle represents circles defined by three noncollinear points. ST_GeodesicString represents arcs defined by a sequence of points interpolated by geodesic curve segments. ST_EllipticalCurve represents a single curve segment having elliptical interpolation. ST_NURBSCurve represents a nonuniform rational BSpline defined by a polynomial. ST_Clothoid represents a single curve segment having clothoid interpolation. ST_SpiralCurve represents a single curve segment having spiral interpolation.

ST_Surface is an abstract type representing 2-dimensional geometries composed by simple surfaces consisting of a single patch whose boundary is specified by one exterior ring and zero or more interior rings if the surface has holes. In the type ST_CurvePolygon, the boundaries are any curve, while in the type ST_Polygon, the boundaries must be linear strings. ST_Triangle, represent polygons composed of three linear strings. ST_PolyhedrlSurface represents surfaces formed by stitching together simple surfaces along their boundaries, while ST_TIN represents polyhedral surfaces composed only of triangles.

ST_GeomCollection represents collections of zero or more ST_Geometry values. ST_MultiPoint represents a collection of single points, not necessarily distinct (i.e., a bag of points). Similarly, ST_MultiCurve represents a bag of ST_Curve and ST_MultiLineString a bag of ST_LineString. Notice that there are no types ST_MultiCircularString and ST_MultiCompoundCurve. The types ST_MultiSurface and ST_MultiPolygon represent, respectively, sets of curve polygons and sets of polygons with linear boundaries. In addition, ST_MultiSurface constrains its values to contain only disjoint surfaces.

The standard also defines a rich set of spatial methods and functions. These can be grouped in several categories.

There are methods that retrieve properties or measures from a geometry. Examples are ST_Boundary for retrieving the boundary of a geometry and ST_Length for the length of a line string of a multiline string.

There are also methods that convert between geometries and external data formats. Three external data formats are supported: well-known text representation (WKT), well-known binary representation (WKB), and Geography Markup Language (GML). For GML, for example, there are functions like ST_LineFromGML or ST_MPointFromGML, which return, respectively, a line or a multipoint value from its GML representation.

There are methods that compare two geometries with respect to their spatial relation. These are ST_Equals, ST_Disjoint, ST_Within, ST_Touches, ST_Crosses, ST_Intersects, ST_Overlaps, and ST_Contains. All these methods return an integer value that can be 1 (true) or 0 (false).

There are also methods that generate new geometries from other ones. The newly generated geometry can be the result of a set operation on two geometries (e.g., ST_Difference, ST_Intersection, ST_Union) or can be calculated by some algorithm applied to a single geometry (e.g., ST_Buffer).

Finally, the SQL/MM standard defines an information schema that provides a mechanism to determine the available spatial features. It consists of the following four views:

1. ST_GEOMETRY_COLUMNS lists all columns in all tables that are of type ST_GEOMETRY or one of its subtypes as well as the optional SRS associated with the column.

2. ST_SPATIAL_REFERENCE_SYSTEMS describes the available SRSs.
3. ST_UNITS_OF_MEASURE describes the different units of measures that can be used, for example, to calculate distances, lengths, or areas.
4. ST_SIZINGS contains the spatial-specific metavariables and their values. An example is the maximum length that can be used for a WKT of a geometry.

To conclude this section, it is important to remark that PostGIS provides a GEOGRAPHY data type, which uses geodetic coordinates instead of Cartesian coordinates. Coordinate points in the GEOGRAPHY type are always represented in the WGS 84 SRS (SRID 4326). Thus, this type can be used to load data using latitude and longitude coordinates. However, as many tools do not yet support the GEOGRAPHY data type, in the remainder of this book we will only cover the GEOMETRY data type.

11.3.3 Raster Model

The data model that we presented in Sect. 11.1.2 is used to represent continuous fields at an abstract level. At a logical level, continuous fields must be represented in a discrete way. For this, we need first to partition the spatial domain into a finite number of elements. This is called a **tessellation**. Then, we must assign a value of the field to a representative point in each partition element. Furthermore, since values of the field are known only at a finite number of points (called sampled points), the values at other points must be inferred using an interpolation function. In practice, different tessellations and different interpolation functions may be used. The most popular representation is the raster tessellation, which supports the **raster model**. This model is structured as an array of cells, where each cell represents the value of an attribute for a real-world location. Usually, cells represent square areas of the underlying space, but other shapes can also be used.

PostGIS introduces a new data type called RASTER that stores raster data in a binary format in PostgreSQL. PostGIS provides functions to manipulate raster data and to combine it with vector data. Rasters are composed of bands, also called channels. Although rasters can have many bands, they are normally limited to four, each one storing integers. For example, a picture such as a JPEG, PNG, or TIFF is generally composed of one to four bands, expressed as the typical red green blue alpha (RGBA) channels. A pixel in raster data is generally modeled as a rectangle with a value for each of its bands. Each rectangle in a raster has a width and a height, both representing meters/feet/degrees of the geographic space in the SRS.

When raster data are stored in PostGIS, the pixels are allocated to a data column of type RASTER, similar to how geometries are stored in a column of type GEOMETRY or GEOGRAPHY. A full raster file can be stored in a single record in a single column or can be split into tiles, where each tile is stored as a separate record. Finally, efficient access to raster data requires these data to be indexed. The RASTER type uses GIST indexes like the GEOMETRY and GEOGRAPHY data types do. GIST indexes use the notion of minimal bounding boxes to define indexed regions in space.

We describe next some of the functions provided by PostGIS to manipulate raster data. For a complete description of all the functions, we refer to the reference manual.

Several functions allow to query the properties of a raster. For example, the function ST_BandNoDataValue has as parameters a raster and a band number and returns the value used to represent cells whose actual values are unknown, referred to as no data. Similarly, the function ST_SetBandNoDataValue sets the value that represents no data in a band. Another function is ST_Value, which returns the value in a location of the raster for a given band. Similarly, the ST_SetValue function returns a new raster, with the value at the specified location set to the argument value.

Other functions convert between rasters and external data formats. For example, the function ST_AsJPEG returns selected bands of the raster as a single JPEG image. Analogously, the functions ST_AsBinary and ST_AsPNG return the binary and PNG representations of the raster, respectively.

Another group of functions converts between rasters and vector formats. The function ST_AsRaster converts a GEOMETRY to a RASTER. To convert a raster to a polygon, the function ST_Polygon is used, which unions all the pixels in a raster that are not equal to the no data value of the band. The function ST_Envelope returns the minimum bounding box of the extent of the raster, represented as a polygon.

There are functions that compare two rasters or a raster and a geometry with respect to their spatial relation. For example, the Boolean function ST_Intersects, which takes two raster bands or a raster band and a geometry as input, returns true if the two raster bands intersect or if the raster intersects the geometry, respectively.

Another group of functions generates new rasters or geometries from other ones. For example, ST_Intersection takes two rasters as arguments and returns another raster. Also, the ST_Union function returns the union of a set of raster tiles into a single raster composed of one band. The extent of the resulting raster is the extent of the whole set.

Finally, there are several aggregation functions for rasters. These include ST_Min4ma, ST_Max4ma, ST_Sum4ma, ST_StdDev4ma, and ST_Mean4ma, which calculate, respectively, the minimum, maximum, sum, mean, or standard deviation of pixel values in a neighborhood.

We finish this section by comparing the functions provided by Post-GIS against the operations defined for the field data type introduced in Sect. 11.1.2.

With respect to the operations that perform the projection over domain and range, we can see that DefSpace and ST_Polygon are equivalent operations and that RangeValues could be easily constructed using ST_Value. With respect to the operations that allow the interaction between domain and range, IsDefinedAt can be constructed using ST_Value and ST_BandNoDataValue. Analogously, HasValue can be constructed with ST_Value, and AtGeometry can be constructed with ST_Value and ST_Intersection, for example. The other operations are not implemented at all or cannot be easily implemented using the currently provided operations. This is the case, for instance, of At, AtMin, and AtMax, and the other operations. The same occurs with the rate of change operations like the partial derivatives. Although the built-in functions like ST_Min4ma compute aggregations in a neighborhood, they do not implement the functionality required by the aggregation operations of Table 11.2 such as the FMin and FMax operations.

11.4   Relational Representation of Spatial Data Warehouses

In this section, we explain how a conceptual multidimensional schema is translated into a relational schema in the presence of spatial data. As an example, Fig. 11.15 shows the relational representation of the GeoNorthwind conceptual schema given in Fig. 11.4. In the figure, the spatial attributes are written in boldface for better readability. We explain next this translation based on the rules given in Sect. 5.3.

11.4.1   Spatial Levels and Attributes

A level is mapped to the relational model using Rule 1 given in Sect. 5.3. However, since in the conceptual model the spatial support is represented implicitly (i.e., using pictograms), spatial levels require an additional attribute for storing the geometry of their members. In addition, both nonspatial and spatial levels may contain spatial attributes. Thus, we need to generalize this rule to account for spatial levels and attributes as follows:

Rule 1S: A level L, provided it is not related to a fact with a one-to-one relationship, is mapped to a table T_L that contains all attributes of the level. A surrogate key may be added to the table, otherwise the identifier of the level will be the key of the table. For each spatial attribute, an appropriate spatial data type must be chosen to store its geometry. Further, if the level is spatial, an additional attribute of a spatial data type is added to represent the geometry of its members. Note that additional attributes will be added to this table when mapping relationships using Rule 3S below.

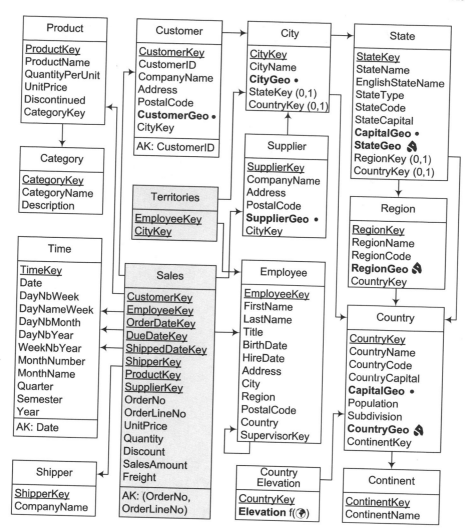

Fig. 11.15 Logical representation of the GeoNorthwind data warehouse in Fig. 11.4

We remark that the abstract spatial types presented in Sect. 11.1.1 must be mapped into corresponding spatial types provided by the implementation platform at hand. For instance, while at the conceptual level the Line data type in Fig. 11.1 represents arbitrary curves, such curves can only be approximated with one of the subtypes of the ST_Curve data type in Fig. 11.14. In addition, current systems differ in the set of spatial types provided. For instance, while PostGIS provides types similar to those of the SQL/MM standard presented in Sect. 11.3.2, Oracle provides a unique data type SDO_Geometry that must be parameterized for defining different types of geometries.

We illustrate the mapping above using the State level shown in Fig. 11.15. The PostGIS definition for this table is given next, where the definition of some columns is elided for readability:

```
CREATE TABLE State (
        StateKey INTEGER PRIMARY KEY NOT NULL,
        StateName VARCHAR (30) NOT NULL,
        ...
        CapitalGeo GEOMETRY(POINT, 4326),
        StateGeo GEOMETRY(POLYGON, 4326),
        ...
        CONSTRAINT CapitalInState
            CHECK(ST_COVERS(StateGeo, CapitalGeo)))
```

To account for the implicit geometry indicated by a pictogram in the conceptual schema, a column StateGeo of type POLYGON is used for storing the geometry of states. Further, the spatial attribute CapitalGeo of type POINT is used for storing the geometry of the capital cities of states. Both spatial columns are defined in the WGS84 SRS, whose identifier in PostGIS is 4326. Finally, notice that a **check constraint** ensures that the geometry of a state covers the geometry of its capital.

Now, we can insert, for example, the state of Florida as follows:

```
INSERT INTO State (StateKey, StateName, ..., CapitalGeo, StateGeo, ...)
VALUES (12345, 'Florida', ..., ST_GeomFromText('POINT(1 -1)'),
        ST_GeomFromText('POLYGON((0 0, 1 1,...,1 -1, 0 0))'), ...);
```

Figure 11.15 illustrates an alternative mapping of spatial attributes. Here, the raster attribute Elevation is not included in table Country, but it is placed instead in another table CountryElevation. This is done for optimization reasons: The raster data could be voluminous and therefore slow down significantly the queries involving the Country level. Moreover, most of those queries will not require the elevation information. Notice that this approach can be used for all spatial attributes.

The table CountryElevation can be created as follows:

```
CREATE TABLE CountryElevation (
        CountryKey INTEGER, Elevation RASTER,
        FOREIGN KEY (CountryKey) REFERENCES Country(CountryKey));
```

The table contains a foreign key to the Country dimension table and an attribute of the RASTER data type. This attribute will store a raster that covers the spatial extent of each country.

11.4.2 Spatial Facts, Measures, and Hierarchies

The mapping of a fact to the relational model is performed using Rule 2 introduced in Sect. 5.3, which we extend here for coping with spatial features:

Rule 2S: A fact F is mapped to a table T_F that includes as attributes all measures of the fact. Further, a surrogate key may be added to the table. Spatial measures must be mapped to attributes having a spatial type. In addition, if the fact has an associated topological constraint, a trigger may be added to ensure that the constraint is satisfied for all fact members. Note that additional attributes will be added to this table when mapping relationships using Rule 3S below.

A relationship is mapped using Rule 3 given in Sect. 5.3. This rule is extended below for coping with spatial features:

Rule 3S: A relationship between either a fact F and a dimension level L or between dimension levels L_P and L_C (standing for the parent and child levels, respectively) can be mapped in three different ways, depending on its cardinalities:

Rule 3a: If the relationship is one-to-one, the table corresponding to the fact (T_F) or to the child level (T_C) is extended with all the attributes of the dimension level or the parent level, respectively. Spatial attributes must be mapped to attributes having a spatial type.

Rule 3b: If the relationship is one-to-many, the table corresponding to the fact (T_F) or to the child level (T_C) is extended with the surrogate key of the table corresponding to the dimension level (T_L) or the parent level (T_P), respectively, that is, there is a foreign key in the fact or child table pointing to the other table.

Rule 3c: If the relationship is many-to-many, a new table T_B (standing for bridge table) is created that contains as attributes the surrogate keys of the tables corresponding to the fact (T_F) and the dimension level (T_L) or the parent (T_P) and child levels (T_C), respectively. If the relationship has a distributing attribute, an additional attribute is added to the table to store this information.

Further, if the relationship has an associated topological constraint, a trigger may be added to ensure that the constraint is satisfied by all instances of the relationship.

For example, applying the above rules to the spatial fact Maintenance given in Fig. 11.6 will result in a table that contains the surrogate keys of the four dimensions Segment, RoadCoating, County, and Time, as well as the corresponding referential integrity constraints. Further, the table contains attributes for the measures Length and CommonArea, where the latter is a spatial attribute. The table can be created as follows:

```
CREATE TABLE Maintenance (
    SegmentKey INTEGER NOT NULL,
    RoadCoatingKey INTEGER NOT NULL,
    CountyKey INTEGER NOT NULL,
    TimeKey INTEGER NOT NULL,
    Length INTEGER NOT NULL,
```

```
CommonArea GEOMETRY(LINESTRING, 4326),
FOREIGN KEY (SegmentKey) REFERENCES Segment(SegmentKey),
/* Other foreign key constraints */ );
```

As an example of mapping of spatial hierarchies, Fig. 11.15 shows the mapping of the relationship between the Region and Country levels in Fig. 11.4. We see that the Region table includes an attribute RegionKey referencing the parent level Country.

11.4.3   Topological Constraints

We conclude this section studying how a topological constraint in a fact or between two spatial levels is mapped to the relational model. These constraints restrict either the geometries of spatial members related to a fact or the geometry of children members with respect to the geometry of their associated parent member. For example, the spatial fact Maintenance in Fig. 11.6 has an Overlaps relationship that states that a segment and a county related to each other in a fact member must overlap. Similarly, in Fig. 11.4, a CoveredBy relationship exists between the Region and Country levels, which indicates that the geometry of a region is covered by the geometry of a country.

The trigger that enforces the topological constraint in the spatial fact Maintenance can be written as follows:

```
CREATE OR REPLACE FUNCTION SegmentOverlapsCounty()
RETURNS TRIGGER AS $SegmentOverlapsCounty$
    DECLARE
        SegmentGeo GEOMETRY;
        CountyGeo GEOMETRY;
    BEGIN
        /* Retrieve the geometries of the associated segment and county */
        SegmentGeo = (SELECT S.SegmentGeo FROM Segment S
            WHERE NEW.SegmentKey = S.SegmentKey);
        CountyGeo = (SELECT C.CountyGeo FROM County C
            WHERE NEW.CountyKey = C.CountyKey);
        /* Raise error if the topological constraint is violated */
        IF NOT ST_OVERLAPS(SegmentGeo, CountyGeo) THEN
            RAISE EXCEPTION 'The segment and the county must overlap';
        END IF;
        RETURN NEW;
    END;
$SegmentOverlapsCounty$ LANGUAGE plpgsql;

CREATE TRIGGER SegmentOverlapsCounty
BEFORE INSERT OR UPDATE ON Maintenance
FOR EACH ROW EXECUTE PROCEDURE SegmentOverlapsCounty();
```

Notice that in the above example, the topological constraint involves only two spatial levels. It is somewhat more complex to enforce a topological constraint that involves more than two spatial dimensions.

A topological constraint between spatial levels can be enforced either at each insertion of a child member or after the insertion of all children members. The choice among these two solutions depends on the kind of topological constraint. For example, a topological constraint stating that a region is located inside the geometry of its country can be enforced each time a city is inserted, while a topological constraint stating that the geometry of a country is the spatial union of all its composing regions must be enforced after all of the regions and the corresponding country have been inserted.

As an example of the first solution, a trigger can be used to enforce the CoveredBy topological constraint between the **Region** and **Country** levels in Fig. 11.4. This trigger should raise an error if the geometry of a region member is not covered by the geometry of its related country member. Otherwise, it should insert the new data into the **Country** table. The trigger is as follows:

```
CREATE OR REPLACE FUNCTION RegionInCountry()
RETURNS TRIGGER AS $RegionInCountry$
    DECLARE
        CountryGeo GEOMETRY;
    BEGIN
        /* Retrieve the geometry of the associated country */
        CountryGeo = (SELECT C.CountryGeo FROM Country C
            WHERE NEW.CountryKey = C.CountryKey);
        /* Raise error if the topological constraint is violated */
        IF NOT ST_COVERS(CountryGeo, NEW.RegionGeo) THEN
            RAISE EXCEPTION 'A region cannot be outside its country';
        END IF;
        RETURN NEW;
    END;
$RegionInCountry$ LANGUAGE plpgsql;

CREATE TRIGGER RegionInCountry
BEFORE INSERT OR UPDATE ON Region
FOR EACH ROW EXECUTE PROCEDURE RegionInCountry();
```

In the second solution, child members are inserted without activating a trigger. When all children members have been inserted, the verification is performed. For the GeoNorthwind case study, suppose that the geometries of **Region** partition the geometry of **Country**. When all regions of a country have been inserted into the warehouse, the following query can be used to look for countries whose regions do not partition the geometry of the country.

```
SELECT CountryKey, CountryName
FROM   Country C
WHERE  NOT ST_EQUALS(C.CountryGeo,
           (SELECT ST_UNION(R.RegionGeo)
            FROM Region R WHERE R.CountryKey = C.CountryKey))
```

11.5 GeoMondrian

GeoMondrian[1] is a spatial OLAP (SOLAP) server. It is a spatially extended version of Pentaho Analysis Services, also known as Mondrian, which we have discussed in Sect. 5.10. The open-source version of GeoMondrian only supports PostGIS-based data warehouses, while the commercial version adds support for Oracle, SQL Server, and MySQL.

GeoMondrian integrates spatial objects into the OLAP data cube structure. It implements a native geometry data type and provides spatial extensions to the MDX query language, thus enabling spatial analysis capabilities into analytical queries. The geospatial extensions to the MDX query language include inline geometry constructors, filtering of members based on topological predicates, spatial calculated members and measures, and calculations based on scalar attributes derived from spatial features.

As it is the case in Mondrian, a cube schema is defined in GeoMondrian using an XML syntax.[2] GeoMondrian adds the Geometry data type for member properties. For example, the spatial hierarchy of the Customer dimension in the GeoNorthwind cube (Fig. 11.4) is defined as follows:

```
<Hierarchy primaryKey="CustomerKey" primaryKeyTable="Customer">
  . . .
  <Level name="Continent" table="Continent" column="ContinentName" />
  <Level name="Country" table="Country" column="CountryName">
    . . .
    <Property name="CountryGeo" column="CountryGeo type="Geometry" />
  </Level>
  <Level name="Region" table="State" column="RegionName">
    . . .
  </Level>
  <Level name="State" table="State" column="StateName">
    . . .
    <Property name="CapitalGeo" column="CapitalGeo" type="Geometry" />
    <Property name="StateGeo"column="StateGeo" type="Geometry" />
  </Level>
  <Level name="City" table="City" column="CityName">
    . . .
    <Property name="CityGeo" column="CityGeo" type="Geometry" />
  </Level>
  <Level name="Customer" table="Customer" column="CompanyName">
    . . .
    <Property name="CustomerGeo" column="CustomerGeo"
      type="Geometry" />
  </Level>
</Hierarchy>
```

---

[1] http://www.spatialytics.org/projects/geomondrian/

[2] Note that in Sect. 5.10 we described Mondrian version 4.0. The current version of GeoMondrian uses version 3.0 of the Mondrian metamodel.

Geometry properties map to PostGIS GEOMETRY columns in the dimension tables. As can be seen, spatial dimensions are typically defined as snowflake dimensions because star schemas induce a redundancy of geometries located at higher levels of a hierarchy, which would require much storage space and would slow down queries.

Once the spatial cube is defined, MDX queries containing spatial predicates and functions can be addressed to GeoMondrian, as we will see in the next section.

11.6 Querying the GeoNorthwind Cube in MDX

We now show through a series of examples how a spatial data warehouse can be queried with MDX. For this, we use the GeoNorthwind data warehouse.

Query 11.1. Total sales in 1997 to customers located in cities that are within an area whose extent is a polygon drawn by the user.

```
SELECT Measures.SalesAmount ON COLUMNS,
        FILTER(Customer.Geography.City.MEMBERS,
        ST_Within(Customer.Geography.CURRENTMEMBER.Properties('CityGeo'),
        ST_GeomFromText('POLYGON ((200.0 50.0, 300.0 50.0,
        300.0 80.0, 200.0 80.0, 200.0 50.0))'))) ON ROWS
FROM    Sales
WHERE OrderDate.[1997]
```

The above query uses the spatial predicate ST_Within to filter members according to their location. The polygon given as argument to the ST_GeomFromText function will be defined by the user with the mouse in a graphical interface showing a map.

Query 11.2. Total sales to customers located in a state that contains the capital city of the country.

```
SELECT { Measures.SalesAmount } ON COLUMNS,
        NON EMPTY FILTER(Customer.Geography.State.MEMBERS,
        ST_Contains(Customer.Geography.CURRENTMEMBER.
        Properties('StateGeo'),Customer.Geography.CURRENTMEMBER.
        PARENT.PARENT.Properties('CapitalGeo'))) ON ROWS
FROM    Sales
```

The above query uses the function ST_Contains to verify that the geometry of a state contains the geometry of the capital of its country.

The following query defines a calculated member that is a geometry.

Query 11.3. Spatial union of the states in the USA where at least one customer placed an order in 1997.

```
WITH MEMBER Measures.GeoUnion AS
        ST_UnionAgg(Customer.Geography.CURRENTMEMBER.CHILDREN,
        'StateGeo')
SELECT { Measures.SalesAmount, Measures.GeoUnion } ON COLUMNS,
        { Customer.Geography.Country.[USA] } ON ROWS
FROM   Sales
WHERE  OrderDate.[1997]
```

Here, we use the function ST_UnionAgg to perform the spatial union of all the states of the USA that satisfy the query condition. The second argument of the function states the name of the property (i.e., StateGeo) containing the geometries that will be aggregated.

Query 11.4. Distance between the customers' locations and the capital of the state in which they are located.

```
WITH MEMBER Measures.Distance AS
        ST_Distance(Customer.Geography.CURRENTMEMBER.
        Properties('CustomerGeo'), Customer.Geography.
        CURRENTMEMBER.PARENT.PARENT.Properties('CapitalGeo'))
SELECT { Measures.Distance } ON COLUMNS,
        Customer.Geography.Customer.MEMBERS ON ROWS
FROM   Sales
```

The above query defines a calculated measure Distance, which is a numerical value obtained by computing with the function ST_Distance the distance from the geometries of the customer and the capital of its state.

Query 11.5. For each customer, total sales amount to its closest supplier.

```
WITH MEMBER Measures.Distance AS
        ST_Distance(
        Customer.Geography.CURRENTMEMBER.Properties('CustomerGeo'),
        Supplier.Geography.CURRENTMEMBER.Properties('SupplierGeo'))
SELECT Measures.SalesAmount ON COLUMNS,
        GENERATE(Customer.Geography.Customer.MEMBERS,
        BOTTOMCOUNT(Customer.Geography.CURRENTMEMBER *
        Supplier.Geography.Supplier.MEMBERS, 1, Measures.Distance)) ON ROWS
FROM   Sales
```

In the above query, we use the GENERATE function to obtain for each customer the closest supplier. The latter is obtained by applying the BOTTOMCOUNT function with respect to the calculated measure Distance.

Query 11.6. Total sales amount for customers that have orders delivered by suppliers such that their locations are less than 200 km from each other.

```
SELECT { Measures.[Sales Amount] } ON COLUMNS,
        GENERATE(Customer.Geography.Customer.MEMBERS,
        FILTER(Customer.Geography.CURRENTMEMBER *
```

```
        Supplier.Geography.Supplier.MEMBERS, ST_Distance(
        Customer.Geography.CURRENTMEMBER.Properties('CustomerGeo'),
        Supplier.Geography.CURRENTMEMBER.Properties('SupplierGeo'))
        < 200 AND Measures.SalesAmount > 0 )) ON ROWS
FROM    Sales
```

This query uses the GENERATE and the FILTER functions to obtain for each customer the suppliers that are at less than 200 km from the customer and such that they are related through at least one order, that is, their SalesAmount measure is greater than 0.

Query 11.7. Distance between the customer and supplier for customers that have orders delivered by suppliers of the same country.

```
WITH MEMBER Measures.CustomerCountry AS
        Customer.Geography.CURRENTMEMBER.PARENT.
        PARENT.PARENT.NAME
     MEMBER Measures.SupplierCountry AS
        Supplier.Geography.CURRENTMEMBER.PARENT.
        PARENT.PARENT.NAME
     MEMBER Measures.Distance AS
        ST_Distance(Customer.Geography.CURRENTMEMBER.
        Properties('CustomerGeo'), Supplier.Geography.
        CURRENTMEMBER.Properties('SupplierGeo'))
SELECT { Measures.Distance } ON COLUMNS,
        GENERATE( Customer.Geography.Customer.MEMBERS,
        FILTER( Customer.Geography.CURRENTMEMBER *
        Supplier.Geography.Supplier.MEMBERS,
        SupplierCountry = CustomerCountry AND
        [Sales Amount] > 0) ) ON ROWS
FROM    Sales
```

In the above query, we use the GENERATE function to obtain for each customer the suppliers located in the same country. For this, we use the FILTER function to keep only couples of customer and supplier located in the same country and such that the customer has an order in which the supplier is involved. Note that the expression Customer.Geography.Customer.MEMBERS, although somehow awkward, first points to the name of the dimension (Customer); then, for this dimension, it looks for the Geography hierarchy and goes up again to look for the Customer, actually the first level in the hierarchy.

Query 11.8. Number of customers from European countries with an area larger than $50,000\,\mathrm{km}^2$.

```
WITH MEMBER Measures.CountryArea AS
        ST_Area(Customer.Geography.CURRENTMEMBER.
        Properties('CountryGeo'))
     MEMBER Measures.CustomerCount AS
        COUNT(EXISTING Customer.Geography.Customer)
```

```
SELECT  Measures.CustomerCount ON COLUMNS,
        FILTER(Customer.Geography.Country.MEMBERS,
        CountryArea > 50000 AND Customer.Geography.
        CURRENTMEMBER.PARENT.NAME = 'Europe') ON ROWS
FROM    Sales
```

In this query, the calculated measure CountryArea uses the function ST_Area for obtaining the area of a country. The calculated measure CustomerCount uses the keyword EXISTING to force the set of customers to be evaluated within the current context, that is, the current country. Finally, the function FILTER allows to select European countries whose area is greater than 50,000.

Query 11.9. For each supplier, number of customers located at more than 100 km from the supplier.

```
WITH MEMBER Measures.CustomerCount AS
        COUNT(FILTER(Supplier.Geography.CURRENTMEMBER *
        Customer.Geography.Customer.MEMBERS, ST_Intersect(ST_Buffer(
        Supplier.Geography.CURRENTMEMBER.Properties('SupplierGeo'), 100)
        Customer.Geography.CURRENTMEMBER.Properties('CustomerGeo'))
        AND Measures.SalesAmount > 0 ))
SELECT { Measures.CustomerCount } ON COLUMNS,
        Supplier.Geography.Supplier.MEMBERS ON ROWS
FROM    Sales
```

The calculated measure CustomerCount uses the function ST_Buffer to produce a circle of 100 km radius centered in the location of the current supplier. The function ST_Intersects then verifies that this circle intersects with the location of the customer. The function FILTER selects for each supplier the customers that satisfy the topological constraint and that are related through at least one order, and, finally, the function COUNT is used to obtain the number of selected customers.

Query 11.10. For each supplier, distance between the location of the supplier and the centroid of the locations of all its customers.

```
WITH MEMBER Measures.CustomerLocations AS
        ST_UnionAgg(FILTER(Customer.Geography.Customer.MEMBERS,
        Measures.SalesAmount > 0 ), 'CustomerGeo'))
    MEMBER Measures.CentroidCustomers AS
        ST_Centroid(CustomerLocations)
    MEMBER Measures.DistanceCentroid AS
        ST_Distance(CentroidCustomers,
        Supplier.Geography.CURRENTMEMBER.Property('SupplierGeo'))
SELECT { Measures.DistanceCentroid } ON COLUMNS,
        Supplier.Geography.Supplier.MEMBERS ON ROWS
FROM    Sales
```

In the calculated measure CustomerLocations, the function FILTER is used for selecting the customers of the current supplier. Then, the ST_UnionAgg function is used for aggregating into a single geometry all the locations of the selected customers. In the calculated measure CentroidCustomers, the function ST_Centroid function is used to compute the centroid of the locations of the customers of the current supplier. Finally, in the calculated measure DistanceCentroid, the distance between the location of the supplier and the centroid of all its customers is computed.

11.7 Querying the GeoNorthwind Data Warehouse in SQL

Analogously to what we did in Chap. 6, we show that MDX queries can also be expressed in SQL. Given that in this book we have covered SQL extensively, we do not comment on the queries, which are straightforward.

Query 11.1. Total sales in 1997 to customers located in cities that are within an area whose extent is a polygon drawn by the user.

```
SELECT    C.CustomerName, SUM(S.SalesAmount)
FROM      Sales S, Customer C, City Y, Time T
WHERE     S.CustomerKey = C.CustomerKey AND C.CityKey = Y.CityKey AND
          S.TimeKey = T.TimeKey AND T.Year = 1997 AND
          ST_Within(C.CityGeo, ST_GeomFromText('POLYGON((200.0 50.0,
          300.0 50.0, 300.0 80.0, 200.0 80.0, 200.0 50.0)))')
GROUP BY  C.CustomerName
```

Query 11.2. Total sales to customers located in a state that contains the capital city of the country.

```
SELECT    C.CustomerName, SUM(S.SalesAmount)
FROM      Sales S, Customer C, City Y, State A, Country O
WHERE     S.CustomerKey = C.CustomerKey AND
          C.CityKey = Y.CityKey AND Y.StateKey = A.StateKey AND
          A.CountryKey = O.CountryKey AND
          ST_Contains(A.StateGeo,O.CapitalGeo)
GROUP BY  C.CustomerName
```

Query 11.3. Spatial union of the states in the USA where at least one customer placed an order in 1997.

```
SELECT ST_Union(DISTINCT A.StateGeo)
FROM   Sales S, Customer C, City Y, State A, Country O, Time T
WHERE  S.CustomerKey = C.CustomerKey AND C.CityKey = Y.CityKey AND
       Y.StateKey = A.StateKey AND A.CountryKey = O.CountryKey AND
       O.CountryName = 'United States' AND
       S.TimeKey = T.TimeKey AND T.Year = 1997
```

Query 11.4. Distance between the customers' locations and the capital of the state in which they are located.

```
SELECT DISTINCT C.CompanyName AS CustomerName,
        ST_Distance(C.CustomerGeo,CS.CapitalGeo) AS Distance
FROM    Sales S, Customer C, City AS CC, State AS CS
WHERE   S.CustomerKey = C.CustomerKey AND
        C.CityKey = CC.CityKey AND CC.StateKey = CS.StateKey
ORDER BY C.CompanyName
```

Query 11.5. For each customer, total sales amount to its closest supplier.

```
SELECT    C.CustomerName, SUM(S.SalesAmount)
FROM      Sales S, Customer C, Supplier U
WHERE     S.CustomerKey = C.CustomerKey AND
          S.SupplierKey = U.SupplierKey AND
          ST_Distance(C.CustomerGeo,U.SupplierGeo) <= (
          SELECT MIN(ST_Distance(C.CustomerGeo,U1.SupplierGeo)
          FROM   Sales S1, Supplier U1
          WHERE S1.CustomerKey = C.CustomerKey AND
                 S1.SupplierKey = U1.SupplierKey )
GROUP BY C.CustomerName
```

Query 11.6. Total sales amount for customers that have orders delivered by suppliers such that their locations are less than 200 km from each other.

```
SELECT    C.CustomerName, SUM(S.SalesAmount)
FROM      Sales S, Customer C, Supplier U
WHERE     S.CustomerKey = C.CustomerKey AND
          S.SupplierKey = U.SupplierKey AND
          ST_Distance(C.CustomerGeo,U.SupplierGeo) < 200
GROUP BY C.CustomerName
```

Query 11.7. Distance between the customer and supplier for customers that have orders delivered by suppliers of the same country.

```
SELECT DISTINCT C.CompanyName AS CustomerName,
        U.CompanyName AS SupplierName,
        ST_Distance(C.CustomerGeo,U.SupplierGeo) AS Distance
FROM    Sales S, Customer C, City AS CC, State AS CS,
        Supplier U, City AS SC, State AS SS
WHERE   S.CustomerKey = C.CustomerKey AND
        C.CityKey = CC.CityKey AND CC.StateKey = CS.StateKey AND
        S.SupplierKey = U.SupplierKey AND U.CityKey = SC.CityKey AND
        SC.StateKey = SS.StateKey AND SS.CountryKey = CS.CountryKey
ORDER BY C.CompanyName, U.CompanyName
```

Query 11.8. Number of customers for European countries with an area larger than $50,000 \, \text{km}^2$.

```
SELECT    C.CountryName, COUNT(DISTINCT S.CustomerKey)
FROM      Sales S, Customer U, City Y, State T, Country C, Continent A
WHERE     S.CustomerKey = U.CustomerKey AND U.CityKey = Y.CityKey AND
          Y.StateKey = T.StateKey AND T.CountryKey = C.CountryKey AND
          ST_Area(C.CountryGeo) > 50000 AND
          C.ContinentKey = A.ContinentKey AND A.ContinentName = 'Europe'
GROUP BY  C.CountryName
```

Query 11.9. For each supplier, number of customers located at more than 100 km from the supplier.

```
SELECT    P.SupplierName, COUNT(DISTINCT C.CustomerKey)
FROM      Sales S, Supplier P, Customer C
WHERE     S.SupplierKey = P.SupplierKey AND
          S.CustomerKey = C.CustomerKey AND
          ST_Distance(P.SupplierGeo,C.CustomerGeo) > 100
GROUP BY  P.SupplierName
```

Query 11.10. For each supplier, distance between the location of the supplier and the centroid of the locations of all its customers.

```
SELECT    P.SupplierName, ST_Distance(P.SupplierGeo,
          ST_Centroid(ST_Union(DISTINCT C.CustomerGeo)))
FROM      Sales S, Supplier P, Customer C
WHERE     S.SupplierKey = P.SupplierKey AND S.CustomerKey = C.CustomerKey
GROUP BY  P.SupplierName
```

11.8 Spatial Data Warehouse Design

In this section, we extend the method studied in Chap. 10 to support spatial data. Recall that the method includes the phases of requirements specification, conceptual design, logical design, and physical design. We revisit these phases, describing how to take spatial support into account. Similar to traditional data warehouse design, this method is independent of the conceptual model used. We will use the MultiDim model extended with spatial data studied in the present chapter.

There is not yet a well-established method for the design of spatial data warehouses. In general, the four phases described for designing traditional data warehouses can be applied for spatial data warehouses. Two main approaches can be distinguished. In the first one, spatial elements are included in the initial conceptual schema. In the other approach, the nonspatial schema is initially developed, and it is augmented afterward with spatial elements. In both cases, the spatially extended conceptual schema is then translated into logical and physical schemas using mapping rules. Nevertheless, owing to the lack of a well-accepted conceptual model for the design of spatial data warehouses, in many situations the phase of conceptual design is skipped, starting the design process with the logical schema.

11.8.1   *Requirements Specification and Conceptual Design*

Like for traditional data warehouses, spatial data warehouses can be designed on the basis of the analysis requirements of the users, the data available in the source systems, or both. This leads to three approaches for spatial data warehouse design, referred to as the analysis-driven, source-driven, and analysis/source-driven approaches.

An aspect that distinguishes spatial data warehouse design from conventional data warehouse design is the need to define when we will consider spatial support during the design process. If spatial support is considered in the early steps of the requirements specification phase, we are in the case of **early inclusion of spatial support**. Otherwise, we are in the case of **late inclusion of spatial support**. As we will see, the choice between these two options depends on the users' knowledge of spatial data features and the presence of spatial data in the source systems. Further, this choice is independent of which of the three approaches above is used. For example, a particular data warehouse project might choose a source-driven approach with early inclusion of spatial support in order to integrate existing spatial applications into a decision-support infrastructure that is used by experts cognizant of spatial databases.

Analysis-Driven Approach

In the analysis-driven approach to spatial data warehouse design, the requirements specification phase is driven by the analysis needs of the users. Figure 11.16a shows the steps required in this approach. As can be seen in that figure, in the first step of the requirements specification phase, users at various management levels are identified to ensure that the requirements will express the goals of the organization. These users will help the developer team to understand the purpose of having a spatial data warehouse and to determine the analysis needs, which are collected in the second step. The information gathered and the corresponding metadata are documented in the third step and serve as a basis for the next phase.

We next analyze how the two design choices for including spatial support affect the requirements and conceptual modeling processes.

Early Inclusion of Spatial Support

In this case, we assume that the users are familiar with concepts related to spatial data, including its manipulation and some kinds of spatial analysis. Therefore, from the beginning of the requirements specification process, the users may be able to express what spatial data they require in order to exploit the features of multidimensional models and to perform various kinds of spatial analysis, and the design process may be performed following the same steps as those for traditional data warehouse design.

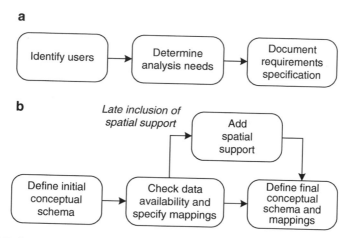

Fig. 11.16 Steps of the analysis-driven approach for spatial data warehouses. (a) Requirements specification phase. (b) Conceptual design phase

The conceptual design phase (Fig. 11.16b) starts with the development of the initial spatial data warehouse schema. Note that this schema already includes spatial elements since we assume that the users are able to refer to spatial data when expressing their specific analysis needs. Therefore, we follow the lower path of Fig. 11.16b. In the following step, we must determine whether the data are available in the source systems. Then, the corresponding mappings with data warehouse elements must be specified. Note, however, that external sources may be needed if the required spatial support does not exist in the source systems. In the last step, the final schema is developed; it includes all data warehouse elements for which the corresponding data exists in the source systems (whether internal or external). Additionally, the final mapping between the two kinds of systems is delivered.

Late Inclusion of Spatial Support

It may happen that users are not familiar with spatial data management or that they prefer to start by expressing their analysis needs related to nonspatial elements and include spatial support later on. In this case, the requirements specification and conceptual-design phases proceed as for a traditional data warehouse, ignoring spatial features until the initial schema is checked with respect to the data available in the source systems. As shown in Fig. 11.16b, prior to the development of the final schema and the corresponding mappings, there is an additional step to add spatial support. In this step, the designers present the conceptual schema to the users and ask them for indications about the spatial support required.

If the MultiDim model is used as a conceptual model for designing a spatial data warehouse, in the first step the designers may consider each level and decide whether that level, some of its attributes, or both should be represented spatially. Then, if a hierarchy includes two related spatial levels, a topological constraint between them may be specified. If a fact relates two or more spatial dimensions, the designers can help the users to determine whether a topological constraint exists between these dimensions. Finally, the inclusion of spatial measures may be considered. Note that the elements of the multidimensional schema could be analyzed in a different order, depending on the designers' skills and their knowledge about spatial data warehouses and the particularities of the conceptual model used. Similar to the previous case, the step of checking data availability may require access to external sources since spatial data may not be present in the underlying source systems. The final schema should include the modified mappings.

As an example, consider the schema in Fig. 4.2, developed for a traditional data warehouse following the method described in Chap. 10. When this schema was shown to the users, they required the possibility to visualize on maps the geographic hierarchies for Customer, Supplier, and Employee dimensions. Figure 11.4 shows the addition of geographic properties to the hierarchies in the initial conceptual schema. We use the spatial extension of the MultiDim model described in Sect. 11.2. The spatial elements are then checked against the data available in the source systems. Since the operational data do not include spatial components, external sources were used to obtain the corresponding information for these spatial hierarchies.

Source-Driven Approach

As explained in Chap. 10, this approach relies on the data in the source systems. Like in the analysis-driven approach, spatial support may be included either early or late in the design process. Since the operational databases are the driving force in this approach, the choice between early or late inclusion of spatial requirements depends on whether these databases are spatial or not.

Early Inclusion of Spatial Support

If the source systems include spatial data, steps similar to those for traditional data warehouse design can be applied. They are indicated in Fig. 11.17a and the lower path of Fig. 11.17b. Requirements specification starts with

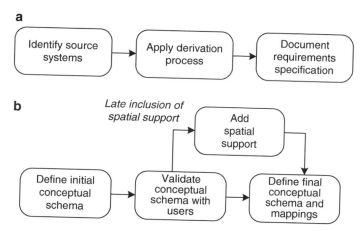

Fig. 11.17 Steps of the source-driven approach for spatial data warehouses. (**a**) Requirements specification phase. (**b**) Conceptual design phase

the identification of the source systems that may serve as data providers for the spatial data warehouse. External sources are not considered at this stage. In the second step, these sources are analyzed to discover multidimensional schema elements. No semiautomatic or automatic procedure has been proposed in the literature for deriving the schema of a spatial data warehouse from the schemas of source systems. Thus, this derivation process should be conducted manually and must rely on the designers' knowledge of the business domain and of spatial data warehouse concepts. The multidimensional schema obtained, as well as the corresponding metadata, are documented in the third step of the requirements specification phase.

In the first step of the conceptual design phase, a conceptual schema with spatial elements is developed. This schema is shown to the users to determine their interest and to identify elements that are important for analysis. The users' recommendations for changes will be reflected in the final schema obtained in the last step, where mappings between the source and data warehouse schemas are also developed.

Late Inclusion of Spatial Support

This case occurs when the source systems do not include spatial data or they do contain spatial data but the derivation process is complex and the designers prefer to focus first on nonspatial elements and to address spatial support later on. Thus, the design process proceeds as for a traditional data warehouse with the addition of a step for adding spatial support. Note that this support is considered only for the previously chosen elements of the multidimensional schema. This is shown in Fig. 11.17a and the upper path of Fig. 11.17b.

If the MultiDim model is used to represent the traditional data warehouse schema, the analysis of which elements can be spatially represented can be conducted in a way similar to that in the analysis-driven approach above. If spatial support is not provided by the underlying operational systems, external sources may deliver the required spatial data. The corresponding mapping should be included as part of the final schema.

We do not include an example to illustrate this approach since such an example would proceed in the same way as for the creation of a schema using the source-driven approach in the case of a traditional data warehouse and for adding spatial support in the analysis-driven approach above.

Analysis/Source-Driven Approach

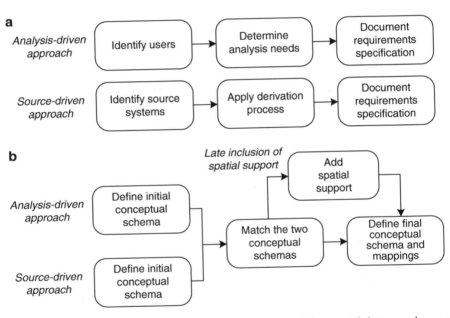

Fig. 11.18 Steps of the analysis/source-driven approach for spatial data warehouses. (a) Requirements specification phase. (b) Conceptual design phase

This approach combines the two previously described approaches which may be used in parallel, as mentioned in Sect. 10.3.5. Two chains of activities, corresponding to the analysis-driven and source-driven approaches, can be distinguished, as it can be seen in Fig. 11.18. The figure shows the steps of the analysis/source-driven approach for spatial data warehouses. Similarly to the previous cases, we propose two different solutions, the choice of which depends on whether the users are familiar with concepts related to spatial data and whether the source systems include spatial data. The discussion about early or late inclusion of spatial support in this approach is analogous to the ones in previous sections, therefore we omit it.

11.8.2 Logical and Physical Design

The logical and physical design of a spatial data warehouse should consider the various aspects mentioned in Sects. 10.5 and 10.6 for traditional data warehouses, which refer to the mapping of a conceptual schema into a logical and a physical schema and to the ETL process, all of these also extensively discussed previously in this book. To avoid redundancy, we do not repeat the explanations here.

11.9 Summary

In this chapter, we studied how data warehouses can be extended with spatial data. For this, we presented a spatial extension of the MultiDim conceptual model with spatial types and field types and defined a set of operations that can be performed upon them. We extended the hierarchies studied in Chaps. 4 and 5 to include spatial data, yielding spatial hierarchies. We also generalized the rules for translating conceptual to logical models to account for spatial data. Then, we addressed the vector and raster models for explaining how spatial abstract data types can be represented at the logical level. As in the rest of the book, we used as example the Northwind data warehouse, which we extended with spatial data. We called this extension the GeoNorthwind data warehouse. We implemented the above concepts using PostGIS, the spatial extension of the PostgreSQL database, and GeoMondrian, the spatial extension of the Mondrian OLAP server. We also showed how the GeoNorthwind data warehouse can be queried using a spatial extension of MDX and with SQL extended with spatial functions. We finally described a method for the design of spatial data warehouses, which extends the method for traditional data warehouse design presented in the previous chapter. As in the traditional case, we presented three different approaches, depending on whether the driving force is the analysis needs, the information in the source systems, or both. For each one of these three approaches, we considered two situations, depending on when spatial data are included in the process.

11.10   Bibliographic Notes

There are many books on spatial databases and geographic information systems (GIS). Popular books in these topics are [174, 187, 229, 234]. SQL/MM, the spatial extension of SQL, is an ISO standard [94], which is also described in [132, 134]. The ISO 19123:2005 standard [93] defines a conceptual schema for coverages, which are logical implementations of continuous fields such as rasters and TINs. A book introducing the main features of PostGIS is [146]. The book [143] describes GRASS, an open-source GIS that includes advanced capabilities for manipulating raster data.

The spatial extension of the MultiDim model presented in this chapter is based on the spatial data types of MADS [155], a spatiotemporal conceptual model, and on the work on field types by the present authors [69, 212, 214]. The notion of SOLAP was introduced in [176], and it is reviewed in [11]. Other relevant work on SOLAP can be found in [13, 14, 224]. A book introducing Mondrian is [10]. Although not much work has been done on the topic of OLAP analysis of continuous fields (see [5, 6]), this kind of data has been under study for many years in GISs. An algebra for fields was defined in the classic book of Tomlin [202] and continued by the work of several authors [24, 34, 138, 154].

Since spatial data warehousing is a relatively recent research area, methodological aspects of their design have not been much addressed in the literature (see, for instance, [63, 64, 125]).

11.11   Review Questions

11.1 What are spatial databases? Describe two complementary ways of modeling spatial data in database applications.

11.2 Describe the various spatial data types at a conceptual level, giving for each one of them an example of its use.

11.3 Define the various topological relationships in terms of the boundary, interior, and exterior of spatial values.

11.4 What are continuous fields? How are they implemented at a conceptual level?

11.5 Give examples of operations associated with field types. Explain the rate-of-change operations for field types.

11.6 Explain why traditional operations must be lifted for field types. Illustrate this with examples.

11.7 Discuss the following concepts: spatial dimension, spatial level, spatial attribute, spatial fact, spatial measure, spatial hierarchy, and topological relationship.

11.8 What are the differences between a spatial level, a spatial level with spatial attributes, and a nonspatial level with spatial attributes?

11.9 Give an example of each of the following spatial hierarchies: balanced, unbalanced, and generalized hierarchies.

11.10 What is the difference between alternative and parallel spatial hierarchies?

11.11 Why are n-ary topological relationships needed in spatial facts? Are such relationships usual in spatial databases?

11.12 How does a spatial measure differ from a numerical measure computed with spatial operations? Does a spatial measure require to be related to spatial dimensions?

11.13 Give an example of a multidimensional schema containing a spatial measure. Transform the spatial measure into a spatial dimension. Compare the two schemas with respect to the various queries that can be addressed to them.

11.14 Define the geoid and the ellipsoid. What are they used for? What are the differences between them? What is a datum?

11.15 What are SRSs?

11.16 What is the difference between the vector and the raster data models for representing spatial data?

11.17 Describe the spatial data types implemented in SQL/MM.

11.18 Describe how field types are implemented in PostGIS. How does this implementation differ from the abstract definition of field types?

11.19 Discuss the mapping rules for translating a spatial MultiDim schema into a relational schema. State the advantages and disadvantages of alternative mappings.

11.20 How is a topological relationship between spatial levels represented in a logical schema?

11.21 How can one check in a logical schema the topological relationship of a fact?

11.22 Describe from a methodological perspective how spatial data can be included in data warehouses.

11.12   Exercises

11.1 Consider the GeoFoodmart cube, whose schema is given in Fig. 11.19. Write in MDX the following queries:

(a) For each store, give the total sales to customers from the same city as the store.

(b) For each store, obtain the ratio between the sales to customers from the same state and its total sales in 2013.

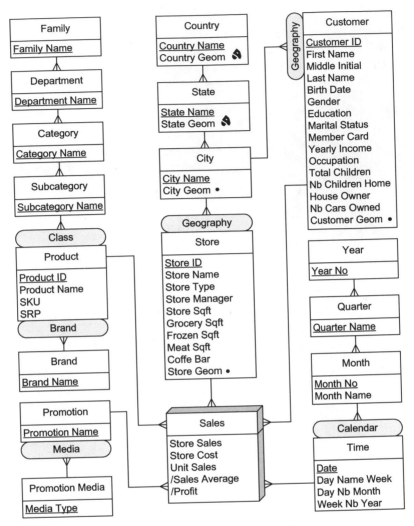

Fig. 11.19 Conceptual schema of the GeoFoodmart cube

(c) Display the unit sales by product brand, considering only sales to customers from a country different from the country of the store.

(d) Display all measures summarized for the stores located in California or Washington, considering only stores in California that are less than 200 km from Los Angeles and stores in Washington that are less than 200 km from Seattle.

(e) Total sales of stores located at less than 5 km from the city center against total sales for all stores in their state.

(f) For each store, list total sales to customers living closer than 10 km from the store against total sales for the store.

(g) For each city, give the store closest to the city center and its best-sold brand name.

(h) Give the spatial union of all the cities that have more than one store with a surface of more than 10,000 square feet.

(i) Give the spatial union of the states such that the average of the total sales by customer in 1997 is greater than $60 per month.

(j) Give the spatial union of all the cities where all customers have purchased for more than $100.

(k) Display the spatial union of the cities whose sales count accounts for more than 5% of all the sales.

11.2 Consider the GeoFoodmart data warehouse, whose relational schema is given in Fig. 11.20. Write in SQL the queries stated in the previous exercise.

11.3 Add spatial data to the data warehouse schema you created as a solution of Ex. 5.9 for the AirCarrier application. You must analyze the dimensions, facts, and measures and define which of them can be extended with spatial features. You should also consider adding continuous field data representing altitude so you can enhance the analysis trying to find a correlation between the results and the elevation of the geographic sites.

11.4 Consider the logical schema obtained as a solution of Ex. 11.3. Using the reverse engineering technique you prefer, produce a multidimensional schema from it.

11.5 Write in MDX the following queries over the schema of the cube obtained in Ex. 11.4:

(a) For each carrier and year, give the number of scheduled and performed flights.

(b) For each airport, give the number of scheduled and performed flights in the last 2 years.

(c) For each carrier and distance group, give the total number of seats sold in 2012 per carrier.

(d) Give the total number of persons arriving to or departing from airports closer than 15 km from the city center in 2012.

(e) Give by year the ratio between flights in airports closer than 15 km from the city center and flights in airports located between 15 and 40 km from the city center.

(f) Display the spatial union of all airports with more than 5,000 departures in 2012.

(g) Display the spatial union of all airports where more than 100 carriers operate.

(h) For cities operated by more than one airport, give the total number of arriving and departing passengers.

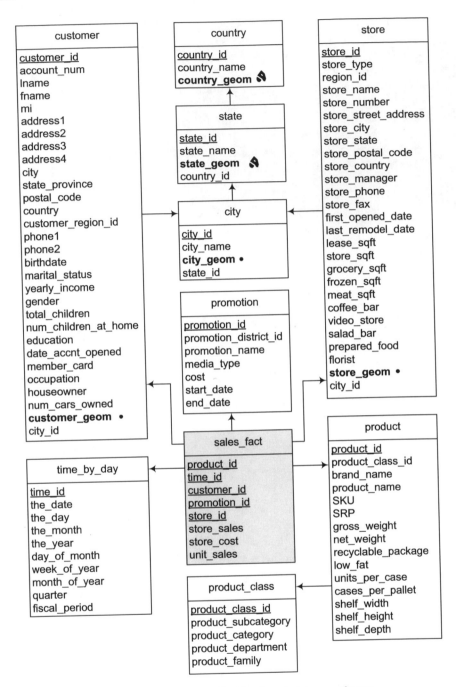

Fig. 11.20 Relational schema of the GeoFoodmart data warehouse

(i) For cities operated by more than one airport, give the total number of arriving and departing passengers at the airport closest to the city center and the ratio between this value and the city total.

(j) Display the spatial union of all airports located at more than 1,000 m above sea level.

(k) Compare the number of departed and scheduled flights for airports located above and below 1,000 m above sea level in 2012.

11.6 Write in SQL the queries of Ex. 11.5 over the logical schema obtained in Ex. 11.3.

Chapter 12
Trajectory Data Warehouses

The previous chapter focused on the analysis of the spatial features of static objects such as stores, cities, or states, where by static we mean that the spatial features of these objects do not change (or change exceptionally) across time. However, there is a wide range of applications that require the analysis of the so-called moving objects, that is, objects that continuously change their position in space and time. This is called mobility data analysis. The interest in mobility data analysis has expanded dramatically with the availability of embedded positioning devices like GPS. With these devices, traffic data, for example, can be captured as a collection of sequences of positioning signals transmitted by the cars' GPS along their itineraries. Since such sequences can be very long, they are often processed by dividing them in segments. For instance, the movement of a car can be segmented with respect to the duration of the time intervals in which it stops at a certain location. These segments of movement are called trajectories, and they are the unit of interest in the analysis of movement data. Trajectory analysis can be applied, for example, in traffic management, which requires to monitor and analyze traffic flows to capture their characteristics. Other applications aim at tracking the position of the users of social networks recorded by the electronic devices they carry, like smartphones or tablets, in order to analyze their behavior. As we have seen throughout this book, data warehouses and OLAP techniques have been successfully used for transforming detailed data into valuable knowledge for decision-making purposes. Extending data warehouses to cope with trajectory data leads to trajectory data warehouses, which we study in this chapter.

We start this chapter in Sect. 12.1 motivating mobility data analysis. Then, in Sect. 12.2, we define temporal types, which provide a way to represent at a conceptual level values that evolve in time, while in Sect. 12.3 we give a possible implementation for these types in PostGIS. In Sect. 12.4, we present the Northwind trajectory data warehouse. Finally, Sect. 12.5 is devoted to querying trajectory data warehouses.

A. Vaisman and E. Zimányi, *Data Warehouse Systems*, Data-Centric
Systems and Applications, DOI 10.1007/978-3-642-54655-6_12,
© Springer-Verlag Berlin Heidelberg 2014

12.1   Mobility Data Analysis

Nowadays, with the massification of positioning devices such as GPS, we are able to collect huge amounts of mobility data, which may be extremely valuable in many application areas. A typical application scenario is the analysis of the activities carried out by tourists in a city. During their stay, tourists visit museums, parks, and several different attractions. They also consume many services like accommodation, restaurants, shops, and so on. From the point of view of an analyst, these tourist places and services are denoted places of interest. A tourist trajectory consists in moving from one place of interest to another, stopping for some time at some of them. Data about these trajectories can be collected and analyzed, for example, to optimize the offer of services or to plan tourist itineraries within the city. As another example, large industrial cities with high car ownership rates are suffering a decrease in their air quality. Normally, stations are located at different points in these cities in order to measure air quality at regular time intervals. It is not hard to guess that the techniques that we have studied in this book can be very useful for understanding and analyzing the evolution of the quality of the air and the effects of corrective measures that the governments may take to keep pollution below certain limits. For example, we can analyze the trajectories followed by cars, trucks, and buses and correlate them with the air quality measures. Or we can study the population being exposed to heavy pollution loads and when this occurs.

In Chap. 11, we have studied how the spatial features of objects can be represented in databases and data warehouses. Although these spatial features can change in time, these changes are typically considered as **discrete**. For example, a parcel can be merged with another one at a certain instant. Similarly, the borders of a state or a country can change in time. In this chapter, we are interested in objects whose spatial features change continuously in time. These are called **moving objects**. While we will deal with moving points in this chapter, many applications must also deal with moving regions, for example, to monitor the trajectory of polluting clouds, or stains in sea bodies, as in our previous example. Trajectories can be represented in a continuous or a discrete way. A **continuous trajectory** is composed of the movement track of an object, occurring within a certain interval, enriched with interpolation functions that allow us to compute, with a reasonable degree of confidence, the spatiotemporal position of the moving object for any instant in this interval. On the other hand, a **discrete trajectory** is composed of the finite sequence of spatiotemporal positions in a certain interval. The main difference between a discrete and a continuous trajectory is that in the former there is no plausible interpolation function between two points. As a typical example, consider the case of a web site of a social network like Foursquare web site.[1] A user checks in at a place at 2 p.m. The next day, she does the same at 1 p.m., and at 4 p.m. she checks in at another place. Interpolation between these three spatiotemporal points will be most likely useless for any application that wants to analyze the movement of this user. However, an application aimed at analyzing the presence of people in a given area may find this information useful. Note that the difference between discrete and continuous trajectories has to do with the application semantics rather than with the time between two consecutive trajectory points. For example, if we want to perform a long-term analysis of the positions of people, then it may be the case that the random check-ins at Foursquare could be considered a continuous trajectory.

Spatiotemporal databases or **moving object databases** store and query the positions of moving objects. For example, a typical query to a moving object database would be "When will the next train from Rome arrive?", which is a query about a moving point. We can also query moving regions and ask questions such as "At which speed is the Amazon rain forest shrinking?". However, these databases do not support analytical queries such as "Total number of deliveries started in Brussels in the last quarter of 2012" or "Average duration of deliveries by city." These queries can be more efficiently handled if mobility data are stored in a data warehouse. Conventional data warehouses can be extended in order to support moving object data, leading to the concept of **spatiotemporal** or **trajectory data warehouses** which, in addition to alphanumeric and spatial data, contain data about the trajectories of moving objects. Trajectories are typically analyzed in conjunction with other data, for instance, spatial data like a road network configuration or continuous field data like temperature, precipitation, or elevation.

Like in Chap. 11, to support spatiotemporal data we make use of a collection of data types that capture the evolution over time of base types and spatial types. We denote these types as temporal, and we study them in detail in the next section.

12.2 Temporal Types

Temporal types represent values that change in time, for instance, to keep track of the evolution of the salaries of employees. Conceptually, temporal types are functions that assign to each instant a value of a particular domain. They are obtained by applying a constructor temporal($\cdot$). Hence, a value of type temporal(real) (e.g., representing the evolution of the salary of an employee) is a continuous function f : instant $\rightarrow$ real.

---

[1]http://www.foursquare.com

In what follows, the time dimension is assumed to represent **valid time**. In the field of **temporal databases**, valid time is the time when the values in a certain tuple are valid in the database, while **transaction time** is the time when a tuple is recorded in the database. For example, if the salary of an employee is recorded in the database on December 28, 2013, this will be stored as its transaction time, but if it holds for the employee from January 1, 2014, the latter date will be recorded as the valid time for this attribute.

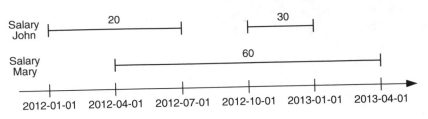

Fig. 12.1 Examples of temporal reals representing the evolution of salaries

Temporal types are partial functions, that is, they may be undefined for certain periods of time. As an example, SalaryJohn and SalaryMary are values of type temporal(real), which represent the evolution of the salary of two employees as depicted in Fig. 12.1. For instance, John has a salary of 20 in the period [2012-01-01, 2012-07-01) and a salary of 30 in the period [2012-10-01, 2013-01-01), while the salary remains undefined in between 2012-07-01 and 2012-09-30. We denote by '⊥' this undefined value. As a convention, we use closed-open intervals.

Table 12.1 Classes of operations on temporal types

Class	Operations
Projection to domain/range	DefTime, RangeValues, Trajectory
Interaction with domain/range	IsDefinedAt, HasValue, AtInstant, AtPeriod, InitialInstant, InitialValue, FinalInstant, FinalValue, At, AtMin, AtMax
Rate of change	Derivative, Speed, Turn
Temporal aggregation	Integral, Duration, Length, TAvg, TVariance, TStDev, TMin, TMax
Lifting	All new operations inferred

Temporal types have an associated set of operations, which can be grouped into several classes, as shown in Table 12.1. We discuss next these operations.

First, there are operations that perform the *projection into the domain and range* of the function defining the temporal type. Operations DefTime and RangeValues return, respectively, the projection of a temporal type into its domain and range. For example, DefTime(SalaryJohn) and RangeValues(SalaryJohn) return, respectively, {[2012-01-01, 2012-07-01), [2012-10-01,

2013-01-01)} and {20,30}. We will explain the Trajectory operation when we discuss the temporal spatial types below.

Another set of operations allows the *interaction with the domain and range*. The IsDefinedAt predicate is used to check whether the temporal function is defined at an instant or is ever defined during a given set of intervals. Analogously, the predicate HasValue checks whether the function ever assumed one of the values given as second argument. The operations AtInstant and AtPeriod restrict the function to a given time or set of time intervals. The operations InitialInstant and InitialValue return, respectively, the first instant at which the function is defined and the corresponding value. The operations FinalInstant and FinalValue are analogous. The Operation At restricts the temporal type to a value or to a range of values in the range of the function. The operations AtMin and AtMax reduce the function to the instants when its value is minimal or maximal, respectively.

For example, IsDefinedAt(SalaryJohn, 2012-06-15) and HasValue (SalaryJohn, 25) result, respectively, in the Boolean values true and false. Furthermore, AtInstant(SalaryJohn, 2012-03-15) and AtInstant(SalaryJohn, 2012-07-15) return, respectively the value 20 and '⊥', because John's salary is undefined at the latter date. Similarly, AtPeriod(SalaryJohn, [2012-04-01, 2012-11-01)) results in a temporal real with value 20 at [2012-04-01, 2012-07-01) and 30 at [2012-10-01, 2012-11-01), where the periods have been projected to the intervals given as parameter of the operation. Further, InitialInstant(SalaryJohn) and InitialValue(SalaryJohn) return 2012-01-01 and 20 which are, respectively, the initial time and value of the temporal value. Moreover, At(SalaryJohn, 20) and At(SalaryJohn, 25) return, respectively, a temporal real with value 20 at [2012-01-01, 2012-07-01) and '⊥', because there is no salary with value 25 whatsoever. Finally, AtMin(SalaryJohn) and AtMax(SalaryJohn) return, respectively, a temporal real with value 20 at [2012-01-01, 2012-07-01) and a temporal real with value 30 at [2012-10-01, 2013-01-01).

An important property of any temporal value is its **rate of change**, computed by the Derivative operation, which takes as argument a temporal integer or real and yields as result a temporal real given by the following expression:

$$f'(t) = \lim_{\delta \to 0} \frac{f(t+\delta) - f(t)}{\delta}.$$

For example, Derivative(SalaryJohn) results in a temporal real with value 0 at [2012-01-01, 2012-07-01) and [2012-10-01, 2013-01-01). The other operations of this class will be described in the context of temporal spatial types later in the chapter.

There are three basic **temporal aggregation operations** that take as argument a temporal integer or real and return a real value. Integral returns the area under the curve defined by the function, Duration returns the duration of the temporal extent on which the function is defined, and Length returns the length of the curve defined by the function. These operations are defined as follows:

- Integral: $\int_T f(x)\, dx$.
- Duration: $\int_T dx$.
- Length: $\int_T \sqrt{1 + \left(\frac{dy}{dx}\right)^2}\, dx$.

From these operations, other derived operations can be defined. These are prefixed with a 'T' (temporal) in order to distinguish them from the usual aggregation operations generalized to temporal types, which we discuss below.

- TAvg: Integral/Duration.
- TVariance: $\int_T \frac{(f(x) - \mathsf{TAvg})^2}{\mathsf{Duration}}\, dx$.
- TStDev: $\sqrt{\mathsf{TVariance}}$.

For example, the operation TAvg computes the weighted average of a temporal value, taking into account the duration in which the function takes a value. In our example, TAvg(SalaryJohn) will yield 23.25, given that John had a salary of 20 during 182 days and a salary of 30 during 92 days. Further, TVariance and TStDev compute the variance and the standard deviation of a temporal type. Finally, TMin and TMax return, respectively, the minimum and maximum value taken by the function. These are obtained by Min(RangeValues(·)) and Max(RangeValues(·)) where Min and Max are the classic operations over numeric values.

The generalization of the operations on nontemporal types to temporal types is called lifting. Lifting an operation over nontemporal types replaces any of its argument types by the respective temporal type and returns a temporal type. As an example, the less than ($<$) operation has lifted versions where one or both of its arguments can be temporal types and the result is a temporal Boolean. Intuitively, the semantics of such lifted operations is that the result is computed at each instant using the nonlifted operation.

Several definitions of an operation may be applied when combining two temporal types defined on different temporal extents. A first solution could be that the result is defined in the *intersection* of both extents and undefined elsewhere. Another solution could be that the result is defined on the *union* of the two extents, and a default value (like 0, for the addition) is used for the extents that belong to only one temporal type. For the lifted operations, we assume that the result is defined in the intersection of both extents.

Analogously, *aggregation* operations can also be lifted. For example, a lifted Avg operation combines a set of temporal reals and results in a new temporal real where the average is computed *at each instant*. As an example, given the two temporal values above, Avg({SalaryJohn, SalaryMary}) gives as result a temporal real whose graphical representation is given in Fig. 12.2.

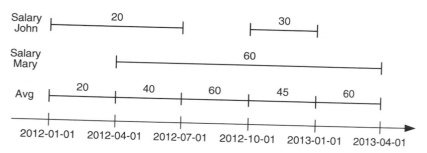

Fig. 12.2 Graphical representation of the temporal average

12.2.1 Temporal Spatial Types

All operations for temporal types discussed so far are also valid for spatial types. For example, a value of type temporal(point), which can represent the trajectory of a truck, is a continuous function $f :$ instant $\rightarrow$ point.

We will present now some of the specific operations of Table 12.1 for the spatial case. We will use as example two temporal points RouteT1 and RouteT2, which keep track of the delivery routes followed by two trucks T1 and T2 on the same day, say, January 10, 2012. A graphical representation of the trajectories of the two trucks is given in Fig. 12.3. We can see, for instance, that truck T1 took 10 min to go from point (0,0) to point (2,2), and then it stopped for 15 min at that point. In this example, we assume a constant speed between pairs of points. Thus, truck T1 traveled a distance of $\sqrt{8} = 2.83$ in 10 min, while truck T2 traveled a distance of $\sqrt{5} = 2.23$ in the first 10 min and a distance of 1 in the following 5 min.

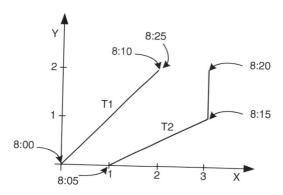

Fig. 12.3 Graphical representation of the trajectories of two trucks

The operation Trajectory projects temporal geometries into the plane (see Table 12.1). The projection of a temporal point into the plane may consist of points and lines, while the projection of a temporal line into the plane may consist of lines and regions. Finally, the projection of a temporal region into the plane consists in a region. In our example, Trajectory(RouteT1) will result in the leftmost line in Fig. 12.3, without any temporal information.

All operations over nontemporal spatial types are lifted to allow any of the arguments to be a temporal type and return a temporal type. As an example, the Distance function, which returns the Cartesian minimum distance between two geometries, has lifted versions where one or both of its arguments can be temporal points and the result is a temporal real. Intuitively, the semantics of such lifted operations is that the result is computed at each instant using the nonlifted operation. That means the lifted Distance function returns the distance between two spatial objects at any given point in time. In our example, Distance(RouteT1, RouteT2) returns a temporal real shown in Fig. 12.4, where, for instance, the function has a value 1.5 at 8:10 and 1.41 at 8:15.

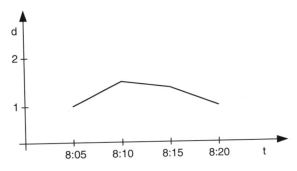

Fig. 12.4 Distance between the trajectories of the two trucks in Fig. 12.3

Topological operations can also be lifted. In this case, the semantics is that the operation returns a temporal Boolean that computes the topological relationship at each instant. For example, Intersects(RouteT1, RouteT2) will return a temporal Boolean with value false during [8:05, 8:20] since the two trucks were never at the same point at any instant of their route.

A common request is to ask whether two temporal points satisfy a topological relationship at a particular instant or at a particular time period. This can be easily obtained by applying first the AtInstant or AtPeriod operations and then by verifying the traditional topological relationship. For example, we could ask if the two trucks T1 and T2 intersected each other at 8:30 with the expression Intersects(AtInstant(RouteT1, 8:30), AtInstant(RouteT2, 8:30)). Notice that here the Intersects operation applied is the nonlifted one. In our example, the result returns false. However, note that the reason could be the imprecision of the measures in time and/or space. One solution to this could be to define a buffer in time and space. This can be stated as follows:

Intersects(Buffer(RouteT1, 0.6, 0:10), Buffer(RouteT2, 0.6, 0:10))

The term Buffer(RouteT1, 0.6, 0:10) defines an elliptic cylinder, or cylindroid, around the trajectory of the truck, with a half-axis of 0.6 over the spatial dimension and a half-axis of 10 min over the temporal dimension. In this case, the initial points of the trajectories RouteT1 and RouteT2 will satisfy the query, since they are at distance 1; that means two circles with radius 0.6 and with centers, respectively, in point (0,0) at 8:00 and in point (1,0) at 8:05 have non-null intersection if the time tolerance is 10 min. The same occurs with the ending points of both trajectories.

As we have seen, *aggregation* operations can also be lifted. For example, Union(RouteT1, RouteT2) will result in a *single* temporal geometry composed of the two lines in Fig. 12.3.

We define four operations for computing the rate of change for points. Operation Speed yields the usual concept of speed of a temporal point at any instant as a temporal real, defined as follows:

$$f'(t) = \lim_{\delta \to 0} \frac{f_{\text{distance}}(f(t + \delta), f(t))}{\delta}.$$

Operation Direction returns the direction of the movement, that is, the angle between the x-axis and the tangent to the trajectory of the moving point. Operation Turn yields the change of direction at any instant, defined as follows:

$$f'(t) = \lim_{\delta \to 0} \frac{f_{\text{direction}}(f(t + \delta), f(t))}{\delta}.$$

Finally, Derivative returns the derivative of the movement as a temporal real. We gave the definition of Derivative in the previous section. Note that we can get the acceleration of a temporal point P by Derivative(Speed(P)). For example:

- Speed(RouteT1) yields a temporal real with values 16.9 at [8:00, 8:10] and 0 at [8:10, 8:25].
- Direction(RouteT1) yields a temporal real with value 45 at [8:00, 8:10].
- Turn(RouteT1) yields a temporal real with value 0 at [8:00, 8:10].
- Derivative(RouteT1) yields a temporal real with value 1 at [8:00, 8:10].

Notice that during the stop of the truck, the direction and turn are undefined.

12.2.2 Temporal Field Types

Temporal fields represent phenomena that vary both on time and space. As shown in Fig. 12.5a, a temporal field can be conceptualized as a function that assigns a value to each point of a spatiotemporal space. Temporal fields are obtained by composing the temporal and field constructors. For example,

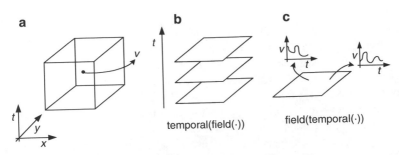

Fig. 12.5 Three possible ways to conceptualize temporal fields

a value of type temporal(field(real)), which defines a function f : instant $\rightarrow$ (point $\rightarrow$ real), can be used to represent temperature, which varies in time and space. Notice that the types temporal(field(real)) (Fig. 12.5b) and field(temporal(real)) (Fig. 12.5c) are equivalent, that is, they associate a real value to a point in a spatiotemporal space.

All operations defined for temporal types apply for temporal fields, although some of them must be redefined, as we will see next. Suppose that Temperature is a temporal field defined over Belgium and covering the period [2010-01-01, 2012-12-31]. DefTime(Temperature) yields the period above, and RangeValues(Temperature) yields the range defined by the minimum and maximum temperature at all instants in the period above and all points located in Belgium. Similarly, AtInstant(Temperature, 2011-01-01 08:00) yields a nontemporal field corresponding to the temperature at that particular instant, while AtPeriod(Temperature, [2012-04-01, 2012-04-03]) returns a temporal field projected over the given interval. Finally, InitialInstant(Temperature) and InitialValue(Temperature) return the first instant for which a temperature is defined, along with the nontemporal field corresponding to that instant.

We have seen that the operations AtMin and AtMax reduce the function defining a temporal value to the instants when its value is minimal or maximal, respectively. These operations have as argument a temporal value and return a temporal value. As temporal fields vary both on space and time, two versions of these operations must be considered, depending on whether the operation is applied instant by instant or point by point. For example, AtMin_t applied to a temporal(field(real)) (see Fig. 12.5b) operates instant by instant and applies the operation AtMin to the field of reals valid at that instant, thus restricting it to the points in space where its value is minimum. On the other hand, AtMin_s applied to a field(temporal(real)) (see Fig. 12.5c) operates point by point and applies the operation AtMin to the temporal real valid at that point, thus restricting it to the instants where its value is minimum.

Similarly, lifted aggregation operations must be renamed to differentiate those that operate on space or on time. For example, Sum_s and Sum_t correspond to the Sum operation lifted in space and in time, respectively.

Thus, given a set of temporal fields t_i representing the number of trucks of type i that are present at a location in space at a particular instant, Sum_s($\{t_i\}$) will result in a temporal field t obtained by applying the operation Sum_t to each point in space, since each point in space defines a temporal real. Similarly, Sum_t($\{t_i\}$) will result in a temporal field t obtained by applying the operation Sum_s to each instant, since each instant defines a field of reals.

Other operations take a temporal field and return either a nontemporal field or a temporal value. This is performed by the global aggregation operations. Suppose we want a nontemporal field giving at each point in space the minimum temperature value at that point ever. For this, we apply the FMin operation that we have seen in Chap. 11. At each point, this operation applies the TMin operation to the temporal real valid at that point yielding a real value. As a result, we obtain a value of type field(real). Analogously, suppose we want a temporal real giving at each instant the minimum temperature value at any point in space. For this, we apply the TMin operation discussed earlier, which at each instant applies the F_Min to the field of reals valid at that instant yielding a real value. As a result, we obtain a value of type temporal(real).

In addition, new spatiotemporal operations have to be defined. For example, operation AtTGeometry restricts the field to a given subset of the spatiotemporal cube defined by a temporal spatial value. In particular, projecting a temporal field to a temporal point will keep only the points in the field that belong to the moving track of the point, that is, a three-dimensional line in the cube. For example, AtTGeometry(Temperature, RouteT1) results in a field defining the temperature during the trajectory of the truck.

12.3 Implementation of Temporal Types in PostGIS

Current DBMSs do not provide support for temporal types. Some prototypes provide this support; the most prominent one is SECONDO, a database system designed at the FernUniversität in Hagen. SECONDO can handle moving objects, that is, continuously changing geometries. In this section, we show a possible implementation in PostgreSQL/PostGIS of the temporal types we presented in Sect. 12.2. Our implementation is based on the approach followed by SECONDO. Nevertheless, the reader should be aware that such temporal types are not yet supported by PostgreSQL/PostGIS. The authors of this book have explored this extension in a prototypical way, based on a preliminary temporal extension of PostgreSQL,[2] which defines a PERIOD data type and its associated operations.

---

[2] Available at http://temporal.projects.pgfoundry.org/

It is worth noting that temporal support has been introduced in the SQL:2011 standard and has been implemented in DB2, Oracle, and Teradata. However, such functionality adds temporality to tables, thus associating a period to each row. However, to cope with the needs of trajectory data warehousing, we need an alternative approach which adds temporality to attributes, thus associating a period to an attribute value.

We have seen that, conceptually, a temporal type is a function from the time domain to a base or spatial type. Thus, for each data type D, where D is a base type (e.g., INTEGER, REAL, or BOOLEAN) or a spatial type (e.g., GEOMETRY or its subtypes), there are associated temporal types T_D(P,Q), where P is either PERIOD or INSTANT and Q is either DATE, TIME, or TIMESTAMP. In other words, P states whether the values are recorded by intervals or by instants, whereas Q represents the granularity at which data are represented in the period or instant P. For example, a type T_INTEGER(PERIOD,DATE) can be used to represent the evolution of the salaries of employees shown in Fig. 12.1. On the other hand, a value of a type T_FLOAT(INSTANT,TIME) can represent, for example, that the temperature was 15.5°C at 8:00 a.m. and was 17°C at 9:00 a.m. In this case, we can use (linear) interpolation functions to compute the value of temperature at any time that is not explicitly recorded. As we have said, the time dimension is assumed to represent **valid time**.

Temporal types are partial functions that may be undefined for certain periods of time. We use the value NULL as undefined value. For example, in Fig. 12.1, the salary of John is NULL between 2012-07-01 and 2012-09-30.

Consider, for example, the following table definition:

```
CREATE TABLE Employees (
        SSN INTEGER PRIMARY KEY,
        FirstName VARCHAR(30),
        LastName VARCHAR(30),
        BirthDate DATE,
        SalaryHist T_INTEGER(PERIOD,DATE) )
```

A tuple can be inserted in this table as follows:

```
INSERT INTO Employee VALUES ( 123456789, 'John', 'Smith', '1980-01-01',
        T_INTEGER( 20 PERIOD('2012-01-01', '2012-07-01'),
                   30 PERIOD('2012-10-01', '2013-01-01') ) )
```

The value of SalaryHist above corresponds to the uppermost value shown in Fig. 12.1. For defining values of temporal types, we use the PERIOD data type defined in the temporal extension of PostgreSQL mentioned above. The periods above define closed-open intervals. Thus, for instance, the value 20 covers the period starting on 2012-01-01 up until the day before 2012-07-01. Note that instead of a continuous function, we use two temporal attributes, FromDate and ToDate, to indicate the validity interval of each tuple. Note also that we use closed-open intervals.

We show next how some of the operations for temporal types defined in Table 12.1 can be expressed extending PostgreSQL/PostGIS. For example, given the above table with the single tuple inserted, the query

```
SELECT DefTime(E.SalaryHist), RangeValues(E.SalaryHist)
FROM   Employee E
```

returns, respectively, the array of periods {PERIOD('2012-01-01', '2012-07-01'), PERIOD('2012-10-01', '2013-01-01')} and the array of integers {20,30}. Here, we use the ARRAY type provided by PostgreSQL. Similarly, the query

```
SELECT AtInstant(E.SalaryHist, '2012-03-15'), AtInstant(E.SalaryHist, '2012-07-15'),
FROM   Employee E
```

will return, respectively, the values 20 and NULL, because the salary of the employee is undefined on 2012-07-15. The following query

```
SELECT AtPeriod(E.SalaryHist, PERIOD('2012-04-01', '2012-11-01'))
FROM   Employee E
```

returns

```
T_INTEGER( 20 PERIOD('2012-04-01', '2012-07-01'),
           30 PERIOD('2012-10-01', '2012-11-01') )
```

where the periods have been projected to the intervals given in the query. Furthermore, the query

```
SELECT AtMin(E.SalaryHist), AtMax(E.SalaryHist)
FROM   Employee E
```

will give as result

```
T_INTEGER(20 PERIOD('2012-01-01', '2012-07-01')
T_INTEGER(30 PERIOD('2012-10-01', '2013-01-01')
```

that is, the minimum and maximum values and the time intervals when they occurred.

We show next the usage of lifted operations. Recall that for these operations, the semantics is such that the nonlifted operation is applied at each instant. For example, assume a second tuple is inserted in table Employee as follows:

```
INSERT INTO Employee VALUES ( T2666, 'Mary', 'Warner', '1980-01-01',
       T_INTEGER( 60 PERIOD('2012-04-01', '2013-03-01') ) )
```

The value of SalaryHist in the tuple above corresponds to the lowermost value shown in Fig. 12.1. Then, the query

```
SELECT E1.SalaryHist < E2.SalaryHist
FROM   Employee E1, Employee E2
WHERE  E1.FirstName = 'John' and E2.FirstName = 'Mary'
```

results in the value

T_BOOLEAN('True' PERIOD('2012-04-01', '2012-07-01')
                    'True' PERIOD('2012-10-01', '2013-01-01'))

Notice that the comparison is performed only on the time instants that are shared by the two temporal values. Similarly, the query

SELECT AVG(E.SalaryHist)
FROM   Employee E

will result in the value

T_REAL(20 PERIOD('2012-01-01', '2013-04-01')
              40 PERIOD('2012-04-01', '2012-10-01')
              60 PERIOD('2012-10-01', '2012-10-01')
              45 PERIOD('2012-10-01', '2013-01-01')
              60 PERIOD('2013-01-01', '2013-04-01'))

A graphical representation of this result was shown in Fig. 12.2.

In order to show the operations for spatial types, we will use the following table, which keeps track of the delivery routes followed by trucks:

CREATE TABLE Delivery (
              TruckId CHAR(6) PRIMARY KEY,
              DeliveryDate DATE,
              Route T_POINT(INSTANT,TIMESTAMP))

We insert now two tuples in this table, containing information of two deliveries performed by two trucks T1 and T2 on the same day, January 10, 2012:

INSERT INTO Delivery VALUES ('T1', '2012-01-10',
              T_POINT(Point(0 0) '08:00', Point(2 2) '08:10', Point(2 2) '08:25'))
INSERT INTO Delivery VALUES ('T2', '2012-01-10',
              T_POINT(Point(1 0) '08:05', Point(3 1) '08:15', Point(3 2) '08:20'))

A graphical representation of the trajectories of the two trucks was shown in Fig. 12.3. As we are working with *continuous trajectories*, we assume linear interpolation between any two consecutive points and a constant speed between pairs of points.

We show next examples of lifted spatial operations. The following query computes the distance of the two trucks at every instant:

SELECT ST_Distance(D1.Route, D2.Route)
FROM   Delivery D1, Delivery D2
WHERE D1.TruckId = T1 AND D2.TruckId = T2

This query returns

T_REAL(1 '08:05', 1.5 '08:10', 1.41 '08:25', 1 '08:20')

whose graphical representation was given in Fig. 12.4. Similarly, the following query computes a buffer of 0.6 km and 10 min around the trajectories:

```
SELECT ST_Buffer(Route, 0.6, 0:10)
FROM    Delivery
```

The result is composed of spatiotemporal cylindroids around the trajectories of the trucks. As we have seen in Sect. 12.2, we can use this operation combined with the lifted intersection topological operation for testing whether the routes of the two trucks intersect, as follows:

```
SELECT ST_Intersects(ST_Buffer(D1.Route, 0.6, 0:10),
        ST_Buffer(D2.Route, 0.6, 0:10))
FROM    Delivery D1, Delivery D2
WHERE  D1.TruckId = T1 AND D2.TruckId = T2
```

Finally, the following query computes the union of two moving points:

```
SELECT ST_Union(D1.Route, D2.Route)
FROM    Delivery D1, Delivery D2
WHERE  D1.TruckId = T1 AND D2.TruckId = T2
```

The result of the query is given next:

```
T_MULTIPOINT(
    ( Point(0 0) '08:00', Point(2 2) '08:10', Point(2 2) '08:25' )
    ( Point(1 0) '08:05', Point(3 1) '08:15', Point(3 2) '08:20' ) )
```

For implementing temporal fields, we use temporal rasters defined by the type T_RASTER(P,Q), where P and Q are defined as above. We give next an example that combines geometries and rasters. For this, we create a table LandPlot describing parcels of land as follows:

```
CREATE TABLE LandPlot (
        Id INT PRIMARY KEY,
        Geom GEOMETRY(POLYGON),
        SoilType RASTER,
        Temp T_RASTER(INSTANT,DATE) )
```

Here, the attribute Geom contains the geometry of the land plot, SoilType contains a raster identifying the kinds of soil in the land plot, and Temp contains a temporal raster reporting the temperatures in the land plot on a daily basis. The query

```
SELECT L.Id, AtPeriod(L.Temp, PERIOD('2012-04-01', '2012-04-04'))
FROM    LandPlot L
```

returns for each land plot a temporal raster with the temperature for each of the 3 days in the interval. Analogously, the following query returns for each land plot the first day at which the temperature is reported and the nontemporal raster of that day:

```
SELECT L.Id, InitialInstant(L.Temp), InitialValue(L.Temp)
FROM    LandPlot L
```

We can see that the operations are applied to temporal fields in the same way as they are applied to other temporal data types. The following query computes for each land plot a nontemporal raster reporting the average temperature during March 2012 at each point in the land plot:

```
SELECT L.Id, AVG_S(AtPeriod(L.Temp, PERIOD('2012-03-01', '2012-04-01')),
FROM   LandPlot L
```

Here, the temperature field is restricted to March 2012 with function AtPeriod. Then, the AVG_S is applied to the resulting temporal raster, which obtains at each point in space the average temperature over the month.

Finally, the following query selects land plots with an average temperature greater than 10°C in March 2012:

```
SELECT L.Id
FROM   LandPlot L
WHERE Favg(Avg_S(AtPeriod(T.Temp, PERIOD('2012-03-01', '2012-04-01')))) > 10
```

In the above query, the temperature field, restricted to March 2012 with the AtPeriod operation, is aggregated with the Avg_S operation resulting in a nontemporal field reporting the average temperature over the month at each point. Then, the field aggregation operation FAvg is applied to obtain the average as a real value, which is then compared to 10.

12.4   The Northwind Trajectory Data Warehouse

We are now ready to study how a conventional data warehouse (or a spatial data warehouse) can be extended with temporal types in order to support the analysis of trajectory data. We will use the Northwind case study in order to introduce the main concepts. Let us state the problem.

The Northwind company wants to build a trajectory data warehouse that keeps track of the deliveries of goods to their customers in order to optimize the shipping costs. Spatial data in the warehouse include the road network, the delivery locations, and the geographical information related to these locations (city, state, country, and area). Nonspatial data include the characteristics of the trucks performing the trajectories. In addition, we have the trajectories followed by the trucks, that means, moving object data. Figure 12.6 shows the conceptual schema depicting the above scenario using the MultiDim model, which we introduced in Chap. 4 and extended to support spatial data in Chap. 11 (although any other conceptual model could be used instead). In order to support spatiotemporal data, we extended the MultiDim model with spatial types and temporal types.

We would like to analyze the deliveries by trucks, days, roads, and delivery locations. Therefore, we need to split the trajectories into **segments** such that each segment is related to a single truck, day, road, start location, and

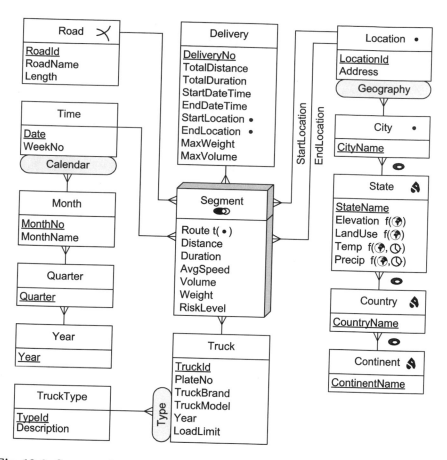

Fig. 12.6 Conceptual schema of the Northwind trajectory data warehouse

end location. Since we need to keep track of all segments belonging to a single delivery, we define an additional dimension Delivery that groups the data belonging to each trajectory as a whole.

As shown in the figure, there is a fact, Segment, which is related to five dimensions: Truck, Time, Road, Delivery, and Location. The fact is related to the Location dimension through two roles: StartLocation and EndLocation. Dimensions are composed of levels and hierarchies. For example, the Road dimension has only one level, and the Location dimension is composed of five levels, with a one-to-many parent-child relationship defined between each couple of levels. Levels have attributes that describe their instances or members. For example, level Road has attributes RoadId, RoadName, and Length. If a level or an attribute is spatial, it has an associated geometry (e.g., point, line, or region) which is indicated by a pictogram, as studied in the previous chapter. In our example, dimensions Road and Location are spatial, and a geometry is associated with each level in both dimensions. On the other hand, StartLocation and EndLocation are spatial attributes of the Delivery dimension, and their geometry is of type point.

There are seven measures attached to the fact Segment: Route, Distance, Duration, AvgSpeed, Volume, Weight, and RiskLevel. The first one, Route, keeps the movement track of the segment. It is a **spatiotemporal measure** of type temporal point, as indicated by the symbol 't(•)'. The other measures are numerical, where Distance, Duration, and AvgSpeed are computed from Route.

Topological constraints are represented using pictograms in facts and in parent-child relationships. For example, the topological constraint in the fact Segment indicates that whenever a road and a location are related in an instance of the relationship, they must overlap. Similarly, the topological constraint in the hierarchy of dimension Location indicates that a location is included in its parent City and similarly for the other parent-child relationships in the hierarchy.

As stated before, the movement tracks within segments are kept in the measure Route, while data describing the whole trajectories are kept in dimension Delivery. Alternatively, we could have represented segments or even whole deliveries in a dimension. Our model is flexible enough to represent various situations, where trajectories can be aggregated along spatial and alphanumeric dimensions or facts can be aggregated over a trajectory dimension. The choice among these representations depends on the queries to be addressed. Indeed, the complexity of the queries and their execution time will depend on how much the information requested is precomputed in measures, as data warehouses are optimized for aggregating measures along dimensions. In other words, although it is possible to aggregate data from dimensions, queries will be more elaborated to write and less efficient to execute.

Finally, the schema in Fig. 12.6 includes several continuous fields. As explained in Chap. 11, *nontemporal* fields are identified by the 'f(◉)' pictogram, while *temporal* ones are identified by the 'f(◉,⊙)' pictogram. There are four field attributes in the State level as follows. Elevation and LandUse are nontemporal fields. The former could be used, for example, to analyze the correlation between speed of trajectories and elevation (or slope), and the latter to select trajectories starting in a residential area and finishing on an industrial area. Further, there are two temporal fields Temp (temperature) and Precip (precipitation). In addition, numerical measures can be calculated from field data. For example, measure RiskLevel, which represents knowledge from domain experts about the relative risk of the segments, can be computed from the measure Route and the four fields. For example, a segment with high speed in descending slopes, in residential areas, with frozen temperatures, or with high precipitation will have high risk level. Fields can also be included as measures in facts, although this is beyond the scope of this chapter.

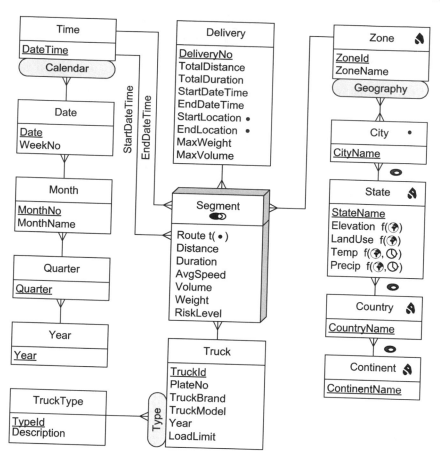

Fig. 12.7 An alternative segmentation of trajectories with respect to delivery zones

The data warehouse of Fig. 12.6 **segments trajectories** with respect to days, roads, trucks, start locations, and end locations. An alternative schema, shown in Fig. 12.7, segments trajectories with respect to the delivery zones in which they occur. Notice that, as stated by the many-to-many relationship between zones and cities, a delivery zone can span several cities, and a city can be split in several delivery zones. Notice also that the time granularity in Figs. 12.6 and 12.7 differs. In the former case, the granularity is day, although we keep the movement track in the Route measure with a timestamp granularity. In the latter case, we relate each segment with its initial and final timestamps. The choice among the two alternative data warehouse schemas depends on application requirements and the typical OLAP queries to be addressed.

When trajectories are used as measures, the problem of aggregation arises. In the examples of Figs. 12.6 and 12.7, we kept the movement track of the trajectory segments in a temporal point. Thus, we can aggregate such segments along the different dimensions. Another use of trajectory aggregation identifies "similar" trajectories and merges them in a class. This aggregation may come together with an aggregate function, which may be the COUNT function in the simplest case, although more complex ones may be used. Thus, we can ask queries like "Total number of trajectories by class," or "List all the trajectories similar to the one followed by truck T1 on November 25, 2012." The main problem consists in adopting an appropriate notion of **trajectory similarity**, through the definition of a similarity measure, for instance, a distance function. The simplest approach to define similarity between two trajectories is viewing them as vectors and using the Euclidean distance as similarity measure. The problem of this technique is that it cannot be easily applied to trajectories having different length or sampling rate, and it is not effective in the presence of noise in the data. A typical way of aggregating trajectories is clustering them together, considering different distance functions or other characteristics (e.g., same starting point, same ending point, etc.). Discovering trajectories with the same pattern is another way of aggregating trajectories.

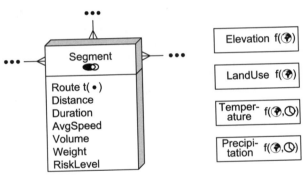

Fig. 12.8 Extending the Northwind trajectory data warehouse with global fields

In Fig. 12.6, we associated the field types to the level State. This allows a more efficient manipulation of fields when the focus of analysis is at the state level. However, as we will see later, for some queries it is necessary to keep the overall fields covering all the space of interest, without partitioning. Figure 12.8 extends our example with such *global* fields. Thus, a global temporal field such as Temperature can be seen as a spatiotemporal cube that associates a real value to any given point in space and time. In this case, such fields are related to facts or dimensions through spatial or spatiotemporal operations.

12.5   Querying the Northwind Trajectory Data Warehouse in SQL

In order to address queries to the Northwind trajectory data warehouse, we first translate the conceptual schema in Fig. 12.6 into a snowflake schema, as shown in Fig. 12.9. To express our queries, we use the temporal types and their associated operations as defined in Sect. 12.3.

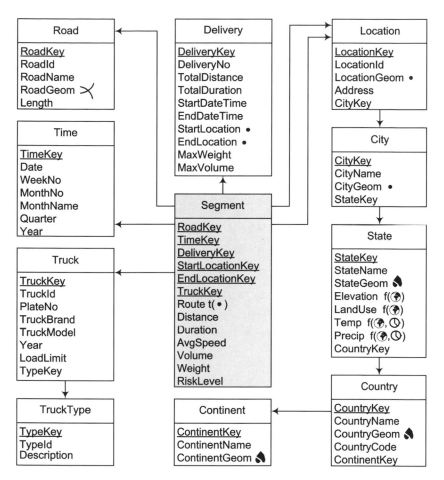

Fig. 12.9 Relational representation of the Northwind trajectory data warehouse in Fig. 12.6

We start with a conventional OLAP query.

Query 12.1. Total number of segments, by road, covered by Volvo trucks in February 2012.

```
SELECT    R.RoadKey, COUNT(*)
FROM      Segment S, Road R, Time T, Truck U
WHERE     S.RoadKey = R.RoadKey AND S.TimeKey = T.TimeKey AND
          S.TruckKey = U.TruckKey AND U.TruckBrand = 'Volvo' AND
          T.Date >= '2012-02-01' AND T.Date < '2012-03-01'
GROUP BY RoadKey
```

This query addresses the fact table **Segment** and some of its associated dimensions. The query does not involve temporal data types, not even geometric characteristics of spatial dimensions. The query can be used to identify the segments most frequently used by Northwind trucks.

We give next an example of an OLAP query involving the **Delivery** dimension and two possible solutions for it.

Query 12.2. Average duration of deliveries that have one segment which started in the city of Brussels in the last quarter of 2012.

```
SELECT AVG(D.TotalDuration)
FROM   Delivery D
WHERE EXISTS (
       SELECT *
       FROM   Segment S, StartLocation L, City C, Time T
       WHERE S.DeliveryKey = D.DeliveryKey AND
             S.StartLocationKey = L.LocationKey AND
             L.CityKey = C.CityKey AND C.CityName = 'Brussels' AND
             S.TimeKey = T.TimeKey AND T.Quarter = 'Q4 2012'
```

Here, for each instance of the **Delivery** dimension, the inner query verifies that at least one segment of the delivery started in the city of Brussels and occurred on the last quarter of 2012. Notice that the total duration of the deliveries is precomputed in the **Delivery** dimension and therefore it is possible to apply the function average to them. If the duration of the whole deliveries must be calculated from the measure **Duration** of the fact table, then the query would be written as follows:

```
WITH DeliveryTotal AS (
       SELECT    D.DeliveryKey, SUM(Duration) AS TotalDuration
       FROM      Delivery D, Segment S
       WHERE     D.DeliveryKey = S.DeliveryKey
       GROUP BY D.DeliveryKey )
SELECT AVG(TotalDuration)
FROM   DeliveryTotal D
WHERE EXISTS (
       SELECT *
       FROM   Segment S, StartLocation L, City C, Time T
       WHERE S.DeliveryKey = D.DeliveryKey AND
             S.StartLocationKey = L.LocationKey AND
             L.CityKey = C.CityKey AND C.CityName = 'Brussels' AND
             S.TimeKey = T.TimeKey AND T.Quarter = 'Q4 2012'
```

In the version above, a temporary table **DeliveryTotal** computes the total duration of a delivery by adding the duration of all its segments. Then, the average is computed as in the previous query. Note that this solution would be used if the information of the deliveries is not precomputed in the Delivery dimension table, that is, if the attribute TotalDuration is not present in such table.

We consider now the spatial data types and their associated operations, which we studied in Chap. 11. These kinds of queries are denoted SOLAP queries. For example, the predicate ST_Intersects can be used to test whether two geometries intersect.

Query 12.3. Number of deliveries in the last quarter of 2012, for each road that intersects Brussels.

```
SELECT    RoadKey, COUNT(DISTINCT DeliveryKey) AS NoDeliveries
FROM      Road R, Delivery D
WHERE     EXISTS (
          SELECT *
          FROM   City C
          WHERE  C.CityName = 'Brussels' AND
                 ST_Intersects(R.RoadGeom,C.CityGeom) ) AND
          EXISTS (
          SELECT *
          FROM   Segment S, Time T
          WHERE  S.RoadKey = R.RoadKey AND
                 S.DeliveryKey = D.DeliveryKey AND
                 S.TimeKey = T.TimeKey AND T.Quarter = 'Q4 2012' )
GROUP BY RoadKey
```

The first inner query selects the roads that intersect the city of Brussels using the ST_Intersects predicate, which determines if a pair of geometries intersect. The second inner query selects the deliveries that have a segment that occurred on the road in the last quarter of 2012. Then, the outer query groups for each road all the selected deliveries and then counts the number of distinct ones.

Spatiotemporal OLAP accounts for the case when the spatial objects evolve over time, that is, they involve temporal spatial types as introduced above. As an example, the following query includes the Route measure, that is, the movement track of a segment.

Query 12.4. For each road, give the geometry of the segments of the road on which at least one delivery passed on May 1, 2012.

```
WITH SegmentTrajs AS (
         SELECT S.SegmentKey, Trajectory(S.Route) AS Trajectory
         FROM   Segment S )
SELECT    R.RoadKey, ST_Union(S.Trajectory)
FROM      Road R, SegmentTraj S, Time T
WHERE     R.RoadKey = R.RoadKey AND S.TimeKey = T.TimeKey AND
          T.Date = '2012-05-01' )
GROUP BY R.RoadKey
```

In the definition of the temporary table SegmentTrajs, we suppose that there is an operation Trajectory (see Table 12.1) that takes as argument a temporal point and returns the line containing all the points traversed by the former. Then, the query performs a spatial union on all the geometries thus obtained. Notice that a function ST_Union that acts as an aggregate function (e.g., as COUNT) is not defined by the OGC, but it is available in PostGIS.

We next present another example of a spatiotemporal OLAP query.

Query 12.5. Number of deliveries that started in Brussels on May 1, 2012.

```
SELECT  COUNT(D.DeliveryKey)
FROM    Delivery D, City C
WHERE   C.CityName = 'Brussels' AND
        CONVERT(DATE, D.StartDateTime) = '2012-05-01' AND
        ST_Intersects(D.StartLocation,C.CityGeom)
```

Notice that since D.StartDateTime returns a timestamp, the CONVERT function is applied for obtaining the corresponding day. The reader could be asking herself/himself that this is actually not a spatiotemporal query. This is, however, because the query takes advantage of the fact that the start time and the start location of trajectories are precomputed in the Delivery dimension. If this were not the case, the query would read

```
WITH DeliveryFull AS (
        SELECT D. DeliveryKey, InitialValue(S.Route) AS StartLocation,
               InitialInstant(S.Route) AS StartDateTime
        FROM   Delivery D, Segment S
        WHERE  D.DeliveryKey = S.DeliveryKey AND NOT EXISTS (
               SELECT *
               FROM   Segment S1
               S1.DeliveryKey = D.DeliveryKey AND
               InitialInstant(S1.Route) < InitialInstant(S.Route) ) )
SELECT COUNT(D.DeliveryKey)
FROM   DeliveryFull D, City C
WHERE  C.CityName = 'Brussels' AND
       CONVERT(DATE, D.StartDateTime) = '2012-05-01' AND
       ST_Intersects(D.StartLocation,C.CityGeom)
```

In the definition of the temporary table DeliveryFull, the functions InitialValue and InitialValue return, respectively, the starting point and the starting instant of the moving point geometry S.Route. The inner query of the temporary table definition ensures that segment S is the first segment of a delivery by verifying that its start time is the smallest among all those of the segments composing the delivery. This is done with the help of function InitialInstant. Finally, the query counts the deliveries that started in the city of Brussels on May 1, 2012. Since attribute StartDateTime is a timestamp, the CONVERT function is applied for obtaining the corresponding day.

Our next example query involves the LandUse field.

Query 12.6. Average duration of the deliveries that started in a residential area and ended in an industrial area on February 1, 2012.

```
SELECT  D.TotalDuration
FROM    Delivery D, Location L1, Location L2, City C1, City C2,
        State S1, State S2
WHERE   CONVERT(DATE,D.StartDateTime) = '2012-02-01' AND
        CONVERT(DATE,D.EndDateTime) = '2012-02-01' AND
        D.StartLocation = L1.LocationGeom AND
        D.EndLocation = L2.LocationGeom AND
        L1.CityKey = C1.CityKey AND L2.CityKey = C2.CityKey AND
        C1.StateKey = S1.StateKey AND C2.StateKey = S2.StateKey AND
        ST_Intersects(D.StartLocation,At(S1.LandUse,'Residential')) AND
        ST_Intersects(D.EndLocation,At(S2.LandUse,'Industrial'))
```

Since it is supposed that attributes StartDateTime and EndDateTime are of type timestamp, the function CONVERT is used for obtaining the corresponding dates. Then, the query selects the members L1 and L2 of the Location level corresponding to the start and end locations of the delivery, and the subsequent joins obtain the correspond states. Further, the function At (see Table 12.1) projects the land use fields of the corresponding states to the values of type residential or industrial. Finally, the function ST_Intersects ensures that the start and end locations of the delivery are included in the filtered rasters. Notice that, as is the case in PostGIS, the ST_Intersects predicate can compute not only if two geometries intersect but also if a geometry and a raster intersect.

The above query involved the (partitioned) land use field in level State. We could have used, instead, the global LandUse field in Fig. 12.8. In this case, the query would be written as follows:

```
SELECT  D.TotalDuration
FROM    Delivery D, LandUse L
WHERE   CONVERT(DATE,D.StartDateTime) = '2012-02-01' AND
        CONVERT(DATE,D.EndDateTime) = '2012-02-01' AND
        ST_Intersects(D.StartLocation,At(L,'Residential')) AND
        ST_Intersects(D.EndLocation,At(L,'Industrial'))
```

In this case, we can see that it is more efficient to use the global field rather than the partitioned field. However, there are cases that working the other way round is more efficient.

Note that the query above does not involve temporal data since it does not mention a temporal geometry such as measure Route nor a temporal field such as Temperature. The next query involves both temporal attributes.

Query 12.7. Average speed and maximum temperature during the segment, for trajectory segments that occurred on February 1, 2012.

```
SELECT  S.SegmentKey, S.AvgSpeed, TMax(AtMGeometry(E,S.Route))
FROM    Segment S, Time T, Temperature E
WHERE   S.TimeKey = T.TimeKey AND T.Date = '2012-02-01'
```

In the query above, we use the global **Temperature** field shown in Fig. 12.8. Otherwise, we would need to make the union of the fields in attribute **Temp** of level **State** for all states traversed by the truck. Function **AtMGeometry** projects the temporal field to the movement track of the segment, resulting in a temporal real. In other words, the function computes the position of the trajectory segment at each time instant, and then from the field valid at that instant, it obtains the temperature. Finally, function **TMax** obtains the maximum temperature value during the segment.

Our next example query involves field aggregation.

Query 12.8. Average temperature by month and by state.

Here, we need an auxiliary function that, given a month and a year, returns the period composed of all the days of the month. The function, denoted **PeriodMonth**, is defined as follows:

```
CREATE OR REPLACE FUNCTION PeriodMonth(Month int, Year int)
RETURNS PERIOD AS $PeriodMonth$
    DECLARE
        PerStart CHAR(10);
        PerEnd CHAR(10);
    BEGIN
        PerStart = CAST($2 as CHAR(4)) || '-' || CAST($1 as CHAR(2)) || '-01';
        IF $1 < 12 THEN
            PerEnd = CAST($2 as CHAR(4)) || '-' || CAST($1+1 as CHAR(2)) || '-01';
        ELSE
            PerEnd = CAST($2+1 as CHAR(4)) || '-01-01'
        END IF;
        RETURN PERIOD(PerStart,PerEnd);
    END;
$PeriodMonth$ LANGUAGE plpgsql;
```

Then, the query is as follows:

```
WITH Month AS (
        SELECT DISTINCT MonthNo, Year
        FROM    Time T )
SELECT S.StateName, M.MonthNo, M.Year,
        FAvg(Avg_S(AtPeriod(S.Temp,PeriodMonth(M.MonthNo, M.Year))))
FROM    State S, Month M
```

Here, it is supposed that the period of time covered by the time dimension is the same as the one in which the temperature temporal field is defined. In the query, a temporary table **Month** is defined in the **WITH** clause containing all months of the **Time** dimension. The main query starts by combining each state with each month. Then, the temperature field of the state is projected to the corresponding month with function **AtPeriod**. Function **Avg_S** is then used to compute the average of the temperature values during the month at each point in the state, resulting in a nontemporal field. Finally, function **FAvg** obtains the average temperature over the nontemporal field, which is a real.

The next query combines a field and a trajectory.

Query 12.9. Deliveries that have driven along more than 50 km of roads at more than 1,000 m of altitude.

```
SELECT  D.DeliveryNumber
FROM    Delivery D
WHERE ( SELECT  SUM(ST_Length(DefSpace(AtGeometry(
                  At(T.Elevation,Range(1000,6000)), Trajectory(S.Route)))))
        FROM    Segment S, State T
        WHERE   S.DeliveryKey = D.DeliveryKey AND
                ST_Intersects(T.StateGeom,Trajectory(S.Route)) ) > 50
```

For each delivery, the inner query collects the composing segments and the states traversed during the segment. This is done by verifying in the WHERE clause that the geometry of the state and the trajectory of the route intersect. Then, for each couple of segment and state, the elevation field of the state is projected to the range of values between 1,000 and 6,000 (it is supposed that the latter is the maximal value) with function At and then projected to the trajectory of the route with function AtGeometry. The part of the route at more than 1,000 m is obtained by function DefSpace, and then the length of this route is computed. The SUM aggregation operation is then used to compute the sum of the lengths of all the obtained routes and finally the outer query verifies that this sum is greater than 50.

The two next queries combine a temporal field and a trajectory.

Query 12.10. Deliveries that have driven along more 50 km on rainy conditions during July 2013 in Belgium.

```
SELECT  D.DeliveryNumber
FROM    Delivery D
WHERE ( SELECT  SUM(ST_Length(DefSpace(AtGeometry(
                  AtPeriod(At(T.Precip,Range(1,100)),
                  PERIOD('2013-07-01','2013-08-01')), Trajectory(S.Route)))))
        FROM    Segment S, State T, Country C
        WHERE   S.DeliveryKey = D.DeliveryKey AND
                T.CountryKey = C.CountryKey AND
                C.CountryName = 'Belgium'
                ST_Intersects(T.StateGeom,Trajectory(S.Route)) ) > 50
```

In the above query, it is supposed that rainy conditions mean between 1 mm (moderate rain) and 100 mm (extreme rain) per hour. For each delivery, the inner query collects the composing segments and the states in Belgium traversed during the segment. Then, for each couple of segment and state, the precipitation field of the state is projected to the range of values between 1 and 100 with function At, then projected to the month of July 2013 with function AtPeriod, and then projected to the trajectory of the route with function AtGeometry. The part of the route satisfying the conditions is obtained by function DefSpace, and then the length of this route is computed. The SUM operation is then used to add up the lengths of all the obtained routes, and finally the outer query verifies that this sum is greater than 50.

Query 12.11. For each delivery, give the total time when it has driven on rainy conditions at more than 70 km/h.

SELECT   D.DeliveryNumber, SUM(Duration(DefTime(AtPeriod(
          AtMGeometry(At(T.Precip,Range(1,100),S.Route)),
          DefTime(At(Speed(S.Route),Range(70,150))))))))
FROM   Delivery D, Segment S, State T
WHERE   S.DeliveryKey = D.DeliveryKey AND
          ST_Intersects(T.StateGeom,Trajectory(S.Route))
GROUP BY D.DeliveryNumber

For each delivery, the composing segments and the states traversed during the segment are collected. Then, for each couple of segment and state, the precipitation field of the state is projected to the range of values between 1 and 100 with function At, then projected to the moving point with function AtMGeometry, and then projected to the period of time in which the speed of the trajectory was between 70 and 150 km/h with function AtPeriod. The function DefTime computes the time period during which the route satisfies the conditions and then the duration of this period is computed. Finally, the SUM operation is used to add up the durations of all the obtained periods.

12.6 Summary

We have discussed data warehousing techniques that applied to trajectory data help to improve the decision-making process. For this, we first defined temporal types, which capture the variation of a value across time. Applying temporal types to spatial data leads to the notion of temporal spatial types, which provide a conceptual view of trajectories. Finally, applying temporal types to field data types produces spatiotemporal field data types, which model temporal continuous fields. At the logical level, we studied how these conceptual data types can be implemented in PostGIS. We presented a concrete case extending the Northwind data warehouse with trajectory data and show how to query this data warehouse using PostGIS extended with temporal types of different kinds.

12.7 Bibliographic Notes

An overall perspective of the current state of the art in trajectory management can be found in the books [173,240]. A state of the art in spatiotemporal data warehousing, OLAP, and mining can be found in [70]. This chapter is based on previous research work on spatiotemporal data warehousing and continuous fields performed by the authors [212,213].

The data type system for temporal types follows the approach of [75]. The system SECONDO developed by Güting et al. is described in [233]. An SQL extension for spatiotemporal data is proposed in [223]. The view of continuous fields as cubes was introduced in [69]. The GeoPKDD trajectory data warehouse, its associated ETL process, and the double-counting problem during aggregation are studied in [151]. A good discussion on trajectory data warehouses is presented in [129, 161]. Analysis tools for trajectory data warehouses can be found in [167]. A survey on spatiotemporal aggregation is given in [222], while a state-of-the-art analysis on trajectory aggregation is provided in [7].

12.8 Review Questions

12.1 What are moving objects? How are they different from spatial objects?

12.2 Give examples of different types of moving objects, and for each of these types, illustrate a scenario in which the analysis of them is important.

12.3 What is a trajectory?

12.4 Discuss different criteria that can be used to segment movement. How do analysis requirements impact on this segmentation?

12.5 What is the difference between continuous and discrete trajectories?

12.6 Define the terms trajectory databases and trajectory data warehouses. Mention the main differences between the two concepts.

12.7 What are temporal types? How are they constructed?

12.8 Define valid time and transaction time.

12.9 Give an example of a temporal base type, a temporal spatial type, and a temporal field type.

12.10 Give examples of operations associated with each of the temporal types in the previous question.

12.11 Explain why traditional operations must be lifted for temporal types. Illustrate this with examples.

12.12 Give a hint about how temporal types can be implemented in a platform such as PostGIS. How does this implementation differ from the abstract definition of temporal types?

12.13 Discuss how temporal types can be added to a multidimensional schema.

12.14 Discuss the implications of including trajectories as dimensions or measures in a data warehouse.

12.15 What does the term similarity of trajectories mean? State why this concept is important in data warehouse context.

12.16 Comment on two different ways to include field types in a multidimensional schema. Give examples of queries that take advantage of one representation over the other.

12.9   Exercises

12.1 Consider the train company application described in Ex. 3.2 and whose
conceptual multidimensional schema was obtained in Ex. 4.3. Add
spatiotemporal data to this schema to transform it into a trajectory
data warehouse. You must analyze the dimensions, facts, and measures,
and define which of them can be extended with spatiotemporal features.

12.2 Transform the conceptual schema obtained as solution for Ex. 12.1
into a relational one. This schema should correspond to the relational
schema without spatiotemporal features obtained in Ex. 5.3.

12.3 Write in SQL the following queries on the relational schema obtained
in Ex. 12.2:

   (a) Give the trip number, origin, and destination of trips that contain
       segments with a duration of more than 3 h and whose length is
       shorter than 200 km.
   (b) Give the trip number, origin, and destination of trips that contain
       at least two segments served by trains from different constructors.
   (c) Give the trip number of trips that cross at least three cities in less
       than 2 h.
   (d) Give the total number of trips that cross at least two country
       borders in less than 4 h.
   (e) Give the average speed by train constructor. This should be
       computed taking the sum of the durations and lengths of all
       segments with the same constructor and obtaining the average. The
       result must be ordered by average speed.
   (f) For each possible number of total segments, give the number of
       trips in each group and the average length, ordered by number of
       segments. The result should look like (5, 50, 85; 4, 30, 75; ...),
       meaning that there are 50 trips with 5 segments with an average
       length of 85 km, 30 trips with 4 segments of average length of 75 km,
       and so on.
   (g) Give the trip number and origin and destination stations for trips
       such that at least one segment of the trip runs for at least 100 km
       within Germany.

12.4 Consider an application that monitors air quality measuring the values
of a set of pollutants (such as particulate matter or sulfur dioxide) at a
fixed number of stations. Measures are collected hourly or daily and are
expressed both in traditional units (like micrograms per cubic meter,
or parts per million) or using an air quality index, which in Europe has
5 levels using a scale from 0 (very low) to greater than 100 (very high).
Stations are typically located alongside roads and obviously located in
districts. Finally, there is also field data corresponding to land use and
temperature.

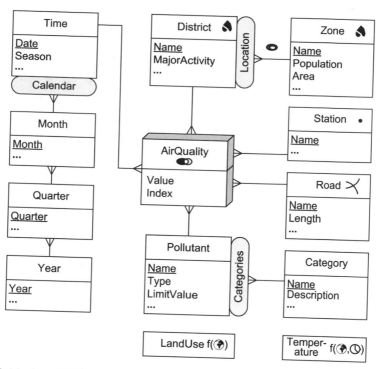

Fig. 12.10 A multidimensional schema for analyzing air quality

The conceptual multidimensional schema of this application is given in Fig. 12.10. Translate the schema into a logical schema.

12.5 Write in SQL the following queries on the relational schema obtained in Ex. 12.4:

(a) For pollutants belonging to the organic category, give the maximum value by station and month.

(b) For stations located on the Autostrada del Sole, give the average values of lead registered in the last quarter of 2010.

(c) For stations located at a distance of at most 1 km of the Autostrada del Sole, give the average values of lead registered in the last quarter of 2010.

(d) For zones with at least 20% of industrial land use, give the average value for carbon monoxide on February 1, 2012.

(e) Roads located in industrial zones, such that the average temperature in 2012 along the road was higher than 20°C.

(f) Maximum temperatures by land use type in 2012.

(g) Maximum temperatures in 2012 in stations where organic pollutants were over the limit more than five times.

12.6 Consider the alternative Northwind trajectory data warehouse given
in Fig. 12.7, which is obtained by partitioning the deliveries into zones
instead of into roads. Translate the conceptual schema into a logical
one.

12.7 Write in SQL the following queries on the relational schema obtained
in Ex. 12.6:

(a) For each truck, give the total number of hours serviced per country.
(b) For each delivery and each zone, give the total time driven in the
zone and the average and maximum speed within the zone.
(c) List the deliveries that started and ended in the same zone and
have passed through a zone different from the former.
(d) Give the deliveries, together with their length, for deliveries that
started in a zone that belongs to two different states and ended in
a zone that belongs to exactly one state.
(e) Total number of deliveries that started in a zone that contains the
city of Brussels, drove for at least 2 h within France, and ended in
a zone belonging to Antwerp.
(f) For each delivery and each zone, give the total number of hours
that the delivery drove within the zone in rainy conditions and at
more than 20°C.
(g) Trucks that drove in March 2012 in zones such that more than 50%
of their area is at more than 1,000 m above sea level.

Chapter 13
New Data Warehouse Technologies

Big data refers to large collections of data that may be unstructured or may grow so large and at such a high pace that it is difficult to manage them with standard database systems or analysis tools. Examples of big data include web logs, radio-frequency identification tags, sensor networks, and social networks, among other ones. It has been reported as of the time of writing this book that 7 and 10 terabytes of data are added and processed, respectively, by Twitter and Facebook every day. Approximately 80% of these data are unstructured, and 90% of them have been created in the last 2 years. Management and analysis of these massive amounts of data demand new solutions that go beyond the traditional processes or software tools. All of these have great implications on the way data warehousing practice is going to be performed in the future. For instance, big data analytics requires in many cases the data latency (the time elapsed between the moment some data are collected and the action based on such data is taken) to be dramatically reduced. Thus, near real-time data management techniques must be developed. Also, external data sources like the semantic web may need to be queried.

Technology has started to give answers to the challenges introduced by big data: massive parallel processing, column-store databas systems, and in-memory database systems (IMDBSs) are some of these answers that we will discuss in this chapter. In Sect. 13.1, we present the MapReduce framework and its most popular implementation, Apache Hadoop. In Sect. 13.2, we study Hive and Pig Latin, two high-level languages that make it easier to write the MapReduce code. We then study two architectures increasingly used in data warehousing: column-store database systems (Sect. 13.3) and IMDBSs (Sect. 13.4). To give a complete picture, in Sect. 13.5 we briefly describe several database systems that exploit the architectures above. We conclude the chapter with a study of real-time data warehousing (Sect. 13.6) and the extraction, loading, and transformation paradigm (ELT), which is challenging the traditional ETL process (Sect. 13.7). These new data

A. Vaisman and E. Zimányi, *Data Warehouse Systems*, Data-Centric Systems and Applications, DOI 10.1007/978-3-642-54655-6_13, © Springer-Verlag Berlin Heidelberg 2014

warehousing paradigms are built on the technologies that we study in the first part of the chapter.

13.1   MapReduce and Hadoop

MapReduce is a processing framework originally developed by Google to perform web search on a very large number of commodity machines. MapReduce can be implemented in many languages over many data formats. It works on the concept of divide and conquer, breaking a task into smaller chunks and processing them in parallel over a collection of identical machines (a cluster). Data in each processor are typically stored in the file system, although data in database management systems (DBMSs) are supported by several extensions, like HadoopDB. A MapReduce program consists of two phases, namely, Map and Reduce, which run in parallel in clustered commodity servers as we will see below.

Among the many MapReduce implementations, the most popular one is **Hadoop**, an open-source framework written in Java. It has the capability to handle structured, unstructured, or semistructured data using commodity hardware, dividing a task into parallel chunks of jobs and data. Hadoop runs on its distributed file system (HDFS) but can also read and write other file systems. Hadoop uses blocks (typically of 128 MB) to store files on the file system. One block of Hadoop may consist of many blocks of the underlying operating system. Moreover, blocks can be replicated in several different nodes. For example, block1 can be stored in node1 and node3, block2 in node2 and node4, and so on. There are two main pieces of software that handle MapReduce jobs:

- The **job tracker** receives all the jobs from clients, schedules the Map and Reduce tasks to appropriate task trackers, monitors failing tasks, and reschedules them to different task tracker nodes. One job tracker exists in each Hadoop cluster.
- The **task trackers** are the modules that execute the job. There are many task trackers in a Hadoop cluster to manage parallelism in Map and Reduce tasks. They continuously send messages to the job tracker to let the latter know that they are alive and asking for a task.

The process and elements involved in a MapReduce job can be succinctly described as follows:

- The MapReduce program tells a job client to run a MapReduce job. The job client sends a message to a job tracker and gets an ID for the job.
- The job client copies the job resources (e.g., a .jar file) to the shared file system, usually HDFS.
- The job client sends a request to the job tracker to start the job. The job tracker computes the ways of splitting the data so that it can send each chunk of job to a different mapper process to maximize throughput.

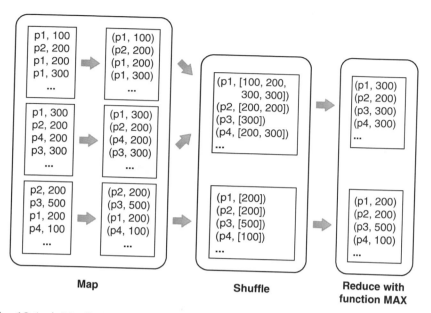

Map   **Shuffle**   **Reduce with function MAX**

Fig. 13.1 A MapReduce process for products

- The job tracker sends a Map task or a Reduce task to a task tracker for execution. The task trackers, based on the job ID, retrieve the job resources from the distributed file system.
- Finally, the task trackers launch a Java virtual machine with a child process which runs the Map or Reduce code.

Figure 13.1 shows an example of how MapReduce works. Consider that orders in the Northwind database come from many sources, each from one country. We are interested in analyzing product sales. The files in this example contain pairs of the form (ProductKey, Quantity). In a Map phase, the input is divided into a list of key-value pairs with the ProductKey as a key and the Quantity as a value. This list is then sent as an input to the so-called Shuffle phase in which it is sorted such that values with the same ProductKey are put together. The output from the shuffle phase is a collection of tuples of the form (key, list-of-values). This is forwarded into a Reduce phase where many different operations like average, sum, or count can be performed. Since the key-list pairs are independent from each other, they can be forwarded to multiple task trackers for parallel execution.

The following table summarizes the format of the input and output of the phases of a MapReduce process:

	Input	Output
Map	(k1,v1)	(List(k2,v2))
Shuffle	(List(k2,v2))	(k2,List(v2))
Reduce	(k2,List(v2))	(List(k3,v3))

13.2   High-Level Languages for Hadoop

Using Hadoop is not easy for end users not familiar with MapReduce. Users need to write MapReduce code even for simple tasks like counting or averaging. A solution for this is to use high-level languages, which allow programmers to work at a higher level of abstraction than in Java or other lower-level languages supported by Hadoop. The most commonly used such languages are Hive and Pig Latin. Both of them are translated into MapReduce jobs, resulting in programs that are much smaller than the equivalent Java ones. Besides, these languages can be extended, for example, writing user-defined functions in Java. This can work the other way round: programs written in high-level languages can be embedded in other languages as well.

13.2.1   Hive

Hive, developed at Facebook, brings the concepts of tables, columns, partitions, and SQL to the Hadoop architecture, keeping the extensibility and flexibility of Hadoop. Hive organizes data in tables and partitions. Like in relational systems, partitions can be defined according to time intervals, allowing Hive to prune data while processing a query. In addition, Hive provides an SQL dialect called Hive Query Language (HiveQL) for querying data stored in a Hadoop cluster. HiveQL is not only a query language but also a data definition and manipulation language. The data definition language is used to create, alter, and delete databases, tables, views, functions, and indexes. The data manipulation language is used to insert, update, and delete at the table level; these operations are not supported at the row level.

The Hive data model includes primitive data types like BOOLEAN and INT and collection data types as STRUCT, MAP, and ARRAY. Collection data types allow, for example, many-to-many relationships to be represented, avoiding foreign key relationships between tables. On the other hand, they introduce data duplication and do not enforce referential integrity. As an example, we show below a simplified representation of table Employees from the Northwind database in Fig. 2.4, where the attributes composing a full address are stored in a STRUCT and the Territories attribute is an ARRAY that contains the set of territory names to which the employee is related. Hive has no control over how data are stored and supports different file and record formats. The table schema is applied while the data are read from storage, implementing what is known as schema on read. The example below includes the file format definition (TEXTFILE in this case) and the delimiter characters needed to parse each record:

```
CREATE TABLE Employees (
        EmployeeID INT, Name STRING,
```

```
Address STRUCT<Street:STRING, City:STRING,
        Region:STRING, PostalCode:STRING, Country:STRING>,
Territories ARRAY<STRING> )
ROW FORMAT
DELIMITED FIELDS TERMINATED BY ','
COLLECTION ITEMS TERMINATED BY '|'
LINES TERMINATED BY '\n'
STORED AS TEXTFILE;
```

HiveQL allows to implement the typical relational operations. The query below performs a projection over the Name and City attributes:

```
SELECT Name, Address.City
FROM    Employees;
```

A selection operation that obtains employees related to more than four territories is expressed as follows:

```
SELECT *
FROM    Employees
WHERE  Size(Territories) > 4;
```

HiveQL supports different join operations, such as INNER JOIN, OUTER JOIN, and LEFT SEMI JOIN, among others. Below, we join tables Employees and Orders:

```
SELECT *
FROM    Employees E JOIN Orders O ON E.EmployeeID = O.EmployeeID
```

HiveQL also supports other SQL-like clauses, for example, GROUP BY, HAVING, and ORDER BY.

Hive also supports computations that go beyond SQL-like languages, for example, generating machine learning models. For this, Hive provides language constructs that allow users to plug in their own transformation scripts in an SQL statement. This is done through the MAP, REDUCE, TRANSFORM, DISTRIBUTE BY, SORT BY, and CLUSTER BY keywords in the SQL extensions. As an example, we show how we can write a Hive program to count the occurrences of products in an input file, like in the example of Fig. 13.1. This is a variant of the typical word count example:

```
CREATE TABLE Products (Content STRING);
FROM          (MAP Products.Content
              USING 'tokenizerScript' AS ProductID, Count
              FROM Products
              CLUSTER BY ProductID) mapOut
              REDUCE mapOut.ProductID, mapOut.Count
              USING 'countScript' AS ProductID, Count;
```

The scripts tokenizerScript and countScript can be implemented in any language, like Python or Java. The former script produces a tuple for each new product in the input; the latter script counts the number of occurrences of each product. The CLUSTER BY clause tells Hive to distribute the Map output (mapOut) to the reducers by hashing on ProductID.

13.2.2 Pig Latin

Pig is a high-level data flow language for querying data stored on HDFS. It was developed at Yahoo! Research and then moved to the Apache Software Foundation. There are three different ways to run Pig: (a) as a script, just by passing the name of the script file to the Pig command; (b) using the grunt command line; and (c) calling Pig from Java in its embedded form. A Pig Latin program is a collection of statements, which can either be an operation or a command. For example, the LOAD operation with a file name as an argument loads data from a file. A command could be an HDFS command used directly within Pig Latin, such as the ls command to list all files in the current directory. The execution of a statement does not necessarily result in a job running on the Hadoop cluster.

Pig does not require schema information, which makes it suitable for unstructured data. If a schema of the data is available, Pig will make use of it, both for error checking and optimization. However, if no schema is available, Pig will still process the data making the best guesses it can. Pig data types can be of two kinds. *Scalar* types are the usual data types, like INTEGER, LONG, FLOAT, and CHARARRAY. On the other hand, three kinds of *complex* types are supported in Pig, namely, TUPLE, BAG, and MAP, where the latter is a set of key-value pairs. For example, depending on schema availability, we can load employee data in several ways as follows:

```
Employees = LOAD 'Employees' AS (Name:chararray, City:chararray, Age:int);
Employees = LOAD 'Employees' AS (Name, City, Age);
Employees = LOAD 'Employees';
```

corresponding, respectively, to whether there is explicit schema and data types, explicit schema without data types, or no schema.

As an example, we show how relational algebra operations can be implemented in Pig, using the Northwind database of Fig. 2.4. We start with the projection. Suppose we have loaded the Employees table into the EmployeeLoad.txt text file:

```
EmployeeLoad = LOAD '/user/northwind/Employees.txt' AS
               (EmployeeID, LastName, FirstName, Title, ... , PhotoPath);
EmployeeData = FOR EACH EmployeeLoad GENERATE
               EmployeeID, LastName, FirstName;
DUMP           EmployeeData;
STORE          EmployeeData INTO '/home/results/projected';
```

Most of the steps are self-explanatory. The GENERATE instruction projects the first three attributes in the file Employees.txt stored in the variable EmployeeLoad.

A selection would be coded as:

```
EmployeeThree = FILTER EmployeeLoad BY EmployeeID == '3';
DUMP            EmployeeThree;
```

Aggregation is also supported in Pig through the GROUP BY operation. Assume we have the EmployeeLoad relation already loaded, and we want to compute aggregates from these data. For this, we have to group the rows into buckets. Over these grouped data, we can then run the aggregate functions. For example, we can group employee data by FirstName:

```
byFirstName = GROUP EmployeeLoad BY FirstName;
```

The result of this operation is a new relation with two columns: one named group and the other one with the name of the original relation. The former contains the schema of the group, in our case a column of CHARARRAY type containing all first names in the original table. This column can be directly accessed as group.FirstName. The second column has the name of the original relation and contains a bag of all the rows in such relation that match the corresponding group, that is, the rows corresponding to employees with the same first name.

The results can be then processed using the classic aggregate functions, for example, COUNT, and the FOREACH operator, which performs a loop over each bag, as follows:

```
FirstNameCount = FOREACH byFirstName GENERATE
                 GROUP AS FirstName
                 COUNT(EmployeeLoad),
```

We conclude with an example of a join operation. We want to join the files storing orders and employees. The join must be performed on two attributes, the ID of the employee and the postal code, in order to obtain the employees that handled orders shipped to the place where they live. Finally, a projection is performed:

```
Employees = LOAD '/user/northwind/Employees.txt' AS
            (EmployeeID, LastName, ... , PhotoPath);
Orders    = LOAD './northwind/Orders.txt' AS
            (OrderID, CustomerID, EmployeeID, ... , ShipCountry);
Joined    = JOIN Employees BY (EmployeeID, PostalCode),
            Orders BY (EmployeeID, ShipPostalCode);
Projected = FOR EACH Joined GENERATE
            Employees::EmployeeID, Employees::PostalCode,
            Orders::CustomerID;
DUMP        Projected;
```

The first two statements load the two files into two variables, Employees and Orders. The JOIN BY statement performs the join, similarly to SQL, and GENERATE performs the projection.

The left and right outer joins are performed in a similar way, adding the keywords LEFT OUTER and RIGHT OUTER, respectively, after the JOIN BY clause. For example, in the query above, we would write JOIN Employees BY (EmployeeID, PostalCode) LEFT OUTER.

13.3   Column-Store Database Systems

So far, we have assumed DBMS architectures with the typical record-oriented storage, where attributes of a record are placed contiguously in disk pages. Thus, a disk page contains a certain number of database tuples, which at the moment of being queried are accessed either sequentially or through some of the indexes studied in Chap. 7. These architectures are appropriate for OLTP systems. For systems oriented to ad hoc querying large amounts of data (like in OLAP), other structures can do better, for example, **column-store databases**, where the values for each column (or attribute) are stored contiguously in the disk pages, such that a disk page will contain a number of database columns. Thus, a database record is scattered into many different disk pages. We study this architecture next.

Figure 13.2a shows the row-store organization, where records are stored in disk pages. Figure 13.2b shows the column-store alternative. In most systems, a page contains a single column. However, if a column does not fit in a page, it will be stored in as many pages as needed. When evaluating a query over a column-store architecture, a DBMS just needs to read the values of the columns involved in the query, thus avoiding to load into memory irrelevant attributes. For example, consider a typical data warehouse query over the Northwind data warehouse as follows:

```
SELECT      CustomerName, SUM(SalesAmount)
FROM        Sales S, Customer C, Product P, Time T, Employee E
WHERE       S.CustomerKey = C.CustomerKey AND
            S.ProductKey = P.ProductKey AND S.TimeKey = T.TimeKey AND
            S.EmployeeKey = E.EmployeeKey AND
            P.Discontinued = 'Yes' AND T.Year= '2012' AND E.City = 'Berlin'
GROUP BY C.CustomerName
```

Depending on the query evaluation strategy, the query above may require accessing all columns of all the tables in the FROM clause, totaling 51 columns. The number of columns can increase considerably in a real-world enterprise data warehouse. However, only 12 of them are actually needed to evaluate this query. Therefore, a row-oriented DBMS will read into main memory a large number of columns that do not contribute to the result and which will probably be pruned by a query optimizer. On the contrary, a column-store database system will just look for the pages containing the columns actually used in the query. Further, it is likely that the values for E.City, T.Year, and P.Discontinued will fit in main memory.

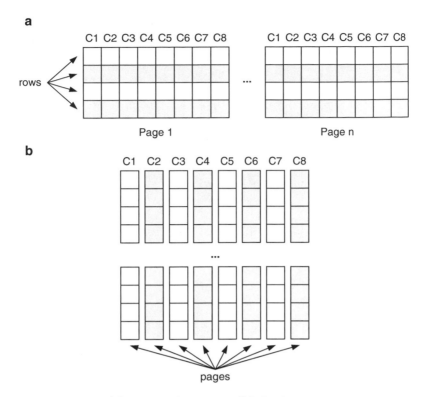

Fig. 13.2 Row-store (**a**) versus column-store (**b**) database systems

To save space, column-store database systems normally store columns in pages in a compressed form. For example, consider the portion of the Sales fact table, shown in Fig. 13.3a. Figure 13.3b–d shows a possible encoding scheme for the columns EmployeeKey, CustomerKey, and ProductKey, respectively. **Compression** is based on run-length encoding, already discussed in Chap. 7. For example, Fig. 13.3b shows a three-column table, with attributes f, v, and l, where f indicates the first of l consecutive records with value v. For instance, the first row in Fig. 13.3b tells that in column EmployeeKey there is a run of length five that starts in the first position and whose value is e1. Analogously, the next record tells that there are three e2 in positions 6–8.

Although efficient for the above scenarios, there are still many problems to be solved by column-store database systems, for example, provide them with capabilities to support updating in an efficient manner, a problem largely solved by mature relational DBMSs (RDBMSs).

a

RowId	EmployeeKey	CustomerKey	ProductKey	...
1	e1	c1	p1	...
2	e1	c1	p4	...
3	e1	c2	p4	...
4	e1	c2	p4	...
5	e1	c2	p4	...
6	e2	c2	p5	...
7	e2	c2	p5	...
8	e2	c2	p1	...
9	e3	c3	p2	...
10	e3	c3	p2	...
...	...	...	...	...

b

f	v	l
1	e1	5
6	e2	3
9	e3	2
...	...	...
...	...	...
...	...	...

c

f	v	l
1	c1	2
3	c2	6
9	c3	2
...	...	...
...	...	...
...	...	...

d

f	v	l
1	p1	1
2	p4	4
6	p5	2
8	p1	1
9	p2	2
...	...	...

Fig. 13.3 Storing columns of a fact table one table per column. (**a**) Fact table Sales.
(**b**) Column EmployeeKey. (**c**) Column CustomerKey. (**d**) Column ProductKey

13.4　In-Memory Database Systems

An IMDBS is a DBMS that stores data in main memory, opposite to
traditional database systems, which store data on persistent media such as
hard disks. Because working with data in memory is much faster than writing
to and reading from a file system, IMDBSs can run applications orders of
magnitude faster. IMDBSs come in many flavors: they can be DBMSs that
only use main memory to load and execute real-time analytics, they can
be used as a cache for disk-based DBMSs, or they can be commercialized
as software–hardware licensed packages, called appliances, particularly for
business intelligence applications. In most cases, they are combined with
column-store technology.

The typical way in which traditional DBMSs operate is based on reading
data from disk to buffer pages located in main memory. When a query is
submitted, data are first fetched in these buffers, and, if not found, new data
are loaded from disk into main memory. If there is an update, the modified
page is marked and written back to disk. The process where disk-based
databases keep frequently accessed records in memory for faster access is

called **caching**. Note, however, that caching only speeds up database reads, while updates or writes must still be written through the cache to disk. Therefore, the performance benefit only applies to a subset of database tasks. In addition, managing the cache is itself a process that requires substantial memory and CPU resources. An IMDBS reduces to a minimum these data transfers, since data are mainly in memory. It follows that the optimization objectives of disk-based database systems are opposed to those of an IMDBS. Traditional DBMSs try to minimize input/output (I/O) using the cache, consuming CPU cycles to maintain this cache. In addition, as we have seen, they keep redundant data, for example, in index structures, to enable direct access to records without the need to go down to the actual data. On the contrary, an IMDBS is designed with the optimization goal of reducing both memory consumption and CPU cycles.

Like traditional DBMSs, typical IMDBSs support the **ACID properties**, namely, atomicity, consistency, isolation, and durability. The first three ones are supported as in traditional DBMSs. Since the main memory is volatile, durability is supported by transaction logging, in which snapshots of the database are called periodically at certain time instants (called **savepoints** or **checkpoints**, depending on the technology and the vendor) and are written to nonvolatile media. If the system fails and must be restarted, the database either rolls back to the last completed transaction or rolls forward to complete any transaction that was in progress when the system failed. IMDBSs also support durability by maintaining one or more copies of the database, which, as in traditional systems, is called **replication**. Nonvolatile RAM provides another means of in-memory database persistence.

Finally, disk-based storage can be applied selectively in an IMDBS. For example, certain record types can be written to disk, while others are managed entirely in memory. Functions specific for disk-based databases, such as cache management, are applied only to records stored on disk, minimizing the impact of these activities over performance and CPU demands.

Figure 13.4 depicts the typical data storage architecture of an IMDBS.[1] The database is stored in main memory, and it is composed of three main parts. The main store contains data stored in a column-oriented fashion. For query optimization reasons, some products also store together groups of columns that are usually accessed together. These are called combined columns. The buffer store is a write-optimized data structure that holds data that have not yet been moved to the main store. That means that a query can need data from both the main store and the buffer. The special data structure of the buffer normally requires more space per record than the main store. Thus, data are periodically moved from the buffer to the main store, a process that requires a merge operation. There are also data structures used to support special features. Examples are inverted indexes

---

[1]This figure is inspired by the SAP HANA architecture (described later in the chapter), although most IMDBSs follow a similar architecture.

Main memory

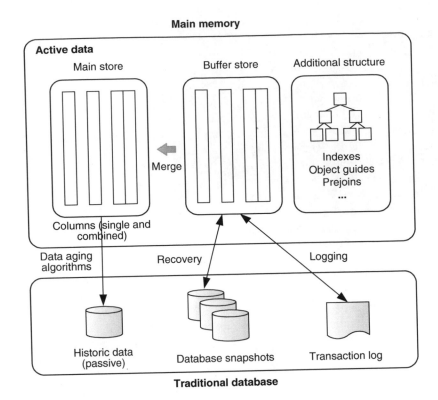

Fig. 13.4 A typical IMDBS architecture

for fast retrieval of low cardinality data, like primary key columns, or object
data guides (in the case of SAP), which allow complex data objects stored
as a hierarchy of elements to be reconstructed. Finally, although data in the
database are stored in main memory, to save memory space, IMDBSs also
store data persistently. This is done as follows. The most recent data are
kept in main memory, since these are the data most likely to be accessed
and/or updated. These data are called **active**. Opposite to this, passive
data are data not currently used by a business process, used mostly for
analytical purposes. Passive data are stored on nonvolatile memory, even
using traditional DBMSs. This supports so-called time-travel queries, which
allow the status of the database as of a certain point in time to be known.
Data partition between active and passive data is performed by **data aging**
algorithms. Nonvolatile memory is also used to guarantee consistency and
recovery under failure: data updates are written in a log file, and database
snapshots are kept in nonvolatile memory, to be read in case of failure. This
combination of main and nonvolatile memory is supposed to allow IMDBSs to
support OLTP transactions and OLAP analysis at the same time. However,
this capability is currently being questioned by researchers and practitioners.

13.5 Representative Systems

We now comment on some representative systems that use column-store and in-memory database technologies. This does not pretend to be an exhaustive list and does not express any preference from the authors about any particular vendor. We just aim at showing how the general architecture and ideas presented above are implemented in real-world products. In this section, we first introduce three examples of column-store database systems, namely, Vertica, MonetDB, and MonetDB/X100. We then show three examples of IMDBSs, namely, SAP HANA, Oracle TimesTen, and Oracle Exalytics. We conclude with Microsoft's approach based on column-store indexes called xVelocity.

13.5.1 Vertica

Vertica[2] is a distributed massively parallel relational DBMS, which is based on the C-Store research project carried out around the year 2005. Although Vertica supports the INSERT, UPDATE, and DELETE SQL operations, it is mainly designed to support analytical workloads. Vertica has a hybrid in-memory/on-disk architecture. This is the main difference with our general architecture in Fig. 13.4, where the main store and buffer store reside in memory and only passive data are stored on disk. Vertica groups data on disk by column rather than by row, with the advantages already commented for analytical queries. Further, data are compressed using different techniques, not only run-length encoding.

Vertica organizes data into sorted subsets of the attributes of a table. These are called projections. Normally, there is one large projection called a super projection (which contains every column in the table) and many small projections. Note that this can be considered analogous to the combined columns in Fig. 13.4. Vertica also supports prejoin projections, although it has been reported that actually they are not frequently used. Vertica has two read- and write-optimized stores, which are somehow variants of the main and buffer stores of Fig. 13.4. The **write-optimized store** (WOS) is an in-memory structure which is optimized for data inserts, deletes, and updates. Data in the WOS are uncompressed, unsorted, and segmented and could be stored in a row- or column-oriented manner. This allows low latency for fast real-time data analysis. The **read-optimized store** (ROS) is a disk-based store where most of the data reside. Data in the ROS are stored as sets of index-value pairs, called ROS containers. Each ROS container is composed of two files per database column: one containing the column itself

---

[2]http://www.vertica.com/

and the other containing the position index. At the ROS, **partitioning** and **segmentation** are applied to facilitate parallelism. The former, also called intra-node partitioning, splits data horizontally, based on data values, for example, by date intervals. Segmentation (also called internode partitioning) splits data across nodes according to a hash key. When the WOS is full, data are moved to the ROS by a **moveout** function. To save space in the ROS, a **mergeout** function is applied (this is analogous to the merge operation in Fig. 13.4).

Finally, although inserts, deletes, and updates are supported, Vertica may not be appropriate for update-intensive applications, like heavy OLTP workloads that, roughly speaking, exceeds 10% of the total load.

13.5.2   *MonetDB*

MonetDB[3] is a column-store IMDBS developed at the Centrum Wiskunde & Informatica (CWI)[4] in the Netherlands. The main characteristics of MonetDB are a columnar storage; a bulk query algebra, which allows fast implementation on modern hardware; cache-conscious algorithms; and new cost models, which account for the cost of memory access.

Usually, in RDBMS query processing, when executing a query plan we typically need to scan a relation R and filter it using a condition ϕ. The format of R is only known at query time; thus, an expression interpreter is needed. The idea of MonetDB is based on the fact that the CPU is basically used to analyze the query expression; thus, processing costs can be reduced by optimizing CPU usage. To simplify query interpretation, the relational algebra was replaced by a simpler algebra.

MonetDB also uses vertical **partitioning**, where each database column is stored in a so-called **binary association table** (BAT). A BAT is a two-column table where the left column is called the head (actually an object identifier) and the right column the tail (the column value). The query language of MonetDB is a column algebra called MIL (Monet Interpreter Language). The parameters of the operators have a fixed format: they are two-column tables or constants. The expression calculated by an operator is also fixed, as well as the format of the result.

However, performance is not optimal since each operation consumes materialized BATs and produces a materialized BAT. Therefore, on the one hand, since it uses a column-at-a-time evaluation technique, MIL does not have the problem of spending 90% of its query execution time in a tuple-at-a-time interpretation overhead, like in traditional RDBMSs, because calculations work on entire BATs, and the layout of these arrays is known at

---

[3]http://www.monetdb.org/
[4]http://www.cwi.nl/

compile time. On the other hand, queries that contain complex calculations over many tuples materialize an entire result column for each function in the expression, even when they are not required in the query result, but just as input to other functions in the expression. If the intermediate results are small, materialization is not actually necessary and produces a large overhead.

13.5.3 MonetDB/X100

To solve the drawbacks of MonetDB, a new query processor, called X100, was devised. Here, columns are fragmented vertically and compressed. These fragments are efficiently processed using a technique called vectorized processing, which operates over small vertical chunks of data items in the cache rather than single records. X100 uses a variant of the relational algebra as query language. The relational operations can process multiple columns at the same time. The primitives of MonetDB/X100 algebra resemble the ones in an extended relational algebra: Scan, Select, Project, Join, Aggr (for aggregation), TopN, and Order. All operators, except for Order, TopN, and Select, return a data flow with the same format as the input. A typical query scans one column at a time, and then the column is passed to the query tree, where the operators above are applied to the data flow.

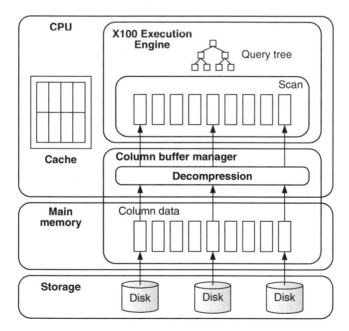

Fig. 13.5 MonetDB/X100 architecture

Figure 13.5 depicts the general **data storage architecture** of MonetDB/X100. All tables are stored in a vertically fragmented form. A storage manager called **column buffer manager** (ColumnBM) was developed. The main difference with MonetDB is that the former stores each BAT in a single contiguous file, while ColumnBM partitions those files in columns (or chunks) and applies compression to optimize the usage of the CPU cache. **Compression** and decompression are managed by the buffer manager. The figure shows also the flow corresponding to each column, from disk until it is scanned by the query processor and passed on to the query tree. Thus, instead of single tuples, entire vectors of values flow upward in the tree. This is called **vectorized execution**. As a consequence, materialization of intermediate results as in MonetDB is not needed. Besides, the entire execution happens within the CPU cache, since this is where the vectors scanned by the query processor are taken from. As shown in Fig. 13.5, main memory is only used as an I/O buffer managed by ColumnBM. This is called **in-cache processing**.

As occurs with many systems, a problem with vertical storage is an increased update cost: a single row update or delete must perform one I/O for each column. MonetDB/X100 avoids this by considering the vertical fragments as objects that do not change. For this, updates are applied to data in so-called delta structures (i.e., structures that store new data). A delete is handled by adding the tuple identifier to a deletion list and an insert as an append in separate delta columns. ColumnBM stores all delta columns together. Thus, both operations only imply one I/O operation. Updates are treated simply as a deletion followed by an insertion. When the column size exceeds a threshold, data storage must be reorganized, which consists in making the vertical storage up to date and the delta columns empty.

13.5.4   SAP HANA

The SAP approach to business intelligence, known as HANA,[5] is based on two main components:

1. The SAP HANA database (also called SAP IMDBS), a hybrid IMDBS that combines row-based, column-based, and object-based technologies, optimized for taking advantage of parallel processing.
2. The SAP HANA appliance (SAP HANA), used for analyzing large volumes of data in real time without the need to materialize aggregations. It is a combination of hardware and software delivered by SAP in cooperation with hardware partners, like IBM.

The core of the SAP HANA database are two relational database engines. The first one is a *column-based engine*, holding tables with large amounts of data that can be aggregated in real time and used in analytical operations. The second one is a *row-based engine*, optimized for row operations, such

---

[5] http://www.saphana.com

as frequent inserts and updates. The latter has a lower compression rate and lower query performance compared to the column-based engine. This architecture allows mixed workloads to be supported in the same server, performing complex analytical computations without the need of materializing tables. Both relational engines support SQL and MDX. Calculations can be performed in the database without moving the data into the application layer, through an SQL script language that can be used to push down data-intensive application logic into the database. Row or column storage can be selected at the time a table is created but can be changed afterward. Both engines share a common persistence layer (the nonvolatile data store in Fig. 13.4), where page management and logging are supported like in traditional databases.

The **data storage architecture** is similar to the generic one depicted in Fig. 13.4, with an optimized column-store area and a nonoptimized buffer area to allow insertions and updates. Insertions, deletions, and updates are handled in HANA following the notion of lifetime management of a data record. A *level L1 delta storage*, organized as a row-oriented storage area, is used for *individual* updates. Bulk updates bypass level L1 and are managed at a *level L2 delta storage*, organized in compressed columns, although it is less optimized than the main storage area. Finally, the main store is the highly compressed in-memory column storage explained above. Typically, records are moved during their life cycle from level L1, to level L2, and to the main store.

Regarding **partitioning**, data are divided into subsets and stored in a cluster of servers, conforming a distributed database. This approach is called scale-out. An individual database table can be placed on different servers within a cluster or can be split into several partitions, either horizontally (a group of rows per partition) or vertically (a group of columns per partition), with each partition residing in a separate server within the cluster.

Atomicity, consistency, and isolation are **ACID properties** that are not affected by in-memory storage. However, as explained above, durability cannot be met by just storing data in main memory since this is volatile storage. To make data persistent, it must reside on nonvolatile storage such as hard drives or flash devices. HANA divides the main memory into pages. When a transaction changes data, the affected pages are marked and written to nonvolatile storage at regular intervals. In addition, a database log captures all changes made by transactions. Each committed transaction generates a log entry that is written to nonvolatile storage, ensuring that all transactions are permanent. SAP HANA stores changed pages at **savepoints**, which are asynchronously written to persistent storage at regular intervals (by default, every 5 min). A transaction does not commit before the corresponding log entry is written to persistent storage, to meet the durability requirement (in traditional database management, this is called write-ahead log). After a power failure, the database can be restarted from the savepoints like a disk-based database: the database logs are applied to restore the changes that were not captured in the savepoints, ensuring that the database can be restored in memory to the same state as before the failure.

Finally, **compression** is performed using data dictionaries. The idea is that each attribute value in a table is replaced by an integer code and the correspondence of codes and values is stored in a dictionary. For example, in the City column of the Customer table, the value Berlin can be encoded as '1', and the tuple (Berlin,1) will be stored in the dictionary. Thus, if needed, the corresponding value (Berlin, in this case) will be accessed just once. Therefore, data movement is reduced without imposing additional CPU load for decompression. The compression factor achieved by this method is highly dependent on the data being compressed. Attributes with few distinct values compress well (e.g., if we have many customers from the same city), while attributes with many distinct values do not benefit as much.

13.5.5   Oracle TimesTen

Oracle TimesTen[6] is an in-memory RDBMS that also supports transaction processing. TimesTen stores all its data in optimized data structures in memory and includes query algorithms designed for in-memory processing.

TimesTen can be used as a stand-alone RDBMS or as an application-tier cache that works together with traditional disk-based RDBMS, for example, the Oracle database itself: existing applications over an Oracle database can use TimesTen to cache a subset of the data to improve response time. In this way, read and write operations can be performed on the cache tables using SQL and PL/SQL with automatic persistence, transactional consistency, and synchronization with the Oracle database. In addition, TimesTen can be used to replicate an entire data warehouse if it fits entirely in memory.

Unlike in traditional DBMSs, where query optimizers are based on disk input/output costs, namely, the number of disk accesses, the cost function of the TimesTen optimizer is based on the cost of evaluating predicates. TimesTen's cache provides range, hash, and bitmap indexes and supports typical join algorithms like nested-loop join and merge-join. Also, the optimizer can create temporary indexes as needed and accepts hints from the user, like in traditional databases.

Two key features of the TimesTen **data storage architecture** are the in-memory database cache and the data aging algorithms. The **in-memory database cache** (IMDB cache) creates a real-time updatable cache where a subset of the tables are loaded. For instance, in the Northwind database, the cache can be used to store recent orders, while data about customers can be stored in a traditional Oracle database. Thus, the information that requires real-time access is stored in the IMDB cache, while the information needed for

---

[6]http://www.oracle.com/us/products/database/timesten/overview/index.html

longer-term analysis, auditing, and archival is stored in the Oracle database. This is analogous to the general architecture depicted in Fig. 13.4. Moreover, the scenario above can be distributed. For example, the Northwind company may have a centralized Oracle database and many applications running at several application server nodes in various countries. To perform analysis of orders and sales in near real time, we may install an IMDB cache database at each node. On the contrary, the customer profiles do not need to be stored at every node. When a node addresses a sales order, the customer's profile is uploaded from the most up-to-date location, which could be either a node or the central database. When the transaction is finished, the customer's profile is updated and stored back into the central database. The IMDB cache can also be used as a read-only cache, for example, to provide fast access to auxiliary data structures, like lookup tables. On the other hand, **data aging** is an operation that removes data that are no longer needed. There are two general types of data aging algorithms: the ones that remove old data based on a timestamp value and the ones that remove the least recently used data.

Like the other systems commented in this chapter, TimesTen uses **compression** of tables at the column level. This mechanism provides space reduction for tables by eliminating duplicate values within columns, improving the performance of SQL queries that must perform full table scans.

Finally, TimesTen achieves **durability** in a similar way as SAP HANA, that is, through transaction logging over a disk-based version of the database. TimesTen maintains the disk-based version using a **checkpoint** operation that occurs in the background, with low impact on database applications. TimesTen also has a blocking checkpoint that does not require transaction log files for recovery and must be initiated by the application. TimesTen uses the transaction log to recover transactions under failure, undo transactions that are rolled back, replicate changes to other TimesTen databases and/or to Oracle tables, and enable applications to detect changes to tables.

In addition to the above, Oracle also commercializes an appliance called **Oracle Exalytics In-Memory Machine**,[7] similar to the SAP HANA appliance studied in Sect. 13.5.4. Exalytics is composed of hardware, business intelligence software, and an Oracle TimesTen IMDBS. The hardware consists in a single server configured for in-memory analytics of business intelligence workloads. Exalytics comes with the Oracle BI Foundation Suite and Essbase, a multidimensional OLAP server enhanced with a more powerful MDX syntax and a high-performance MDX query engine. Oracle Exalytics complements the Oracle Exadata Database Machine, which supports high performance for both OLAP and OLTP applications.

---

[7] http://www.oracle.com/us/solutions/ent-performance-bi/business-intelligence/exalytics-bi-machine/overview/index.html

13.5.6   SQL Server xVelocity

Microsoft's approach to column-store technology differs from the ones described above. Microsoft decided to keep SQL Server as its only database product and to incorporate the column-store technology in the form of an optional index. Microsoft SQL Server includes a collection of in-memory and memory-optimized data management technologies denoted xVelocity.[8] The **xVelocity in-memory analytics engine**, formerly known as **VertiPaq**, is an in-memory column-store engine for analytic queries, which uses the four main techniques we discussed above: columnar storage, compression techniques, in-memory caching, and highly parallel data scanning and aggregation algorithms. The xVelocity engine works with the *tabular* models of PowerPivot for Excel, SharePoint, and Analysis Services, but not with the *multidimensional* and data mining tools of Analysis Services.

The xVelocity engine provides **column-store indexes**, which aim at enhancing query processing in SQL Server data warehouses. Each column is stored separately as in a column-store database. In addition, xVelocity includes a vector-based query execution technology called **batch processing** to further speed up query processing. Data are brought to a memory-optimized cache on demand, although full in-memory query performance is achieved when all data needed by a query is already in main memory. The xVelocity column-store index groups and stores data for each column and then joins all the columns to complete the whole index. The SQL Server query processor can then take advantage of this kind of index to significantly improve query execution time.

A key feature of column-store indexes is that they are built in into SQL Server, which is a general-purpose row-store RDBMS, and the indexes can be defined as any other one. Given the performance gain which this approach achieves for many kinds of data warehouse queries, we can even get rid of the need of building and maintaining summary tables. However, these features come together with some limitations we discuss later.

The syntax for creating a column-store index was introduced in Chap. 7. As an example, we index the columns of the Sales fact table in the Northwind data warehouse as follows:

```
CREATE NONCLUSTERED COLUMNSTORE INDEX CSIdx_Sales
    ON Sales (ProductKey, EmployeeKey, CustomerKey);
```

Column-store indexes are organized as follows. The Sales fact table is stored as groups of rows. Given the column-store index defined above, for each row group and each column, a segment is built containing each column in a group in compressed form. That means, in our example, if the table contains ten groups, there will be thirty segments of compressed data. Each segment is

---

[8] http://msdn.microsoft.com/en-us/library/hh922900.aspx

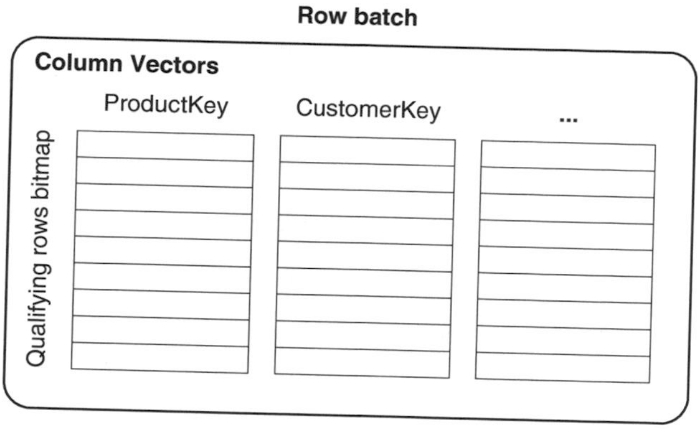

Row batch

Fig. 13.6 Row batch query processing

stored in a BLOB (binary large object). There is also a **segment directory** allowing to quickly find all segments of a given column. In addition, the directory contains metadata, like number of rows, minimum and maximum values, and so on.

The main element in **batch processing** is the row batch (see Fig. 13.6), an object that contains about one thousand rows. Each column within the batch is represented internally as a vector of fixed size elements. There is an additional vector denoted qualifying rows bitmap vector used as follows. For example, to evaluate a condition such as ProductKey < 1, we need to scan the column ProductKey in the batch, perform the comparison, and, for each qualifying element, set the corresponding bit in the qualifying rows vector. Efficient vector-based algorithms reduce the CPU overhead of database operations. It is reported that this reduction can be of up to forty times compared with row-based processing methods.

It is worth remarking that SQL Server column-store indexes and column-based query processing are optimized for typical queries in data warehouses with a large fact table and small- to medium-sized dimension tables, following a star schema configuration. Since these queries include a star join, selection predicates over dimension attributes, and a final aggregation, they typically return a small result set. However, when the result set is large (e.g., if data are not aggregated or there is no join or filtering), performance may be poor since batch processing is not applied, and the benefit from the column-store index is just due to compression and the scanning of fewer columns. Performance may decrease when (a) two large tables are joined so that they require large hash tables that do not fit into memory and must be dumped to disk; (b) many columns are returned, and thus most of the column-store index must be retrieved; and (c) a join condition over a column-store indexed table includes more than one column.

In SQL Server, a table over which a column-store index has been defined cannot be updated. To overcome this problem, some ad hoc techniques can be applied. For example, we can drop the column-store index; perform the required INSERT, DELETE, or UPDATE operations; and then rebuild the column-store index. Of course, building the index on large tables can be costly, and if this procedure has to be followed on a regular basis, it may not be plausible. As another option, we can allocate data identified as static (or rarely changing) into a main table with a column-store index defined over it. Recent data, which are likely to change, can be stored into a separate table with the same schema but which does not have a column-store index defined. Then, we can apply the updates. Note that this requires rewriting a query as two queries, one against each table, and then combining the two result sets with UNION ALL. The updating technique above shows one of the trade-offs of having column storage as an index in a row-oriented database: the ad hoc updating procedures described are performed automatically in most of the other products we described in this chapter. On the other hand, those products are normally not appropriate for heavy transactional workloads.

13.6   Real-Time Data Warehouses

Many current data warehousing applications must handle large volumes of concurrent requests while maintaining adequate query response time and must scale up as the data volume and number of users grow. This is quite different from the early days of data warehousing, when just a few number of users accessed the data warehouse. Moreover, most of these applications need to remain continuously available, without a refreshing time window. These applications require a new approach to the extraction, transformation, and loading (ETL) process studied in Chap. 8. Recall that ETL processes periodically pull data from source systems to refresh the data warehouse. This process is acceptable for many real-world data warehousing applications. However, the new database technologies studied in this chapter make nowadays possible to achieve real-time data warehouses, where there are continuous data warehouse feeds from production systems, and at the same time obtain consistent, reliable data analysis results.

As studied in this book, the life cycle of a data record in a business intelligence environment starts with a business event taking place. ETL processes then deliver the event record to the data warehouse. Finally, analytical processing turns the data into information to help the decision-making process, and a business decision leads to a corresponding action. To approach real time, the time elapsed between the event and its consequent action, called the **data latency**, needs to be minimized. Making rapid decisions based on large volumes of data requires achieving low data latency, sometimes at the expense of potential data inconsistency (e.g., late and/or missing data) and specialized hardware. In the general case, it is the data acquisition process that introduces most of the data latency.

Note that data latency requirements differ between application scenarios. For example, collaborative filtering, with queries such as "People who like X also like Y," requires a data freshness in the range of hours, while fraud detection, for instance, in credit card usage, needs a data latency in the order of minutes or seconds. However, most applications do not require these stringent latency levels. In these cases, the common strategy in practice consists just in increasing the frequency of ETL operations using so-called mini-batch ETL processes, for example, loading data every 10 min.

Several strategies have been devised to achieve real-time ETL for reducing data latency. The simplest one, which requires the least effort in terms of changes to existing architectures, is the one called **near real-time ETL**, which simply increases the frequency of ETL processes. Most of the research work in the field follows this approach. However, this is not enough when data latency must be drastically reduced.

A classic solution to reduce data latency consists in defining **real-time partitions** for fact tables. In this case, real-time and static data are stored in separate tables. Real-time partitions are subject to special update and query rules and must have the same schema as the fact tables. Ideally, they must:

- Contain all updates occurred since the last refresh of the fact table.
- Have the same granularity as the fact table.
- Be lightly indexed in order to efficiently handle input data.
- Support high-performance querying.

Query tools should be able to distinguish between both kinds of tables and know where to find data. That means these tools must formulate a query over the static fact tables and the real-time partitions. This capability is not always achieved by commercial tools, however. Note also that this technique is orthogonal to the database technology used. Thus, real-time partitions could be stored in traditional RDBMS, column-store database systems, or IMDBSs.

There are three types of real-time partitions depending on their granularity, which can be transaction, periodic snapshot, and accumulating snapshot granularity. We explain these types next.

A *transaction-granularity* real-time partition contains one record for each individual transaction in the source system since the beginning of the recording period. The real-time partition has the same structure as its underlying static fact table, but it just contains the transactions that have occurred since the last data warehouse refresh. In addition, the real-time partition should not be indexed in order to be always ready for loading. Although the static fact tables are usually big and heavily indexed, real-time partitions may fit in main memory, and thus, there is no need of indexing them. As an example, let us consider a simplified version of the Sales fact table below.

TimeKey	EmployeeKey	CustomerKey	ProductKey	SalesAmount
t1	e1	c1	p1	100
t2	e2	c2	p1	150
t3	e1	c3	p3	210
t4	e2	c4	p4	80

Suppose that this table is refreshed once a day and that we need current fact data. We show below a transaction-granularity real-time partition, called Partition_Sales, storing the transactions that occurred during the last day, which have not been loaded into the fact table.

TimeKey	EmployeeKey	CustomerKey	ProductKey	SalesAmount
t5	e1	c1	p1	30
t6	e2	c2	p1	125
t7	e3	c3	p3	300

A query asking for total sales by employee and customer would need to access both tables, as follows:

```
SELECT    EmployeeKey, CustomerKey, SUM(SalesAmount)
FROM      (SELECT      EmployeeKey, CustomerKey,
                       SUM(SalesAmount) AS SalesAmount
           FROM        Employee E, Customer C, Sales S
           WHERE       E.EmployeeKey = S.EmployeeKey AND
                       C.CustomerKey = S.CustomerKey
           GROUP BY    EmployeeKey, CustomerKey
           UNION
           SELECT      EmployeeKey, CustomerKey,
                       SUM(SalesAmount) AS SalesAmount
           FROM        Employee E, Customer C, Partition_Sales S
           WHERE       E.EmployeeKey = S.EmployeeKey AND
                       C.CustomerKey = S.CustomerKey
           GROUP BY    EmployeeKey, CustomerKey) AS FactFull
GROUP BY FactFull.EmployeeKey, FactFull.CustomerKey
```

A *periodic-snapshot* real-time partition is related to a fact table with coarser granularity (e.g., week). The real-time partition contains all transactions of the current snapshot period (in this case, the current week). Data are added continuously to this partition and summarized at the granularity of the fact table until the period completes, thus maintaining a rolling summarization of the data that has not yet been loaded into the static table. Suppose that in the simplified Sales fact table above the time granularity is week. As new orders arrive, we perform in the real-time partition a rolling summarization of the measure SalesAmount for the combination of employee, customer, product, and week. This means that the partition contains summarized data up to the current moment of the week. When the week closes, the partition is loaded to the fact table.

Finally, *accumulating snapshot* real-time partitions are used for short processes, like order handling. The real-time partition accumulates frequent updates of facts, and the fact table is refreshed with the last version of these facts. For example, suppose that in the Northwind case study the Sales fact table is refreshed once a day. This table contains records about order lines, and their data (e.g., the due date or the quantity) can change during a day. These updates are performed on the real-time partition, which typically is small and can fit in main memory. At the end of the day, the records in the partition are loaded into the fact table.

There are several alternative approaches for achieving real-time data warehouses, which make use of the real-time partitions studied above. One of such approaches is called **direct trickle feed**, where new data from operational sources are continuously fed into the data warehouse. This is done by either inserting data in the fact tables or into separate real-time partitions of the fact tables. A variant of this strategy, which addresses the mixed workload problem (i.e., updates and queries over the same table), is called **trickle and flip**. Here, data are continuously fed into staging tables that are an exact copy of the warehouse tables. Periodically, feeding is stopped, and the copy is swapped with the fact table, bringing the data warehouse up to date. Another strategy called **real-time data caching** avoids mixed workload problems: a real-time data cache consists in a dedicated database server for loading, storing, and processing real-time data. In-memory database technologies studied in this chapter could be used when we have large volumes of real-time data (in the order of hundreds or thousands of changes per second) or extremely fast query performance requirements. In this case, real-time data are loaded into the cache as they arrive from the source system. A drawback of this strategy is that, since the real-time and historical data are separately stored, when a query involves both kinds of data, the evaluation could be costly.

We have commented above that not all applications have the same latency requirements. In many situations, part of the data must be loaded quickly after arrival, while other parts can be loaded at regular intervals. However, there are many situations where we would like data to be loaded when needed, but not necessarily before that. **Right-time data warehousing** follows this approach. Here, right time may vary from right now (i.e., real time) to several minutes or hours, depending on the required data latency. The key idea is that data are loaded when needed, avoiding the cost of providing real time when it is not actually needed.

The **RiTE** (Right-Time ETL) system is a middleware aimed at achieving right-time data warehousing. In RiTE, a data producer continuously inserts data into a data warehouse in bulk fashion, and, at the same time, data warehouse user queries get access to fresh data on demand. The main component of the RiTE architecture is called the *catalyst*, a software module which provides intermediate storage in main memory for data warehouse tables selected by the user. More in detail, a data *consumer* (transparently to the user) tells the catalyst which rows from a table should be ready for querying, defining a time period (e.g., "I need all data from at most 10 min ago"). Then, the catalyst requests the data to the producer, and when data are received they are stored in main memory. These noncommited and nonpersistent data thus become available to the consumer, who accesses them through table functions. Other data are bulk loaded directly to the data warehouse. Eventually, the data at the catalyst are committed and moved to their final target, the physical data warehouse tables. Note that in this scheme, only data needed in real time are queried from the memory tables, while data with coarser latency can be queried directly from the data warehouse, and all these happens transparently to the user.

Besides the catalyst, there are two modules: the producer and the consumer. In the former, and also at every consumer, specialized database drivers are located. The driver at the producer handles INSERT and COMMIT operations. The consumer uses a specialized JDBC database driver that registers and deregisters with the catalyst, indicating which rows from the memory tables are used. Rows are fetched from the catalyst by using a PostgreSQL table function (a stored procedure returning a set of rows).

13.7   Extraction, Loading, and Transformation

New paradigms are emerging in the data warehouse domain, many of them sustained in the possibilities offered by the technologies studied in this chapter. One of them, called the **MAD analysis**, promotes a change in the way data analytics is being performed. This paradigm claims for a *magnetic*, *agile*, and *deep* analysis. The term *magnetic* refers to the ability to "attract" data sources. In the traditional data warehouse methodology studied in this book, new data sources are not incorporated into the data warehouse until they are carefully cleansed and integrated. In some sense, this approach is said to "repel" new data sources. This may not be appropriate, for example, when external and volatile data sources need to be considered, for example, in a semantic web scenario that we will present in Chap. 14. In the MAD approach, a data warehouse is required to be "magnetic", that is, it should attract all the data sources regardless their data quality. The term *agile* calls for a data warehouse that, instead of a careful and detailed design, allows analysts to rapidly and easily load and produce data. Finally, the term *deep* refers to the use of modern data analysis techniques and statistical methods that go beyond the typical OLAP operations. This amounts to incorporate techniques like the ones studied in Chap. 9, which also requires large amounts of data to be loaded into the warehouse. In addition to the above, we have seen that many applications require real-time, near-real-time, or right-time

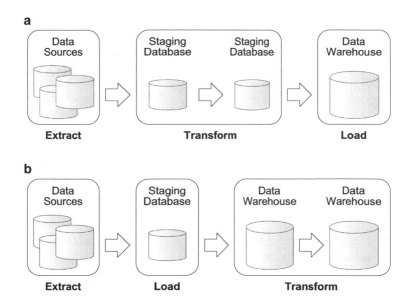

Fig. 13.7 (**a**) Extraction, transformation, and loading (ETL) process. (**b**) Extraction, loading, and transformation (ELT) process

data warehousing. Further, the amount of operational data produced daily is constantly increasing due, among other reasons, to business globalization and the explosion of the number of transactions over the web. In this scenario, it is likely that the time needed to refresh the data warehouse using the traditional ETL process exceeds the allocated updating window.

The above discussion aims at explaining why some practitioners and vendors are proposing a different data loading paradigm: the *extraction, loading, and transformation* (ELT) process. We discuss this next.

Consider Fig. 13.7, which provides a detailed look of the data staging phase in the back-end tier of the architecture depicted in Fig. 3.5. The figure shows that during the ETL process, data are loaded from the sources into a staging database, where the necessary data transformations occur, as described in Chap. 8. After this process, the transformed data are loaded into the data warehouse. The process guarantees that only data relevant to the solution will be extracted and processed, potentially reducing development, extraction, and processing overhead. This also, in some sense, simplifies the management of data security and therefore the data administration overhead. On the other hand, accounting just for relevant data implies that any future requirements that may need data not included in the original design will need to be added to the ETL routines. This may lead to important redevelopment tasks. Besides, the use of third-party tools to implement ETL processes requires learning of new scripting languages and processes.

On the other hand, the new requirements discussed at the beginning of this section led to the ELT paradigm, depicted in Fig. 13.7b. Here, data are extracted from the data sources into the staging database using any available data connectivity tool not just specialized ETL middleware. At this staging database, integrity and business rule checks can be applied, and relevant corrections can be made. After this, the source data are loaded into the warehouse, which provides a validated off-line copy of the source data in the data warehouse. Once in the warehouse, transformations are performed to take the data to their target output format. We can see that while ETL transformation happens at the ETL tool, ELT transformation happens at the *database*. In this way, the extraction and loading processes can be isolated from the transformation process, allowing the user to include data that may be needed in the future. Even the whole data source could be loaded into the warehouse. This, combined with the isolation of the transformation process, means that future requirements can easily be incorporated into the warehouse structure, minimizing the risk of a project. Further, the tools provided with the database engine can be used for this process, reducing the need to implement and learn specialized ETL tools.

We must keep in mind that ELT is an emerging paradigm that, although promising, still needs to be developed further. This paradigm relies, in part, in high-speed data loading, probably using large parallel DBMSs, for example, taking advantage of technologies like MapReduce, studied in Sect. 13.1.

13.8   Summary

We have studied the changes that big data analytics requirements are introducing in the data warehousing world and the answers that the academia and the industry have devised for them. We presented the MapReduce model and its most popular implementation, Hadoop. We also presented two high-level query languages for Hadoop, namely, Pig Latin and HiveQL. We also studied two database architectures that are gaining momentum in data warehousing and business intelligence: column-store databases and IMDBSs. We described the main characteristics of some of the database systems based on these technologies: Vertica, MonetDB, SAP HANA, Oracle TimesTen, and Microsoft xVelocity. Finally, we discussed two modern paradigms increasingly used in data warehousing and business intelligence: real-time data warehousing and ELT. Both paradigms are possible thanks to the technologies studied in this chapter.

13.9 Bibliographic Notes

There is a wide corpus of academic literature and industrial white papers on the topics covered in this chapter. An interesting study about the new requirements for data warehousing is given in [193]. The authors of this book explore new challenges in data warehousing in [215], where also many references can be found. The work by Dean et al. [36] gives a good description of MapReduce. Hadoop is described, for example, in [226]. Hive is discussed in [25, 201] and Pig Latin in [61]. A discussion on MapReduce and column-store databases is provided in [195]. An example of the use of MapReduce in the ETL process is given in [118]. C-Store, one of the first column-store databases, is discussed in [194]. Its commercial version Vertica is studied in [111]. MonetDB is reviewed in [89]. IMDBSs are studied in [164], where SAP HANA is also discussed. Oracle TimesTen is described in [109]. There are several works on real-time data warehousing and real-time ETL [21,185,220]. Real-time partitions are discussed in the books [102,103]. The notion of right-time data warehousing is proposed in [200]. The ELT approach has been introduced in a paper by Cohen et al. [33].

13.10 Review Questions

13.1 What is big data? How can we characterize this notion?
13.2 What are the challenges that big data poses to the future of data warehousing?
13.3 Describe the main characteristics of the MapReduce paradigm.
13.4 Describe the main features of Hadoop.
13.5 What is Hive? What is Pig Latin? Compare Hive and Pig Latin proposing dimensions for this comparison.
13.6 Explain the main characteristics of column-store databases.
13.7 How do column-store databases achieve better efficiency than row-store databases in the case of data warehouses? Is this the case for OLTP databases?
13.8 How do column-store database systems compress the data?
13.9 What are IMDBSs? Which kinds of them have we studied in this chapter?
13.10 What are business intelligence appliances?
13.11 How do optimization techniques differ between IMDBSs and disk-based database systems?
13.12 Describe a typical IMDBS architecture.
13.13 Describe similarities and differences between SAP HANA, MonetDB, and Vertica.

13.14 How do IMDBSs guarantee the ACID properties? Give an answer for each property.

13.15 What is the main difference between the approach of SQL Server's xVelocity and the systems above?

13.16 What are real-time data warehouses? Explain the different alternatives for modeling real-time fact tables.

13.17 How can we achieve real-time ETL? Do we always need real-time ETL? Why? Explain.

13.18 Explain the concept of right-time data warehouses and how it differs from real-time data warehouses. Explain an approach to achieve right-time data warehouses.

13.19 How does ELT differ from ETL? Choose an application scenario you are familiar with for motivating the use of ELT.

13.11   Exercises

13.1 Consider that the Northwind database has been loaded into the HDFS. We want to implement the relational algebra operations over this database using Pig Latin as follows:

(a) Express the projection over the last name of the Employees table.
(b) Express the selection of EmployeeID=3 on the Employees table.
(c) Over the Orders table, obtain the number of deliveries grouped by shipper.
(d) List the Orders table in descending order of ShipName.
(e) Perform the natural join between the Orders and Employee tables on EmployeeID.
(f) Perform the left outer join between the Orders and Employee tables on PostalCode and ShipPostalCode on Orders.
(g) Same as (e) for the right outer join, but joining also by EmployeeID.

13.2 Using the Northwind database of Ex. 13.1:

(a) Define the database in HiveQL.
(b) Express the queries of Ex. 13.1 in HiveQL.

13.3 Consider the Northwind database and the following query:

```
SELECT    CustomerName, SUM(SalesAmount)
FROM      Sales S, Customer C, Product P, Time T, Employee E
WHERE     S.CustomerKey = C.CustomerKey AND
          S.ProductKey = P.ProductKey AND
          P.Discontinued = 'Yes' AND
          S.TimeKey = T.TimeKey AND T.Year = '2012' AND
          S.EmployeeKey = E.EmployeeKey AND E.City = 'Berlin'
GROUP BY C.CustomerName
```

Assume that there are 100,000 tuples in the Sales fact table, 2,000 in Customer, 30,000 in Product, 500 in Time, and 1,000 in Employee. The Northwind database is stored in a column-store database system. Each disk block has a size of 1 MB. You can assume all data you consider necessary to answer the following questions:

- How many disk access will take the evaluation of the query above?
- Assume a row-oriented database, with a block size of 32 K. What would be the answer to the previous question?

Chapter 14
Data Warehouses and the Semantic Web

The availability of enormous amounts of data from many different domains is producing a shift in the way data warehousing practices are being carried out. Massive-scale data sources are becoming common, posing new challenges to data warehouse practitioners and researchers. The semantic web, where large amounts of data are being stored daily, is a promising scenario for data analysis in a near future. As large repositories of semantically annotated data become available, new opportunities for enhancing current decision-support systems will appear. In this scenario, two approaches are clearly identified. One focuses on automating multidimensional design, using semantic web artifacts, for example, existing ontologies. In this approach, data warehouses are (semi)automatically designed using available metadata and then populated with semantic web data. The other approach aims at analyzing large amounts of semantic web data using OLAP tools. In this chapter, we tackle the latter approach, which requires the definition of a precise vocabulary allowing to represent OLAP data on the semantic web. Over this vocabulary, multidimensional models and OLAP operations for the semantic web can be defined. Currently, there are two proposals in this direction. On the one hand, the data cube vocabulary (also denoted QB) follows statistical data models. On the other hand, the QB4OLAP vocabulary follows closely the classic multidimensional models for OLAP studied in this book.

In this chapter, we first introduce in Sect. 14.1 the basic semantic web concepts, including the RDF and RDFS data models, together with a study of RDF representation of relational data and a review of R2RML, the standard language to define mappings from relational to RDF data. In Sect. 14.2, we give an introduction to SPARQL, the standard query language for RDF data. In Sect. 14.3, we discuss the representation and querying of multidimensional data in RDF, including an in-depth discussion of the QB and QB4OLAP vocabularies. We continue in Sect. 14.4 showing how the Northwind data cube can be represented using both vocabularies. We conclude in Sect. 14.5 by showing how to query the QB4OLAP representation of the Northwind data warehouse in SPARQL.

A. Vaisman and E. Zimányi, *Data Warehouse Systems*, Data-Centric Systems and Applications, DOI 10.1007/978-3-642-54655-6_14,
© Springer-Verlag Berlin Heidelberg 2014

14.1   Semantic Web

The **semantic web** is a proposal oriented to represent web content in a machine-processable way. The basic layer for data representation on the semantic web recommended by the World Wide Web Consortium (W3C) is the resource description framework (RDF). In a semantic web scenario, domain ontologies are used to define a common terminology for the concepts involved in a particular domain. These ontologies are expressed in RDF or in languages defined on top of RDF like the Web Ontology Language (OWL)[1] and are especially useful for describing unstructured, semistructured, and text data. Many applications attach metadata and semantic annotations to the information they produce (e.g., in medical applications, medical images, and laboratory tests). We expect that, in the near future, large repositories of semantically annotated data will be available, opening new opportunities for enhancing current decision-support systems.

14.1.1   Introduction to RDF and RDFS

The **resource description framework** (RDF)[2] is a formal language for describing structured information. One of the main goals of RDF is to enable the composition of distributed data to allow data exchange over the web. To uniquely identify resources, RDF uses **internationalized resource identifiers** (IRIs). IRIs generalize the concept of **universal resource locators** (URLs) since they do not necessarily refer to resources located on the web. Further, IRIs generalize the concept of the **uniform resource identifiers** (URIs): while URIs are limited to a subset of the ASCII character set, IRIs may contain Unicode characters.

RDF can be used to express assertions over resources. These assertions are expressed in the form of *subject-predicate-object* triples, where *subject* are resources or *blank nodes*, *predicate* are resources, and *object* are resources or *literals* (i.e., data values). Blank nodes are used to represent resources without an IRI, typically with a structural function, for example, to group a set of statements. A set of RDF triples or *RDF data set* can be seen as a directed graph where subjects and objects are nodes and predicates are arcs.

RDF provides a way to express statements about resources using named properties and values. However, sometimes it is also needed to define kinds or classes of resources and the specific properties describing those resources. A set of reserved words, called **RDF Schema** (RDFS),[3] is used to define

---

[1] http://www.w3.org/2004/OWL/

[2] http://www.w3.org/TR/rdf11-concepts/

[3] http://www.w3.org/TR/rdf-schema/

properties and represent relationships between resources, adding semantics to the terms in a vocabulary. Intuitively, RDF allows us to describe instances, while RDFS adds schema information to those instances. A comprehensive study of the formal semantics of RDFS is beyond the scope of the book, but we provide below the basic concepts we will use in the next sections.

Among the many terms in the RDFS vocabulary, the fragment which represents the essential features of RDF is the subset composed of the following terms: rdf:type, rdf:Class, rdfs:Resource, rdfs:Property, rdfs:range, rdfs:domain, rdfs:subClassOf, and rdfs:subPropertyOf. For example, a triple Employee rdf:type Class tells that Employee is a class that aggregates objects of the same kind, in this case employees (we leave syntactic issues to be presented later, since actually all resources must be defined using IRIs). The triple Davolio rdf:type Employee tells that Davolio is a member of the class Employee. The term rdfs:Resource denotes the class of all resources, and rdf:Property the class of all properties. Importantly, class membership is not exclusive, since a resource may belong to several different classes. Elements belonging to the class rdf:Property represent relationships between resources, used in the predicate part of RDF triples. For example, hasSalary can be defined as a property of an employee using the statement hasSalary rdf:type rdf:Property. The predicate rdfs:subClassOf allows us to define generalization relationships between classes. For example, the triple TemporaryEmployee rdf:subClassOf Employee tells that every temporary employee is also an employee. Analogously, the predicate rdfs:subPropertyOf allows us to define generalization relationships between properties. For example, hasLowSalary rdfs:subPropertyof hasSalary indicates a subproperty to describe employees with low salaries. A rule system can be defined using these and other predicates, thus allowing to infer knowledge from an RDF graph. The RDF Semantics[4] specification defines a precise semantics and corresponding complete systems of inference rules for RDF and RDFS. Finally, let us remark that, in general, triples representing schema and instance data coexist in RDF data sets.

14.1.2 RDF Serializations

An RDF graph is a collection of triples given in any order, which suggests many ways of serialization. Two widely used notations are **RDF/XML**,[5] which defines an XML syntax for RDF, and **Turtle**,[6] which provides a simple way of representing RDF triples.

---

[4] http://www.w3.org/TR/rdf11-mt/
[5] http://www.w3.org/TR/rdf-syntax-grammar/
[6] http://www.w3.org/TR/turtle/

542   14   Data Warehouses and the Semantic Web

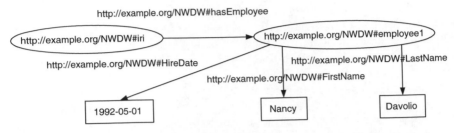

Fig. 14.1 An example of an RDF graph

Figure 14.1 depicts an RDF graph representing an employee of the
Northwind company, her first name, last name, and hire date. The following
piece of RDF/XML code describes this graph.

```
<xml version "1.0" encoding= "utf8"?>
<rdf:RDF
    xmlns:rdf="http://www.w3.org/1999/02/22-rdf-syntax-ns#"
    xmlns:ex="http://example.org/NWDW#">
    <rdf:Description rdf:about="http://example.org/NWDW#iri">
        <ex:hasEmployee>
            <rdf:Description rdf:about="http://example.org/NWDW#employee1">
                <ex:FirstName>Nancy</ex:FirstName>
                <ex:LastName>Davolio</ex:LastName>
                <ex:HireDate>1992-05-01</ex:HireDate>
            </rdf:Description>
        </ex:hasEmployee>
    </rdf:Description>
</rdf:RDF>
```

The first line is the typical XML heading line, and the document starts
with the RDF element. The xmlns attribute is used to define XML namespaces
composed of a prefix and an IRI, making the text less verbose. The subject
and object of the triple representing the company and its employee are within
Description elements, where the attribute rdf:about indicates the IRIs of the
resources. The ex prefix refers to the Northwind data warehouse.

The same triple will be written as follows using Turtle:

```
@prefix rdf: <http://www.w3.org/1999/02/22-rdf-syntax-ns#> .
@prefix ex: <http://example.org/NWDW#> .

ex:iri ex:hasEmployee ex:employee1 .
ex:employee1 rdf:type ex:Employee ; ex:FirstName "Nancy" ;
    ex:LastName "Davolio" ; ex:HireDate "1992-05-01" .
```

Note that Turtle provides a much simpler, less verbose syntax, compared to
RDF/XML, so we use Turtle in the remainder of the chapter.

Data types are supported in RDF through the XML data type system.
For example, by default ex:HireDate would be interpreted as a string value
rather than a date value. To explicitly define the data types for the example
above, we would write in Turtle:

@prefix rdf: <http://www.w3.org/1999/02/22-rdf-syntax-ns#> .
@prefix ex: <http://example.org/NWDW#> .
@prefix xsd: <http://www.w3.org/2001/XMLSchema#> .
ex:iri ex:hasEmployee ex:employee1 .
ex:employee1 rdf:type ex:Employee ; ex:FirstName "Nancy"^^xsd:string ;
    ex:LastName "Davolio"^^xsd:string ; ex:HireDate "1992-05-01"^^xsd:date .

To further simplify the notation, Turtle allows rdf:type to be replaced with 'a'. Thus, instead of

ex:employee1 rdf:type ex:Employee ;

we could write

ex:employee1 a ex:Employee ;

Also, the xml:lang attribute allows us to indicate the language of the text in the triple. For example, to indicate that the name of the employee is an English name, we may write in Turtle:

ex:employee1 ex:FirstName "Nancy"@en ; ex:LastName "Davolio"@en .

Finally, blank nodes are represented either explicitly with a blank node identifier of the form _:name or with no name using square brackets. The latter is used if the identifier is not needed elsewhere in the document. For example, the following triples state that the employee identified by ex:employee1, who corresponds to Nancy Davolio in the triples above, has a supervisor who is an employee called Andrew Fuller:

ex:employee1 a ex:Employee ;
    ex:Supervisor [a ex:Employee ; ex:FirstName "Andrew" ; ex:LastName "Fuller"] .

In this case, the blank node is used as object, and this object is an anonymous resource; we are not interested in who this person is.

A blank node can be used as subject in triples. If we need to use the blank node in other part of the document, we may use the following Turtle notation:

ex:employee1 a ex:Employee ; ex:Supervisor _:employee2 .
_:employee2 a ex:Employee ; ex:FirstName "Andrew"; ex:LastName "Fuller" .

14.1.3 RDF Representation of Relational Data

In this section, we describe how relational data can be represented in RDF in order to be used and shared on the semantic web.

Suppose that the Northwind company wants to share their warehouse data on the web, for example, to be accessible to all their branches. The Northwind data warehouse is stored in a relational database. For our example, we will use the Sales fact table and the Product dimension table of Fig. 14.2, which are simplified versions of the corresponding data warehouse tables. Note that we added an identifier SalesKey for each tuple in the Sales fact table.

a

SalesKey	ProductKey	CustomerKey	TimeKey	Quantity
s1	p1	c1	t1	100
s2	p1	c2	t2	100
...	...	...	...	...

b

ProductKey	ProductName	QuantityPerUnit	UnitPrice	Discontinued	CategoryName
p1	prod1	25	60	No	c1
p2	prod2	45	60	No	c1
...	...	...	...	...	...

Fig. 14.2 An excerpt of a simplified version of the Northwind data warehouse. (a) Sales fact table. (b) Product dimension table

The World Wide Web Consortium (W3C) has proposed two ways of mapping relational data to RDF: the direct mapping and the R2RML mapping, which we present next.

Direct Mapping

The **direct mapping**[7] defines an RDF graph representation of the data in a relational database. This mapping takes as input the schema and instance of a relational database and produces an RDF graph called the *direct graph*, whose triples are formed concatenating column names and values with a **base IRI**. In the examples below, the base IRI is <http://example.org/>. The mapping also accounts for the foreign keys in the databases being mapped. The direct mapping for the Sales fact table and the Product dimension table in Fig. 14.2 results in an RDF graph, from which we show below some triples:

```
@base <http://example.org/>
@prefix rdf:<http://www.w3.org/1999/02/22-rdf-syntax-ns#>

<Sales/SalesKey="s1"> rdf:type <Sales> .
<Sales/SalesKey="s1"> <Sales#SalesKey> "s1" .
<Sales/SalesKey="s1"> <Sales#ProductKey> "p1" .
<Sales/SalesKey="s1"> <Sales#ref-ProductKey> <Product/ProductKey="p1"> .
<Sales/SalesKey="s1"> <Sales#CustomerKey> "c1" .
<Sales/SalesKey="s1"> <Sales#ref-CustomerKey>
        <Customer/CustomerKey="c1"> .
<Sales/SalesKey="s1"> <Sales#TimeKey> "t1" .
<Sales/SalesKey="s1"> <Sales#ref-TimeKey> <Time/TimeKey="t1"> .
<Sales/SalesKey="s1"> <Sales#Quantity> "100" .
...
```

----

[7]http://www.w3.org/TR/rdb-direct-mapping/

```
<Product/ProductKey="p1"> rdf:type <Product> .
<Product/ProductKey="p1"> <Product#ProductKey> "p1" .
<Product/ProductKey="p1"> <Sales#ProductName> "prod1" .
<Product/ProductKey="p1"> <Sales#QuantityPerUnit> "25" .
<Product/ProductKey="p1"> <Sales#UnitPrice> "60" .
<Product/ProductKey="p1"> <Sales#Discontinued> "No" .
<Product/ProductKey="p1"> <Sales#CategoryKey> "c1" .
<Product/ProductKey="p1"> <Sales#ref-CategoryKey>
      <Category/CategoryKey="c1"> .
. . .
```

Each row in Sales produces a set of triples with a common subject. The subject is an IRI formed from the concatenation of the base IRI, the table name, the primary key column name (SalesKey), and the primary key value (s1 for the first tuple). The predicate for each column is an IRI formed as the concatenation of the base IRI, the table name, and the column name. The values are RDF literals taken from the column values. Each foreign key produces a triple with a predicate composed of the foreign key column names, the referenced table, and the referenced column names. The object of these triples is the row identifier for the referenced triple. The reference row identifiers must coincide with the subject used for the triples generated from the referenced row. For example, the triple

<Sales/SalesKey="s1"> <Sales#ref-ProductKey> <Product/ProductKey="p1">

tells that the subject (the first row in Sales) contains a foreign key in the column ProductKey (the predicate in the triple) which refers to the triple identified in the object (the triple whose subject is <Product/ProductKey="p1">).

As can be seen, the direct mapping is very straightforward, although rigid, in the sense that it does not allow any kind of customization. Indeed, the structure of the resulting RDF graph directly reflects the structure of the database, the target RDF vocabulary directly reflects the names of database schema elements, and neither the structure nor the vocabulary can be changed.

R2RML Mapping

R2RML[8] is a language for expressing mappings from relational databases to RDF data sets. Such mappings provide the ability to view relational data in RDF using a customized structure and vocabulary. As with the direct mapping, an R2RML mapping results in an RDF graph.

An R2RML mapping is an RDF graph written in Turtle syntax, called the *mapping document*. The main object of an R2RML mapping is the so-called *triples map*. Each triples map is a collection of triples, composed of a

---

[8]http://www.w3.org/TR/r2rml

logical table, a *subject map*, and zero or more *predicate object maps*. A logical table is either a base table or a view (using the predicate rr:tableName) or an SQL query (using the predicate rr:sqlQuery). A predicate object map is composed of a predicate map and an object map. Subject maps, predicate maps, and object maps are either constants (rr:constant), column-based maps (rr:column), or template-based maps (rr:template). Templates use brace-enclosed column names as placeholders. As an example, Fig. 14.3 shows how a portion of the dimension table Product is mapped to RDF using R2RML. This mapping can be then applied to any instance of the table to produce the triples. We next show the mapping document, which, together with the instance of the table, will produce the RDF graph:

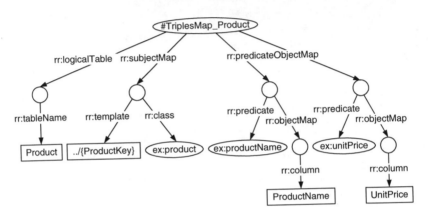

Fig. 14.3 R2RML mapping of the Product dimension

```
@prefix rr: <http://www.w3.org/ns/r2rml#> .
@prefix rdf: <http://www.w3.org/1999/02/22-rdf-syntax-ns#> .
@prefix rdfs: <http://www.w3.org/2000/01/rdf-schema#> .
@prefix ex: <http://example.org/> .

<#TriplesMap_Product>
    a rr:TriplesMap ;
    rr:logicalTable [ rr:tableName "Product" ] ;
    rr:subjectMap [
        rr:template "http://example.org/product/{ProductKey}" ;
        rr:class ex:product ] ;
    rr:predicateObjectMap [
        rr:predicate ex:productName ;
        rr:objectMap [ rr:column "ProductName" ; rr:language "en" ] ; ] ;
    rr:predicateObjectMap [
        rr:predicate ex:unitPrice ;
        rr:objectMap [ rr:column "UnitPrice" ; rr:datatype rdfs:integer ] ; ] .
```

The triples map above (corresponding to the table Product) is called <#TriplesMap_Product>. The logical table is the table Product, and the subject is the template for the key, ProductKey. Applied to the input table, this will produce the subject of the triples. For each such subject, the predicate-object mapping will produce the mapping of the columns we wish to map. For example, rr:predicate ex:productName will map the column ProductName. Note that this procedure allows us to customize the name of the column, for example, according to a given vocabulary. Below, we show some of the triples produced by this mapping when applied to the table Product in Fig. 14.2b:

```
<http://example.org/product/p1>
    a <http://example.org/product> ;
    <http://example.org/productName> "prod1"@en ;
    <http://example.org/unitPrice> "60"^^
        <http://www.w3.org/2000/01/rdf-schema#integer>
    .... ;
```

Foreign keys are handled through *referencing object maps*, which use the subjects of another triples map as the objects generated by a predicate-object map:

```
<#TriplesMap_Sales>
    rr:predicateObjectMap [
        rr:predicate ex:product ;
        rr:objectMap [
            rr:parentTriplesMap <#TriplesMap_Product> ;
            rr:joinCondition [
                rr:child "ProductKey" ;
                rr:parent "ProductKey" ] ; ] ; ] .
```

The rr:parentTriplesMap predicate references an existing triples map in the same mapping file that generates the desired resource. In the example above, in the mapping file for the Sales fact table, when mapping the foreign key for the table Product, we reference the mapping for the latter (which we have called <#TriplesMap_Product>). The join condition (rr:joinCondition) contains two elements, namely, rr:child and rr:parent. The former is associated with a column name of the logical table of the triples map containing the referencing object map. The latter is associated with a logical column name of the referenced triples map.

14.2 SPARQL

SPARQL[9] is the standard query language for RDF graphs. SPARQL queries are built using variables, which are denoted using either '?' or '$' as a prefix, although the former is normally used. The query evaluation mechanism of

---

[9]http://www.w3.org/TR/sparql11-query/

SPARQL is based on subgraph matching, where the selection criteria is expressed as a graph pattern. This pattern is matched against an RDF graph instantiating the variables in the query.

In what follows, we will work with the Northwind data warehouse represented as an RDF graph, as studied in Sect. 14.1.3. Let us analyze the following SPARQL query, which asks for names and hire date of employees:

```
PREFIX ex:<http://example.org/NWDW#>
PREFIX rdf:<http://www.w3.org/1999/02/22-rdf-syntax-ns#>

SELECT ?firstName ?lastName ?hireDate
WHERE { ?emp a ex:Employee .
        ?emp ex:Employee#FirstName ?firstName .
        ?emp ex:Employee#LastName ?lastName .
        ?emp ex:Employee#HireDate ?hireDate . }
```

There are three parts in the query. A sequence of PREFIX clauses declare the namespaces. The SELECT clause indicates the format of the result. The WHERE clause in this case contains a graph pattern composed of four triples in Turtle notation. The triples in the query are matched against the triples in an RDF graph that instantiates the variables in the pattern. In our case, this is the default RDF graph that represents the Northwind data warehouse. If we want to include other graphs, a FROM clause must be added, followed by a list of named graphs. As we have seen, the query above (without the prefix part) can be more succinctly written as follows:

```
SELECT ?firstName ?lastName ?hireDate
WHERE { ?emp a ex:Employee ; ex:Employee#FirstName ?firstName ;
        ex:Employee#LastName ?lastName ; ex:Employee#HireDate ?hireDate . }
```

To evaluate the above query, we instantiate the variable ?emp with an IRI whose type is http://example.org/NWDW#Employee. Then, we look if there is a triple with the same subject and property ex:Employee#FirstName, and, if so, we instantiate the variable ?firstName. We proceed similarly to instantiate the other variables in the query and return the result. Note that in this case the result of the query is not an RDF graph, but a set of literals. Alternatively, the CONSTRUCT clause can be used to return an RDF graph built by substituting variables in a set of triple templates.

From now on, we omit the prefix clauses in queries for brevity. The keyword DISTINCT must be used to remove duplicates in the result. For example, the following query returns the cities of the Northwind customers, without duplicates:

```
SELECT DISTINCT ?city
WHERE { ?customer a ex:Customer ; ex:Customer#City ?city . }
```

The FILTER keyword selects patterns that meet a certain condition. For example, the query "First name and last name of the employees hired between 1992 and 1994" reads in SPARQL as follows:

```
SELECT ?firstName ?lastName
WHERE { ?emp a ex:Employee ; ex:Employee#FirstName ?firstName ;
        ex:Employee#LastName ?lastName ; ex:Employee#HireDate ?hireDate .
        FILTER( ?hireDate >= "1992-01-01"^^xsd:date &&
        ?hireDate <= "1994-12-31"^^xsd:date) }
```

Filter conditions are Boolean expressions constructed using the logical connectives && (and), || (or), and ! (not).

The FILTER keyword can be combined with the NOT EXISTS keyword to test the absence of a pattern. For example, the query "First name and last name of employees without supervisor" reads in SPARQL as follows:

```
SELECT ?firstName ?lastName
WHERE { ?emp a ex:Employee ; ex:Employee#FirstName ?firstName ;
        ex:Employee#LastName ?lastName .
        FILTER NOT EXISTS { ?emp ex:Employee#Supervisor ?sup . } }
```

The OPTIONAL keyword is used to specify a graph pattern for which the values will be shown if they are found. For example, the query "First and last name of employees, along with the first and last name of her supervisor, if she has one" can be written in SPARQL as follows:

```
SELECT ?empFirstName ?empLastName ?supFirstName ?supLastName
WHERE { ?emp a ex:Employee ; ex:Employee#FirstName ?empFirstName ;
        ex:Employee#LastName ?empLastName .
        OPTIONAL { ?emp ex:Employee#Supervisor ?sup .
                   ?sup a ex:Employee ; ex:Employee#FirstName ?supFirstName ;
                   ex:Employee#LastName ?supLastName . } }
```

Notice that the OPTIONAL keyword behaves in a way similar to an outer join in SQL.

Aggregation and Sorting in SPARQL

Aggregate functions summarize information from multiple triple patterns into a single one. SPARQL provides the usual aggregate functions COUNT, SUM, MAX, MIN, and AVG. In addition, along the lines of SQL, before summarization, triples may be grouped using the GROUP BY keyword, and then the aggregate function is applied to every group. Furthermore, filtering of groups may also be performed with the HAVING keyword, like it is done with the FILTER clause for ungrouped sets. Finally, the result can be sorted with the ORDER BY clause, where every attribute in the list can be ordered either in ascending or descending order by specifying ASC or DESC, respectively.

Consider the query "Total number of orders handled by each employee, in descending order of number of orders. Only list employees that handled more than 100 orders." This query is expressed in SPARQL as follows:

```
SELECT      ?emp (COUNT(DISTINCT ?orderNo) AS ?ordersByEmployee)
WHERE       { ?sales a ex:Sales ; ex:Sales#Employee ?emp ;
              ex:Sales#OrderNo ?orderNo .
              ?emp a ex:Employee . }
GROUP BY ?emp
HAVING      COUNT(DISTINCT ?orderNo) > 100
ORDER BY DESC(COUNT(DISTINCT ?orderNo))
```

The GROUP BY clause collects the orders associated with each employee, the HAVING clause keeps only the employees who have more than 100 distinct orders, and the ORDER BY clause orders the result in descending order according to the number of orders.

Consider now the query "For customers from San Francisco, list the total quantity of each product ordered. Order the result by customer key, in ascending order, and by quantity of products ordered, in descending order."

```
SELECT      ?cust ?prod (SUM(?qty) AS ?totalQty)
WHERE       { ?sales a ex:Sales ; ex:Sales#Customer ?cust ;
              ex:Sales#Product ?prod ; ex:Sales#Quantity ?qty .
              ?cust a ex:Customer ; ?ex:Customer#City ?city .
              ?city a ex:City ; ex:City#Name ?cityName .
              FILTER(?cityName = "San Francisco") }
GROUP BY ?cust ?prod
ORDER BY ASC(?cust) DESC(?totalQty)
```

This query defines a graph pattern linking sales to customers and cities. Prior to grouping, we need to find the triples satisfying the graph pattern and select the customers from San Francisco. We then group by pairs of ?cust and ?prod and, for each group, take the sum of the attribute ?qty. Finally, the resulting triples are ordered.

Subqueries

In SPARQL, a subquery is used to look for a certain value in a database and then use this value in a comparison condition. A subquery is a query enclosed into curly braces used within a WHERE clause. The external query is called the outer query.

As an example, let us consider the query "For each customer compute the maximum sales amount among all her orders." The query is written as follows:

```
SELECT      ?cust (MAX(?totalSales) as ?maxSales)
WHERE       { {
              SELECT      ?cust ?orderNo (SUM(?sales) as ?totalSales)
              WHERE       { ?sales a ex:Sales ; ex:Sales#Customer ?cust ;
                            ex:Sales#OrderNo ?orderNo ; ex:Sales#SalesAmount ?sales .
                            ?cust a ex:Customer . }
              GROUP BY ?cust ?orderNo } }
GROUP BY ?cust
```

The inner query computes the total sales amount for each customer and order. Then, in the outer query, for each customer we select the maximum sales amount among all its orders.

Subqueries are commonly used with the UNION and MINUS keywords. The UNION combines graph patterns so that one of several alternative graph patterns may match. For example, the query "Products that have been ordered by customers from San Francisco or supplied by suppliers from San Jose" can be written as follows:

```
SELECT DISTINCT ?prodName
WHERE { {
        SELECT ?prod
        WHERE { ?sales a ex:Sales ; ex:Sales#Product ?prod ;
                ex:Sales#Customer ?cust .
                ?cust a ex:Customer ; ex:Customer#City ?custCity .
                ?custCity a ex:City ; ex:City#Name ?custCityName .
                FILTER(?custCityName = "San Francisco") } }
        UNION {
        SELECT ?prod
        WHERE { ?sales a ex:Sales ; ex:Sales#Product ?prod ;
                ex:Sales#Supplier ?sup .
                ?sup a ex:Supplier ; ex:Supplier#City ?supCity .
                ?supCity a ex:City ; ex:City#Name ?supCityName .
                FILTER(?supCityName = "San Jose") } } }
```

Analogously, the MINUS operation computes the difference between the results of two subqueries. An example is the query: "Products that have not been ordered by customers from San Francisco," which can be written as follows:

```
SELECT DISTINCT ?prod
WHERE { ?sales a ex:Sales ; ex:Sales#Product ?prod .
        MINUS { {
        SELECT ?prod
        WHERE { ?sales a ex:Sales ; ex:Sales#Product ?prod ;
                ex:Sales#Customer ?cust .
                ?cust a ex:Customer ; ex:Customer#City ?city .
                ?city a ex:City ; ex:City#Name ?cityName .
                FILTER(?cityName = "San Francisco") } } } }
```

The inner query computes the products ordered by customers from San Francisco. The outer query obtains all products that have been ordered and subtracts from them the products obtained in the inner query.

14.3 RDF Representation of Multidimensional Data

We are now ready to study two approaches to represent multidimensional data in RDF, namely, QB and QB4OLAP. Suppose that the Northwind company wants to analyze sales data against economic and demographic data, published as open data on the web. Instead of loading and maintaining those data permanently in the local data warehouse, it could be more efficient to either temporarily load them into the warehouse for analysis or to operate over a cube directly in RDF format, as we will study in the next sections. Being able to publish data cubes in RDF will also allow the company to publish data over the web to be shared by all the company branches.

In our study, we will use an ontology from the Ordnance Survey containing administrative geography and civil voting areas in Great Britain.[10] In this ontology, the administrative units are defined as classes, and the geographic relationship between them is defined through properties. For example, GovernmentOfficeRegion (GOR) and UnitaryAuthority (UA) are classes, while hasGORCode, hasUACode, and hasName are properties. The relationship between UA, GOR, and countries (in the UK) is given at the instance level, rather than at the schema level. For instance, the Unitary Authority of Reading, with code 00MC, is contained in the South East Government Office Region. As an example, we show below a portion of the ontology corresponding to Reading:

```
@prefix rdf: <http://www.w3.org/1999/02/22-rdf-syntax-ns#>
@prefix id: <http://data.ordnancesurvey.co.uk/id/>
@prefix admgeo: <http://data.ordnancesurvey.co.uk/ontology/admingeo/>
@prefix skos: <http://www.w3.org/2004/02/skos/core#>

<http://data.ordnancesurvey.co.uk/id/7000000000038895>
    a admgeo:Borough ; a admgeo:UnitaryAuthority ;
    rdf:label "The Borough of Reading" ; admgeo:gssCode "E06000038" ;
    admgeo:hasAreaCode "UTA" ; admgeo:hasUACode "00MC" ;
    skos:prefLabel "The Borough of Reading" .
```

The IRI in the fifth line represents the resource (Reading), and it is the subject of the triples formed with the predicate-object pairs below it (telling, e.g., that the area code of Reading is UTA).

In addition, associated with the geographic data above, we have yearly data about household in the UK. With these data, we build a data cube denoted HouseholdCS with a measure Household and two dimensions, Geography and Time. Dimension Geography is organized into the following hierarchy of levels: UnitaryAuthority → GovernmentOfficeRegion → Country → All. We show examples of instances in Fig. 14.4. Dimension Time has the hierarchy Year → All. Figure 14.5 shows an instance of this data cube, in tabular format. For example, a cell corresponding to the household in Reading in 2006 has value 58. In the next sections, we show how this data cube can be defined in RDF.

---

[10]http://data.ordnancesurvey.co.uk/ontology/admingeo/

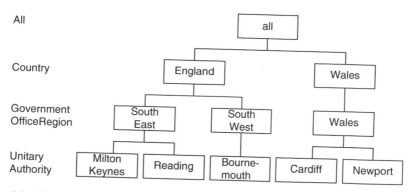

Fig. 14.4 Examples of instances of the dimension Geography

Country	GOR	UA	Year		
			2006	2007	2008
England	South East	Milton Keynes	92	94	96
		Reading	58	58	60
	South West	Bournemouth	71	72	73
Wales	Wales	Cardiff	132.1	134.2	136.7
		Newport	58.7		59.6

Fig. 14.5 An instance of the HouseholdCS data cube in tabular format

14.3.1 RDF Data Cube Vocabulary

The **RDF data cube vocabulary**[11] or QB provides the means to publish statistical data and metadata on the web using RDF. This vocabulary is compatible with the cube model underlying the Statistical Data and Metadata eXchange (SDMX)[12] standard, an ISO standard for exchanging and sharing statistical data and metadata among organizations. Figure 14.6 depicts the QB vocabulary. Capitalized terms represent RDF classes, and noncapitalized terms represent RDF properties. Classes in external vocabularies are depicted in light gray font in Fig. 14.6.

QB provides constructs to represent the structure and instances of statistical data. A data structure definition (DSD), defined as an instance of the class qb:DataStructureDefinition, specifies the schema of a data set, defined as an instance of the class qb:DataSet. This structure can be shared among different data sets. The DSD of a data set is defined by means of the qb:structure property. The DSD has component properties for representing

---

[11]http://www.w3.org/TR/vocab-data-cube/
[12]http://sdmx.org/?page_id=10

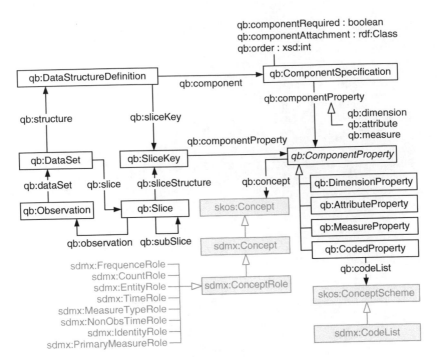

Fig. 14.6 Outline of the QB vocabulary

dimensions, measures, and attributes, called qb:dimension, qb:measure, and qb:attribute, respectively. Component specifications are linked to DSDs via the property qb:component. For example, the schema of the HouseholdCS data cube of Fig. 14.5 can be defined as follows:

```
ex:Geography a qb:DimensionProperty, qb:CodedProperty .
ex:Time a qb:DimensionProperty, qb:CodedProperty .
ex:Household a qb:MeasureProperty .
ex:HouseholdCS a qb:DataStructureDefinition ;
    qb:component [qb:dimension ex:Geography] ;
    qb:component [qb:dimension ex:Time] ;
    qb:component [qb:measure ex:Household] ;
    qb:component [qb:attribute sdmx-attribute:unitMeasure] .
```

For clarity, we omit above the declaration of the prefixes. First, the Geography and Time dimensions as well as the Household measure are defined. Then, the data cube schema, called ex:HouseholdCS, is declared as an instance of qb:DataStructureDefinition. Dimensions, measures, and attributes are defined using the qb:component property and using blank nodes.

Observations, which are instances of qb:Observation, represent points in a multidimensional data space. They are grouped in data sets by means of the qb:dataSet property. An observation is linked to a value in each dimension of the DSD using properties defined as instances of qb:DimensionProperty.

A set of measure values and attributes is associated with an observation using the properties qb:MeasureProperty and qb:AttributeProperty in the DSD, respectively. An instance of the above cube is defined as follows:

```
ex:dataset-hh a qb:DataSet ; rdfs:label "Household in UK"@en ;
    qb:structure ex:HouseholdCS .
ex:o1 a qb:Observation ; qb:dataSet ex:dataset-hh ; ex:Geography ns0:00mc ;
    ex:Time <http://dbpedia.org/resource/2007> ; ex:Household 58 ;
    sdmx-attribute:unitMeasure <http://dbpedia.org/resource/Thousand> .
```

Here, we define a data set ex:dataset-hh, whose structure is ex:HouseholdCS. The observation ex:o1 belongs to this data set. Values for the dimensions are also given. Note that the year 2007 is represented using an IRI.

QB provides the qb:concept property, which links components to the concept they represent. The latter are modeled using the skos:Concept class defined in the SKOS[13] (Simple Knowledge Organization System) vocabulary.

Multidimensional Data Representation in QB

QB does not provide a mechanism to represent a multidimensional schema, but it allows us to represent hierarchical relationships between members of dimension levels using the SKOS vocabulary. A *SKOS concept scheme* defines the semantic relationships between concepts. Concepts are linked to the concept schemes they belong to via the skos:inScheme property. For example, skos:broader and skos:narrower enable the representation of hierarchical relationships. For instance, the triple country skos:narrower region represents a hierarchical relationship where region is at a lower level than country. To provide an entry point to the broader/narrower concept hierarchies, SKOS defines a skos:hasTopConcept property. Thus, hierarchical relationships between dimension members are represented in QB as an instance of qb:DimensionProperty with an associated skos:ConceptScheme. Particular concepts in the concept scheme can be associated with the property skos:hasTopConcept, indicating that these values correspond to members at the highest level of granularity in the dimension hierarchy. Members at lower levels of granularity can be reached using the skos:narrower property. All of the above imply that dimension members in QB may only be navigated from higher granularity concepts down to finer granularity concepts. Note that in general common OLAP operations (except drill down) traverse dimension hierarchies in the opposite direction.

We show next an excerpt of a dimension Geography constructed from the Ordnance Survey ontology introduced above, represented using QB:

```
ex:Geography a qb:DimensionProperty, qb:CodedProperty ; qb:codeList ex:geo .
ex:geo a skos:ConceptScheme ; skos:hasTopConcept ns2:921 .
```

---

[13]http://www.w3.org/2009/08/skos-reference/skos.html

ns2:921 a adgeo:Country ; rdfs:label "England"@en ;
    skos:inScheme ex:geo ; skos:narrower ns1:J .
ns1:J a adgeo:GovernmentOfficeRegion ; rdfs:label "South East"@en ;
    skos:inScheme ex:geo ; skos:narrower ns0:00mc .
ns0:00mc a adgeo:UnitaryAuthority ; rdfs:label "The Borough of Reading"@en ;
    skos:inScheme ex:geo .

The dimension is denoted ex:Geography, and it is defined as member of the classes qb:DimensionProperty and qb:CodedProperty. This dimension is associated to a concept scheme ex:geo, a member of the class skos:ConceptScheme, using the qb:codeList property. Intuitively, this code list represents the set of values of the dimension, organized hierarchically using the concept scheme. The dimension member ns2:921 is defined as the top concept in ex:geo using the property skos:hasTopConcept. It is also stated that such element is an instance of the adgeo:Country class, labeled England. Hierarchical relationships between members are stated using the skos:narrower property, from the most general concepts down to most specific ones, namely, from adgeo:Country through adgeo:GovernmentOfficeRegion to adgeo:UnitaryAuthority. We remark, once more, that the hierarchical relationships are given at the instance level.

OLAP Operations over QB

In a multidimensional model, facts represent points in a multidimensional space, where dimension coordinates are given at the lowest levels of each participating dimension (we have seen, however, in Chaps. 4 and 5, that we may sometimes have facts at different granularities). The QB specification allows observations at different granularity levels to coexist in a data set, which makes the OLAP operations difficult to implement. A solution could be to split the original observations into different data sets, each one containing observations at the same granularity level, which is not possible, since aggregation levels are not modeled in QB, as we have already seen. As a consequence, the QB vocabulary does not provide direct support for OLAP operations. Moreover, the possibility of implementing OLAP operations over data represented using QB has some limitations, described next.

The *roll-up* operation is not supported in QB because of the following. First, rolling-up requires traversing a dimension hierarchy from a base level up to a target level. Since dimension levels are not modeled in QB, this navigation is not supported. Second, the relationship between level members is modeled from the most general concept down to more specific concepts. Finally, aggregate functions for each measure are not modeled, and these functions are needed to implement the roll-up operation. Although in OLAP tools, each measure is associated with an aggregation function, this is not addressed in QB. Analogous observations apply to the *drill-down* operation.

Slicing is not supported in QB due to the fact that aggregate functions for a given measure are not modeled, and these functions are required to reduce to a single value the dimension to be dropped, as explained in Chap. 3.

Dicing is supported by QB. For instance, the FILTER clause in SPARQL can be used to implement a dicing condition.

Given the limitations commented above, in order to be able to define and implement OLAP operations, we must extend QB to support dimension hierarchies. We next explain how this can be done.

14.3.2   QB4OLAP Vocabulary

The **QB4OLAP vocabulary**[14] aims at giving a solution to the problems of the QB vocabulary discussed in the previous section. Multidimensional data can be published in QB4OLAP from scratch, or data already published using QB can be extended with dimension levels, level members, dimension hierarchies, and the association of aggregate functions to measures without affecting the existing observations. Therefore, data cubes already published using QB can also be represented using QB4OLAP without affecting existing applications developed over QB data cubes.

Figure 14.7 depicts the QB4OLAP vocabulary. Classes and properties added to QB (with prefix qb4o) are depicted with light gray background and black font. The class qb4o:LevelProperty models dimension levels. Relations between dimension levels are represented using the property qb4o:parentLevel. Level members are represented as instances of the class qb4o:LevelMember, and relations between them can be expressed using the property skos:broader. Level attributes are defined via the qb4o:hasAttribute property. Level properties are stated in the data structure definition. The class qb4o:AggregateFunction represents aggregate functions. The association between measures and aggregate functions is represented using the property qb4o:hasAggregateFunction. This property, together with the concept of component sets, allows a given measure to be associated with different aggregate functions in different cubes.

Multidimensional Data Representation in QB4OLAP

We next show how QB4OLAP can be used to publish multidimensional data from scratch. The definition of the schema of the Geography dimension using QB4OLAP is shown next:

```
ex:Geography a qb:DimensionProperty .
ex:UnitaryAuthority a qb4o:LevelProperty ; qb4o:inDimension ex:Geography ;
    qb4o:parentLevel ex:GovernmentOfficeRegion .
ex:GovernmentOfficeRegion a qb4o:LevelProperty ; qb4o:inDimension ex:Geography ;
    qb4o:parentLevel ex:Country .
```

---

[14]http://purl.org/qb4olap/cubes

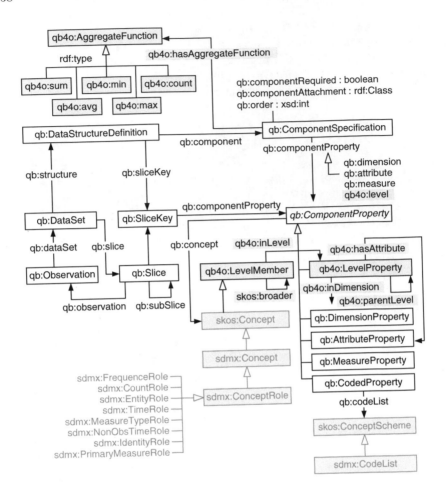

Fig. 14.7 Outline of the QB4OLAP vocabulary

ex:Country a qb4o:LevelProperty ; qb4o:inDimension ex:Geography ;
    skos:closeMatch adgeo:Country .

The levels ex:UnitaryAuthority, ex:GovernmentOfficeRegion, and ex:Country are defined as instances of the class qb4o:LevelProperty, and the relationship between them is defined by the property qb4o:parentLevel.

An instance of the Geography dimension is shown next:

ns0:00mc qb4o:inLevel ex:UnitaryAuthority ;
    rdfs:label "The Borough of Reading"@en ; skos:broader ns1:J .
ns1:J qb4o:inLevel ex:GovernmentOfficeRegion ;
    rdfs:label "South East"@en ; skos:broader ns2:921 .
ns2:921 qb4o:inLevel ex:Country ; rdfs:label "England"@en .

The property qb4o:inLevel indicates the level in the hierarchy to which belongs a level member, while skos:broader defines the parent of a level member. For instance, it is stated that the member ns1:J belongs to level ex:GovernmentOfficeRegion and that such member aggregates over the member ns2:921 in level ex:Country. Note that the dimension instances are treated analogously to QB, using the SKOS vocabulary.

The data cube of Fig. 14.5 can be represented using QB4OLAP as follows:

```
ex:Geography a qb:DimensionProperty .
ex:Time a qb:DimensionProperty .
ex:Year a qb4o:LevelProperty ; skos:closeMatch db:Year ; qb4o:inDimension ex:Time .
ex:Household a qb:MeasureProperty .
ex:HouseholdCS a qb:DataStructureDefinition ;
    qb:component [qb4o:level ex:UnitaryAuthority] ;
    qb:component [qb4o:level ex:Year] ;
    qb:component [qb:measure ex:Household ; qb4o:hasAggregateFunction qb4o:sum] .
```

There are some relevant differences with the QB data cube shown in the previous section. The data cube schema is declared as an instance of the class qb:DataStructureDefinition. The level property qb4o:level is used to specify the levels in the cube schema. For example, the triple ex:HouseholdCS qb:component [qb4o:level ex:Year] tells that ex:Year is a level of the cube. Analogously, the triple ex:Household a qb:MeasureProperty tells that ex:Household is a measure in the cube, like in QB. In addition, the aggregate function corresponding to this measure is defined using the property qb4o:hasAggregateFunction.

An instance of the cube is represented in QB4OLAP as follows:

```
ex:dataset-hh a qb:DataSet ; qb:structure ex:HouseholdCS ;
    rdfs:label "Household in UK"@en .
ex:o1 a qb:Observation ; qb:dataSet ex:dataset-hh ;
    ex:UnitaryAuthority ns0:00mc ; ex:Year db:2007 ; ex:Household 58 .
```

The data set ex:dataset-hh is defined as an instance of the class qb:DataSet, linked to the data cube using the property qb:structure. Further, an observation ex:o1 is defined as an instance of the class qb:Observation. The instance represents the cell in the cube with values ns0:00mc for UA, 2007 for Year, and 58 for the measure Household. Note that observations are defined using QB classes and properties. Therefore, the observations in an existing cube expressed in QB do not need to be changed in order to express the cube in QB4OLAP.

OLAP Operations over QB4OLAP

We now show a possible implementation of some of the OLAP operations over a data cube defined using the QB4OLAP vocabulary. The operations are written in SPARQL.

We start with the ROLLUP operation. As an example, consider the query "Total household by Government Office Region." This is expressed using the operations introduced in Chap. 3 as

ROLLUP(HouseholdCS, Geography → GOR, SUM(Household)).

The structure of the result represented as a QB4OLAP schema denoted by ex:HouseholdByGOR is shown next:

```
ex:HouseholdByGOR a qb:DataStructureDefinition ;
    qb:component [qb4o:level ex:GovernmentOfficeRegion] ;
    qb:component [qb4o:level ex:Year] ;
    qb:component [qb:measure ex:Household ; qb4o:hasAggregateFunction qb4o:sum] .
ex:dataset-hh1 a qb:DataSet ; rdfs:label "Household in UK by GOR"@en ;
    qb:structure ex:HouseholdByGOR .
```

The SPARQL query that implements the operation is shown next:

```
CONSTRUCT { ?id a qb:Observation ; qb:dataSet ex:dataset-hh1 ; ex:Year ?year ;
            ex:GovernmentOfficeRegion ?gor ; ex:Household ?sumHhold . }
WHERE      { {
            SELECT ?gor ?year (SUM(?hhold) AS ?sumHhold)
                   (iri(concat("http://example.org/hhold#Roll-upGOR-",
                   strafter(?gor, "http://example.org/hhold#"), "-",
                   strafter(?year, "http://example.org/hhold#"))) AS ?id)
            WHERE { ?o qb:dataSet ex:dataset-hh ; ex:Year ?year ;
                    ex:Household ?hhold ; ex:UnitaryAuthority ?ua .
                    ?ua skos:broader ?gor .
                    ?gor qb4o:inLevel ex:GovernmentOfficeRegion . }
            GROUP BY ?gor ?year } }
```

In the WHERE clause of the subquery, a graph pattern matching is performed. From the matching triples, the values that instantiate the ?gor and ?year variables are returned and aggregated in the SELECT clause. It is important to remark that new IRIs must be generated to identify each one of the new observations resulting from the application of the operation. This is done in the SELECT clause of the subquery with the strafter function, which returns the substring of the first parameter that appears after the string in the second parameter. Further, in the outer query, the CONSTRUCT clause is used since it returns a graph, opposite to the SELECT clause, which returns literals.

Let us consider now the following slice operation:

SLICE(Sales, Geography, Country="England"),

which drops the dimension Geography by fixing a value in it. As in the previous case, we first need to define the schema of the resulting cube as follows:

```
ex:HouseholdSlice a qb:DataStructureDefinition ;
    qb:component [qb4o:level ex:Year] ;
    qb:component [qb:measure ex:Household ; qb4o:hasAggregateFunction qb4o:sum] .
ex:dataset-hh2 a qb:DataSet ; rdfs:label "Household in England by Year"@en ;
    qb:structure ex:HouseholdSlice .
```

We denote this cube as ex:HouseholdSlice. We can see that the resulting cube has only the Time dimension (level ex:Year) and the ex:Household measure. The SPARQL query that implements the slice operation is shown next:

```
CONSTRUCT { ?id a qb:Observation ; qb:dataSet ex:dataset-hh2 ; ex:Year ?year ;
            ex:Household ?sumHhold . }
WHERE      { {
            SELECT ?year (SUM(?hhold) AS ?sumHhold)
            (iri(concat("http://example.org/hhold#SliceGeo_",
            strafter(?year, "http://example.org/hhold#"))) AS ?id)
            WHERE { ?o qb:dataSet ex:dataset-hh ; ex:Year ?year ;
            ex:UnitaryAuthority ?ua ; ex:Household ?hhold .
            ?ua: qb4o:inLevel ex:UnitaryAuthority ; skos:broader ?gor .
            ?gor: qb4o:inLevel ex:GovernmentOfficeRegion ;
            skos:broader ?country .
            ?country: qb4o:inLevel ex:Country ; rdfs:label ?countryLabel .
            FILTER(?countryLabel = "England"@en) }
            GROUP BY ?year } }
```

Since observations are at the granularity of unitary authority, in the subquery we must roll up to the country level. Then, the FILTER condition implements the slice operation. The SELECT clause of the subquery aggregates all observations pertaining to England at the year level. As in the previous query, the IRIs of the new query are generated in the SELECT clause of the subquery.

Finally, consider the following dice operation:

DICE(HouseholdCS, Time.Year > 2007),

which obtains a subcube from the HouseholdCS data cube containing only data from 2007 onward. This is implemented by the following query:

```
CONSTRUCT { ?id a qb:Observation ; qb:dataSet ex:dataset-hh ;
            ex:Year ?year ; ex:UnitaryAuthority ?ua ; ex:Household ?hhold . }
WHERE      { {
            SELECT ?ua ?year ?hhold
            (iri(concat("http://example.org/hhold#Dice_",
            strafter(?ua, "http://example.org/hhold#"), "_",
            strafter(?year, "http://example.org/hhold#"))) AS ?id)
            WHERE { ?o qb:dataSet ex:dataset-hh ; ex:Year ?year ;
            ex:Household ?hhold ; ex:UnitaryAuthority ?ua .
            FILTER (?year >= 2007) } } }
```

As shown above, the dice condition is implemented by the FILTER clause. Note that the output schema is identical to the cube schema.

14.4 Representation of the Northwind Cube in QB4OLAP

In this section, we show how the Northwind data cube can be represented in RDF using the QB4OLAP vocabulary. The Northwind data cube has been introduced in Fig. 4.2. We show it again in Fig. 14.8 to ease readability.

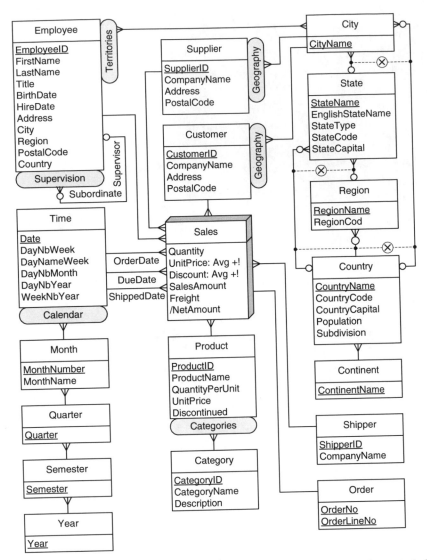

Fig. 14.8 Conceptual schema of the Northwind data warehouse (repeated from Fig. 4.2)

We start by defining the namespace prefixes as follows:

```
@prefix qb: <http://purl.org/linked-data/cube#>.
@prefix qb4o: <http://purl.org/qb4olap/cubes#> .
@prefix nw: <http://dwbook.org/cubes/schemas/northwind#> .
@prefix nwi: <http://dwbook.org/cubes/instances/northwind#> .
@prefix rdf: <http://www.w3.org/1999/02/22-rdf-syntax-ns#> .
@prefix rdfs: <http://www.w3.org/2000/01/rdf-schema#> .
@prefix sdmx-concept: <http://purl.org/linked-data/sdmx/2009/concept#> .
```

@prefix sdmx-dimension: <http://purl.org/linked-data/sdmx/2009/dimension#> .
@prefix skos: <http://www.w3.org/2004/02/skos/core#> .
@prefix db: <http://dbpedia.org/resource/> .

Dimensions are defined using the property qb:DimensionProperty as follows:

```
nw:Employee a rdf:Property, qb:DimensionProperty ; rdfs:label "Employee"@en .
nw:OrderDate a rdf:Property, qb:DimensionProperty ; rdfs:label "Order Date"@en ;
    rdfs:subPropertyOf sdmx-dimension:refPeriod ;
    qb:concept sdmx-concept:refPeriod .
nw:DueDate a rdf:Property, qb:DimensionProperty ; rdfs:label "Due Date"@en ;
    rdfs:subPropertyOf sdmx-dimension:refPeriod ;
    qb:concept sdmx-concept:refPeriod .
nw:ShippedDate a rdf:Property, qb:DimensionProperty ;
    rdfs:label "Shipped Date"@en ; rdfs:subPropertyOf sdmx-dimension:refPeriod ;
    qb:concept sdmx-concept:refPeriod .
nw:Product a rdf:Property, qb:DimensionProperty ; rdfs:label "Product"@en .
nw:Order a rdf:Property, qb:DimensionProperty ; rdfs:label "Order"@en .
nw:Shipper a rdf:Property, qb:DimensionProperty ; rdfs:label "Shipper"@en .
nw:Customer a rdf:Property, qb:DimensionProperty ; rdfs:label "Customer"@en .
nw:Supplier a rdf:Property, qb:DimensionProperty ; rdfs:label "Suppliers"@en .
```

A cube is defined using the property qb:DataStructureDefinition, and its dimensions are defined using the property qb4o:level, as follows:

```
nw:Northwind a qb:DataStructureDefinition ;
    qb:component [qb4o:level nw:Employee] ;
    qb:component [qb4o:level nw:OrderDate] ;
    qb:component [qb4o:level nw:DueDate] ;
    qb:component [qb4o:level nw:ShippedDate] ;
    qb:component [qb4o:level nw:Product] ;
    qb:component [qb4o:level nw:Order] ;
    qb:component [qb4o:level nw:Shipper] ;
    qb:component [qb4o:level nw:Supplier] ;
    qb:component [qb4o:level nw:Customer] ;
```

Measures are defined using the property qb:measure, where the aggregate function associated with each measure is defined using the property qb4o:hasAggregateFunction:

```
    qb:component [qb:measure nw:Quantity ;
        qb4o:hasAggregateFunction qb4o:sum] ;
    qb:component [qb:measure nw:UnitPrice ;
        qb4o:hasAggregateFunction qb4o:avg] ;
    qb:component [qb:measure nw:Discount ;
        qb4o:hasAggregateFunction qb4o:avg] ;
    qb:component [qb:measure nw:SalesAmount ;
        qb4o:hasAggregateFunction qb4o:sum] ;
    qb:component [qb:measure nw:Freight ;
        qb4o:hasAggregateFunction qb4o:sum] ;
    qb:component [qb:measure nw:NetAmount ;
        qb4o:hasAggregateFunction qb4o:sum] .
```

Next, we use the Product dimension to illustrate how to define dimensions. The attributes of the levels are defined with the property qb:AttributeProperty as follows:

```
nw:ProductKey a qb:AttributeProperty ; rdfs:comment "Product Key"@en .
nw:ProductName a qb:AttributeProperty ; rdfs:comment "Product Name"@en .
nw:QuantityPerUnit a qb:AttributeProperty ; rdfs:comment "Quantity per Unit"@en .
nw:UnitPrice a qb:AttributeProperty ; rdfs:comment "Unit Price"@en .
nw:Discontinued a qb:AttributeProperty ; rdfs:comment "Discontinued"@en .
nw:CategoryName a qb:AttributeProperty ; rdfs:comment "Category Name"@en .
nw:Description a qb:AttributeProperty ; rdfs:comment "Description"@en .
```

A dimension is defined with the property qb:DimensionProperty. A dimension level is defined with the property qb4o:LevelProperty, and the associated dimension is defined with the property qb4o:inDimension. The property qb4o:hasAttribute is used to associate the attributes with a dimension level. The definition of the Product dimension is shown next:

```
nw:ProductDim a rdf:Property, qb:DimensionProperty ;
    rdfs:label "Product Dimension"@en ;
nw:Product a qb4o:LevelProperty ; qb4o:inDimension nw:ProductDim ;
    qb4o:hasAttribute nw:ProductKey ; qb4o:hasAttribute nw:ProductName ;
    qb4o:hasAttribute nw:QuantityPerUnit ; qb4o:hasAttribute nw:Discontinued ;
    qb4o:parentLevel nw:Category .
nw:Category a qb4o:LevelProperty ; qb4o:inDimension nw:ProductDim ;
    qb4o:hasAttribute nw:CategoryName ; qb4o:hasAttribute nw:Description .
```

The other dimensions and levels are defined analogously.

14.5   Querying the Northwind Cube in SPARQL

Given the schema of the Northwind cube in Fig. 14.8 expressed in QB4OLAP, we revisit the queries of Sect. 4.4 in SPARQL.

Query 14.1. Total sales amount per customer, year, and product category.

```
SELECT ?custName ?catName ?yearNo (SUM(?sales) AS ?totalSales)
WHERE { ?o qb:dataSet nwi:dataset1 ; nw:Customer ?cust ;
        nw:OrderDate ?odate ; nw:Product ?prod ; nw:SalesAmount ?sales .
    ?cust qb4o:inLevel nw:Customer ; nw:companyName ?custName .
    ?odate qb4o:inLevel nw:OrderDate ; skos:broader ?month .
    ?month qb4o:inLevel nw:Month ; skos:broader ?quarter .
    ?quarter qb4o:inLevel nw:Quarter ; skos:broader ?sem .
    ?sem qb4o:inLevel nw:Semester ; skos:broader ?year .
    ?year qb4o:inLevel nw:Year ; nw:year ?yearNo .
    ?prod qb4o:inLevel nw:Product ; skos:broader ?cat .
    ?cat qb4o:inLevel nw:Category ; nw:categoryName ?catName . }
GROUP BY ?custName ?catName ?yearNo
ORDER BY ?custName ?catName ?yearNo
```

In this query, we select the customer, order date, product, and sales amount of all sales, roll up the date to the year level, roll up the product to the category level, and aggregate the sales amount measure.

Query 14.2. Yearly sales amount for each pair of customer country and supplier countries.

```
SELECT ?custCountryName ?supCountryName ?yearNo (SUM(?sales) AS ?totalSales)
WHERE { ?o qb:dataSet nwi:dataset1 ; nw:Customer ?cust ; nw:Supplier ?sup ;
        nw:OrderDate ?odate ; nw:SalesAmount ?sales .
    ?cust qb4o:inLevel nw:Customer ; skos:broader ?custCity .
    ?custCity qb4o:inLevel nw:City ; skos:broader ?custState .
    ?custState qb4o:inLevel nw:State .
    { ?custState skos:broader ?custRegion .
    ?custRegion qb4o:inLevel nw:Region ; skos:broader ?custCountry . }
    UNION { ?custState skos:broader ?custCountry . }
    ?custCountry qb4o:inLevel nw:Country ; nw:countryName ?custCountryName.
    ?sup qb4o:inLevel nw:Supplier ; skos:broader ?supCity .
    ?supCity qb4o:inLevel nw:City ; skos:broader ?supState .
    ?supState qb4o:inLevel nw:State .
    { ?supState skos:broader ?supRegion .
    ?supRegion qb4o:inLevel nw:Region ; skos:broader ?supCountry . }
    UNION { ?supState skos:broader ?supCountry . }
    ?supCountry qb4o:inLevel nw:Country ; nw:countryName ?supCountryName.
    ?odate qb4o:inLevel nw:OrderDate ; skos:broader ?month .
    ?month qb4o:inLevel nw:Month ; skos:broader ?quarter .
    ?quarter qb4o:inLevel nw:Quarter ; skos:broader ?sem .
    ?sem qb4o:inLevel nw:Semester ; skos:broader ?year .
    ?year qb4o:inLevel nw:Year ; nw:year ?yearNo . }
GROUP BY ?custCountryName ?supCountryName ?yearNo
ORDER BY ?custCountryName ?supCountryName ?yearNo
```

The above query performs a roll-up of the customer and supplier dimensions to the country level and a roll-up of the order date to the year level and then aggregates the measure sales amount. Since a state rolls up to either a region or a country, the patterns between curly brackets before and after the UNION operator are needed to take into account both alternative aggregation paths.

Query 14.3. Monthly sales by customer state compared to those of the previous year.

```
SELECT ?stateName ?yearNo ?monthNo ?totalSales ?salesPrevYear
WHERE {
    # Monthly sales by state
    { SELECT ?stateName ?yearNo ?monthNo (SUM(?sales) AS ?totalSales)
    WHERE { ?o qb:dataSet nwi:dataset1 ; nw:Customer ?cust ;
        nw:OrderDate ?odate ; nw:SalesAmount ?sales .
        ?cust qb4o:inLevel nw:Customer ; skos:broader ?city .
        ?city qb4o:inLevel nw:City ; skos:broader ?state .
        ?state qb4o:inLevel nw:State ; nw:stateName ?stateName .
        ?odate qb4o:inLevel nw:OrderDate ; skos:broader ?month .
        ?month qb4o:inLevel nw:Month ; skos:broader ?quarter ;
```

```
            nw:monthNumber ?monthNo .
            ?quarter qb4o:inLevel nw:Quarter ; skos:broader ?sem .
            ?sem qb4o:inLevel nw:Semester ; skos:broader ?year .
            ?year qb4o:inLevel nw:Year ; nw:year ?yearNo . }
    GROUP BY ?stateName ?yearNo ?monthNo }
    # Monthly sales by state for the previous year
    OPTIONAL {
    { SELECT ?stateName ?yearNo1 ?monthNo
            (SUM(?sales1) AS ?salesPrevYear)
      WHERE { ?o1 qb:dataSet nwi:dataset1 ; nw:Customer ?cust1 ;
            nw:OrderDate ?odate1 ; nw:SalesAmount ?sales1 .
            ?cust1 qb4o:inLevel nw:Customer ; skos:broader ?city1 .
            ?city1 qb4o:inLevel nw:City ; skos:broader ?state .
            ?state qb4o:inLevel nw:State ; nw:stateName ?stateName .
            ?odate1 qb4o:inLevel nw:OrderDate ; skos:broader ?month1 .
            ?month1 qb4o:inLevel nw:Month ; skos:broader ?quarter1 ;
            nw:monthNumber ?monthNo .
            ?quarter1 qb4o:inLevel nw:Quarter ; skos:broader ?sem1 .
            ?sem1 qb4o:inLevel nw:Semester ; skos:broader ?year1 .
            ?year1 qb4o:inLevel nw:Year ; nw:year ?yearNo1 . }
      GROUP BY ?stateName ?yearNo1 ?monthNo }
      FILTER ( ?yearNo = ?yearNo1 + 1) } }
    ORDER BY ?stateName ?yearNo ?monthNo
```

The first inner query computes the monthly sales by state by rolling up the customer dimension to the state level and the order date dimension to the month level. Then, after the OPTIONAL keyword, the second inner query computes again the monthly sales by state. The FILTER condition makes the join of the two inner queries relating the sales amount of a month and that of the corresponding month of the previous year.

Query 14.4. Monthly sales growth per product, that is, total sales per product compared to those of the previous month.

```
SELECT ?prodName ?yearNo ?monthNo ?totalSales ?prevMonthSales
        (?totalSales - ?prevMonthSales AS ?salesGrowth)
WHERE {
        # Monthly sales by product
        { SELECT ?prodName ?yearNo ?monthNo (SUM(?sales) AS ?totalSales)
          WHERE { ?o qb:dataSet nwi:dataset1 ; nw:Product ?prod ;
                nw:OrderDate ?odate ; nw:SalesAmount ?sales .
                ?prod qb4o:inLevel nw:Product ; nw:productName ?prodName .
                ?odate qb4o:inLevel nw:OrderDate ; skos:broader ?month .
                ?month qb4o:inLevel nw:Month ; nw:monthNumber ?monthNo ;
                skos:broader ?quarter .
                ?quarter qb4o:inLevel nw:Quarter ; skos:broader ?sem .
                ?sem qb4o:inLevel nw:Semester ; skos:broader ?year .
                ?year qb4o:inLevel nw:Year ; nw:year ?yearNo . }
        GROUP BY ?prodName ?yearNo ?monthNo }
        # Monthly sales by product for the previous month
        OPTIONAL {
        { SELECT ?prodName ?yearNo1 ?monthNo1
                (SUM(?sales1) AS ?prevMonthSales)
```

```
WHERE { ?o1 qb:dataSet nwi:dataset1 ; nw:Product ?prod ;
        nw:OrderDate ?odate1 ; nw:SalesAmount ?sales1 .
        ?prod qb4o:inLevel nw:Product ; nw:productName ?prodName .
        ?odate1 qb4o:inLevel nw:OrderDate ; skos:broader ?month1 .
        ?month1 qb4o:inLevel nw:Month ; nw:monthNumber ?monthNo1 ;
        skos:broader ?quarter1 .
        ?quarter1 qb4o:inLevel nw:Quarter ; skos:broader ?sem1 .
        ?sem1 qb4o:inLevel nw:Semester ; skos:broader ?year1 .
        ?year1 qb4o:inLevel nw:Year ; nw:year ?yearNo1 . }
      GROUP BY ?prodName ?yearNo1 ?monthNo1 }
      FILTER( ( (?monthNo = ?monthNo1 + 1) && (?yearNo = ?yearNo1) ) ||
      ( (?monthNo = 1) && (?monthNo1 = 12) &&
      (?yearNo = ?yearNo1+1) ) ) } }
ORDER BY ?prodName ?yearNo ?monthNo
```

The first inner query computes the monthly sales by product. Then, after the OPTIONAL keyword, the second inner query computes again the monthly sales by product. The FILTER condition makes the join of the two inner queries relating the sales amount of a month and that of the previous month. The condition must take into account whether the previous month is in the same year or in the previous year.

Query 14.5. Three best-selling employees.

```
SELECT ?fName ?lName (SUM(?sales) AS ?totalSales)
WHERE { ?o qb:dataSet nwi:dataset1 ; nw:Employee ?emp ; nw:SalesAmount ?sales .
        ?emp qb4o:inLevel nw:Employee ; nw:firstName ?fName ;
        nw:lastName ?lName . }
GROUP BY ?fName ?lName
ORDER BY DESC (?totalSales)
LIMIT 3
```

This query computes the total sales by employee, sorts them in descending order of total sales, and keeps the first three results.

Query 14.6. Best-selling employee per product and year.

```
SELECT ?prodName ?yearNo ?maxSales ?fName ?lName
WHERE {
    # Maximum employee sales per product and year
    { SELECT ?prodName ?yearNo (MAX(?totalSales) as ?maxSales)
    WHERE {
        { SELECT ?prodName ?yearNo ?emp (SUM(?sales) AS ?totalSales)
        WHERE { ?o qb:dataSet nwi:dataset1 ; nw:Product ?prod ;
        nw:OrderDate ?odate ; nw:Employee ?emp ;
        nw:SalesAmount ?sales .
        ?prod qb4o:inLevel nw:Product ; nw:productName ?prodName .
        ?emp qb4o:inLevel nw:Employee .
        ?odate qb4o:inLevel nw:OrderDate ; skos:broader ?month .
        ?month qb4o:inLevel nw:Month ; skos:broader ?quarter .
        ?quarter qb4o:inLevel nw:Quarter ; skos:broader ?sem .
        ?sem qb4o:inLevel nw:Semester ; skos:broader ?year .
        ?year qb4o:inLevel nw:Year ; nw:year ?yearNo . }
        GROUP BY ?prodName ?yearNo ?emp } }
```

```
    GROUP BY ?prodName ?yearNo }
    # Sales per product, year, and employee
    { SELECT ?prodName ?yearNo ?fName ?lName
              (SUM(?sales1) AS ?empSales)
    WHERE { ?o1 qb:dataSet nwi:dataset1 ; nw:Product ?prod ;
              nw:OrderDate ?odate1 ; nw:Employee ?emp1 ;
              nw:SalesAmount ?sales1 .
              ?prod qb4o:inLevel nw:Product ; nw:productName ?prodName .
              ?emp1 qb4o:inLevel nw:Employee ; nw:firstName ?fName ;
              nw:lastName ?lName .
              ?odate1 qb4o:inLevel nw:OrderDate ; skos:broader ?month1 .
              ?month1 qb4o:inLevel nw:Month ; skos:broader ?quarter1 .
              ?quarter1 qb4o:inLevel nw:Quarter ; skos:broader ?sem1 .
              ?sem1 qb4o:inLevel nw:Semester ; skos:broader ?year .
              ?year qb4o:inLevel nw:Year ; nw:year ?yearNo . }
    GROUP BY ?prodName ?yearNo ?fName ?lName }
    FILTER ( ?maxSales = ?empSales ) }
ORDER BY ?prodName ?yearNo
```

The first inner query computes the maximum employee sales by product and year. Then, the second inner query computes the sales per product, year, and employee. The FILTER condition makes the join of the two inner queries relating the maximum sales with the employee that realized those sales.

Query 14.7. Countries that account for top 50% of the sales amount.

For simplicity, in this query we compute the top 50% of the sales amount by state, instead of by country. In this case, we must not take care of the fact that states roll up to either regions or countries. This can be taken care by using a UNION operator as was we did in Query 14.2.

```
SELECT ?stateName ?totalSales ?cumSales
WHERE { ?state qb4o:inLevel nw:State ; nw:stateName ?stateName .
        # Total sales and cumulative sales by state
        { SELECT ?state ?totalSales (SUM(?totalSales1) AS ?cumSales)
        WHERE {
                # Total sales by state
                { SELECT ?state (SUM(?sales) AS ?totalSales)
                WHERE { ?o qb:dataSet nwi:dataset1 ; nw:Customer ?cust ;
                        nw:SalesAmount ?sales .
                        ?cust qb4o:inLevel nw:Customer ; skos:broader ?city .
                        ?city qb4o:inLevel nw:City ; skos:broader ?state .
                        ?state qb4o:inLevel nw:State . }
                GROUP BY ?state }
                # Total sales by state
                { SELECT ?state1 (SUM(?sales1) AS ?totalSales1)
                WHERE { ?o qb:dataSet nwi:dataset1 ; nw:Customer ?cust1 ;
                        nw:SalesAmount ?sales1 .
                        ?cust1 qb4o:inLevel nw:Customer ; skos:broader ?city1 .
                        ?city1 qb4o:inLevel nw:City ; skos:broader ?state1 .
                        ?state1 qb4o:inLevel nw:State . }
                GROUP BY ?state1 }
                FILTER ( ?totalSales <= ?totalSales1 ) }
        GROUP BY ?state ?totalSales }
```

```
# Minimum cumulative sales >= 50% of the overall sales
{ SELECT (MIN(?cumSales2) AS ?threshold)
WHERE {
    # 50% of the overall sales
    { SELECT (0.5 * SUM(?sales) AS ?halfOverallSales)
    WHERE { ?o qb:dataSet nwi:dataset1 ;
            nw:SalesAmount ?sales . } }
    # Total sales and cumulative sales by state
    { SELECT ?state2 ?totalSales2
              (SUM(?totalSales3) AS ?cumSales2)
    WHERE {
        { SELECT ?state2 (SUM(?sales2) AS ?totalSales2)
        WHERE { ?o2 qb:dataSet nwi:dataset1 ;
        nw:Customer ?cust2 ; nw:SalesAmount ?sales2 .
        ?cust2 qb4o:inLevel nw:Customer ; skos:broader ?city2 .
        ?city2 qb4o:inLevel nw:City ; skos:broader ?state2 .
        ?state2 qb4o:inLevel nw:State . }
        GROUP BY ?state2 }
        { SELECT ?state3 (SUM(?sales3) AS ?totalSales3)
        WHERE { ?o3 qb:dataSet nwi:dataset1 ;
        nw:Customer ?cust3 ; nw:SalesAmount ?sales3 .
        ?cust3 qb4o:inLevel nw:Customer ; skos:broader ?city3 .
        ?city3 qb4o:inLevel nw:City ; skos:broader ?state3 .
        ?state3 qb4o:inLevel nw:State . }
        GROUP BY ?state3 }
        FILTER ( ?totalSales2 <= ?totalSales3 ) }
        GROUP BY ?state2 ?totalSales2 }
        FILTER(?cumSales2 >= ?halfOverallSales) } }
        FILTER(?cumSales <= ?threshold) }
ORDER BY DESC(?totalSales)
```

The first inner query computes for each country the total sales and the cumulative sales of all countries having total sales greater than or equal to the total sales of the country. The second inner query computes the threshold value, which represents the minimum cumulative sales greater than or equal to the 50% of the overall sales. Finally, the FILTER selects all countries whose cumulative sales are less than or equal to the threshold value.

Query 14.8. Total sales and average monthly sales by employee and year.

```
SELECT ?fName ?lName ?yearNo (SUM(?monthlySales) AS ?totalSales)
        (AVG(?monthlySales) AS ?avgMonthlySales)
WHERE {
    # Monthly sales by employee
    { SELECT ?fName ?lName ?month (SUM(?sales) AS ?monthlySales)
    WHERE { ?o qb:dataSet nwi:dataset1 ; nw:Employee ?emp ;
    nw:OrderDate ?odate ; nw:SalesAmount ?sales .
    ?emp qb4o:inLevel nw:Employee ; nw:firstName ?fName ;
    nw:lastName ?lName .
    ?odate qb4o:inLevel nw:OrderDate ; skos:broader ?month .
    ?month qb4o:inLevel nw:Month . }
    GROUP BY ?fName ?lName ?month }
    ?month skos:broader ?quarter .
```

```
        ?quarter qb4o:inLevel nw:Quarter ; skos:broader ?sem .
        ?sem qb4o:inLevel nw:Semester ; skos:broader ?year .
        ?year qb4o:inLevel nw:Year ; nw:year ?yearNo . }
GROUP BY ?fName ?lName ?yearNo
ORDER BY ?fName ?lName ?yearNo
```

In the query above, the inner query computes the total sales amount by employee and month. The outer query rolls up the previous result to the year level while computing the total yearly sales and the average monthly sales.

Query 14.9. Total sales amount and total discount amount per product and month.

```
SELECT ?prodName ?yearNo ?monthNo (SUM(?sales) AS ?totalSales)
        (SUM(?unitPrice * ?qty * ?disc) AS ?totalDiscAmount)
WHERE { ?o qb:dataSet nwi:dataset1 ; nw:Product ?prod ;
        nw:OrderDate ?odate ; nw:SalesAmount ?sales ;
        nw:Quantity ?qty ; nw:Discount ?disc ; nw:UnitPrice ?unitPrice .
        ?prod qb4o:inLevel nw:Product ; nw:productName ?prodName .
        ?odate qb4o:inLevel nw:OrderDate ; skos:broader ?month .
        ?month qb4o:inLevel nw:Month ; nw:monthNumber ?monthNo ;
        skos:broader ?quarter .
        ?quarter qb4o:inLevel nw:Quarter ; skos:broader ?sem .
        ?sem qb4o:inLevel nw:Semester ; skos:broader ?year .
        ?year qb4o:inLevel nw:Year ; nw:year ?yearNo . }
GROUP BY ?prodName ?yearNo ?monthNo
ORDER BY ?prodName ?yearNo ?monthNo
```

In this query, we roll up to the month level and then compute the requested measures.

Query 14.10. Monthly year-to-date sales for each product category.

```
SELECT ?catName ?yearNo ?monthNo (SUM(?totalSales1) AS ?YTDSales)
WHERE { ?cat qb4o:inLevel nw:Category ; nw:categoryName ?catName .
        ?month qb4o:inLevel nw:Month ; nw:monthNumber ?monthNo ;
        skos:broader ?quarter .
        ?quarter qb4o:inLevel nw:Quarter ; skos:broader ?sem .
        ?sem qb4o:inLevel nw:Semester ; skos:broader ?year .
        ?year qb4o:inLevel nw:Year ; nw:year ?yearNo.
        { SELECT ?catName ?yearNo ?monthNo1 (SUM(?sales1) AS ?totalSales1)
        WHERE { ?o1 qb:dataSet nwi:dataset1 ; nw:Product ?prod1 ;
                nw:OrderDate ?odate1 ; nw:SalesAmount ?sales1 .
                ?prod1 qb4o:inLevel nw:Product ; skos:broader ?cat1 .
                ?cat1 qb4o:inLevel nw:Category ; nw:categoryName ?catName .
                ?odate1 qb4o:inLevel nw:OrderDate ; skos:broader ?month1 .
                ?month1 qb4o:inLevel nw:Month ; nw:monthNumber ?monthNo1 ;
                skos:broader ?quarter1 .
                ?quarter1 qb4o:inLevel nw:Quarter ; skos:broader ?sem1 .
                ?sem1 qb4o:inLevel nw:Semester ; skos:broader ?year1 .
                ?year1 qb4o:inLevel nw:Year ; nw:year ?yearNo. }
        GROUP BY ?catName ?yearNo ?monthNo1 }
        FILTER( ?monthNo >= ?monthNo1 ) }
GROUP BY ?catName ?yearNo ?monthNo
ORDER BY ?catName ?yearNo ?monthNo
```

This query starts by selecting the category, month, and year levels. Then, for each category, month, and year, the query selects all facts whose order date is in the same year but whose month is less than or equal to the current month.

Query 14.11. Moving average over the last 3 months of the sales amount by product category.

```
SELECT ?catName ?yearNo ?monthNo (AVG(?totalSales1) AS ?MovAvgSales)
WHERE { ?cat qb4o:inLevel nw:Category ; nw:categoryName ?catName .
   ?month qb4o:inLevel nw:Month ; nw:monthNumber ?monthNo ;
   skos:broader ?quarter .
   ?quarter qb4o:inLevel nw:Quarter ; skos:broader ?sem .
   ?sem qb4o:inLevel nw:Semester ; skos:broader ?year .
   ?year qb4o:inLevel nw:Year ; nw:year ?yearNo.
   OPTIONAL {
   { SELECT ?catName ?yearNo1 ?monthNo1 (SUM(?sales1) AS ?totalSales1)
   WHERE { ?o1 qb:dataSet nwi:dataset1 ; nw:Product ?prod1 ;
         nw:OrderDate ?odate1 ; nw:SalesAmount ?sales1 .
      ?prod1 qb4o:inLevel nw:Product ; skos:broader ?cat1 .
      ?cat1 qb4o:inLevel nw:Category ; nw:categoryName ?catName .
      ?odate1 qb4o:inLevel nw:OrderDate ; skos:broader ?month1 .
      ?month1 qb4o:inLevel nw:Month ; nw:monthNumber ?monthNo1 ;
      skos:broader ?quarter1 .
      ?quarter1 qb4o:inLevel nw:Quarter ; skos:broader ?sem1 .
      ?sem1 qb4o:inLevel nw:Semester ; skos:broader ?year1 .
      ?year1 qb4o:inLevel nw:Year ; nw:year ?yearNo1. }
   GROUP BY ?catName ?yearNo1 ?monthNo1 }
   FILTER( (( ?monthNo >= 3 && ?yearNo = ?yearNo1 &&
   ?monthNo >= ?monthNo1 && ?monthNo-2 <= ?monthNo1 ) ||
   ( ?monthNo = 2 && (( ?yearNo = ?yearNo1 && ?monthNo1 <= 2 ) ||
   ( ?yearNo = ?yearNo1+1 && ?monthNo1 = 12 ))) ||
   ( ?monthNo - 1 && ((?yearNo = ?yearNo1 && ?monthNo1 = 1 ) ||
   (?yearNo = ?yearNo1+1 && ?monthNo1 >= 11 ))))) } }
GROUP BY ?catName ?yearNo ?monthNo
ORDER BY ?catName ?yearNo ?monthNo
```

This query starts by selecting the category, month, and year levels. Then, for each category, month, and year, the query selects all facts whose order date is within a 3-month window from the current month. This selection involves an elaborated condition in the **FILTER** clause, which covers three cases, depending on whether the month is March or later, the month is February, or the month is January.

Query 14.12. Personal sales amount made by an employee compared with the total sales amount made by herself and her subordinates during 1997.

```
SELECT ?fName ?lName ?persSales ?subordSales
WHERE { ?emp qb4o:inLevel nw:Employee; nw:firstName ?fName ;
   nw:lastName ?lName .
   { SELECT ?emp (SUM(?sales) AS ?persSales)
   WHERE { ?o qb:dataSet nwi:dataset1 ; nw:Employee ?emp ;
         nw:OrderDate ?odate ; nw:SalesAmount ?sales .
```

```
        ?odate qb4o:inLevel nw:OrderDate ; skos:broader ?month .
        ?month qb4o:inLevel nw:Month ; skos:broader ?quarter .
        ?quarter qb4o:inLevel nw:Quarter ; skos:broader ?sem .
        ?sem qb4o:inLevel nw:Semester ; skos:broader ?year .
        ?year qb4o:inLevel nw:Year ; nw:year ?yearNo .
        FILTER(?yearNo = 1997) }
    GROUP BY ?emp }
    { SELECT ?emp (SUM(?sales1) AS ?subordSales)
    WHERE { ?subord nw:supervisor* ?emp .
        ?o1 qb:dataSet nwi:dataset1 ; nw:Employee ?subord ;
        nw:OrderDate ?odate1 ; nw:SalesAmount ?sales .
        ?odate1 qb4o:inLevel nw:OrderDate ; skos:broader ?month1 .
        ?month1 qb4o:inLevel nw:Month ; skos:broader ?quarter1 .
        ?quarter1 qb4o:inLevel nw:Quarter ; skos:broader ?sem1 .
        ?sem1 qb4o:inLevel nw:Semester ; skos:broader ?year1 .
        ?year1 qb4o:inLevel nw:Year ; nw:year ?yearNo1 .
        FILTER(?yearNo1 = 1997) }
    GROUP BY ?emp } }
ORDER BY ?emp
```

The first inner query computes by employee the personal sales in 1997.
The second inner query exploits the recursive hierarchy **Supervision** with
a property path expression in SPARQL. The '*' character states that the
transitive closure of the supervision hierarchy must be taken into account for
obtaining all subordinates of an employee. Then, the sales in 1997 of all these
subordinates are aggregated.

Query 14.13. Total sales amount, number of products, and sum of the
quantities sold for each order.

```
SELECT ?orderNo (SUM(?sales) AS ?totalSales)
        (COUNT(?prod) AS ?nbProducts) (SUM(?qty) AS ?nbUnits)
WHERE { ?o qb:dataSet nwi:dataset1 ; nw:Order ?order ;
        nw:Product ?prod ; nw:SalesAmount ?sales ; nw:Quantity ?qty .
        ?order qb4o:inLevel nw:Order ; nw:orderNo ?orderNo . }
GROUP BY ?orderNo
ORDER BY ?orderNo
```

In this query, we group sales by order number and then compute the requested
measures.

Query 14.14. For each month, total number of orders, total sales amount,
and average sales amount by order.

```
SELECT ?yearNo ?monthNo (COUNT(?orderNo) AS ?nbOrders)
        (SUM(?totalSales) AS ?totalSalesMonth)
        (AVG(?totalSales) AS ?avgSalesOrder)
WHERE {
        { SELECT ?orderNo ?odate (SUM(?sales) AS ?totalSales)
        WHERE { ?o qb:dataSet nwi:dataset1 ; nw:Order ?order ;
                nw:OrderDate ?odate ; nw:SalesAmount ?sales .
                ?order qb4o:inLevel nw:Order ; nw:orderNo ?orderNo . }
        GROUP BY ?orderNo ?odate }
```

?odate qb4o:inLevel nw:OrderDate ; skos:broader ?month .
?month qb4o:inLevel nw:Month ; nw:monthNumber ?monthNo ;
skos:broader ?quarter .
?quarter qb4o:inLevel nw:Quarter ; skos:broader ?sem .
?sem qb4o:inLevel nw:Semester ; skos:broader ?year .
?year qb4o:inLevel nw:Year ; nw:year ?yearNo . }
GROUP BY ?yearNo ?monthNo
ORDER BY ?yearNo ?monthNo

Here, the inner query computes the total sales by order. The outer query then
rolls up the previous result to the month level and computes the requested
measures.

Query 14.15. For each employee, total sales amount, number of cities, and
number of states to which she is assigned.

SELECT ?fName ?lName (SUM(?sales)/COUNT(DISTINCT ?city) AS ?totalSales)
  (COUNT(DISTINCT ?city) AS ?noCities)
  (COUNT(DISTINCT ?state) AS ?noStates)
WHERE { ?o qb:dataSet nwi:dataset1 ; nw:Employee ?emp ; nw:SalesAmount ?sales .
  ?emp qb4o:inLevel nw:Employee ; nw:firstName ?fName ;
  nw:lastName ?lName ; skos:broader ?city .
  ?city qb4o:inLevel nw:City ; skos:broader ?state .
  ?state qb4o:inLevel nw:State . }
GROUP BY ?fName ?lName
ORDER BY ?fName ?lName

Recall that there is a many-to-many relationship between employees and
cities. Thus, the above query rolls up to the city and state levels and then
groups the result by employee. Then, in the SELECT clause, we sum the sales
amount measure and divide it by the number of distinct cities assigned to an
employee. This solves the double-counting problem to which we referred in
Sect. 4.2.6.

14.6 Summary

In this chapter, we studied how OLAP techniques can be applied over the
semantic web. We first introduced the main concepts of RDF and RDFS,
the languages used to represent data and metadata on the semantic web,
and SPARQL, the standard language to query such data. Then, we studied
how to represent relational data in RDF. We then showed how OLAP
techniques can be directly applied to RDF data sets without the need of first
transforming semantic web data into OLAP data cubes. For this, we need
vocabularies that allow us to represent OLAP data and metadata. We studied
and compared two of these vocabularies: the Data Cube Vocabulary (QB) and
the QB4OLAP vocabulary. We studied the limitations of the former when
trying to define the OLAP operations and showed, based on a portion of a

real-world case study, how these operations can be implemented in SPARQL. Finally, we applied QB4OLAP to the Northwind data cube and query the resulting RDF cube using SPARQL.

14.7 Bibliographic Notes

There are many books explaining the basics of the semantic web, for example, [82]. A book entirely devoted to SPARQL is [41]. At the time of writing this book, there is no much work on the topic of applying OLAP directly over RDF data. Section 14.3 of this chapter is based on research work by Etcheverry and Vaisman on QB4OLAP [52, 53]. Kämpgen and Harth [99] also propose to apply OLAP operations on top of QB, although this approach does not solve the limitations discussed in this chapter regarding the absence of dimension structure in QB. In a sequel [100], the same authors proposed to load statistical linked data into an RDF triple store and to answer OLAP queries using SPARQL. For this, they implement an OLAP to SPARQL engine which translates OLAP queries into SPARQL.

We also mentioned that another research approach studies how to extract multidimensional data from the semantic web, and then analyze these data using traditional OLAP techniques. The methods to do this are based on ontologies, which allow us to extract data in a semiautomatic fashion. The idea is to use ontologies to identify facts and dimensions that can populate a data cube. We briefly mention next some of this work.

Niinimäki and Niemi [145] use ontology mapping to convert data sources to RDF and then query this RDF data with SPARQL to populate the OLAP schema. The ETL process is guided by the ontology. In addition, the authors create an OLAP ontology, somehow similar to the vocabularies discussed in this chapter. Ontologies are expressed in RDF and OWL. Along the same lines, Romero and Abelló [180] address the design of the data warehouse starting from an OWL ontology that describes the data sources. They identify the dimensions that characterize a central concept under analysis (the fact concept) by looking for concepts connected to it through one-to-many relationships. The same idea is used for discovering the different levels of the dimension hierarchies, starting from the concept that represents the base level. The output of the method is a star or snowflake schema that guarantees the summarizability of the data, suitable to be instantiated in a traditional multidimensional database. Finally, Nebot and Berlanga [142] proposed a semiautomatic method for extracting semantic data on demand into a multidimensional database. In this way, data could be analyzed using traditional OLAP techniques. Here, the authors assume that data are represented as an OWL ontology. A portion of this ontology contains the application and domain ontology axioms, while the other part contains the actual instance store. A multidimensional schema must first be created from the requirements and the knowledge that can be inferred from the ontologies. This schema is then semiautomatically populated from the ontology.

14.8 Review Questions

14.1 What are the two main approaches to perform OLAP analysis with semantic web data?

14.2 Briefly describe RDF and RDFS and their main constructs.

14.3 Give an example of the RDF/XML and Turtle serializations of RDF data.

14.4 What is SPARQL? How does its semantics differ from the one of SQL?

14.5 Give an example of a SPARQL query, describe its elements, and discuss how it will be evaluated.

14.6 Explain the two standard approaches to represent relational data in RDF. How do they differ from each other?

14.7 How can we represent multidimensional data in RDF?

14.8 Briefly explain the data cube vocabulary QB.

14.9 How can hierarchies be represented in QB?

14.10 Is it possible to perform a roll-up operation on data represented in QB?

14.11 How does the QB4OLAP vocabulary overcome the limitations above?

14.12 Analyze and discuss the implementation of roll-up in QB4OLAP.

14.13 Explain how to perform OLAP queries in SPARQL.

14.9 Exercises

14.1 Given the Northwind data cube, show the QB representation of the Sales fact. Provide at least two observations.

14.2 Given the Northwind data cube, show the QB4OLAP representation of the dimension Customer.

14.3 Do the same as Ex. 14.2 for the dimension Employee.

14.4 Write the R2RML mapping that represents the Northwind data warehouse using the QB4OLAP vocabulary.

14.5 Show the SPARQL query implementing the operation

ROLLUP(Northwind, Product → Category, SUM(SalesAmount)).

14.6 Show the SPARQL query implementing the operation

SLICE(Northwind, Customer, City='Paris').

Sales

product_id	time_id	customer_id	promotion_id	store_id	store_sales	store_cost	unit_sales
219	738	567	0	1	7.16	2.4344	3
684	738	567	0	1	12.88	5.0232	2
551	739	639	7	2	5.20	2.236	4

Product

product_id	product_name	brand_name	product_class_id
219	Best Choice Corn Chips	Best Choice	12
551	Fast Low Fat Chips	Fast	12
684	Gorilla Blueberry Yogurt	Gorilla	6

Product_class

product_class_id	product_subcategory	product_category	product_department	product_family
6	Yogurt	Dairy	Dairy	Food
12	Chips	Snack Foods	Snack Foods	Food

Time_by_day

time_id	the_date	the_day	the_month	the_year	day_of_month	week_of_year	month_of_year	quarter
738	1998-01-07	Wednesday	January	1998	7	4	1	Q1
739	1998-01-08	Thursday	January	1998	8	4	1	Q1

Customer

cust_id	fname	mi	lname	city	state	country	marital_status	yearly_income	gender	education
567	Charles	L.	Christensen	Santa Fe	DF	Mexico	S	$50K-$70K	F	Bachelors
639	Michael	J.	Troyer	Kirkland	WA	USA	M	$30K-$50K	M	High School

Promotion

prom_id	prom_name	media_type
0	No Promotion	No Media
7	Fantastic Discounts	Sunday paper, Radio, TV

Store

store_id	store_type	store_name	store_city	store_state	store_country	store_sqft
1	Supermarket	Store 1	Acapulco	Guerrero	Mexico	23593
2	Small Grocery	Store 2	Bellingham	WA	USA	28206

Fig. 14.9 An instance of the Foodmart data warehouse

14.7 Represent the Foodmart cube schema using the QB4OLAP vocabulary.

14.8 Consider the Foodmart table instances given in Fig. 14.9a. Represent sales facts as observations, adhering to the Data Structure Definition specified in the previous exercise.

14.9 Write in SPARQL the queries over the Foodmart cube given in Ex. 4.9.

Chapter 15
Conclusion

In this book, we have provided an in-depth coverage of the most relevant topics in data warehouse design and implementation. Even though in Chaps. 11–14 we covered advanced and very recent developments, there are many other important ones that have been consciously left out for space reasons in favor of mature technologies. We conclude this book with some brief comments on these topics, which we believe will become increasingly relevant in the near future. We refer to a recent book [144] where further perspectives on business intelligence can be found.

15.1 Temporal Data Warehouses

Inmon's classic definition of data warehouses, presented in Sect. 1.1, mentions their nonvolatile and time-varying characteristics. However, in traditional data warehouses, these features apply only to measures, not to dimensions. Indeed, although data warehouses include a time dimension that is used for aggregation (using the roll-up operation) or for filtering (using the slice and dice operations), the time dimension cannot be used to keep track of changes in other dimensions, for example, when a product changes its category. This situation leaves to the application layer the responsibility of representing changes in dimensions. **Temporal data warehouses** aim at solving this problem by extending the data definition and manipulation languages with temporal semantics. In a temporal data warehouse, changes may occur at the *instance level* (as in the example of the product changing its category mentioned above) or at a *schema level*, for example, when a dimension level is added or deleted. Moreover, when the bottom level of a dimension is added or deleted, the associated fact table is affected, and its schema must be modified. All of these changes must be automatically handled by the data definition language. The semantics of the query language must also account for these changes to produce the correct aggregations.

A. Vaisman and E. Zimányi, *Data Warehouse Systems*, Data-Centric
Systems and Applications, DOI 10.1007/978-3-642-54655-6_15,
© Springer-Verlag Berlin Heidelberg 2014

Temporal data warehouses aim at applying the results of many years of research in **temporal databases** to the data warehouse field. Temporal databases provide structures and mechanisms for representing and managing information that varies over time. In short, temporal databases allow past or future data to be stored in a database as well as the time instants when the changes in these data occurred or will occur. Thus, temporal databases enable users to know the evolution of information required for solving complex problems in many application domains in which time is naturally present, for example, land management, financial, and healthcare applications.

Temporal data warehouses raise many issues, including consistent aggregation in the presence of time-varying data, temporal queries, storage methods, and temporal view materialization. Further, very little attention has been given by the research community to the conceptual and logical modeling of temporal data warehouses or to the analysis of the temporal support that should be included in data warehouses. Some of these issues have been addressed in the literature to various extents.

Golfarelli and Rizzi provide a survey of temporal data warehouses [66]. With a focus on *conceptual modeling* of temporal data warehouses, Malinowski and Zimányi [124, 127] introduced time-varying (i.e., temporal) data types for keeping the history of data warehouse dimensions and extended the MultiDim model studied in this book to address temporal data warehouses. Also, translation rules from the conceptual to the relational and object-relational models are given. *Logical data models* have also been proposed for temporal data warehouses [42–44, 136, 137]. For example, Mendelzon and Vaisman [136, 137] introduced TOLAP, a data model and query language where the schema and the instances of the relationships between levels in a hierarchy are timestamped with their validity intervals. These timestamps define how dimension-level members are aggregated. In this way, we can aggregate measures according to the dimension schema and instances that existed when the corresponding facts occurred.

It is worth remarking that slowly changing dimensions, studied in Chap. 5, address the problem above in a limited way and are only one variant of temporal data warehouses. Further, the slowly changing dimensions solutions do not take into account all the research that has been done in the field of temporal databases. We have seen that some of the solutions for slowly changing dimensions do not preserve the entire history of the data and are difficult to implement. One of the main differences between the temporal models discussed above and the slowly changing dimensions approach is that the semantics of the updates to dimension hierarchies is ignored by the latter. Thus, the valid path at a certain instant in a temporal hierarchy must be computed manually at the moment of writing the query rather than being accounted for automatically by the query language.

Another approach to temporal data warehousing is multiversioning. For example, Ravat et al. [170] defined a multiversion multidimensional model that consists of a set of star versions, each one associated with a temporal interval and including one version for a fact and one version for each dimension associated with a fact. Whenever changes to dimensions or facts occur at the schema level, a new star version is created. A similar approach was taken by Wrembel and Bebel [230], where each change at the schema or instance level results in the creation of a new schema version even though that version has the same structure as the original one in the case of changes at the instance level. Other proposals on this topic are, for example, [31, 140, 208, 231]. The subtle interrelationship between temporal data warehouses and multiversioning still needs to be investigated. For example, a schema update of a source table may trigger a change in the data warehouse schema, hence a new data warehouse version is created. However, it would not be reliable to create a new data warehouse version each time an instance changes. For this, timestamping the association between levels would clearly be a better option. On the other hand, if the data source were a temporal database, a temporal data warehouse that accounts for instance and schema changes appears natural.

In spite of the progress made in the field, temporal databases have not been adopted by database practitioners, and as a consequence, the same occurs in the data warehouse field. This is the main reason why we did not include temporal data warehouses in this book. However, it is worth noting that the last version of the SQL standard released in 2011 has temporal facilities. Further, current database management systems such as Oracle, Teradata, and DB2 also provide temporal support. The availability of such features implies that temporal data warehouse systems will become a reality in the near future, but for that to happen, temporal databases need to become more used than they have been so far.

15.2 3D/4D Spatial Data Warehouses

In our study of spatial and spatiotemporal data warehouses (Chaps. 11 and 12), we had not addressed their extension to manage three- and four-dimensional (3D/4D) objects, which would lead to **3D/4D spatial data warehouses**.

Many modern applications require the integration of 2D and 3D spatial data (see a comprehensive review in [20]). For example, applications such as facility management and disaster management in cities require not only information about the locations but also information about the interior of buildings. In cadastral surveys and insurance, the volume of a building might also be of interest. In spite of the need of such integration between the 2D and 3D worlds, typically the 2D world is digitally represented as a map and the 3D world as a 3D model, both being implemented in completely different data models and minimally integrated. However, nothing should prevent to integrate a 2D city map with a 3D city model in a spatial database by using a unified modeling approach.

Further, in recent years, we have witnessed an increasing interest in 4D (i.e., 3D plus time) spatial database systems. For example, there is an urgent need to move from old 2D cadastral systems to 4D ones [40]. Climate modeling and disaster prevention are other applications that depend on 4D modeling. In most cases, going from a 3D to a 2D model is possible, but moving up from 2D to 3D or 4D is not. Therefore, 3D geomodeling is a research area that is urgently required to produce new 3D/4D geoinformation systems. Further, the design and implementation of geometric and topological database operations for moving 3D (i.e., 4D) objects is a focus of interest for research and industry. Although several conceptual models supporting 3D objects have been proposed in the literature considering both geometrical and topological aspects (e.g., [106, 112, 241]), no current database management system supports 3D topological models, yet many support 2D topologies. A key need for this consists in developing spatial indexes for topological models.

In summary, the directions in this field are the seamless integration between 2D and 3D data models to be usable in both worlds and the development of 3D/4D geographic information systems. A step in this direction is CityGML,[1] an open information model for representing, storing, and exchanging 3D city and landscape models. CityGML is implemented as an application schema for the Geography Markup Language (GML) [110], the standard for spatial data exchange issued by the Open Geospatial Consortium, and provides a standard for describing the geometry, topology, and semantics of 3D objects. CityGML is highly scalable supporting not only buildings but also whole sites, districts, cities, regions, and countries. CityGML provides 3D content, allowing visualization through several applications, but it also allows users to share virtual 3D city and landscape models for sophisticated analysis, for example, environmental simulations, energy demand analysis, city management, and disaster management. As an example, the application of CityGML to a case study in the Netherlands can be found in [216]. There is a series of conferences specifically devoted to 3D GeoInformation. The volumes of these conferences are published by Springer, the last one being [165].

Given the discussion above, the reader should at this point not be surprised to know that very few publications have addressed the combination of data warehouses and 3D objects. As an example, the BioMap data warehouse [121, 122] integrates biological data sources in order to provide integrated sequence/structure/function resources that support analysis, mining, and visualization of functional genomic data. Extending conceptual models for data warehousing in this direction requires first the definition of 3D spatial

---

[1] http://www.citygml.org/

data types, 3D topological operators, and spatial operations and functions that can operate on 3D data types. After that, issues such as the aggregation of spatial measures should be addressed. Thus, there is fertile land for research in the field of 3D spatial data warehouses. Combining these with trajectory data warehouses such as the ones we studied in Chap. 12 would lead to 4D spatial data warehouses.

Another important issue in this respect is to cope with **multiple representations** of spatial data, which means to allow the same real-world object to have several geometries. Dealing with multiple representations is a common requirement in spatial databases, in particular as a consequence of dealing with multiple levels of spatial resolution. This is also an important aspect in data warehouses since spatial data may be integrated from source systems containing data at various different spatial resolutions. In this book, we have implicitly assumed that we have selected one representation from those available. However, we may need to support multiple representations in a multidimensional model. Again, conceptual models should be extended to allow multiple representations of spatial data, as it is the case for the spatiotemporal model MADS [155]. However, this raises some important issues. For example, if levels forming a hierarchy can have multiple representations, additional conditions are necessary to establish meaningful roll-up and drill-down operations.

15.3 Text Analytics and Text Data Warehouses

Other topics that we envision to be important in the future are **text analytics** and **text data warehouses**. This follows clearly from statistics that report that only 20% of corporate data are in transactional systems and the remaining 80% are in other formats, mainly text [171, 206]. In addition, the advent of social media has produced enormous amounts of text data, and the tools studied in Chap. 13 have made possible the analysis of these data. Text data warehouses can help to perform this task, as we explain next.

Automatic extraction of structured information from text has been studied for a long time. There are two main approaches for information extraction: the machine learning approach and the rule-based one. Most systems in both categories were built for academic settings to be used by specialists and are, in general, not scalable to heavy workloads.

In the machine learning approach, techniques like the ones studied in Chap. 9 are used. For example, automatic text classification has been extensively addressed mainly using supervised learning techniques, where predefined category labels are assigned to documents. Examples are the Rocchio algorithm, k-nearest neighbor, decision trees, naïve Bayes algorithm, neural networks, and support vector machines, among other ones. More recently, the combination of different learning methods is increasingly being used. A survey of these techniques can be found in [54].

An example of a rule-based information extraction system is SystemT-IE [107,172], a result from research carried out at the IBM Almaden Research Center. This system is now included as part of the InfoSphere BigInsights suite of products. SystemT-IE comes with an SQL-like declarative language denoted Annotation Query Language (AQL) [30] for specifying text analytics extraction programs (called extractors) with rule semantics. Extractors obtain structured information from unstructured or semistructured text. For this, AQL extends SQL with the EXTRACT statement. Data in AQL are stored in relations where all tuples have the same schema, analogous to SQL relational tables. In addition, AQL includes statements for creating tables, views, user-defined functions, and dictionaries. However, AQL does not support advanced SQL features like correlated subqueries and recursive queries. After the extractors are generated, an optimizer produces an efficient execution plan for them in the form of an annotation operator graph. The plan is finally executed by a runtime engine, which takes advantage of parallel architectures.

Information extraction techniques like the one introduced above can be used to populate a data warehouse for multidimensional text analysis using OLAP. Typically, an ETL process will extract textual data from various sources and, after cleansing and transformation, will load such data into the warehouse. The phases of this process will include textual data and metadata extraction from documents; transformation of the extracted data through classic text retrieval techniques like cleaning texts, stemming, term weighting, language modeling, and so on; and loading the data resulting from the transformation phase into the data warehouse. In a recent book [92], W.H. Inmon details, at a high abstraction level, the tasks required to be performed by an ETL process for text data warehouses.

We next discuss some proposals in the field of text data warehouses.

In one of the earliest works in the field, Tseng and Chou [206] propose a document warehouse for multidimensional analysis of textual data. Their approach is to combine text processing with numeric OLAP processing. For this, they organize unstructured documents into structured data consisting of dimensions, hierarchies, facts, and measures. Dimensions are composed of a hierarchy of keywords referring to a concept, which are obtained using text mining tools. Facts include the identifiers of the documents under analysis and the number of times that a combination of keywords appears in such documents. For example, suppose we are analyzing documents in order to discover products and cities appearing together. A hierarchy of keywords referring to products can be represented in a Product dimension with schema (ProductKey, Keyword, KeywordLevel, Parent), where ProductKey is the surrogate key of the keyword, Keyword is a word in the document, KeywordLevel is the level of Keyword in the hierarchy, and Parent is the parent KeywordLevel. For example, a hierarchy of keywords such as TV → Appliance

→ All Products can be represented by the tuples (p1, All Products, 1, 1), (p2, Appliance, 2, 1), and (p3, TV, 3, 2). The last tuple tells, for instance, that the TV keyword belongs to the hierarchy level 3 and its parent is in level 2. Dimension City would be analogous and could contain, for example, a tuple (c4, Brussels, 3, 2). The fact table is composed of the keys from the dimensions Product and City, the identifier of a document containing a combination of a product and a city, and the number of times that this combination appears in the document. For example, a tuple in the fact table can be $(p3, c4, d_1, 3)$, indicating that the combination of keywords TV and Brussels appears three times in document d_1. Over this structure, OLAP operations can be performed as usual.

In [117], Lin et al. present the notion of *Text Cube*, a data cube for textual data, while in [39] Ding et al. study the problem of keyword-based top-k search in text cubes, that is, given a keyword query, find the top-k most relevant cells in a text cube. The text cube contains both structural information (i.e., conventional dimensions) and textual information. Thus, a text cube is a traditional OLAP data cube extended to summarize and navigate structured and unstructured text data. A cell in the text cube aggregates a set of documents that contain a combination of keywords and attribute values on the cube dimensions. For example, suppose we want to analyze reviews of television models. We can design a text cube with schema (Brand, Model, Price, Review), where the first three attributes are dimensions and the last one is the measure representing the review documents. Consider three cells in the cube, namely, c_1:(Sony, S1, 400, $\{d_1\}$), c_2 : (Sony, S2, 800, $\{d_2\}$), and c_3 : (Panasonic, P1, 400, $\{d_3\}$). Also, assume that documents d_1, d_2, and d_3 contain the keywords {light, cheap, modern}, {expensive, modern}, and {cheap, durable}, respectively. If a user wants to find out the cells in the cube that are most relevant to the keywords cheap and durable, the answer will be c_3 since the review includes the two terms. Cells can also be aggregated. For example, cells c_1 and c_3 above have as parent cell $(*, *, 400, \{d_1, d_2\})$, which contains the reviews aggregated by price. Aggregated cells can also be included in the answer to a query by analyzing the keywords present in the union of the documents.

There are other approaches along similar lines, like the ones of Zhang et al. [237,238], where the authors introduce the notion of *Topic Cube*, which combines OLAP with a probabilistic topic model. We omit the description of these proposals here.

15.4 Multimedia Data Warehouses

New and complex kinds of data are posing new challenges to data analysis. For example, we would like to perform OLAP operations over image or music data and, in general, over multimedia data. For this, **multimedia**

data warehouses must be designed in a way similar to traditional data warehouses. Possible dimensions for image and video data can be the size of the image or video, the width and height of the frames, the creation date, and so on. Many of these dimensions also apply to other kinds of multimedia data.

The main problem in multimedia data warehouses is their high dimensionality. This is due to the fact that multimedia objects like images are represented in a database by descriptors, which can be of two types: content-based (or feature) descriptors and description-based (or textual) descriptors. The former represent the intrinsic content of data (like color, texture, or shape). The latter represent alphanumeric data like acquisition date, author, topic, and so on. Most of the content-based descriptors are set oriented rather than single valued. This would have as a consequence, for example, that we may need to define each different color as a dimension. Given this high-dimensional scenario, the main challenge is to be able to perform multimedia analysis in reasonable execution time.

Image OLAP aims at supporting multidimensional on-line analysis of image data. An example of the efforts in this field is the work by Jin et al. [97], who proposed *Visual Cube* to perform multidimensional OLAP on image collections such as web images indexed by search engines, product images (e.g., from online shops), and photos shared on social networks. Visual Cube defines two kinds of dimensions: metainformation dimensions such as date, title, file name, owner, URL, tag, description, and GPS location and visual dimensions (based on image visual features) such as image size, major colors, face dimension (indicating the existence of faces), and a color/texture histogram. To solve the dimensionality problem commented above, the authors propose two kinds of schemes, namely, a multiple-dimension scheme (MDS) and a single-dimension scheme (SDS). In an MDS representation, each possible value of a feature is considered a dimension. For example, Sunny can be a dimension. Each record corresponding to an image of a sunny day will contain a '1' in this dimension. On the other hand, in an SDS representation, the many possible features will be replaced by a dimension denoted Tag. Thus, an image of a sunny day will contain the value sunny on the Tag dimension. In addition, a set-valued attribute will contain the identifiers of the images with that feature, and a single-valued attribute will contain the total number of such identifiers. The measures in Visual Cube can be a representative image in a cluster or the number of elements in such a cluster. Clusters are computed using techniques like the ones studied in Chap. 9. Records in a cluster have a combination of descriptors corresponding to the cube dimensions. In this way, OLAP operations can be performed. For example, drill-down can be performed by clicking on an image to find others in the cluster. Open questions are, for example, efficient evaluation of top-k queries (given a query cell, find the top-k similar cells measured by the similarity of their images) and incremental update of Visual Cube (given new images, efficiently update the cube).

In the medical domain (as is also the case, e.g., in bioinformatics), multimedia data constitute valuable information for the decision-making process. Arigon et al. [8, 9] have applied the idea of multimedia data warehouses for analyzing electrocardiograms (ECGs). This work aims at extending clinical decision-support systems with multimedia information. This requirement poses many challenges. On the one hand, advanced modeling features such as those studied in this book are needed. Examples include the support of complex hierarchies (a pathology could belong to many classes), many-to-many relationships (a patient may have many pathologies and vice versa), and so on. On the other hand, complex multimedia data, and probably also textual data, must be supported. To deal with these data, first users need to develop efficient algorithms (e.g., based on signal or image processing, pattern recognition, statistical methodologies, among other ones) in order to transform the initial raw data (e.g., an ECG or an X-ray) into data descriptors. Selecting an appropriate set of descriptors is a challenge and depends on the domain under analysis. In the work we are commenting, the authors use the star and snowflake schemas as modeling tools. In these schemas, the dimensions are the descriptors of these data. There are three dimensions related to the patient: principal pathology, age, and gender (description-based descriptors) and two dimensions related to ECG acquisition: time and technology. Finally, two dimensions are related to the content of the ECGs: the QT duration (the time after the ventricles are repolarized) and the noise level (content-based descriptors). The fact table is composed of the foreign key of such descriptors and the ECG signal. Thus, we can, for example, count the number of ECGs that have a given characteristics, or compute an average over a list of ECGs that have a given characteristics in order to obtain a "medium ECG". Note the similarity to the Visual Cube approach described above.

Along similar lines, **music data warehouses** are starting to attract the attention of researchers and the industry, arising from the interest in so-called music information retrieval. The work by Deliège and Pedersen [37,38] envisions an extension of data warehouse technologies to music warehouses that integrate a large variety of music-related information, including both low-level features and high-level musical information. The authors define a music warehouse as a dedicated data warehouse optimized for storing and analyzing music content. The work analyzes the features that a music warehouse must support and the dimensions that a music cube must contain, including a classification of music metadata in four categories: (a) editorial, which covers administrative and historical information; (b) cultural, defined as knowledge produced by the environment (like reviews, for instance); (c) acoustic, which refers to acoustic features, like spectral analysis, or wavelets, which describe the music content; and (d) physical, which refers to the storage medium. Music data warehouses can be built based on these characteristics.

There are many open issues to solve in order to make music warehouses a reality. Further, there is still no clear data model and query language. Finally, the authors identify ten challenges for music warehouses. Some of them are the definition of appropriate aggregation functions for acoustic data, precision-aware retrieval, support of various kinds of hierarchies, and integration of new data types. As it can be seen, most of the problems already solved in traditional data warehouses are still open in the music setting, thus opening an interesting research field for the years to come.

15.5 Graph Analytics and Graph Data Warehouses

Graph analytics has been steadily gaining momentum in the data management community in recent years since many real-world applications are naturally modeled as graphs, in particular in the domain of social network analysis. A graph database management system [178] is a database management system that allows creating, reading, updating, and deleting a graph data model. Some systems use native graph storage, which means they are optimized and designed for storing and managing graph data structures. Others serialize the graph data into a relational or an object-relational database. Graph databases provide better support for graph data management than relational databases. This is mainly due to the fact that relational databases deal just implicitly with connected data, while graph databases store actual graphs. Representative graph databases like Neo4J[2] and Titan[3] have their own data model. They also have their own query language, called Cypher and Gremlin, respectively.

Given the extensive use of graphs to represent practical problems, multidimensional analysis of graph data and **graph data warehouses** are promising fields for research and application development. There is a need to perform graph analysis from different perspectives and at multiple granularities. This poses new challenges to the traditional OLAP technology. Graphs whose nodes are of the same kind are referred to as *homogeneous*. *Heterogeneous* graphs, on the other hand, can have nodes of different kinds. We next comment on some proposals based on homogeneous graphs since work on heterogeneous graphs (e.g., [235]) is at a preliminary stage.

A first framework and classification of OLAP for graphs was proposed in [28,29]. This framework, called *Graph OLAP*, presents a multidimensional and multilevel view of graphs. As an example, consider a set of authors working in a given field, say data warehouses. If two persons coauthored x papers in a conference, say DaWaK 2009, then a link is added between

---

them, which has a collaboration frequency attribute x. For every conference in every year, we may have a coauthor graph describing the collaboration patterns among researchers. Thus, each graph can be viewed as a snapshot of the overall collaboration network. These graphs can be aggregated in an OLAP style. For instance, we can aggregate graphs in order to obtain collaborations by conference type and year for all pairs of authors. For this, we must aggregate the nodes and edges in each snapshot graph according to the conference type (like database conferences) and the year. For example, if there is a link between two authors in the SIGMOD and VLDB conferences, the nodes and the edge will be in the aggregated graph corresponding to the conference type Databases. More complex patterns can be obtained, for example, by merging the authors belonging to the same institution, enabling to obtain patterns of collaboration between researchers of the same institutions.

Taking the above concepts into account, in Graph OLAP, dimensions are classified as *informational* and *topological*. The former are close to the traditional OLAP dimension hierarchies using information of the snapshot levels, for example, Conference → Field → All. They can be used to aggregate and organize snapshots as explained above. On the other hand, topological dimensions can be used for operating on nodes and edges within individual networks. For example, a hierarchy for authors like AuthorId → Institution will belong to a topological dimension since author institutions do not define snapshots. These definitions yield two different kinds of Graph OLAP operations. A roll-up over an informational dimension overlays and joins snapshots (but does not change the objects), while a roll-up over a topological dimension merges nodes in a snapshot, modifying its structure.

Graph Cube [239] is a model for graph data warehouses that supports OLAP queries on large multidimensional networks, accounting for both attribute aggregation and structure summarization of the networks. A multi-dimensional network consists of a collection of vertices, each containing a set of multidimensional attributes describing the nodes' properties. For example, in a social network, the nodes can represent persons, and multidimensional attributes may include UserID, Gender, City, etc. Thus, multidimensional attributes in the graph vertices define the dimensions of the graph cube. Measures are aggregated graphs summarized according to some criteria. Note that the problem here is different from Graph OLAP, where there are several snapshots. In Graph Cube, we have only one large network, thus we have a graph summarization problem. For example, suppose that we have a small social network with three nodes. Two of them correspond to male individuals in the network, while the third corresponds to a female. A graph that summarizes the connections between genders will have two nodes, one labeled male and the other labeled female. The edges between them will be annotated with the number of connections of some kind. For instance, if in the original graph there were two connections between two male persons (in both directions), the summarized graph will contain a cycle over the male node, annotated with a '2'. If there was just one connection between a woman and a man, there will be an edge between nodes male and female annotated with a '1'.

Note that from a modeling point of view, there is no agreement upon a conceptual model for graph databases. To fill this gap, in [62] the authors introduce a conceptual model for graph databases, oriented to allow analysts to perform data analysis over graphs not only in an OLAP style but also using more sophisticated analysis like data mining, for instance. For this, as usual, measures and dimensions must be defined. The authors identified two kinds of measures: informational measures, which are calculated from the attributes of the edges and nodes, and structural measures, which result from the algorithms performed on the structural properties of the graph. A structural measure could be, for instance, a subgraph containing the shortest path between two nodes or a numerical value computing the length of the path. Graph evolution is central to this model. This would allow, for example, to study the evolution of the shortest path between users and products or the shortest path between two members of a group in a social network.

Appendix A
Graphical Notation

In the following, we summarize the graphical notation used in this book.

A.1 Entity-Relationship Model

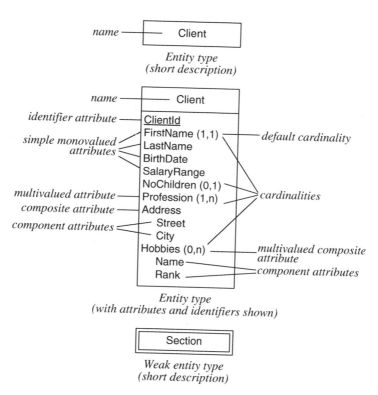

A. Vaisman and E. Zimányi, *Data Warehouse Systems*, Data-Centric
Systems and Applications, DOI 10.1007/978-3-642-54655-6,
© Springer-Verlag Berlin Heidelberg 2014

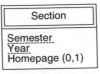

Weak entity type
(with attributes and partial identifiers shown)

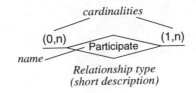

Relationship type
(short description)

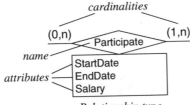

Relationship type
(with attributes shown)

Identifying relationship type
(short description)

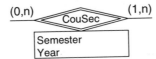

Identifying relationship type
(with attributes shown)

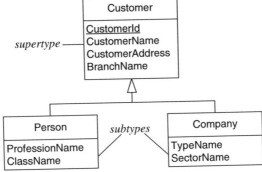

Generalization/specialization
relationship type

A.2   Relational Model

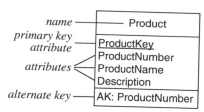

Relational table
(with attributes and keys shown)

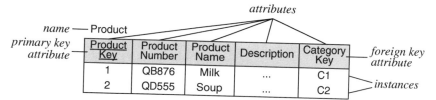

Referential integrity

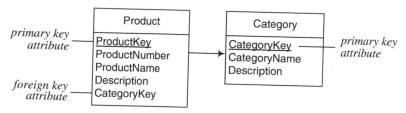

Relational table with instances

A.3   MultiDim Model for Data Warehouses

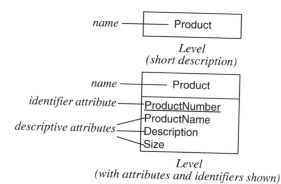

Level
(short description)

Level
(with attributes and identifiers shown)

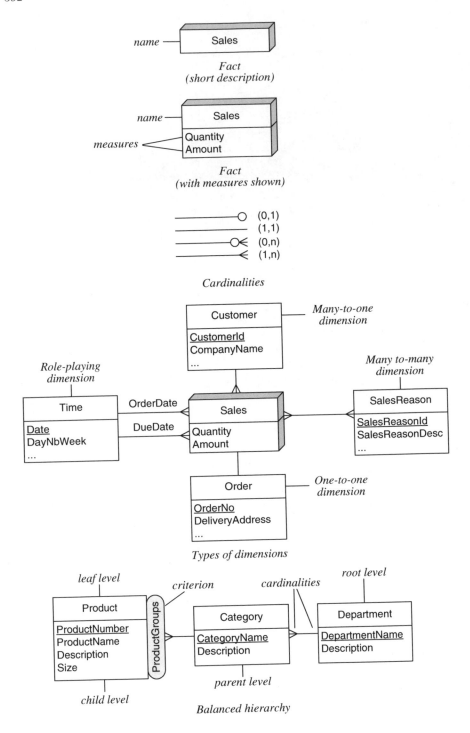

Fact
(short description)

Fact
(with measures shown)

Cardinalities

Types of dimensions

Balanced hierarchy

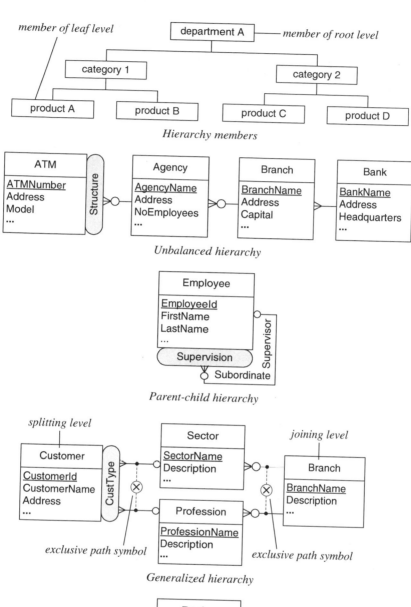

member of leaf level   department A   *member of root level*

category 1   category 2

product A   product B   product C   product D

Hierarchy members

ATM
ATMNumber
Address
Model
...

Structure

Agency
AgencyName
Address
NoEmployees
...

Branch
BranchName
Address
Capital
...

Bank
BankName
Address
Headquarters
...

Unbalanced hierarchy

Employee
EmployeeId
FirstName
LastName
...

Supervision

Supervisor

Subordinate

Parent-child hierarchy

splitting level

Customer
CustomerId
CustomerName
Address
...

CustType

Sector
SectorName
Description
...

joining level

Branch
BranchName
Description
...

Profession
ProfessionName
Description
...

exclusive path symbol

exclusive path symbol

Generalized hierarchy

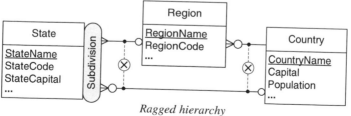

State
StateName
StateCode
StateCapital
...

Subdivision

Region
RegionName
RegionCode
...

Country
CountryName
Capital
Population
...

Ragged hierarchy

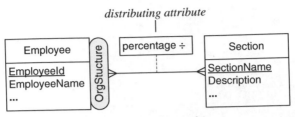

Nonstrict hierarchy

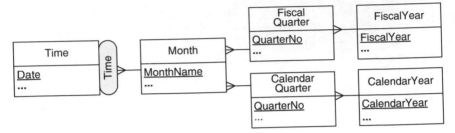

Alternative hierarchy

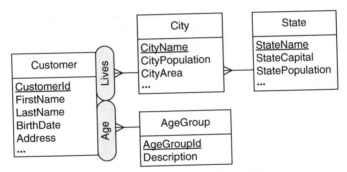

Parallel independant hierarchies

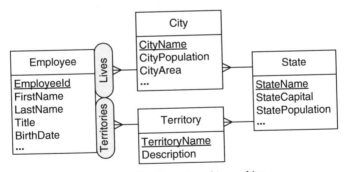

Parallel dependant hierarchies

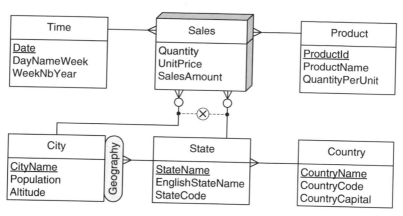

Fact with multiple granularities

A.4 MultiDim Model for Spatial Data Warehouses

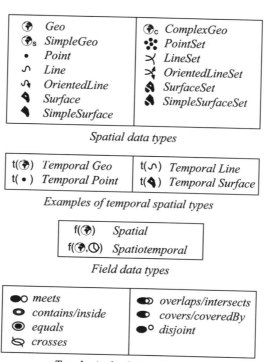

Spatial data types

Examples of temporal spatial types

Field data types

Topological relationship types

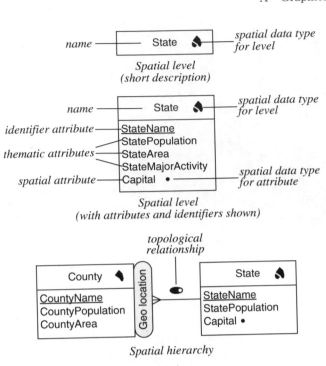

name ──── State 🌢 ── *spatial data type for level*

Spatial level
(short description)

name ──── State 🌢 ── *spatial data type for level*

identifier attribute ── StateName
── StatePopulation
thematic attributes ── StateArea
── StateMajorActivity
spatial attribute ── Capital • ── *spatial data type for attribute*

Spatial level
(with attributes and identifiers shown)

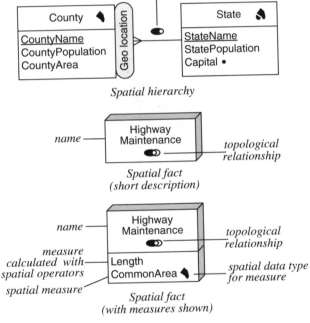

topological relationship

County 🌢   State 🌢
CountyName   StateName
CountyPopulation StatePopulation
CountyArea   Capital •

Geo location

Spatial hierarchy

name ── Highway Maintenance ── *topological relationship*

Spatial fact
(short description)

name ── Highway Maintenance ── *topological relationship*

measure calculated with spatial operators ── Length
CommonArea 🌢 ── *spatial data type for measure*
spatial measure

Spatial fact
(with measures shown)

A.5   BPMN Notation for ETL

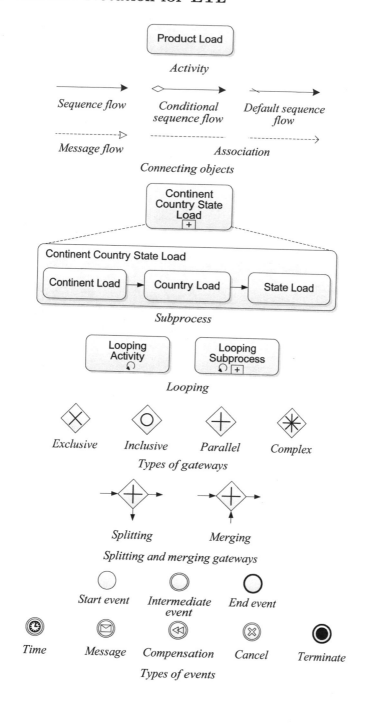

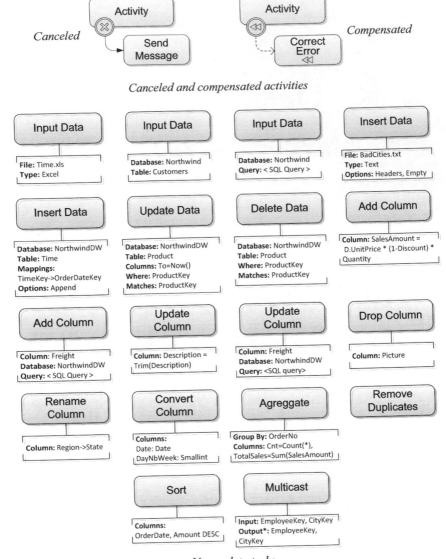

Canceled and compensated activities

Unary data tasks

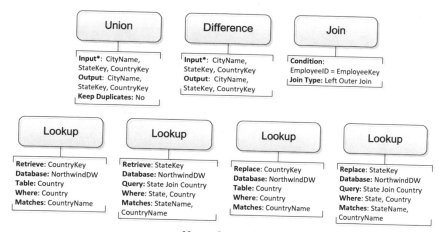

N-ary data tasks

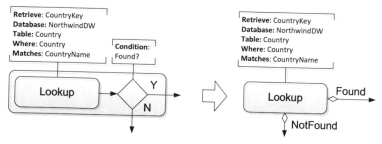

Shorthand notation for lookup

References

1. A. Abelló, J. Samos, F. Saltor, YAM² (Yet Another Multidimensional Model): an extension of UML. Inf. Syst. **32**(6), 541–567 (2006)
2. S. Agarwal, R. Agrawal, P. Deshpande, A. Gupta, J.F. Naughton, R. Ramakrishnan, S. Sarawagi, On the computation of multidimensional aggregates, in *Proceedings of the 22nd International Conference on Very Large Data Bases, VLDB'96* (Morgan Kaufmann, 1996), pp. 506–521
3. R. Agrawal, R. Srikant, Fast algorithms for mining association rules in large databases, in *Proceedings of the 20th International Conference on Very Large Data Bases, VLDB'94* (Morgan Kaufmann, 1994), pp. 487–499
4. R. Agrawal, R. Srikant, Mining sequential patterns, in *Proceedings of the 11th International Conference on Data Engineering, ICDE'95* (IEEE Computer Society Press, 1995), pp. 3–14
5. T.O. Ahmed, M. Miquel, Multidimensional structures dedicated to continuous spatiotemporal phenomena, in *Proceedings of the 22nd British National Conference on Databases, BNCOD 2005*. Lecture Notes on Computer Science, vol. 3567 (Springer, 2005), pp. 29–40
6. T.O. Ahmed, M. Miquel, R. Laurini, Supporting decision making for spatiotemporal phenomena, in *Proceedings of the 3rd International Conference on Information Technology: Research and Education, ITRE*, 2005, pp. 440–444
7. G. Andrienko, N. Andrienko, A general framework for using aggregation in visual exploration of movement data. Cartographic J. **47**(1), 22–40 (2010)
8. A. Arigon, A. Tchounikine, M. Miquel, Handling multiple points of view in a multimedia data warehouse. ACM Trans. Multimedia Comput. Commun. Appl. **2**(3), 199–218 (2006)
9. A. Arigon, A. Tchounikine, M. Miquel, Multimedia data warehouses: a multiversion model and a medical application. Multimedia Tools Appl. **35**(1), 91–108 (2007)
10. W.D. Back, N. Goodman, J. Hyde, *Mondrian in Action: Open Source Business Analytics* (Manning Publications Co., 2013)
11. Y. Bédard, S. Rivest, M. Proulx, Spatial online analytical processing (SOLAP): concepts, architectures, and solutions from a geomatics engineering perspective, in *Data Warehouses and OLAP: Concepts, Architectures and Solutions*, ed. by R. Wrembel, C. Koncilia (IRM Press, 2007), chapter 13, pp. 298–319
12. L. Bellatreche, M. Schneider, H. Lorinquer, M.K. Mohania, Bringing together partitioning, materialized views and indexes to optimize performance of relational data warehouses, in *Proceedings of the 6th International Conference on*

A. Vaisman and E. Zimányi, *Data Warehouse Systems*, Data-Centric Systems and Applications, DOI 10.1007/978-3-642-54655-6,
© Springer-Verlag Berlin Heidelberg 2014

Data Warehousing and Knowledge Discovery, DaWaK'04. Lecture Notes in Computer Science, vol. 3181 (Springer, 2004), pp. 15–25

13. S. Bimonte, M. Miquel, When spatial analysis meets OLAP: multidimensional model and operators. Int. J. Data Warehouse Mining **6**(4), 33–60 (2010)

14. S. Bimonte, M. Bertolotto, J. Gensel, O. Boussaid, Spatial OLAP and map generalization: model and algebra. Int. J. Data Warehouse Mining **8**(1), 24–51 (2012)

15. M. Böhnlein, A. Ulbrich-vom Ende, Deriving initial data warehouses structures from the conceptual data models of the underlying operational information systems, in *Proceedings of the 2nd ACM International Workshop on Data Warehousing and OLAP, DOLAP'99* (ACM, 1999), pp. 15–21

16. A. Bonifati, F. Cattaneo, S. Ceri, A. Fuggetta, S. Paraboschi, Designing data marts for data warehouses. ACM Trans. Software Eng. Methodol. **10**(4), 452–483 (2001)

17. G. Booch, I. Jacobson, J. Rumbaugh, *The Unified Modeling Language: User Guide*, 2nd edn. (Addison-Wesley, 2005)

18. R. Bouman, J. van Dongen, *Pentaho Solutions: Business Intelligence and Data Warehousing with Pentaho and MySQL* (Wiley, 2009)

19. J. Bowen, *Getting Started with Talend Open Studio for Data Integration* (Packt Publishing, 2012)

20. M. Breunig, S. Zlatanova, 3D geo-database research: retrospective and future directions. Comput. Geosciences **37**(7), 791–803 (2011)

21. R.M. Bruckner, B. List, J. Schiefer, Striving towards near real-time data integration for data warehouses, in *Proceedings of the 4th International Conference on Data Warehousing and Knowledge Discovery, DaWaK'02*. Lecture Notes in Computer Science, vol. 2454 (Springer, 2002), pp. 317–326

22. L. Cabibbo, R. Torlone, Querying multidimensional databases, in *Proceedings of the 6th International Workshop on Database Programming Languages*. Lecture Notes in Computer Science, vol. 1396 (Springer, 1997), pp. 319–335

23. L. Cabibbo, R. Torlone, A logical approach to multidimensional databases, in *Proceedings of the 6th International Conference on Extending Database Technology, EDBT'98*. Lecture Notes in Computer Science, vol. 1377 (Springer, 1998), pp. 183–197

24. G. Câmara, D. Palomo, R.C.M. de Souza, F. de Oliveira, O. Regina, Towards a generalized map algebra: principles and data types, in *Proceedings of VII Brazilian Symposium on Geoinformatics, GeoInfo 2005* (2005), pp. 66–81

25. E. Capriolo, D. Wampler, J. Rutherglen, *Programming Hive* (O'Reilly Media, 2012)

26. M. Casters, R. Bouman, J. van Dongen, *Pentaho Kettle Solutions: Building Open Source ETL Solutions with Pentaho Data Integration* (Wiley, 2010)

27. J. Celko. *Analytics and OLAP in SQL* (Morgan Kaufmann, 2006)

28. C. Chen, X. Yan, F. Zhu, J. Han, P.S. Yu, Graph OLAP: towards online analytical processing on graphs, in *Proceedings of the 8th IEEE International Conference on Data Mining, ICDM 2008* (IEEE Computer Society Press, 2008), pp. 103–112

29. C. Chen, X. Yan, F. Zhu, J. Han, P.S. Yu, Graph OLAP: a multi-dimensional framework for graph data analysis. Knowledge Inf. Syst. **21**(1), 41–63 (2009)

30. L. Chiticariu, R. Krishnamurthy, Y. Li, S. Raghavan, F. Reiss, S. Vaithyanathan, SystemT: an algebraic approach to declarative information extraction, in *Proceedings of the 48th Annual Meeting of the Association for Computational Linguistics, ACL 2010* (The Association for Computer Linguistics, 2010), pp. 128–137

31. J. Chmiel, T. Morzy, R. Wrembel, Multiversion join index for multiversion data warehouse. Inf. Software Technol. **51**(1), 98–108 (2009)

32. C. Ciferri, R. Ciferri, L.I. Gómez, M. Schneider, A.A. Vaisman, E. Zimányi, Cube algebra: a generic user-centric model and query language for OLAP cubes. Int. J. Data Warehousing Mining **9**(2), 39–65 (2013)

33. J. Cohen, B. Dolan, M. Dunlap, J.M. Hellerstein, C. Welton, MAD skills: new analysis practices for big data. Proc. VLDB Endowment **2**(2), 1481–1492 (2009)

34. J.P. Cordeiro, G. Câmara, U.F. Moura, C.C. Barbosa, F. Almeida, Algebraic formalism over maps, in *Proceedings of VII Brazilian Symposium on Geoinformatics, GeoInfo 2005* (2005), pp. 49–65

35. L. Davidson, J.M. Moss, *Pro SQL Server 2012 Relational Database Design and Implementation.* (APress, 2012)

36. J. Dean, S. Ghemawat, MapReduce: a flexible data processing tool. Commun. ACM **53**(1), 72–77 (2010)

37. F. Deliège, T.B. Pedersen, Music warehouses: challenges for the next generation of music search engines, in *Proceedings of the 1st International Workshop on Learning the Semantics of Audio Signals, LSAS 2006*, 1996, pp. 95–105

38. F. Deliège, T.B. Pedersen, Fuzzy song sets for music warehouses, in *Proceedings of the 8th International Conference on Music Information Retrieval, ISMIR 2007* (Austrian Computer Society, 2007), pp. 21–26

39. B. Ding, B. Zhao, C.X. Lin, J. Han, C. Zhai, A.N. Srivastava, N.C. Oza, Efficient keyword-based search for top-k cells in text cube. IEEE Trans. Knowledge Data Eng. **23**(12), 1795–1810 (2011)

40. F. Döner, R. Thompson, J. Stoter, Ch. Lemmen, P. van Oosterom, H. Ploeger, S. Zlatanova, Solutions for 4D cadastre - with a case study on utility networks. Int. J. Geographical Inf. Sci. **25**(7), 1173–1189 (2011)

41. B. DuCharme, *Learning SPARQL: Querying and Updating with SPARQL 1.1*, 2nd edn. (O'Reilly Media, 2013)

42. J. Eder, C. Koncilia, Changes of dimension data in temporal data warehouses, in *Proceedings of the 3rd International Conference on Data Warehousing and Knowledge Discovery, DaWaK'01*. Lecture Notes in Computer Science, vol. 2114 (Springer, 2001), pp. 284–293

43. J. Eder, C. Koncilia, T. Morzy, The COMET metamodel for temporal data warehouses, in *Proceedings of the 14th International Conference on Advanced Information Systems Engineering, CAiSE'02*. Lecture Notes in Computer Science, vol. 2348 (Springer, 2002), pp. 83–99

44. J. Eder, K. Wiggisser, Modeling transformations between versions of a temporal data warehouse, in *Proceedings of the ER 2008 Workshops*. Lecture Notes in Computer Science, vol. 5232 (Springer, 2008), pp. 68–77

45. Z. El Akkaoui, E. Zimányi, Defining ETL workflows using BPMN and BPEL, in *Proceedings of the 12th ACM International Workshop on Data Warehousing and OLAP, DOLAP 2009* (ACM, 2009), pp. 41–48

46. Z. El Akkaoui, E. Zimányi, J.-N. Mazón, J. Trujillo, A model-driven framework for ETL process development, in *Proceedings of the 14th ACM International Workshop on Data Warehousing and OLAP, DOLAP 2011* (ACM, 2011), pp. 45–52

47. Z. El Akkaoui, J.-N. Mazón, A.A. Vaisman, E. Zimányi, BPMN-based conceptual modeling of ETL processes, in *Proceedings of the 14th International Conference on Data Warehousing and Knowledge Discovery, DaWaK 2012*. Lecture Notes in Computer Science, vol. 7448 (Springer, 2012), pp. 1–14

48. Z. El Akkaoui, E. Zimányi, J.-N. Mazón, J. Trujillo, A BPMN-based design and maintenance framework for ETL processes. Int. J. Data Warehousing Mining **9**(3), 46–72 (2013)

49. R. Elmasri, S. Navathe, *Fundamentals of Database Systems*, 6th edn. (Addison-Wesley, 2011)

50. N. Enriquez, S.S. Rathore, *Discovering Business Intelligence Using MicroStrategy 9* (Packt Publishing, 2013)
51. M. Ester, H.-P. Kriegel, J. Sander, X. Xu, A density-based algorithm for discovering clusters in large spatial databases with noise, in *Proceedings of the 2nd International Conference on Knowledge Discovery and Data Mining, KDD-96* (AAAI Press, 1996), pp. 226–231
52. L. Etcheverry, A.A. Vaisman, Enhancing OLAP analysis with web cubes, in *Proceedings of the 9th Extended Semantic Web Conference, ESWC 2012.* Lecture Notes in Computer Science, vol. 7295 (Springer, 2012), pp. 469–483
53. L. Etcheverry, A.A. Vaisman, QB4OLAP: a vocabulary for OLAP cubes on the semantic web, in *Proceedings of the Third International Workshop on Consuming Linked Data, COLD 2012.* CEUR Workshop Proceedings, vol. 905. CEUR-WS.org, 2012
54. R. Farkas, *Machine Learning Techniques for Applied Information Extraction.* Ph.D. thesis, University of Szeged, 2009
55. S. Few, Dashboard confusion. Intell. Enterprise **7**, 14–15 (2004)
56. S. Few, *Information Dashboard Design: The Effective Visual Communication of Data.* (O'Reilly Media, 2006)
57. M. García Mattío, D.R. Bernabeu, *Pentaho 5.0 Reporting by Example: Beginner's Guide* (Packt Publishing, 2013)
58. H. Garcia-Molina, J.D. Ullman, J. Widom, *Database Systems: The Complete Book*, 2nd edn. (Prentice Hall, 2008)
59. M.N. Garofalakis, R. Rastogi, K. Shim, SPIRIT: sequential pattern mining with regular expression constraints, in *Proceedings of the 25th International Conference on Very Large Data Bases, VLDB'99* (Morgan Kaufmann, 1999), pp. 223–234
60. M.N. Garofalakis, R. Rastogi, K. Shim, Mining sequential patterns with regular expression constraints. IEEE Trans. Knowledge Data Eng. **14**(3), 530–552 (2002)
61. A. Gates, *Programming Pig* (O'Reilly Media, 2011)
62. A. Ghrab, S. Skhiri, S. Jouili, E. Zimányi, An analytics-aware conceptual model for evolving graphs, in *Proceedings of the 15th International Conference on Data Warehousing and Knowledge Discovery, DaWaK'13.* Lecture Notes in Computer Science (Springer, 2013), pp. 1–12
63. O. Glorio, J. Trujillo, An MDA approach for the development of spatial data warehouses, in *Proceedings of the 10th International Conference on Data Warehousing and Knowledge Discovery, DaWaK'08.* Lecture Notes in Computer Science, vol. 5182 (Springer, 2008), pp. 23–32
64. O. Glorio, J.-N. Mazón, I. Garrigós, J. Trujillo, A personalization process for spatial data warehouse development. Decis. Support Syst. **52**(4), 884–898 (2012)
65. M. Golfarelli, S. Rizzi, A methodological framework for data warehouse design, in *Proceedings of the 1st ACM International Workshop on Data Warehousing and OLAP, DOLAP'98* (ACM, 1998), pp. 3–9
66. M. Golfarelli, S. Rizzi, A survey on temporal data warehousing. Int. J. Data Warehouse Mining **5**(1), 1–17 (2009)
67. M. Golfarelli, S. Rizzi, *Data Warehouse Design: Modern Principles and Methodologies* (McGraw-Hill, 2009)
68. M. Golfarelli, D. Maio, S. Rizzi, Conceptual design of data warehouses from E/R schemes, in *Proceedings of the 31st Hawaii International Conference on System Sciences, HICSS-31* (IEEE Computer Society Press, 1998), pp. 334–343
69. L.I. Gómez, S. Gómez, A.A. Vaisman, A generic data model and query language for spatiotemporal OLAP cube analysis, in *Proceedings of the 15th International Conference on Extending Database Technology, EDBT 2012* (ACM, 2012), pp. 300–311

70. L.I. Gómez, B. Kuijpers, B. Moelans, A.A. Vaisman, A state-of-the-art in spatio-temporal data warehousing, OLAP and mining, in *Integrations of Data Warehousing, Data Mining and Database Technologies: Innovative Approaches*, ed. by D. Taniar, L. Chen (IGI Global, 2011), chapter 9, pp. 200–236

71. I. Gorbach, A. Berger, E. Melomed, *Microsoft SQL Server 2008 Analysis Services Unleashed* (Pearson Education, 2009)

72. J. Gray, S. Chaudhuri, A. Basworth, A. Layman, D. Reichart, M. Venkatrao, F. Pellow, H. Pirahesh, Data cube: a relational aggregation operator generalizing group-by, cross-tab, and sub-totals. Data Mining Knowledge Discov. **1**(1), 29–53 (1997)

73. A. Gupta, I.S. Mumick, V.S. Subrahmanian, Maintaining views incrementally, in *Proceedings of the ACM SIGMOD International Conference on Management of Data, SIGMOD'93* (ACM, 1993), pp. 157–166

74. A. Gupta, I.S. Mumick, Maintenance of materialized views: Problems, techniques, and applications. IEEE Data Eng. Bull. **18**(2), 3–18 (1995)

75. R.H. Güting, M. Schneider, *Moving Objects Databases* (Morgan Kaufmann, 2005)

76. J. Han, J. Pei, Y. Yin, Mining frequent patterns without candidate generation, in *Proceedings of the ACM SIGMOD International Conference on Management of Data, SIGMOD'00* (ACM, 2000), pp. 1–12

77. J. Han, M. Kamber, J. Pei, *Data Mining: Concepts and Techniques*, 3rd edn. (Morgan Kaufmann, 2011)

78. V. Harinarayan, A. Rajaraman, J.D. Ullman, Implementing data cubes efficiently, in *Proceedings of the 1996 ACM SIGMOD International Conference on Management of Data* (ACM, 1996), pp. 205–216

79. S. Harinath, R. Pihlgren, D.G.-Y. Lee, J. Sirmon, R.M. Bruckner, *Professional Microsoft SQL Server 2012 Analysis Services with MDX and DAX* (Wrox, 2012)

80. D. Hecksel, B. Wheeler, P. Boyd-Bowman, J. Testut, D. Gray, C. Dupupet, *Getting Started with Oracle Data Integrator 11g: A Hands-on Tutorial* (Packt Publishing, 2012)

81. I. Hilgefort, *Reporting and Analysis with SAP BusinessObjects*, 2nd edn. (SAP Press, 2012)

82. P. Hitzler, M. Krotzsch, S. Rudolph, *Foundations of Semantic Web Technologies* (CRC Press, 2011)

83. C. Howson, F. Newbould, *SAP BusinessObjects BI 4.0 The Complete Reference*, 3rd edn. (McGraw-Hill, 2012)

84. C.A. Hurtado, C. Gutierrez, Handling structural heterogeneity in OLAP, in *Data Warehouses and OLAP: Concepts, Architectures and Solutions*, ed. by R. Wrembel, C. Koncilia (IRM Press, 2007), chapter 2, pp. 27–57

85. C.A. Hurtado, C. Gutierrez, A. Mendelzon, Capturing summarizability with integrity constraints in OLAP. ACM Trans. Database Syst. **30**(3), 854–886 (2005)

86. C.A. Hurtado, A. Mendelzon, Reasoning about summarizabiliy in heterogeneous multidimensional schemas, in *Proceedings of the 8th International Conference on Database Theory, ICDT'01*. Lecture Notes in Computer Science, vol. 1973 (Springer, 2001), pp. 375–389

87. C.A. Hurtado, A. Mendelzon, OLAP dimension constraints, in *Proceedings of the 3rd ACM SIGACT-SIGMOD Symposium on Principles of Database Systems, PODS'02* (ACM, 2002), pp. 375–389

88. B. Hüsemann, J. Lechtenbörger, G. Vossen, Conceptual data warehouse design, in *Proceedings of the 2nd International Workshop on Design and Management of Data Warehouses, DMDW'00*, CEUR Workshop Proceedings, 2000, p. 6

89. S. Idreos, F. Groffen, N. Nes, S. Manegold, K.S. Mullender, M.L. Kersten, MonetDB: two decades of research in column-oriented database architectures. IEEE Data Eng. Bull. **35**(1), 40–45 (2012)

90. W.H. Inmon, *Building the Data Warehouse* (Wiley, 2002)

91. W.H. Inmon, C. Imhoff, R. Sousa, *Corporate Information Factory*, 2nd edn. (Wiley, 2001)

92. W.H. Inmon, K. Krishnan, *Building the Unstructured Data Warehouse* (Technics Publications, LLC, 2011)

93. ISO TC 211, Geographic Information – Schema for Coverage Geometry and Functions: ISO 19123:2005 (2005)

94. ISO/IEC JTC 1/SC 32, Information Technology – Database languages – SQL Multimedia and Application Packages – Part 3: Spatial: ISO/IEC 13249-3:2011, 4th edn. (2011)

95. H. Jagadish, L. Lakshmanan, D. Srivastava, What can hierarchies do for data warehouses, in *Proceedings of the 25th International Conference on Very Large Data Bases, VLDB'99* (Morgan Kaufmann, 1999), pp. 530–541

96. M. Jarke, M. Lanzerini, C. Quix, T. Sellis, P. Vassiliadis, Quality-driven data warehouse design, in *Fundamentals of Data Warehouses*, 2nd edn. (Springer, 2003), pp. 165–179

97. X. Jin, J. Han, L. Cao, J. Luo, B. Ding, C.X. Lin, Visual cube and on-line analytical processing of images, in *Proceedings of the 19th ACM Conference on Information and Knowledge Management, CIKM 2010* (ACM, 2010), pp. 849–858

98. M. Jürgens, *Index Structures for Data Warehouses*. Lecture Notes in Computer Science, vol. 1859 (Springer, 2002)

99. B. Kämpgen, A. Harth, Transforming statistical linked data for use in OLAP systems, in *Proceedings the 7th International Conference on Semantic Systems, I-SEMANTICS 2011*. (ACM, 2011), pp. 33–40

100. B. Kämpgen, A. Harth, No size fits all: Running the star schema benchmark with SPARQL and RDF aggregate views, in *Proceedings of the 10th International Conference on the Semantic Web, ESWC 2013*. Lecture Notes in Computer Science, vol. 7882 (Springer, 2013), pp. 290–304

101. L. Kaufman, P.J. Rousseeuw, *Finding Groups in Data: An Introduction to Cluster Analysis* (Wiley, 1990)

102. R. Kimball, J. Caserta, *The Data Warehouse ETL Toolkit: Practical Techniques for Extracting, Cleaning, Conforming, and Delivering Data* (Wiley, 2004)

103. R. Kimball, M. Ross, *The Data Warehouse Toolkit: The Complete Guide to Dimensional Modeling*, 3rd edn. (Wiley, 2013)

104. R. Kimball, L. Reeves, M. Ross, W. Thornthwaite, *The Data Warehouse Lifecycle Toolkit: Expert Methods for Designing, Developing, and Deploying Data Warehouses* (Wiley, 1998)

105. B. Knight, E. Veerman, J.M. Moss, M. Davis, C. Rock, *Professional Microsoft SQL Server 2012 Integration Services* (Wrox, 2012)

106. T. Kolbe, R. Gröger, Towards unified 3D city models, in *Proceedings of ISPRS Commission IV Joint Workshop on Challenges in Geospatial Analysis, Integration and Visualization II*, 2003

107. R. Krishnamurthy, Y. Li, S. Raghavan, F. Reiss, S. Vaithyanathan, H. Zhu, SystemT: a system for declarative information extraction. SIGMOD Rec. **37**(4), 7–13 (2008)

108. K. Kulkarni, J.-E. Michels, Temporal features in SQL:2011. SIGMOD Rec. **41**(3), 34–43 (2012)

109. T. Lahiri, M.-A. Neimat, S. Folkman, Oracle TimesTen: an in-memory database for enterprise applications. IEEE Data Eng. Bull. **36**(2), 6–13 (2013)

110. R. Lake, D. Burggraf, M. Trninic, L. Rae, *Geography Mark-Up Language: Foundation for the Geo-Web* (Wiley, 2004)

111. A. Lamb, M. Fuller, R. Varadarajan, N. Tran, B. Vandier, L. Doshi, C. Bear, The Vertica analytic database: C-Store 7 years later. Proc. VLDB **5**(12), 1790–1801 (2012)

112. S. Larrivée, Y. Bédard, J. Pouliot, How to enrich the semantics of geospatial databases by properly expressing 3D objects in a conceptual model, in *Proceedings of the OTM 2005 Workshops: On the Move to Meaningful Internet Systems.* Lecture Notes in Computer Science, vol. 3762 (Springer, 2005), pp. 999–1008

113. J. Lechtenbörger, G. Vossen, Multidimensional normal forms for data warehouse design. Inf. Syst. **28**(5), 415–434 (2003)

114. W. Lehner, J. Albrecht, H. Wedekind, Normal forms for multidimensional databases, in *Proceedings of the 10th International Conference on Scientific and Statistical Database Management, SSDBM'98* (IEEE Computer Society Press, 1998), pp. 63–72

115. H. Lenz, A. Shoshani, Summarizability in OLAP and statistical databases, in *Proceedings of the 9th International Conference on Scientific and Statistical Database Management, SSDBM'97* (IEEE Computer Society Press, 1997), pp. 132–143

116. S.S. Lightstone, T.J. Teorey, T. Nadeau, *Physical Database Design: The Database Professional's Guide to Exploiting Indexes, Views, Storage, and More*, 4th edn. (Morgan Kaufmann, 2007)

117. C.X. Lin, B. Ding, J. Han, F. Zhu, B. Zhao, Text Cube: computing IR measures for multidimensional text database analysis, in *Proceedings of the 8th IEEE International Conference on Data Mining, ICDM 2008* (IEEE Computer Society Press, 2008), pp. 905–910

118. X. Liu, C. Thomsen, T.B. Pedersen, MapReduce-based dimensional ETL made easy. Proc. VLDB Endowment **5**(1), 1882–1885 (2012)

119. S. Luján-Mora, J. Trujillo, A comprehensive method for data warehouse design, in *Proceedings of the 5th International Workshop on Design and Management of Data Warehouses, DMDW'03.* CEUR Workshop Proceedings, 2003

120. S. Luján-Mora, J. Trujillo, I.-Y. Song, A UML profile for multidimensional modeling in data warehouses. Data Knowledge Eng. **59**(3), 725–769 (2006)

121. M. Maibaum, G. Rimon, C. Orengo, N. Martin, A. Poulovasillis, BioMap: gene family based integration of heterogeneous biological databases using AutoMed metadata, in *Proceedings of the 15th International Workshop on Database and Expert Systems Applications, DEXA'04* (IEEE Computer Society Press, 2004), pp. 384–388

122. M. Maibaum, L. Zamboulis, G. Rimon, C. Orengo, N. Martin, A. Poulovasillis, Cluster based integration of heterogeneous biological databases using the AutoMed toolkit, in *Proceedings of the 2nd International Workshop on Data Integration in the Life Sciences, DILS 2005.* Lecture Notes in Computer Science, vol. 3615 (Springer, 2005), pp. 191–207

123. E. Malinowski, E. Zimányi, Hierarchies in a multidimensional model: from conceptual modeling to logical representation. Data Knowledge Eng. **59**(2), 348–377 (2006)

124. E. Malinowski, E. Zimányi, Inclusion of time-varying measures in temporal data warehouses, in *Proceedings of the 8th International Conference on Enterprise Information Systems, ICEIS'06*, 2006, pp. 181–186

125. E. Malinowski, E. Zimányi, Requirements specification and conceptual modeling for spatial data warehouses, in *Proceedings of the OTM 2006 Workshops: On the Move to Meaningful Internet Systems.* Lecture Notes in Computer Science, vol. 4277 (Springer, 2006), pp. 1616–1625

126. E. Malinowski, E. Zimányi, *Advanced Data Warehouse Design: From Conventional to Spatial and Temporal Applications* (Springer, 2008)
127. E. Malinowski, E. Zimányi, A conceptual model for temporal data warehouses and its transformation to the ER and object-relational models. Data Knowledge Eng. **64**(1), 101–133 (2008)
128. I. Mami, Z. Bellahsene, A survey of view selection methods. SIGMOD Rec. **41**(1), 20–29 (2012)
129. G. Marketos, E. Frentzos, I. Ntoutsi, N. Pelekis, A. Raffaetà, Y. Theodoridis, Building real-world trajectory warehouses, in *Proceedings of the 7th ACM International Workshop on Data Engineering for Wireless and Mobile Access* (ACM, 2008), pp. 8–15
130. J.-N. Mazón, J. Trujillo, M. Serrano, M. Piattini, Designing data warehouses: From business requirement analysis to multidimensional modeling, in *Proceedings of the 1st International Workshop on Requirements Engineering for Business Need and IT Alignment, REBN'05*, 2005, pp. 44–53
131. M. Mehta, R. Agrawal, J. Rissanen, SLIQ: a fast scalable classifier for data mining, in *Proceedings of the 5th International Conference on Extending Database Technology, EDBT'96*. Lecture Notes in Computer Science, vol. 1057 (Springer, 1996), pp. 18–32
132. J. Melton, *Advanced SQL:1999. Understanding Object-Relational and Other Advanced Features* (Morgan Kaufmann, 2003)
133. J. Melton, SQL:2003 has been published. SIGMOD Rec. **33**(1), 119–125 (2003)
134. J. Melton, A. Eisenberg, SQL multimedia and application packages (SQL/MM). SIGMOD Rec. **30**(4), 97–102 (2001)
135. J. Melton, A. Simon, *SQL:1999. Understanding Relational Language Components* (Morgan Kaufmann, 2002)
136. A. Mendelzon, A.A. Vaisman, Temporal queries in OLAP, in *Proceedings of the 26th International Conference on Very Large Data Bases, VLDB'00* (Morgan Kaufmann, 2000), pp. 243–253
137. A. Mendelzon, A.A. Vaisman, Time in multidimensional databases, in *Multidimensional Databases: Problems and Solutions*, ed. by M. Rafanelli (Idea Group, 2003), pp. 166–199
138. J. Mennis, R. Viger, C.D. Tomlin, Cubic map algebra functions for spatio-temporal analysis. Cartography Geographic Inf. Sci. **32**(1), 17–32 (2005)
139. D. Moraschi, *Business Intelligence with MicroStrategy Cookbook* (Packt Publishing, 2012)
140. T. Morzy, R. Wrembel, On querying versions of multiversion data warehouse, in *Proceedings of the 7th ACM International Workshop on Data Warehousing and OLAP, DOLAP'04* (ACM, 2004), pp. 92–101
141. I.S. Mumick, D. Quass, B.S. Mumick, Maintenance of data cubes and summary tables in a warehouse, in *Proceedings of the ACM SIGMOD International Conference on Management of Data, SIGMOD'97* (ACM, 1997), pp. 100–111
142. V. Nebot, R. Berlanga Llavori, Building data warehouses with semantic web data. Decis. Support Syst. **52**(4), 853–868 (2011)
143. M. Neteler, H. Mitasova, *Open Source GIS: A GRASS GIS Approach*, 3rd edn. (Springer, 2008)
144. R.T. Ng et al., *Perspectives on Business Intelligence*. Synthesis Lectures on Data Management (Morgan & Claypool, 2013)
145. M. Niinimäki, T. Niemi, An ETL process for OLAP using RDF/OWL ontologies, in *Journal on Data Semantics XIII*, ed. by S. Spaccapietra, E. Zimányi, I.-Y. Song. Lecture Notes in Computer Science, vol. 1396 (Springer, 2009), pp. 97–119
146. R.O. Obe, L.S. Hsu, *PostGIS in Action*, 2nd edn. (Manning Publications Co., 2014)

147. K. Oehler, J. Gruenes, C. Ilacqua, *IBM Cognos TM1: The Official Guide* (McGraw-Hill, 2012)
148. A. Olivé, *Conceptual Modeling of Information Systems* (Springer, 2007)
149. P.E. O'Neil, Model 204 architecture and performance, in *Proceedings of the 2nd International Workshop on High Performance Transaction Systems.* Lecture Notes in Computer Science, vol. 359 (Springer, 1989), pp. 40–59
150. E. O'Neil, G. Graefe, Multi-table joins through bitmapped join indices. SIGMOD Rec. **24**(3), 8–11 (1995)
151. S. Orlando, R. Orsini, A. Raffaetà, A. Roncato, C. Silvestri, Spatio-temporal aggregations in trajectory data warehouses. J. Comput. Sci. Eng. **1**(2), 211–232 (2007)
152. F. Paim, J. Castro, DWARF: an approach for requirements definition and management of data warehouse systems, in *Proceedings of the 11th IEEE International Requirements Engineering Conference, RE'03* (IEEE Computer Society Press, 2003), pp. 75–84
153. F. Paim, A. Carvalho, J. Castro, Towards a methodology for requirements analysis of data warehouse systems, in *Proceedings of the 16th Brazilian Symposium on Software Engineering, SBES'02*, 2002, pp. 1–16
154. L. Paolino, G. Tortora, M. Sebillo, G. Vitiello, R. Laurini, Phenomena: a visual query language for continuous fields, in *Proceedings of the 11th ACM Symposium on Advances in Geographic Information Systems, ACM-GIS'03* (ACM, 2003), pp. 147–153
155. C. Parent, S. Spaccapietra, E. Zimányi, *Conceptual Modeling for Traditional and Spatio-Temporal Applications: The MADS Approach* (Springer, 2006)
156. D. Parmenter, *Key Performance Indicators (KPI): Developing, Implementing, and Using Winning KPIs*, 2nd edn. (Wiley, 2010)
157. M.R. Patil, F. Thia, *Pentaho for Big Data Analytics* (Packt Publishing, 2013)
158. T.B. Pedersen, Managing complex multidimensional data, in *Proceedings of the 2nd European Business Intelligence Summer School, eBISS 2012.* Lecture Notes in Business Information Processing, vol. 138 (Springer, 2012), pp. 1–28
159. T.B. Pedersen, C.S. Jensen, C.E. Dyreson, Extending practical pre-aggregation in on-line analytical processing, in *Proceedings of the 25th International Conference on Very Large Data Bases, VLDB'99* (Morgan Kaufmann, 1999), pp. 663–674
160. T.B. Pedersen, C.S. Jensen, C. Dyreson, A foundation for capturing and querying complex multidimensional data. Inf. Syst. **26**(5), 383–423 (2001)
161. N. Pelekis, A. Raffaetà, M.L. Damiani, C. Vangenot, G. Marketos, E. Frentzos, I. Ntoutsi, Y. Theodoridis, Towards trajectory data warehouses, in *Mobility, Data Mining and Privacy: Geographic Knowledge Discovery*, ed. by F. Giannotti, D. Pedreschi (Springer, 2008), Chapter 9, pp. 189–211
162. R. Person, *Balanced Scorecards and Operational Dashboards with Microsoft Excel*, 2nd edn. (Wiley, 2013)
163. T. Piasevoli, *MDX with Microsoft SQL Server 2008 R2 Analysis Services Cookbook* (Packt Publishing, 2011)
164. H. Plattner, A. Zeier, *In-Memory Data Management: Technology and Applications*, 2nd edn. (Morgan Kaufmann, 2012)
165. J. Pouliot, S. Daniel, F. Hubert, A. Zamyadi (eds.), *Progress and New Trends in 3D Geoinformation Sciences.* (Springer, 2013)
166. E. Pourabbas, M. Rafanelli, Hierarchies, in *Multidimensional Databases: Problems and Solutions*, ed. by M. Rafanelli (Idea Group, 2003), pp. 91–115
167. A. Raffaetà, L. Leonardi, G. Marketos, G. Andrienko, N. Andrienko, E. Frentzos, N. Giatrakos, S. Orlando, N. Pelekis, A. Roncato, C. Silvestri, Visual mobility analysis using T-Warehouse. Int. J. Data Warehousing Mining **7**(1), 1–23 (2011)

168. R. Ramakrishnan, J. Gehrke, *Database Management Systems*, 3rd edn. (McGraw-Hill, 2003)
169. N.H. Rasmussen, C.Y. Chen, M. Bansal, *Business Dashboards: A Visual Catalog for Design and Deployment* (Wiley, 2009)
170. F. Ravat, O. Teste, G. Zurfluh, A multiversion-based multidimensional model, in *Proceedings of the 8th International Conference on Data Warehousing and Knowledge Discovery, DaWaK'06*. Lecture Notes in Computer Science, vol. 4081 (Springer, 2006), pp. 65–74
171. F. Ravat, O. Teste, R. Tournier, G. Zurfluh, Top_Keyword: an aggregation function for textual document OLAP, in *Proceedings of the 10th International Conference on Data Warehousing and Knowledge Discovery, DaWaK'08*. Lecture Notes in Computer Science, vol. 5182 (Springer, 2008), pp. 55–64
172. F. Reiss, S. Raghavan, R. Krishnamurthy, H. Zhu, S. Vaithyanathan, An algebraic approach to rule-based information extraction, in *Proceedings of the 24th International Conference on Data Engineering, ICDE'08* (IEEE Computer Society Press, 2008), pp. 933–942
173. C. Renso, S. Spaccapietra, E. Zimányi (eds.), *Mobility Data: Modeling, Management, and Understanding* (Cambridge Press, 2013)
174. P. Rigaux, M. Scholl, A. Voisard, *Spatial Databases with Application to GIS* (Morgan Kaufmann, 2002)
175. M. Rittman, *Oracle Business Intelligence 11g Developers Guide* (McGraw-Hill/Osborne Media, 2012)
176. S. Rivest, Y. Bédard, P. Marchand, Toward better support for spatial decision making: defining the characteristics of spatial on-line analytical processing (SOLAP). Geomatica **55**(4), 539–555 (2001)
177. S. Rizzi, E. Saltarelli, View materialization vs. indexing: balancing space constraints in data warehouse design, in *Proceedings of the 15th International Conference on Advanced Information Systems Engineering, CAiSE'03*. Lecture Notes in Computer Science, vol. 2681 (Springer, 2003), pp. 502–519
178. I. Robinson, J. Webber, E. Eifrem, *Graph Databases* (O'Reilly Media, 2013)
179. M.C. Roldán, *Pentaho Data Integration: Beginner's Guide*, 2nd edn. (Packt Publishing, 2013)
180. O. Romero, A. Abelló, Automating multidimensional design from ontologies, in *Proceedings of the 10th ACM International Workshop on Data Warehousing and OLAP, DOLAP'07* (ACM, 2007), pp. 1–8
181. O. Romero, A. Abelló, On the need of a reference algebra for OLAP, in *Proceedings of the 9th International Conference on Data Warehousing and Knowledge Discovery, DaWaK'07*. Lecture Notes in Computer Science, vol. 4654 (Springer, 2007), pp. 99–110
182. M. Russo, A. Ferrari, C. Webb, *Expert Cube Development with Microsoft SQL Server 2008 Analysis Services* (Packt Publishing, 2009)
183. M. Russo, A. Ferrari, C. Webb, *Microsoft SQL Server 2012 Analysis Services: The BISM Tabular Model.* (Microsoft Press, 2012)
184. C. Sapia, M. Blaschka, G. Höfling, B. Dinter, Extending the E/R model for multidimensional paradigm, in *Proceedings of the 17th International Conference on Conceptual Modeling, ER'98*. Lecture Notes in Computer Science, vol. 1507 (Springer, 1998), pp. 105–116
185. D.A. Schneider, Practical considerations for real-time business intelligence, in *Proceedings of the 1st International Workshop on Business Intelligence for the Real-Time Enterprises, BIRTE'06*. Lecture Notes in Computer Science, vol. 4365 (Springer, 2007), pp. 1–3
186. J.C. Shafer, R. Agrawal, M. Mehta, SPRINT: a scalable parallel classifier for data mining, in *Proceedings of the 22nd International Conference on Very Large Data Bases, VLDB'96* (Morgan Kaufmann, 1996), pp. 544–555

187. S. Shekhar, S. Chawla, *Spatial Databases: A Tour* (Prentice Hall, 2003)

188. A. Simitsis, Mapping conceptual to logical models for ETL processes, in *Proceedings of the 8th ACM International Workshop on Data Warehousing and OLAP, DOLAP'05* (ACM, 2005), pp. 67–76

189. B.C. Smith, C.R. Clay, *Microsoft SQL Server 2008 MDX Step by Step* (Microsoft Press, 2009)

190. R. Srikant, R. Agrawal, Mining generalized association rules, in *Proceedings of the 21st International Conference on Very Large Data Bases, VLDB'95* (Morgan Kaufmann, 1995), pp. 407–419

191. R. Srikant, R. Agrawal, Mining sequential patterns: generalizations and performance improvements, in *Proceedings of the 5th International Conference on Extending Database Technology, EDBT'96*. Lecture Notes in Computer Science, vol. 1057 (Springer, 1996), pp. 3–17

192. K. Stockinger, K. Wu, Bitmap indices for data warehouses, in *Data Warehouses and OLAP: Concepts, Architectures and Solutions*, ed. by R. Wrembel, C. Koncilia (IRM Press, 2007), chapter 7, pp. 157–178

193. M. Stonebraker, Stonebraker on data warehouses. Commun. ACM **54**(5), 10–11 (2011)

194. M. Stonebraker, D.J. Abadi, A. Batkin, X. Chen, M. Cherniack, M. Ferreira, E. Lau, A. Lin, S. Madden, E. O'Neil, P. O'Neil, A. Rasin, N. Tran, S. Zdonik, C-Store: a column-oriented DBMS, in *Proceedings of the 31st International Conference on Very Large Data Bases, VLDB'05* (Morgan Kaufmann, 2005), pp. 553–564

195. M. Stonebraker, D.J. Abadi, D.J. DeWitt, S. Madden, E. Paulson, A. Pavlo, A. Rasin, MapReduce and parallel DBMSs: friends or foes? Commun. ACM **53**(1), 64–71 (2010)

196. P.-N. Tan, M. Steinbach, V. Kumar, *Introduction to Data Mining*, 2nd edn. (Addison-Wesley, 2013)

197. A. Tennick, *Practical MDX Queries: For Microsoft SQL Server Analysis Services 2008* (McGraw-Hill, 2010)

198. T.J. Teorey, S.S. Lightstone, T. Nadeau, H.V. Jagadish, *Database Modeling and Design: Logical Design*, 5th edn. (Morgan Kaufmann, 2011)

199. C. Thomsen, T.B. Pedersen, A survey of open source tools for business intelligence, in *Integrations of Data Warehousing, Data Mining and Database Technologies: Innovative Approaches*, ed. by D. Taniar, L. Chen (IGI Global, 2011), chapter 10, pp. 237–257

200. C.S. Thomsen, T.B. Pedersen, W. Lehner, RiTE: providing on-demand data for right-time data warehousing, in *Proceedings of the 24th International Conference on Data Engineering, ICDE'08* (IEEE Computer Society Press, 2008), pp. 456–465

201. A. Thusoo, J.S. Sarma, N. Jain, Z. Shao, P. Chakka, N. Zhangand, S. Anthony, H. Liu, R. Murthy, Hive: a petabyte scale data warehouse using Hadoop, in *Proceedings of the 26th International Conference on Data Engineering, ICDE 2010* (IEEE, Computer Society Press 2010), pp. 996–1005

202. D. Tomlin, *Geographic Information Systems and Cartographic Modeling* (Prentice Hall, 1990)

203. R. Torlone, Conceptual multidimensional models, in *Multidimensional Databases: Problems and Solutions*, ed. by M. Rafanelli (Idea Group, 2003), pp. 69–90

204. J. Trujillo, M. Palomar, J. Gomez, I.-Y. Song, Designing data warehouses with OO conceptual models. IEEE Comput. **34**(12), 66–75 (2001)

205. N. Tryfona, F. Busborg, J. Borch, StarER: a conceptual model for data warehouse design, in *Proceedings of the 2nd ACM International Workshop on Data Warehousing and OLAP, DOLAP'99* (ACM, 1999), pp. 3–8

206. F.S.C. Tseng, A.Y.H. Chou, The concept of document warehousing for multidimensional modeling of textual-based business intelligence. Decis. Support Syst. **42**(2), 727–744 (2006)

207. A. Tsois, N. Karayannidis, T. Sellis, MAC: conceptual data modelling for OLAP, in *Proceedings of the 3rd International Workshop on Design and Management of Data Warehouses, DMDW'01.* CEUR Workshop Proceedings, 2001, p. 5

208. I.Z. Turki, F.G. Jedidi, R. Bouaziz, Multiversion data warehouse constraints, in *Proceedings of the 13th ACM International Workshop on Data Warehousing and OLAP, DOLAP 2010* (ACM, 2010), pp. 11–18

209. P. Turley, R.M. Bruckner, T. Silva, K. Withee, G. Paisley, *Professional Microsoft SQL Server 2012 Reporting Services* (Wrox, 2012)

210. A.A. Vaisman, Data quality-based requirements elicitation for decision support systems, in *Data Warehouses and OLAP: Concepts, Architectures and Solutions*, ed. by R. Wrembel, C. Koncilia (IRM Press, 2007), chapter 16, pp. 58–86

211. A.A. Vaisman, An introduction to business process modeling, in *Proceedings of the 2nd European Business Intelligence Summer School, eBISS 2012.* Lecture Notes in Business Information Processing, vol. 138 (Springer, 2012), pp. 29–61

212. A.A. Vaisman, E. Zimányi, A multidimensional model representing continuous fields in spatial data warehouses, in *Proceedings of the 17th ACM SIGSPATIAL Symposium on Advances in Geographic Information Systems, ACM-GIS'09* (ACM, 2009), pp. 168–177

213. A.A. Vaisman, E. Zimányi, What is spatio-temporal data warehousing? in *Proceedings of the 11th International Conference on Data Warehousing and Knowledge Discovery, DaWaK'09.* Lecture Notes in Computer Science, vol. 5691 (Springer, 2009), pp. 9–23

214. A.A. Vaisman, E. Zimányi, Physical design and implementation of spatial data warehouses supporting continuous fields, in *Proceedings of the 12th International Conference on Data Warehousing and Knowledge Discovery, DaWaK'10.* Lecture Notes in Computer Science, vol. 6263 (Springer, 2010), pp. 25–39

215. A.A. Vaisman, Esteban Zimányi, Data warehouses: next challenges, in *Proceedings of the 1st European Business Intelligence Summer School, eBISS 2011.* Lecture Notes in Business Information Processing, vol. 96 (Springer, 2011), pp. 1–26

216. L. van den Brink, J. Stoter, S. Zlatanova, Establishing a national standard for 3D topographic data compliant to CityGML. Int. J. Geographical Inf. Sci. **27**(1), 92–113 (2013)

217. A. van Lamsweerde, *Requirements Engineering: From System Goals to UML Models to Software Specifications* (Wiley, 2009)

218. Y. Vasiliev, *Oracle Business Intelligence: The Condensed Guide to Analysis and Reporting* (Packt Publishing, 2010)

219. P. Vassiliadis, A survey of extract-transform-load technology, in *Integrations of Data Warehousing, Data Mining and Database Technologies: Innovative Approaches*, ed. by D. Taniar, L. Chen (IGI Global, 2011), chapter 8, pp. 171–199

220. P. Vassiliadis, A. Simitsis, Near real time ETL, in *New Trends in Data Warehousing and Data Analysis*, ed. by S. Kozielski, R. Wrembel. Annals of Information Systems, vol. 3 (Springer, 2008), pp. 16–50

221. P. Vassiliadis, A. Simitsis, S. Skiadopoulos, Conceptual modeling for ETL processes, in *Proceedings of the 5th ACM International Workshop on Data Warehousing and OLAP, DOLAP'02* (ACM, 2002), pp. 14–21

222. I.F. Vega López, R.T. Snodgrass, B. Moon, Spatiotemporal aggregate computation: a survey. IEEE Trans. Knowledge Data Eng. **17**(2), 271–286 (2005)

223. J. Viqueira, N. Lorentzos, SQL extension for spatio-temporal data. VLDB J. **16**(2), 179–200 (2007)

224. G. Viswanathan, M. Schneider, On the requirements for user-centric spatial data warehousing and SOLAP, in *Proceedings of the DASFAA 2011 Workshops*, Lecture Notes in Computer Science, vol. 6637 (Springer, 2011), pp. 144–155

225. D. Volitich, G. Ruppert, *IBM Cognos Business Intelligence 10: The Official Guide* (McGraw-Hill, 2010)

226. T. White, *Hadoop: The Definitive Guide*, 3rd edn. (O'Reilly Media, 2012)

227. M. Whitehorn, R. Zare, M. Pasumansky, *Fast Track to MDX*, 2nd edn. (Springer, 2005)

228. I.H. Witten, E. Frank, M.A. Hall, *Data Mining: Practical Machine Learning Tools and Techniques*, 3rd edn. (Morgan Kaufmann, 2011)

229. M. Worboys, M. Duckham, *GIS: A Computing Perspective*, 2nd edn. (CRC Press, 2004)

230. R. Wrembel, B. Bebel, Metadata management in a multiversion data warehouse, in *Journal on Data Semantics VIII*, ed. by S. Spaccapietra et al. Lecture Notes in Computer Science, vol. 4380 (Springer, 2007), pp. 118–157

231. R. Wrembel, T. Morzy, Managing and querying version of multiversion data warehouse, in *Proceedings of the 10th International Conference on Extending Database Technology, EDBT'06*. Lecture Notes in Computer Science, vol. 3896 (Springer, 2006), pp. 1121–1124

232. K. Wu, E. J. Otoo, A. Shoshani, Optimizing bitmap indices with efficient compression. ACM Trans. Database Syst. **31**(1), 1–38 (2006)

233. J. Xu, R.H. Güting, A generic data model for moving objects. GeoInformatica **17**(1), 125–172 (2013)

234. A.K.W. Yeung, G.B. Hall, *Spatial Database Systems: Design, Implementation and Project Management*. GeoJournal Library, vol. 87 (Springer, 2007)

235. M. Yin, B. Wu, Z. Zeng, HMGraph OLAP: a novel framework for multi-dimensional heterogeneous network analysis, in *Proceedings of the 15th ACM International Workshop on Data Warehousing and OLAP, DOLAP 2012* (ACM, 2012), pp. 137–144

236. F. Zemke, What's new in SQL:2011. SIGMOD Rec. **41**(1), 67–73 (2012)

237. D. Zhang, C.X. Zhai, J. Han, Topic cube: topic modeling for OLAP on multidimensional text databases, in *Proceedings of the SIAM International Conference on Data Mining, SDM 2009*, 2009, pp. 1123–1134

238. D. Zhang, C.X. Zhai, J. Han, A.N. Srivastava, N.C. Oza, Topic modeling for OLAP on multidimensional text databases: topic cube and its applications. Stat. Anal. Data Mining **2**(5–6), 378–395 (2009)

239. P. Zhao, X. Li, D. Xin, J. Han, Graph Cube: on warehousing and OLAP multidimensional networks, in *Proceedings of the ACM SIGMOD International Conference on Management of Data, SIGMOD 2011* (ACM, 2011), pp. 853–864

240. Y. Zheng, X. Zhou (eds.), *Computing with Spatial Trajectories* (Springer, 2011)

241. S. Zlatanova, On 3D topological relationships, in *Proceedings of the 11th International Conference on Database and Expert Systems Applications, DEXA'00*. Lecture Notes in Computer Science, vol. 1873 (Springer, 2000), pp. 913–924

Index

ACID properties
  in in-memory databases, 517
  in Oracle TimesTen, 525
  in SAP HANA, 523
Additive measures, 58, 93
Ad hoc queries, 79
Agglomerative algorithm, 338
Algebraic measures, 59
Alternate keys, 23
Alternative hierarchies, 98–99
  in Analysis Services, 160
  logical representation, 134
  spatial, 439
Analysis-driven design, 81, 387, 415–416
  conceptual design, 402–407, 462–464
  requirements specification, 389–395,
    462–464
Analysis Services, 82, 152–163
  attribute hierarchies, 155
  Business Intelligence Semantic Model,
    82
  data members, 159
  data mining, 350–362
  data source views, 152
  data sources, 152
  diagrams, 153
  fact dimensions, 154
  HOLAP storage, 271
  implementation of hierarchies,
    158–161
  key performance indicators (KPIs),
    366–370
  many-to-many dimensions, 154,
    158
  measure groups, 161
  measures, 161
  MOLAP storage, 271

multilevel or user-defined hierarchies,
  155
named calculations, 152
named queries, 152
parent-child hierarchies, 159
partitioning, 269–273
physical design, 269–275
query performance, 274–275
ragged hierarchies, 160
reference dimensions, 154
regular dimensions, 154, 155
ROLAP storage, 270
role-playing dimensions, 154
semiadditive measures, 161
Analysis/source-driven design, 81, 387,
  417–418
  conceptual design, 409–410, 466–467
  requirements specification, 401–402,
    466–467
Analytical dashboards, 372
Apriori algorithm, 340
Association rules, 338–347
  in Analysis Services, 359–362
  confidence, 339
  defined, 339
  hierarchical, 343
  interesting rules, 339
  itemset, 339
  pattern growth mining, 344–347
  support, 339
Attribute hierarchies
  in Analysis Services, 155
  in Mondrian, 168
Attributes, 18
  derived, 19
  of dimensions, 55
  of levels, 91

A. Vaisman and E. Zimányi, *Data Warehouse Systems*, Data-Centric
Systems and Applications, DOI 10.1007/978-3-642-54655-6,
© Springer-Verlag Berlin Heidelberg 2014

Printed by Printforce, the Netherlands